1987

THE
REAGAN
EXPERIMENT

THE CHANGING DOMESTIC PRIORITIES SERIES

Listed below are the titles published to date in the Changing Domestic Priorities Series.

THE REAGAN EXPERIMENT
An Examination of Economic and Social Policies under the Reagan Administration (1982)

HOUSING ASSISTANCE FOR OLDER AMERICANS
The Reagan Prescription (1982)

MEDICAID IN THE REAGAN ERA
Federal Policy and State Choices (1982)

THE REAGAN EXPERIMENT

An Examination of Economic and Social
Policies under the Reagan Administration

John L. Palmer
Isabel V. Sawhill

Editors

A Report of The Urban Institute's
Changing Domestic Priorities Project

THE URBAN INSTITUTE PRESS · WASHINGTON, D.C.

Advisory Board of the
Changing Domestic Priorities Project

CONTENTS

FOREWORD   xv

ACKNOWLEDGMENTS   xvii

1. PERSPECTIVES ON THE REAGAN EXPERIMENT/   1
   John L. Palmer, Isabel V. Sawhill

   Responding to Public Concerns   2
   The Program for Economic Recovery   4
   The Federal Partnership with State-Local
       Governments and the Nonprofit Sector   10
   The Shift in Social Policy   14
   Taking Stock   22

PART ONE
THE PROGRAM FOR ECONOMIC RECOVERY

2. ECONOMIC POLICY/*Isabel V. Sawhill*   31

   The Legacy of the 1970s   32
   The Administration's Economic Strategy   36
   Early Reactions   42
   Monetary Restraint and Inflation   46
   Fiscal Policy, Deficits, and the Economy   53
   Conclusions   57

3. BUDGET POLICY/*John L. Palmer, Gregory B. Mills*   59

   Historical Trends in the Federal Budget: 1956-1981 61
   President Reagan's Budget Program   67
   The Tax and Spending Changes Enacted during 1981   76
   The Changed Budget Outlook and Its Consequences   83
   Conclusions   94

4. TAX POLICY/*Charles R. Hulten, June A. O'Neill*   97

   Background   99
   The Economic Recovery Tax Act of 1981   109
   Economic Impacts   115
   Conclusions   127

5. REGULATORY POLICY/*George C. Eads, Michael Fix*   129

   The Reagan Administration's Regulatory Philosophy   130
   The Precedents for the Reagan Program   133
   The Reagan Administration's Strategy for Regulatory Relief   136
   Regulatory Reform in Practice: Deregulating Transportation   142
   The Reagan Regulatory Relief Program: A Framework for
     Evaluation   145
   Concluding Observations on the Reagan Program's First Year   152

PART TWO
THE RELATIONSHIP OF THE FEDERAL GOVERNMENT TO
THE STATE-LOCAL AND NONPROFIT SECTORS

6. THE STATE AND LOCAL SECTOR/*George E. Peterson*   157

   The New Federalism in Perspective   159
   Block Grants and the State Response   170
   State Tax and Budget Actions   183
   Conclusions   196
   Appendix: State Budget Adjustments   198

7. THE NONPROFIT SECTOR/*Lester M. Salamon,*
  Alan J. Abramson   219

   What is the Nonprofit Sector?   221
   The Economic Recovery Program and the Nonprofit Sector:
     The Theory   222
   The Economic Recovery Program and the Nonprofit Sector:
     The Realities   230
   The Impacts in Reality: Early Indications   241
   Conclusions   242

PART THREE

THE SHIFT IN SOCIAL POLICY

8. EMPLOYMENT, TRAINING, AND ECONOMIC
   DEVELOPMENT/*Marc Bendick, Jr.*   247

      The Nature of Structural Employment Problems   248
      To What Extent Can Prosperity Solve Structural Employment
         Problems?   251
      The Administration's Policy Initiatives   254
      Conclusions   267

9. HEALTH/*Judith Feder, John Holahan, Randall R. Bovbjerg,
   Jack Hadley*   271

      Historical Review   272
      Budget Reductions and Program Changes   278
      Reforms to Promote Efficiency and Limit Health Costs   297
      Conclusions   303

10. SOCIAL SERVICES/*Michael F. Gutowski, Jeffrey J. Koshel*   307

      Historical Development in Social Services   308
      Social Services within a Changing Federal Budget   313
      Issues   322

11. EDUCATION/*June A. O'Neill, Margaret C. Simms*   329

      Elementary, Secondary, and Vocational Education   331
      Higher Education   344

12. INCOME SECURITY/*James R. Storey*   361

      Policy Development Prior to 1981   363
      Policy Changes under President Reagan   372
      Consequences of Policy Changes   380
      Conclusions   391

13. HOUSING AND COMMUNITY DEVELOPMENT/
    Raymond J. Struyk, John A. Tuccillo, James P. Zais   393

        Selected Developments, 1974-1980   396
        Change during the Reagan Administration   403
        Summary   413

14. TRANSPORTATION/*Ronald F. Kirby, Carol T. Everett*   419

        Issues in the Federal Financing of Transportation   420
        The Reagan Initiatives   426
        Responses to Date   433
        Conclusion   435

PART FOUR
IMPACTS ON PEOPLE AND PLACES

15. REGIONAL IMPACTS/*Thomas Muller*   441

        Regional Fiscal Flows in the Pre-Reagan Period   443
        The Change in Regional Fiscal Flows under the Reagan
            Administration   446
        Personal Income and Employment   454
        Conclusions   455

16. THE ECONOMIC WELL-BEING OF FAMILIES AND
    INDIVIDUALS/*Lee Bawden, Frank Levy*   459

        Recent Trends in Living Standards and Income Distribution 461
        Policy Changes   468
        Effects on Economic Well-being   471
        Conclusions   482

APPENDIX   485

NOTES   495

ABOUT THE AUTHORS   525

TABLES

2-1	Performance of the Economy by Decade	34
2-2	The Administration's Economic Forecasts	41
2-3	Selected Economic Indicators, 1980–1982	44
2-4	Selected Measures of Inflation and Labor Compensation Since 1979	51
2-5	Deficit Projections	53
3-1	Government Expenditures as a Percentage of Gross National Product, FY 1956–FY 1981	62
3-2	Distribution of Federal Budget Outlays, FY 1956–FY 1981	65
3-3	Reagan Administration Budget Projections, March 1981	68
3-4	Congressional Budget Office Baseline Budget Projections, July 1981	69
3-5	Effect on Federal Budget Outlays of President Reagan's Budget Program, by Major Budget Category	74
3-6	Effect on Federal Budget Outlays of President Reagan's 1983 Budget Program, by Domestic Program Area	75
3-7	Effect on Federal Budget Outlays of Policy Changes in the First Eighteen Months of the Reagan Administration, by Major Budget Category	80
3-8	Effect on Federal Budget Outlays of Policy Changes in the First Eighteen Months of the Reagan Administration, by Domestic Program Area	82
3-9	Congressional Budget Office Baseline Budget Projections, with the Defense Proposals in President Reagan's 1983 Budget, February 1982	84
3-10	Differences between the CBO Baseline Budget Projections of July 1981 and February 1982 for FY 1982 and FY 1986	86
3-11	Deficit Estimates under President Reagan's 1983 Budget	88
3-12	Effect on the FY 1986 Baseline Deficit of Various Deficit Reduction Measures	90
3-13	Deficit Reduction Measures in the FY 1983 First Concurrent Budget Resolution	93
4-1	Federal, State, and Local Government Receipts as a Percentage of Gross National Product, 1929–1981	100
4-2	Change in the Tax Base and Nontaxed Portions of Income: 1948, 1969, 1978	102
4-3	Marginal Personal Income Tax Rates for Four-Person Families, Selected Years, 1960–1984	104
4-4	Average Federal Tax Rates for Four-Person Families, Selected Years, 1960–1984	105
4-5	Effective Corporate Tax Rates	112
4-6	Revenue Effects of the Economic Recovery Tax Act of 1981, Administration and Congressional Budget Office Estimates, by Fiscal Year	113
4-7	Projections of Federal Tax Receipts by Source, under Current Law and Prior Laws, by Fiscal Year	114

4-8   Change in Individual Income Tax Liability and in After-Tax Income
       under Assumed Changes in the Tax Law   117
4-9   Federal Tax Liabilities and Income: Simulated 1984 Distributions   119
6-1   Revenue Sources, State and Local Governments   162
6-2   Block Grant Summary   172
6-3   Attempts to Strengthen Legislative Role in Allocating Federal Grants,
       1981–1982   177
6-4   State Use of Block Grant Transfers   178
6-5   Summary of Block Grant Replacement   180
6-6   Number of State Measures Implementing Tax Actions, by Type and
       Year, 1978–1982   185
6-7   California Tax Relief, FY 1976–FY 1983   186
6-8   Characteristics of States Grouped by FY 1982 Budget Condition   189
7-1   The Charitable Nonprofit Sector in the U.S., 1977   222
7-2   Federal Outlays in Fields Where Nonprofit Organizations Are Active,
       FY 1981 Outlays   226
7-3   Projected Changes in Federal Spending in Fields Where Nonprofit
       Organizations Are Active, FY 1981–FY 1985   227
7-4   Reductions in Federal Outlays in Comparison with Nonprofit Ex-
       penditures in Fields of Interest to Nonprofit Organizations in FY
       1982 and FY 1983   229
7-5   Federal Government Support as a Share of Total Nonprofit Reve-
       nues, Excluding Religion, 1981   233
7-6   Projected Changes in Revenues of Nonprofit Organizations from
       Federal Sources, FY 1981–FY 1985   235
7-7   Levels of Increase in Private Giving Required to Hold Nonprofit
       Organizations at 1981 Spending Levels After Taking Account of
       Inflation and Budget Cuts, 1982–1985   236
7-8   Projected Private Individual Giving under the 1981 Tax Law and
       Pre-1981 Law, 1981–1984   238
8-1   Federal Obligations for Selected Employment, Training, and Eco-
       nomic Development Programs, FY 1981–FY 1983   255
8-2   The Cost Effectiveness of Various CETA Activities in Enhancing
       the Postprogram Earnings of Disadvantaged Adult Workers   257
8-3   Characteristics of Participants in Programs under the Comprehensive
       Employment and Training Act, FY 1980   259
9-1   The Federal Health Budget: Calendar 1965–1980   275
9-2   Federal Health Expenditures: Estimated Effects of Changes Enacted
       by the 97th Congress   279
9-3   Health Expenditures: Estimated Effects of Changes Proposed in the
       1983 Budget   281
9-4   Block Grant Structure: Proposed vs. Final Form   292
9-5   Block Grant Spending vs. Prior Categorical Spending   294
10-1   Federal Funding for Major Social Services Programs, FY 1975–
       FY 1981   311
10-2   Changes in Federal Funding for Major Social Services Programs
       under the Reagan Administration   314
10-3   Effects of Omnibus Budget Reconciliation Act of 1981 on Texas
       Social Services Budget   317

10-4   Comparison of Federal Expenditures on Income Security and Health
        Programs with Federal Expenditures on Social Services, FY 1962–
        FY 1982   323
11-1   Federal Funding for Elementary, Secondary, and Vocational
        Education for FY 1981   333
11-2   Federal Funding for Elementary, Secondary, and Vocational
        Education for FY 1982   337
11-3   Federal Funding for Elementary, Secondary, and Vocational
        Education for FY 1983   339
11-4   Percentage of Men Enrolled in College and in the Armed Forces
        and Percentage of Women Enrolled in College, by Age   350
11-5   Federal Outlays on Student Assistance for Higher Education,
        FY 1974–FY 1985   352
12-1   Federal Outlays for Income Security Programs, 1935–1980   364
12-2   Selected Tax Expenditures for Income Security Purposes, 1970–
        1980   367
12-3   Baseline Income Security Outlays and Enacted Savings Projected
        to 1984, by Program   374
12-4   Policy Changes and Proposals to Reduce Benefits for Welfare
        Recipients with Earnings   377
12-5   Estimated Income Security Tax Expenditures for Fiscal Years 1981
        and 1983 and Percentage Change, for Selected Tax Expenditures   379
12-6   Changes in Mean 1979 Income, Program Eligibility, and Poverty
        Status Due to Welfare Benefit Reductions, for Selected Recipient
        Groups   381
13-1   Objectives of U.S. Housing Policy, Rationale, and Associated
        Programs   394
13-2   Number of Assistance Commitments Made and Program Mixes,
        HUD Housing Assistance Programs, FY 1975–FY 1982   398
13-3   Summary of Federal Housing and Community Development
        Financing in FY 1981   402
13-4   Estimated Percentage Reductions in Subsidies to Current Housing
        Program Participants from Changes Enacted in 1981 or Proposed
        for Enactment in 1982   411
13-5   Summary of Changing Federal Housing Activities, FY 1981–
        FY 1987   415
13-6   Summary of the Consistency of Major Actions or Proposals with
        Four Objectives   416
14-1   Governmental Expenditures on Transportation, FY 1980   421
14-2   Proposed and Actual Changes in Federal Budget Authority for
        Selected Transportation Programs   427
14-3   Proposed and Actual Changes in Federal Outlays for Selected Trans-
        portation Programs   428
15-1   Total and per Capita Federal Revenue and Expenditure Flow in
        FY 1980   445
15-2   Regional Distribution of Reductions in Domestic Programs, FY 1982   448
15-3   Regional Distribution of Defense Contracts and Subcontracts   450
15-4   Regional Distribution of Increased Defense Outlays, FY 1982   451
15-5   Regional Distribution of Estimated Tax Reductions, FY 1982   452

15-6   Regional Fiscal Flows Attributable to Changes in Tax and Spending
         Policies, FY 1982 and FY 1986   453
16-1   The Distribution of Family Income for 1960, 1970, and 1979   463
16-2   Distribution of Families by Type, 1960–1979   464
16-3   Selected Statistics on Median Family Incomes   464
16-4   Statistics on the Poverty Population for 1960, 1970, and 1979   465
16-5   Estimated Reductions in FY 1984 Outlays, for Payments to Indi-
         viduals and Families Resulting from 1981 Congressional Actions   469
16-6   Change in Household Income Distributed by Type of Policy Change,
         by Income Class, Calendar Year 1984   474
16-7   Effect of Economic Recovery Tax Act on Taxes Paid by Households
         in 1984, by Income Class, under Two Alternative Measures   476
16-8   Effect of 1981 Changes in Personal Income Taxes, AFDC, and Food
         Stamps on the Incomes of Families, by Income Class   478
16-9   Effect of 1981 Changes in Income Taxes, AFDC, and Food Stamps
         on AFDC Families, by Poverty Level   479
16-10   Effects of Growth Assumptions and 1981 Policy Changes on the
         Average Real Incomes of Families, 1980 to 1984   481
A-1   Federal Outlays as a Percentage of Gross National Product,
         FY 1956–FY 1981   485
A-2   Federal Outlays by Domestic Program Area, FY 1966–FY 1981   486
A-3   Federal Taxes, Outlays, and the Budget Deficit, FY 1956–FY 1981   487
A-4   Congressional Budget Office Baseline Budget Projections, by Major
         Budget Category, July 1981   488
A-5   Total Tax Receipts as Percentage of Gross Domestic Product, OECD
         Member Countries, 1955–1980   489
A-6   Distribution of Personal Income Tax Returns, by Marginal Rate of
         Tax, 1961 and 1979   490
A-7   Changes in Tax-Exempt Levels of Income Compared to the Poverty
         Threshold, by Filing Status and Number of Dependents, 1948–
         1984   491
A-8   Effective Tax Rates on Depreciable Assets Used in Nonresidential
         Business, 1952–1979   492
A-9   Distribution of Nondefense Program Reductions, by Region and
         State, FY 1982   493

FIGURES

2-1   Two Scenarios: Crowding-In vs. Crowding-Out   56
4-1   Historical Corporate Tax Rates, 1952–1980   107
4-2   Net Investment Shares and Marginal Tax Rates, 1952-1979   124

FOREWORD

In 1982 The Urban Institute began a three-year project to examine the shifts in economic and social policies occurring under the Reagan administration. This book is the first product of that effort.

When President Reagan assumed office in January 1981, the nation faced high inflation, sluggish economic growth, rapidly rising federal expenditures, and an inadequate defense budget. In response, the president proposed a comprehensive plan designed to bolster the nation's economy, strengthen its defense, and reduce the role of government. Major shifts in federal regulation, tax, and budget policies were advanced. Many of the domestic responsibilities that the federal government had assumed over the past several decades were to be eliminated, reduced, or transferred to state and local governments and to the private sector.

With the initial stages of President Reagan's program already enacted by the Congress, a process of substantial change is now underway. These changes warrant careful examination for two reasons: first, this is the beginning of a multiyear process. The impact of most shifts in federal policy is uncertain: unforeseen developments and unintended consequences are inevitable. Objective analysis and timely feedback of the effects of these changes will contribute to informed consideration by the public and better decisions by policy makers over the next several years.

Second, the United States is embarking upon an experiment with economic and social policy, perhaps as significant as the New Deal. The Reagan administration has raised fundamental questions about the appropriate role of government in national life. Its program starts with distinct premises about economic and social behavior. Because these premises have far-reaching implications for the character of public policy, a rigorous and impartial assessment of this experiment is in order.

The Changing Domestic Priorities project is designed to help meet these needs. This research effort, the initial funding for which was provided by the Ford Foundation and the John D. and Catherine T. MacArthur Foundation, complements the Institute's long-standing work in assessing the consequences of public actions. It draws heavily upon the accumulated expertise of Institute staff and other researchers, as well as on an established tradition of objective public policy analysis. The project is broad in scope and thus relies heavily on collaborative research to capture the interactions between policy changes and public responses.

The Changing Domestic Priorities project has three objectives:

- to monitor and interpret significant shifts in economic and social policy;
- to determine the actual and likely consequences of these shifts; and
- to explore the implications and alternatives for further public actions.

This book is aimed primarily at the first of these three objectives. It explores the magnitude and significance of the shifts in federal policy that took place during the first eighteen months of the Reagan administration, as well as many of the policies that the president proposed for subsequent consideration. Insofar as it has been possible, the book discusses the impacts of these changes thus far on people, places, and institutions. Where sufficient research exists, likely future impacts are projected.

This examination contains no prescriptions. It does provide information and insight to the public and to national and local leaders, to help them understand the issues and evaluate the means for achieving various public purposes. Over the next several years, the Changing Domestic Priorities project will continue to measure and interpret the results of the redirection in federal policy. This first report will be followed by a series of detailed studies in various areas of interest, such as health, education, income security, and state and local governments. A second overview volume synthesizing the project's findings will be published in 1984.

I want to express my appreciation for the assistance and support provided by our funding sponsors, our board of advisors, and numerous outside scholars and public officials who gave generously of their time and wisdom. The views expressed herein are the authors' and should not be attributed to The Urban Institute, its trustees, its funding sources, or the members of the advisory board of this project.

William Gorham
President
The Urban Institute

ACKNOWLEDGMENTS

This book is a collective and collaborative effort of the authors of the several chapters, their secretaries, The Urban Institute Press, and the Institute's general research and administrative support staff. We are grateful for their extraordinary efforts and the good humor and patience they exhibited under considerable time pressure. In addition, we would like to thank Ann Guillot and Timmy Napolitano for their assistance in coordinating the numerous parts of this project, and Gregory Mills for his general analytical support in all phases of this project.

This book has benefited from the comments provided by members of our "Changing Domestic Priorities" Advisory Board and numerous other outside readers. We thank them as well as the Ford Foundation and the John D. and Catherine T. MacArthur Foundation whose grants made the book possible.

John L. Palmer
Isabel V. Sawhill

CHAPTER 1

PERSPECTIVES ON THE REAGAN EXPERIMENT

John L. Palmer
Isabel V. Sawhill

President Reagan took office in 1981 with a plan to "put the nation on a fundamentally different course—a course leading to less inflation, more growth, and a brighter future for all of our citizens."[1] He pledged not only to revive the economy but also to improve the nation's defense capability and to transfer significant powers and responsibilities to state and local governments and to the private sector.

In setting these objectives, the president crystallized some emerging popular perceptions about the nation's problems. This much was to be expected. What was not expected was how fast and how far he would attempt to alter the course of federal policy. A counterrevolution is underway, after a half century of growing federal efforts to stabilize the economy, insure individuals against misfortune, redistribute income and opportunity, and respond to other perceived national needs. The nucleus of this counterrevolution is a philosophy of more limited government. Its articulation by a popular new president has sparked a fresh debate about the purposes of government and

[We are greatly indebted to the other authors of this volume for providing the information on which much of this chapter is based and for their comments on earlier drafts. We are also indebted to George E. Peterson, Robert D. Reischauer, and Gregory B. Mills for their assistance in the preparation of this chapter. Any opinions expressed herein are our own.]

the ability of individuals and institutions to advance in an environment of diminished federal assistance.

Translating new ideas into action requires congressional approval and continued public support. During his first year in office the president was remarkably successful in securing congressional enactment of his proposals. Thus, the Reagan experiment was firmly launched.

The major purpose of this book is to place the president's policies in perspective. Particular attention is given to their historical antecedents, rationale, preliminary impacts, and issues raised for further public debate. The focus is on changes in economic and social policy. Little attention is given to defense, foreign affairs, the environment, or natural resources. As the first publication in an ongoing examination of changing domestic priorities, this book is intended to chronicle policy developments during the first eighteen months of the Reagan administration and to sharpen understanding of their magnitude and significance.

This chapter first provides historical background on the issues and then draws heavily on the other chapters in the volume to describe the shifts in policy and, where possible, their likely impacts. A concluding section assesses the significance of the Reagan experiment.

Responding to Public Concerns

Any president taking office in 1981 would have had to respond, in some degree, to the public's concerns about the economy, national security, the growth of spending and taxes, and the ability of government to solve social problems.

The economy performed more poorly during the 1970s than during the 1960s. The 1970s were a decade of unprecedented peacetime inflation and slow productivity growth. The causes of the economy's lackluster performance remained a matter of debate, with some economists blaming oil and food price shocks, and others overly stimulative fiscal and monetary policies. There was virtually unanimous belief that something needed to be done.

By 1980 there was bipartisan support for greater defense spending. The share of the federal budget devoted to defense had declined from over one-half in the 1950s to less than one-quarter in 1976. In the late 1970s Congress began to authorize a modest defense build-up, and President Carter in his last budget proposed 5 percent annual increases in inflation-adjusted defense spending. Thus, military expenditures would certainly have increased no matter which of the major presidential candidates had been elected in 1980.

The debate has focused more on the size of the increase and how to translate such spending increases into greater military preparedness and greater national security.

Despite the economic reversals of the 1970s, the United States remained one of the most affluent of all nations—a country that could afford to expand its defense sector, maintain its domestic commitments, and still have a lower tax burden than most other industrialized nations. In 1980 the United States ranked fourteenth among twenty-four industrialized countries in terms of total taxes paid as a proportion of gross domestic product. Nevertheless, the public sector's spending (state, local, and federal) as a proportion of Gross National Product (GNP) in the United States had crept up from about one-quarter in the mid-1950s to almost one-third by 1981, largely because of increasing federal expenditures. Americans felt that government programs and regulations had proliferated unnecessarily and that taxes were too high. They demanded—and got—fiscal retrenchment at the state and local level. Since 1977 more than half the states have passed tax or spending limitations, the best-known example being California's approval of Proposition 13 in 1978.

Questions also had been raised about the federal government's ability to solve social problems. The New Deal created worker- and employer-funded programs to protect employees and their families against loss of income due to incapacity, death, retirement, or unemployment. During the 1960s the federal government moved beyond insuring workers against loss of income to address more difficult and more chronic forms of poverty through programs that ranged from cash transfers to health care, nutrition assistance, subsidized housing, compensatory education, and manpower training. Yet, fifteen years after the War on Poverty and Great Society programs had been initiated, few of the high expectations of their proponents had been realized. To be sure, more generous income transfers helped to reduce the incidence of poverty from 17.3 percent in 1965 to 11.6 percent in 1979 (or even lower if noncash benefits are considered). These programs also eliminated the greater risk of poverty faced by the aged and greatly improved the access of the poor and elderly to decent medical care. Nevertheless, the public seemed to feel that too much money was being spent on such programs, sometimes with too little effect, and that too large a proportion of the population had become dependent on federal assistance, weakening the incentives for them to make it on their own.

In earlier administrations, attempts to reduce such dependency through education and training had produced some successful programs, such as the Job Corps, Head Start, and compensatory education under Title I of the Elementary and Secondary Education Act. Still, overall impacts on the distribution of income, the level of unemployment among the disadvantaged, or the amount of welfare dependency were difficult to discern. Finally, concern that recipients would not use cash assistance responsibly led to the growth of "in-kind" benefits and social services, with some inevitable loss of individual freedom and the emergence of provider groups with an interest in maintaining these services.

Not only individuals but also state and local governments were becoming more dependent on federal assistance. Federal aid grew from $11 billion in 1965 to $91 billion in 1980. State and local governments increasingly became the administrative agents for carrying out federal mandates. The number of federal categorical grant programs grew from under 200 to about 500 during this period. These arrangements helped equalize fiscal burdens for different areas of the country, while leaving the delivery of services in local hands. However, they threatened governments' accountability to the voters, as one level of government collected the taxes to pay for services provided by another. Meaningful federal oversight also became more difficult. State and local officials felt that the proliferation of programs and regulations seriously constrained their ability to efficiently deliver public services. In lobbying for fewer restrictions, they indicated a willingness to accept ninety cents of untied aid in place of a dollar of categorical assistance.

The business sector also felt hampered by the explosive growth of federal regulations during the 1960s and 1970s in such areas as occupational health and safety, the environment, equal employment opportunity, and product safety. In addition, inflation eroded the value of business tax write-offs and squeezed after-tax profits. While there was no clear evidence that regulation or taxes were a major cause of the productivity slowdown, such burdens created uncertainty and distress for the business community. This led to increasing business support for policies to control inflation, reduce regulation, and provide more generous depreciation write-offs.

Many of the foregoing problems had been addressed by the Carter administration. However, President Carter was hampered by both his style and his constituency from acting strongly on these matters. Thus, the public perceived the efforts of his administration to be inadequate. By contrast, Ronald Reagan had a coherent set of philosophical principles for addressing the nation's problems and a talent for communicating his vision of the country's future.

The Program for Economic Recovery

In February 1981 the new administration unveiled its Program for Economic Recovery. The plan called for a stable and restrictive monetary policy, a much lower rate of growth in federal spending, a reduction in personal and business taxes, and substantial regulatory relief. These components of the administration's overall plan are analyzed in part 1 (chapters 2 through 5). Each element of the program was designed to reduce the role of government in the economy. A more limited federal presence was advocated largely because of its perceived benefits for overall economic performance.

Embedded within this economic program was a fundamentally conservative social philosophy for the responsibilities of the federal government in promoting the general welfare and redressing inequalities among citizens and fiscal disparities among communities. However, the administration wanted its policies to be judged not so much on their philosophical merits as on their economic results. In fact, by yoking its social agenda to economic performance, the administration secured a degree of public and legislative support for its program that otherwise might not have been forthcoming. However, in doing so it subjected its economic policies to a high standard of performance and created expectations for a revitalized economy that have yet to be met.

Economic Policy

The administration's economic policy rests on a mixture of theories. "Monetarism" requires that the Federal Reserve limit the growth of the money supply in order to reduce inflation while "supply side" economics calls for a reduction in taxes to provide greater incentives to work, save, and invest. Based on the presumed success of these strategies, the administration issued an economic forecast in early 1981 that proved to be extremely optimistic. There was no supply side miracle leading to economic recovery, but the tight monetary policy endorsed by the administration led to a recession. The business downturn, along with some fortuitous softening of oil and food prices, produced a substantial drop in the rate of inflation.

The long-term benefits of living in a noninflationary world may be substantial, but the short-term costs of eliminating inflation are high. They are estimated in chapter 2 of this volume to be $1.2 trillion in lost output and income over a period of perhaps five to ten years (the equivalent of $15,000 per household). About a fifth of these costs have already been paid as the result of keeping the economy somewhat depressed since early 1980. The remainder represents the additional output and income that would have to be sacrificed if inflation were to be virtually eliminated over the next few years. Along with less growth of output and income comes high unemployment, lower profits, and a shrinking revenue base for all levels of government.

Thus far, a very restrictive monetary policy has been the dominant influence on the economy, drowning out any supply side response to the tax cut enacted in 1981. The administration's tax policy may eventually have a significant impact on work, savings, and investment and so could improve the economy's long-term growth potential. The main result of tax policy to date, however, has been to enlarge future deficits. If such deficits persist, they will reduce the pool of savings available for business investment, as the federal government borrows these savings to finance its own debt. This possibility weakens the likelihood that the tax cut will improve the economy's future growth rate.

The most fundamental change in economic policy was the administration's rejection of any use of countercyclical stabilization policy in the firm belief that such policies had proved ineffective. Since 1946 the federal government has had a commitment to use fiscal and monetary policy to maintain high employment and stable prices. While such activist policies were somewhat discredited during the 1970s and have always been controversial because of their presumed inflationary consequences, real output and employment have been much more stable since 1946 than in the first half of the century. Businesses and workers have benefited from this climate of greater stability. If the administration maintains its policy of nonintervention, these groups will no longer be able to plan on the federal government being a silent partner in providing jobs and markets and thereby limiting economic risks.

Budget Policy

Failure of the economy to recover as quickly and strongly as initially predicted made it impossible to balance the budget while simultaneously reducing taxes and increasing defense spending, even with large domestic spending reductions. Early in 1981 the president had been able to promise simultaneous pursuit of these objectives by virtue of his optimistic predictions for the economy.

Based on these economic predictions, the Congress enacted a multiyear tax cut even larger than the president had proposed. It also adopted the president's defense proposals in full and passed cuts in nondefense spending that were only slightly less than those initially requested by the president. These cuts reduced program outlays in fiscal year (FY) 1982 by $32 billion below the spending projected under prior policies. The relative size of these outlay reductions will grow each year, amounting to $55 billion in FY 1986.

Despite the reductions in nondefense programs, these enacted tax and spending changes, along with the failure of the economy to respond to the new policies, dramatically raised future deficit projections. By late 1981 it was clear, even to the administration, that its various budget goals were not compatible. In response to this changed outlook, the president presented his

1983 budget proposals to Congress in early 1982, pledging continued support for the 1981 tax cuts and planned defense build-up but abandoning the goal of a balanced budget by 1984. The president sought to hold projected deficits below $100 billion primarily through additional domestic program cuts—even larger than he had previously proposed—and through continued reliance on optimistic economic assumptions.

In marked contrast to the previous year, Congress rejected the president's request as a starting point for its own 1983 budget deliberations. Congress is now embarked on a long-term deficit reduction program that will take several years to fully define and implement. In preliminary action on the 1983 budget, Congress passed a resolution calling for substantial tax increases and non-defense program cuts, modest reductions in the planned defense build-up, and major management savings. It also assumed that interest rates would drop considerably in response to these deficit reduction measures, lowering the cost of financing the federal debt and thus further reducing projected deficits. While congressional estimates suggest that such a scheme would bring down the deficit to about $60 billion by FY 1986, a more realistic projection of such policies points toward a 1986 deficit of over $130 billion (see table 3-13).

Although the spending changes enacted in 1981 have begun to realign federal budget priorities as the president wished, they did not curtail the major sources of nondefense spending growth. Federal outlays are estimated to be a higher percentage of GNP in FY 1982 (24.2) than they were in FY 1981 (23.1) and are expected to stay at historically high peacetime levels under current policies. This failure to restrain the growth of federal expenditures, in combination with the large tax cut, has introduced a long-term structural imbalance between spending and revenues.

The long-term budget dilemma is truly sobering. Balancing the budget within the next five years would require a combination of revenue increases and program spending reductions that by FY 1986 would have to reach an annual level in excess of $225 billion, or more than 5 percent of projected GNP. If a strong and sustained economic recovery is not underway by the fall of 1982, the budget imbalance will worsen.

Eliminating deficits will necessitate a combination of tax increases, cut-backs in planned defense outlays, and considerable spending restraint in do-mestic programs. However, tax increases and defense reductions will require that President Reagan retreat from his original policy objectives, while sub-stantial domestic spending restraint will require that Congress overcome strong political opposition to cuts in Social Security and Medicare. The difficulty of reaching legislative compromises on such issues will result in pressure to tolerate continuing large deficits.

Tax Policy

The long-term deficits that became the focus of so much attention in 1982 were largely caused by the Economic Recovery Tax Act (ERTA) of 1981. This law, which gave the largest tax cut in the nation's history, is estimated to result in a cumulative revenue loss of almost $300 billion by the end of 1984 and over $1 trillion by the end of 1987. A substantial portion of this cut, however, will simply offset the increase in tax burdens that otherwise would have occurred over the next few years as inflation and higher standards of living push people's incomes into higher tax brackets—a process called "bracket creep."

ERTA has three objectives: to provide relief from bracket creep, to promote economic growth, and to reduce the size of government. With respect to tax relief, at currently forecasted rates of inflation, ERTA will reduce the ratio of federal receipts to GNP from 21 percent in 1981 to around 18 percent in the mid-1980s, a ratio not experienced since the mid-1970s. The largest part of ERTA is the three-stage reduction in individual income tax rates which cumulates to 23 percent by 1984. This reduction will more than offset the bracket creep anticipated between 1980 and 1984 for the average taxpayer, but for some—those with larger families and lower incomes—the failure to adjust upward personal exemptions and the zero bracket amount (standard deduction) means that a rollback of effective rates to 1980 levels will not occur.

The impact of ERTA on the rate of economic growth depends on how it affects work, savings, and investment decisions. Because the personal income tax cut is partially an offset to bracket creep and thus lowers effective rates only modestly, and because taxes do not appear to have powerful effects on individual work and savings decisions, a large response in these areas should not be anticipated.

The cuts in business taxes are relatively deeper and are targeted on new investment. Their impact on effective tax rates depends on future inflation. At an 8 percent annual rate of inflation, ERTA will yield a reduction in the effective corporate tax rate on plant and equipment from 40 percent to 18 percent by 1986. At lower rates of inflation, the corporate income tax would be effectively eliminated for many firms. Per dollar of revenue loss, these business tax cuts—in the form of accelerated depreciation and a more generous investment tax credit—have a larger "supply side" impact on GNP than do personal tax cuts. Thus, a smaller overall tax reduction, but one more heavily concentrated on business, would have improved economic growth and produced a smaller budget deficit than did ERTA.

Thus far, the recession and high interest rates have overwhelmed any response of investment to lower taxes. But these tax policies are long-term measures, and an immediate response was never very likely.

ERTA's impact on the size of government remains to be seen. However, as noted earlier, it is largely responsible for projected deficits and has certainly increased pressures to reduce or restrain spending. Moreover, indexing the personal income tax for inflation beginning in 1985 means that new revenues will no longer be automatically available to finance government growth. Thus, competition between the federal government and the private sector for scarce credit and real resources will intensify.

Regulatory Policy

The administration proposed that regulatory relief be given a role in economic policy rivaling that assigned to budget, tax, and monetary policy. Its campaign to cut federal regulations was based on a belief that regulation was a significant factor in the decline of American productivity, and that the federal government had improperly intruded into the affairs of private individuals, state and local governments, and business.

To date the administration's regulatory relief campaign has employed six strategies. They are (1) the withdrawal and revision of proposed and existing administrative regulations, (2) expanded White House oversight of the regulatory process and the required use of cost-benefit analysis for all proposed regulations, (3) severe budget and personnel cuts in regulatory enforcement agencies, (4) a general relaxation of federal enforcement efforts through the dismissal or settlement of legal actions brought against parties formerly believed to be in violation of federal laws, (5) the elimination of rules that constrain state and local government actions and the further transfer of enforcement authority to lower levels of government, and (6) the appointment of administration officials who are sympathetic to the regulatory relief goals.

Several conclusions emerge from examining the regulatory relief program to date. First, the administration's goals are sometimes in conflict. For example, imposing more stringent validation requirements on state and local governments providing Aid to Families with Dependent Children (AFDC) and subsidized lunches seems to contradict the administration's interest in regulatory relief in general and devolution of federal authority in particular. Second, by relying on an administrative rather than a legislative approach to regulatory relief, the administration's efforts are more vulnerable to legal or political challenge. Thus, early gains may be difficult to sustain, and expec-

tations of regulated parties may not change as fast as hoped, especially since
the cost savings provided to business appear to be less than claimed. Without
legislation and without a federal presence to override the diversity of state
regulations, the regulatory environment remains complex and uncertain. Third,
the administration has made some progress in substituting more flexible and
innovative marketlike incentives for "command and control" regulation, although it has not pushed as hard as might have been expected, given its
commitment to regulatory reform.

The Federal Partnership with State-Local
Governments and the Nonprofit Sector

It is one thing for the federal government to change its own policies. It
is quite another for the federal government to alter the character of services
actually received by citizens. In the domestic sphere, at least, the federal
government itself delivers very few services. Rather, it relies on a vast array
of third parties—states, cities, counties, community organizations, social
service agencies, and the like.

When the federal government changes its budget priorities, these other
organizations must decide how they will react. In principle, they could offset
the federal budget cutbacks by supplementing spending from their own resources. Or they could pass on the federal budget reductions, allowing them
to become reductions in all public and quasipublic spending. Part 2 (chapters
6 and 7) of this volume discusses the impacts of federal policy shifts on state
and local governments and nonprofit organizations.

The administration has endorsed a special interpretation of the federal
government's past relations with the state-local and nonprofit sectors. This
interpretation holds that the federal government has improperly supplanted—
"usurped" is the term sometimes used—the roles of both lower levels of
government and nonprofit organizations. In the administration's view the
financial dependence of these organizations on the federal government has
stripped them of vitality. The federal presence has distorted local priorities,
lessened administrative accountability, and suffocated the growth of institutions which are closer to the citizenry than is Washington.

This view presumes that the federal government can strengthen the state-
local and nonprofit sectors by withdrawing from many of its current activities.
If the federal government has taken over responsibilities that the citizenry
once did either voluntarily or through local government, the federal government can help to restore these same functions to citizens by relinquishing
them and the taxes necessary to finance them. This is what the president has

proposed to do in his New Federalism plan and in his efforts to revitalize the voluntary sector.

Viewing the federal government as a competitor with other organized associations is a distinctly conservative perspective. It contrasts with the cooperative model of federal relations. The ties to the federal government that the president condemns were developed in the belief that they fostered a constructive partnership between Washington and the states and localities and between the public and nonprofit sectors. Eliminating this "cooperative federalism" is a fundamental and controversial element of the Reagan experiment.

The State and Local Sector

During the 1960s and 1970s state and local governments became closely tied to the federal government. Until recently, federal grants-in-aid were the fastest growing part of state and local budgets. Federal funding consisted predominantly of matching grants restricted to narrowly defined purposes and requiring local financial participation. As a result, states and localities were not only financially dependent on the federal government but became cost-sharing partners with Washington in such basic programs as Medicaid, AFDC, highway construction, and schooling for disadvantaged children. Though lower levels of government managed these programs, their purposes were defined in part at the federal level and constraints on local discretion were built into the federal grant structure.

President Reagan's agenda for changing federal relations with state and local governments has both short-term and long-term elements. In the short run, grants-in-aid to lower levels of government are singled out for the sharpest spending reductions. This is principally a budget-cutting strategy, but it is also a vehicle for federal withdrawal from selected program areas. Simultaneously, the administration has launched an effort to expand local budget flexibility by simplifying grant administration and removing grant regulations. It has consolidated categorical grants into less restrictive block grants.

The administration also has moved to sever the direct funding link between the federal government and localities. During the 1970s the fastest-growing form of federal aid was direct assistance to cities, counties, and other units of local government. Local aid was built into the General Revenue Sharing program and became a hallmark of the Carter administration's urban policy. The Reagan philosophy holds that the federal government should deal principally with the states. The block grants designate the states as aid recipients for many programs that formerly were funded directly through cities or local nonprofit organizations. Freedom to design their own local aid policies is one of the flexibilities that states are to acquire under the Reagan grant reform.

For the long term, the administration proposes sorting out public functions by level of government in order to restore the "traditional" separation of responsibilities. Federal, state, and local governments would become almost fully responsible for financing their own services—a relationship that the Reagan administration views as essential to restoring public accountability. The administration proposes two specific devices for achieving this sorting out. The first is a "swap" of major programs, with Medicaid to be assumed by the federal government and AFDC assigned to the states. The second is a "turnback" of some thirty to forty other programs (beyond those already proposed for block grants) to the states. By 1991 federal aid to state and local governments would be almost as low a share of these governments' budgets as in 1933.

The fundamental elements in the short-term strategy are the block grants. In FY 1982, the Congress consolidated seventy-seven categorical programs into nine block grants. Further block grants have been proposed by the president for FY 1983. Although the budgetary scale of the initial block grants is not large, the states' reaction to them provides the first glimpse of their probable response to the entire New Federalism agenda.

So far, states have been reluctant to compensate for federal funds lost through block granting. Based on findings from a sample of twenty-five states (see table 6-5), state replacement funding was most common within the Social Services Block Grant, but even here only eight states replaced some or all of the lost federal funds in FY 1982, and only eight states replaced some of the further FY 1983 losses. For the other block grants, the extent of replacement was still lower. The fiscal condition of the states appears to have been the dominant consideration in replacement decisions. States with large positive budget balances often have stepped in with state supplementation, even if they do not have a history of high human service spending. In contrast, states under fiscal pressure have not replaced federal funds even when they historically have had high spending commitments.

State governments as a group are now laboring under severe budgetary pressure. A faltering economy, the legacy of tax reductions enacted over the period 1978-1981, the constraints of voter-imposed revenue limitations, and federal aid cutbacks combined in FY 1982 and FY 1983 to force states into making their greatest budget adjustments in decades. The states' budget reserves, so robust a few years ago, have now been largely exhausted.

This underlying fiscal condition carries great significance for the eventual impact of the administration's federalism program. Federal grant reductions at this moment are much more likely to produce net reductions in public spending than would have been the case three years ago, or might be the case three years in the future. The leanness of state budget positions leaves little choice but to pass on the greater part of federal grant reductions as net spending reductions. If it is part of the administration's agenda to trim all public spending, its experiment could not have been launched at a more propitious moment—painful though the coincidence of fiscal blows is for states and localities.

The Nonprofit Sector

There are over 100,000 private, nonprofit service organizations in the United States. They deliver most of the country's hospital care, much of the higher education, and a considerable portion of the social services (such as foster care and family counseling). They are also the principal channel for a host of cultural, civic, and community-organization activites. These organizations received, on average, about two-fifths of their income from the federal government in 1981. The federal government's support of the nonprofit sector now exceeds all of private giving combined, whether from individuals (exclusive of giving for sacramental religious purposes), corporations, or foundations.

With its strong ties to the federal government, the nonprofit sector has been buffeted by federal budget reductions. The administration's proposals would reduce the income available to nonprofits by an estimated $35 billion (1981 dollars) between FY 1981 and FY 1985. This is about a one-fifth reduction in the amount of income nonprofits could normally have expected to receive from the federal government and between 5 and 10 percent of the total expected budget for the nonprofit sector over this period. These cuts are concentrated most heavily on social welfare and community development organizations, where the revenue loss will be on the order of one-quarter of their expected budgets. These are the very groups that will be under greatest pressure to replace the public services targeted for elimination.

The administration hopes that the growth in private giving will offset much of the reduction in federal support for the nonprofit sector. There is little question that federal budget reductions will place increased demands on the nonprofit sector. But the scale of giving that would be required makes such replacement improbable. Simply to hold constant the real value of nonprofits' resources in the face of the proposed federal cutbacks, private charitable contributions would have to jump over $4 billion or 22 percent in 1982, and an average of more than $13 billion or 40 percent annually over the period 1983-1985. This increase in charitable donations would have to occur at a time when federal tax changes have raised the after-tax costs of private contributions.

One can exaggerate the importance of dollars, of course. The shift in federal policy may stimulate far greater self-reliance and innovation within the state-local and nonprofit sectors at the same time that it diminishes their resources. But federal withdrawal from the policy and financial partnership with these sectors will require fundamental institutional change.

The Shift in Social Policy

With the commitment to expand the nation's defense capability and reduce tax burdens, it was a foregone conclusion that nondefense programs would be cut. The president's practical need to make room in the budget coincided with his goal to reduce the federal role in domestic policy. He proposed changes that cut deep and wide. Many of these have already been enacted by Congress or implemented through executive action. As a result, the nation is engaged in a retrenchment and reformation of social policy, the details of which are described in part 3 (chapters 8 to 14).

The Pattern of Budget Reductions

Federal nondefense programs fall into three broad categories: benefit payments to individuals, grants to state and local governments, and other federal operations. Spending for these purposes totaled $432 billion in FY 1981. The great bulk of this spending (about $320 billion) was for cash or in-kind transfer payments to individuals. These are generally paid under "entitlement programs," whose outlays generally increase automatically with inflation and the growth of eligible populations. A small share of these transfer payments (about one-fifth) is for programs targeted on the low-income population. The remainder is primarily spent on social insurance programs, particularly Social Security and Medicare. Other federal nondefense program spending is "discretionary"; that is, funds are appropriated each year by Congress. In FY 1981 grants to state and local governments accounted for roughly half of this discretionary spending, and other federal operations accounted for the remainder.

The reductions in nondefense program spending enacted in the FY 1982 budget process were spread across all program areas. Discretionary grants to state and local governments were cut most (15 percent below levels they would have reached under prior policies). Other federal operations were reduced somewhat less. Benefit payments for individuals were reduced the least (by only 4 percent). However, the cuts were much larger for the low-income assistance programs than for social insurance programs (see table 3-7 for more details).

Reductions from prior policy levels in specific areas of domestic policy range from 2 percent for veterans benefits to more than 47 percent for employment and training in FY 1982 (see table 3-8). Despite these sizable reductions, spending for most domestic policy areas will continue to grow unless further reductions are made. This growth will be vastly larger for the income security and health areas, which are dominated by Social Security, Medicare, and other cash-transfer and health-financing entitlement programs, than for the other areas of domestic activity largely comprised of discretionary programs. As a result, a continuously growing share of federal domestic spending will be devoted to social insurance and other health care financing programs. Social Security and Medicare alone are now projected to account for over one-half of all domestic program spending by FY 1986. This mainly reflects expected general inflation and even greater increases in per capita health care costs, as well as growth in the aged population.

President Reagan's 1983 budget proposed additional reductions in domestic spending even larger than those enacted as part of the 1982 budget. These proposed cuts have a similar pattern to that of the ones already enacted and further extend the thrust of the 1982 budget changes.

Social Program Changes

The philosophy of a reduced federal role has been translated into policy in different ways in different social program areas. The nature of the changes is detailed in part 3 for seven areas: income security; health; social services; transportation; housing and community development; employment, training, and economic development; and education. It is impossible to summarize the myriad of policy shifts. For an overview, however, the majority of them can be categorized under three broad themes.

Shifting Responsibility to State and Local Governments. The largest share of the enacted and proposed social policy changes is embodied in the proposals mentioned earlier for the withdrawal of the federal government in favor of increased administrative, financial, and policy-setting responsibility at lower levels of government. In the long run the New Federalism would eliminate the federal role in all but a few of the areas where federal grants-in-aid now exist.

In his 1982 budget, the president proposed the consolidation of over ninety categorical programs into four block grants: two in health, one in education, and one in social services and income assistance. Congress acceded to the consolidation of seventy-seven programs into nine block grants: four in health, one in education, and four in the social services area. Several of these block grants, such as the ones for primary health care and low-income energy assistance, are little more than a relabeling of a preexisting large categorical program. The others reflect far more substantial consolidation. The president's FY 1983 budget proposed further consolidation affecting over forty additional categorical grant programs, which would either be added to the existing block grants or folded into seven new ones. Affected areas include employment and training as well as those in the FY 1982 block grant proposals.

Other short-term actions by the administration are being taken to transfer responsibilities to, or increase the administrative flexibility of, state and local governments. For example, it has increased the administrative discretion of states in certain aspects of the AFDC program and granted them greater leeway in setting rates for providers in the Medicaid program. It also has eliminated regulations such as those requiring special facilities for the handicapped, and recommended phasing out federal financial support for urban and secondary roads.

Greater Reliance on the Private Sector and on Market Mechanisms. A second set of social policy changes involves greater reliance on the private sector and market-oriented approaches for accomplishing public purposes. In some areas the administration argues either that there is no legitimate federal concern or that any attempt at federal intervention is more likely to exacerbate social problems than to improve them. Some policy changes that were defended on these grounds and enacted by Congress include the sale of Conrail to the private sector and the elimination of public service employment under the Comprehensive Employment and Training Act (CETA), certain payments under impact aid for elementary and secondary education, and medical care for merchant seamen. Other proposed changes would end subsidies for physician education, legal services, and Health Maintenance Organizations (HMOs).

In other areas, where the administration proposes the continuation of a federal role, it has argued that policies relying upon freedom of choice and market incentives will be more successful in achieving desired social objectives. Thus the administration has moved to reduce greatly federal regulation of housing finance and to increase user fees for water and air transportation. Furthermore, it has proposed tuition tax credits to promote private school alternatives for elementary and secondary education and a mix of tax, expenditure, and regulatory incentives to promote economic development of distressed urban areas (enterprise zones). The administration also has advocated (though not formally proposed) reform of health care financing involving more reliance on competition to restrain rising costs. This would be implemented by reducing tax subsidies for privately financed health insurance and by prepayment schemes for publicly financed health insurance.

Narrower Targeting of Benefits to Individuals. A third set of policy changes involves the reduction or elimination of what the administration has characterized as unintended or undesirable benefits for individuals. These changes typically confine income-related assistance programs to the poorest recipients and those whom society generally does not expect to work (the ''truly needy''). Examples of enacted changes in benefit programs not targeted on the low-income population include the reduction of extended unemployment insurance benefits, the elimination under Social Security of the minimum benefit for new recipients and of dependents' and survivors' benefits for college students, and the reduction of the in-school subsidy and the imposition of a needs test (for high-income families) in the Guaranteed Student Loan (GSL) program. Other proposed changes would increase patient cost-sharing in Medicare and further tighten the needs test in the GSL program.

Examples of already enacted changes limiting income-related assistance are restrictions on gross income, and more limited deductions for child care, work expenses, and earned income in the AFDC and Food Stamp programs; tightening of income eligibility restrictions in the school lunch program; and lowering of income limits and raising the contribution rate required of housing assistance recipients. Proposed changes include further benefit reductions in most of these programs as well as in the Supplemental Security Income (SSI) program for the aged, blind, and disabled and in Pell Grants providing needs-tested financial aid for postsecondary education.

In short, fewer individuals will be eligible for many benefit programs, and the benefits of many of those still eligible will be reduced.

Assessing the Shift in Social Policy

How should this retrenchment be viewed? Beyond the savings achieved to hold down the federal deficit, will the new design of social policy contribute to or detract from social welfare? In working toward some answers to these questions, the authors of part 3 assess information about past program performance and likely consequences of the changes. Only a few general observations are offered here.

Some of the program changes proposed by the Reagan administration have long-standing antecedents and were widely considered meritorious. Several had been advocated by earlier administrations, usually for reasons that went beyond simple budgetary considerations. Examples are reductions in the guaranteed student loan subsidy and support for physician education, reduced reliance on new construction in housing assistance programs, and the scaling back of public service employment.

Other proposals, although representing a more marked departure from past presidential policies, were fully developed prior to the Reagan administration and had considerable bipartisan support. Examples of these are the reduction of direct federal housing finance operations and greater user fees for many transportation services.

Several measures reduced or eliminated programs that many policy makers and analysts had criticized as being of dubious effectiveness although such cutbacks had not been proposed by previous administrations. Examples include the Professional Standards Review Organizations (PSROs) and certificates of need programs in health, trade adjustment assistance, and several small regional economic development programs.

Not all of the proposed program changes, by any means, reflect such consensus. Many programs that were cut had either a record of proven social effectiveness or were new approaches with a strong promise of success. Examples of these are immunization grants, the Job Corps, the nutrition program for low-income pregnant women, infants, and children (WIC), compensatory education for disadvantaged children, and the new child welfare services program.

Other programs were proposed for broad cuts where trimming and restructuring were needed. Examples are the large Social Security benefit cuts for early and new retirees and the cap on increases in federal Medicaid grants to states, both of which Congress quickly rejected, and the across-the-board reductions in CETA training programs that Congress did enact.

And some of the program changes are gambles that could jeopardize stated purposes. Among these are the major reductions in income-related benefit payments, which were done in a manner that creates major work disincentives for the near-poor and working-poor. Rather than the hoped for greater independence, these changes could increase vulnerability of these groups to economic dependency.

Finally, the administration has pressed the view that many social programs should be fully financed and managed at lower levels of government. However, poverty and other social problems are unequally distributed geographically. There is little incentive for a state with a relatively large concentration of such problems or a limited fiscal capacity to impose the necessary taxes to pay for even effective programs. Even if they wished to provide greater assistance, governors and state legislatures cannot afford to allow their tax burdens to get too far out of line with those in other states if they want to maintain their attractiveness as places to live and conduct business. There also are fears that relatively high levels of assistance to the poor might attract a larger dependent population.

Thus, if the nation wants to be sure that adequate attention is being paid to certain social problems, such as poverty or schooling for disadvantaged children, more federal involvement than is envisioned by the president may prove essential. Moreover, the timing of any shift in federal responsibilities is quite important. Because state governments are currently facing severe budgetary shortfalls due to the recession, this period is the worst of times in which to ask them to weigh choices about which social programs should be maintained at the state level.

Impact on People and Places

The ultimate concern of public policy is the well-being of people. In the short run, some degree of public sacrifice was inevitable if the Reagan administration was to deal effectively with problems such as high inflation and inadequate defense that faced the nation in 1981. Yet the magnitude, duration, and distribution of the needed sacrifices—such as more unemployment and fewer government benefits—were unclear and a cause for great concern. The administration hoped that its economic program would work quickly, require only modest sacrifices, and hence be judged by end results. Rich and poor alike were to benefit from the increased income and employment flowing from renewed growth. As these expectations have faded, the questions of who is bearing the burden and who is reaping the benefits of the new policies grow more salient.

Answering these questions accurately is difficult. The direct impacts of a tax cut or a reduction in welfare benefits on individual or family income can be easily measured. The indirect impacts, however, are harder to ascertain and often can be more important. These indirect effects flow from the impacts of the policy changes on the economy and through the incentives they provide for individuals or institutions to change their behavior.

Thus far the consequences of the 1981-1982 recession have far outweighed the impacts of the tax reductions, the defense build-up, and the domestic budget cuts. By mid-1982 civilian employment and real hourly earnings were no higher than they had been in 1980, and the unemployment rate had risen by more than two percentage points. After adjustment for inflation, median family income declined by 3.5 percent during 1981. And the incidence of poverty increased from 13.2 percent in 1980 to 14.0 percent in 1981, its highest level since 1967.

The recession also has severely restricted the ability of state and local governments to pay for current services. Many states have been obliged to raise tax rates, negating much of the federal government's tax relief. For example, Ohio's temporary state tax increases will offset over half of the second round of the federal income tax cut in that state.

The impacts of the current policy shifts are distributed unequally among people and places. Part 4 (chapters 15 and 16) examines the likely impact of the changes in federal policy on the fiscal health of geographic regions and on the economic well-being of individuals and families.

The Fiscal Impacts on Regions

The federal taxes paid by the individuals and businesses of a region generally do not match the federal expenditures made within that region. This imbalance can exacerbate or ameliorate economic disparities caused by other factors. Since the 1930s federal tax and spending policies generally have served to redistribute income and economic activity from the more affluent northern states to the once much poorer states in the South and West. However, with the rapid growth of the Sunbelt in recent years, these impacts have become more controversial. Older industrial areas with stagnating economies have become concerned that federal activities are inadvertently worsening the disparities in regional economic growth.

The administration's policies, in fact, will aggravate the imbalance in regional growth. The per capita tax reductions enjoyed by the West and the energy-rich states, such as Texas, in the West South-Central region will be greater than those experienced in other regions, particularly low-income states, such as Kentucky, in the East South-Central region. The domestic program cuts that have already been enacted will reduce per capita federal spending most acutely in the North. These losses will be particularly large in states with generous social programs, such as New York and Massachusetts, and states where farm price supports are important, such as North and South Dakota and Nebraska.

During 1982 increased defense outlays offset about one-quarter of the reductions in domestic program expenditures. This proportion will probably increase over time. Unlike the tax cut and the domestic program reductions, which will affect every county in the nation, increased defense spending will be concentrated in a few areas. Almost four-fifths of the added defense outlays will be spent on aircraft, ships, and other weapons systems. This spending will particularly benefit states in the Pacific and New England areas, as well as a few other states that traditionally benefit from military procurements. The Appalachian region and most other noncoastal states will receive few additional dollars.

The initial impact of President Reagan's tax and spending policies will be to widen the economic disparities between wealthy areas, such as the Pacific and New England regions, and the less affluent states of the South. Similarly, the more economically vibrant areas of the West and Southwest should gain from these policies at the expense of the stagnant Midwest. As one would expect, there are exceptions to these patterns. Oregon, for example, will experience more adverse effects than its neighbors, while Connecticut will benefit more from added defense outlays than other northern states. However, on balance these changes add further fuel to the "Sunbelt-Frostbelt" debate and keep alive the fundamental question about the extent to which federal policy should be sensitive to differing regional impacts.

Impacts on Family and Individual Incomes

The tax cut reduced rates for everyone but maintained the existing levels for personal exemptions, standard deductions, and the earned income tax credit (which provides a special credit to low-income families with earnings). This combination, together with the lowering of the maximum tax rate on unearned income from 70 to 50 percent, skews the tax relief toward higher-income taxpayers and, with inflation, results in increased tax burdens for many low-income families. Moreover, the cuts to date in benefit payments and other grant programs disproportionately affect those below the average income level.

The net effect of these tax and social program cuts through 1984 will be to provide no significant overall change in the purchasing power of those with incomes below $15,000, modest increases for the broad middle class, and substantial gains for higher-income families. Within the bottom group, those receiving benefit payments of one sort or another are likely to find themselves worse off—particularly those AFDC and Food Stamp families with earnings.

This picture of the direct effects of the 1981 tax cuts and 1982 budget spending cuts on personal incomes does not include the consequences of the overall performance of the economy. As mentioned earlier, the recession has reduced average family income. Research has also shown that recessions disproportionately affect low-income, two-parent families.

But how will people fare after the economy revives? If no other tax and spending changes are enacted and if the economy grows as rapidly as the administration assumes, the purchasing power of the average family will be about 5 percent higher in 1984 than in 1980. On the other hand, a weaker recovery from the 1981-1982 recession will leave the average family no better off in 1984 than in 1980.

While the gains from any economic growth would benefit households at all income levels, such gains are unlikely to offset the losses in transfer payments and, in some cases, the increased tax burdens experienced by many low-income families. Thus, even if the administration's policy changes result in a healthy economy by 1984, many low-income households will be worse off than in 1980, while high-income households will be much better off. One reason that low-income households do not benefit more from growth is that an increasing proportion is headed by single parents, usually women, with little attachment to the labor force.

This picture of the consequences of the current policy shifts is tentative and incomplete for several reasons. First, the additional expenditure reductions and tax increases that undoubtedly will be enacted to reduce future federal budget deficits will further decrease the purchasing power of the average family. (Also, these changes could have distributional implications different from the initial tax and spending changes.) Second, the changes in tax and transfer policy could create incentives for people to behave differently—to work harder, to save more, or to give more to charity. While most evidence suggests that such responses will be weak, the new policies could change behavior enough to moderately affect the income distribution. Third, the responses of state and local governments and nonprofit institutions must be taken into account.

Finally, the rate of long-term economic growth will be a critical determinant of the economic well-being of individuals and families. If the administration's overall policies successfully promote long-term economic growth, then most people will be better off for these policies. The low-income population will benefit to some degree from the trickle-down effect, but these benefits will be limited since this group is increasingly comprised of people unable to work. Even under the best of conditions, the welfare of millions still will depend heavily on the adequacy of public transfer programs.

Taking Stock

Three aspects of the Reagan administration's economic and social policies are particularly noteworthy. The first is the experiment in supply side policies that was offered as a solution to the country's economic problems. The second is the shift in social philosophy as fundamental as was the New Deal. The third is the efforts of the administration to leave behind a more effective set of federal programs and policies than it inherited from its predecessors.

The Reagan Economic Program

The Reagan economic program promised more than could be delivered. It proved impossible to increase defense spending, reduce tax burdens, and balance the budget simultaneously. The president has had to abandon the third objective and compromise somewhat on the other two. Nor did it prove possible to lower inflation and promote economic growth without an intervening recession. The president's supply side economic policies may help the economy eventually achieve a long-term rate of growth higher than under more conventional economic policies. However, this remains a highly speculative proposition.

From the start, it was doubtful that the performance of the economy could accommodate the goals of increasing defense, reducing taxes, and balancing the budget. The likely inconsistency of these goals had been widely noted during the presidential campaign and the first year of the Reagan administration, but the president disarmed his critics with optimistic economic projections based on supply side theories. These theories are at the heart of the Reagan experiment in economic policy, differentiating it from traditional Republican policies advocating balanced budgets achieved through more equal reductions in taxes and spending. But the application of the theory failed to produce either the expected short-run recovery or the additional revenues needed to finance tax relief and military spending. A new course must now be charted through unknown and risky territory.

Unless Congress takes corrective action, the country will experience continued and growing budget deficits of unprecedented magnitude. Their elimination will require some combination of major modifications in taxes, the defense build-up, and the social insurance safety net. The specific approach taken will affect the size and shape of the public sector over the next several decades.

Although the most immediate and concrete result of experimenting with supply side economics is larger budget deficits, there are other probable consequences. These include some loss of credibility for the administration, high interest rates (pushing deficits still higher as the cost of financing the debt escalates), and potential government absorption of savings that otherwise could fund business investment. High interest rates increase the risk that recovery from the 1981-1982 recession will be neither strong nor sustained. This possibility, in conjunction with growing federal claims on private savings, means that the long-run effects of the administration's economic policies on productivity and growth could be adverse.

Another consequence of the supply side experiment may be a faster contraction of the federal government's domestic activities, as the deficits create continuing pressures for spending restraint. While President Reagan's supply side experiment may not have worked in the short-run, it could still contribute to the achievement of his long-term goals for social policy.

The Reagan Counterrevolution

For the most part, the changes enacted to date do not turn back the clock in federal policy very far. To be sure, in some social program areas, such as employment and training, federal spending has returned to where it stood prior to the Great Society and the decade of rapid growth in federal social spending under Presidents Johnson and Nixon. However, in most policy areas these changes represent a return to the early 1970s. By 1985 they will result in federal domestic spending as a percentage of GNP at about the same level that prevailed in 1974-1975; tax burdens will be lowered to the levels prevailing in the early 1970s. Similarly, based on federal spending changes to date, the federal share of total state and local budgets will still be comparable to its level in the mid-1970s, and the degree of grant consolidation and flexibility introduced into the overall grants-in-aid system will be relatively modest.

On the other hand, the president's proposals call for far more change. They have also raised fundamental questions about the roles and responsibilities of different levels of government and the amount of equalizing of income and opportunity that government should attempt. For the past half century no one has so successfully focused public debate on these issues. It is at this philosophical level, and in the administration's pending proposals, that President Reagan's program is best understood as a counterrevolution. The shift in philosophy is manifest in the administration's position on three issues: the contribution of government to economic and social welfare, the relationship of the federal government to other sectors, and the definition of the social safety net.

The past fifty years have been a period during which the discovery of a problem always seemed to lead to the search for a government solution. President Roosevelt's New Deal was followed by Truman's Fair Deal, Kennedy's New Frontier, Johnson's Great Society, and Nixon's New Economic Policy. The trend of growing federal policy interventions, whether in the form of spending or other policies (for example, wage and price controls) persisted through both Republican and Democratic administrations.

In contrast, the current administration believes that government is more often the problem than the solution. The administration may yet achieve its objective of eliminating "big government" if the tax cut is followed by severe domestic spending restraint by the Congress and if the recession and earlier fiscal limitations cause state and local governments to ratify the federal spending cuts. How this prospect is viewed depends on the extent to which one believes government has ameliorated or exacerbated various economic and social problems.

One does not have to accept the administration's argument that the federal government is the problem to have a favorable view of the retrenchments it has advocated. The rapid expansion in federal domestic spending and related activities brought with it excesses and inefficiencies. President Carter, despite his strong commitment to a leaner and more efficient government, had little success in achieving it. Many of the benefits and programs that were sharply curtailed or eliminated in the 1982 budget were of dubious value. It is likely that the only way that most of these budget cuts could have been accomplished was by administering a shock to the political system as President Reagan did.

The second and related shift in philosophy involves a new conception of the federal government's relationships with state and local governments, with the nonprofit sector, and with the business sector. Each is to be given maximum freedom to pursue its own agenda. The price of this freedom is less financial assistance from the federal government and perhaps a less stable economic environment. While nonprofit organizations have much to lose and little to gain, the business community and state and local governments are more ambivalent about these proposed arrangements. The administration's rejection of an active economic stabilization role for government and its New Federalism proposals would restore economic policy and intergovernmental relations to their status before the New Deal. Some commentators view these proposals as a convenient diversion from immediate budget and economic problems. However, they have been a philosophical constant in Ronald Reagan's political career, and it would be a fundamental misjudgment to underestimate his resolve on these issues.

A third dimension of the counterrevolution can be found in the administration's conception of the social safety net. Although its definitions have not always been clear or consistent, the administration has implicitly rejected the idea that the federal government has a commitment to assist the poor regardless of the reasons for their poverty. Those to be protected by the social safety net—the aged, disabled, poor mothers with very young children, and the short-term unemployed—are considered deserving of assistance, largely because the administration (and most of the public) believes that these groups should not be expected to work. Excluded from the safety net are those who can work but whose earnings still leave them with chronically or temporarily inadequate incomes. This group has had its assistance radically cut or eliminated. The Food Stamp program, for example—a close substitute for a broad-based income support system—has been cut substantially; and AFDC benefits for working mothers have been virtually eliminated.

At a programmatic level, these shifts express a New Deal concept of "the deserving poor" and reject the expanded objectives of the 1960s War on Poverty. At a more philosophical level, they involve a retreat from egalitarian values that had attracted growing and often bipartisan support over the past twenty years. As the president's 1982 *Economic Report* notes, one of the administration's basic tenets is that "income redistribution is not a compelling justification in the 1980s for Federal taxing and spending programs."[2] Some people may reject this basic tenet, but others may support the administration for one of two reasons. First, they may feel that the battle against poverty and inequality has gone too far in principle. Second, they may believe that government tax and income security programs reduce incentives to work and save, thereby sapping individual resourcefulness and the vitality of the economy.

The latter view has been a continuing theme in presidential statements. Few would argue that government taxes and spending do not affect people's behavior, but the magnitude and significance of these effects are disputed. For the most part, research suggests that the changes in tax and income security programs advocated by the president will not have substantial aggregate behavioral effects. Moreover, even if they do, many people still feel that a little less efficiency is a price worth paying for a little more economic security. To achieve its goals of reducing government expenditures and improving economic growth, it was not essential for the administration to propose spending and tax changes calling for disproportionate sacrifices on the part of the poor. By doing so, the president has opened himself to the criticism that his policies are unfair.

The successful implementation of the Reagan counterrevolution will require much deeper cuts in government expenditures and a turnback of responsibilities to state and local governments as proposed under the president's New Federalism. The extent to which this will be achieved is unclear. It will depend in part on whether the administration can command public support in the face of a weakened economy.

The Reagan Government

Responsible governance at the federal level entails a careful sorting of good from bad policies. This sorting requires more than ideology or a set of principles, though these are essential. It also must be based on two other factors—an understanding of the problems and the effectiveness of current and proposed policies in dealing with them, and improvement in the design and administration of whatever policies the federal government chooses to support.

The Reagan administration has put forth some new ideas and has already implemented significant changes in program structure. Many more changes are on the administration's agenda or will be thrust upon it by events. It is too soon to determine the extent to which these program reforms will lead to a more effective federal government. However, the way in which the administration attends to these programmatic concerns will determine the extent to which it leaves behind a better government than the one it inherited. A few examples will illustrate this point.

First and most importantly, there is now a long-term imbalance in the federal budget. Currently projected deficits will not disappear without radical surgery. Whether the administration and the Congress choose to operate on taxes, on the defense budget, on middle-class entitlements, or (as seems likely) on all three, they will have to make tough choices about the shape and not just the size of these changes. Achievable savings from reductions in waste, fraud, and abuse cannot fill more than a fraction of the need.

On the expenditure side, Social Security and Medicare are currently projected to account for about two-thirds of the growth in nondefense program expenditures between now and 1987. Thus far, the administration has focused on short-term budgetary savings and has done little to come to grips with the role that these two programs might play in any effort to restrain long-term spending growth. It mishandled its initial opportunity to achieve reform of the Social Security system when it advanced a proposal that was neither well-formulated nor politically realistic. As a result, Social Security became an even more highly politicized issue, and the prospects for timely, constructive reform were diminished.

The major factor driving Medicare expenditures is health care cost inflation. The administration has yet to address this problem. Congress currently is being forced to take the lead in Medicare reimbursement reform even though it is not well-suited to formulate the kind of complex policy change that will be necessary.

On the tax front, ERTA was devoted to reducing personal and business tax rates without any broadening of the tax base. Combining base broadening with rate reduction is usually the best way to overcome political opposition to loophole closing. By divorcing rate reductions from loophole closing, the administration lost an opportunity to improve the tax system. However, this obviously speeded passage of the bill, and the fact that the administration and various members of Congress have now expressed interest in some form of a "flat tax" suggests that structural reforms may yet be advanced.

So far, structural reform has generally taken a back seat to enactment of the Program for Economic Recovery. The administration has argued—quite correctly—that economic recovery and long-term growth are important prerequisites to achieving other goals. However, the design of its tax, expenditure, and regulatory proposals has not always been consistent with its economic growth objectives. Programs aimed at developing human resources (education, training, and social services) and improving public infrastructure (highways, mass transit, and economic development) were disproportionately cut rather than maintained or reformed. Three-quarters of the tax relief under ERTA was allocated to individuals rather than to businesses, thereby encouraging consumption relatively more than investment. Tax rates were cut, but little was done to change provisions that divert resources from productive activities and lead to inefficient decisions. Regulations have been curbed, but because these changes were accomplished administratively and not through legislation, the regulatory environment remains uncertain.

Conclusion

The Reagan administration's goals are clear. Its strategies are still evolving. An administration that is less than two years old has time to rethink and refine its strategies. The current one appears to be involved in just such an exercise, although concerns about appearing inconsistent may have slowed the process or kept much of it from public view.

The success of the Reagan government in leaving behind a more effective set of programs and policies than it inherited—in areas where there is a continuing federal role—will depend largely on how effectively it deals with the many needs for structural reform. The Reagan experiment with economic policy has clearly not worked in the short run and is unlikely to live up to the administration's expectations for the long run. The Reagan counterrevolution in social and economic policy is potentially profound but still in its infancy.

However, the already enacted changes in taxes and spending are substantial. And they, in combination with deficits and other consequences of the economy's poor performance, are requiring major adjustments by individuals, institutions, and all levels of government. Thus, even if the economic experiment is altered or the counterrevolution proceeds no further, their legacy will extend well beyond President Reagan's term in office.

PART ONE

THE PROGRAM FOR ECONOMIC RECOVERY

Chapter 2

ECONOMIC POLICY

Isabel V. Sawhill

The economy performed poorly during the decade of the 1970s. There was too much inflation and too little productivity growth. The reasons for this poor performance have been a source of disagreement among economists, but by the end of the decade the public had tired of complex explanations and was looking for fresh ideas and new leadership.

Ronald Reagan responded to this need. He rejected the conventional view that a country cannot have price stability and full employment at the same time and rallied the voters around a new vision of national prosperity with benefits for rich and poor alike. The success of his administration will be judged largely on its ability to deliver on these promises—or at least to do better than its predecessors.

[The author wishes to thank Nancy Barrett, Peter Clark, Frank de Leeuw, Lawrence Klein, Patrick O'Keefe, Van Ooms, Robert Solow, Herbert Stein, and her colleagues at The Urban Institute for their comments on a previous draft. She also benefited from the reactions of participants at a conference sponsored by the Institute and the National Academy of Sciences in June 1982. Comments from Barry Bosworth and Robert J. Gordon were especially useful. Martin Anderson and Otto Eckstein provided fresh perspectives on the issue of uncertainty in economic forecasts.]

The president's economic objectives—to curb inflation, reduce unemployment, and improve productivity growth—were similar to those which any administration would have placed high on the nation's agenda in 1981. But the proposed strategy for achieving these objectives—a four-point program of budget, tax, regulatory, and monetary policies—was an unconventional mixture of monetarist doctrines and untested supply side theories.

It was supply side theory that provided the stated rationale for the tax cut of 1981. The purpose of the tax cut is to increase savings, investment, and work effort and to revive the economy's lagging rate of growth. Thus far, its major effect has been to produce unexpectedly large deficits.

Less visible, but of far greater significance for understanding recent economic events, is the more orthodox part of the package: a monetary policy designed to reduce inflation. It is monetary and not fiscal policy that is responsible for both the current recession and some of the recent progress in bringing inflation under control. It may also explain why interest rates are so high.

In its examination of current economic policy, this chapter begins with a brief review of recent economic trends and then describes the administration's "Program for Economic Recovery." It examines the performance of the economy during 1981 and early 1982 after the new policies were put in place. Finally, it analyzes the administration's monetary and fiscal policies, giving particular attention to the impact of monetary restraint on inflation and the effects of large budget deficits on the economy. More detailed descriptions of the administration's budget, tax, and regulatory policies are included in the next three chapters.

It is too soon to judge the impact of the president's program on the economy's long-term growth. So far, the public has exhibited a remarkable willingness to pay the short-run costs associated with a recession and high interest rates in the hope that long-term improvement in the economy's performance will result. The public needs to know when these benefits will materialize and what their likely magnitude will be. Some of the possible long-term benefits from the 1981 tax cut are given greater attention in chapter 4.

The Legacy of the 1970s

It is important to understand the economic situation that the current administration inherited when it took office in 1981. Accordingly, this section provides a brief review of economic developments during the 1970s and of current disagreements among economists about the reasons for the generally poor performance of the economy.

A Retrospective View of the Problems

The 1970s were a decade of unprecedented peacetime inflation. They were also a period of high unemployment and slow productivity growth. But despite these problems, the average citizen was substantially better off at the end than at the beginning of the decade. The most salient facts about the decade may be summarized as follows (table 2-1):

- As measured by the Consumer Price Index (CPI), the price level more than doubled over the decade. This was about four times as large an increase as occurred during the 1950s and 1960s.

- After adjustment for inflation, total output (and income) increased by 36 percent, substantially less than during the 1960s but about equal to the record for the 1950s.

- The relatively satisfactory rate of growth in output was achieved, in part, because of a dramatic increase in employment over the decade of the 1970s, reflecting a large influx of women and youth into the labor force. At the same time, productivity, or output per hour worked, grew at less than half the rate experienced during the 1950s and 1960s, and real earnings per worker grew at an equally slow pace.

- Unemployment rates averaged 6.2 percent for the decade compared to 4.5 percent in the 1950s and 4.8 percent in the 1960s. Some of this increase may have been related to the changing composition of the labor force, but even among adult males the unemployment rate was substantially higher than it had been during the two prior decades. In part, this was because the economy experienced considerable cyclical instability over the decade. However, periodic recessions and high unemployment did little to moderate the rate of inflation, which became higher and higher at each cyclical peak.

- In spite of high rates of inflation and unemployment, most people's incomes kept pace with rising prices. Moreover, as a result of smaller families and a higher proportion of the adult population at work (58.5 percent in 1980 vs. 56.1 percent in 1970), by the end of the decade the average citizen was substantially better off in strictly economic terms.[1] On an inflation-adjusted basis, after-tax income per person grew by 23 percent during the 1970s compared to 35 percent during the 1960s and 15 percent during the 1950s.

In short, it was not a bad ten years when put in historical perspective. But there were a number of economic problems that became more serious as the decade progressed. These included inflation, unemployment, and declining productivity growth.

TABLE 2–1

PERFORMANCE OF THE ECONOMY BY DECADE

	1950s	1960s	1970s
Inflation (percentage increase in the CPI)	20	31	112
Growth (percentage increase in real GNP)	38	49	36
Productivity (percentage increase in output per hour in private business sector)	32	33	15
Employment (percentage increase in number employed)	11	20	27
Unemployment (average rate for all workers)	4.5	4.8	6.2
Unemployment (average rate for adult males)	3.9	3.6	4.5
Standard of living (percentage increase in per capita real disposable personal income)	15	35	23

SOURCE: *Economic Report of the President* (Washington, D.C.: Government Printing Office (GPO), 1982), tables B-52 (p. 291), B-2 (p. 234), B-40 (p. 278), B-30 (p. 268), B-31 (p. 269), B-24 (p. 261).

NOTE: Decade increases calculated from three-year averages centered on 1950, 1960, 1970, and 1980.

Competing Economic Theories and Explanations for Stagflation

Within the economics profession, currently there are two competing theories of how the economy works. Each leads to a different interpretation of the events of the 1970s.

The first, the neo-Keynesian view, stresses that wages and prices do not respond quickly and fully to changes in demand and supply and that, as a result, shortages or surpluses of goods and labor can accumulate over protracted periods. The most egregious surplus occurs when there are more people looking for work than there are jobs available. While flexible wages should eliminate any involuntary unemployment, there are various factors that make such adjustments (especially downward adjustments) unlikely. These include long-term wage contracts, the fixed costs involved in hiring and training employees, equity-based pay practices, the knowledge that the government is committed to reducing unemployment, and the availability of income support for the unemployed. These impediments to wage and price flexibility, it is argued, make it very costly to reduce inflation using demand restraint alone and make wage-price controls or some other type of incomes policy appear quite attractive.[2]

The neo-Keynesians recognize that there were periods during the 1970s (such as 1972-1973) when demand was excessive enough to create inflationary pressures, but they give considerably more weight to the role of oil, food, and other "supply shocks" in ratcheting up the rate of inflation over the decade.[3] In a world of "sticky" wages and prices, a rise in prices in one sector of the economy is not necessarily offset by declines in other sectors. Thus, the price shocks which occurred in 1973-1974, and again in 1979-1980, added directly to inflation, and through their effects on cost-of-living adjustments, expectations, and the economy's cost structure became part of the ongoing wage-price spiral. Moreover, because higher prices placed a drain on consumer purchasing power not compensated for by a more relaxed monetary policy, the economy entered a recession after each "supply shock" episode (in 1974-1975 and again in 1980).

This explanation of stagflation can be contrasted with a second view of the world, that held by mainstream monetarists. This group puts greater faith in the ability of markets to adjust to demand-supply imbalances without causing inflation and unemployment. Instead, it is policy errors that bear the major responsibility for the legacy of stagflation.[4] The argument is that continual attempts to stimulate the economy have had no permanent effects on output or employment but have served to increase the inflation rate over the decade.

According to this view, a government-induced increase in total spending may initially bid up prices faster than wage rates, lowering real wages and encouraging businesses to expand in response to higher profits. But once workers realize that, as a result of inflation, they are less well off than before, they demand more compensation. Thus, labor costs rise again, making it impossible to sustain the initial gains in output and employment but leaving a permanently higher wage-price spiral in their wake.

Those who accept this diagnosis of the problem believe that the solution is for the government to avoid "stop-go" monetary and fiscal policies. They believe that most unemployment is voluntary and that the inflation of the 1970s was due to excessive growth of the money supply.

To summarize, the neo-Keynesians believe that the market is the problem (because wages and prices are inflexible) and that the government should be part of the solution. The mainstream monetarists believe that the government is the problem (because it creates too much money) and that more reliance on the market is the primary solution. At present, both sets of views have a respectable following within the economics profession.

Like most conservatives, many members of the Reagan administration subscribed to a monetarist view of the world and firmly rejected an activist "Keynesian" policy. However, as we shall see, they grafted onto this mainstream monetarist model not only some less orthodox supply side theories but also a more extreme version of monetarism which emphasizes the possibility of radically revising people's expectations. This latter theory is called "rational expectations."

The supply side plank was primarily a response to the productivity problem.[5] Even more than high rates of inflation and unemployment, lagging productivity growth remains a phenomenon in search of an explanation. In spite of much careful research, there is no real consensus about the relative importance of different factors in explaining the recent slowdown in productivity growth. One economist has constructed an "average opinion" about the causes of the slowdown, based on a large number of studies, each of which tends to single out one or two specific explanations for the problem.[6] In this synthesis, 14 percent of the blame for the post-1973 slowdown is assigned to slower capital formation, 5 percent of the blame goes to the shifting mix of the labor force, 9 percent to rising energy costs, 9 percent to increased regulation of business, 5 percent to a reduction in research and development activity, and 14 percent to sectoral shifts in economic activity. This leaves almost half (44 percent) of the slowdown unexplained.

Challenge for the 1980s

It was these problems of double-digit inflation, high unemployment, and lagging productivity growth that President Reagan faced when he took office in early 1981. As the foregoing review indicates, the problems are serious. At the same time, they are poorly understood. Economists have become increasingly embroiled in doctrinal disputes in recent years, and some have made extravagant claims for their own views. But most are genuinely puzzled by one or more aspects of recent economic history and cautious about prescribing simple remedies. Not surprisingly, the public has become increasingly confused and ready to respond to new leadership. Thus, the time was ripe in 1981 for a new experiment in economic policy.

The Administration's Economic Strategy

The new administration's economic program, as announced on February 18, 1981, called for a fundamental shift in the role of government in the economy that included a major reduction in personal and business taxes, a much lower rate of growth in federal spending, a program of regulatory reform and relief, and a new commitment to a stable monetary policy.

This section addresses two questions relating to these proposals:

- How are they supposed to work to solve the problems of inflation, unemployment, and slow growth?

- What were their anticipated results as embedded in the administration's economic forecasts?

Rationale

The administration's economic strategy rests solidly on the premise that individual initiative and unfettered markets will produce the best possible outcomes.[7] While unregulated markets do not always produce completely satisfactory results, these results may be the best that are achievable. Thus, the four elements in the Reagan plan are all designed to reduce the role of government in economic life.

Beyond being held together by a certain amount of libertarian glue, the proposals are based on an odd blending of supply side, monetarist, and rational expectations views. To be sure, the relative emphasis given to each has varied somewhat among different administration officials and has shifted over time.

The newest and most controversial ingredient in the package is the supply side view, which President Reagan adopted during his campaign and appears to continue to support.[8] Supply side economics emphasizes the role of relative prices in providing incentives for individuals to engage in various activities. A cut in marginal tax rates increases the fraction of each dollar of extra wage or interest income that taxpayers can keep and thus the reward for working or for saving. Similarly, more generous depreciation allowances and other tax breaks provide incentives for greater business investment. In addition, lower tax rates should stem the flow of resources into relatively unproductive tax shelters. These ideas have a respectable intellectual history and are not a matter of dispute among most economists. It is the postulated speed and magnitude of supply side effects that are controversial.

A tax-induced rise in savings, investment, and work effort is expected to stimulate a high rate of economic growth. It is argued that such growth need not be inflationary as long as any resulting budget deficits are not financed by the creation of new money, and that growth may actually lower inflation if unit labor costs fall in response to higher productivity. One extreme view (usually attributed to Arthur Laffer) is that the tax cuts can be self-financing. A less extreme position assumes that the increased revenues resulting from a higher level of economic activity will help to reduce the deficit and that a larger volume of savings—induced by lower marginal tax rates at every level of income—will be available to finance some portion of the remaining deficit. The proposed reduction in government expenditures also serves to contain the deficit.

While the supply side tax cuts are expected to release the long-term productive potential of the economy, monetary restraint is expected to restore price stability. The monetarists believe that a steady reduction in money supply growth is the best way to bring down the existing rate of inflation. Most doubt that this can be done quickly or without an interim period of slow growth and high unemployment. However, these transition costs can be reduced if businessmen, workers, and investors are quickly persuaded that the government is firmly committed to its current campaign against inflation, and that they can therefore afford to accept lower prices, wages, and interest rates. Once this occurs, more of the reduced money growth can support increased output and employment in place of continued inflation.

To effect a less painful transition, it is essential to establish the credibility of the policy and to change people's expectations as rapidly as possible. Once people understand that the rules of the economic game have changed—that government will no longer increase spending to bail out failing companies or provide jobs for unemployed workers—then businesses will restrain prices and workers will moderate their wage demands to avoid these unpleasant consequences. These psychological considerations underscore the importance of establishing firm monetary targets, of putting a multiyear tax cut in place immediately, and of not retreating from these policies at the first sign of trouble.[9] If expectations do not adjust quickly and a recession intervenes, then patience, and not a shift in policy, is required. Consistency is part of the strategy, and it is long-term results that count.

In summary, the administration's program is based on the supply side idea that one can increase growth by reducing taxes (and removing burdensome regulation), the monetarist view that one can curb inflation by a steady reduction in money growth, and the rational expectations view that a change in the policy rules can cause this disinflation to occur rapidly.

It is interesting to speculate about why the administration chose this particular mix of policies rather than adhering to the mainstream monetarist and "balance-the-budget" ideas that have traditionally guided Republican administrations. The answer may lie in the political salability of a policy mix that promises less inflation, more employment, and higher growth—all at the same time—and thereby avoids the need to explicitly address the tough trade-offs among these goals that most economists believe exist, at least in the short run. But this raises questions about whether this experiment with a new policy mix will work. Moreover, if it should fail, public confidence in government's ability to deal with the country's economic problems might be further damaged.

Anticipated Results

Like many administrations, the current one began with rosy predictions of what its economic program would accomplish. On February 18, 1981 in presenting the proposals to Congress, the president stated:

If enacted in full, this program can help America create 13 million new jobs, nearly 3 million more than we would have without these measures.[10]

And on March 10, 1981 in a second message to Congress, he noted:

Our tax proposal will, if enacted, have an immediate impact on the economic vitality of the nation, where even a slight improvement can produce dramatic results. For example, a 2 percent increase in economic growth will add $60 billion to our GNP in one year alone.[11]

Finally, on July 27, 1981, in a televised speech, the president said:

For 19 out of the last 20 years, the federal government has spent more than it took in. There will be another large deficit in this present year which ends September 30th. But with our program in place, it won't be quite as big as it might have been and starting next year, the deficits will get smaller until in just a few years the budget can be balanced.

He went on to note that the program was already beginning to have positive results:

The rate of inflation is no longer in double-digit figures. The dollar has regained strength in the international money markets and businessmen and investors are making decisions with regard to industrial development, modernization and expansion, all of this based on anticipation of our program being adopted and put into operation.[12]

A certain amount of rhetorical overstatement is standard fare in presidential speech making, but this president was more skillful than most in using his persuasive powers to rally public support for his program. By late February 1981, 71 percent of those responding to an Associated Press/ NBC News poll were in favor of cutting federal income tax rates 10 percent a year for three years—a much higher proportion than just a few months earlier;[13] and in August 1981, most of what the president had proposed was enacted. (More details on the 1981 budget and tax legislation are included in chapters 3 and 4.)

A more precise and closely watched indicator of what an administration hopes to accomplish is its own economic forecasts. These, too, often tend to be overly optimistic, but this administration's forecasts have been more controversial than most.

The initial Office of Management and Budget model runs, prepared early in 1981, showed that the president's program would produce deficits ranging from $82 billion in 1982 to $116 billion in 1984. Budget Director Stockman rejected these conventional estimates as "absurdities" and turned to outside sources for help in preparing a set of projections that would more adequately reflect the administration's supply side perspective. He predicted these new projections would "set off a wide-open debate on how the economy works, a great battle over the conventional theories of economic performance."[14]

This 1981 battle over economic assumptions was followed by a second one in early 1982 as the president's first regular budget and economic reports were prepared and submitted to the Congress. In his State of the Union address on January 26, 1982, the president made clear that he had little confidence in any of the numbers, that "there are too many imponderables for anyone to predict deficits or surpluses several years ahead with any degree of accuracy." In fact, long-term forecasts have usually turned out to be highly inaccurate although short-term forecasts (over one to two years) have a somewhat better record of performance.[15] However, the range of uncertainty around the numbers is large. It has been estimated, for example, that the average annual federal deficit for fiscal years 1982-1984 could range between $97 billion and $170 billion because of "normal" forecasting errors.[16]

Whether accurate or not, such forecasts are required by law and their implications for outlay and revenue projections and the size of the deficit tend to overwhelm the effects of policy changes that are under administration or congressional control. For example, changes in economic assumptions between March 1981 and February 1982 increased the administration's forecast of the 1982 deficit by $56.9 billion (from $42.7 to $98.6 billion).

One factor motivating any administration to make optimistic predictions, but especially an administration concerned with the psychology of the marketplace, is the fear that the release of bad news will unsettle financial markets and subvert the achievement of its goals. But, this strategy trades off a possible short-term improvement in expectations for a long-term reduction in credibility, and if the short-term benefits fail to materialize, it can turn out to be quite costly, both politically and economically. The 1981 tax cut, for example, which was based on 1981's economic projections, is largely responsible for the deficits anticipated over the next several years. These deficits, in turn, have created enormous political difficulties for the 1982 Congress and threatened to derail the budget process.

Table 2-2 presents the administration's projections for 1981-1984 and indicates how the forecast has varied as new information has become available.[17] The table indicates the following:

- In early 1981, the administration was predicting modest growth and only a slight decline in inflation for the year. The economy ended up performing more poorly than expected on the growth front and better than expected on the inflation front.

- In early 1982, the administration revised its earlier forecast. The downward revisions in growth rates for 1982 are more consistent with the Federal Reserve's tight monetary policy, but total spending is still predicted to be higher than in 1981. As already noted, the

TABLE 2-2

THE ADMINISTRATION'S ECONOMIC FORECASTS

	Actual		Forecast										
			1981		1982			1983			1984		
	1980	1981	3/81	7/81	3/81	7/81	2/82	3/81	7/81	2/82	3/81	7/81	2/82
Percentage change, 4th quarter over 4th quarter													
Nominal GNP	9.4	9.3	11.0	11.8	13.3	12.9	10.4	11.8	11.8	11.0	10.1	10.1	10.0
Real GNP (1972 dollars)	-0.3	0.7	1.4	2.5	5.2	5.2	3.0	4.9	4.6	5.2	4.5	4.5	4.9
GNP deflator	9.8	8.6	9.5	9.1	7.7	7.3	7.2	6.6	6.9	5.5	5.7	5.5	4.9
CPI	12.6	9.4	10.5	8.6	7.2	6.2	6.6	6.0	5.6	5.1	5.1	4.8	4.7
Level													
Unemployment rate													
Annual average	7.1	7.6	7.8	7.5	7.2	7.3	8.9	6.6	6.6	7.9	6.4	6.2	7.1
4th quarter	7.5	8.4	7.7	7.7	7.0	7.0	8.4	6.5	6.5	7.6	6.3	6.2	6.8
Interest rate, 91-day													
Treasury bills	11.5	14.1	11.1	13.6	8.9	10.5	11.7	7.8	7.5	10.5	7.0	6.8	9.5
Budget deficit (−) or surplus													
Billions of dollars	−60	−76	−55	−56	−45	−43	−99	−23	−23	−92	+1	+1	−83
Percentage of GNP	2.3	2.6	1.9	1.9	1.4	1.3	3.1	0.6	0.6	2.6	a	a	2.1

SOURCE: Office of Management and Budget, *Fiscal Year 1982 Budget Revisions* (Washington, D.C.: GPO, March 1981); Office of Management and Budget, *Mid-Session Review of the 1982 Budget* (Washington, D.C.: GPO, July 1981); Office of Management and Budget, *Budget of the United States Government, Fiscal Year 1983* (Washington, D.C.: GPO, February 1982).

a. Less than 0.05 percent.

change in economic assumptions between March 1981 and Febuary 1982 increased the projected 1982 deficit by about $57 billion.

- During 1982, unemployment is expected to average close to 9 percent for the year as a whole but to fall to 8.4 percent by the last quarter. Interest rates are expected to fall in line with inflation and to be about 2.5 percentage points lower than in 1981.

- For 1983 and 1984, dollar GNP growth is assumed to remain in the 10 to 11 percent range with an increasing proportion of total spending going to support greater output growth rather than rising prices. By 1984, the inflation rate is expected to subside to about 5 percent while real GNP growth is also predicted to be about 5 percent. The unemployment rate drops substantially but remains in the neighborhood of 7 percent. The 1984 deficit remains above $80 billion or 2.1 percent of GNP.

All in all, it is an optimistic set of projections.

Early Reactions

The response of most economists and Wall Street experts to the administration's economic plan and to the early forecasts of its predicted effects was one of skepticism.[18] After enactment of the spending and tax bills in the summer, financial markets failed to respond positively. Between passage of the tax bill and Labor Day, the stock market fell precipitously and long-term bond rates moved up. These developments suggested that the desired revision of expectations was not taking place as quickly as had been hoped. On October 1, 1981, the *Wall Street Journal*, long a supporter of the "new economics," observed editorially that "the expectational effect has not materialized." During the same week, Norman B. Ture, Treasury under secretary for economic and tax affairs, was quoted as saying, "If there's been any major disappointment, it's been the failure of the financial markets to revise their expectations."[19] It was becoming increasingly clear to the administration that expectations would only change in response to real economic events, not because of mere announcements of policy shifts or even legislative successes. As the 1982 *Economic Report of the President* stated, "Credibility must be earned by performance."[20]

At the same time, the Federal Reserve maintained a tight rein over the money supply through 1981 and ended up undershooting its own targets. The most closely watched measure of the money supply grew by only 2.3 percent over the year, well under the targeted range of 3.5 to 6.0 percent. While a call for a gradual reduction in monetary growth had been part of the Program for Economic Recovery, this degree of restraint was somewhat greater than the administration had wanted.[21] Minor disagreements aside, the general result was quite predictable. Because inflationary expectations and behavior had not been eliminated, all of the small rise in total money spending permitted by the Federal Reserve went to accommodate the continued rise in wages and prices with little left over to support an expansion of output and employment. Thus, the economy entered a recession in July 1981. Real output, which had been expanding somewhat erratically since the last recession had ended in the middle of 1980, plummeted toward the end of the year; and the unemployment rate which had been in the neighborhood of 7 to 7.5 percent through most of this same period rose sharply to 8.3 percent in the fourth quarter, a harbinger of still higher rates to come (table 2-3).

The fact that the promised expansion failed to occur raised questions about the speed and magnitude of the hoped for supply side effects. While the cuts in personal tax rates did not go into effect until October, the business tax cuts were retroactive to January 1, 1981. However, with utilization of existing plant and equipment running far below normal levels, and long-term interest rates hanging high, business investment plans remained sluggish. In early 1982, nonfarm businesses reported that they planned to decrease expenditures on new plant and equipment (adjusted for inflation) for the year as a whole. Subsequent quarterly surveys have shown further downward adjustments in business investment plans.

If it was predictable that tight monetary policy would produce a recession in the absence of a sharp revision in expectations or a supply side miracle, it was equally predictable that a recession would help to bring down the rate of inflation. After rising by 10.9 percent between the third quarter of 1980 and the third quarter of 1981, the Consumer Price Index (CPI) increased at an annual rate of 7.7 percent in the fourth quarter of 1981 and has continued to fall erratically since that time. Some of the good news was related to what was happening to food and energy prices, but the gains were broader than this and suggested that the monetary plank of the administration's program was working well. (A more detailed discussion of recent wage and price developments will be found in this chapter under "Monetary Restraint and Inflation.") The Federal Reserve's commitment to bring inflation under control through a gradual deceleration of the money supply predates the current administration and has helped to keep the economy soft, at least since early 1980. However, its resolve was undoubtedly strengthened by the current administration's endorsement of an antiinflationary monetary policy.

The combination of recession and lower inflation has had another result: much larger deficits than originally anticipated. While large deficits would persist under current law even if the economy were to stay on a high-em-

TABLE 2–3

SELECTED ECONOMIC INDICATORS, 1970–1982

	Annual Average			Quarterly Data[a]					
	1970–1979	1980	1981	1981:I	1981:II	1981:III	1981:IV	1982:I	1982:II
Percentage change in GNP (1972 dollars)	3.2	–0.4	1.9	7.9	–1.5	2.2	–5.3	–5.1	1.7
Unemployment rate (all workers)	6.2	7.1	7.6	7.4	7.4	7.4	8.3	8.8	9.5
Capacity utilization rate in manufacturing	81.7	79.1	78.5	79.9	79.8	79.3	74.8	71.6	70.3
Aaa corporate bond yields	8.2	11.9	14.2	13.2	14.0	14.9	14.6	15.0	14.5
Percentage change in expenditures for new plant and equipment, nonfarm business (1972 dollars)	3.4	0.8	0.0	11.6	–6.4	7.7	–8.5	–2.0	–9.4[b]
Percentage change in Consumer Price Index (all urban consumers)	7.1	13.5	10.4	11.0	7.8	11.8	7.7	3.2	4.6
Percentage change in per capita disposable personal income (1972 dollars)	2.4	–0.9	1.5	2.9	–0.3	3.4	0.2	–2.8	2.3

SOURCE: *Economic Report of the President*, 1982; Bureau of Labor Statistics; and Federal Reserve Board.
a. All quarterly figures are seasonally adjusted. Percentage changes are calculated from the preceding period and then annualized.
b. Planned.

ployment growth path, poor economic performance has greatly exacerbated the problem. These deficits, in turn, have unsettled financial markets and are believed by many to be one reason long-term interest rates have not declined. Whatever their cause, high interest rates could choke off any revival of growth after the 1981-1982 recession has run its course.

High interest rates are not only retarding recovery at home but also stifling the world economy as other countries are forced to deflate in concert with the United States to defend the value of their currencies. The resulting slowdown in growth rates among developed countries has helped to reduce oil and other commodity prices, but it has also put the industrialized nations on a dangerous path toward worldwide slump and renewed protectionism.

It is these gloomy forecasts for both domestic and worldwide recovery that have focused attention on the problem of high interest rates in the United States. While rates have come down since early 1981, they have not declined as much as inflation, leaving real rates at historically high levels. Some observers believe that progress in eliminating future deficits, by calming fears of excessive public borrowing and inflation, will bring rates down. Others believe that it is a combination of tight monetary policy, the volatility of rates associated with the Federal Reserve's post-1979 policy of targeting on the money supply, and financial deregulation that are more responsible for the current situation. If they are right, then reducing deficits will not necessarily bring down interest rates; a shift in monetary policy will be needed as well. Still another possibility is that real interest rates are high because people have not yet adjusted to the fact that inflation has declined. In this case, it is only a matter of time until rates come down, and no shift in policy is necessarily required. The extent to which each of these explanations for high interest rates is correct is simply not known.

In sum, the administration's record to date is a mixed one. On the one hand, the rate of inflation has been substantially reduced. On the other, the economy has been depressed with unemployment and interest rates at postwar highs. By the end of 1981, the average citizen was a little better off than at the beginning of the year, although per capita income (after adjustment for inflation and taxes) did not grow as rapidly as during the 1970s (table 2-3).

Continued progress on the inflation front should permit an increasing proportion of total spending to support an expansion of output and employment, helping to revive the economy. Thus, a critical factor will be the speed with which the process of disinflation occurs, with further progress largely dependent on what happens to wages. A continued deceleration of prices to a basic rate of 3 or 4 percent a year would permit a healthy rate of real growth even within the context of current restraints on the growth of the money supply.

At the same time, the prospects of large deficits in combination with continued monetary restraint have put fiscal and monetary policy on a collision course with potentially serious consequences for real interest rates and credit-sensitive sectors of the economy. The implications for both the strength of the short-term recovery and long-term growth are still unclear but do not seem particularly promising. Much will depend on the success of White House and congressional actions to bring the budget under control and the Federal Reserve's willingness to finance an expansion in the face of continuing concerns about inflation. It is worth emphasizing that all three will be involved in determining the fate of the economy. The critical nature of the Federal Reserve's role, in particular, is not well appreciated by the general public.

This preliminary assessment raises a number of issues which need to be addressed in greater detail. First, how effective is monetary restraint in bringing inflation under control, and what costs does this impose on the economy? Second, what are the implications of the large deficits currently projected for the next few years? Third, granted that the supply side tax cuts have not had much visible impact to date, what is the expected long-term response to these measures? And fourth, how is the program of regulatory relief likely to affect the economy?

The remainder of this chapter addresses the first two of these issues. The effects of the supply side tax cuts and the program of regulatory relief are likely to be longer term and are thus more difficult to assess at this time. However, further discussion of each of these issues is included in chapters 4 and 5 of this volume.

Monetary Restraint and Inflation

Stripped of its supply side mantle, the administration's economic policy rests on the traditional monetarist view that reducing inflation requires a reduction in the rate of growth of the money supply to a level consistent with the economy's long-term, noninflationary growth path.

A number of issues arise in attempting to evaluate such a policy including (1) the extent to which the Federal Reserve will be diverted from this mission by the need to pursue other objectives, such as reducing unemployment or financing the government's debt; (2) the Federal Reserve's ability to control the money supply, and the link between the money supply and total spending on goods and services; and (3) the time it will take for a reduction in total spending to translate into a drop in the rate of inflation, the role expectations play in this process, and the costs imposed on the economy in the interim.

After a brief discussion of each of these topics, this section concludes with a review of recent progress in bringing inflation under control.

Federal Reserve Objectives

Both the administration and the Federal Reserve are in favor of using monetary policy to effect a rather rapid reduction in inflation—what one economist has called "gradualism with perceptible speed."[22] However, the administration has occasionally criticized the Federal Reserve for not implementing this policy more smoothly and consistently and for decelerating money supply growth even faster than the administration had planned.[23]

On the other hand, using monetary policy for short-run stabilization purposes is firmly rejected.[24] While this is usually put in terms of the failures of "fine tuning" and the administration's determination not to repeat the mistakes of the past, it appears that "gross tuning" is rejected as well. Thus, no adjustment of monetary policy in response to the 1981-1982 recession was contemplated in spite of the fact that real interest rates and unemployment exceeded their postwar peaks. Presumably this benign neglect is related to the monetarists' commitment to reduce inflation at whatever cost and their concern about reigniting inflationary expectations and not just to their dislike of interventionist policies.

The Federal Reserve's policy stance has led to considerable frustration among those who believe that the policy's negative side effects—high interest rates, an overvalued dollar, and sluggish growth at home and abroad—are an excessive price to pay in the battle against inflation. For example, the Chairman of the Joint Economic Committee, Henry Reuss, has called for a binding congressional resolution instructing the Federal Reserve to return to the money targets implied by the original Program for Economic Recovery and asking it to meet these less stringent targets on a two-year rather than an annual basis.[25] Western European leaders, credit-sensitive industries, homeowners, farmers, and small businessmen also tend to favor a relaxation of monetary policy. Whether the Federal Reserve can resist these pressures remains to be seen.

Concern that the Federal Reserve will be diverted from the long-term objective of reducing inflation by the need to respond to these pressures has resurrected some of the old arguments about "rules vs. discretion" in monetary policy. The ultimate "rule" would be a return to some form of the gold standard, tying the currency to the supply of this asset and attempting to eliminate any scope for human decision making. Short of this a constitutionally or statutorily based rule could be imposed on the Federal Reserve. Both of these options are discussed in the 1982 *Economic Report of the President* and rejected in favor of a steady, noninflationary rate of growth in the money supply.[26] But just as seemingly uncontrollable deficits have brought renewed calls for a balanced budget amendment, fears that the Federal Reserve will "monetize" the deficit may keep such ideas alive even though they have little following among economists.

Money and Spending

The Federal Reserve cannot directly control the rate of inflation or, for that matter, the level of total spending in the economy (that is, nominal GNP). What the Federal Reserve can control is the reserves supplied to the banking system through its own purchases and sales of government securities and the amount of reserves it requires banks to hold against their deposits (which together make up what is called "the adjusted monetary base"). To a much lesser extent, it can also control the money supply—especially "narrower" forms of money such as M-1 (which includes currency plus checkable deposits) as opposed to "broader" forms such as M-3 (which includes, in addition, savings accounts, money market mutual fund shares, repurchase agreements, and time deposits).

Whether changes in the money supply then translate into a predictable change in total spending depends on what is happening to money velocity— the number of times each dollar is used during a year to support final expenditures by individuals and businesses. Between 1975 and 1981, M-1 velocity increased at an average rate of 3.6 percent a year but with considerable year-to-year variation around the average. These increases in money turnover are the result of the generally high interest rates that prevailed during this period and of new financial instruments and practices. Both have encouraged or enabled businesses and households to economize on their cash balances.

A number of economists view this ability of the public to use the existing money supply more or less intensively as a serious flaw in the monetarist prescription for controlling inflation.[27] They argue that financial and nonfinancial institutions invent new forms of money almost as fast as the Federal Reserve brings old forms under control. Money market mutual funds, for example, which are offered by nondepository institutions (e.g., stockbrokers) and thus are not subject to Federal Reserve control, grew from a value of $4 billion in December 1975 to $185 billion in December 1981. These innovations mean that the Federal Reserve's control over final spending is imperfect and that monetary targets must be adjusted to take shifts in velocity into account. If they are not, then wide swings in interest rates are a predictable result.

Partly because of these shifts in velocity but also because it might be less confusing to the public, several leading economists have suggested that the Federal Reserve announce its annual targets in terms of the desired growth of nominal GNP or even in terms of its ultimate objective: the reduction of inflation.[28] It is argued that this would have more influence on inflationary expectations than current Federal Reserve announcements which focus on a bevy of Ms with continually changing definitions. The monetarist members of the current administration, on the other hand, believe that the relationships between narrow measures of M and economic activity are relatively stable or predictable and that having too many targets permits too much policy discretion and confuses markets; they favor an emphasis on the M-1 targets or on the adjusted monetary base.[29]

A related issue is the period of time over which the targets should be met. Financial columnists attach significance to weekly and monthly money supply numbers, a practice that economists of all persuasions decry, but there is serious disagreement about whether quarterly growth rates can or should be brought into line with the announced annual targets. The Federal Reserve has argued that quarterly deviations are unimportant as long as the annual targets are achieved. The current administration, on the other hand, has complained about the volatility of money supply growth, arguing that this has unsettled markets and helped to keep interest rates high.[30]

Time Frames and Economic Costs

There is little doubt that monetary restraint can reduce inflation. At issue is how long it will take, the price that will be paid in terms of lost output and employment, whether the benefits are sustainable, and whether they are worth the costs. Probably no set of issues divides economists more than these.

One group of economists (the rational expectations school) argues that a well-advertised monetary policy has all of its effects on the rate of inflation and none on the "real economy," even in the short run, because individuals can anticipate the effects of a policy of restraint and make the needed adjustments in their own behavior to avoid any adverse consequences. Workers, for example, will accept lower wages rather than suffer from a prolonged period of unemployment, and businessmen will lower prices rather than incur a slump in sales. According to this view, the fight against inflation can be both short and quite painless.[31]

Neo-Keynesians, in contrast, contend that monetary restraint will have its major impacts on output and employment. Because wage and price adjustments in a modern economy are sluggish, and respond only slightly, if at all, to economic slack, current policies are a prescription for a deep and prolonged recession. According to one review of the historical evidence, it takes an extra point of measured unemployment sustained for a year to reduce the rate of wage inflation by one-third to one-half point a year. By this estimate, it would take four years of 8 percent unemployment to reduce inflation by four percentage points. The cumulative cost would be $600 to $700 billion in lost output and income, or $9,000 per family.[32]

Midway between these two camps are the "mainstream monetarists" who believe that a period of slack will be needed to bring down the rate of inflation but that the benefits are well worth the short-term costs. Establishing the credibility of the policy or convincing people that they are living in a new policy "regime" can shorten the time it will take to conquer inflation and reduce but not eliminate the costs.

It is this latter view that is now espoused by a number of economists within the administration. However, there has been reluctance on the part of the president and some of his advisers to admit that controlling inflation is likely to be a painful process for some period of time. Forecasts of high rates of nominal and real growth for the next several years are inconsistent with a tight monetary policy and the need to put the economy through a recession in order to win the war against inflation. If the Federal Reserve continues to gradually decelerate the growth of the money supply by about half a percentage point a year, assuming velocity increases at its normal rate, nominal GNP growth would end up three or four points below its officially projected level for 1983 and 1984.[33] Overly optimistic projections, and the public statements that accompany them, may even undermine the credibility of the antiinflation strategy and increase the time it takes for it to have beneficial effects.

The 1982 *Economic Report of the President* clearly articulates the view that inflationary expectations that have been built up over a number of years take time to respond to a change in economic conditions.[34] The monetarist members of the administration estimate that it will take one and a half to two years to see significant positive results on the inflation front and three to five years to eliminate the problem.[35] It is not clear what the base period for these estimates should be. If the base period is the fall of 1979, when the Federal Reserve first adopted a monetarist policy, inflation should be well under control before the next presidential election, according to this view.

Recent Price and Wage Developments

Recent developments provide us with some new opportunities to test the validity of the rational expectations, the neo-Keynesian, and the mainstream monetarist views. As we have seen, there was no immediate shift in expectations or elimination of inflation as a result of the Reagan program; however, progress is being made.

The CPI, which had been rising at an annual rate of 11.2 percent when the administration took office, increased by 7.6 percent between the first quarter of 1981 and the first quarter of 1982 (table 2-4). Much of this gain, however, was related to the improved behavior of volatile elements in the CPI, such as housing costs, food, and energy. Food prices, which had in-

TABLE 2–4

SELECTED MEASURES OF INFLATION AND LABOR COMPENSATION SINCE 1979
(Percentage changes from same quarter in preceding year)

	CPI All Items	CPI Less Food, Energy, and Housing Costs[a]	Hourly Earnings Index (All Industries)	Employment Cost Index (Wages and Salaries, All Workers)
1979 I	9.8	7.3	8.2	7.8
II	10.7	7.4	7.9	7.6
III	11.7	7.2	8.1	7.7
IV	12.7	7.3	8.1	8.7
1980 I	14.3	8.2	8.4	9.1
II	14.4	8.7	9.1	9.3
III	12.9	9.2	9.2	9.4
IV	12.6	9.9	9.7	9.0
1981 I	11.2	9.3	9.8	9.4
II	9.8	9.3	9.4	9.3
III	10.9	9.8	9.2	9.1
IV	9.6	9.5	8.4	8.8
1982 I	7.6	8.9	7.8	8.1

SOURCE: Bureau of Labor Statistics.

a. Special Index 7 as estimated by the BLS excludes home purchases, finance, taxes, and insurance, food, and energy.

creased at double-digit levels in 1978 and 1979, rose by 8.6 percent in 1980 and 7.9 percent in 1981. Energy prices, which had been rising at 25 to 30 percent in 1979 and 1980, dropped back to 13 percent for 1981 as a whole with actual decreases toward the end of the year.[36] Thus, when one examines the CPI excluding these factors, the drop in the inflation rate is much less— only 0.4 percentage points since the first quarter of 1981.

Consumer and business expectations of inflation have also slowed. However, for the first time since the data have been collected, consumers are more pessimistic about long-term than about short-term rates of inflation, suggesting that they do not believe recent gains are permanent.[37]

Continued progress in bringing down the rate of inflation will depend on what happens to wages. Labor costs represent about two-thirds of total costs for most businesses, and prices are generally set as a mark-up over costs. Profits are being squeezed now as the rate of increase in prices falls more rapidly than that of wages, but this pattern cannot be permanently sustained.

There has been a significant slowdown in money wage gains in recent quarters (table 2-4).[38] The hourly earnings index was rising by 2 percentage points less in early 1982 than in early 1981, and the rate of increase in the employment cost index fell by 1.3 percentage points over the same period.[39] Data on 1981 wage settlements in contracts covering 1,000 workers or more show wage adjustments averaging 7.9 percent per year over the life of the contract, the largest annual increase since 1975.[40] Although there have been wage and benefit concessions in such industries as autos, trucking, petroleum refining, and meatpacking, these may reflect the special circumstances facing these industries (foreign competition, deregulation, falling oil prices, and technological change) as much as they do the state of the economy. Still, continued slack and the delayed influence of a slower rate of inflation on cost-of-living adjustments should cause further wage deceleration.

How does the disinflation that has occurred to date compare to what the rational expectations, neo-Keynesian, and mainstream monetarist schools would predict? Clearly, there is no support here for the "rational expectations" idea that inflation adjusts immediately to a shift in policy. Rather, the question is whether inflation has fallen more rapidly than the standard neo-Keynesian model of wage and price behavior would predict—providing support for the monetarist notion that a firm and credible shift in policy can reduce the costs of disinflation. Thus far, there is little or no evidence that businessmen or workers are behaving differently than in the past. Predictions using a standard neo-Keynesian model are capable of fully explaining the recent decline in the rate of inflation.[41]

What have these gains on the inflation front cost to date? If it is assumed that a full-employment economy would have entailed keeping the unemployment rate around 6 percent since the beginning of 1980, then we have forfeited about $200 billion in GNP and increased the federal deficit by about $50 billion as the result of maintaining a soft economy over this period (from the first quarter of 1980 through the first quarter of 1982).[42] This is only the first installment on what may be a protracted period of economic slack so the total costs of reducing inflation cannot yet be known. Some neo-Keynesian models put the cost of lowering inflation by another five percentage points at around $1,000 billion.[43] Whether the benefits of living in a noninflationary economy are commensurate with these costs is difficult to judge. It is also possible that people do not yet realize that the rules of the economic policy game have changed. Once they do, the process of disinflation may occur more rapidly and be less expensive than these estimates suggest.

Finally, it should be noted that new inflationary pressures almost inevitably accompany an economic recovery.[44] So unless the economy is kept in a permanently depressed state, or structural reforms are introduced, the problem of inflation will not go away.

Fiscal Policy, Deficits, and the Economy

The centerpiece of the administration's economic policy was the multi-year tax cuts for individuals and businesses. These were accompanied by attempts to restrain the growth of nondefense spending, but the net effect has been to produce an enormous amount of red ink (see chapter 3 for further details). As of mid-1982, deficits averaging $210 billion a year between 1983 and 1985 were projected (table 2-5). Although it is clear that Congress will not allow deficits of this magnitude to occur, the problem will not be easily solved, especially over the short run. What, then, is the significance of these deficits? To what extent will they provide additional stimulus to the economy over the next few years? And, will the Treasury's need to finance the deficit keep interest rates high and possibly choke off investment?

Stimulus for the Economy

When the level of economic activity falls off, revenues automatically decline and expenditures (for unemployment insurance and other benefit programs) automatically rise. As a rough rule of thumb, each extra percentage point of unemployment increases the deficit by about $27 billion. Thus, the deficits observed in any year reflect, as well as influence, the level of economic activity. It is only by estimating the deficit under constant economic conditions

TABLE 2–5

DEFICIT PROJECTIONS
(In $ billions)

	Actual 1981	Projected 1982	1983	1984	1985
Budget deficit					
Current policies[a]	58	119	182	216	233
Administration proposals	58	114	130	127	116
High-employment budget deficit					
Current policies[a]	25	40	108	153	175
Administration proposals	25	34	54	63	57

SOURCE: Committee on the Budget, House of Representatives, *First Concurrent Resolution on the Budget—Fiscal Year 1983* (Washington, D.C.: GPO, 1982), p. 58.
a. Current policy represents tax and spending measures in place as of May 1982, plus the administration's defense program.

(as with the so-called "high-employment deficit") that one can get a sense for the degree of economic stimulus inherent in any fiscal policy.

Estimates of the high-employment deficit prepared by the staff of the House Budget Committee (table 2-5) indicate the following:

- Holding economic conditions constant, there is a *rising* deficit between now and 1985 and thus some net stimulus for the economy. Even if all of the administration's proposals were enacted, the high-employment deficit would increase over time.

- Fiscal policy was not particularly expansionary in 1982. It becomes much more stimulative in 1983 and in 1984. (The degree of stimulus is measured by looking at the change in the high-employment deficit from year to year.)

- In 1982, about two-thirds of the deficit is the result of weakness in the economy; and only about one-third is "structural." However, the structural deficit gets worse in future years.

The message is clear: the current deficit (for 1982) is not a problem. Even the $68 billion increase in the high-employment deficit that would occur between 1982 and 1983 in the absence of congressional action would not necessarily be inappropriate—given the depressed state of the economy.[45] However, as the economy approaches full employment, large and growing deficits become increasingly troublesome. If financed by the Federal Reserve (a much feared but unlikely outcome), these deficits would be inflationary. If not, they would still be likely to crowd out investment.

Impacts on Interest Rates and Investment

Assuming that the Federal Reserve does not accommodate the Treasury's need for credit, deficits mean the government must compete with private borrowers for funds. If the supply of credit is not sufficient to meet the needs of both groups, interest rates will rise and crowd the marginal private borrower (as well as state and local governments) out of the market. Over the long run, then, deficits do have implications for the economy's rate of growth.

Combined with a declining savings rate, the rising deficits (as a percentage of GNP) of recent years have meant that the federal government has, in fact, claimed an increasing share of total available credit.[46] Large projected deficits for 1982 and beyond have raised concerns that the share will rise still further and discourage business investment.

During the 1970s, an average of 16.7 percent of GNP was saved (in the form of personal savings, corporate retained earnings, and depreciation).

Federal deficits absorbed a little over 10 percent of these savings with the remainder being available for private investment. The administration projects a 1984 deficit that is only a little larger (as a percentage of GNP) than those that prevailed in the 1970s. In addition, it expects that the savings rate will rise from 16.7 percent to 19.1 percent by 1984. This is based on a presumption that most of the business tax cut and about half of the personal tax cut will be saved and that the personal savings rate will increase from 5 to 7 percent.[47] These rates are well within the bounds of historical experience. When taxes were cut in early 1964, the personal savings rate rose from 5.4 percent in 1963 to 8.1 percent in 1967. However, this increase probably owed more to the fact that disposable incomes were growing rapidly (under such circumstances consumers adjust their spending rates with a lag) than to the drop in marginal tax rates per se. The evidence reviewed in chapter 4 suggests that it may be risky to assume that the savings rate would increase this much on a permanent basis. However, if savings did respond this dramatically, then in spite of somewhat higher deficits, the share of GNP available for private investment would rise above the level of the 1970s, generating an additional $91 billion in investment funds between 1982 and 1984.[48] This is labeled the "crowding-in scenario" in figure 2-1.

An alternative, less optimistic set of projections is also presented and labeled the "crowding-out" scenario in figure 2-1. It assumes that the savings rate remains at its 1970s level and that the administration's 1983 budget proposals are not adopted. Under this scenario the share of GNP available for private investment remains well below the 1970s average and deficits absorb an additional $280 billion in potential investment funds between 1982 and 1984.[49]

Whether the supply of savings will actually be a constraining factor over this period depends on what happens to business investment plans. With capacity utilization rates in manufacturing in the neighborhood of 70 percent in mid-1982 (compared to a 1970s average of 82 percent), businesses have little incentive to make new expenditures. While economists still disagree about the determinants of investment, many believe that spending on plant and equipment is more sensitive to operating rates than to the cost of capital, especially over the short run.[50] According to this view, a deficit reduction program that brought down interest rates over the next year or two but at the price of a still more depresssed economy would have few, if any, beneficial effects on investment. To be fully effective, such a strategy would have to be accompanied by a more stimulative monetary policy. According to another view, the current combination of a loose fiscal policy and a tight monetary policy is conducive to greater business investment. The argument is that high interest rates disproportionately discourage investment in "unproductive"

FIGURE 2-1

TWO SCENARIOS: CROWDING-IN VERSUS CROWDING-OUT

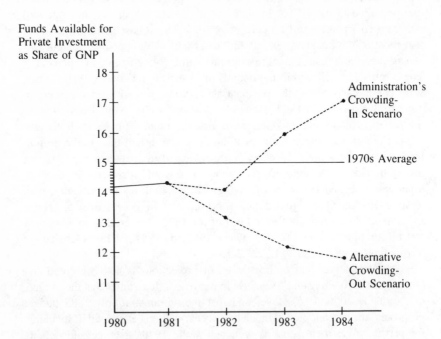

Funds Available for
Private Investment
as Share of GNP

SOURCE: Author's calculations.
    NOTE: Crowding-in scenario based on administration's savings assumptions and deficit pro-
jections; alternative crowding-out scenario based on historical savings rate and CBO deficit
projections.

assets such as housing and consumer durables, freeing up funds for plant and
equipment.[51]

To summarize, fiscal policy is having little impact on the economy in
1982 but will produce large and growing "structural" deficits in the years
ahead. It is commonly believed that reducing these long-term deficits would
lower interest rates and revive the economy in 1982-1983. However, as
emphasized earlier, no one knows why interest rates are currently so high;
triple-digit deficits are only one of the several possible explanations. Thus,
it should not be assumed that a deficit reduction program will produce an
immediate improvement in the economy.

The implications of these structural deficits for long-term economic growth
are much clearer. If allowed to persist, they may absorb savings that could
otherwise be devoted to private investment and undermine the administration's
growth objectives.

Conclusions

Economic performance deteriorated over the decade of the 1970s and set the stage for a new experiment in economic policy. The policy put in place in 1981 is an amalgam of supply side and traditional monetarist beliefs about how the economy works. Its most important elements are a multiyear tax cut and strong support for the restrictive monetary policy that has been in operation since the end of 1979.

Thus far, inflation is responding to the monetarist prescription. However, wages and prices appear to be no more responsive to economic slack than they were during the 1970s, making this a painful process. Monitoring wage and price developments over the next several years will help to establish whether the new policies are leading to greater wage and price flexibility than in the past.

The reduction in inflation has come at the cost of a depressed economy, widespread unemployment, and a substantial loss of real output and income. Moreover, the recession, together with high interest rates, has cast a pall over investment spending and drowned out any possible supply side response to the 1981 tax cut. However, no one should have expected these incentives to affect people's behavior quickly. They are long-term growth measures whose ultimate effects will not be known for many years.

One thing is clear: the tax cuts in combination with the defense build-up have produced unacceptable deficits, and it now appears that some mid-course corrections will be needed on this front. Options for reducing deficits are considered in chapter 3, but the magnitude of the problem suggests that a large part of the supply side economic plank may have to be shelved. If this should occur, then what would remain is a very traditional set of con-servative economic policies. Such policies have always given more weight to reducing inflation than to maintaining or expanding employment and output.

What have these policies meant for the average citizen thus far? Despite the recession, the average person's standard of living improved during the president's first year in office, although the improvement was minimal and the distribution of gains and losses was not evenly shared (see chapter 16). Perhaps people will take this small improvement as a sign that real incomes can rise even when money incomes are growing more slowly than previously. This realization could lead to further moderation in wage demands and bring the inflation rate down still faster, setting the stage for renewed growth.

Probably the biggest imponderable is whether the renewed growth will be sustainable and what will happen to inflation once the economy revives. Can a repeat of the policy errors and supply shocks that produced the inflation of the 1970s be avoided? Will a new era of price stability and growth follow the stagflation of the 1970s in the same way that the prosperity of the 1960s followed the recession-prone 1950s? Or have economic and social institutions changed in ways that make this less likely? The administration's policies have been so self-confidently based on a firmly held set of beliefs about supply side measures that little thought has been given to these broader issues. A willingness to address them would be a healthy addition to current discussions.

Chapter 3

BUDGET POLICY

John L. Palmer
Gregory B. Mills

Several basic concerns about the functioning of government were central to the 1980 presidential campaign. How far should the responsibilities of the public sector extend, and how should they be divided between the federal government and state and local governments? What should be the relative emphasis in federal financial support between defense and domestic activities? To what extent should the federal government employ deficit financing? As a presidential candidate, Ronald Reagan expressed strong views on all these issues.

Budget policy plays the central role in defining the nature and extent of federal activity, and it has been President Reagan's major tool for pursuing his policy objectives. Soon after assuming office, he presented to the Congress a long-term federal budget program that embodied dramatic changes from past trends. It called for substantial outlay reductions, major tax cuts, and a rapidly declining deficit. Large increases in defense spending were proposed, while domestic programs were to be sharply curtailed, with greater authority provided to state and local governments. Simultaneous accomplishment of these goals was highly dependent upon the immediate success of his Program for Economic Recovery.

By December 1981 Congress had enacted most of the president's 1982 budget requests with surprising ease and speed.[1] It passed a massive tax cut,

sizable reductions in domestic programs, and the first installment of his defense build-up. However, these changes, along with the failure of the economy
to respond to the new policies, dramatically raised future deficit projections.
It became clear even to the administration that the various budget goals were
not compatible.

In response to this changed outlook, the president's 1983 budget request
proposed even deeper domestic program cuts, while largely adhering to the
enacted tax cuts and defense build-up and accepting a continuation of deficits
at unprecedented levels. There was virtual unanimity in Congress that this
general approach was unacceptable. In marked contrast to the previous year,
Congress rejected the president's request as a starting point for its own 1983
budget deliberations. It is now embarked on a long-term deficit reduction
program that will take several years to fully define and implement.

This chapter focuses on the federal budget—how it has already changed
and may change further under the Reagan administration. It first describes
the historical trends in federal spending and revenues. Second, it discusses
the Reagan administration's budgetary program, how this program departs
from the past, and what it implies for the future funding of domestic programs.
Third, this chapter examines the tax and spending changes enacted by Congress during 1981. Although they were not as large as generally reported,
the effects of the domestic spending reductions on the 1982 budget were
sizable and will become proportionately larger over time. By 1986 the cuts
in entitlement programs targeted on the low-income population will reduce
benefits by about 10 percent. Hardest hit, however, were grants to state and
local governments and other federal nondefense operations, which by 1986
will be reduced by 20-25 percent below their prior service levels as a result
of the congressional actions during 1981.

In combination with the military build-up, these domestic spending reductions have begun the shift in federal budget priorities that the president
sought. However, they did not curtail the major sources of spending growth;
no effective restraint on the overall long-run growth of federal expenditures
has yet been implemented. The large tax cut thus introduced a major structural
imbalance between projected federal spending and revenues. Alternative approaches to eliminating long-term deficits and restoring budgetary balance
can yield widely differing outcomes with respect to the future size and role
of the federal government. The final part of this chapter considers this new
budgetary outlook, how it came about, some of the longer-term strategic
issues at stake in the continuing budget debates, and initial congressional
action on the 1983 budget.

Historical Trends in the Federal Budget: 1956-1981

During the quarter century preceding the Reagan administration, government expenditures in the United States increased nearly tenfold. When one accounts for the effect on outlays of both inflation and unemployment, the upward trend in federal spending was far less dramatic but still substantial. More striking was the shifting composition of federal spending away from defense outlays, which only kept pace with inflation, and toward domestic outlays, whose rapid growth was fueled by programs that provide benefit payments to individuals. Despite an increasing burden of federal taxes, the rise in outlays throughout the 1970s led to larger deficits and an increasing budget share devoted to interest payments on the national debt. These fiscal realities resulted in a widely shared consensus that taxes should be reduced and that real defense spending should be increased—but that deficits also should be reduced. Whoever assumed office as president in January 1981 would face a likely set of budgetary objectives that could only be pursued through restraint on nondefense spending.

The Size and Growth of Government Spending

Public expenditures—federal, state, and local—grew substantially during the twenty-five years preceding the Reagan administration. Since the mid-1970s, federal spending growth has led the expansion of total public spending. Whether the pace of federal spending growth should be viewed with alarm has been much debated; there is no clear answer to the question, "How much is too much?"

Measured in nominal terms, the sum of federal, state, and local government spending grew from $99 billion in 1956 to $925 billion in 1981. Both the federal component and the state and local component experienced a nearly tenfold increase. Of course, this was a period of generally rising prices and an expanding population. It is conventional to control for these price and scale effects by expressing public expenditures as a percentage of Gross National Product (GNP). On this basis, government spending rose from 24 percent in 1956 to 32 percent in 1981 (table 3-1). Over one-third of the rise in the federal GNP share from 17.1 percent to 23.7 percent was due to increased grants to state and local governments, reflecting a more active federal role in shaping the pattern of state and local expenditures. Since the

TABLE 3–1

GOVERNMENT EXPENDITURES AS A PERCENTAGE OF GROSS NATIONAL PRODUCT
(FY 1956–FY 1981)

Federal Fiscal Year[a]	Total Government Expenditures	State and Local Expenditures from Own Revenue[b]	Federal Expenditures (Budget and Off-Budget)		
			Total	Grants to State and Local Governments	All Other
FY 1956	24.1	7.0	17.1	0.8	16.3
FY 1961	27.5	8.3	19.2	1.3	17.9
FY 1966	27.1	8.5	18.6	1.8	16.8
FY 1971	30.6	10.2	20.4	2.6	17.8
FY 1976	32.9	10.2	22.7	3.5	19.2
FY 1981	32.4	8.6	23.7	3.2	20.5
Increase from FY 1956 to FY 1981	8.3	1.6	6.6	2.4	4.2

SOURCE: Office of Management and Budget, "Total Government Finances," February 1982, p. 4; and Office of Management and Budget, "Federal Grants-In-Aid to State and Local Governments," March 1982, p. 5.

a. Fiscal years end on June 30 for 1956 through 1976 and on September 30 for 1981.
b. Net of nontax receipts, computed on a national income accounts basis by federal fiscal year.

mid-1970s, state and local spending, both including and excluding federal grants, has actually declined as a percentage of GNP. This recent drop in the state and local share of GNP was approximately offset by the continued rise in the federal share, leading to total public expenditures remaining roughly constant as a percentage of GNP.

On several accounts, however, the federal spending growth indicated in table 3-1—a rise in GNP share of 6.6 percentage points between 1956 and 1981—is a questionable measure of the expansion in federal program activity.[2] To the extent that the prices paid by the federal government have risen more rapidly than general prices in the economy, the real increase in government activity is overstated. Second, the interest component of federal outlays does not represent current government services but rather the financing of prior spending. Third, the observed levels of both federal outlays and GNP are sensitive to the business cycle. During periods of high unemployment, outlays increase as transfer payments rise, while GNP falls as capacity utilization declines. A comparison between any two years thus may not accurately reflect the underlying trend.[3]

The three adjustments just implied—using inflation-corrected amounts for both outlays and GNP, excluding net interest outlays, and assuming full employment—yield a series of GNP shares for federal expenditures that increase by only 1.3 percentage points, from 17.6 percent in 1956 to 18.9 percent in 1981, with no change between 1976 and 1981 (table A-1). By this measure there was only very modest relative growth in federal program activity. However, this is of little consolation to anyone concerned about financing burdens imposed by a rapidly growing amount of total federal spending.

The Changing Composition of Federal Spending

As federal outlays crept upward as a percentage of GNP, the growth experienced by different components of the budget varied considerably. Between 1956 and 1981, the budget share devoted to national defense declined from 56.4 percent to 24.3 percent. Growth in nondefense spending was due largely to a dramatic rise in cash assistance and in-kind benefits provided directly to individuals, with other domestic programs contributing less strongly to the upward spending trend. This differential pattern of growth is best understood by focusing on the major categories of federal spending, for which data will be presented throughout this chapter.

"National defense" encompasses all activities related to the common defense and security of the United States, most importantly the compensation paid to military and civilian defense personnel, the expenses of operating and maintaining military installations, and the costs of procuring military hardware.

"Benefit payments for individuals" includes cash or in-kind income transfers to individuals or families for which no current service is rendered. Nearly all such benefits are paid under entitlement programs, whereby any applicant meeting the eligibility criteria must receive payment. Program outlays are thus not constrained by the congressional appropriation process but are determined by the combination of program rules and changing economic and demographic conditions. The "low-income assistance" component includes those programs that are targeted on the low-income population, usually through an explicit means test. Medicaid, Food Stamps, Aid to Families with Dependent Children (AFDC), and Supplemental Security Income (SSI) are currently the largest such programs. All other programs providing benefit payments to individuals are in the "social insurance and other" component. Social Security and Medicare now constitute nearly three-fourths of this component and over half of total benefit payments for individuals.[4]

"All other grants to state and local governments" includes federal aid for all functions exclusive of income transfers. Such activities include highway and sewer construction, urban mass transit, community development, social services, employment and training, and elementary and secondary education. "Net interest" consists largely of interest paid on the public debt and on tax refunds, net of interest received by federal trust funds. "Other federal operations" includes all remaining budget outlays, ranging from farm price supports to foreign aid to the general operations of the government.

The twenty-five years of federal budget history preceding the Reagan administration showed a steady decline through the mid-1970s in the share of the budget devoted to national defense and an increase throughout the period in the shares associated with benefit payments for individuals and net interest (table 3-2). Adjusted for inflation, defense spending actually declined between the mid-1950s and the mid-1970s. This trend was reversed under the Carter administration, as real defense outlays grew following 1977 and the budget share for defense stabilized at 24 percent.

The remaining two budget aggregates, other grants to state and local governments and other federal operations, each grew as a share of the budget through the mid-1970s and then declined slightly through 1981. The expansion in federal grants occurred through a proliferation of categorical domestic programs, growing in number from less than 150 in 1960 to about 500 in 1980. These grant programs were created to assist state and local governments to meet their needs or to encourage them to address national priorities.[5] (For more detail on the recent growth of federal outlays by domestic program area, see table A-2.)

Any explanation of the rise in federal spending between 1956 and 1981 must focus primarily upon the growth in benefit payments for individuals.

TABLE 3-2

DISTRIBUTION OF FEDERAL BUDGET OUTLAYS
(FY 1956–FY 1981)

	FY 1956	FY 1961	FY 1966	FY 1971	FY 1976	FY 1981
	Percentage of Total Budget Outlays					
National defense	56.4	47.7	40.7	36.1	24.5	24.3
Benefit payments for individuals	21.0	28.0	26.9	37.4	48.5	48.2
Low-income assistance	(3.7)	(4.3)	(4.8)	(7.4)	(10.2)	(10.3)
Social insurance and other	(17.3)	(23.6)	(22.1)	(30.0)	(38.3)	(37.9)
Other grants to state and local governments	2.9	4.3	6.2	8.1	10.4	8.3
Net interest	7.2	6.9	7.0	7.1	7.3	10.5
Other federal operations	12.5	13.2	19.1	11.3	9.3	8.7
Total	100.0	100.0	100.0	100.0	100.0	100.0
Addendum						
Total grants to state and local governments	5.3	7.3	9.6	13.4	16.2	14.4

SOURCE: Office of Management and Budget, "Federal Government Finances," February 1982, pp. 60–63; and Office of Management and Budget, "Payments for Individuals," February 1982, pp. 33–72.

NOTE: In this and subsequent tables in this chapter, totals may not add due to rounding.

Low-income assistance exhibited faster real growth than other benefit payments, but the social insurance programs contributed a much larger dollar amount to the rising budget total. The growth in benefit programs was due to a series of six broad and interrelated policy and demographic factors. It is useful to review them briefly to understand how much upward pressure on such federal expenditures could be expected through the 1980s.

First, new programs were introduced to meet specific income needs. Among the more important ones were Medicare, Medicaid, low-income housing assistance, and guaranteed student loans. Second, the eligibility provisions of existing programs were liberalized, extending coverage to a wider population. Third, economic and demographic shifts led to larger numbers of eligible persons, apart from the more generous eligibility rules. The increase in the number of elderly persons, single-parent families, and unemployed persons meant larger numbers of potential recipients. Fourth, the "participation rate" among those eligible for benefits rose in most programs. Fifth, benefit levels per recipient steadily increased, in part because of inflation. Several major real benefit increases occurred in Social Security. Programs explicitly indexed to a measure of price change experienced automatic nominal increases. Expenditures in the health financing programs rose with benefit expansions and rapidly inflating medical care costs. Finally, more generous federal matching provisions were adopted, with states bearing a smaller share of program expenditures. The extreme example of this was the federalization in 1974 of basic benefits to the aged, blind, and disabled under the Supplemental Security Income program.

For several reasons, it was unlikely that the prior rapid growth rate for benefit payments to individuals would have continued through the 1980s under any administration. Entering the decade, the growth in the population segments comprised of elderly persons and single-parent families was subsiding. Program participation rates had reached levels high enough that possible further growth from this source was quite limited. Finally, political support for new programs, expanded eligibility, and higher real benefit levels was diminishing. This was due to many factors, including fiscal limitations and public perceptions that there was little unmet need and that federal programs were an inefficient means of addressing any such residual needs.

Financing Federal Expenditures: Taxes and Borrowing

The federal government can finance its spending in two ways—by taxing or borrowing. Despite the increasing burden of federal taxes through the last decade, revenue growth has lagged increasingly behind the rise in federal outlays. This has led to an increasing reliance upon debt financing and, as noted earlier, a growing share of total outlays for interest payments.

Federal tax receipts increased as a share of GNP from 18.1 percent in 1956 to 21.0 percent in 1981, rising very slowly throughout most of the period and then more rapidly in the latter part. This occurred despite periodic cuts in personal income tax rates to offset the movement of taxpayers into higher tax brackets because of both inflation and real income growth. Contrasted with this upward trend was the downward movement in the percentage of federal budget outlays financed through tax revenues (table A-3). During 1956-1970, receipts exceeded 90 percent of budget outlays in thirteen of fifteen fiscal years. During 1971-1981, however, receipts exceeded 90 percent of outlays in only four of eleven fiscal years. As a percentage of GNP, the average federal budget deficit rose more or less continuously over the period 1956-1980, from 0.3 in 1956-1960 to 2.4 in 1976-1980. The cumulative effect of these budget deficits, along with increases in off-budget outlays and interest rates, caused net interest payments to jump from 7.3 percent of budget outlays in 1976 to 10.5 percent by 1981.

The Outlook in 1981

Recent federal budget history contained much that Ronald Reagan had campaigned against in 1980 and sought to reverse as president. In fact, the budget would have posed difficult dilemmas for any administration in the 1980s. Federal expenditures as a percentage of GNP had grown rapidly in the late 1970s, after increasing very gradually since the mid-1950s. Although much of this acceleration was due to stagflation, not underlying program trends that would maintain this expansion in a healthy economy, the growing momentum of federal spending nevertheless posed a problem.

The ratio of federal taxes to GNP had also crept up, but revenues increasingly fell short of expenditures through the 1970s. Another in the series of periodic tax cuts was clearly in order for the early 1980s, but it would have to be accompanied by greater spending restraint if it were not to result in a continued upward drift in the federal tax burden or high risk of large deficits. It also was evident that the burden of any such spending restraint would have to fall primarily on nondefense spending, since Congress (and the Carter administration) had recently initiated a program of real defense growth planned to be sustained well into the 1980s.

President Reagan's Budget Program

President Reagan's desire to reverse past budget trends was strongly reflected in the five-year budget plan he presented as part of the Program for Economic Recovery. He proposed to reduce substantially federal expenditures and revenues as a percentage of GNP, while accommodating a defense build-up much larger than that adopted by Congress under President Carter. Expenditure growth was to be restrained more than revenue growth, leading to a balanced budget by 1984. The deepest cuts were proposed for discretionary domestic programs, especially those funded through grants to state and local governments. Requested reductions in benefit payments to individuals were more modest, with low-income assistance bearing a far larger relative share than social insurance programs. As a result, the defense share of the budget would increase substantially through the 1980s, while the share for benefit payments to individuals would remain roughly constant and the share for other domestic activities would decline dramatically.

Economic Assumptions and Budget Projections

President Reagan's economic and budget policies and projections were inextricably interdependent from the outset. He argued that a sizable decrease in the rate of growth of federal spending was essential to the success of his economic policies. This success, in turn, was critical to achieving his desired budget outcomes. In addition to assuming full passage of the president's tax and spending proposals, the budget projections made by the administration in early 1981 assumed a rapid, strong, and sustained revitalization of the economy (table 3-3). Many outside observers argued that this economic optimism was unfounded and that the budget projections were therefore unrealistic. Indeed, a March 1981 reestimate of the administration's proposals under a set of economic assumptions more in accord with those of most private economic forecasters showed a deficit of $49 billion in 1984, rather than a balanced budget.[6] However, the administration adhered to its economic

TABLE 3–3

REAGAN ADMINISTRATION BUDGET PROJECTIONS, MARCH 1981

	FY 1981	FY 1982	FY 1983	FY 1984	FY 1985	FY 1986
	Billions of Dollars					
Revenues	600.3	650.3	709.1	770.7	849.9	940.2
Outlays	655.2	695.3	732.0	770.2	844.0	912.0
Deficit (−) or surplus	−54.9	−45.0	−22.8	0.5	5.8	28.2
	Percentage of GNP					
Revenues	21.1	20.4	19.7	19.3	19.3	19.5
Outlays	23.0	21.8	20.3	19.3	19.2	19.0
Deficit (−) or surplus	−1.9	−1.4	−0.6	0.0	0.1	0.5

SOURCE: Office of Management and Budget, *Fiscal Year 1982 Budget Revisions*, March 1981, p. 11.

assumptions, which were largely adopted by Congress in deciding on the 1982 budget.

To understand how the president's initial tax and spending proposals were expected to change the budget outlook, it is helpful to compare the administration's initial budget projections to the baseline budget projections published by the Congressional Budget Office (CBO) in July 1981 (table 3-4). The latter projections were provided to Congress to assist in its deliberations over the 1982 budget and were based upon economic assumptions that differed from the administration's only with respect to interest rates. (Congress requested that CBO use a similar optimistic set of economic assumptions, both because there was great reluctance to imply that the president's economic program would not work and because it made their politically difficult budget choices easier.) By definition, baseline projections assume no change in the prevailing policies, with adjustments for inflation in all programs whether or not required by current law.[7] Their purpose is not to predict what is expected to happen but to provide a reference point against which the effects of policy changes can be estimated. Thus, these CBO baseline estimates essentially held constant the real level of services that could be bought with 1981 spending authority, whereas the administration's estimates embodied its proposed policy changes.

With no change in policies, the CBO projected revenues to grow faster than GNP and expenditures slower than GNP. This would produce a small surplus for 1983 and larger ones thereafter. In contrast, the administration's proposed tax cut was estimated to cause a sizable decline in revenues as a percentage of GNP. Despite the defense build-up, the administration also projected that its proposed nondefense reductions would cause federal outlays to fall to 19.0 percent of GNP in 1986, compared to CBO's baseline estimate

TABLE 3–4

CONGRESSIONAL BUDGET OFFICE BASELINE BUDGET PROJECTIONS, JULY 1981

	FY 1981	FY 1982	FY 1983	FY 1984	FY 1985	FY 1986
	Billions of Dollars					
Revenues	611.9	709.1	810.2	919.6	1,033.2	1,158.8
Outlays	659.8	738.7	792.5	843.3	894.9	949.9
Deficit (−) or surplus	−47.9	−29.6	17.7	76.3	138.3	208.9
	Percentage of GNP					
Revenues	21.4	22.0	22.3	22.8	23.3	23.9
Outlays	23.1	22.9	21.8	20.9	20.2	19.6
Deficit (−) or surplus	−1.7	−0.9	0.5	1.9	3.1	4.3

SOURCE: Congressional Budget Office, *Baseline Budget Projections: Fiscal Years 1982–1986* (Washington, D.C.: GPO, 1981), p. 10.

of 19.6 percent. In fact, had the CBO used economic and technical assumptions identical to the administration's, its baseline projection also would have shown expenditures near 19 percent of GNP in 1986. Thus, the administration required only negligible nondefense expenditure reductions from the prevailing baseline to achieve its 1986 outlay target of 19 percent of GNP, as long as real defense outlays were not to increase faster than the 3 percent annual rate contained in the CBO baseline. However, larger nondefense cuts were necessary to accommodate the much more rapid defense growth requested by the president.

Revenues

The centerpiece of President Reagan's tax cut proposal was the three-year, across-the-board reduction in individual income tax rates. A sizable business tax cut was also included.[8]

Two things about this tax cut proposal are noteworthy. First, it was estimated to reduce the overall burden of federal taxes from its 1980 level, though not drastically. The administration's 1984 revenue projection, 19.3 percent of GNP, was still slightly above the ratio of taxes to GNP that prevailed throughout most of the 1970s. Much of the tax cut was needed simply to offset the projected continued increase in tax burdens shown in the CBO baseline estimates. As noted earlier, Congress would probably have passed a sizable tax cut in 1981, whether or not Ronald Reagan had become president. However, its magnitude might have been lower and its distribution probably different.

Second, President Reagan adopted the multiyear Kemp-Roth tax cut proposal not only for its embodiment of supply side economics, but also because he viewed it as a means of restraining expenditure growth. Given the desire to balance the budget, a tax cut that lowers the projected ratio of revenues to GNP below that of projected expenditures to GNP leads to considerable pressure for expenditure cuts. In fact, the size and timing of the budget cuts initially proposed by President Reagan were largely dictated by his adoption of the Kemp-Roth tax cut and by his objective of a balanced budget in 1984, rather than by any independent view of the desired level of federal spending.

Expenditures

President Reagan's early budget proposals called for nondefense spending reductions in excess of $40 billion in 1982, growing to nearly $100 billion in 1986—about 5 and 10 percent, respectively, of the July 1981 CBO baseline projections for total budget outlays. His defense request was for annual real growth of outlays of nearly 9 percent throughout the 1980s. Total outlays, which in real terms had grown over the past twenty-five years slightly faster than GNP, were projected to grow at about half the rate of GNP. In the next paragraphs the stated criteria used to guide the development of the specific domestic reductions are presented, followed by a discussion of the effects of the president's proposals on particular areas of the federal budget.

The Specific Cuts and Their Rationale. In its Program for Economic Recovery, the administration set forward nine specific guidelines for the proposed domestic budget cuts.[9]

1. *Preserve the social safety net.* In addition to rebuilding the nation's defense capabilities, the administration's other overriding budget priority was to maintain the "social safety net" intended to protect the elderly, unemployed, poor, and veterans. The major programs identified in the social safety net were Social Security, Medicare, basic unemployment benefits, SSI, AFDC, and veterans income security and health care. They were to be spared from any cuts that would affect the most needy. This principle was largely honored in the cuts originally specified but was observed less in later proposals.

2. *Revise entitlements to eliminate unintended benefits.* The administration identified entitlement programs, particularly those newly added or greatly expanded during the 1970s, as the major source of the unrestrained federal growth that threatened eventual fiscal distress. More substantial cuts were proposed for those entitlement programs not in the social safety net, such as Medicaid, food and nutrition, extended unemployment benefits, trade adjustment assistance, and housing assistance. These cuts "were designed to eliminate excesses, overlaps, and unintended benefits . . . and to . . . refocus benefits on the truly needy and retarget programs on their intended purposes."

3. *Reduce subsidies to middle- and upper-income groups.* These subsidies were identified as a low priority for federal spending. It was also argued that paring them back would "arrest what has heretofore been an unfortunate national drift toward the universalization of social benefits." Programs targeted for cutbacks under this criterion were school lunches, student aid, and housing finance.

4. *Recover allocable costs with user fees.* For federal activities that provide direct economic benefits to specific groups, the administration proposed to shift more of the costs onto those who benefit. Proposals here included the imposition or increase of user fees for inland waterways, airports, and Coast Guard services.

5. *Apply sound economic criteria to economic subsidy programs.* The administration proposed major reductions in federal grants and other subsidies that serve to alleviate economic hardships on specific sectors and populations, because of their presumed undesirable distortions of the market economy.

Programs targeted for reductions under this criterion were public service employment, subsidies for new energy technologies, community development, operating subsidies for mass transit, and certain agriculture support and credit activities.

6. *Stretch out and retarget public sector capital investment programs.* These were identified as desirable federal activities that must be squeezed in order to contribute to the overall need for budget reductions. Such programs included water resource projects, waste treatment facilities, highways, mass transit, and airports.

7. *Consolidate categorical grant programs into block grants.* As a first step toward streamlining the federal system of financial assistance to state and local governments and returning greater authority to state and local governments, President Reagan in 1981 proposed the consolidation of seventy-seven categorical programs in the social, education, and health services areas into five block grants. Reduced funding levels were justified partially on the presumed savings from lower administrative costs and more efficient service delivery. In 1982 the president requested further program consolidations into block grants with additional funding cutbacks. He also unveiled his "New Federalism" proposal for a major realignment of federal-state fiscal and programmatic responsibilities in the grant-in-aid system, with considerable long-run savings to the federal budget.

8. *Reduce federal overhead, personnel costs, and program waste and inefficiencies.* The administration proposed to evaluate and tighten many aspects of federal administration and management. Major cost-saving initiatives pertained to federal employment, debt collection and management, leasing of the Outer Continental Shelf, surplus property disposal, employee travel, waste and abuse, and receipt collection.

9. *Impose fiscal restraint on other programs of national interest.* This was a catch-all category for other programs that the administration considered either of low priority or of dubious merit. Areas targeted here were the arts and humanities and science and technology.

These criteria reflect a mix of some concerns cited by earlier administrations in support of specific budget reduction measures and other ideas (such as the social safety net) that more uniquely expressed the Reagan administration's budget philosophy. In some cases, they did not govern the selection of program cuts as much as they served simply as a convenient categorization for specific proposals.

The Effects on Major Spending Categories. The effect of the defense build-up and the nondefense reductions proposed by the president would be to increase substantially the defense share of total outlays at the expense of nondefense program outlays other than payments for individuals. This compositional shift is best illustrated by comparing the pattern of actual outlays in 1981 with that for 1986 implied by the president's 1983 budget proposals (table 3-5).[10] President Reagan's budget program called for defense spending to rise from 24.3 percent of the budget in 1981 to 35.8 percent in 1986. Real defense outlays were to increase at an annual rate of close to 9 percent, compared to the 5 percent proposed by the outgoing Carter administration and the 3 percent in CBO's baseline projections. (The CBO baseline projections for comparable budget categories are shown in table A-4.) While the defense plan called for a very sizable increase, it would serve only to restore the defense share to its level of the early 1970s, still considerably less than the level prior to the rapid expansion in nondefense expenditures in the late 1960s.[11]

Under the president's budget proposals, payments for individuals would grow at an annual real rate of less than one percent between 1981 and 1986. This compares to an annual rate of 8 percent over the past twenty-five years and a projected 3 percent annual real growth between 1981 and 1986 under the policies he inherited. This marked reduction in growth under the baseline scenario occurs, as noted earlier in this chapter, because several of the factors that fueled past increases are no longer relevant. The administration's proposals called for benefit payments to maintain their share of total program outlays from 1981 through 1986. However, a major shift would occur in the composition of this spending category. Means-tested programs were targeted for substantial cuts; outlays for low-income assistance programs would be reduced by nearly 20 percent in real terms from 1981 to 1986. Meanwhile, social insurance and other programs would continue to grow at an annual real rate of 2 percent.

Much of the burden for accommodating the rapid defense growth, while still providing for a sizable decline in total outlays as a percentage of GNP, thus would fall on the remaining two nondefense program categories—other grants to state and local governments and other federal operations. Under President Reagan's budget proposals, both these categories were projected to experience large real declines. By 1986 the "other grants" category would be reduced to nearly half its 1981 level in real terms. Over the same period, real spending on other federal operations would be reduced to less than 30 percent of its prior level.[12]

The Effects on Domestic Programs. The president's budget proposals called for truly dramatic spending reductions in specific areas of domestic policy. As a result of the severe cutbacks proposed for the grants to state and local governments and other federal operations, all of the program areas not dominated by entitlement programs would receive large reductions by 1986 from their 1981 levels of funding (table 3-6). Unadjusted for inflation, these

TABLE 3–5

EFFECT ON FEDERAL BUDGET OUTLAYS OF PRESIDENT REAGAN'S BUDGET PROGRAM, BY MAJOR BUDGET CATEGORY

	FY 1981 Outlays, Actual		FY 1986 Outlays, President Reagan's 1983 Budget		Annual Rate of Growth, FY 1981 to FY 1986	
	Billions of Dollars	Budget Share (%)	Billions of Dollars	Budget Share (%)	Nominal (%)	Real (%)
National defense	159.8	24.3	331.7	35.8	15.7	8.7
Benefit payments for individuals	316.6	48.2	434.9	46.9	6.6	0.9
Low-income assistance	(67.4)	(10.3)	(71.3)	(7.7)	(1.1)	(−4.2)
Social insurance and other	(249.2)	(37.9)	(363.6)	(39.2)	(7.8)	(2.0)
Other grants to state and local governments	54.8	8.3	40.3	4.3	−6.0	−12.0
Net interest	68.7	10.5	99.3	10.7	7.6	1.7
Other federal operations	57.4	8.7	21.0	2.3	−18.2	−22.2
Expenditures	(73.9)	(11.2)	(54.0)	(5.8)	(−6.1)	(−10.7)
Offsetting receipts	(−16.5)	(−2.5)	(−33.0)	(−3.6)	(14.9)	(9.2)
Total	657.2	100.0	927.0	100.0	7.1	1.0
Addendum						
Total grants to state and local governments	94.8	14.4	84.7	9.1	−2.2	−7.8

SOURCE: Office of Management and Budget, "Federal Government Finances," February 1982, pp. 63 and 69, and authors' decomposition of the benefit payments category.

TABLE 3–6

EFFECT ON FEDERAL BUDGET OUTLAYS OF PRESIDENT REAGAN'S 1983 BUDGET PROGRAM, BY DOMESTIC PROGRAM AREA

	FY 1981 Outlays		FY 1986 Outlays		Change in Outlays, FY 1981 to FY 1986 (%)
	Billions of Dollars	Domestic Budget Share (%)	Billions of Dollars	Domestic Budget Share (%)	
Income security[a]	218.1	49.3	295.4	56.4	35.4
Low-income assistance	(35.9)	(8.1)	(34.4)	(6.6)	(−4.2)
Social insurance and other	(182.2)	(41.2)	(261.0)	(49.8)	(43.2)
Health	66.0	14.9	102.4	19.5	55.2
Education	15.1	3.4	8.8	1.7	−41.7
Social services	6.5	1.5	5.0	1.0	−23.1
Employment and training	9.8	2.2	3.6	0.7	−63.3
Housing and community development[b]	12.7	2.9	12.4	2.4	−2.4
Transportation	23.3	5.3	19.6	3.7	−15.9
Veterans benefits	23.0	5.2	27.9	5.3	21.3
Revenue sharing	6.9	1.6	7.3	1.4	5.8
Other domestic programs[c]	61.1	13.8	42.1	8.0	−31.1
Total[d]	442.5	100.0	524.5	100.0	18.5

SOURCE: Office of Management and Budget, "Federal Government Finances," February 1982, pp. 27–49.

a. Excludes housing assistance.

b. Includes mortgage credit, thrift insurance, community development, and housing assistance to individuals.

c. Includes general science, space, and technology; energy; natural resources and environment; agriculture; commerce; regional development; administration of justice; and general government.

d. The total and its components are all gross of any offsetting receipts and net of allowances.

reductions in outlays range from 2 percent for transportation to over 60 percent for employment and training.[13] Since an increase in prices of over 30 percent was projected for the time period, the percentage reduction in actual service levels implied by these figures is much greater.

Although income security, health, and veterans benefits would fare much better than other categories, veterans benefits would decline modestly after adjusting for inflation. Those income security programs that are targeted on low-income families and individuals, such as AFDC and Food Stamps, would decline in real value by about one-fourth. The health area, which is dominated by Medicare and Medicaid, would experience a large nominal increase, despite modest cuts in these financing programs and much larger percentage cuts in the health services programs. This results from an expanding Medicare-eligible population and presumed increases in per capita health care costs well in excess of the general rate of inflation.

One particularly notable result of the proposed shift of priorities reflected in these spending proposals is that federal domestic activities would become increasingly dominated by cash transfer and health financing programs. These constituted less than 70 percent of the domestic program outlays in 1981 but would rise to nearly 80 percent by 1986 under the administration's plans.

The Tax and Spending Changes Enacted during 1981

The first year of congressional action on the administration's program was widely acknowledged as a momentous political victory for President Reagan. Congress passed a multiyear tax cut that was even more generous than the president's proposal. It also enacted spending changes in the 1982 budget that granted President Reagan most of what he requested. The first phase of his planned defense build-up was approved. Domestic program expenditures were reduced from their baseline levels by nearly 6 percent in 1982 and more so in subsequent years, through specific cuts that followed closely the president's proposals. However, because of their consequences for future deficits and interest outlays, the net effect of these spending changes and the tax cut was to increase future total outlays well above their prior baselines.

The Tax Cut

The multiyear tax cut that Congress passed in the Economic Recovery Tax Act of 1981 contained a 25 percent across-the-board reduction in personal income tax rates, as opposed to the 30 percent reduction the president had originally requested. Through other provisions, the Congress granted reductions in individual or corporate taxes beyond the specific cuts sought by the president. Most important was the indexing in 1985 of the individual income tax structure, whereby personal exemptions, the zero bracket amount, and bracket widths would be adjusted annually for inflation. Such other provisions were largely ones that the president strongly supported and had intended to seek in some form through a subsequent tax bill.

The result was a tax cut that was significantly more generous than the president's proposal. CBO estimated the revenue loss at over $1 trillion for the first six years, growing as a percentage of GNP from 1.2 percent in 1982 to 5.4 percent in 1986 and 5.9 percent in 1987. This compares to its prior estimate of the president's proposed tax cut of 1.6 percent of GNP in 1982 and 4.1 percent of GNP in 1986.

The Defense Increases and Nondefense Reductions

President Reagan's 1982 budget request submitted in March 1981 was for a defense outlay increase of $8 billion in 1982 and nondefense program outlay reductions of just over $40 billion as compared to a current policy baseline.[14] The Congress, through the Omnibus Budget Reconciliation Act passed in June 1981, granted the president his defense request and reduced nondefense program outlays by an amount that CBO estimated at nearly $33 billion.

In September 1981 the administration estimated that an additional $16 billion in deficit reduction measures was necessary to achieve its original objectives for the 1982 budget. This additional request occurred in part because the congressional reconciliation process had achieved outlay reductions below the president's original proposals. However, the major reason was an upward estimate in uncontrollable spending—primarily interest on the debt (due to the failure of interest rates to fall as forecast by the administration) and farm price supports. To offset the rising deficit estimates, the president proposed additional spending cuts of $13 billion and tax increases of $3 billion. The majority of the spending cuts were to result from a 12 percent reduction in most nondefense discretionary areas; the other components were a $2 billion reduction in defense outlays and a $2.6 billion cut in entitlement programs. The Congress accepted the president's defense modification but granted a smaller reduction in nondefense appropriations, estimated by CBO to further reduce program outlays by about $10 billion. The administration never specified the entitlement cuts for 1982 and also delayed its tax proposals until submission of the president's 1983 budget plan.

By all accounts, the president was tremendously successful in accomplishing his 1982 spending objectives; he got most of the changes he requested from Congress. However, precise estimates of these changes are difficult because of their differential effects on budget authority and outlays, shifting economic and technical assumptions, the different bases against which they might be measured, and subsequent actions and obfuscation on the part of Congress. A reasonably accurate picture can be constructed, though, on the basis of adjusted CBO data. This is done in the remainder of this section for the overall magnitude of the spending changes and their distribution by broad outlay components and by domestic social program categories. In each case, estimates are presented for both 1982 and 1986 in order to provide a sense of both the immediate and longer-term consequences.

The Overall Magnitude of the Spending Changes. Congress approved an increase in defense outlays of approximately $7.3 billion in 1982, growing to $33.1 billion in 1986. Nondefense program reductions are estimated at $31.6 billion or 6.4 percent of their baseline expenditures for 1982, growing to $54.8 billion or 8.2 percent of their baseline expenditures for 1986.[15]

The $7.3 billion increase in 1982 defense outlays reflects a much larger— nearly $20 billion—increase in 1982 defense budget authority. Not all of this increase in authority is spent immediately, since much of it is earmarked for items such as military hardware that take years to procure. Congress also approved plans (subject to review and ratification in following years) for additional large increases in defense budget authority for 1983 and 1984 above the prior baseline but did not explicitly address subsequent years. The $33.1 billion estimated increase in 1986 defense outlays reflects these higher budget authority targets for 1983 and 1984 but makes no assumptions about a continued increased build-up. The administration's original defense plans called for an increase in outlays over the prior baseline which grows to over $80 billion in 1986. Thus, congressional action on the 1982 budget set a policy course that was consistent with the president's long-run request but represented only a first installment.

While the congressional estimates of legislative action through December 1981 showed nondefense program reductions of about $43 billion for FY 1982, the actual impact on 1982 federal spending will be much smaller. Under great pressure to maximize the apparent size of the reductions in nondefense outlays for 1982, Congress made certain accounting shifts and mandated technical assumptions that led CBO's reported numbers to substantially exaggerate the impact of nondefense reductions. Largest among these was the shift of the strategic petroleum reserve to off-budget status. A budget "savings" of $3.7 billion was thus credited, even though neither the overall level of federal spending nor the total deficit was affected. However, the most egregious example of specious savings was the shift of $685 million in Medicare payments from the first month of FY 1982 to the last month of FY 1981, so that it would show up as 1982 budget savings. Congress had done just the reverse the year before when it wanted to show cuts in the 1981 budget. Thus, credit was taken twice for a nonexistent reduction.

The $31.6 billion estimate of 1982 nondefense program spending reductions used in this analysis excludes such questionable savings. It also reflects more recent (and realistic) economic and technical assumptions than those embodied in the July 1981 CBO baseline, and accounts for subsequent congressional actions through June 1982.[16]

Thus, while the reductions in nondefense spending in the 1982 budget were substantial, they were less than what was generally reported. Furthermore, recall that these reductions are measured from a baseline that assumes discretionary programs would be increased to compensate for inflation, even though this would require explicit congressional action to increase budget authority. Had this inflation adjustment not been assumed, the reductions would have been estimated at $12 billion to $15 billion rather than $31.6 billion.

The estimated nondefense spending reductions grow from 1982 to 1986 not only in absolute terms, but also as a percentage of the pre-Reagan baseline, from 6.4 percent in 1982 to 8.2 percent in 1986. This is due to the lagged effect of changes in budget authority on the level of outlays in nondefense discretionary programs. Congress reduces outlays for these programs by reducing budget authority, thus limiting the extent to which agencies may enter into obligations that would result in future outlays. For many programs reduced budget authority translates immediately into reduced outlays, since the funds typically purchase products (such as meals for the elderly) or services (such as Park Service rangers) that are immediately provided. However, in such cases as transportation or housing, where long-term capital investment projects are undertaken, many years pass before a current reduction in budget authority leads to a commensurate reduction in outlays. Current outlays in these programs are determined much more by past congressional actions. Thus, the longer-term outlay implications of reduced budget authority in discretionary nondefense programs are more severe than the immediate ones.

The Effects of the Policy Changes on Major Spending Categories. All of the broad nondefense program categories absorbed a substantial share of the reductions from the 1982 baseline, as shown in table 3-7. However, in proportional terms the reductions are far larger for grants to state and local governments and other federal operations than for benefit payments for individuals. And the proportional reduction in low-income assistance programs is more than twice that in other payments for individuals.

Because of the much larger reduction in 1982 budget authority than outlays, the outlay reductions in other federal operations and other grants to state and local governments nearly double as a percentage of their baselines between 1982 and 1986. Other grants to state and local governments will be reduced to only 75 percent of their 1986 baseline levels. In contrast, the proportional reduction in payments to individuals remains constant between

TABLE 3-7

EFFECT ON FEDERAL BUDGET OUTLAYS OF POLICY CHANGES IN THE FIRST EIGHTEEN MONTHS OF THE REAGAN ADMINISTRATION, BY MAJOR BUDGET CATEGORY

| | Baseline Outlays, Billions of Dollars | | Enacted Changes, Relative to Baseline | | | | Budget Share (%) | |
| | | | Billions of Dollars | | Percentage of Baseline | | Pre-change | Post-change |
	FY 1982	FY 1986	FY 1982	FY 1986	FY 1982	FY 1986	FY 1982	FY 1986
National defense	182.8	252.5	7.3	33.1	4.0	13.1	23.9	27.1
Benefit payments for individuals	366.4	511.1	−15.1	−20.8	−4.1	−4.1	48.0	46.6
Low-income assistance	(74.9)	(104.3)	(−5.5)	(−10.2)	(−7.3)	(−9.8)	(9.8)	(8.9)
Social insurance and other	(291.5)	(406.8)	(−9.6)	(−10.6)	(−3.3)	(−2.6)	(38.2)	(37.6)
Other grants to state and local governments	57.7	71.8	−8.4	−18.0	−14.6	−25.1	7.6	5.1
Net interest	83.9	93.8	1.1	61.7	1.3	65.8	11.0	14.8
Due to nondefense outlay reductions	--	--	(−2.5)	(−25.8)	--	--	--	--
Due to defense increases and tax cuts	--	--	(3.6)	(87.5)	--	--	--	--
Other federal operations	72.5	83.2	−8.1	−16.0	−11.2	−19.2	9.5	6.4
Total	763.3	1,012.4	−23.2	40.0	−3.0	4.0	100.0	100.0
Addendum								
Total nondefense programs (excludes net interest)	496.6	666.1	−31.6	−54.8	−6.4	−8.2	65.1	58.1
Total grants to state and local governments	104.8	136.2	−13.7	−22.9	−13.1	−16.8	13.7	10.8

SOURCE: Estimates made by the authors, based upon data from the Congressional Budget Office.

1982 and 1986. The reductions in social insurance and other programs decline in significance, offsetting an increase in the proportional reductions in low-income assistance from 7.3 percent in 1982 to 9.8 percent in 1986.

Due to the combination of the nondefense spending cuts and defense increases enacted during 1981, the shares of total outlays of the broad expenditure categories shift in the direction the administration proposed—with defense increasing its share at the expense of nondefense programs other than payments for individuals. Despite the magnitude of the spending changes, however, the shift achieved solely on the basis of the 1982 budget changes is mild compared to what the administration has proposed to accomplish from further nondefense cuts and continued increases in defense appropriations.

The Effects of Spending Reductions on Domestic Programs. Total domestic program spending was reduced by 5.8 percent from its baseline for 1982 as a result of the budget cuts.[17] All areas (except revenue sharing) were affected, though the depth of the reductions differs considerably (table 3-8). The cut of nearly one-half in employment and training programs was by far the largest. Health, veterans benefits, and the income security programs not targeted on the low-income population all received quite small percentage cuts. Reductions in the other program areas ranged from 6 to 16 percent in 1982.

By 1986 the effects of the spending reductions are larger (8.2 percent of baseline) and are distributed somewhat differently. The reductions in the education, transportation, and "other" categories roughly double as a percentage of baseline outlays, while the reductions for income security and veterans benefits increase by one-half. On the other hand, the reductions in health and social services are roughly the same in 1986 as in 1982 as a proportion of baseline outlays. While the actual outlay reduction in housing and community development declines in significance between 1982 and 1986, this is misleading as an indicator of the ultimate, very substantial consequences of the congressional actions during 1981. There were severe reductions in budget authority for low-income housing assistance whose effects will not be fully felt for thirty years.[18] The combined effect of all these spending reductions is to increase the share of total domestic program spending going to cash transfers and health care financing (income security, health, and veterans benefits) at the expense of all other domestic program areas.

The Consequences for Total Outlays

So far this discussion has focused on the direct outlay effects of the defense increases and the nondefense cuts. These spending changes, along

TABLE 3-8

EFFECT ON FEDERAL BUDGET OUTLAYS OF POLICY CHANGES IN THE FIRST EIGHTEEN MONTHS OF THE REAGAN ADMINISTRATION, BY DOMESTIC PROGRAM AREA

	Baseline Outlays, Billions of Dollars		Enacted Changes, Relative to Baseline				Domestic Budget Share (%)	
			Billions of Dollars		Percentage of Baseline		Pre-change	Post-change
	FY 1982	FY 1986	FY 1982	FY 1986	FY 1982	FY 1986	FY 1982	FY 1986
Income security[a]	253.7	340.7	-9.8	-18.3	-3.9	-5.4	50.5	52.3
Low-income assistance	(40.3)	(51.1)	(-4.2)	(-6.3)	(-10.4)	(-12.3)	(8.0)	(7.3)
Social insurance and other	(214.1)	(289.6)	(-5.6)	(-12.0)	(-2.3)	(-4.1)	(42.6)	(45.1)
Health	79.5	132.4	-2.5	-4.3	-3.1	-3.2	15.8	20.8
Education	17.1	23.6	-2.7	-6.8	-15.8	-28.8	3.4	2.7
Social services	6.9	8.4	-0.6	-0.8	-8.7	-9.5	1.4	1.2
Employment and training	11.6	15.0	-5.5	-7.9	-47.4	-52.6	2.3	1.2
Housing and community development[b]	17.3	23.4	-2.0	-1.4	-11.6	-6.0	3.4	3.6
Transportation	22.5	27.8	-1.4	-4.2	-6.2	-15.1	4.5	3.8
Veterans benefits	24.2	28.4	-0.5	-0.9	-2.1	-3.2	4.8	4.5
Revenue sharing	6.4	7.9	0.1	0.2	1.6	2.5	1.3	1.3
Other domestic programs[c]	62.2	63.2	-4.4	-10.5	-7.1	-16.6	12.4	8.6
Total[d]	502.1	670.8	-29.3[e]	-54.9[e]	-5.8	-8.2	100.0	100.0

SOURCE: Estimates made by the authors, based upon data from the Congressional Budget Office.

a. Excludes housing assistance.

b. Includes mortgage credit, thrift insurance, community development, and housing assistance to individuals.

c. Includes general science, space, and technology; energy; natural resources and environment; agriculture; commerce; regional development; administration of justice; and general government.

d. The total and its components are all gross of offsetting receipts and net of allowances.

e. Differs from the total nondefense estimate shown in Table 3–7 due to the exclusion here of any changes in international affairs, allowances, with the tax cut, also have an indirect outlay impact because they alter deficit financing needs and thus affect net interest payments. This effect, also shown in table 3-7, is minor for 1982, adding only $1.1 billion to baseline outlays. This is the net of a $2.5 billion reduction in interest due to the deficit-reducing consequences of the nondefense cuts and a $3.6 billion increase in interest due to the deficit-increasing consequences of the defense build-up and tax cut. However, by 1986 this combined net effect on interest is quite large ($61.7 billion), due to the cumulative effect of policy changes on deficits for 1982 through 1986—and leads to an increase in the net interest share of the total budget from 11 percent in 1982 to nearly 15 percent in 1986. Over this time period, the consequences of the tax cut for interest payments become increasingly dominant.

When all of these direct and indirect effects are taken into account, the tax and spending changes enacted by Congress during 1981 serve to lower 1982 budget outlays by $23.2 billion or 3 percent of their baseline level. By 1986 the direction of this effect reverses, and they actually *add* $40 billion or 4 percent to total baseline outlays. This surprising result and other factors combined to produce a dramatic shift in the long-term budget outlook.

The Changed Budget Outlook and Its Consequences

As attention shifted from the 1982 budget to the new long-term budget outlook, it became clear that budget prospects were radically different from that of any previous experience. Under the new policies, baseline projections showed growing deficits of unprecedented magnitude throughout the 1980s. The unexpected size of the tax cut, combined with the poor performance of the economy, was largely responsible for a budget outlook far worse than anticipated. Failure of the 1982 budget reductions to effectively restrain the growth of nondefense spending also was a major contributing factor. If the budget is to be balanced by 1986, a combination of program expenditure reductions and tax increases totaling about 5 percent of GNP is required, starting with the 1983 budget. This cannot be accomplished without additional domestic program reductions two to three times as large as those enacted during 1981, unless President Reagan largely abandons his tax reduction and defense build-up objectives.

The Changed Budget Outlook

The February 1982 CBO baseline projections, when amended to include the president's defense program, reflect a severe structural imbalance between current federal tax and spending policies (table 3-9). Revenues decline continuously as a percentage of GNP—rapidly at first, because of the personal income tax rate reductions, and then more gradually after 1984. Outlays reach a new peacetime high in excess of 24 percent of GNP in 1982 and maintain that level throughout the projection period. The result is a series of rapidly expanding, triple-digit deficits that reach $293 billion (6.4 percent of projected GNP) in 1986. The economic and technical assumptions underlying the projections are generally less optimistic than those used during 1981. However, evolving economic realities suggest that even the revised assumptions may be too optimistic and that the projections still understate the level of baseline deficits.

Because such deficits are beyond the range of relevant historical experience, their consequences are highly uncertain. (The largest post-World War II deficit was 4.0 percent of GNP in 1976.) However, economists, financial

TABLE 3–9

CONGRESSIONAL BUDGET OFFICE BASELINE BUDGET PROJECTIONS, WITH THE
DEFENSE PROPOSALS IN PRESIDENT REAGAN'S 1983 BUDGET, FEBRUARY 1982

	FY 1981	FY 1982	FY 1983	FY 1984	FY 1985	FY 1986
	Billions of Dollars					
Revenues	602.6	631.3	651.6	701.1	763.1	817.9
Outlays	660.5	740.9	819.0	908.1	1,007.6	1,110.5
Deficit (−) or surplus[a]	−57.9	−109.6	−167.4	−207.0	−244.5	−292.6
	Percentage of GNP					
Revenues	21.1	20.6	19.0	18.5	18.3	18.0
Outlays	23.1	24.2	23.9	24.0	24.2	24.4
Deficit (−) or surplus[a]	−2.0	−3.6	−4.9	−5.5	−5.9	−6.4

SOURCES: Congressional Budget Office, *Baseline Budget Projections for Fiscal Years 1983–1987* (Washington, D.C.: GPO, 1982), p. xvii; and Congressional Budget Office, *An Analysis of the President's Budgetary Proposals for Fiscal Year 1983* (Washington, D.C.: GPO, 1982), p. 66. The impact of the president's defense proposals in 1986 has been approximated from the latter report, which reestimates the president's budget only through 1985. The impact on net interest outlays of the higher defense spending was estimated by the authors.

a. Congress adopted a slightly different set of economic and technical assumptions than those underlying these projections during negotiations over the first concurrent budget resolution for FY 1983. Those assumptions yield a pattern of deficits somewhat higher than those shown here for FY 1982–1984 ($182.0 billion in FY 1983) and somewhat lower than those in FY 1985–1986.

experts, and politicians of nearly all persuasions consider this a recipe for continued economic distress, if not disaster. As discussed in chapter 2, the most prevalent concern is that the federal government's requirements for debt financing would place excessive demands on credit markets. Under the current tight monetary policy, this would sustain real interest rates at such high levels that private borrowing and investment would be discouraged and the potential growth rate of the economy markedly slowed. Alternatively, the Federal Reserve Bank could adopt a more expansive monetary policy to accommodate both federal and private borrowing at lower interest rates, at some risk of reigniting inflation.[19]

How did this predicament arise? The shift in the deficit picture between CBO's July 1981 and February 1982 baseline projections (including the president's defense request in the latter) is enormous—2.6 percent of GNP in 1982 and a staggering 11.0 percent of GNP in 1986. To what extent was this the result of the tax cuts, the defense build-up, the changed economic outlook, or other factors? Answers to these questions are helpful in understanding the debate over future budget strategies.

The Shift in the Revenue Outlook. The shift in the revenue side of the budget accounts for two-thirds of the swing in the 1986 deficit of 11.0 percent of GNP. The tax cut, which reduces estimated revenues by 5.4 percent of GNP in 1986, is the dominant factor. Slower economic growth and lower inflation lead to projected revenue losses of another 2.1 percent of GNP (table 3-10).

When the administration's original proposal was presented in 1981, serious concerns were raised about the wisdom of enacting such a large, multiyear tax cut before corresponding expenditure cuts were passed and before the nature of the economic recovery became clear. Nevertheless, the long-term tax reduction finally approved by Congress and the president was substantially larger than the president's original proposal. Critics of this tax cut have questioned whether such a large and permanent revenue loss was a responsible policy, given the sensitivity to economic conditions of both spending and revenues, the uncertain economic outlook, and the administration's highly optimistic 1981 economic forecast.

The tax cut essentially removed any maneuvering room on the revenue side to offset the consequences of the poorer-than-projected economic performance, short of Congress taking explicit action to raise taxes. In the past, the revenue side of the budget always contributed substantially to the self-correction of deficits in long-term projections, since taxes would rise as a percentage of GNP as the latter expanded. Greater pressure now has been placed on reductions in federal spending in order to control projected deficits. This is presumably what the administration and most congressional conser-

TABLE 3-10

DIFFERENCES BETWEEN THE CBO BASELINE BUDGET PROJECTIONS OF JULY 1981
AND FEBRUARY 1982,
FOR FY 1982 AND FY 1986

	Billions of Dollars		Percentage of GNP[a]	
	FY 1982	FY 1986	FY 1982	FY 1986
Revenues				
February 1982 projection	631	818	20.6	18.0
July 1981 projection	709	1,159	22.0	25.4
Difference	−78	−341	−2.5	−7.5
Economic and technical				
assumptions	(−39)	(−97)	(−1.3)	(−2.1)
Policy changes	(−39)	(−244)	(−1.3)	(−5.4)
Outlays				
February 1982 projection[b]	741	1,111	24.2	24.4
July 1981 projection	739	950	24.1	20.9
Difference	2	161	0.1	3.5
Economic and technical				
assumptions	(25)	(63)	(0.8)	(1.4)
Policy changes[c]	(−23)	(98)	(−0.8)	(2.2)
Deficit (−) or surplus				
February 1982 projection	−110	−293	−3.6	−6.4
July 1981 projection	−30	209	−1.0	4.6
Difference	−80	502	−2.6	11.0
Economic and technical				
assumptions	(−64)	(−160)	(−2.1)	(3.5)
Policy changes	(−16)	(−342)	(−0.5)	(7.5)

SOURCES: Tables 3–4, 3–6, and 3–7. Revenue losses associated with the Economic Recovery
Tax Act of 1981 are from the Congressional Budget Office, *Baseline Budget Projections for Fiscal Years 1983–1987* (Washington, D.C.: GPO, 1982), p. 25.
  a. As percentage of February 1982 CBO estimate of GNP for the corresponding fiscal year.
  b. Assumes adoption of the defense proposals in President Reagan's 1983 budget.
  c. Any interaction in the effects of changes in economic assumptions and policies is attributed
to the policy changes. For example, the impact on net interest outlays of higher defense spending
and lower revenues is estimated at the interest rates projected in February 1982.

vatives had in mind—and may explain why they were willing to approve a
tax cut that made the budget vulnerable to such huge deficits.

The Shift in the Spending Outlook. Outlay changes contributed marginally to the swing in the 1982 deficit picture and very substantially (3.5
percent of GNP) to that in 1986. Estimated spending for 1982 rose by $25

billion over the old baseline due simply to worse-than-predicted economic conditions and reestimates in programs not subject to specific spending limits. The four major contributing factors here were the effects of higher health care cost inflation on Medicare and Medicaid, higher unemployment on unemployment insurance, lower farm incomes on farm price supports, and higher interest rates on interest payments. By 1986 such changes in economic and technical assumptions lead to estimated outlay increases of $63 billion, more than twice as much as in 1982. (Nearly $20 billion of this is due to upward revisions in the rate of health care cost inflation, particularly for hospital costs, despite a downward revision in the overall rate of inflation.) The startling fact is that these "uncontrollable" spending increases are greater than the spending reductions resulting from the domestic program cuts.[20]

Of equal significance for 1986 is that policy changes adopted during 1981 add $98 billion to projected outlays. This reflects the $40 billion increase resulting from congressional actions as discussed at the end of the last section plus an estimated $58 billion in additional outlays resulting from continued implementation of the president's requested military build-up ($48 billion in defense outlays and $10 billion in interest payments).

The specific numbers shown in long-term baseline budget projections can change substantially depending upon what economic, technical, and defense build-up assumptions are made. However, the general picture is not changed by altering these assumptions within wide and reasonable ranges. President Reagan vowed to bring federal expenditures under control and sharply restrain their rate of growth. Despite the unprecedented reductions in the 1982 budget, he failed completely in these efforts through this first budget cycle of his administration. The cuts did little to restrain the major sources of nondefense program growth, and the tax cut and defense build-up greatly added to future deficit projections.

The president cannot be held responsible for the extensive automatic growth of domestic program spending under current policies; it was built in before he assumed office. However, both the administration and Congress can be faulted for approving such a large tax cut and defense build-up, while failing also to adopt measures to restrain domestic spending growth in any fundamental way.

Deficit Reduction Strategies

In his 1983 budget proposals, President Reagan responded to this changed long-term budget outlook in three ways: (1) he adhered more or less to his

original tax reduction and defense spending objectives; (2) he abandoned his
objective of a balanced budget within the five-year projection period; and
(3) he sought to hold projected deficits below $100 billion through domestic
cuts even deeper than those he originally proposed and through continued use
of highly optimistic economic and technical assumptions. Using the economic
and technical assumptions underlying its February 1982 baseline projections,
CBO estimated that full adoption of the president's proposals would result in
a budget deficit above $100 billion in 1983 and even higher in subsequent
years (table 3-11).[21] In stark contrast to the 1982 budget, both parties in
Congress quickly rejected the president's 1983 budget as a point of departure
for their deliberations, viewing the projected deficits as politically intolerable
if not economically disastrous.

To agree on the undesirability of large deficits, however, is not to agree
on how to eliminate them. The near unanimity that Congress displayed in
rejecting the president's amended long-run budget strategy belied the deeply
differing views as to which mix of deficit reduction measures is preferable.

TABLE 3-11

DEFICIT ESTIMATES UNDER PRESIDENT REAGAN'S 1983 BUDGET

	FY 1982	FY 1983	FY 1984	FY 1985
Administration baseline deficit with proposed defense spending growth[a]	101	146	165	168
Less: Proposed revenue increases[a]	—	–13	–19	–18
Proposed spending reductions[a]	–3	–43	–65	–81
Total deficit reductions[a]	–3	–56	–84	–99
Plus: Proposed spending increases[a]	—	2	2	3
Administration deficit target[a]	99	92	83	72
CBO estimate of deficit under the administration's budget[b]	111	121	129	140

SOURCE: Congressional Budget Office, *An Analysis of the President's Budgetary Proposals for Fiscal Year 1983* (Washington, D.C.: GPO, 1982), p. 6.

a. Based upon the administration's economic and technical assumptions; does not reflect the
April 1982 OMB budget update, which added approximately $10 billion annually to the 1983–
1985 outlay and deficit estimates.

b. Involves reestimates of the administration's specific revenue increase and spending reduction measures, as well as different economic assumptions.

Congress embarked on its 1983 budget deliberations in what promised to be the first of several years of overriding emphasis on deficit reduction. In doing so, it faced a political task of herculean proportions. Accepting the president's defense proposals, the February 1982 CBO baseline projections indicate that, in order to approach a balanced budget by 1986, the Congress would need to enact a combination of tax increases and program outlay reductions starting in 1983 that exceed $225 billion, or 5 percent of GNP, by 1986. (Lower interest payments would reduce the deficit by about another $55 billion, leaving only a $13 billion deficit, given the $293 billion baseline deficit estimate).[22]

In order to design a deficit reduction program of this magnitude, fundamental issues and tradeoffs have to be addressed. How much should come from increased revenues versus reduced spending? (Stated differently, how much should the size of the federal government be pared?) What should be the allocation of federal spending between defense and nondefense programs? Within the domestic area, what proportion of the reductions should be borne by the high-growth entitlement programs versus the discretionary programs that were cut more deeply in the 1982 budget? To what extent should further reductions in low-income assistance or grants to state and local governments be avoided?

To illuminate the strategic options, consider two extreme alternatives, based on the estimates in table 3-12. On the one hand, 1986 taxes could be increased from the projected February 1982 baseline level of 18 percent of GNP to 21 percent—the level that prevailed when President Reagan assumed office. In addition, the defense build-up could be scaled back to the 5 percent annual real growth advocated by the Carter administration. This would represent a full retreat by the president from his two remaining major budgetary objectives (having already abandoned his objective of a balanced budget). However, achieving the deficit target would still require reductions in nondefense programs of $50 billion, about as large as those enacted in the first round of budget cutting in 1981.

On the other hand, taxes might be increased to only 19 percent of GNP—President Reagan's target in his original tax proposal and the level prevailing throughout the 1970s—and the defense build-up scaled back modestly to, say, an annual rate of 7 percent real growth. (The president's 1983 budget proposed revenue increases amounting to about 0.4 percent of GNP by 1986 and a negligible scaleback in defense outlays.) Nevertheless, the deficit target would require additional domestic program reductions of about $120 billion— more than double those achieved during 1981.

What is the potential for additional reductions in nondefense programs?[23] As noted earlier, the share of domestic spending going to discretionary pro-

TABLE 3–12

EFFECT ON THE FY 1986 BASELINE DEFICIT OF VARIOUS DEFICIT REDUCTION
MEASURES

	Reduction to the FY 1986 Baseline Deficit (Billions of Dollars)
Revenue Increases	
Eliminate or postpone (beyond 1986) the July 1983 tax cut	44
Eliminate or postpone (beyond 1986) the indexing provisions to be effective in 1985	30
Increase revenues by one percent of GNP, through other means	45
Outlay Reductions	
Defense reductions (excluding defense pay raises and military retirement)	
Restrain annual real growth to 7 percent	15
Restrain annual real growth to 5 percent	40
Lower automatic cost-of-living adjustments in entitlement programs (including military retirement)[a]	
Delay July 1983 Social Security increase by three months and index all programs by 2 percentage points less than CPI	19
Delay July 1983 Social Security increase by three months and index all programs by 4 percentage points less than CPI	27
Other entitlement reductions	
Adopt all proposals in the administration's 1983 budget[b]	20–25
Federal pay restraint (including defense pay raises)	
Limit annual adjustments to 4 percent	14
Management savings	5–10
Other nondefense outlay reductions	
Freeze all discretionary programs through FY 1986 at FY 1982 levels	27
Net interest savings	
Reduce debt service through revenue increases or expenditure reductions amounting to one percent of GNP by FY 1986	11

SOURCE: Congressional Budget Office, *Reducing the Federal Deficit: Strategies and Options* (Washington, D.C.: GPO, 1982) and authors' own estimates.
   a.   Excludes low-income assistance. Inclusion of such programs would add only a few billion dollars of savings.
   b.   Assumes that several proposals for FY 1983 do not go into effect until FY 1984.

grams is scheduled to decline substantially as a result of the 1982 budget cuts. Outlays for other grants to state and local governments and other federal operations comprise less than 20 percent of 1986 nondefense program outlays in the February 1982 baseline projections and account for only 5 percent of the growth in these outlays between 1982 and 1986. One possibility frequently discussed in Congress would be a total freeze on the discretionary programs, so that they are held at 1982 nominal levels and not adjusted, even for inflation, through 1986. Combined with very substantial federal pay restraint and certain other management initiatives, this could result in 1986 outlay reductions of about $50 billion, or slightly more than one percent of GNP. This would constitute a 25 percent reduction from projected outlays based on service levels of pre-Reagan policies, on top of the 20-25 percent drop enacted in the 1982 budget. Thus, any effort to reduce domestic outlays by substantially more than one percent of GNP must focus on benefit payments for individuals, if it is not to greatly worsen fiscal pressures on state and local governments and severely cripple other federal operations.

The 1986 level of low-income assistance was reduced by 10 percent through action on the 1982 budget. This, in combination with their small share of baseline nondefense program outlays in 1986 (less than 20 percent), leaves little scope for substantial additional cuts that will not fundamentally affect the ability of these programs to serve the most needy people in our society. Another 10 percent cut in low-income assistance would yield less than $10 billion in 1986. This suggests that much of the burden of any deep cuts in domestic programs should be borne by the other benefit payment programs that were more favorably treated in the 1982 budget reductions.

These social insurance and related programs primarily finance health care and provide disability and retirement pensions for Social Security recipients, veterans, and federal workers. The Social Security and Medicare programs dominate this outlay category, as they do the entire domestic budget. Together they comprise more than half of 1986 baseline domestic program expenditures and more than two-thirds of the projected growth in these expenditures between 1982 and 1986.

There are two general approaches to restraining the growth of benefit payment programs. The first is to make structural changes that will reduce either the number of eligible people or the cost of benefits available to those who become eligible. The amount of savings that can be achieved through this approach can be considerable in the long run but is likely to be much more limited within a five-year budget horizon. This is because any proposal for reform that is likely to gather sufficient political support must be phased in over time, in order not to disadvantage current or prospective recipients or be otherwise disruptive. It is difficult to capture congressional interest in such changes, except in times of extreme budgetary pressure when they provide little assistance to the immediate problem. Nevertheless, if substantial long-term restraint on the growth of domestic expenditures is sought, the Congress must be willing to take such actions even without the incentive of major short-term savings.[24]

The second approach for restraining the growth of benefit payment programs is to reduce COLAs in the cash programs and increase beneficiary cost-sharing in Medicare. These changes have the advantage of producing substantial and immediate impacts on the level of spending. They also impose small benefit reductions on the entire recipient population, rather than concentrating the burden on a lesser number. While such steps would substantially reduce the deficit, they are by themselves not a panacea for the long-term deficit problem. A package of domestic program cuts combining fairly restrictive COLA limitations with cuts in low-income assistance as large as the administration proposed in its 1983 budget and other reductions in selected social insurance programs (including increased cost-sharing in Medicare) would yield a deficit reduction of only about 2 percent of GNP in 1986.

Congressional Action on the 1983 Budget

In June 1982 Congress passed its first concurrent budget resolution for FY 1983. This resolution set target levels for 1983 through 1985 for spending by functional budget category and for total revenues. It also specified the amounts of deficit reduction to be achieved by the relevant congressional committees through subsequent legislative action. Congress's paramount concern was to reduce future deficits by as much as was politically feasible. By the Budget Committees' estimates, the prescribed spending reductions and revenue increases, if fully implemented, would reduce the deficit to $104 billion in 1983 and to even lower levels in succeeding years. To understand the longer-term budgetary implications of this preliminary action on the 1983 budget, it is instructive to examine its potential impact for 1986 (table 3-13).

Based upon a projection of the Budget Committees' estimates, the action prescribed in the budget resolution would reduce the estimated 1986 baseline deficit by $210 billion. However, Congress chose to adopt very favorable assumptions with respect to the magnitude of the deficit reduction to be achieved through restraint on defense and entitlement spending and through management savings. Congress also assumed that interest rates would decline by 5.1 percentage points over the calendar period 1983-1985 as a result of the deficit reduction scheme, whereas CBO had forecast only a 2.6 percentage point decline over this time period. These assumptions account for $49 million, or nearly one-quarter, of the deficit reduction amount claimed by the Congress. In addition, the Budget Committees adopted a slightly revised economic forecast, plus the administration's estimates of baseline revenues and baseline defense spending. These result in a baseline deficit for 1986 of $274 billion as opposed to the $293 billion estimate based on CBO's earlier projections (table 3-9), leading to a deficit estimate of $64 billion if the budget resolution measures are implemented.

TABLE 3–13

DEFICIT REDUCTION MEASURES IN THE FY 1983 FIRST CONCURRENT BUDGET
RESOLUTION

	Consequences for FY 1986 Budget (Billions of Dollars)	
	Projection of Budget Committee Estimates[a]	Alternative Estimates[b]
Baseline deficit	274[c]	293[d]
Deficit reductions		
Revenue increases (taxes and user fees)	–47	–47
Defense reductions	–12	–10
Lower automatic cost-of-living adjustments in entitlement programs	–4	–4
Other entitlement reductions	–12	–11
Federal pay restraint	–15	–14
Management savings	–14	–7
Other nondefense outlay reductions	–30	–30
Net interest savings		
Due to lower interest rates	–36	0
Due to lower deficits	–40	–37
Total	–210	–160
Remaining deficit	64	133

SOURCES: Senate Budget Committee, Congressional Budget Office, Office of Management and Budget, and authors' own estimates.

a. These projections assume a continuation through FY 1986 of the pattern of FY 1983–1985 deficit reductions contained in the budget resolution. Where specific policies were implied by the resolution, available estimates from CBO and OMB have been used.

b. These estimates are based upon CBO's economic and technical assumptions, plus some reestimates by the authors. In particular, they reflect CBO technical differences with respect to defense reductions, Civil Service retirement, and accelerated leasing of the Outer Continental Shelf. Furthermore, the authors have assumed that only half of the management savings (excluding off-shore leasing) would be achieved through implementation of such measures as specified by the Budget Committees. Finally, the authors have assumed no reduction in interest rates between FY 1982 and FY 1986 beyond the 2.9 percentage point decline in ninety-day Treasury bill rates contained in CBO's economic forecast of February 1982.

c. This projection reflects the administration's baseline revenue estimate, which is approximately $20 billion above that associated with the economic and technical assumptions in the CBO February 1982 baseline projections. The difference is almost entirely due to technical differences between CBO and the Treasury Department in estimated revenues.

d. From table 3–9.

An alternative, and probably more realistic, 1986 budget deficit estimate of $133 billion, over twice as large as the congressional estimate, is shown in the second column of table 3-13. It also assumes implementation of the deficit reduction measures implied by the first concurrent resolution, but it uses CBO's technical reestimates of several of the program spending reductions, and an estimate of management savings that is more consistent with past experience with these types of measures. This alternative estimate indicates that full implementation of the prescribed measures would eliminate slightly more than one-half of the previously estimated long-term baseline deficit. About one-half of the $123 billion in direct deficit savings due to policy changes (as opposed to interest savings) would come from revenue increases (with tax increases of one percent of GNP) and defense outlay reductions. Nondefense cuts would be as large as those made in conjunction with the 1982 budget. Grants to state and local governments and other federal operations would once again bear a disproportionate share of the burden. Entitlement programs not targeted on the low-income population would again be reduced proportionately less than low-income assistance and by far less than all other nondefense spending.

The composition of the deficit reductions specified in the budget resolution is thus largely consistent with the administration's initial long-run budget objectives. Although it has generally not been recognized as such, this would appear to signal a political victory for the president in the second round of budget decisions under his administration as considerable as that achieved in the first round. It is also clear, however, that several more rounds of deficit reductions will be necessary to restore fully a balance between federal spending and revenues.

Conclusions

In the course of President Reagan's legislative victories during 1981, it appeared that the fundamental issues concerning the size and financing of the government, and the allocation of resources among competing alternatives, had been confronted and largely resolved. As the 1983 budget cycle approached, however, it became all too clear that this resolution was ephemeral. Final congressional action on the 1983 budget undoubtedly will narrow the range of uncertainty, but several subsequent budget cycles will have to pass before the critical choices adopted by Congress to address the long-term budgetary dilemma are fully evident. So far President Reagan has been remarkably successful in achieving congressional acquiescence to his long-term spending and revenue priorities.

However, the assessment in this chapter of alternatives for eliminating the long-term deficit carries a clear message: a politically viable deficit-elimination program is likely to require a substantial retreat by the president from his original defense and tax objectives. In addition, very sizable further reductions in domestic spending will be necessary, including cuts in the politically sensitive Social Security and Medicare programs. However, there is still considerable latitude for tradeoffs among tax increases, scaling back of the planned defense build-up, and reductions in nondefense spending. The extreme political difficulty of the choices involved will continue to result in considerable pressure both to engage in unrealistic forecasting in order to postpone the painful reckoning and to tolerate substantial, continuing deficits. The range of conceivable political compromises encompasses widely varying outcomes as to the functioning of the economy, the size of government, and the allocation of public resources over the next several decades. Rarely has the nation confronted fiscal choices with such important long-term consequences. Faced with these prospects, it will not be surprising if the president and the various factions of Congress continue to find it difficult to reach agreement over the next several years.

Chapter 4

Tax Policy

Charles R. Hulten
June A. O'Neill

The Reagan administration came to office at a time when many Americans were questioning whether they wanted more government and the additional taxes to pay for it. Taxes are never popular, but the 1970s were marked by overt taxpayer discontent. In several states voters placed limits on state taxing power, and a federal tax limitation movement took root.[1] Public opinion polls also showed signs of increasing resistance to higher federal taxes. Over the period 1972 to 1981, the Advisory Council on Intergovernmental Relations found a significant rise in the percentage of citizens citing the federal income tax as the "worst tax—that is, the least fair."[2]

Recent years have also witnessed greater interest in the impact of taxes on incentives to work, save, and invest. Economists have always been sensitive to the tradeoff between the use of the tax system to redistribute income and the effects of the resulting tax structure on economic efficiency. In the past it was assumed, however, that the efficiency costs of redistribution were

[The authors would like to thank Don Fullerton, Harvey Galper, Richard Musgrave, Rudolph Penner, Hyman Sanders, Eugene Steuerle, Lawrence Summers, Emil Sunley, Eric Toder, James Verdier, and numerous colleagues for commenting on earlier drafts of this chapter. They would also like to thank Janice McCallum and Carolyn O'Brien for their valuable assistance.]

small, at least at the level of taxation then imposed. More recently it has been argued that the economic impacts of high tax rates may be substantial.

By the early 1980s support for a federal tax cut had grown for several reasons. First, taxpayers had seen inflation raise their incomes and push them into higher tax brackets—a process called "bracket creep." Second, some viewed a tax cut as a way to curb the growth in federal expenditures, on the assumption that rising deficits would not be tolerated. Third, after a decade of poor productivity growth, considerable support existed for policies that would promote economic growth, and tax incentives were seen as a major way to stimulate growth.

Large-scale tax reduction was a central element of the Reagan campaign and has continued to be a major feature of the administration's policies. In his first major address to Congress on February 18, 1981, President Reagan outlined his administration's tax proposals, the main parts of which called for a reduction in personal income tax rates by 10 percent a year for a three-year period and a sharp increase of depreciation allowances for business.

The Economic Recovery Tax Act (ERTA) of 1981 is built largely on the administration's proposals, although some significant changes and additions were made, as will be discussed later. In its final form ERTA passed in the Senate by 67 to 8 votes and in the House by 282 to 95 votes and was signed into law on August 13, 1981.

The strength of the growing sentiment against rising taxes is reflected in the ease with which ERTA was passed. Yet ERTA has already aroused considerable controversy. The administration believes that the cuts will significantly spur individuals to work harder, to increase their saving, and to invest in more productive activities. Critics have been skeptical that these so-called supply side effects will be large and have argued that the cuts are largely a windfall to the rich at the expense of the poor. The question also has been raised whether the nation can afford the full ERTA tax cut, given projections of large future deficits and the difficulty of making major cuts in government spending.

This chapter addresses these issues. It reviews the recent development of the nation's tax system and that of other developed countries, giving particular attention to individual and business income taxes in the United States. It discusses specific provisions of ERTA and how they will affect families and individuals at different income levels. Finally, the effects of taxes on work, savings, and investment are evaluated. The implications of the tax cut for budget policy and its effects on the economy are discussed in chapters 2 and 3.

Background

The ERTA tax cuts were to a large degree a reaction to past trends in federal taxes. This section reviews these trends. After a brief overview of the tax system, individual and corporation income taxes will be considered in more detail.

Historical Overview

How much have taxes grown? In particular, what has happened to federal, state, and local revenues as a percentage of the Gross National Product (GNP) over the period 1929 through 1981? The following points (based on the data in table 4-1) are salient:

1. The share of total government receipts in GNP tripled from 1929 through 1981, rising from 11 to 33 percent; three-fifths of this rise occurred from 1929 through 1945 and was associated with the increase in the size of the federal government during the Great Depression and World War II.

2. State and local governments collected most of the nation's taxes before World War II, accounting for two-thirds of all government revenues in 1929. During World War II, however, the state and local government share declined. By 1945 federal revenues accounted for 80 percent of all government receipts. Between 1947 and 1977 state and local government taxes grew steadily as a percentage of GNP but have declined somewhat since then, reflecting state and local tax cuts and tax limitation legislation (as discussed in chapter 6).

3. Federal taxes remained relatively stable as a percentage of GNP during most of the post-World War II period, rising temporarily during the Korean and Vietnam wars but generally fluctuating between 18 and 19 percent of GNP. More recently, federal receipts have risen above this range—from 18.5 percent of GNP in 1975 to 21.4 percent in 1981—a movement that may not be dramatic, but is nonetheless noteworthy for a peacetime period.

4. The composition of federal taxes has undergone two important changes. One is the decline in the corporate income tax as a source of federal revenues—from more than one-quarter of federal receipts during the 1950s to 11 percent in 1981. The other is the rise in Social Security

TABLE 4–1

FEDERAL, STATE, AND LOCAL GOVERNMENT RECEIPTS AS A PERCENTAGE OF GROSS NATIONAL PRODUCT, 1929–1981

Year	GNP (In $ billions)	Total Receipts %	Federal Government					State and Local Government[c] %
			Total %	Individual Income Taxes %	Social Security[a] %	Corporate Income Taxes %	Other Taxes and Revenues[b] %	
1929	103.4	10.9	3.7	—	—	—	—	7.3
1933	55.8	16.7	4.8	—	—	—	—	11.8
1940	100.0	17.7	8.6	—	—	—	—	9.1
1945	212.4	25.0	20.0	—	—	—	—	5.0
1947	233.1	24.4	18.5	8.1	0.9	4.6	4.9	5.9
1949	258.3	21.6	15.0	6.0	0.9	3.7	4.4	6.7
1950	286.5	24.1	17.5	6.1	1.1	6.0	4.3	6.6
1952	348.0	25.2	19.3	8.6	1.3	5.3	4.1	6.5
1955	400.0	25.3	18.2	7.6	1.7	5.3	3.6	7.1
1960	506.5	27.5	19.0	8.3	2.5	4.2	4.0	8.6
1963	596.7	28.2	19.2	8.2	2.7	4.1	4.2	9.1
1965	691.1	27.2	18.0	7.4	2.6	4.2	3.8	9.3
1969	944.0	31.4	20.9	9.7	4.1	3.8	3.3	10.6
1971	1,077.6	29.9	18.4	8.0	4.1	3.1	3.2	11.5
1975	1,549.2	30.4	18.5	7.8	5.0	2.8	2.9	11.9
1976	1,718.0	31.3	19.3	8.2	5.0	3.2	2.9	12.0
1977	1,918.0	31.6	19.6	8.5	4.9	3.2	3.0	12.0
1978	2,156.1	31.6	20.0	8.8	5.1	3.3	2.8	11.6
1979	2,413.9	31.7	20.5	9.4	5.3	3.1	2.7	11.2
1980	2,626.1	31.9	20.6	9.6	5.4	2.7	2.9	11.3
1981	2,922.2	32.7	21.4	9.9	5.8	2.3	3.4	11.3

SOURCES: Council of Economic Advisers, Economic Report of the President, 1982; Eugene Steuerle and Michael Hartzmark, "Individual Income Taxation 1947–79," National Tax Journal, vol. 34 (June 1981), pp. 145–166, table A–1; and unpublished data from the Bureau of Economic Analysis for 1980 and 1981.

a. Includes railroad retirement taxes.

b. Includes excise taxes, custom duties, estate and gift taxes, and other taxes, and nontax receipts.

c. Excludes federal grants in aid.

taxes, which increased from 5 percent of federal revenues in 1947 to 28 percent in 1981.

Comparison with Other Developed Countries

Despite the outcry against high taxes in the United States, taxes in this country are quite low compared with those in many other developed countries. Among eighteen of the member countries of the Organization for Economic Cooperation and Development (OECD), the United States ranked fourteenth in total tax receipts as a percentage of Gross Domestic Product (GDP) in 1980 (table A-5). Moreover, the increase in the ratio of tax receipts to GDP was smaller in the United States than in most OECD countries over the period 1955-1980. Sweden, currently the frontrunner, collected 50 percent of its GDP in taxes in 1980 compared with only 26 percent in 1955. However, tax growth in Sweden as well as in most of the OECD countries slowed considerably during the late 1970s.

The Individual Income Tax

At one time the individual income tax affected only a small percentage of the population.[3] It is now the most important source of federal revenue, accounting for 46 percent of all receipts in 1981. There has been a decline since 1969 in the proportion of total income subject to the tax, as the various types of deductions, exclusions, and exemptions have changed in relative importance. In addition, average and marginal tax rates have risen for many families because periodic tax-rate reductions have not been sufficient to counter the inflation-induced bracket creep. Between 1970 and 1980 the marginal and average tax rates of middle-income, four-person families rose by 20 and 23 percent, respectively.

The Tax Base. When the Reagan administration took office, it focused on reducing tax rates rather than on overhauling the tax system as a whole. However, interest is increasingly being expressed in some form of a "flat tax" that would combine rate reduction with a broadening of the tax base (the amount of income subject to tax).

The tax base has never been much more than half of personal income (table 4-2). In 1948 the tax base was 36 percent of personal income; it rose to a high of 51 percent of personal income in 1969, but had slipped back to 44 percent by 1978. These changes in the size of the tax base are the net result of changes in the importance of the various taxed and untaxed components of income. On the one hand, the tax base has been eroded by increases in deductions and exclusions, which rose from 19 percent of personal income

TABLE 4-2

CHANGE IN THE TAX BASE AND NONTAXED PORTIONS OF INCOME: 1948, 1969, 1978
(Percentage of personal income)

Income Item	1948	1969	1978	1948–1969	1969–1978
				Change in tax base	
Income taxed at a positive rate (tax base)	35.8	51.0	43.5	+15.2	−7.5
				Change in base due to increase or decrease in income item	
Nontaxed income					
Exclusions from AGI	10.7	13.5	18.4	−2.8	−4.9
Nontaxable transfers[a]	4.9	5.3	8.2	−0.4	−2.9
Labor fringe benefits[b]	1.2	3.5	5.2	−2.3	−1.7
Other[c]	4.7	4.7	5.1	0.0	−0.4
Itemized deductions	3.3	10.1	9.1	−6.8	+1.0
Standard deductions[d]	4.6	2.4	6.7	+2.2	−4.3
Personal exemptions on taxable returns	24.4	14.1	7.7	+10.3	+6.4
Income offset by credits[e]	—	0.5	5.2	−0.5	−4.7
AGI of nontaxable individuals, unreported AGI, and reconciliation[f]	21.3	8.5	9.4	+12.8	−0.9

SOURCE: Derived from Eugene Steuerle and Michael Hartzmark, "Individual Income Taxation
1947–79," tables A–2 and A–3.
   a.   Includes Social Security retirement, disability and health transfers, and railroad retirement
transfers, less personal contributions, plus all other federal transfers except military pay and
taxable government pensions.
   b.   Employer contributions to pension, profit sharing, group health, life insurance, and other
benefits.
   c.   Other exempted personal income such as contributions to IRAs, exempt interest income,
moving expenses, and other business expenses.
   d.   Zero bracket amount in 1978.
   e.   See Steuerle and Hartzmark for method of derivation.
   f.   Includes reconciliation of conceptual differences between adjusted gross income (AGI) as
measured by the Bureau of Economic Analysis and AGI as reported to the IRS.

in 1948 to 34 percent of personal income by 1978. On the other hand, the
growth in deductions and exclusions after 1948 was more than offset by a
sharp decline in the importance of personal exemptions, which formerly had
played a major role in reducing the tax base. This change was mainly due to
the erosion of the value of the exemption by inflation during a period when
incomes were rising even faster than inflation.[4] The decline in the value of

the personal exemption has also resulted in an increase in the proportion of the population required to file tax returns. Finally, the decline in self-employment and the rising importance of wage and salary income has increased the share of income subject to withholding and, therefore, more readily reported. Thus, over the period 1948 through 1978 there was a net rise in the tax base.

Tax Rates. The tax base interacts with the statutory rate structure to determine the proportion of income paid by individuals and families. The fairness of a tax system is usually judged by looking at how this proportion (the average tax rate) varies among different population groups. The efficiency or incentive aspects of the tax system, however, depend more on the additional tax paid on each added dollar of income (the marginal tax rate). One problem is that efforts to make the system more progressive (by increasing the average tax rate for persons with higher incomes) frequently result in higher marginal tax rates.

In 1961, 10 percent of tax returns had a marginal rate exceeding 22 percent, and 70 percent had rates of 20 to 22 percent (table A-6). During the late 1960s and the 1970s real income growth, combined with inflation, pushed a larger percentage of taxpayers into high marginal tax brackets, while legislation lowered rates at the bottom. By 1979, 35 percent of tax returns had a marginal rate exceeding 22 percent, while 36 percent had rates of 16 percent or less.

Looking at the change in marginal tax rates for four-person families, one again finds rising marginal tax rates over the period 1960 to 1980 for middle- and upper-income families (table 4-3). The increase was particularly great for higher-income families. Those with twice the median income experienced a rise in marginal rates from 22 percent in 1960 to 43 percent in 1980, but at one-half the median, rates were somewhat lower in 1980 than in 1960.

What has happened to average tax rates over this period? Again, an examination of taxes calculated for married couples with two children at different points in the income distribution shows that average tax rates have increased considerably since 1960 at all income levels (table 4-4). Over the past decade, a typical middle-income family of four found their tax rate rising from 9.3 percent to 11.4 percent, an increase of 23 percent. The rise is even greater when Social Security taxes are included. The same family found their tax burden from both sources increasing from 12.6 to 17.5 percent, or by 39 percent.

Much of this increase in tax rates occurred because inflation moved families into higher tax brackets, but inflation also raised tax rates by affecting the personal exemption and the zero bracket amount (ZBA; formerly called the standard deduction). In 1948 the personal exemption was $600, which in

TABLE 4–3

MARGINAL PERSONAL INCOME TAX RATES FOR FOUR-PERSON FAMILIES, SELECTED
YEARS, 1960–1984[a]
(Percentage)

| | Family Income | | |
Year	*One-Half Median Income*	*Median Income*	*Twice Median Income*
1960	20	20	22
1965	14	17	22
1970	15	20	26
1975	17	22	32
1980	18	24	43
Under Economic Recovery Tax Act of 1981			
1981	18	28	42
1984	16	25	38
Under 1980 Tax Law			
1981	18	28	43
1984	21	32	49

SOURCE: U.S. Department of the Treasury, Office of Tax Analysis.
   a.   Excludes Social Security taxes and state and local income taxes.

terms of 1981 dollars would be $2,267. The current exemption, however, is
$1,000. The zero bracket amount has been increased more frequently than
the personal exemption, particularly during the 1970s. It provides an adjustment for marital status but not for family size. The ZBA and the exemption
are fixed until 1985, when they will be indexed.

Together, the exemptions and the ZBA determine the tax-exempt level
of income for individuals and families of different size and marital status.
Tax-exempt levels were high enough to exclude most large families below
the poverty line from taxation during the period 1948 through 1978, but they
have slipped further and further below the poverty threshold since 1978 and
will continue to do so until they are indexed in 1985 (table A-7). Tax-exempt
levels for single persons and for couples with no dependents were very low
relative to the poverty threshold in the earlier years but have risen as the ZBA
was increased by legislation. As a consequence, average tax rates for single
taxpayers and childless couples have increased much less sharply than have
rates for large families.

Business Income Taxation

Although effective tax rates for individuals have risen since 1960, those
for corporations have fallen over the same period. In both cases, inflation-

TABLE 4–4

AVERAGE FEDERAL TAX RATES FOR FOUR-PERSON FAMILIES, SELECTED YEARS, 1960–1984[a]

Year	Income Tax Rates			Combined Income and Social Security Tax Rates		
	One-Half Median Income	Median Income	Twice Median Income	One-Half Median Income	Median Income	Twice Median Income
1960	2.8	7.8	12.1	5.8	10.1	13.2
1965	3.3	7.1	11.1	6.9	9.3	12.2
1970	6.6	9.3	13.5	11.4	12.6	15.2
1975	4.2	9.6	14.9	10.1	14.8	17.5
1978	4.7	11.1	17.4	10.8	16.3	20.0
1979	5.1	10.8	17.2	11.2	16.9	20.4
1980	6.0	11.4	18.2	12.1	17.5	21.5
Under Economic Recovery Tax Act of 1981						
1981	6.8	11.8	19.1	13.5	18.5	22.9
1984	6.7	10.3	16.7	13.4	17.0	20.8
Under 1980 Tax Law						
1981	6.9	11.9	19.4	13.6	18.6	23.2
1984	8.7	13.4	21.7	15.4	20.1	25.8

a.   Authors' calculations assume itemized expenses amounting to 23 percent of adjusted gross income (AGI) in all years, except for those at one-half the median income level, for whom the standard deduction is assumed. Examples refer to a one-earner husband-wife family in all years. Median income for a four-person family was $6,295 in 1960, $7,800 in 1965, $11,165 in 1970, $15,848 in 1975, $20,428 in 1978, $22,422 in 1979, and $24,332 in 1980. Income was projected based on the administration's inflation forecast given in the 1983 budget. All income is treated as earned taxable income. Only the employee share of Social Security taxes is included.

induced increases in effective rates have been offset periodically by tax law changes. However, more emphasis has been placed on investment tax credits and accelerated depreciation deductions rather than tax-rate changes in order to accomplish the objective of lowering effective corporate tax rates. Many believe this to be a more effective way to stimulate new investment and thereby improve productivity, since the benefits of a tax rate reduction are spread over the entire corporate sector while tax credits and accelerated depreciation are targeted directly to the decision to invest in plant and equipment.

The past three decades have seen four major reforms in the way business income is taxed: in 1954 accelerated depreciation was adopted; in 1962 the investment tax credit (ITC) was initiated and depreciation write-off periods were shortened; in 1971 write-off periods were again shortened and the ITC made permanent; and in 1981 write-off periods were shortened still further and the rate of the ITC was generally increased with the passage of ERTA.

Each change has had the effect of reducing the effective tax rate on corporate income.

The corporate income tax was established in 1909 as a one percent tax on corporate profits in excess of $5,000. In calculating taxable income, corporations were allowed to deduct a "reasonable allowance" for the "wear, tear, and obsolescence" of capital assets used up in the production of income. Between 1909 and 1945, the corporate tax rate rose dramatically, reaching a maximum marginal rate of 52 percent in 1950. At this higher tax rate the question of what constituted a reasonable depreciation allowance became a pressing issue. The existing pre-World War II treatment was widely believed to be inadequate because of the high obsolescence rate of capital put in place during the war. As a result, the tax code was revised in 1954 to allow new accelerated depreciation patterns in addition to the straightline method that allocates costs evenly over the life of the asset. Because the accelerated methods resulted in larger depreciation deductions in the early years of an asset's life, the present value of the deductions was generally increased, even though the total amount ultimately deducted was unchanged.

The increased present value of the depreciation allowances under the accelerated forms of depreciation translated into lower effective tax rates on corporate income. These tax rates are shown in figure 4-1 for the period 1952 through 1980 (see also table A-8).[5] Three different tax concepts are used. The marginal corporate tax rate on income from new plant and equipment represents the tax rate paid on income from a new equity-financed investment after a tax law goes into effect. It takes into account the impact of inflation in eroding the value of historical cost-depreciation deductions, the benefits associated with accelerated depreciation in excess of true (or economic) depreciation, and the value of investment tax credits. These factors, together with the fact that not all income is taxed at the top marginal rate, cause the marginal tax rate to differ from the maximum statutory rate. The average effective corporate tax rates shown in figure 4-1 are the ratio of total taxes paid on all income to pretax corporate profits. This average tax rate differs from the marginal tax rate in that it captures taxes paid on income from old as well as new assets. The average corporate tax rate thus represents the effects of past tax laws. It also covers income from more types of corporate assets: land, inventories, and intangible assets as well as plant and equipment.[6]

The sluggish growth of the late 1950s brought forth renewed calls for progrowth tax incentives. Legislation in 1962 established a new set of guideline lives that shortened depreciation write-off periods by 30 to 40 percent.[7] The year 1962 also saw the introduction of a 7 percent investment tax credit

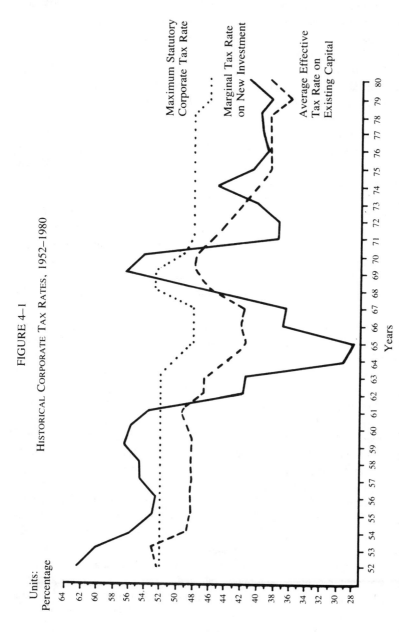

FIGURE 4–1

HISTORICAL CORPORATE TAX RATES, 1952–1980

Units: Percentage

Years

Maximum Statutory Corporate Tax Rate

Marginal Tax Rate on New Investment

Average Effective Tax Rate on Existing Capital

SOURCE: U.S. Department of Commerce, Bureau of Economic Analysis, *The National Income and Product Accounts of the United States, 1929–1976. Statistical Tables* (Washington, D.C.: GPO, 1981), table 1.13; and C. R. Hulten, J. W. Robertson, S. M. Davies, unpublished. Tax rates refer to the nonresidential, nonfinancial segment of the corporate sector.

for machinery and equipment.[8] This credit conferred an immediate cost advantage to equipment relative to most structures. The top marginal rate of the corporate tax was also reduced in 1964—from 52 percent to 50 percent—and was further reduced to 48 percent in 1965.

The effects of these changes can be seen in figure 4-1. The marginal corporate rate on new plant and equipment fell by almost half—from 53.1 percent in 1961 to 27.7 percent in 1965. The average rate also declined, but by less than the change in the marginal rate, and both rates fell below the nominal statutory rate.

The Vietnam War years of 1966 through 1969 were a period of rising business tax rates. The ITC was suspended between October 1966 and March 1967 and was repealed in 1969. The marginal corporate rate more than doubled between 1965 and 1969, and both marginal and average rates returned to approximately their pre-1962 levels. The recession of 1970, however, led once more to a reversal in corporate tax policy, and 1971 saw the restoration of the ITC for equipment and the introduction of an Asset Depreciation Range (ADR) system of depreciation allowances that permitted a 20 percent shortening of guideline lives for equipment (structures were not included in ADR). As a result the marginal corporate tax rate fell from 54.1 percent in 1970 to 37.5 percent in 1971.

The trend in effective tax rates after 1971 was dominated by the rising rate of inflation. Depreciation allowances have always been restricted to the original cost of the capital asset, and during inflationary periods replacement cost exceeds original cost; thus depreciation deductions do not reflect the value of the capital used up in production.[9]

The impact of inflation on effective tax rates is evident in figure 4-1. The marginal corporate tax rate crept upward from 37.5 percent in 1971 to 45 percent in 1974. In 1975 the ITC was increased to 10 percent, and in 1979 the top statutory rate was reduced to 46 percent. The effect of these changes was to stabilize both the marginal and average effective tax rates at approximately the 40 percent level.

Overall, the 1952-1980 period saw a decline in the rate corporate income was taxed. The actual path of the marginal corporate tax rate, however, was far from smooth. Recessions typically brought about reductions, whereas expansions generally produced increases in marginal effective tax rates. This period was also characterized by the tendency to use accelerated depreciation and tax credits, rather than major rate reductions, as a way to stimulate investment spending. This tendency, which was maintained by ERTA, meant that tax relief was targeted to depreciable assets (plant and equipment) rather than to all sources of corporate income.

The Economic Recovery Tax Act of 1981

One result of the bracket creep and lagging productivity growth of the 1970s was, as it had been in the past, strong pressure to reduce both individual and business taxes. In fact, some type of tax cut would most likely have been enacted by Congress in 1981 under any president. This section summarizes the specific provisions of the individual and corporate income tax cuts enacted as part of ERTA and then discusses the overall size of the tax reductions.

Individual Income Tax Provisions

The forerunner of the individual income tax provisions in ERTA was the tax cut first proposed by Representative Jack Kemp (R.-N.Y.) and Senator William Roth (R.-Del.) in 1978 (H.R. 8333 and S. 1860, respectively), which called for a one-third reduction in personal income tax rates to be phased in over three years. Subsequent versions of the Kemp-Roth bill altered the structure of the tax cut and reduced its size somewhat. The Reagan administration's original proposal, calling for an across-the-board reduction in tax rates of 10 percent a year for each of three years, was clearly modeled after these later versions of the Kemp-Roth bill. The distinctive feature retained from the first Kemp-Roth bill is a commitment to a succession of large tax cuts despite uncertainties about inflation and the state of the economy.

As passed, the 1981 tax act (ERTA) provides a fairly close substitute for the rate reductions in the Reagan proposal: 5 percent in the first year and 10 percent in each of the next two years, which yields cumulative reductions in individual income tax rates of 1.25 percent in 1981, 10 percent in 1982, 19 percent in 1983, and 23 percent in 1984 and subsequent years. In addition, the top marginal rate on income other than earnings was reduced from 70 percent to 50 percent as of January 1, 1982, bringing it down to the same level as the maximum rate on earned income that had prevailed under prior law. As a result of this last change, the maximum rate of tax on capital gains was also reduced—from 28 percent to 20 percent.[10]

Starting in 1985, ERTA will provide more permanent insurance against the effects of future inflation by indexing the individual income tax structure. That is, the income tax brackets, the ZBA, and the personal exemption will all be adjusted automatically for changes in the Consumer Price Index (CPI). However, until 1985 the ZBA and the personal exemption will be fixed at their 1979 levels and will therefore erode in value with inflation.

Another significant ERTA change provides a tax deduction to two-earner married couples equal to 5 percent of the lower earner's wages in 1982 (up to $30,000 of earnings) and 10 percent in 1983 and thereafter. The child care tax credit is liberalized by increasing the amount of employment-related child care expenses eligible for the credit. The rate of the child care credit will vary by income level, with lower income families receiving a larger benefit.

A deduction for charitable contributions made by individual taxpayers who do not itemize deductions is to be phased in over a five-year period. Estate and gift tax exemptions are increased, and tax rates on these items reduced. For surviving spouses the inheritance tax is eliminated.

Other provisions are aimed at increasing savings. These include extending eligibility for individual retirement accounts (IRAs) to workers covered under employer-sponsored pension plans, and permitting deductions for contributions to an IRA of up to $2,000 per worker per year. The limit on deductions made by self-employed workers for a Keogh retirement plan is raised from $7,500 to $15,000, and a one-time exclusion of $1,000 for interest received on "all savers" certificates issued by banks and other financial institutions is allowed for the period October 1, 1981 to December 31, 1982.

The effects of the basic rate reduction provisions on the marginal and average tax rates of families are discussed in more detail later in this chapter.

Corporate Income Tax Provisions

During the late 1970s business groups endorsed the "10-5-3" proposal that eventually became, in modified form, the centerpiece of the business tax cut in ERTA. The 10-5-3 proposal gained bipartisan congressional support and was introduced as a bill (H.R. 4646) in 1979 by Representatives Barber B. Conable (R.-N.Y.) and James R. Jones (D.-Okla.).

The 10-5-3 proposal called for assets to be grouped into three categories for the purpose of determining depreciation deductions. Autos and light trucks were assigned a three-year write-off period, other machinery and equipment a five-year period, and structures a ten-year period. These write-off periods were considerably shorter (except for autos) than allowable guideline lives under the ADR system then in existence. In fact, 80 percent of the 130 ADR equipment classes had a minimum tax life of more than five years, and 40 percent had a tax life of more than ten years. The ten-year permissible tax life for structures was also much shorter than the thirty-seven year average tax life actually found to be in use by a 1971 Department of the Treasury study.[11] The rate of the ITC was also increased under the 10-5-3 proposal.

The need for a substantial reduction in business income taxes was perceived by many groups, and several alternatives to the 10-5-3 plan were proposed.[12] The election of Ronald Reagan, however, shifted attention back to the 10-5-3 proposal. The basic structure of the 10-5-3 proposal was adopted into ERTA with some modifications, such as the lengthening of most structures' tax lives to fifteen years. "Safe harbor leasing" provisions were also introduced, increasing the generosity of the package. Safe harbor leasing is a device that permits the sale of unused tax credits and depreciation deductions. It allows a company with no tax liability to sell a depreciable asset (for tax purposes only) and then to lease it back. The purchaser-lessor receives the benefit of the ITC and depreciation deductions, and when these are exhausted the asset is sold back to the original owner. The original owner-lessee is thus able to receive immediate tax benefits even though no taxable income is present.

The new package was called the Accelerated Cost Recovery System (ACRS). The impact of the ACRS on the effective tax rates of figure 4-1 is shown in table 4-5. At an 8 percent annual rate of inflation ERTA will yield a cut in the effective corporate tax rate on plant and equipment from 40 percent to 18 percent by 1986, when it is fully phased in. The largest cut goes to equipment—twenty-eight percentage points—while structures receive only an eleven percentage point cut. At lower rates of inflation the effective tax rate actually becomes negative, implying that ACRS is a subsidy to depreciable assets rather than a tax. This feature of ERTA is one of the most interesting and controversial aspects of the tax cut.

How Big Is the Tax Cut?

The ERTA tax reductions are often depicted as enormous. However, the adjective used to describe the tax cut depends on the choice of a point of comparison as well as on the economic assumptions used to make the estimates.

Estimates of the size of the tax cut made by both the administration and the Congressional Budget Office (CBO) are based on the difference in revenue flows under ERTA and under the tax code in effect prior to ERTA (table 4-6). Based on this comparison the tax loss is indeed enormous. The loss in federal revenues will amount to $286 billion by 1987 according to the administration and $294 billion according to CBO, figures that would be 5.8 percent and 5.9 percent of GNP, respectively.

Without a change in the tax code, inflation would have continued to push individuals into higher tax brackets and would have eroded the value of business depreciation deductions. The administration's 1983 budget projects a cumulative increase in consumer prices of 25 percent between 1981 and 1985. (CBO projects a 31 percent increase for the same period.) Because of inflation, a world without legislated tax reductions is a world of substantial tax increases (table 4-7). Under the pre-ERTA law, it is estimated that the

TABLE 4–5

EFFECTIVE CORPORATE TAX RATES
(Percentage)

Industry Division	1980 Tax Law			ACRS		
	Total	Equipment	Plant	Total	Equipment	Plant
Agriculture	28.6	24.8	46.2	8.7	1.7	40.5
Mining	50.4	32.2	59.1	33.3	1.3	48.6
Construction	28.2	26.2	54.3	8.2	2.3	43.5
Manufacturing	36.6	28.8	54.5	14.3	1.4	43.7
Transportation, communication, and utilities	42.3	43.6	40.4	18.4	12.6	27.0
Trade	37.3	29.3	50.1	17.5	3.4	40.1
Finance and insurance	38.8	28.7	50.0	20.7	3.1	40.0
Services	38.5	27.8	50.4	20.5	3.1	39.9
Total nonresidential business	39.6	33.7	49.5	17.8	5.5	38.5

SOURCE: C. R. Hulten, J. W. Robertson, S. M. Davies, unpublished. Rates refer to Accelerated Cost Recovery System (ACRS) when fully phased in and assume an 8 percent expected rate of inflation.

TABLE 4–6

REVENUE EFFECTS OF THE ECONOMIC RECOVERY TAX ACT OF 1981 (ERTA), ADMINISTRATION AND CONGRESSIONAL BUDGET OFFICE ESTIMATES, BY FISCAL YEAR

(In $ billions)

	Actual 1981	Projections					
		1982	1983	1984	1985	1986	1987
Total Federal Receipts							
Administration							
Prior law	600	665	745	843	955	1,073	1,193
ERTA	599	626	653	704	778	843	907
Difference	—	–39	–92	–139	–177	–230	–286
CBO							
Prior law	605	670	747	849	982	1,062	1,176
ERTA	603	631	652	701	763	818	882
Difference	–2	–39	–95	–148	–189	–244	–294
Revenue loss as percentage of GNP[a]							
Administration	—	1.2	2.7	3.7	4.2	5.1	5.8
CBO	—	1.3	2.8	3.9	4.5	5.4	5.9

SOURCE: Office of Management and Budget, *Budget of the United States Government, Fiscal Year 1983,* Baseline Projections for Fiscal Years 1983–1987 (Washington, D.C.: GPO, 1982).

a. Calculated as the difference between prior law and ERTA revenues as a percentage of GNP, using the GNP estimates projected by the administration and CBO for their respective estimates of the dollar value loss.

individual income tax would rise to almost 12 percent of GNP in FY 1985, up from 10 percent in 1981, and the corporate tax would rise to 2.6 percent of GNP, up from 2.1 percent, over the same period. The effect of ERTA is to reverse the upward push of inflation on individual tax rates, bringing them back to the lower levels of the mid-1970s. The corporate tax, however, is projected to remain below the level of the 1970s. As a whole, under ERTA federal receipts are projected by the CBO to fall to 18.3 percent of GNP in 1985 and 17.7 percent in 1987, or 2.8 and 3.4 percentage points, respectively, below the federal tax share of GNP actually reached in 1981.

CBO estimates of the extent to which ERTA offsets the effects of inflation indicate that almost half of the rate reductions by 1984 will simply offset bracket creep from October 1, 1981.[13] If the revenue loss estimate is adjusted for the effects of inflation on the individual income tax, the loss is reduced to 2.3 percent of GNP by 1984, which is still large but less dramatic than the estimate of 3.9 percent shown in table 4-6. The Kennedy-Johnson tax cut of 1964 was enacted in a period of very low inflation—not much above one percent a year; it was estimated to have amounted to about 2.2 percent of

TABLE 4–7

Projections of Federal Tax Receipts by Source, under Current Law and Prior Laws, by Fiscal Year

Fiscal Year	GNP (In $ billions)	Total Receipts	Federal Receipts as Percentage of GNP				
			Individual Income Taxes	Corporate Income Taxes	Social Insurance Taxes	Excise Taxes	Other Tax and Non-tax Revenues
Actual							
1971	1,032	18.3	8.4	2.6	4.7	1.6	1.0
1975	1,480	18.9	8.3	2.7	5.7	1.1	1.0
1981	2,859	21.0	10.0	2.1	6.4	1.4	1.0
Projected[a]							
Current law (1981 tax act)							
1982	3,082	20.3	9.7	1.5	6.7	1.4	1.0
1983	3,434	19.0	8.8	1.6	6.5	1.2	0.9
1984	3,792	18.6	8.4	1.8	6.4	1.1	0.9
1985	4,164	18.7	8.6	1.8	6.6	0.9[b]	0.8
Prior law (1978 tax act)							
1982	3,082	21.6	10.6	1.8	6.7	1.4	1.0
1983	3,434	21.7	11.0	2.0	6.5	1.2	1.0
1984	3,792	22.2	11.4	2.4	6.4	1.1	0.9
1985	4,164	22.9	11.9	2.6	6.6	1.0[b]	0.9

SOURCES: 1983 *Budget*, pp. 3–32, 4–10, 9–60; Council of Economic Advisers, *Economic Report to the President*, 1982, table B–69, table B–72.

a. Based on administration estimates.
b. Assumes extension of the highway trust fund taxes that are scheduled to expire on September 30, 1984.

GNP.[14] If the standard of comparison is the extent to which ERTA is expected to reduce real effective tax rates below their 1981 levels, then ERTA's effect by 1984 would seem to be only slightly larger than the 1964 tax cut.

All of these estimates are based on certain assumptions about the rate of inflation through 1984 (as well as changes in other economic variables). If inflation and nominal income growth differ from these assumptions, then these measures of revenue loss will be wrong. At very low rates of inflation, little of the tax cut would go to offset continuing bracket creep, and the real cut in taxes would be closer to the 23 percent statutory cut. The nature of the 1981 tax cut, which sets out a series of rate reductions in nominal terms over a multiyear period following several years of unusually high inflation, makes the actual magnitude of the cut extremely hard to predict.

Economic Impacts

In evaluating changes in tax policy, two broad questions are usually asked: is the change fair, and how does it affect the economy's performance, that is, the allocation of resources and the rate of economic growth? This section uses these two criteria, equity and efficiency, to evaluate the changes introduced by ERTA.

Equity

Two aspects of a tax system contribute to perceptions of its fairness: the extent to which persons with equal ability to pay are assessed equal tax burdens, and the way the tax burden is shared among those with different abilities to pay.

Most people agree that equals should be treated equally. Controversy arises, however, when one tries to define equals, and measurement problems may prevent using agreed-upon definitions in practice. Currently, money income received during the year is the basic standard for determining ability to pay, although it has been tempered by deductions, exemptions, and income exclusions. The extent to which these adjustments improve or worsen tax equity is a much-debated issue and one that will likely move to the forefront as the issue of broadening the tax base becomes more prominent.

ERTA takes a small first step toward addressing a longstanding equity issue in the tax treatment of the family by providing a deduction based on the earnings of the lower-earning spouse. In so doing, it recognizes that one-earner and two-earner married couples with equal money incomes may not have equal ability to pay. The one-earner couple benefits from tax-free income in the form of goods and services produced in the home by the full-time homemaker. The total real income of the two-earner couple is more fully taxable, however, because more of it is in the form of observable market income. The second-earner deduction responds to this inequity by providing a small tax break for two-earner couples. At the same time it partially remedies the problem known as the "marriage penalty"—that is, the tax incentive for two people to remain single if each has significant earnings.[15] Other provisions of ERTA also affect the treatment of "equals." By failing to adjust the personal exemption for inflation until it is indexed in 1985, ERTA provides less tax relief to families with more dependents, continuing the trend of recent years. Raising the exemption is costly, having an increase of $100 is estimated to reduce revenues by $5 billion. Furthermore, the extent to which the personal exemption should be liberalized on equity grounds is a controversial issue.[16]

In general, ERTA did not address the issue of broadening the tax base, for example, by taxing fringe benefits or reducing tax deductions and closing tax shelters. Such structural tax changes are difficult to achieve because one person's notion of a proper adjustment for ability to pay is another's notion of an inappropriate subsidy.

In the United States a progressive income tax structure is used to divide the tax burden among those with unequal ability to pay. The extent of progressivity desired, however, is a controversial subject, and one about which Americans seem to be ambivalent. On the one hand, the statutory rate structure has generally called for considerable progressivity; but on the other hand, there are ample opportunities for reducing taxable income so that effective progressivity is substantially lessened. The impact of ERTA on the progressivity of the tax structure has been one of the most hotly debated aspects of the tax cut. Critics of ERTA argue that it is a rich man's tax cut, while supporters of ERTA note that it is an across-the-board tax cut and is therefore relatively neutral in its effects.

Which of these views is correct? The answer depends to a large extent on how one interprets the question. Several ways of looking at the issue are presented in table 4-8. When the situations of four-person families at different points in the income distribution are contrasted under ERTA and under prior law, two aspects of the distribution of the tax burden stand out:

- ERTA cuts the tax liabilities of all income groups by about the same percentage (example a in table 4-8). This is what is meant by an across-the-board tax cut and in this sense the tax cut is neutral.

- After-tax incomes rise by a greater percentage the higher the income level (example d). This is the point made by those who feel that the

TABLE 4–8

Change in Individual Income Tax Liability and in After-Tax Income under Assumed Changes in the Tax Law, Four-Person Families by Income, 1981 and 1984

	One-Half Median Income[a]	Median Income	Twice Median Income
Tax liability (1981 dollars)			
(a) 1984—under old law	1,144	3,524	11,414
1984—under ERTA	881	2,709	8,784
Percentage change	−23.0	−23.1	−23.0
(b) 1981—under old law	907	3,130	10,204
1984—under old law	1,144	3,524	11,414
Percentage change	+26.1	+12.6	+11.9
(c) 1981—under old law	907	3,130	10,204
1984—under ERTA	881	2,709	8,784
Percentage change	−2.9	−13.5	−13.9
After-tax income (1981 dollars)			
(d) 1984—under old law	12,006	22,775	41,184
1984—under ERTA	12,269	23,590	43,814
Percentage change	+2.1	+3.6	+6.4
(e) 1981—under old law	12,243	23,169	42,394
1984—under old law	12,006	22,775	41,184
Percentage change	−1.9	−1.7	−2.9
(f) 1981—under old law	12,243	23,169	42,394
1984—under ERTA	12,269	23,590	43,814
Percentage change	+0.2	+1.8	+3.3

Source: See table 4–4.

a. Assumes standard deduction. All other groups are assumed to have deductions of 23 percent of AGI.

tax burden was cut unfairly. It is, however, a direct consequence of the arithmetic of progressive taxes. At higher income levels taxes account for a larger share of income. An equal percentage reduction in taxes for all income groups will therefore always increase the after-tax incomes of those at higher income levels by a greater percentage than for those at lower income levels. In this sense the rich benefit more than the poor from an across-the-board tax cut.

Under a progressive tax system the only way to adopt a tax cut that increases the after-tax income of all groups by the same percentage would be to reduce tax liabilities by a smaller percentage amount the higher the income. For example, a family with twice the median income would have to be given a tax cut of 7.6 percent instead of 23 percent if the increase in their after-tax income was to be held to the 2.1 percent increase attained by those at one-half the median. Such a policy would, however, widen the spread of marginal tax rates. This is what occurred over much of the 1960s and early 1970s, when tax relief was concentrated at lower income levels, and inflation was allowed to raise marginal rates at income levels above the median. An across-the-board tax cut reduces the spread in marginal tax rates, but at the expense of less equalization of after-tax incomes.

In the absence of inflation the effects of ERTA would be largely captured by the above comparisons. However, inflation is not expected to be negligible, and since it affects tax liabilities differently at different income levels, it must be taken into account (at least until 1985, when the individual income tax structure will be indexed). Assuming that the 1980 tax law remained in effect, inflation alone would have raised taxes, and this increase would be proportionately more at the lowest income level, in large part because of the erosion of the personal exemption (example b in table 4-8). However, inflation would reduce after-tax income most for the highest income group (example e). The other examples (c and f) show the changes in tax liabilities and after-tax income between 1981 and 1984, allowing the effects of both ERTA and inflation to operate. Although bracket creep reduces the 23 percent tax cut for all groups, the failure to adjust the exemptions weakens the effect of ERTA most at the lowest income level. Thus, because of inflation, those with lower incomes do not obtain as much benefit from ERTA as do those with higher incomes.

The cases reviewed in table 4-8 refer to hypothetical four-person families with incomes derived entirely from the earnings of one spouse. The table takes no account of the differential impact of ERTA on other types of families or individuals, and it ignores unearned income and the ERTA provisions that apply to such income. The Urban Institute's tax and transfer model has been used to simulate the effects of ERTA, combined with Social Security taxes, on the entire population of families and individuals in 1984.[17]

Although much the same story about the workings of the tax cut is told with the simulations reported in table 4-9 as with the simple hypothetical cases presented in table 4-8, some additional information is provided with the more comprehensive data. While taxes are significantly lower in 1984 under ERTA compared to what they would have been under the 1980 law, close to 60 percent of the drop in average effective tax rates simply offsets

TABLE 4-9

FEDERAL TAX LIABILITIES AND INCOME: SIMULATED 1984 DISTRIBUTIONS UNDER ERTA AND OTHER SCENARIOS[a]

Posttax 1984 Income[c] (In dollars)	Percentage of Families and Unrelated Individuals	Percentage of Pretax Income	Percentage of After-Tax Income			Effective Tax Rate[b]		
			Under 1980 Law[d]	Under ERTA[e]	Under Indexed 1980 Structure[f]	Under 1980 Law[d]	Under ERTA[e]	Under Indexed 1980 Structure[f]
Under 5,000	6.9	0.7	0.9	0.9	0.9	2.6	2.5	2.2
5,000–9,999	15.3	4.3	5.3	5.0	5.1	5.6	4.7	4.2
10,000–14,999	14.4	6.8	7.8	7.5	7.7	11.9	9.6	9.9
15,000–19,999	13.3	9.4	10.4	10.1	10.2	16.1	12.8	13.9
20,000–24,999	11.9	11.2	11.8	12.1	11.7	19.7	15.6	17.3
25,000–34,999	18.7	24.7	24.2	24.1	24.2	25.3	20.5	22.3
35,000–49,999	12.8	23.4	22.4	22.8	22.6	27.1	20.7	23.3
50,000–69,999	5.3	14.1	12.7	13.2	12.9	31.4	23.4	27.1
70,000 and over	1.3	5.4	4.5	4.8	4.6	35.6	26.4	31.5
Total	100.0	100.0	100.0	100.0	100.0	23.7	18.5	20.6

a. Estimates are based on The Urban Institute's TRIM2 data file, which ages a sample of the population and its income to 1984. The economic assumptions used for aging are those of the high growth path. See chapter 16 for details.

b. Social Security and personal income taxes as a percentage of pretax income. Capital gains are estimated.

c. Includes all cash transfers plus the value of the Food Stamp bonus. Excludes Social Security and income taxes.

d. Simulates the effect of tax provisions prior to the 1981 tax act without indexing the tax brackets, the personal exemption, or any other parameter.

e. Simulates the effect of ERTA tax schedules. The second-earner deduction of the top rate on unearned income to 50 percent are reflected. The child care credit is not included.

f. Simulates the effect of the 1980 tax structure indexed to 1984. The personal exemption, the zero bracket, and all other tax brackets and the earned income tax credit (EITC) are all indexed by changes in the CPI from 1980 to 1984. Otherwise the pre-ERTA provisions are maintained—i.e., no second-earner deduction and the top rate on unearned income is left at 70 percent.

the effect of inflation on tax liabilities between 1980 and 1984. Consistent with table 4-8, at the lowest income levels ERTA does not compensate for inflation;[18] at the highest income levels the "real" reduction in tax liability is 16 percent. Contributing to this result is the reduction in the top rate on unearned income from 70 percent to 50 percent and the cut in the capital gains tax rate. Both cuts benefit high-income groups disproportionately. The degree of progressivity of the personal income tax is somewhat less under ERTA than it would have been under 1980 law. In 1984 upper-income house-holds ($50,000 or more of after-tax income) end up with 18 percent of after-tax income under ERTA as compared to the 17.2 percent they would have had under 1980 tax law. Lower-income households ($10,000 or less of after-tax income) end up with 5.9 percent of after-tax income under ERTA as compared with the 6.2 percent they would have had under prior law. Similarly, ERTA reduces effective tax rates most among those with higher incomes. In evaluating these changes it should be noted, however, that the measurement of effective tax burdens is subject to considerable conceptual and statistical problems, and that these problems are likely to be greatest at the highest and lowest income levels.[19]

In the final analysis the answer to the question of whether ERTA does or does not improve the distribution of the tax burden rests on a value judgment concerning how much equalizing society wishes to impose on itself through taxation.

Effects on Resource Allocation and Economic Growth

As described in chapter 2, the 1970s saw high inflation and unusually slow productivity growth. Improvements in labor productivity dropped from an annual growth rate of 3.2 percent for 1948-1965, to 2.3 percent for 1965-1973, to 1.1 percent for 1973-1978.[20] For the past three years productivity growth almost ceased. The passage of ERTA was motivated, in part, by a desire to reverse this trend.

Can tax cuts spur investment, technological advance, and other sources of productivity growth? The popularized views of "supply siders" stress that high tax rates have produced such inefficient economic behavior that a tax cut, by correcting these inefficiencies, would produce quick and percep-tible effects on economic growth. Such expectations of rapid success have obviously not been fulfilled. The economy in 1982 has been dominated by a recession, and the enactment of tax cuts has clearly not been sufficient to offset the effects of high interest rates and depressed demand (see chapter 2). This does not mean that ERTA will not have positive effects in the long run. Most economists believe that it takes time for the impact of such policy changes to be fully felt, and in the case of ERTA the importance of these time lags is enhanced by the fact that many provisions of the act are to be phased in as late as 1986.

What can be said about long-run prospects for economic growth under ERTA? In answering this question, it is important to consider what economists know—and don't know—about the impact of taxes on economic activity. Two general effects have been identified. One is the potential gains arising from removing the distorting influence of taxes on the allocation of resources, including choices between work and leisure. These distortions affect the efficiency with which existing resources are used. The other potential effect is the impact of a tax reduction on choices between current and future consumption—that is, on the amount of saving and investment. This effect influences the rate of economic growth.

Taxes and Work Effort. A tax reduction increases take-home pay per hour worked and provides an incentive to work more.[21] In the short run, individuals typically do not have much leeway in adjusting their work hours. Over the long run, however, individuals may respond to a tax cut by allocating less time to untaxed activities like leisure or work in the home and more time to regular labor market participation (by entering the labor force, increasing hours on a current job, changing jobs, or taking a second job). In addition to hours of work, a tax cut may affect the type of occupation chosen, the amount of training and schooling undertaken, and the age of retirement.

How big a labor supply response can one expect from a tax cut? The overall labor force participation rate, which had been fairly stable over most of the post-World War II period, rose from 62 percent to 64 percent between 1975 and 1981, even though marginal tax rates increased over the same period. Although this comparison suggests that rising tax rates do not discourage work, this comparison fails to take into account other factors influencing labor force participation and does not prove that tax-rate changes have no long-run effects.[22] An analysis that holds "other things the same" is needed to determine the effects.

Most empirical research has suggested that the number of hours worked a year by men in their prime years is quite insensitive to changes in wage rates.[23] Some recent research, which has explicitly taken into account the effects of the progressivity of the income tax on work effort, has concluded that the tax reduced the hours worked by the average married man by 8 percent in 1975.[24] This study estimated that replacing the current progressive income tax system with one that was more nearly proportional but that raised the same total revenues would remove most of the work disincentive effects.

The literature has been almost unanimous in concluding that women, particularly married women, are more responsive to both wage-rate and tax-

rate changes. The middle range of estimates suggests that a 10 percent reduction in the tax rate would increase hours worked by married women by 4
or 5 percent, but several studies have found responses that are at least twice
as large.[25] The reason for this relatively high response is that women have
been more likely to specialize in home activities than men and thus have
broader alternatives to holding a job.

The labor supply response to a tax cut like ERTA should thus be greater
for women than for men. This conclusion is reinforced by the structure of
ERTA, which contains a provision that particularly benefits married women—
the 10 percent second-earner deduction. One recent study estimates that in
response to the second-earner deduction, married women would increase their
hours of work by 2.2 percent.[26] This increase would be sufficient to restore
one-third of the revenue loss attributed to the 10 percent deduction. The supply
side response in this case is not large enough to claim that this portion of the
tax cut would be self-financing, but it is large enough to illustrate the potential
importance of behavioral responses to the tax cut.

The actual size of the labor supply response to ERTA depends on the
magnitude of the tax cut as well as on the effect that a tax cut of a given size
has on the number of hours worked. Using the higher estimate for men given
in the study described in the previous paragraph and the middle estimate for
women, it has been estimated that the 23 percent across-the-board tax reduction would increase men's hours of work by about 2 to 2.5 percent and
married women's hours of work by 8 to 9 percent. This estimate is relevant
if the size of the tax cut is measured as the full statutory cut. However, as
already noted, much of the cut simply offsets the effects of inflation. A cut
that reduces effective tax rates to the level of the mid-1970s, as ERTA is
projected to do, is not likely to have large observable effects on labor supply.
It would, however, prevent any decline in work effort that could have occurred
had tax rates been allowed to rise.

Only recently has economic research turned to the long-run effects of
taxes on occupational choice, age of retirement, and training and other job-
related investments. Some evidence suggests that the age of retirement and
the extent of on-the-job training may be affected by taxes, but the magnitude
of these effects has not been well established.[27] One effect of high taxes may
be to cause individuals to seek work in jobs where their remuneration is
nonmonetary (in the form of amenities) or where the possibility of receiving
untaxed forms of income (fringe benefits, food, shelter) is greater. A tax
reduction may thus improve overall efficiency even if the increase in hours
worked is not dramatic.

Taxes, Savings, and Investment. Capital formation occurs when households, businesses, and governments save more and when this additional do-

mestic saving is translated into investment. Capital formation in the business sector can also be increased without additional saving if funds are channeled away from households and governments (i.e., away from investment in housing, consumer durables, and government debt) or are attracted from overseas. Finally, capital can be effectively increased if it is used more efficiently within the business sector.

How do taxes affect saving and investment? A tax cut, in principle, can increase the total supply of personal saving by increasing the after-tax return to saving. But the empirical evidence on saving is even less conclusive than the evidence on labor supply responses. One study estimates that a 10 percent change in the after-tax rate of return would increase saving by 4 percent;[28] another states that saving might increase by as much as 15 to 30 percent;[29] and a third suggests that there would be little or no effect.[30] The divergence of results is simply too wide for a consensus. The picture is further complicated by the fact that personal saving constitutes only 40 percent of gross saving, with business saving accounting for most of the rest. The cut in corporate taxes under ERTA will increase both retained earnings and depreciation, adding directly to business saving.

Although the overall impact of ERTA on saving is extremely difficult to predict, it is worth noting that the gross rate of saving in the United States has remained remarkably constant over the post-World War II period. This does not mean that the gross saving rate is invariant to changes in tax policy, but the high degree of stability over such a long period does suggest that changes in the saving rate are hard to achieve.

Tax policy can also influence the desired level of investment. Most economists agree that in the long run funds flow to the investment alternative with the highest risk-adjusted after-tax rate of return. A cut in taxes will tend to raise the return to all capital and selectively benefit investment alternatives that are relatively favored by the tax cut. The short-run and intermediate effects of a tax cut are more debatable, however. If companies are underutilizing existing plant and equipment to a high degree, a tax cut is likely to have little impact until the slack is reduced. Moreover, it takes time to order and produce new plant and equipment, so a tax cut should not be expected to have immediate results even under favorable circumstances.

What then is the prospect that ERTA will increase investment in the business sector? The paradigm for the current tax cut is the Kennedy-Johnson tax cut of the early 1960s, which seems to have had a positive impact on investment. Figure 4-2 shows the effect of this earlier cut, in which the marginal effective corporate tax rate is shown in conjunction with the share of net business fixed investment in real GNP. It is evident that this share rose sharply in the mid-1960s at the same time that the effective tax rate was

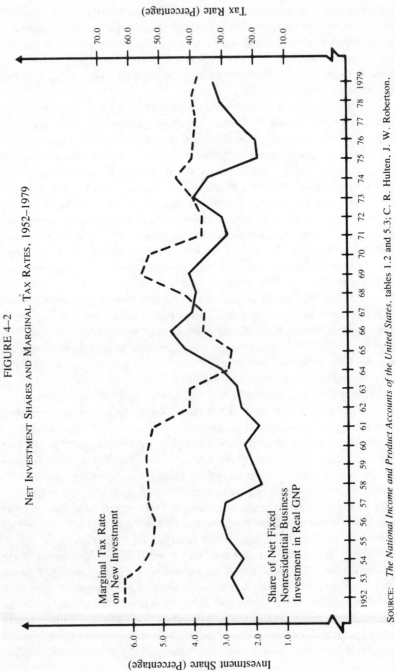

FIGURE 4–2

NET INVESTMENT SHARES AND MARGINAL TAX RATES, 1952–1979

SOURCE: *The National Income and Product Accounts of the United States*, tables 1.2 and 5.3; C. R. Hulten, J. W. Robertson, and S. M. Davies, unpublished.

falling. Then as the tax rate rose in the late 1960s, the share of net investment fell. The two series do not track well in the 1970s, but this was a period of stagflation, price controls, and energy shocks. In general, such simple comparisons between business tax changes and investment may be misleading because other factors may be playing critical roles. For example, changes in the growth rate of real GNP can have powerful impacts on the level of net business investment, and the relatively stable output growth of the late 1960s may have contributed to the rapid growth in investment spending.[31]

The efficiency with which the existing supply of capital is allocated is also an important tax issue.[32] Income from capital has been subject to vastly different tax rates according to (1) the sector in which it originated, (2) the type of asset from which it originated, and (3) the method by which it is distributed. Income originating in the corporate sector is subject to the corporate income tax, and dividends and realized capital gains are taxed again under the individual income tax. "Income" originating in the household sector, on the other hand, is largely in the form of the services derived from owner-occupied housing and consumer durables and thus escapes taxation entirely. Capital income originating in the state and local government sector also escapes taxation. Income originating in the noncorporate business sector is taxed under the individual income tax but not under the corporate tax, and even in the corporate business sector effective tax rates vary greatly across industries (see table 4-5).

Effective tax rates vary across assets even within a given industry. Depreciable assets have traditionally been accorded the advantage of accelerated depreciation and tax credits, whereas income accruing to land, inventories, and entrepreneurial effort has not. Furthermore, the tax code contains many special opportunities for sheltering income from taxation—investment in oil and gas drilling, for example—that create differential tax treatment across different types of assets.

The result has been a crazy-quilt pattern of taxation on the return to capital and a strong potential for tax-induced distortions in the allocation of capital. ERTA confronts this problem in several ways. A general tax cut, for example, will ultimately tend to reduce these tax-induced distortions. Moreover, the fall in effective corporate tax rates under ERTA reduces the differential treatment of income originating in the corporate sector and the lightly taxed capital income of the household and the state-local government sectors. ERTA can thus be expected to improve the allocation of resources.[33] The allocation within sectors is another matter. The business tax cuts in ERTA involve an increase in the investment tax credit and the acceleration of depreciation allowances; thus ERTA increases the differential treatment of depreciable assets and other types of corporate assets. Furthermore, the effective tax rates of table 4-5 indicate that the differential treatment of structures and equipment is widened. Under prior law the effective tax rate on plant was sixteen percentage points higher than on equipment. Under ERTA it is thirty-three points higher.[34]

Changes in the rate of inflation can also contribute to an inefficient allocation of resources. Although ERTA will introduce indexing in the personal income tax starting in 1985, the corporate tax will remain unindexed. Any future change in inflation will therefore continue to change the real value of depreciation deductions and put uneven pressure on effective tax rates.

One method of inflation proofing the corporate income tax has been put forward by Harvard professors Alan Auerbach and Dale W. Jorgenson.[35] They propose a "first year recovery allowance" scheme, under which (1) depreciation deductions are equal to true ("economic") depreciation costs, (2) the present value of the deductions is calculated using an inflation-adjusted rate of discount, (3) a deduction based on this present value is taken when the asset is acquired, and (4) no deductions are taken in subsequent years. Another approach would be to allow firms to write off the cost of their investments immediately. This alternative, called "expensing," results in effective marginal tax rates of zero, since capital is in effect treated as a current input like labor. The absence of a tax on the marginal asset means that no tax-induced distortions are present, although this result requires that interest on the debt used to finance the purchase of the asset not be taken as a tax deduction. The expensing alternative also solves the inflation problem by putting capital on a current account basis and moves the tax system toward a consumption (rather than an income) base.

Overall Effects on Economic Growth

Economists have not been able to settle the question of how taxes affect economic activity. The estimated responsiveness of labor supply, saving, and investment to changes in taxes have varied greatly across studies.

Nonetheless, certain boundaries can be established as a guide to making policy judgments about the effects of taxes. The most extreme supply side view—that a tax cut would induce so much growth that it would pay for itself (by increasing the tax base)—has been shown to imply either implausibly high labor supply responses or unrealistically high initial tax rates.[36] Using "best guess" estimates of the responsiveness of saving, investment, and labor supply, the tax rate on labor income would have to exceed 70 percent initially in order for a tax cut to be self-financing. This initial tax rate is considerably greater than the actual 25 percent tax rate on labor income estimated for 1977-1978.[37] If, on the other hand, the initially prevailing tax rate is equal to 25 percent, then the required responsiveness of labor supply is about ten times greater than the best guess estimate.

It is thus implausible that tax reductions as in ERTA would cause such increases in economic activity as to be self-financing. Nevertheless, supply side responses may promote improved resource allocation and substantially higher economic growth. A rough idea of the magnitude of possible effects is provided by simulations of the impact of tax cuts on potential GNP. Using available assumptions about the effects of personal income taxes on hours of work, and of business taxes on investment, one study has simulated the effect of various tax cut measures on potential GNP (while neutralizing the demand side effects through assumed reductions in government spending).[38] These simulations indicate that a 10 percent revenue loss through a personal tax cut results in 1.6 percent more in real GNP five years later, while a corporate rate cut of equal magnitude provides a 3.8 percent GNP increase. Investment tax credits and accelerated depreciation schemes produce still larger gains. These estimates do not, however, incorporate a saving supply response to individual rate cuts; nor do they attempt to measure the efficiency gains from improvements in resource allocation.

Conclusions

The 1981 tax act provided for a multiyear, large-scale cut in individual income and business taxes. The act had three objectives: (1) to provide tax relief from inflation-induced bracket creep, (2) to promote economic growth, and efficient resource allocation and (3) to reduce the size of government. At this time the extent to which these objectives will be achieved cannot be known.[39] However, based on this chapter's review of tax policy changes, the following observations can be made.

With respect to tax relief, the largest part of ERTA is the three-stage reduction in individual income tax rates, which will cumulate to 23 percent by 1984. At currently forecasted rates of inflation, these reductions will more than offset the bracket creep anticipated between 1980 and 1984 for the average taxpayer, but for some—those with larger families and with lower incomes—the cut will not be sufficient to roll back effective rates to 1980 levels. If the price level continues to rise less rapidly than forecast, as it has in the first half of 1982, then tax relief could be greater than now envisioned.

The impact of the tax cuts on economic growth depends on how work, saving, and investment decisions are made in response to tax changes. Most economists believe that such incentives operate over a long period and that the current recession is likely to dominate economic growth in the short run. Although quantitative evidence on the longer-run impacts is not as abundant or as conclusive as one might wish, a reduction in marginal tax rates should improve resource allocation and increase economic growth. However, because much of the individual income tax cut reverses bracket creep, one should not expect to observe significant changes from current levels of labor supply except by married women, who are receiving a larger cut and who are more responsive to tax changes.

The cuts in business tax rates are relatively larger and more targeted to business fixed investment. Thus they may induce a more significant response. However, while they were partly motivated by the impact of inflation on effective tax rates, but they do nothing to inflation proof corporate taxes. The rate of inflation will thus continue to interact with the current tax system to produce arbitrary tax burdens and to impair economic efficiency through its effects on risk and uncertainty. Thus, unless inflation is brought under control, investment may remain somewhat depressed for this reason alone. On the other hand, once inflation is eliminated the business tax cuts may be viewed as overly generous. At a zero rate of inflation corporate income taxes for many firms are effectively repealed.

The presumption that tax cuts can be used as a tool to reduce the size of government is based on a political judgment that rising deficits would not be tolerated and that tax increases (once the tax cut was passed) would be more unpalatable to the electorate than would expenditure cuts. As discussed in chapter 3, the outcome of the budgetary battle is still a matter of conjecture.

ERTA has been criticized for two reasons. Some have said that a bigger payoff in terms of efficiency and growth could have been achieved with the same revenue cost had more structural reforms been instituted. Others have labeled ERTA unfair. At a technical level the first criticism is undoubtedly correct. This chapter has alluded to alternative proposals for individual and business tax cuts that may well have been more effective than ERTA. Changing the tax system is, however, as much a political as a technical exercise, and structural reforms would require more extensive debate and analysis than that which preceded ERTA.

The unfairness charge has no answer because equity is a judgmental matter. Those who define equity by progressivity and give little weight to efficiency arguments may consider ERTA inequitable. The degree of progressivity in the rate structure will be lessened as a result of ERTA and its interaction with inflation. The individual income tax, however, remains progressive; families at twice the median income will have an average tax rate 2.5 times as high as families at one-half the median. Moreover, some may feel that the redistributive benefits achieved with the current tax system are not great enough to compensate for the efficiency losses. This is an area where tradeoffs exist. An informed public debate on these issues will help in making these tradeoffs in the future.

CHAPTER 5

REGULATORY POLICY

George C. Eads
Michael Fix

Ronald Reagan campaigned for office on a platform committed to cutting federal regulations. The campaign focused on social regulations in areas such as health, the environment, and civil rights, all of which had grown rapidly during the 1960s and 1970s. Significantly, the Reagan program was labeled regulatory relief, not regulatory reform, and it became one of the pillars of the administration's plan to revitalize the American economy. Indeed, actions designed to demonstrate a real dedication to regulatory relief were taken by the president immediately upon taking office and were heavily publicized throughout his administration's first year.

Reagan was not the first president to assign a prominent place on his administration's agenda to cutting back federal rules and regulations. But he was the first to give such a program equal billing with the other central elements of a macroeconomic strategy: tax, budget, and monetary policies. Other presidents, however, had acknowledged the linkage between reduced regulation and improved macroeconomic performance. For example, President Ford based his requirement that an inflation impact statement accompany "major" proposed rules and regulations on the premise that excessive and poorly conceived rules contributed to business cost pressures and therefore to inflation.

This premise found support in the work of respected economists,[1] who had determined that regulation was contributing to the nation's poor productivity performance. But the conclusion that most economists had reached by the late 1970s was that although well-reasoned and well-executed regulatory reform would improve the economy's efficiency and functioning—and would therefore improve macroeconomic performance—gains would be modest and would be realized only over the long run.

This "mainstream" consensus was reflected in the January 1980 *Annual Report of the President's Council of Economic Advisers*. In a review of the sources of the productivity slowdown (estimated to be about 1.5 percentage points), the council found regulation's contribution to be modest but not trivial:

> The diversion of resources to comply with government regulation may have accounted for as much as three-tenths of a percentage point of the decline, although the impact has not been so large in recent years.[2]

The council concluded that although there were factors that at least partially offset regulation's productivity-depressing effects, a role for regulatory reform remained:

> Many of these regulations have, of course, improved the quality of our environment and the health and safety of workers and consumers, and have provided benefits that are not measured in business output and productivity statistics. But regulation has not always provided these in the most effective and efficient manner, and there is ample room for improvement.[3]

President Reagan chose to reject this view of the modest macroeconomic potential of regulatory reform and assigned regulatory relief a central place in his administration's strategy to "revitalize" the American economy. Why did he do this? Has the regulatory relief effort produced the results expected of it during the administration's first year? What will be the longer-term consequences of the Reagan administration's regulatory effort? These are the questions this chapter seeks to answer.

The chapter begins by outlining the Reagan regulatory philosophy. It then briefly sketches the emergence of regulatory reform as a national issue and the way in which it found expression in the policies of the Nixon, Ford, and Carter administrations. Next, the administration's strategies for implementing the regulatory relief program are described. The chapter then turns to a description of the program's effects on industry and consumers, focusing on a single sector—transportation. Finally, a framework is suggested for evaluating the Reagan program, and some initial assessments are provided.

The Reagan Administration's Regulatory Philosophy

The administration's emphasis on regulatory relief derives from both pragmatic and ideological concerns. At its root, however, is a philosophical mistrust of government's attempts to control private conduct through regulation.

High-level White House officials, most prominently Murray Weidenbaum, chairman of the Council of Economic Advisers (CEA), have long argued that the costs associated with regulation—especially social regulation[4]—were contributing to the nation's poor economic performance by absorbing resources that otherwise would flow to "productive" investments. They have also alleged that a general belief that regulation would continue to grow was contributing to inflationary expectations—expectations the administration would have to curb if it were to reduce inflation significantly. Thus, the importance assigned to immediate and highly visible regulatory relief in the famous "Dunkirk" memo of David Stockman, director of the Office of Management and Budget, is not surprising. That memo states,

> A dramatic, substantial *rescission* of the regulatory burden is needed for the short term cash flow relief it will provide to business firms and the long term signal it will provide to corporate investment planners. A major "regulatory ventilation" will do as much to boost business confidence as tax and fiscal measures.[5]

Reagan administration officials, however, have been troubled by more than regulation's costs. The growth in social regulation is viewed as yet another manifestation of the federal government's intrusion into private decision making. Administration officials believe that federal rule makers have involved the government in the minutiae of business decision making, have imposed unwanted paperwork burdens, and have prescribed private behavior in areas previously left to the discretion of private citizens or to rules set by common law. This relatively new, expanded federal regulatory presence is opposed by administration officials on the grounds of both efficiency and ideology.

The administration does acknowledge that in certain areas—such as worker safety and environmental protection—a limited federal regulatory role is necessary. But, in doing so, it narrowly defines the instances where federal intervention will be tolerated. For example, the 1982 *Annual Report of the Council of Economic Advisers* states that no adequate justification can be found for much of the detailed safety regulation developed during the 1970s:

> Many government programs, such as detailed safety regulations or the provision of specific goods (rather than money) to the poor, are best described as paternalistic. . . . This administration rejects paternalism as a basis for policy.[6]

Instead, the administration has declared its preference for private methods of control such as insurance, voluntary standard setting, and private litigation.

Where the need for a federal regulatory presence can be justified, the administration has announced that this authority should be exercised in as nonintrusive a manner as possible. Accordingly, it prefers the operation of market-like regulatory mechanisms and supports regulatory techniques that provide regulated parties with maximum flexibility—such as mandating standards of performance (e.g., levels of pollutants) rather than ways of achieving them. In addition, Reagan administration officials clearly prefer enforcement strategies that target "bad apples" with a history of noncompliance instead of across-the-board monitoring.

Finally, the administration views the growth of federal regulation as a prime example of authority lodged at inappropriate levels of government. Federal agencies are viewed as remote and insensitive to local conditions. Thus, when regulation is necessary, the administration believes it should be administered whenever possible by state and local authorities or by private, third-party, standard-setting organizations (such as the Underwriters Laboratory). Further, it believes that regulations used to channel federal funds to achieve federally endorsed social objectives should be sharply reduced, if not eliminated.

An exception to the administration's aversion to federally imposed constraints on state and local spending is the use of regulatory standards to limit potential fraud or abuse in social welfare programs. As a result, the enactment of strict federal rules setting eligibility standards for Aid to Families with Dependent Children (AFDC) and Food Stamps was deemed entirely appropriate by administration officials, despite the administrative burden they imposed on local program officers.

The administration's concerns over the effects of regulation on the economy have not been limited to social regulation. Economic regulation is also viewed as costly and an unwarranted intrusion into the affairs of business. Initiatives undertaken in this area include the phasing out of crude oil price and allocation controls, the disavowal of legislation designed to give the president standby authority to impose such controls in the event of a severe oil supply disruption, and support for Federal Communications Commission (FCC) efforts to relax the conditions under which it grants radio and television franchises.

Perhaps the most significant change in economic regulatory policy witnessed so far has been a sharp shift in attitudes toward the economic dangers posed by big business and the appropriate occasions for invoking antitrust laws. Among the efforts taken to modify the use of antitrust laws have been a retreat from Carter administration attempts to obtain legislation restricting corporate acquisitions by oil companies; the canceling of a federal probe of concentration in the auto industry; and, most importantly, the settlement of the AT&T and IBM antitrust cases.

To sum up, the Reagan administration's regulatory philosophy appears to be that a generally diminished federal regulatory presence is preferable except in isolated cases. Less regulation will improve business cash flow, help break inflationary expectations, get the government out of second guessing business as well as state and local governments, and increase individual freedom.

The Precedents for the Reagan Program

An extraordinary burst in social regulation occurred in the 1960s and 1970s. The period, however, was not marked by a conspicuous deterioration in the areas subject to regulatory expansion. Monopoly power did not increase; profits, although high, were not exorbitant by conventional standards. The nature and consequences of environmental spillovers were increasingly recognized, but ambient concentrations of many important pollutants appeared to have fallen, at least through the 1960s; information available to consumers was no more misleading than it had been; and "excessive competition" remained the justification looking for a single valid example.[7]

Whatever the reality, it is evident that public concern about such matters as environmental degradation, unsafe products, unhealthy workplaces, and "unjust" profits clearly have increased over the past two decades. Moreover, the public's concern about these problems shows no signs of having abated, if public opinion polls can be trusted.[8]

If the public appears to support regulation's goals, why has Ronald Reagan—and indeed every president since Richard Nixon—found it useful to campaign against regulation? Because the public does not like regulation *in practice*. People have become sensitized to its costs—costs that can be measured in the tens (and, by some accounts, even the hundreds) of billions of dollars per year. They resent its paperwork, which requires billions of work hours per year to complete. They resent being "hassled" by federal inspectors and being told what they can and cannot do by "Washington bureaucrats."

Attempts to reform and even reduce regulation did not originate with President Reagan. Indeed, his program is best viewed against the historical backdrop of the efforts of his three predecessors. Each faced the same critical issues: how far to exert presidential authority over the independent and executive branch regulatory agencies; how to resolve the conflict between regulatory goals and competing economic claims; whether and how far to push for legislative changes in regulatory mandates; how to divide regulatory responsibilities between the federal government and the states; and what kind of people to appoint to regulatory posts.

The Nixon Administration's Quality of Life Review

Much of the expansion of regulatory authority that President Reagan is trying to bring under control originated under President Nixon. To be sure, a number of the most important initiatives—such as the creation of the National Highway Traffic Safety Administration (NHTSA) and the Occupational Safety and Health Administration (OSHA)—were principally initiatives of the Congress. But for various complex reasons, the Nixon administration acquiesced in, or loaned support to, many of these efforts. And, of course, the Nixon administration was responsible for what was perhaps the greatest expansion of regulatory authority ever witnessed in peacetime—the imposition of wage and price controls.[9]

In addition, it was the Nixon administration that first began to grapple seriously with the problems of controlling the federal regulatory apparatus. White House concern over proliferating federal regulations and their costs surfaced in 1971, when senior officials in the Nixon administration grew concerned over regulations being churned out by the recently formed Environmental Protection Agency (EPA). In an attempt to contain those costs and rein in the agency, White House staff established the Quality of Life Review Program. Under the program, the Office of Management and Budget (OMB) reviewed regulations proposed by executive branch agencies, together with supporting analyses, *prior* to their required publication in the *Federal Register;* then they circulated the proposed rules for interagency comment. Although memoranda issued by OMB Director George Schultz indicated that the Quality of Life Review was to apply to all executive branch agencies issuing "social" regulations, in practice only EPA was singled out for examination.

Not surprisingly, the Quality of Life Review Program—which survived (though in reduced form) through the Ford administration—provoked both controversy and acrimony. The program's opponents considered it an arbitrary and intrusive arrogation of power by the White House—a criticism that has haunted all subsequent White House oversight efforts. Supporters of the Quality of Life Review claimed that it speeded the development of an independent analytic capacity within EPA and forced the agency to coordinate its rulemaking activities with industry and interested agencies earlier, and more effectively, than had been the case.

Innovations during the Ford Administration

Mounting concern over the suspected costs of regulation and their relationship to inflation resulted in two goals during the Ford administration: further reform of the regulatory process and, more significantly, economic deregulation. Ford's regulatory management initiatives required agencies to expressly consider the costs of proposed regulations, vested increased oversight authority in OMB, and expanded the capacity of the executive branch to determine the cost-effectiveness of proposed rules.

The Ford administration also began in earnest the economic deregulation of transportation. During his brief term, Ford issued presidential messages calling for the deregulation of the airline,[10] railroad,[11] and trucking industries[12] and introduced legislation designed to increase rate-setting flexibility and to reduce barriers to entry. Although strong industry and union lobbying kept Congress from passing airline or trucking bills, modest legislative progress was made toward rail deregulation with the enactment of the 1976 Railroad Revitalization and Regulatory Reform Act.

The Carter Regulatory Reform Program

Jimmy Carter, like Ronald Reagan, placed regulatory reform high on his policy agenda. The Carter program had three principal objectives: improved regulatory management, economic deregulation, and the adoption of less-intrusive regulatory techniques.

In the area of regulatory management, Carter pursued the goals of further centralizing and coordinating regulatory oversight, developing cost-based review standards, increasing the executive department's capacity to assess regulatory impacts, reducing paperwork, and expanding citizen participation in the rule-making process.

Carter's initiatives in the area of economic deregulation were particularly significant. Among the legislative victories of his administration were the Airline Deregulation Act of 1978 (P.L. 95-504), the Motor Carrier Act of 1980 (P.L. 96-296), and the Staggers Act (P.L. 96-448), which substantially deregulated the railroad industry. Each bill was, to a degree, a successor to earlier Ford administration deregulatory attempts because each sought to lower barriers to entry and increase price competition.

The Carter administration also began a governmentwide campaign for the adoption of innovative regulatory techniques. The Carter staff saw part of its mission to be the "selling" of alternatives to traditional "command and control" regulatory strategies to agency personnel and the imparting of a new federal regulatory philosophy. The alternative strategies were to be applied when regulation was appropriate, but current techniques were viewed as inefficient.

The administration-backed approach reflected, among other things, a willingness to substitute incentives for constraints, standards set by third parties for governmental standards, and flexible compliance goals for rigid standards. Moreover, this approach revealed a growing faith in the ability of markets to allocate resources efficiently and a correlative distrust in the efficacy of "command and control" regulations.

The Status of Regulatory Reform by the End of 1980

As a result of actions throughout the 1970s and 1980, important advances in regulatory management, economic deregulation, and the implementation of innovative techniques had been realized. However, regulation was still perceived to be out of control. Whether this was in fact correct is irrelevant—Ronald Reagan was able to capitalize on that widespread belief.

The Reagan Administration's Strategy for Regulatory Relief

Viewed with the benefit of a year's hindsight, the Reagan administration's strategy for regulatory relief, both implicit and explicit, seems to have consisted of the following elements:

1. The elimination, modification, or postponement of dozens of administrative regulations and the promulgation of relatively few new regulatory initiatives.
2. Reform of the regulatory process through increased White House oversight and the imposition, except where expressly prohibited by law, of a rigid cost-benefit standard by which all existing and proposed rules are to be judged.
3. The appointment of agency heads sympathetic to the president's regulatory values and the removal and transfer of senior, and in some cases, middle-level agency personnel to obtain vigorous staff support for the administration's regulatory objectives.
4. Substantial budget and personnel reductions within federal regulatory agencies and departments.
5. The dismissal or settlement of legal actions against parties formerly believed to be in violation of federal laws and the initiation of comparatively few new enforcement activities.
6. The elimination or modification of federal regulations affecting state or local governments and the consolidation of numerous federal categorical grant programs into block grants.

The Regulatory Freeze and Its Aftermath

Perhaps the most highly publicized of all the administration's initiatives was the withdrawal, postponement, and modification of dozens of administrative regulations. This began with the suspension, on January 28, 1981, of nearly 200 "midnight regulations." Two classes of rules were affected—those that had only been proposed (and, hence, needed only to be withdrawn), and those promulgated in final form that had not gone into effect (and were, therefore, suspended pending review). According to the administration, of the 172 rules caught in the freeze, 112 were eventually allowed to take effect without substantial change. Twelve were put into effect after substantial changes had been made, and 18 were withdrawn or otherwise suspended. The remaining 30 are currently undergoing more thorough review.[13]

To date, the administration has not undertaken any major new rule-making initiatives. ("New" is used here to indicate development of rules that address previously unregulated matters or actors.) To illustrate, as of April 1, 1982, the Bureau of Consumer Protection of the Federal Trade Commission had proposed no new trade regulations since the Reagan administration took office and had launched no new investigations of trade practices likely to result in future rule makings. Indeed, CEA Chairman Weidenbaum has noted this lull in regulatory activity in his recent speeches, comparing its importance to the critical clue in a Sherlock Holmes mystery—the dog that *didn't* bark.

Administration officials have repeatedly pointed to three indices to demonstrate the direction and success of their regulatory efforts: (a) a 33 percent decline for the first ten months of 1981 in the number of pages printed in the *Federal Register* compared to the same period in 1980; (b) a 25 percent decrease in the total number of rules published compared to 1980 figures; and (c) a 50 percent reduction in the number of major rules issued over the same period.[14] The number of pages printed in the *Federal Register* in any given year may be a questionable measure of regulatory activity for a number of reasons. First, the *Federal Register* can, and has at various times, been modified by changes in typeface, elimination of blank pages, changes in page size, and, most importantly, changes in the relative detail used to describe proposed rule makings. Second, agencies have substantial discretion regarding what they choose to publish in the *Federal Register*.[15] In sum, however, there does appear to have been a real overall decrease in *new* regulatory actions during the administration's first year.

Regulatory Oversight and Management during the Reagan Administration

The president's regulatory management program consists of three major elements—the designation of a uniform cost-effectiveness standard that virtually all new regulations must meet; the formal centralization of regulatory oversight authority for all executive department agencies within the White House-controlled Office of Management and Budget; and the creation of a

highly visible regulatory reform advocacy group—the President's Task Force
on Regulatory Relief—to be staffed by a newly formed Office of Information
and Regulatory Affairs (OIRA).

On January 22, 1981, almost immediately after taking office, President
Reagan announced the formation of his Task Force on Regulatory Relief, a
cabinet-level regulatory appeals group to be chaired by the vice president.
The task force is responsible for the following:

- Reviewing major regulatory proposals by executive branch agencies,
  especially proposals that appear to have major policy significance
- Assessing executive branch regulations currently on the books, especially those that are burdensome to the national economy or to key
  industrial sectors
- Overseeing the development of legislative proposals in response to
  congressional timetables (e.g., the Clean Air Act) and codifying the
  president's views on the appropriate roles and objectives of regulatory
  agencies[16]

OIRA, which staffs the task force, has roughly ninety staff positions. It
has review authority over all proposed executive department agency rules.
Moreover, it oversees the Paperwork Reduction Act and the Regulatory Flexibility Act. Some commentators have questioned whether OIRA has the capacity to take on such a formidable set of responsibilities.

On February 17, 1981, the president issued a detailed executive order
that set out the most significant features of his regulatory management plan—
systematic cost-effectiveness analysis and centralization of oversight authority.[17] The order states that no final rule may be published unless it is determined that the potential benefits to society outweigh their projected costs,
and that the chosen regulatory alternative maximizes net social benefits while
minimizing net social costs. Proposed rules must also take into account "the
condition of the particular industries affected by regulations, the condition of
the national economy, and other regulatory actions contemplated for the future."

The order requires that a Regulatory Impact Analysis (RIA) be prepared
and accompany all proposed and final rules designated as "major."[18] Each
RIA must describe the potential costs and benefits of the proposed rule and
suggest alternative approaches. Although RIAs must be made available to the
public, they need not be printed in the *Federal Register*.

The order establishes OMB as the focal point of presidential oversight
by requiring that all *proposed major rules* be submitted to OMB's director
sixty days before publication in the *Federal Register* and that all *final major
rules* be submitted thirty days before publication. All *nonmajor rules* must
be submitted ten days before publication to the director of OMB at both the
proposed and final stages. Thus OMB, or more specifically, OIRA, passes

judgment on the appropriateness of each proposed regulation at least twice before it becomes law. Moreover, the director of OMB is authorized to designate major rules for review and to establish schedules for the reviews and analyses. In addition, the order requires that all executive agencies begin reviewing *existing major regulations* to determine the extent to which they conform to the standards elaborated elsewhere in the directive.

A quantitative overview of the administration's efforts during 1981 reveals that as of December 31, OMB had been sent 2,803 rules for review; 2,446 rules (87 percent) had been approved without change, and 138 (5 percent) had been approved with minor changes; 95 rules (3 percent) were returned to the agencies for major changes (often a proxy for effective termination) or were withdrawn; and 43 (2 percent) of the 2,803 rules reviewed were classified as major, 22 of which were supported by RIAs.[19]

Personnel Actions

As have all presidents, Ronald Reagan has appointed like-minded individuals to cabinet and subcabinet level posts. Accordingly, the strong antiregulatory tone of the administration is reflected in the philosophies and backgrounds of his appointees.

This administration is also not unusual in that the match between available regulatory posts, the preferred candidates' political and philosophical leanings, and their professional backgrounds was often imperfect. However, the Reagan administration may be atypical in its sometimes explicit preference for candidates with no substantive experience in the general regulatory area of the agency or department to which they have been appointed. For example, it has been reported that one of the qualifications for the top job at the National Highway Traffic Safety Administration was a lack of experience in highway safety. The selection of Ray Peck, formerly director of regulatory affairs for the National Coal Association, satisfied that criterion.[20]

Given the president's political philosophy, it is not surprising that his appointments have often been drawn from the regulated industries themselves. An example is the appointment of John Shad as chairman of the Securities and Exchange Commission; Shad was formerly the vice chairman of E.F. Hutton and Company. Somewhat more surprising was the appointment of individuals who had had a direct adversarial relationship with the agency they were slated to head. The most prominent example is Secretary of the Interior James Watt's litigation on behalf of the Denver-based Mountain States Legal Foundation. The administration's willingness to remove, replace, or relocate midlevel regulatory staff in order to alter agency priorities is also somewhat unusual.[21]

Budget and Staff Reductions

The regulatory relief program, like other areas of administration policy, is being implemented in part through targeted budget cuts and resulting personnel reductions. Indeed, the executive branch and the independent agencies charged with administering federal social and economic regulations have been subject to sharp personnel reductions. In most instances personnel and support losses have substantially exceeded governmentwide staff reduction levels. For example, the president's 1983 budget proposes sharp reductions from 1981 staffing levels in the Department of the Interior's Office of Surface Mining (38 percent), the Consumer Protection Agency (29 percent), OSHA (22 percent), and the Federal Trade Commission (22 percent).[22]

Reduction of Agency Enforcement Efforts

Agency budget cuts and resulting staff reductions seem to be compatible with the administration's goal of altering federal regulatory enforcement practices across a number of program areas. The administration has repeatedly indicated that it is eager to shift greater enforcement responsibility to the states; to rely, where possible, on negotiation rather than litigation in disposing of violations; and to rely increasingly on voluntary monitoring and compliance with federal regulations.

Sharp reductions in the enforcement activities of most federal agencies have been reported in the past year. In 1980, for example, the special litigation section of the civil rights division of the Justice Department filed twenty-nine suits to protect the rights of prison inmates, mental patients, the physically handicapped, and persons who suffer discrimination in public accommodations. In 1981 no such suits were filed.[23] Similarly, in 1980 the general litigation section of Justice's civil rights division filed twenty-two suits to enforce school desegregation laws. In 1981 that number fell to ten.[24]

To implement its changed enforcement strategies during the Reagan administration's first year, the EPA has

- Abolished its enforcement office, splitting its functions among several different offices[25]
- Asked the Justice Department to drop forty-nine pending enforcement actions claiming, among other things, that enforcement should be referred to the states, that the cases were insignificant or stale, or that the named facilities were now in compliance with the law[26]
- Reduced the average number of cases EPA refers annually to the Justice Department for prosecution from 200 to 30[27]

The number of formal investigations into potential car defects by the National Highway Traffic Safety Administration fell from fifteen during the last year of the Carter administration to four during the first nine months of President Reagan's term.[28] At the same time, the Occupational Safety and Health Administration's average monthly inspections declined 17 percent, while the average monthly number of serious citations issued dropped 27 percent.[29]

Under current law, the federal government pays the states to inspect nursing homes for compliance with federal standards in areas such as medical care and patient's rights. Homes must satisfy federal standards to participate in Medicare or Medicaid. Sharp cuts in federal payments to states for nursing home inspections, however, have led to staff reductions and substantially diminished state enforcement efforts. California officials note that the state has lost $2.9 million of the $8 million it was receiving in federal funds and has cut its enforcement staff from 395 to 291 persons.[30] Thus, budget cuts have led not only to a decline in federal enforcement of federal standards but a reduction in state enforcement of federal standards.

Redefining the Federal-State Relationship in Regulation

Another focus of the administration's efforts has been federal intergovernmental rules. Twenty-five of the 100 regulations originally slated for review by the President's Task Force on Regulatory Relief directly affected state and local governments. The administration's program of regulatory federalism is founded on two principles: a profound mistrust of strong centralized government, and a belief that program management and administration is more cost-effective at lower rather than higher levels of government. In addition, the deregulatory program serves the political purpose of appeasing state and local officials forced to reduce services or raise taxes as a result of cuts in federal assistance.

The administration's initiatives in this area have taken two forms. The most prominent has been the congressionally ordered establishment of nine block grant programs, consolidating fifty-seven separate federal aid efforts. This action enabled the federal government to eliminate hundreds of pages of associated regulations. The other major initiatives have been accomplished through the traditional administrative process and overseen by the Task Force on Regulatory Relief, OIRA, and the agencies. The block grant initiatives are discussed in chapter 6. The remainder of this section will concentrate on the administrative actions.

To date, the task force has focused on a number of crosscutting regulations which in the past have been singled out by state and local administrators as being particularly burdensome.[31] Among these are prevailing wage standards, federal nondiscrimination policies pertaining to the handicapped, federally prescribed nondiscrimination policies in employment, and many of the most significant environmental and land use initiatives undertaken by the federal government in the 1970s. Perhaps the most highly touted administration action to date in the intergovernmental area was its withdrawal of the Carter administration's proposed bilingual education rules, which, it is claimed, will save state and local governments $1 billion to $3 billion.

Regulatory Reform in Practice: Deregulating Transportation

A brief description of the administration's strategies in the general area of transportation will convey some sense of the direction and ambition of the regulatory relief program. For the purposes of this chapter, this example also demonstrates the translation of strategies and philosophy into concrete programs.

Transportation is an area that has long been subject to economic regulation and has, in recent years, come increasingly under the purview of the new "social regulations." The economic regulation of the various common carrier modes—airlines, railroads, trucking, pipelines, and barges—as already noted, has been sharply reduced over the past few years. By contrast, the automobile industry has been subjected to an increasing amount of "social" regulation. Automobiles have been one of the nation's largest sources of air pollution; a principal cause of accidental death, injury, and property damage; and major users of petroleum products. Concern with environmental protection, safer and more reliable consumer products, and energy conservation have all led to an increasingly regulated auto industry.

The Administration's Auto Package

At the time the Reagan administration took office, the American auto industry was experiencing a severe slump in sales, high unemployment, and an eroding share of the total market. Among the new administration's first regulatory actions was the announced rescission of thirty-four proposed regulations that addressed emission control, safety, and fuel economy objectives. The aggregate capital cost savings provided the industry were estimated at $1.3 billion over five years. Reagan officials claimed that consumers, in turn, would save $8 billion over the same period.

The auto industry was also a major beneficiary of the administration's tax bill, which provided accelerated depreciation schedules for investments in plant and equipment, and which provided unprofitable firms the opportunity to sell unused tax credits to other more profitable entities.

Providing broad regulatory relief for the auto industry was a logical policy move for the administration for three reasons. First, there was the requisite motive: regulatory relief offered a means of assistance that would preserve the simplicity of the tax bill, provide an alternative to trade restrictions, and permit continued firmness in the area of monetary restraint. Moreover, broad regulatory relief for the auto industry could be assembled into a visible "package" for publicity purposes. Second, the means appeared to exist for broad deregulation of the auto industry. In the cases of safety regulations and emission controls for trucks and diesel vehicles, the administration believed it had the necessary legal authority at the administrative or agency level to alter policy without having to navigate the legislative process. Finally, there was opportunity; the Carter administration had left office with a substantial number of regulations pending that appeared peculiarly vulnerable to summary administrative action.

The regulations to be withdrawn or modified fell primarily in two areas: safety and emission control. Among the safety regulations that were rescinded, delayed, or canceled by the National Highway Traffic Safety Administration were the following:

- The required installation of passive restraint systems (airbags or automatic belts)
- Bumper standards intended to withstand crashes of up to five miles per hour
- Standards for objects such as roof pillars that obstruct a driver's field of vision
- Standards that would make speedometers tamper-proof
- Regulations that would upgrade braking requirements for new light trucks, buses, and vans
- Rules on low-tire-pressure warning indicators for cars, trucks, and buses

Among the emission control rules proposed by EPA were regulations that would do the following:

- Relax emission standards for some truck pollutants
- Relax the percentage of vehicles tested on assembly lines that must meet federal emission standards
- Promote self-certification practices for new vehicles
- Permit the implementation of a fleet averaging or "mobile bubble" concept in calculating vehicle emissions
- Postpone the application of federal air pollution standards for auto industry paint shop operations

In addition, the administration signaled its intent not to propose any post-1985 fuel economy standards.

Tension among the administration's general policy goals is particularly evident in the auto safety area. These goals include the implementation of more cost-effective regulations, the avoidance of undue governmental paternalism, and the provision of regulatory relief to industry. Assuming, as some economists do, that by far the most cost-effective solution to auto safety is the mandatory installation of passive restraints (airbags or automatic seat belts), why did the administration retreat from full implementation of the rule? NHTSA officials claim that one rationale for their action was the fact that passive belts—the industry's preferred option—would be detachable and would not be used by consumers. However, it appears that the overriding reason the requirement was withdrawn was because passive restraints represent precisely the kind of governmental paternalism that the Reagan administration has expressly rejected. Thus, despite the fact that benefits arguably exceeded costs, cost-effectiveness proved an insufficient rationale for going forward with the regulation.

Economic Regulation at the Interstate Commerce Commission

The clash between ideology and political pragmatism is also evident in regulation of common carriers. Early in the Reagan presidency, nationwide attention began to focus on the issue of continued deregulation of the transportation industry by the Interstate Commerce Commission (ICC). It appears that the administration's call for broad economic deregulation has been heeded only partially within that agency—and indeed some commentators have noted that the president himself may have supported a slowdown of the deregulation efforts put in place by the Carter administration.[32]

At the heart of the debate is the new chairman of the ICC, Reese Taylor. Taylor has been criticized for backpedaling on trucking deregulation. A report issued by the Joint Economic Committee of the Congress found that under Taylor's leadership the ICC had

- Rejected rate reductions while expressing concern over "predatory pricing"
- Hired more regulatory staff and shown an inclination to hold hearings on applications, often at great expense to would-be entrants into the trucking business
- Granted narrow operating rights to applicants for trucking authority rather than allowing them freedom to expand beyond immediate markets
- Failed to appeal in a timely fashion a ruling by the U.S. Court of Appeals for the Fifth Circuit that struck down the agency's liberalized certification policies for common carriers[33]

Critics assert that the bloom is off trucking deregulation largely because of intense political pressure brought by the major carriers, their industry association (the American Trucking Association), and the Teamsters Union. These groups have been unhappy about the consequences of deregulation as increased entry, service innovation, and price competition have led to falling freight rates. Lower rates, in turn, have eroded the monopoly positions of some major carriers as well as the union and have necessitated Teamster wage concessions.

Commission officials note that ICC actions are perfectly consistent with the language of the Motor Carrier Act, which, they claim, does not entirely eliminate the protectionist goals of the pre-deregulation era. Moreover, they assert that the agency is extending the deregulation of the railroads begun under President Carter. These claims are supported by a recent unanimous commission decision on a final rule permitting merged railroads to lower rates and offer faster service than was formerly possible.[34]

Here again, one can see conflicting tendencies in the regulatory relief program. If the administration's critics are correct, promotion of the interests of a targeted beneficiary—the Teamsters—superseded the conflicting goal of furthering economic deregulation. Where no such comparably potent beneficiary has existed—as in the intercity bus or rail industry—progress toward deregulation has continued apace.

The Reagan Regulatory Relief Program: A Framework for Evaluation

The administration's goals for its regulatory relief program can be grouped into three broad categories: the program must fulfill its assigned role in the economic "game plan"; it must advance the administration's commitment to reduce the federal presence in the economy; and it must demonstrate the administration's desire to redefine the federal-state-local government relationship. These are ambitious and, in some cases, long-term goals. Although it is far too early to tell whether they will be fully met, certain aspects of the program were intended to have short-run—indeed, almost immediate—effects. Thus, it is reasonable to ask even at this relatively early date whether these expectations have been met. Moreover, it is possible to suggest a general framework within which the entire regulatory relief program might eventually be judged.

Regulation's Place in the Economic Game Plan

As was noted at the beginning of this chapter, regulatory relief was given an extremely important role to play in the administration's plan to revitalize the economy, a role as central as tax and fiscal measures. *Actual* rescissions in regulations were to reduce businesses' short-term cash flow requirements significantly, thereby increasing their ability to undertake "productive" investment. *Anticipated* changes in the volume and stringency of future regulations were to be important elements in boosting business confidence and breaking inflationary expectations.

Assessing the program's success with regard to the objective of improving corporate cash flow is complicated by the difficulty of defining an appropriate baseline against which to measure the cost reductions and by problems in estimating claimed savings. Evaluating the regulatory relief program's success in altering expectations is similarly complicated by problems inherent in measuring expectations.

Improvement in Corporate Cash Flow. The regulatory freeze delayed promulgation of several regulations and led, on occasion, to the promulgation of rules modified in ways that may lower compliance costs. Further, the overall pace of issuing new regulations did decrease markedly during the administration's first year in office, and enforcement actions undertaken by regulatory agencies declined significantly. All of these things probably reduced regulatory compliance costs, but by how much?

The administration has claimed that the savings just from the freeze and its immediate aftermath amounted to at least $5 billion in annual expenses and $15 billion in future capital investment. No estimates have been made by the administration of the dollar impact of its entire first-year effort, but the total would undoubtedly run much higher than the figures just cited.

These claims of cost savings have been skeptically received for a number of reasons. For one thing, savings from regulations that the Carter administration had merely proposed but not promulgated have been folded into the administration's estimates of overall savings. It is impossible to know the extent to which the cost of these regulations would have been reduced prior to their final promulgation—if indeed all had been promulgated. Even more problematic is determining what industry anticipated to be the cost of these future regulations. Over the last several years, business has become much more sophisticated at "reading" the regulatory process. Thus, it is unlikely that many firms had set aside, even for planning purposes, the full amount estimated as the cost of these proposed regulations.

Where existing regulations were modified or rescinded, estimated costs are more credible. But even here, problems arise in calculating the resulting savings. First, when an already-promulgated regulation is rolled back, business is likely to have invested some money in preparing to comply with it. These costs are "sunk"—they cannot be recovered. Estimates of the savings from regulatory rescission should take these "sunk" costs into account. As far as can be determined, the administration's figures do not.

Calculating the savings that result from reduced enforcement is even more difficult. Although some businesses may take advantage of reduced enforcement to lower compliance costs, others—aware of the risk of private or state legal action or concerned about their general corporate image—may not alter their behavior. Paradoxically, it is important to the Reagan administration's overall regulatory relief strategy to be able to claim that reduced enforcement resources have not generated widespread noncompliance. Otherwise, a congressional backlash may result.

The plain fact is that no one really knows how widespread compliance with regulations was even before the Reagan regulatory relief program began. Enforcement programs have lacked strategic goals and measures of success. Thus, we do not have a baseline against which to measure changes.

Altering Inflationary Expectations. Regardless of the short-run cash flow improvement arising from regulatory relief, a sincere belief on the part of business that the regulatory "game" has changed can help to alter inflationary expectations in a significant way.

Although inflationary expectations are a highly subjective phenomenon, little understood by economists, two points can be made about their relationship to regulatory change. First, expectational changes must ultimately confront reality. If regulatory relief is to play a major role in reducing inflationary expectations, businessmen are going to have to experience genuine cost savings.

Second, if they don't, then exaggerated claims that the regulatory picture has totally changed and that extremely large cost savings can be expected may undermine the credibility of the entire regulatory reform movement and regulatory reform's potential impact on the economy.

To sum up, the administration has been able to convince much of industry to announce its support for the regulatory relief program. The effort has cut costs, though by an unknown amount, and appears to have convinced businessmen that the regulatory game has changed—at least somewhat. But how much the game has actually changed has yet to be determined.

Reducing the Federal Presence in the Economy

The administration has made much of the growth of the gross national product (GNP) share absorbed by the federal government. But the growth of the federal presence is not measured merely by the level of GNP absorbed. As the administration has observed time and again, the spread of regulation has included the federal government in private decision making to an extent far greater than its GNP share reflects. Indeed, a single-minded concentration on GNP share reduction, if reflected in the substitution of nonbudgeted items such as regulation for budgeted items, would be meaningless or, more likely, counterproductive.

This chapter has already discussed the administration's reliance on the administrative process in reducing regulatory burdens. The discussion noted that, by and large, their efforts have not involved statutory change. This approach is understandable because statutory change takes time, and time was one thing the administration believed was in short supply when it entered office.

Moreover, the regulatory authority and latitude available even under relatively tightly worded statutes are not generally appreciated. The areas of activity to which regulations can be applied; the nature and stringency of the regulatory burden imposed; and the degree to which regulations, once established, will be enforced can all be subject to administrative action. Further, reviewing courts are generally reluctant to second-guess the head of an administration agency, provided procedural requirements have been carefully followed.[35] The appointment of regulators determined to use every bit of flexibility to write lenient regulations and to enforce them as leniently as the law permits will produce results that differ substantially from a more activist approach to regulation drafting and enforcement. The Reagan administration's appointment of "permissive" regulators will, if maintained over a long enough time, surely result in a significantly reduced federal regulatory presence.

Such a strategy involves several significant risks. First, changing regulatory personnel rather than statutes works only if the newly appointed regulators know just how far they can go without overstepping their legal bounds. Examples existed in previous administrations of regulators who failed to heed the advice of their general counsels, or who appointed less than fully competent individuals and found their attempts to reduce regulatory burdens on industry overturned.

A second risk of relying too heavily on a strategy of administrative regulatory relief is that a "disaster" can occur (or can be made to appear to have occurred), leading Congress to tighten up considerably on the latitude it grants an agency. Sustained controversy over Interior Secretary James Watt's stewardship over federal lands, or fears that EPA Director Anne Gorsuch is not being sufficiently aggressive in dealing with the discharge of toxic wastes, could eventually lead Congress to reduce the discretion these administrators currently enjoy. After all, as already noted, public concern with "overregulation" still seems to be accompanied by strong public support for the achievement of regulation's most important goals. If Reagan administration regulators appear to be abusing their discretion, and plausible claims of resulting harm can be made, then legislative attempts to force regulatory action are predictable. A related problem associated with relying on an administrative approach—one particularly bound up in the issue of enforcement—is the potential for selective application. Perceptions that similarly situated businesses or individuals are being dissimilarly treated are likely to lead to legal challenges that could also threaten current regulatory initiatives.

The third risk of an administrative relief approach is that it takes time to demonstrate that relief has occurred. As noted, mere claims that "the game has changed" do not necessarily convince businessmen that change has occurred. A change in statute is visible (though perhaps the public overrates it), while a change in the administration of an existing statute is less obvious.

Ultimately, therefore, significant regulatory relief is liable to require significant statutory change. But such change is by no means assured, even in a Republican-controlled Congress. The perception that Reagan appointees have not made a good faith effort to enforce the law, do not understand the statutes they administer, or have been inept in dealing with Congress, all could undermine the possibility for substantial statutory change.

One important strategy for reducing federal intrusiveness in private sector decision making is the use of alternatives to inflexible, inefficient "command and control" regulatory techniques. Indeed, the administration is on record as supporting the use of these less-intrusive techniques.

One achievement in this regard is the administration's strong effort—after overcoming initial skepticism on the part of the EPA administrator—to obtain liberalized rules for emissions trading. Emissions trading allows industry to reduce emissions beyond established pollution standards at one source, where control is relatively cheap, and to use the emission reduction credit to satisfy pollution standards at another source, where control is more expensive.[36] This effort, like many other regulatory reform efforts, goes back several years. But there can be no doubt that the Reagan administration has been able to move the policy faster, if not further, than the Carter administration could have hoped. In this case, a dedication to broadening the policy to the maximum extent possible, coupled with a thorough understanding on the part of professional-level bureaucrats of how to make the program work, has been responsible for its success. It is probably fair to say that the emissions trading concept has been taken about as far as possible under the 1977 Clean Air Act. Another area in which the administration appears to be promoting the use of market-like regulatory tools, is the "averaging" of fleetwide emissions of certain pollutants, constituting, in effect, a performance standard.

Another achievement is OSHA's attempt to reduce regulatory "hassle" by "targeting" workplace inspections. To be sure, the standard against which this effort is to be measured is not high because the old "nontargeted" OSHA approach is not generally thought to have produced positive results.

In other instances, the administration has appeared less enthusiastic about adopting innovative techniques. EPA's efforts to move the concept of marketable permits from the status of an economic curiosity to an accepted regulatory technique have foundered for lack of high-level support. Aside from the controlled trading, averaging, and targeted inspection examples cited, there is little systematic effort to·adopt less-intrusive forms of regulation.

This situation is not entirely unpredictable. As noted earlier, the Reagan administration is philosophically opposed to much federal regulation. The development of less-intrusive methods of regulation flies in the face of this philosophy—it implies that regulation may be necessary. At the very least, Reagan regulatory officials are wary of developing techniques that would make regulation more tolerable.

Even under the Reagan philosophy, regulation will continue to exist. The concerns of administration officials notwithstanding, the government's ability to conspicuously reduce the "hassle factor" of regulation will help determine the ultimate success of the administration's regulatory relief effort— especially in the eyes of the general public.

The Regulatory Relief Program and the "New Federalism"

Although reducing the *amount* of federal regulation is important to the Reagan administration, righting the regulatory balance between the federal government and state and local governments is also of concern. This strategy has taken two directions: a reduction in the degree to which the federal government attempts to impose its social preferences on states and localities through regulation; and a shift in responsibility for regulation to units better able to sense the needs of citizens (including businesses). The first of these entails less regulation overall; the second, an alternative governmental source of rules.

Although federally prescribed standards for state and local service delivery are widespread, a number of intergovernmental regulations have proven particularly controversial. For example, federal rules on transportation for handicapped persons prompted an outright declaration of future noncompliance by New York City officials and a general outcry from city transit administrators across the country. Attempts by President Carter's Interior Department to control access to federal lands in the West are credited with sparking a "sagebrush rebellion." The Carter Education Department's attempts to specify bilingual education standards for local school districts were widely criticized.

In each of these cases, the Reagan administration has moved to respond to such criticisms, though its success has been limited. Interior Secretary Watt's proposal to change coal and oil leasing rules and the procedures by which lands are designated as wilderness areas set off a storm of criticism, even in states where the "sagebrush rebellion" commanded the largest political following. On the other hand, however, Education Secretary Terrel Bell's suspension of the Carter bilingual regulations and his broader moves to reduce the power of the Education Department (even to the point of eliminating it as a cabinet-level agency) are seen as signals of reduced federal interference in state efforts to control educational programs—signals favorably received by many local officals.

The administration's estimates of cost savings produced by its efforts at regulatory federalism, like its claims of business savings, may be substantially overstated for two reasons. Consider the large savings reported earlier, $1 billion to $3 billion per year, said to result from the administration's suspension of the Carter administration's bilingual regulation. First, these figures appear to represent *total* program costs, not *incremental* costs. Only incremental costs—or the expenses that would not have been incurred but for federal regulations—measure potential savings to local governments. Many school districts would offer substantial bilingual education programs in the absence of any federal mandate because of the size and political power of their non-English-speaking populations, or because local educators believe bilingual training to be professionally sound. In other instances local educational agencies may be compelled by state law to offer bilingual education.

Second, these budget figures may understate the extent to which legislative and judicial support exists for bilingual education. Accordingly, the legal residue of existing federal regulations, federal and state statutes, and case law that remains in the wake of the withdrawal of the proposed bilingual education rules may remove the possibility of substantial savings through program elimination or modifications.[37]

Statutory obstacles to sweeping regulatory change pose real problems in the intergovernmental area because many of the most important federal acts establish with some specificity the reach and authority of federal power in regulating a designated area. Thus, real regulatory relief for state and local officials may have to await congressional rather than administrative action.

A recent series of articles in the *Washington Post* suggest that regulatory relief may be coming more slowly to the public sector than it has to the private sector.[38] These articles, based on interviews with local officials in the town of Appleton, Wisconsin, found that the Reagan initiatives had had little tangible impact on the burden reported by government officials and townspeople as previously documented during the Carter administration.

There is, of course, no assurance that Appleton's experience is representative. Conversations with Dallas city officials revealed that EPA-approved relaxation of state stream standards would save the city approximately $100 million in the construction of new wastewater treatment facilities. The changes in standards permitted the city to build new facilities that treat wastewater at the secondary rather than the more complex and expensive tertiary level. Conversations with officials in Newark and Cincinnati revealed no comparable cost savings resulting from the deregulatory efforts because, unlike Dallas, neither Cincinnati nor Newark is experiencing population growth. Accordingly, no similar expansion of sewage treatment capacity is called for. Thus, it could be the case that fast-growing jurisdictions that are undertaking capital expansion programs may reap substantial savings from relaxation of federal environmental standards in ways not available to older, stable, or declining jurisdictions such as Appleton.

It appears that the administration may be willing to abandon its goal of removing the federal government from local affairs when it conflicts with other objectives. The most prominent example of this is the administration-sponsored provision in the Omnibus Reconciliation Act (P.L. 97-35) that set a statutory limit on the amount of assets a household could own and still remain eligible for AFDC. Not only was the prior limit lowered (from $2,000 to $1,000) and expressed by statute rather than by rule, but also the authority to designate items to be excluded from consideration was transferred from the states to the U.S. Department of Health and Human Services.[39] Local officials have complained that the new federal standards have proven both burdensome and expensive.

The issue of state autonomy cuts two ways. For example, OSHA and a coalition of industry groups recently succeeded (over the objections of Reagan's OMB) in forcing the proposal of *federal* chemical labeling standards for toxics present in the workplace. Their victory owed to a widespread fear that a proliferation of inconsistent state-mandated chemical labeling requirements would prove more costly than uniform federal standards. Early Reagan promises to eliminate EPA's much-criticized noise office have also run up against the federal preemption problem. In fact, industry is having second thoughts concerning the wisdom of state rather than federal regulation. Transportation Secretary Drew Lewis has served notice of his intention to fight local airport noise ordinances on the grounds that they constitute an unreasonable burden on interstate commerce. In short, the proper degree of state autonomy as far as regulation is concerned is still very much an open question.

Concluding Observations on the Reagan Program's First Year

The fact that the Reagan administration's program, unlike those of its predecessors, is labeled "regulatory relief" rather than "regulatory reform" is no accident. It is the administration's view that, for all their efforts, previous programs of reform have failed to reduce the regulatory burden, in part because their commitment was only half-hearted.

Lack of will may indeed have been a problem. For all their interest in reforming regulation, most officials in previous administrations appeared to believe that government had a significant role in controlling private sector activity and in assuring citizens a minimum level of amenities, regardless of where they lived. They saw regulation as a legitimate though clumsy and overused tool for achieving these ends. Officials in the Reagan administration appear to view regulation in a more negative light, narrowly defining the occasions when its use would be legitimate.

However, this administration's strong commitment to regulatory relief has not been matched by commensurate action. Looking back, it seems the political capital needed to achieve the administration's tax and budget objectives, coupled with the procedural opportunities provided by the Carter administration's legacy of midnight rules, dictated that an administrative rather than a legislative approach be taken to regulatory relief. This reliance on an administrative strategy raises the issue of the sustainability of the administration's efforts. By forgoing whatever political opportunities were available to make legislative changes, the regulatory relief program has been made more vulnerable to legal assaults and political challenge. As a result it is likely to be less capable of influencing business costs and expectations of inflation. The problems with a purely administrative approach are illustrated by a recent U.S. Court of Appeals decision invalidating the rescission of NHTSA's passive restraint standards[40]—the centerpiece of the administration's efforts to bring regulatory relief to the auto industry.

Thus, as the program moves beyond its first year, the euphoria has died and the complex task of institutionalizing the changes that Reagan promised has begun. The belief that deregulation could have an immediate and visible impact on the economy has faded. The direction that regulatory change takes in the future, however, may still contribute in an important way to the ultimate success or failure of the Reagan effort to revitalize the economy.

PART TWO

THE RELATIONSHIP OF THE FEDERAL GOVERNMENT TO THE STATE-LOCAL AND NONPROFIT SECTORS

Chapter 6

THE STATE AND LOCAL SECTOR

George E. Peterson

Domestic policy in the United States is the product of implicit partnerships between different levels of government. When the federal government changes its priorities, as the Reagan administration has done, states and localities must decide how they will react. In principle these governments could absorb federal budget cutbacks by supplementing public spending with their own resources and could enlarge their program responsibilities to compensate for those relinquished by Washington. Or they could refrain from supplementation, allowing the federal budget reductions to become reductions in all government activity.

States and localities are not merely reactive partners. Their budget initiatives have as great an impact on domestic policy as the federal government's. Well before the 1980 presidential election, state and local governments had embarked on their own revolution of tax reductions. Although the election

[The author gratefully acknowledges the contributions of Barbara A. Davis, Albert Fries, and Fred Teitlebaum. Information on state budget adjustments in FY 1982 and FY 1983 is drawn in part from a joint survey by the National Conference of State Legislatures and The Urban Institute and reported in Steven D. Gold, Karen M. Benker, and George E. Peterson, *State Budget Actions in 1982*.]

gave national ratification to what until then had been a state and local phenomenon, it also threw the federal government into direct competition with
states and localities for providing tax relief. The problems created by this
competition to reduce tax burdens have been exacerbated by the recession,
which has made it impossible for all levels of government simultaneously to
keep their promises of tax cuts.

This chapter begins by considering the administration's short- and long-
term strategies for changing federal relations. During the presidential campaign Ronald Reagan argued that the policy partnership between the federal
government and state and local governments had gone awry. He revived this
theme in his 1982 State of the Union address and budget message: "During
the past 20 years, what had been a classic division of functions between the
Federal Government and the States and localities has become a confused
mess. Traditional understandings about the roles of each level of government
have been violated." The president promised "to clear up this mess" and
said he was launching a "major effort to restore American federalism."[1] In
the long run the Reagan policy involves a fundamental sorting out of responsibilities by level of government in which many federal government
functions and some revenue sources are to be returned to the states. Although
the ultimate fate of the federalism proposals is uncertain, the president clearly
has succeeded in his goal of stimulating fresh consideration of how to divide
domestic policy responsibilities among federal, state, and local governments.

In the short run the administration has given priority to reversing the
historical growth in federal aid to state and local governments while providing
them with greater flexibility in spending federal dollars. The primary vehicle
for achieving this flexibility has been reform of the grants-in-aid structure
through the introduction of block grants. The details of the federal budget
reductions and grant consolidations and their program impacts in specific
areas of social policy are discussed in part 3 of this volume. The second
section of this chapter considers the common themes that run through the
changes in grant design and the initial reactions by the states to the greater
flexibility but lower funding levels of the block grants.

The third section of this chapter adopts the perspective of the state-local
partners in domestic policy production. It considers the major changes in state
tax and spending policies that have occurred since the mid-1970s and fits
state budgets for FY 1982 and FY 1983 within this recent history. Most states
face local versions of the federal budget dilemma; under current economic
conditions they cannot balance their budgets at desired program levels, given
the tax-rate reductions they have made. The choices that states are now making
in resolving this dilemma will determine their capacity for absorbing the
various federalism initiatives and help establish the ultimate impact of federal

policy changes, as these changes work their way through all levels of government.[2]

The New Federalism in Perspective

In its federalism proposals the administration has provided a road map of its desired dealings with state and local governments over the next decade. These proposals represent a major political and philosophical departure from the prevailing view and practice of federalism as it has evolved since the 1930s. The specifics of the long-term proposals are certain to be altered—indeed, they had already undergone significant modification by June 1982, when this chapter was written. Whether the broad goals of the New Federalism will eventually be endorsed by Congress or whether any version of the sorting out of program responsibilities will be found that is acceptable to both the administration and the states remain matters of speculation. Nonetheless, the New Federalism proposals spell out the administration's cumulative intentions. The grant changes that have been made to date, while sometimes appearing to be no more than convenient devices for achieving federal budget reductions, have been consistent with the New Federalism principles.

The depth of the transformation in state-local relations that the administration proposes is best illustrated by a single comparison. In 1980 federal aid constituted almost 25 percent of state and local expenditures.[3] If all the administration's proposals were to come to fruition by 1991—a scant decade and a year later—the federal aid share in state and local budgets would be reduced to 3 to 4 percent.

This reduction in the federal presence would be achieved by a combination of grant cutbacks, program swaps, and federal withdrawal from shared funding arrangements. A disengagement of this scale would not only reverse the last two decades of federal intrusion into state and local affairs, which President Reagan lamented in his budget message, but would reduce the federal role in state and local budgets to levels unknown since 1933.[4] The proposed policy turnabout is even more remarkable since it reverses a trend toward deeper intermixing of the responsibilities and financing of different levels of government, which seemingly had commanded bipartisan support since World War II.

State and Local Expenditure Trends

From 1951 to 1975 the state and local sector was one of the premier growth sectors in the American economy. Real spending by that sector grew in each of those years, even when adjusted for population growth. Over that quarter-century the share of state and local expenditures in the Gross National Product (GNP) almost doubled, rising from 7.9 percent in 1951 to a high of 15.0 percent in 1975. This growth far outpaced the growth in federal spending. During the last decade of that period, almost one-quarter of all new jobs created in the American economy were generated by state and local governments.

Impressive and persistent as this growth curve was, it was fueled by different policy priorities in different periods. The early 1950s witnessed a building surge in the public sector, supported by the need to catch up on capital programs that had been postponed during the war and to accommodate the incipient baby boom. School and highway construction led public spending. During the 1960s, when real spending growth for state and local governments reached its peak, school operating costs lodged the principal claim on budget expansions. The last wave of the baby boom carried tax increases before it and left in its wake an educational sector destined to struggle with the consequences of enrollment decline.

The most distinctive characteristic of state and local spending growth through much of the 1970s was the emergence of these governments as the administrative *agents* for carrying out federal policy. State and local governments have been cost-sharing partners in one of the most rapidly growing domestic programs, Medicaid, which is administered by the states but strongly regulated by Washington. States administer the jointly financed Aid to Families with Dependent Children (AFDC) as well as other federally financed social welfare programs. The 1974-1975 recession brought perhaps the purest application of state and local governments' role as administrative agent. Almost all of the federal government's program of countercyclical stimulation in response to the recession was assigned to the state and local sector for management, including principal responsibility for operating temporary public service jobs programs under 100 percent federal funding.

It is remarkable in retrospect how abruptly the historical growth of the state and local sector was halted. With a single exception, in every year since 1976 real total spending in the sector has grown at a slower rate than in *any* year during the previous quarter-century. Real per capita spending by state and local governments, which had jumped by 44 percent between 1965 and 1975, has fallen since then. The share of state and local spending in the GNP declined by two full percentage points between 1975 and 1981, from 15.0 percent to 13.0 percent, and has continued its decline into 1982.

The slowdown in state and local spending has been given permanence by state constitutional amendments and other formal measures limiting future spending growth. No fewer than twenty-five states have passed new statewide tax or spending limitations since 1977,[5] the most famous measure being California's approval of Proposition 13 in June 1978. Most of these measures have been redundant in the short run. Political opposition to taxes and spending has proved stronger than the limits written into state constitutions. However, the limitations have given permanent expression to public preferences on spending matters and made it impossible for elected officials to return to business as usual in the sector, even if they had been so inclined.

Paying for Sectoral Growth

It is likely that taxpayer resistance to state and local spending would have been encountered earlier had these governments had to pay for their own growth. As it was, much of the financing came from federal assistance. Throughout the 1960s and early 1970s federal aid grew much faster than state and local own-source revenues (see table 6-1). The strongest surge in federal assistance came in 1972 with the introduction of general revenue sharing. The influx of federal dollars at that time built up surpluses so much that state and local government tax relief was possible in the next few years. Between 1973 and 1975 growth of own-source revenues fell below their historical growth path. Net reductions in the state and local tax structure occurred for the first time in decades.

When the hiatus of relative tax relief came to an end in 1976-1977, the taxpayer rebellion broke out. Proposition 13 was a protest against the resumption of spiraling state and local tax burdens. The effectiveness of this tax revolt is demonstrated by the drop in state-local revenues as a percentage of personal income from its high of 15.0 in 1977 to 13.7 by 1980. Throughout most of the 1970s opinion polls consistently indicated that the public believed that local property taxes constituted the most onerous tax burden.[6] Only after the achievement of large-scale property tax relief and other state and local tax reductions in 1978-1980 did the public turn its full attention to the federal government, supporting President Reagan's push for major federal tax cuts.

Another aspect of the state and local tax revolt deserves notice. The state and local sector entered the 1970s with a tax structure whose revenue yields grew automatically with inflation. Most estimates for this period indicate that a one percent increase in national income would automatically generate about a one percent increase in total state and local tax yields.[7] Despite this and despite the rapid growth of federal aid, state and local governments for a good part of the 1970s continued to raise tax rates, generating still more revenue for public spending. The extra revenues produced by tax-rate changes ranged from $2.0 billion to $4.3 billion per year in the late 1960s and early

TABLE 6–1

REVENUE SOURCES, STATE AND LOCAL GOVERNMENTS, 1960–1981

Calendar Year	(1) Own-Source Revenues[a] (In Current $ Billions)	(2) Percentage Growth from Previous Year	(3) Federal Aid Revenues, (In Current $ Billions)	(4) Percentage Growth from Previous Year	(5) Own-Source Revenues as Percentage of Personal Income	(6) Estimated Change in Tax Revenues from Tax Rate Changes[b] (In Current $ Billions)
1960	43.4	10.3[c]	6.5	21.9[c]	10.8	1.2[c]
1965	64.0	9.5[c]	11.1	14.2[c]	11.8	0.8[c]
1970	111.9	14.7[c]	24.4	24.0[c]	13.7	2.1[c]
1971	124.0	11.7	29.0	18.9	14.3	4.1
1972	140.8	13.5	37.5	29.3	14.8	4.3
1973	154.4	9.7	40.6	8.3	14.5	-3.2
1974	167.5	8.5	43.9	8.1	14.3	-2.7
1975	183.1	9.3	54.6	24.4	14.5	0
1976	206.7	12.9	61.1	11.9	14.9	3.3
1977	230.5	11.5	67.5	10.5	15.0	0.8
1978	250.1	8.5	77.3	14.5	14.5	-9.0
1979	270.8	8.3	80.4	4.0	13.9	-13.9
1980	296.0	9.3	88.0	9.5	13.7	-7.1
1981	329.8	11.4	87.2	-0.9	13.7	-1.7

SOURCES: Columns 1 through 5: computed from National Income and Product Accounts (NIPA), *1982 Economic Report of the President*, table B–77, except for 1981, where revised NIPA data used, *Survey of Current Business, April 1982*, table 3.3. Column 6: Office of State and Local Finance, U.S. Department of the Treasury, as presented in Robert W. Rafuse, Jr. "The Outlook for State-Local Finance under the New Federalism." (Paper presented at a conference sponsored by the New York State Legislative Commission on State-Local Relations and the Nelson A. Rockefeller College of Public Affairs and Policy, State University of New York at Albany, April 27, 1982).

a. Taxes, fees and charges, contributions to social insurance funds, and "other." Sector revenues exceed sector expenditures because of the surpluses in social insurance and other funds.

b. Computed as difference between total tax revenue growth and tax revenue growth predicted from constant tax-rate structure based on elasticities found in economic literature (1.6 for individual income tax, 1.2 for corporate income tax, 1.1 for general sales tax, 0.6 for selective sales tax, and 0.9 for property tax and other).

c. Average for preceding five years.

1970s and again reached this level in the mid-1970s after the injection of general revenue sharing monies had been absorbed.[8]

The rush of tax relief after 1978 not only resulted in considerable lowering of tax rates but also greatly reduced the automatic revenue growth of the state-local tax system. The third section of this chapter discusses the unprecedented lowering of tax rates that occurred during this period, as well as the revamping of tax structures that took place to limit the growth of tax yields in response to inflation. These initiatives succeeded in keeping tax revenue growth between 1978 and 1980 far below personal income growth and returned to taxpayers an estimated $7 billion to $14 billion per year through state and local tax-rate reductions.

The FY 1982 Reagan budget revisions thus were imposed on a state and local sector that was in the midst of its own tax and spending revolution. The sector's real growth had been halted in 1976, and large tax relief had been granted annually since 1978. By cutting its tax structure and grants-in-aid as severely as it has done, the federal government has put state and local politicians in a difficult position. If these governments continue to press forward with their own programs of tax relief, they will face cumulative revenue impacts that will be much greater than before, since federal policy now adds to rather than dampens the sector's own tax reductions. On the other hand, state and local officials can abandon tax relief and try to preserve spending programs in the face of the federal government's new policies. In doing so they run the risk that credit for listening to taxpayer demands will pass to Washington.

The Reagan Program: Short Term

The immediate policies of the Reagan administration toward state and local governments are embodied in its FY 1982 and FY 1983 budgets. They involve deep reductions in grants-in-aid funding, simplified grants administration and regulation, and consolidation of numerous categorical grants into a few larger block grants.

Grants-in-aid Funding. From a federal budget perspective the administration's first priority has been to curtail grants-in-aid outlays (see chapter 3). The administration's revised FY 1982 budget proposed cutting grants support 13.4 percent from the proposed Carter FY 1982 budget level of just under $100 billion. Grant outlays in FY 1982, after congressional action, are estimated to have fallen 3.7 percent from actual FY 1981 levels.

Achieving a slowdown in federal aid growth has been an avowed objective of federal budgetary policy since at least the presidency of Gerald

Ford. Year in and year out since 1974, federal budgets have projected that
next year grants-in-aid would end their strong growth, or at the very least
would do so net of temporary programs such as countercyclical assistance.
In reality little slowing of grants growth occurred until 1981. The resolve to
restrain grant expenditures seemingly disappeared in the face of economic
recession, with its increase in entitlement claims and pressures for countercyclical aid, or in the face of congressional action to expand federal assistance
for social purposes unrelated to current economic conditions. It is true that
starting in FY 1979, with the phase-out of the federal countercyclical programs, grant funding slowed its course. But before FY 1981 this slowdown
resulted almost exclusively from closing out temporary antirecession programs.[9] It was in the last year of the Carter administration that the first serious
steps to change the permanent grant picture were taken. General revenue
sharing payments to state governments were eliminated for FY 1981 in recognition of the states' strong fiscal positions.

From this perspective the Reagan grants-in-aid budget for FY 1982,
although it brought a sharp reversal in actual funding, represented a less
drastic departure from the stated long-term intentions of earlier administrations. The truly distinguishing feature of the Reagan budget strategy has been
the cumulative and intensifying pressure it has placed on grants-in-aid funding.
After receiving the greater part of the reductions it sought in the FY 1982
budget, the administration returned to Congress with new budget proposals
that would reduce grant outlays by an additional 10 percent for FY 1983.

Of equal significance have been actions the administration did *not* take.
In sharp contrast to the last major recession, when the administration and
Congress competed with each other in the design of "emergency" countercyclical assistance to state and local governments, the 1981-1982 recession
brought virtually no proposals for countercyclical aid and no indication what-
soever that the administration would consider deviating from its grant reduction strategy to provide temporary antirecession assistance.

Federal Overload and Grant Decongestion. At the same time the
administration has sought to reduce the federal grants-in-aid budget, it has
sought to simplify grant administration and regulation. In 1962 there were
estimated to be 160 federal formula or project grants to state and local governments. By 1967 there were 379, and by 1980, roughly 500. In management
terms alone, this grant structure is believed by many to have left the federal
government with more duties than it can perform effectively. In testifying
before the House Manpower and Housing Subcommittee, David Stockman,
director of the Office of Management and Budget (OMB), argued that program
decentralization was necessary to ease the administrative strain on the federal
system:

We are overloaded at the national level. We simply can't make wise decisions on the thousands of issues that come before us. There has to be a better division of labor and a redelegation of decision making to lower levels of government.[10]

The administration has tackled congestion in the grant system in the most direct way possible—by terminating grant programs and consolidating others into block grants. Sixty-two federal aid programs—more than one-tenth of all federal grants—were simply eliminated from the most recent federal grants catalog on the grounds that no more funds would be provided for them.

A special review was ordered of the restrictions and mandates built into federal grants with the purpose of giving grant recipients more discretion over spending priorities. This has resulted in such decisions as to remove the rule requiring that 75 percent of Community Development Block Grant (CDBG) funds be targeted to low- and moderate-income citizens, and a formal proposal to delegate to state bodies responsibility for setting the standards to be met in federally supported road repairs. Grant regulations also have been rewritten to relax federal auditing and reporting requirements.

Block Grants. The third leg of the administration's short-term strategy has been program consolidation into block grants. Block grants are consistent with four of the administration's announced objectives in overhauling the grants-in-aid system. First, they are meant to reduce the administrative complexity of the grant structure. Second, they take a step toward restoring the central role of the states in the intergovernmental system. Third, in their pure form they remove the federal matching incentives that have stimulated state and local spending in the past. Most importantly, block grants support the principle of state discretion over the uses of their resources and provide the bridge to total turnback of program responsibility and revenues that the administration desires.

The principle of block granting is not new. It was part of the Nixon redesign of the grants system, also called in its time New Federalism. Block grants then, as now, were intended to give recipient governments more program flexibility by removing categorical prescriptions for grant purposes, while still spelling out the general policy areas for which federal funds could be used. The block grant agenda advanced by Richard Nixon, and after him Gerald Ford, was in some respects more ambitious than that proposed by Ronald Reagan. Together with general revenue sharing the Nixon proposals for block granting by functional areas would have raised the share of broadly discretionary grants in the federal aid mix from its level of 2 percent in FY 1971 to 45 percent when totally in place. In contrast, the proposals in President Reagan's FY 1983 budget on top of the block grant package passed by Congress for FY 1982 would raise the share of broad-based and general purpose grants only from 17.8 percent in FY 1981 to 25.4 percent in FY 1983.

In budget terms the block grants thus far have been of modest scale. The policy attention given to them might seem to be exaggerated were it not for their power as precedents. The administration has stated its intention to press forward with more block grant proposals and did so in the FY 1983 budget, in which it recommended seven further block grants to Congress. Should the plans for a fundamental sorting out of government responsibilities flounder amid congressional or state opposition, the administration can be expected to redouble its efforts at block granting as a partially acceptable substitute. The details of the administration's block grant initiatives, and the states' responses to them, are the subject of the next section of this chapter.

The Reagan Program: Long Term

To the administration, block grants are not an end in themselves but the bridge to a fundamental realignment of the federal system. Central to the Reagan critique of federalism is the contention that federal relations have been abused by the practice of shared administration and shared financing of domestic programs. Consequently, in its New Federalism initiatives the administration has proposed a decade-long plan for reallocating government responsibilities in a way that leaves each level of government with quite separate and clearly assigned functions and, to the maximum extent possible, its own sources of funding to meet these responsibilities.

The mechanisms for achieving this separation of functions and financing are what the administration has called a program swap and turnback. In its original form the swap would have given the federal government exclusive responsibility for administering and financing Medicaid while assigning to the states full responsibility for the Aid to Families with Dependent Children and Food Stamps. In later versions of the proposal, the Food Stamp program was pulled out to remain a federal responsibility.

The turnback proposal consists of some forty grants-in-aid programs, including the block grants already passed by Congress, for which specific federal funding would be terminated and the responsibility returned to states or localities. These programs constitute a major part of the federal grants-in-aid system, involving $30 billion to $33 billion at the administration's proposed FY 1983 funding levels. In exchange for accepting the turnback, the states could tap into a federal trust fund created to provide transitional financing through 1987 for the programs being turned back.

As originally proposed the trust fund would have consisted of revenues from the federal windfall oil profits tax and federal excise taxes on tobacco, alcohol, gasoline, and telephone service. Beginning in 1988 the trust fund would be reduced by 25 percent each year until its complete elimination in 1991. Between 1988 and 1991 the states would be free to pick up the programs relinquished by the federal government or not do so, and would be free to reimpose at the state level taxes of the type that the federal government was phasing out. In later versions of the turnback, the windfall oil profits tax was dropped from the tax bundle in recognition of the fact that reimposition of an equivalent tax was a realistic option only for the handful of states with oil production. Interim general fund support would replace this element of the turnback financing.

Shortly after announcing the New Federalism proposals, the administration began protracted negotiations with state and local representatives over their content. The National Governors Association, the National Conference of State Legislatures, and local representatives all have endorsed the principle of program and revenue turnbacks and federal assumption of Medicaid. Discussion has centered around the adequacy of the interim financing provided by the trust fund, the speed with which federal funding would be withdrawn starting in 1988, and the appropriateness of welfare support as a state responsibility.

Dual Federalism. Although the eventual fate of the New Federalism proposals remains uncertain, the administration undoubtedly has achieved one of its goals—to stimulate debate over the proper nature of American federalism.[11] At the heart of New Federalism is the radical principle that there should be a strict separation of federal from state and local program responsibilities and financing. This policy has been dubbed "dual federalism." Its emergence as a philosophy for redirecting federal relations has been remarkably swift. When Ronald Reagan campaigned for the 1976 presidential nomination, his proposal to turn back $90 billion of domestic programs to the states was treated as an extremist gaffe. It is a tribute to the president's ability to frame national policy debate that both his account of the nature of traditional federalism and his prescription for the future of federalism now command authority, if not general assent.

The principles of dual federalism are perhaps most instructively contrasted with those of mixed or "cooperative" federalism, as captured by Morton Grodzins' famous marble-cake analogy.[12] Grodzins argued that it was a vast oversimplification to view federal relations as consisting of three separate layers of responsibilities—federal, state, and local. A far more accurate image than such a three-layer cake was the "rainbow or marble cake, characterized by an inseparable mingling of differently colored ingredients." Grodzins argued that, like the swirls of color in a marble cake, the functions of different levels of government were inextricably woven together through mixed financing arrangements and shared program responsibilities.

The sharing of functional responsibilities until recently has been thought to be not only an inescapable but also a desirable part of contemporary federalism. Each of the programs proposed in the past for federal funding assistance has been asserted to have a national as well as a state or local interest and therefore to be appropriate for mixed financing. For those programs that were predominantly national in design and funding, mixed federalism had the additional benefit of permitting decentralized administration.

The notion of dual federalism challenges both the descriptive and prescriptive basis of this account. Its proponents concede that the marble-cake metaphor may have been accurate in 1960. They contend that a marble cake is too benign an image for the tangled federal relations that the Reagan administration inherited. But they look to an earlier historical reference point for their statement of federal principles. The Reagan program for fiscal federalism in 1991 resembles nothing so closely as the reality of fiscal federalism in 1933. That was the last year in which federal aid to state and local governments was as low a share of these governments' budgets as is now proposed for 1991, and it was the last year without significant federal-state mixing of social program financing. The intervening half-century that saw the creation of the intergovernmental nexus in support of social programs, and in the process made the federal government the dominant member of the federal partnership, is treated in the Reagan account as a distortion of traditional federalism.[13]

The principle of dual federalism has encountered its greatest philosophical resistance when used to rationalize the return to states of the nation's basic welfare program, Aid to Families with Dependent Children. Even many conservative spokesmen have argued that determination of welfare support levels should not be entrusted to states and made hostage to the potential competition between states to reduce tax burdens.[14] There is fear, too, that the differences among states in fiscal capacity may force them into adopting undesirably divergent welfare support levels if they are made to bear the full cost of welfare.

In its discussions with state organizations, the administration has moved to accommodate to some degree both of these objections. It has accepted the principle of a national floor on AFDC benefit levels. It also has indicated that it might accept, as part of an overall swap and turnback package, measures that provide compensatory federal assistance to states with low taxing capacities.

The States' Role in Domestic Policy. Under the Reagan version of sorting out, more domestic policy responsibility would be assigned to the states. State governments are presumed to be in closer touch with the demands of the local electorate, more responsive to the popular will, and more efficient in program administration. Public opinion appears to support this reorientation toward the states. A recent Gallup Poll (October 1981) revealed that, "By a 67 to 15% vote, survey respondents believe the state governments are more understanding than the federal government of the real needs of the people. By a similar 67 to 18% margin, the public feels their state government is more likely than the federal government to administer social programs efficiently."[15]

The administration's desire to return authority to the states is motivated not only by the virtues of state governments but by the belief that devolution of responsibility will weaken the interest groups that lobby for domestic social programs. The president is reported to have been quite blunt on this point. In a meeting with Republican members of the House Appropriations Committee, he is quoted as saying:

> It's far easier for people to come to Washington to get their social programs. It would be a hell of a lot tougher if we diffuse them and send them back to the states. All their friends and connections are in Washington.[16]

The principle of state preeminence here reinforces conservative convictions about government spending. As bodies closer to the majority will and less subject to recipient group lobbying, the states are thought to be better able to resist demands for social spending.[17]

Fiscal Impact of New Federalism. From a fiscal perspective the key issue surrounding the New Federalism is whether the state and local sector can absorb the program transfers and grant cutbacks that the administration proposes without massive increases in its own tax structure. The administration maintains that this is possible. Its estimates indicate that the state and local sector could maintain its current inflation-adjusted levels of spending per capita in the face of federal aid losses, and even generate growing surpluses, *if* the administration's 1982 economic projections for the 1980s are realized and *if* state and local tax yields respond to economic growth and inflation as they did in the early 1970s.[18]

There are two major elements of risk in these projections. First, they are extremely sensitive to the real rate of economic growth. The administration projects 3.7 percent annual real growth over the period 1981-1987 and continued robust growth beyond that period. This permits state and local revenues to grow strongly relative to costs. If, by contrast, real growth occurs at the lower rate of the 1970s, the state and local sector cannot absorb the New Federalism without major tax or spending adjustments.

Second, past studies of the revenue responsiveness of the state and local tax structure almost certainly overestimate the growth inherent in the current tax structure. Nine states now index their personal income taxes. Many have established arbitrary ceilings to the growth in annual property tax revenues. These steps have lowered the "automatic" growth of state and local tax yields.

In sum, the New Federalism would create the same sort of economic gamble for state and local budgets that the federal tax cuts did for the federal budget. *If* real economic growth occurs at the highly favorable rates assumed by the administration, the state and local sector would find itself able to absorb the New Federalism without great strain. Otherwise, the shifts in program responsibility and funding would force state and local governments into large-scale tax increases or large-scale spending reductions in order to maintain the budget balances that most are required to have by state law.

Block Grants and the State Response

Of all the grants-in-aid changes contained in the FY 1982 budget, the block grant consolidations are the most revealing of what the continued pursuit of the Reagan administration's notions of federalism would yield. First, they provide an important precedent. Whatever the fate of the New Federalism discussions, new block grant proposals almost certainly will continue to be placed before Congress. Second, they offer a philosophical bridge to the full turnback of federal program responsibilities. The block grants embody in miniature most of the principles of the New Federalism. All of the programs folded into the 1982 block grants have been designated for eventual return to the states. Most importantly, the states' responses to the block grants and accompanying funding cuts provide the first glimpse of how the states are likely to react to the full set of New Federalism initiatives.

The Reagan Approach to Block Grants

Although the block grant form is not novel, several common themes run through the Reagan block grants that set them apart from their predecessors (see table 6-2).

Reduced Funding. All of the block grants, as initially adopted, traded greater policy discretion and administrative flexibility for less funding.[19] This approach stands in marked contrast to the previous attempts to introduce block grants during the Nixon and Ford administrations, when it was thought that increased funding was the price that had to be paid to buy structural reform. To the Reagan administration, greater grant flexibility has been a way of making budget cuts more palatable.

At the beginning of the FY 1982 budget debate, some administration spokesmen went so far as to assert that the 25 percent reductions in program funding recommended for the block grants would be fully compensated by the removal of federal constraints on the uses of funds and reductions in regulatory red tape. In testifying before the Senate Subcommittee on Intergovernmental Relations, OMB Deputy Director Edwin L. Harper stated:

> The block grant designs must be viewed in the context of the total budget. To accomplish the goals of the Economic Recovery Program, it was clear that an immediate reduction in the growth of federal assistance was essential. In order for the states to ensure that these reductions could occur without causing reductions in service levels, we quickly realized that massive reductions in program prescriptiveness and administrative requirements had to accompany budget cuts. Our block grant proposals are designed to satisfy this objective.[20]

The value of flexibility was acknowledged early in the budget discussions by the National Governors Association and the National Conference of State Legislatures when they put forward their own proposals to trade block grant consolidations and regulatory relaxation for 10 percent funding cuts. The administration subsequently retreated from the strong assertion that block granting could hold recipients harmless in the face of 25 percent cuts, affirming only that the greater flexibility of the block grants would cushion part of the blow from reduced funding.

State Role. All of the block grants designate state governments as the recipients of funding. In several cases this designation supplants earlier arrangements under which program funds were paid directly to local governments or to nongovernmental entities. Perhaps the most basic reorientation of this kind affects the state-directed portion of the Community Development Block Grant, in which states are now authorized to design their own programs for assisting local governments, superseding a direct federal-local relationship under the old small cities discretionary grant program. State governments also replace a wide variety of other local authorities, including county governments, community health centers, and local education agencies, as original recipients of funding under other block grants. Altogether, of the seventy-seven categorical programs consolidated into block grants, forty-seven formerly delivered federal funds directly to localities.

A number of pass-through limitations were imposed by Congress to prevent the block grants from becoming vehicles for terminating local programs formerly dependent on federal aid. States must pass through at least 80 percent of the Elementary and Secondary Education Block Grant to local education agencies. Funding is mandated for formerly federally supported community mental health centers through FY 1984 under the Alcohol, Drug Abuse, and Mental Health Block Grant, and for community health centers in

TABLE 6–2

BLOCK GRANT SUMMARY
(In $ millions)

Block Grant	(1) FY 1982 Appropriations	(2) Percentage Change from FY 1981 Appropriations	(3) Date Available for State Assumption	(4) Number of Consolidated Programs[a]	(5) Number of States Accepting Block Grant (As of April 1, 1982)	(6) Matching and Maintenance of Effort Requirements	(7) Transfer Provisions
Alcohol, drug abuse, and mental health	428.1	−20.8	Oct. 1981	10 Categoricals	49	Federal funds will be used to supplement not supplant nonfederal	7% can be transferred for specified health purposes
Community services	336.5	−35.9	Oct. 1981	7 Categoricals	38	None	5% to energy, Head Start, or Older Americans Act
State community development	States administered approximately 900 of total block of 3,456.0	—	Feb. 1982	1 Discretionary	37	10% state match if state elects to distribute funds	None
Maternal and child health	347.5	−23.5	Oct. 1981	9 Categoricals	48	$3 state for each $4 federal	None

Program	Col 1	Col 2	Col 3	37 Categoricals	Automatic transfer	Expenditures to be at least 90% of level for 2nd prior FY, federal funds must supplement	None
Elementary and secondary education	470.7[b]	−10.5[c]	July 1982	37 Categoricals	Automatic transfer	Expenditures to be at least 90% of level for 2nd prior FY, federal funds must supplement	None
Low-income home energy assistance	1,869	+6.6	Oct. 1981	1 Categorical	Automatic transfer	None	10% to social services, community services, and health
Primary care	246.3[d]	−23.9	Oct. 1982	2 Categoricals	Not yet available	FY 1983: 20% state match, FY 1984: 33 1/3% match	None
Preventive health services	81.6	−12.4	Oct. 1981	1 Block and 6 Categoricals	48	Federal funds must supplement	7% to health
Social services	2,400.0	−19.8	Oct. 1981	1 Block and 1 Categorical	Automatic transfer	None	10% to health or energy block

SOURCE: Column 1: Third Continuing Budget Resolution, as shown in *Budget of the United States Government, Fiscal Year 1983*, Appendix; Column 2: Department of Health and Human Services and *U.S. Budget*, Special Analysis H; Columns (3), (6), (7): Block grant legislation; Column 4: Advisory Commission on Intergovernmental Relations, *A Catalog of Federal Grant-in-Aid Programs to State and Local Governments*, Appendix A (ACIR, M-133, Feb., 1982); Column 5: Federal agencies' records.

a. The reported number of programs consolidated into the block grants differs with program definition. This listing is derived from Office of Management and Budget, *Catalog of Federal Grant Assistance*.

b. Includes consolidations under chapter 2 of the Education Consolidation and Improvement Act of 1981 (a), (b), (c), (d).

c. This program is advance-funded. Therefore, federal budget reductions do not affect state spending until next fiscal year.

d. Block grant not available to states until FY 1983. Appropriation total is for programs to be consolidated.

FY 1983 under the Primary Care Block Grant. The earmarking provisions of
the Community Services Block Grant also require pass-throughs to local
groups. Finally, if states do not meet four special conditions, the Community
Development Block Grant reverts to direct federal-local payment.

Transfers between Blocks. An important innovation in several of the
Reagan block grants is the option to transfer funds from one to another, up
to a specified ceiling. This provision not only enlarges states' budget flexibility
in the short run but is one of the more obvious "bridge" elements linking
the present interim grant forms to the more sweeping removal of restraints
proposed for the future. As originally proposed by the administration, transfers
between all of the health and human services block grants would have been
possible. In the end, limited transfers were permitted for five.

Matching Incentives. The pure block grant form eliminates matching
requirements. One of the stated intentions of the Reagan administration has
been to eliminate the incentives to public spending inherent in the categorical
matching grant structure. However, Congress acted to retain spending support
for particular functions by preserving state matching requirements or maintenance of effort requirements in several of the block grants.

Regulatory and Reporting Reforms. From the beginning the Reagan
administration emphasized its desire to simplify and limit federal regulation
of the block grants. The interim final rules issued by the Department of Health
and Human Services for its seven block grants reflect the new regulatory
posture:

> The Secretary has determined that the Department should implement the block grant
> programs in a manner that is fully consistent with the Congressional intent to enlarge
> the states' ability to control use of the funds involved. Accordingly, to the extent
> possible, we will not burden the states' administration of the programs with defi-
> nitions of permissible and prohibited activities, procedural rules, paperwork and
> recordkeeping requirements, or other regulatory provisions. The states will, for the
> most part, be subject only to the statutory requirements, and the Department will
> carry out its functions with due regard for the limited nature of the role that Congress
> has assigned to us.[21]

State Reaction to the Block Grants

Congressional approval of the block grants shifted the initiative to the
states. States have had to decide how they would react politically, administratively, and budgetarily to the new block grants. Their decisions have been
complicated by the realization that the block grants were not a one-time
initiative for FY 1982. More block grants and steeper funding cuts were
promised for FY 1983. Most observers foresee a cumulative shift to the block
grant instrument throughout the 1980s, giving the initial reaction of states
considerable weight as precedent.

Block Grant Acceptance. Formal transfer of the block grants to state management has been made swiftly. Two of the human services block grants that involved relatively little consolidation or change in structure from earlier programs (social services and low-income home energy assistance) were automatically transferred to the states, as was the education block grant. The states were offered a choice for the remaining grants. A state could either accept administration of the block grants or could elect to have the grants remain as categoricals for a period with continued administrative responsibilities by the responsible federal agency. In such cases the state would be charged an administration fee. Most states have chosen to accept full grant management at the earliest possible date. Where they have not done so, the explanation usually lies in institutional impediments at the state level rather than objections to the principles of block consolidation or state management.

The occasional difficulties encountered in block grant acceptance illustrate some of the differences in state fiscal operations that will continue to place limits on reform of the intergovernmental grant system. States were required to designate a single state agency to be responsible for administration of each block grant. Often, the categoricals consolidated into a block grant had previously been administered by different state agencies. Disputes among agencies as to who should inherit the block grant sometimes delayed acceptance. This was especially true in states where the legislature must participate in decisions about changes in grant administration, but where it was not scheduled to be in session near the initial acceptance period.

Implementation of the block grants in Texas exemplifies these administrative difficulties.[22] Texas enthusiastically supported the shift toward state administrative responsibility, complaining only that the 1981 federal legislation did not go far enough. Despite this acceptance the state was unable to accept certain block grants and had difficulty in accepting others due to a series of riders attached by the state legislature to the FY 1982-1983 biennial budget. The legislature adjourned in June of 1981 and was not scheduled to reconvene until the spring of 1983. The riders thus represented the legislature's attempt to influence the block grant decisions while it was out of session. Most restrictive were provisions stipulating that (1) no federal funds could be expended for programs and activities that were not already included in the legislative budget; (2) any state funds appropriated to match federal dollars would be reduced proportionately to the reduction in federal funds and could not be reallocated; and (3) unless a state financial management committee was approved by the voters (it was not), no expenditure of federal funds was allowed that would require consolidation in a single agency of funding authority that had previously been divided among several agencies.

These provisions greatly hampered efforts at the executive level to accept the block grants. The legislative rider forbidding executive consolidation of funding authority led to protracted negotiations with the federal government over the designation of a nominal "sole state agency" that could pass through funds to other agencies. Because of the Texas legislature's stipulation that no federal funds could be expended for programs or activities not already in the state budget, the state found itself unable to accept the block grants for community services or community development. The programs in these blocks had previously gone to other organizations or to other levels of government.

State Executive-Legislative Conflict. Disputes over block grant acceptance, where they have occurred, usually have been symptomatic of a larger competition between the governor and the state legislature over the ability to decide how federal grants will be allocated. In the past, as long as almost all federal program grants were categorical, there was relatively little state discretion over the uses to which federal monies were put. Most state legislatures ceded authority over grant allocations to the executive branch without too much consideration. This trend was reinforced by federal regulations that often required that an executive branch agency serve as grant recipient.[23] In recent years, however, the legislative branch began to reassert its interest in allocating federal aid dollars. Adoption of the FY 1982 block grants, and the prospect that much greater opportunities will exist for allocating federal funds in the future, has accelerated the assertion of legislative authority. Most often this has taken the form of legislative insistence that federal funds be appropriated for program purposes in the same way as the state's own funds or that joint executive-legislative committees be empowered to make decisions regarding the allocation of federal block grants.

Table 6-3 contains a sampling of the forms that this assertion of state legislative authority has taken. Few political patterns are evident in the states' jockeying over block grant powers. The conflict has been primarily institutional, a desire on the part of the legislatures to enlarge their budgetary authority.

Transfers between Block Grants. Most states have availed themselves of the option of transferring funds between block grants. The most common direction of movement has been from the low-income home energy assistance block to the social services block. Thirty-three states transferred funds out of energy assistance, of which twenty-six moved all or part of the transfers into social services (table 6-4). In part this direction of transfer reflects the states' desire to shift funds, wherever possible, from more narrowly defined program areas to more expansive ones, where greater flexibility for program selection exists. The energy assistance block grant also suffered the least initial funding reduction and then was supplemented by Congress in February 1982 to a level above that of FY 1981. This treatment contrasted sharply with funding reductions for the other block grants. Energy assistance also served as a con-

TABLE 6–3

<small>ATTEMPTS TO STRENGTHEN LEGISLATIVE ROLE IN ALLOCATING FEDERAL GRANTS,</small>
1981–1982

State	Action
Colorado	Republican legislature passed budget bill that "appropriates" block grant funds for program purposes. Democratic governor, under guise of line veto, struck all language relating to legislative "appropriation" of block grants. Legislature failed to override by one vote. Legislature has challenged governor's veto authority in legal suit.
Connecticut	Legislature passed bill requiring governor to submit a block grant spending plan. Continues recent trend toward legislative appropriation of federal funds.
Kentucky	Legislature overrode governor's veto, passed bills giving legislative committees authority to review block grant plans and expenditures, maintain grant allocation role between sessions.
Massachusetts	1981 legislation requires legislative appropriation of all federal grant funds. Bill vetoed by governor, overridden by legislature.
New Mexico	Legislature created federal funds reduction study committee. Governor vetoed bill that would have required all grant spending adjustments to be reviewed by legislative finance committee.
New York	Legislative leadership brought court case asserting that expenditure of federal funds without legislative appropriation was unconstitutional. State Court of Appeals ruled in favor of legislative appropriation. Legislation in 1981 implemented this requirement and set up senate-assembly review panel for grants. In 1982 governor vetoed even stronger legislative control as "unnecessarily restrict[ing] Executive discretion relative to Federal block grants." Override vote pending.
Oklahoma	Law creates joint committee on federal funds made up of ten members of legislature to approve expenditure plans for block grants, review all grant applications.
Tennessee	Legislature tried to create a state funding board (three legislative appointees, two gubernatorial appointees) to approve grant allocations. House passed, governor opposed, Senate never voted.
Wisconsin	Democratic legislature included provision in budget to establish committee to hold hearings and formulate allocations for block grants. Republican governor vetoed.

SOURCES: Barbara Yondorf and Karen Benker, *Block Grants: A New Chance for Legislatures to Oversee Federal Funds,* Legislative Finance Paper no. 15 (Denver, Colo.: National Conference of State Legislatures, February 1982); Jean Lawson and Carl W. Stenberg, "Rebalanced Federalism: The States' Role and Response," in *Intergovernmental Perspective* (Washington, D.C.: Advisory Commission on Intergovernmental Relations, winter 1982); Urban Institute survey.

TABLE 6–4

STATE USE OF BLOCK GRANT TRANSFERS[a]
(As of March 31, 1982)

State	Energy Assistance	Alcohol, Drug Abuse, and Mental Health	Preventive Services	Community Services	Social Services
Total states transferring out[b]	33	2	4	4	1
Total states transferring in[b]	0	10	1	3	26

SOURCE: U.S. Department of Health and Human Services, "Preliminary Information on Implementation of Health and Human Services Block Grants" (May 1982).

a. The four block grants excluded from the table do not have transfer provisions.

b. Transfers out do not equal transfers in because of multiple transfers in both directions and because of transfers outside block grants to Older Americans Act and Head Start program.

venient "bank" for the states. Because of the seasonality of states' energy demands, this block grant was the only one for which the Department of Health and Human Services permitted immediate cash drawdown instead of quarterly expenditure allocations. The grant therefore was a natural one to be tapped for cash transfers to other parts of the states' budgets.

States' Replacement Funding. Have the states acted to replace federal cutbacks in the block grant programs? Will the administration's grant reductions end up as costs shifted to the state and local sector, or will they produce a reduction in total spending at all levels of government? Some indications of states' reactions are available, although it is too early to offer definitive answers to these questions.

State officials have had to prepare their budgets amid great uncertainty as to federal aid policy. In drawing up their FY 1982 budgets (for the fiscal year beginning in July 1981), the states had to guess about the ultimate shape of the 1982 federal budget. This process has been repeated for the states' FY 1983 budgets, with still more uncertainty as to how much of the additional grant reductions the president proposed for FY 1983 Congress would accept. In the short run states' adjustments were further complicated by the overlap of state and federal fiscal years. For the first quarter of FY 1982 (July through September 1981), states typically could spend funds that remained under the old categoricals while planning commitments for the new block grant funds that would become available October 1.

Despite these complications the states' reactions to federal block grants have been better documented than their reactions to most other federal grant initiatives. Because of the acknowledged importance of the block grants and the contest between the executive and legislative branches over block grant disposition, many states have drawn up explicit block grant budgets. Supplemental budgets often were adopted in mid-year once congressional action on the block grants situation was clarified. An element of political posturing may creep into these budgets, as the states seek to dramatize or downplay their replacement funding, depending on the political point they wish to make. But overall there is better than usual evidence on state policies in replacing federal funds.

The Urban Institute conducted a survey of twenty-five states to determine block grant funding decisions in FY 1982 and FY 1983. The sample was chosen to be representative of the regional, political, and fiscal characteristics of all states. The findings are summarized in table 6-5 for five of the seven block grants that became effective in FY 1982.[24] The numerator of each fraction in the table is the additional state funding allocated to replace lost federal funds. The denominator is the total federal aid loss. For FY 1983 both figures are *additional* changes from the new base established in FY 1982. The FY 1983 federal aid losses are those projected by the states in their own budget planning.

Several conclusions emerge from the survey. First, the overall rate of state funding replacement has been low. The highest rates of replacement are to be found in social services, in which eight of the twenty-five states in FY 1982 and eight in FY 1983 augmented their own funding to offset federal funding reductions. Even where replacement has occurred, it has generally filled in for only a small share of federal funds and on a highly selective basis (e.g., to preserve day care services). For the other block grants, replacement is still less frequent. Blanket assertions that the states have failed to replace federal funding for the block grants, however, are exaggerated.

Second, the magnitude of dollars involved is not large, especially when judged in relation to the other budget adjustments states are being forced to make. Several states reported that block grant funding decisions so far have received relatively little attention from either the executive or legislative branch.

Third, states' decisions about replacement funding from their own resources were highly consistent with their policies toward transfer of federal funds between blocks. Most of the states using their own funds to augment social services, for example, also transferred other block grant funds into the social services block. This pattern suggests a budget strategy wherein the flexibility provided by interblock transfers is fully exhausted before tapping the states' own resources.

Fourth, none of the states in the sample currently in most severe fiscal difficulty (Michigan, Minnesota, Ohio, and Oregon) committed themselves

TABLE 6–5

SUMMARY OF BLOCK GRANT REPLACEMENT: NEW STATE FUNDS/LOST FEDERAL FUNDS

0 = NO REPLACEMENT

(In $ millions)

	Social Services		Low-income Energy Assistance		Preventive Health		Alcohol, Drug Abuse, and Mental Health		Maternal and Child Health	
	FY 1982	FY 1983	FY 1982[a]	FY 1983	FY 1982	FY 1983	FY 1982	FY 1983	FY 1982	FY 1983
States with Some Replacement										
Colorado	2.3/5.9	2.3/6.6	0	0	0.3/?	0.4/?	0	0	0.5/0.6	0.3/0.8
Florida	3.0/16.8	3.6/19.1	0	0	0	0	0	0	0	0.3/1.5
Idaho	0	0.3/0.8	0	0	0	0	0	0	0	0
Illinois	20.4/36.0	0[c]	0	0	0.2/0.4	0[c]	0	0	2.6/5.2	0[c]
Kansas	0.3/3.0	0.6/?	0	0	0	0.1/?	0	2.8/?	0	0
Kentucky	0	5.0/6.5	0	0	0	0	0	0	0	0
Maryland	2.0/9.9	0[c]	0	0	0	0	0.2/?	0	0.1/?	0[b]
New Jersey	7.0/13.1	4.3/6.0	0	6.1/?	0	0	0	0	0	0
New Mexico	0	1.2[d]/0.8[c]	0	0	0	0.2/0.5	0	0.3/3.0	0	0.3/?

Oklahoma	5.0/5.0	0[c]	0	0	0	0	0.9[d]/0.4	0.6/0.6	1.6/1.6
Oregon	2.7/5.4	0[c]	0	0.5/1.0	0[c]	0	0	0	0
Vermont	0	0.8/1.5	0	0	.03/.06	0	0	0	.36/.42
No. of states with some replacement	8	8	1	3	4	1	3	4	5

Alabama
Arizona
California[c]
Hawaii

States with No Replacement

Indiana	Missouri
Massachusetts	New York[f]
Michigan	Ohio
Minnesota	Texas
	Utah

Total sample = 25

SOURCE: Urban Institute survey, from state budgets, supplemental budgets, and unpublished state budget analyses. FY 1982: includes supplemental budget adjustments through May 1982; actual federal grant levels (state fiscal year). FY 1983: Adopted budgets through May 31; governor's budget proposals where budget not adopted as of May 31; state projections of federal grant levels. State replacement funding does *not* include transfers between federal block grants .

a. No decrease in federal funding levels for FY 1982.

b. State has not projected magnitude of FY 1983 federal aid cut.

c. FY 1982 replacement continued in FY 1983; no additional replacement.

d. Total increase in state funding exceeds FY 1983 federal aid reduction; state funds will replace FY 1982 federal cuts as well.

e. California did not accept in FY 1982 the Preventive Health Block Grant, the Alcohol, Drug Abuse, and Mental Health Block Grant or the Maternal and Child Health Block Grant.

f. New York did not accept in FY 1982 the Maternal and Child Health Block Grant.

to *any* new replacement funding in FY 1983, although Oregon did provide replacement in social services and preventive health in FY 1982. Follow-up investigation for Nebraska, Washington and Wisconsin, the three other states under necessity of severe budget adjustments but not in the original sample, also revealed no replacement activity.

Fifth, the states with relatively high levels of historical spending on human services (for example, New York, California, Michigan, Minnesota, and Massachusetts) do not display a tendency toward replacement. None of these states replaced lost federal funds in any of the block grants for either FY 1982 or FY 1983. All of these states presently find themselves under some degree of fiscal strain. In contrast, several states with historically low human services spending and currently good fiscal positions did act to provide funding supplements. Of the six sample states identified as being in good budget position (Colorado, Hawaii, Kansas, New Mexico, Oklahoma, and Texas), four made substantial funding replacements in FY 1983.[25] This suggests that the budget and reserve positions of states have been the most important short-term factors influencing block grant replacement decisions.

Block Grants to Localities. The example set by the federal government in using block grants to cushion funding reductions has held understandable appeal for state governments wrestling with their own budgetary problems. A number of governors seized upon the block grant model in proposing changes in state aid to local governments for FY 1983. Although the governors emphasized that their intent was to bring the flexibility of New Federalism to local levels of government, they almost always followed the federal strategy of coupling block grants with funding reductions or at least causing abrupt funding slowdowns in previously fast-growing grant programs. The interest groups most affected by block grant consolidations, however, had had time to regroup from their congressional defeats and were much more effective in resisting block granting in state legislatures than they had been in resisting the FY 1982 federal block grants.

The pressures for block granting are illustrated by the actions of the Washington state legislature, which passed a special education block grant for the FY 1982 and FY 1983 biennium. The block grant consolidated more than a dozen special education programs, allowing local authorities far greater discretion over the use of funds. It was the budget crunch in the state that was responsible for the block grant concept's winning favor. The increased flexibility of the block grant was meant to compensate local jurisdictions for a 12 percent reduction in funding from the previous biennium.

An even more direct example of state imitation of the federal grant structure is provided by Pennsylvania. It adopted an adult services block grant for FY 1983 as a means of passing on to counties part of the funding reductions the state suffered from the federal social services block grant cuts. Several other states used the momentum of the federal block grants to simplify state-to-county allocation formulas and enhance county discretion over use of state funds.

Two of the most publicized state block grant proposals were developed for education by Governor Matheson of Utah and Governor Thornburgh of Pennsylvania. Both sought to build directly on the attention given to federal block granting. Both proposals were rejected by the state legislatures. Leading the opposition were education groups who feared that block grant consolidation would lead to slower funding growth and the disappearance of funding protection for special education programs and special category pupils. In both cases the weight given to special category pupils in local aid allocations would have been reduced and state mandates for special education programs relaxed.

State Tax and Budget Actions

The Reagan administration's plan to return to the states responsibility for many domestic programs comes at a special moment in the states' own fiscal histories. State and local governments were the first to encounter the taxpayer revolt. Over the three years 1978 to 1980 state governments cut their tax rates by an unprecedented extent and accelerated their programs of property tax relief for local governments. The assault on traditional tax structures continued into 1981, albeit at a reduced pace. Under the best of economic circumstances, these tax reductions would have placed a degree of strain on state budgets. Coupled with economic recession, they have precipitated the need for some of the most severe budgetary adjustments since the Depression. The scale of these adjustments has prevented many states from filling in for federal program reductions and often has relegated the debate over federal funding impacts to a second or third order of importance. For at least the next year or two, state budget decisions will continue to be dominated by the states' own fiscal conditions. The states' attempts to restore budgetary balance will largely determine their response to the federal aid cutbacks and establish the context within which the New Federalism agenda will be considered for most of the 1980s.

The Era of Tax Relief

The period 1978-1980 stands as a rebuttal to those who maintain that the dreadnought of government cannot alter its course except with excruciating slowness. The shift in tax and spending policy accomplished at the state and local level in these years is fully on a scale with what the Reagan administration has proposed for the federal government.

Although taxpayer resistance to state and local spending had many antecedents, it was the passage of Proposition 13 in California, effective with the beginning of FY 1978, that triggered the rush to reduce state and local tax burdens. The message behind Proposition 13 was sufficiently ambiguous to generate a wide range of tax-cutting responses in other states. Many states interpreted Proposition 13 as a protest against property taxation and redoubled their efforts to limit local property taxes, either on their own initiative or under mandates from taxpayer referendums.

Other states saw in Proposition 13 a warning against the accumulation of budgetary surpluses of the kind that the state of California had compiled. These states hastened to return their surpluses to taxpayers through one-time tax rebates or permanent reductions in tax structures before voters took matters into their own hands. Still other states interpreted Proposition 13 as a protest against taxes that automatically escalated with inflation (the initiative had been preceded by record-breaking increases in California property values, assessments, and property tax bills). They used the momentum Proposition 13 provided to "index" the most inflation-prone of state taxes—the personal income tax.

The outburst of state tax relief between 1978 and 1980 saw twelve states reduce their general income tax rates and nine states index their income tax systems. Forty-three different states adopted new limitations on local property taxes or new property tax relief plans. These actions are summarized in table 6-6. Five examples follow to illustrate the different routes states took to achieve tax relief:[26]

California. No state has done more than California to unburden its tax structure (see table 6-7). In just four years the state has moved from having one of the nation's highest ratios of taxes to personal income to a position very near the mean of all states. Proposition 13 limited property taxes in the state to one percent of market value and limited assessment growth, except upon sale of property, to 2 percent annually. According to state estimates Proposition 13 will have saved California taxpayers $35 billion in property tax bills through FY 1983. It is by no means the only tax and spending limitation affecting the state, however. Proposition 4, a state and local spending limitation effective in FY 1981, restricts the growth of tax-supported appropriations to the rise in the California Consumer Price Index (CCPI) combined with the population growth rate. So far this limit has not been binding.

California also has indexed the state personal income tax. Brackets were indexed in 1978 and exemptions in 1979. Originally brackets were raised at

TABLE 6–6

NUMBER OF STATE MEASURES IMPLEMENTING TAX ACTIONS,
BY TYPE AND YEAR, 1978–1982

Tax Action	1978	1979	1980	1981	Spring 1982
Personal income tax					
Reductions					
Indexation	3	4	2	0	0[a]
General rates	4	6	2	3	0
Specific rates	3	3	0	0	0
Total major measures	10	13	4	3	0
Increases					
Indexation	0	0	0[b]	1[b,c]	0[b]
General rates	2	0	0	0[d]	5[e]
Specific rates	0	0	0	1	0
Total major measures	2	0	0	2	5
Property tax					
New statewide limitation on levies, rates, or assessment growth	7	9	7	4	—
New property tax relief	20	21	19	17	—
Sales tax					
Reductions					
Across-the-board	1	0	0	1	0
Base contraction (food, drugs, or medical— exemption or reduced rates)	9	12	2	3	—
Total measures	10	12	2	4	—
Increases					
Across-the-board, permanent	0	0	1	3	4
Temporary and extension of temporary	1	1	3	3	—
Base expansion	3	1	0	3	1
Total measures	4	2	4	9	—

SOURCES: Urban Institute survey; Federation of Tax Administrators; National Conference of State Legislatures.

a. Excludes California's successful referendum initiative to continue full tax-bracket indexing.

b. Excludes Oregon's postponement of implementation of its indexation statute.

c. Includes Minnesota's reduction in its indexation program.

d. Excludes Rhode Island, which raised its "piggy-back" income tax from 19 percent to 19.2 percent of federal tax liability. Due to changes in federal personal income tax law, receipts will be less than from a fixed-rate structure.

e. Excludes Vermont, which raised its "piggy-back" income tax from 23 percent of federal tax liability to 24 percent, for less than full effect of federal changes. Includes Nebraska, which raised its piggy-back income tax from 15 percent to 17 percent of federal tax liability, resulting in a net revenue increase.

TABLE 6–7

CALIFORNIA TAX RELIEF,
FY 1976–FY 1983
(In $ millions)

Local property tax relief	
Proposition 13	35,000
Homeowners' exemption	3,948
Inventory exemption	3,249
Open space	119
Total local property tax relief	42,316
State tax relief	
Personal income tax	
Indexing	7,992
Other	1,132
Renter property tax credit	2,129
Senior citizens' property tax relief	561
Business taxes	341
Inheritance and gift taxes	271
Energy credits	292
Other	542
Total state tax relief	13,260

SOURCE: State of California, *FY 1983 Budget Summary.*

a rate three points below the CCPI, but the state implemented full indexation in 1980 and 1981. A statewide referendum in June 1982 mandated continuation of full indexation despite the budget imbalance the state faced.

Colorado. Since 1977 Colorado has been a virtual laboratory of tax relief. State general fund spending is limited by a 1977 statute to no more than 7 percent per annum growth. Any additional revenues received, after allowance for carrying modest balances, must be returned in the form of tax relief. Although Colorado's 7 percent limit has enough loopholes not to be fully binding (school aid payments, for example, have been interpreted as property tax relief for purposes of the statute), it has had a strong impact on the state's spending and tax relief policies.

In 1978 Colorado indexed its income tax structure. The state annually sets a percentage rate by which the standard deduction, personal exemption, and tax-rate brackets are adjusted. Indexation has been supplemented by a number of other tax relief measures, both temporary and permanent. A 10 percent income tax credit was granted in FY 1980, raised to 20 percent in FY 1981, and set at 16 percent in FY 1982. The state sales tax on food and home heating fuels was dropped. The investment tax credit for business was expanded and school property tax relief widened. All in all, fifty-two different tax relief measures were passed by the 1978-1981 sessions of the Colorado legislature. By FY 1982 they had reduced annual revenues by an amount equal to one-quarter of the state's actual budget.

Hawaii. Hawaii has chosen to provide tax relief through a series of one-time returns of revenue rather than through permanent reductions in its tax structure. The state is required to hold a constitutional convention every ten years. The most recent convention was held in 1978 and enacted both a revenue return requirement and a spending limitation. The state is now required to return revenue to taxpayers whenever the general fund ending balance is 5 percent or more of general fund revenues for two consecutive years. In FY 1980 and FY 1981 the state ended the year with general fund balances of more than 16 and 19 percent of revenues, respectively, putting into operation the revenue-return requirement. For the 1981 tax year the state provided a one-time tax credit of $100 per exemption regardless of household income. The most recent session of the state legislature enacted a one-time credit of $25 per exemption for 1982 tax payments.

Minnesota. Until recently Minnesota was the scene of strenuous tax-relief competition between the legislature, which is controlled by the Democratic Farm Labor (DFL) party and the governor, a Republican. Historically, the DFL has worked to provide large-scale property tax relief. A series of legislative actions has created an unusually complicated property tax relief posture in which the state limits local property tax rates, limits local spending growth financed by property taxation, and has rebated 58 percent of property tax bills for most residential property taxpayers. Rebate entitlements for school taxes will total some $345 million in FY 1983. Governor Quie, in contrast, campaigned in 1978 on a platform of lower income tax rates for individuals and business. He succeeded in indexing the state's income tax, at an estimated cumulative revenue loss thus far of $1.2 billion. The DFL and Republican competition to establish tax relief made it especially difficult for the state to address its FY 1982 and FY 1983 budget shortfalls.

New York. In the mid-1970s New York State had the highest tax burdens of any state in the nation except Alaska, both in per capita terms and as a percentage of personal income. It was the fiscal and economic crisis of 1975-1976 that made tax reduction the state's policy priority. Tax reductions have been focused primarily on the personal income tax and business taxation. Prior to 1977 the maximum personal income tax rate was 15 percent plus a 2.5 percent surcharge. The surcharge was repealed in 1977, and the top marginal rate gradually reduced from 15 percent to 10 percent. This change in the progressivity of the tax structure was meant to appeal to business investors. It also has had the effect of partial indexation, reducing the exposure of individual tax burdens to inflationary increases in household income.

Despite the diversity of states' tax-cutting behavior, certain general patterns are evident. States with the highest overall tax burdens in relation to personal income were most likely to make major reductions in their tax structures, especially for personal income taxation. Eleven of the thirteen states reducing their income tax rates and seven of the nine states indexing their income tax systems had tax burdens above the median for all states in 1978.[27] Part of the pressure for tax relief in these states came from fear that high tax rates would render business activities noncompetitive.

The 1978-1980 era of tax relief not only lowered the states' overall tax structures but tilted the state and local sector's tax mix away from property taxation and toward income and sales taxation. In 1977 sales tax receipts by state and local governments surpassed property tax receipts for the first time in the nation's history ($63.9 billion to $62.4 billion). By 1981 sales taxes generated $20 billion more per year in revenues than did property taxes. The growth in revenues from fees and charges has also outpaced the growth in revenue from traditional tax sources. Opinion polls indicate that if further state and local revenues must be raised, taxpayers prefer that this pattern continue.

State Fiscal Conditions

The tax cutting of state governments was made possible by their robust reserve positions. These have now been eroded. As a result states have become highly vulnerable to the effects of economic recession on current revenues. The extent of budget deterioration can be seen from states' general fund balances. For all states in the aggregate, year-ending balances fell from $11.7 billion in FY 1980 to $6.5 billion in FY 1981 and were projected by state budget officers in the middle of FY 1982 to fall to $2.4 billion by the end of the fiscal year.[28] The latter projection may overstate the deterioration in actual balances, since it omits the remedial actions that many states have had to take. But the direction and precipitousness of the trend are unmistakable.

States can be grouped into three broad categories according to their current fiscal or budgetary condition. The states in our sample have been classified in this manner in table 6-8. In the "good" group are states with strong surplus balances or equivalent budget protection. All of the sample states, except Colorado, classified as "good" project general fund reserves at the end of FY 1982 of roughly 10 percent or more of general fund expenditures. Colorado is prevented from accumulating reserves by its revenue limitation. However, the state's permanent revenue sources are growing explosively, and the state at any time can choose to halt its series of one-time tax credits that return revenues to taxpayers, as it in fact did in FY 1983.

TABLE 6-8

CHARACTERISTICS OF STATES GROUPED BY FY 1982 BUDGET CONDITION

	(1) Projected Year-End FY 1982 General Fund Balance as Percentage of General Fund Expenditures	(2) Unemployment Rate (Feb. 1982)	(3) Governor's Party	(4) Legislative Party[a]	(5) Budget Cycle[b]
Good budget condition					
Colorado	3.4[c,d]	6.7	D	R	A
Hawaii	14.1	5.5	D	D	B2
Kansas	10.4	5.8	D	R	A
New Mexico	15.6	7.5	D	D	A
Oklahoma	25.2	4.9	D	D	A
Texas	9.8	7.8	R	D	B2
Fair budget condition					
Alabama	1.1	13.9	D	D	A
Arizona	2.8	7.9	D	R	A
California	0.6	9.6	D	D	A
Florida	7.9	7.1	D	D	B2
Idaho	1.4	12.0	D	R	A
Illinois	1.8	10.1	R	D/R	A
Indiana	2.6	13.3	R	R	B2
Kentucky	1.0[d]	11.5	D	D	B1
Maryland	5.0	9.8	D	D	A
Massachusetts	0.6	8.3	D	D	A
Missouri	5.1	10.1	R	D	A
New Jersey	2.2	9.3	R	D	A
New York	0.1	8.0	D	R/D	A
Utah	1.5	9.1	D	R	A
Vermont	0.0	8.7	R	R	A

TABLE 6–8 (continued)

CHARACTERISTICS OF STATES GROUPED BY FY 1982 BUDGET CONDITION

	(1) Projected Year-End FY 1982 General Fund Balance as Percentage of General Fund Expenditures	(2) Unemployment Rate (Feb. 1982)	(3) Governor's Party	(4) Legislative Party[a]	(5) Budget Cycle[b]
Poor budget condition					
Michigan	0.0	16.1	R	D	A
Minnesota	−13.9	7.7	R	D	B2
Nebraska[e]	−2.7	6.3	R	Nonpartisan	A
Ohio	0.0	12.2	R	R/D	B2
Oregon	−4.1	12.4	R	D	B2
Washington[e]	−4.8	12.9	R	R	B2
Wisconsin[e]	1.2	9.7	R	D	B2

SOURCES: Column 1: National Governors Association and National Association of State Budget Officers (NASBO), *Fiscal Survey of the States, 1981-82* (Washington, D.C.: National Governors Association, June 1982). Column 2: U.S. Department of Labor, *Employment and Earnings, May 1982* (Washington, D.C.: GPO), table D-1. Columns 3-5: Urban Institute and National Conference of State Legislatures survey.

a. D = Democrat; R = Republican; D/R = Senate is Democratic; Assembly or House is Republican.
b. A = annual; B1 = FY 1983 is first year of biennium; B2 = FY 1983 is second year of biennium.
c. Maximum general fund reserve permitted under state law (equals 4.0 percent of general fund spending for direct state programs).
d. Includes reserve funds not counted as general fund balances in NASBO survey.
e. Not in twenty-five-state representative sample; added to provide further information on "poor" states.

States classified as being in "poor" budgetary condition face the prospect of ending FY 1982 with negative balances or would do so were it not for extreme last-minute budget adjustments or accounting manipulations. The remaining states have been classified as in "fair" condition. Any classification of this type involves some arbitrariness, but for the most part the differences between state budget positions are plain. To provide additional perspective on the states confronting the most severe budget adjustments, three other "poor" states—Nebraska, Washington, and Wisconsin—were added to the representative sample of twenty-five states used throughout the chapter.

Unemployment and Region. The influence of economic conditions on budgets is evident from the state groupings. The "good" condition states all enjoy well-below-average unemployment rates. They tend to be clustered in the energy-producing parts of the country. The "poor" condition states tend to have higher-than-average unemployment rates and to be clustered in the North Central and Pacific Northwest regions. These regions have been hardest hit by the problems of heavy manufacturing and construction-related industries, respectively. Minnesota and Nebraska are conspicuous exceptions to the association between unemployment rates and budget condition. Although both states have suffered from the recession, their budgetary difficulties have been out of proportion with the problems of the underlying economy.

Severance Taxes. The ability to levy severance taxes on oil, gas, or coal production has emerged as perhaps the most important difference in states' taxing capacity in the 1980s. With only one exception, *all* of the states ending FY 1981 with general fund balances in excess of 15 percent of general fund spending rely heavily on severance taxation.[29] The single exception is Hawaii, which benefits from its own form of tax exporting through the tourist trade. The extreme and growing importance of severance taxation to states' fiscal conditions has significance for the design of New Federalism turnbacks. One of the main objectives of states without severance tax possibilities has been to establish the principle that there should be differential federal aid to states to compensate for differential access to severance taxes. This is held to be especially important if fundamental programs like AFDC are to be returned to the states for financing.

Politics and Budget Cycles. Every budget has its political dimensions. It is a peculiarity of the classification of sample states that all of the states in "poor" budget condition have Republican governors. Of the six states in this class with partisan legislatures, five have at least one legislative house controlled by Democrats. The sixth state—Washington—had split legislative control for part of the governor's term.

These differences in budget condition do not reflect a systematic difference in executive or legislative ability by party affiliation. But they may reflect a systematic tendency for Republican governors to have been more optimistic in projecting FY 1982 economic recovery when drawing up their budgets. Budgetary shortfalls on the revenue side have been greatest in these states. The party conflict between the executive and legislative branches also has hampered efforts to make emergency changes that would reestablish balance in state budgets. Three governors of states classified in "poor" condition—Milliken of Michigan, Quie of Minnesota, and Dreyfus of Wisconsin—have announced they will not stand for reelection, largely because of their states' fiscal difficulties and the problems of dealing with state legislatures during budgetary retrenchment.

The uncertainty surrounding state revenue estimates has been exacerbated in those states where FY 1983 is the second year of a biennial budget cycle. Few persons of any political coloration foresaw in the spring of 1981 the depth or extent of the national recession. The states that had to make two-year revenue forecasts at that time have faced the most severe subsequent budget adjustments. This is illustrated by the preponderance of states in the second year of a biennial budget cycle in the "poor" category of table 6-8.

State Budget Adjustments in FY 1982 and FY 1983

A faltering economy, the legacy of past tax reductions, the need to compensate local governments for their revenue limitations, and federal aid cutbacks all combined in FY 1982 and FY 1983 to force states into making their greatest budget adjustments in decades. The very magnitude and abruptness of the budget revisions help reveal state policy priorities. The diversity of state budget responses defies easy generalization. Summaries of the principal budget actions and policy issues for the sample states are given in the appendix to this chapter. This section identifies several themes to be found in the summaries.

Reversal of Tax Relief. The era of state and local tax relief has come to a resounding halt, at least temporarily. The majority of states have been obliged to raise tax rates for FY 1983. Wherever possible, states have limited their rate increases to minor taxes. But as of mid-June 1982, five states—Michigan, Minnesota, Nebraska, Ohio, and Oregon—had made major increases in their personal income tax rates. Another five states—Florida, Nebraska, Vermont, Washington, and Wisconsin—had made major sales tax expansions. There were no broad tax reductions.

Some of the state tax increases have been large enough to offset the greater part of the 10 percent federal income tax reduction taking effect July 1, 1982. Ohio's 25 percent income tax surcharge and increase in rates for taxpayers earning $80,000 or more, for example, was estimated by the Ohio legislative budget office to offset 50 to 84 percent of the federal income tax cut, depending upon tax bracket.

One tax issue that almost all states had to address was their response to changes in the federal tax structure. The forty-four states with corporate income taxes stood to lose revenue by conforming to the Accelerated Cost Recovery System (ACRS) adopted for the federal tax code. Previously every state except California allowed companies and individuals to depreciate property for state purposes in the same way that it was depreciated for federal purposes. As of mid-June 1982, seventeen states had conformed to ACRS without raising their tax rates, six states had conformed while raising corporate tax rates, and seventeen states had decoupled from federal depreciation standards, though some planned future reconsideration of their actions.[30]

It is interesting to compare the mix of tax increases and appropriations reductions used to balance budgets in the states facing the most severe deficits. At one extreme is Wisconsin, with $416 million of FY 1982 tax increases and other general fund revenue increases but under $50 million of budget cuts. Nebraska also balanced its budget primarily through revenue increases, raising its personal income tax, along with its corporate income tax, general sales tax, and cigarette tax. Minnesota and Michigan both raised taxes by less than they reduced spending when balancing their budgets (Michigan favored spending cuts by a five to three margin). Ohio, Oregon, and Washington all relied on tax increases for somewhat more than half their total budget adjustments. In every state, however, tax increases were viewed as a last resort. They were approved only after broad budget reductions, either in the same budget year or the preceding one.

Deferral of Budget Problems. In coping with FY 1982 and FY 1983 budget problems, no budget strategy has been more common than to postpone the problems insofar as possible. States have displayed an impressive imagination in this regard. California, Illinois, and Michigan have skipped or lowered contributions to their state employee pension systems. Indiana and Kentucky suspended refund payments on personal income taxes until the start of the new fiscal year. A number of states have accelerated withholding of income or sales taxes, in order to generate cash that would balance the FY 1982 budget. They have deferred to FY 1983 or later payments on outstanding obligations, including aid to local governments. Most of the major tax increases enacted to balance budgets have been announced as temporary surcharges that will terminate at a given date.

If, as the states hope, economic recovery is swift and vigorous, these deferrals of budget problems will prove to have been prudent. But they borrow against future budgets as surely as does short-term debt. Should the economy continue to falter, the states will find that the steps taken to balance accounts in FY 1982 will jeopardize future budget stability.

Welfare Spending. Most states have attempted to protect social welfare spending from the full force of their budget reductions. As hard hit as it has been by recession, the state of Michigan made the decision not to curtail welfare and Medicaid eligibility, despite $266 million in unforeseen welfare costs in FY 1982 attributable to high unemployment. The basic social welfare system has been kept intact as part of the state's response to recession. The same strategy has been followed in Ohio, Minnesota, and Washington. Oregon is an apparent exception. It has made severe reductions in AFDC and Medicaid eligibility and has also reduced AFDC benefit levels. But these changes were carried out in 1980. They represent a shift in political philosophy—the state revised all welfare programs to pay less than the minimum wage and maximize work incentives—rather than a response to budgetary pressure.

Without exception, states have passed on the tightening of AFDC income eligibility initiated by the federal government. For many states, control of Medicaid costs has become one of the most urgent priorities, as they seek to remove the pressure on the rest of the budget created by Medicaid deficits. Few states have raised welfare benefits and some, like California, have taken special action to override the cost-of-living adjustments that would automatically take place under state law. But the appendix to this chapter shows that welfare programs in general have been cut less than the rest of the state budget where severe revisions have been necessary.

Education. Another function receiving budget protection has been basic aid to elementary and secondary education. The preferential treatment given basic school aid stands in contrast with budgeting for special education programs, which in many states has been targeted for spending cutbacks. The reassessment of special education aid by the states has been supported by federal education block grant policies and regulatory relaxation.

State policy toward education aid has become inextricably bound up with state policy toward property tax relief. Many states now tie their school assistance programs to limits on local property taxation or deliver ''school'' funding directly to taxpayers by rebating part of their school tax payments. Some of the states in the worst fiscal condition have begun to rescind parts of their property tax relief programs. Oregon, in two special budget-balancing sessions of the legislature, cut the maximum payment under its homestead property tax relief plan from $800 to $215. Minnesota also reversed more than a decade of deepening property tax relief, affirming that the state had gone too far in substituting state revenues raised through the income tax for local property taxes. Its cutbacks in school aid and property tax relief were accompanied by an easing of controls on local property tax rates, with the intent of encouraging localities to raise property taxes to replace state funds. It is estimated that Minnesota property tax revenues will jump by 24 percent in FY 1983.

Other Priorities. Governors in a number of states designated long-run capital plans for repair and improvement of the state's infrastructure facilities as a budget priority. Typically, they proposed new gas or other taxes to finance a capital rebuilding plan. More often than not, state legislatures reduced funding for these long-run plans. This sequence was followed in New York, New Jersey, Colorado, Maryland, Virginia, and other states.

The single fastest-growing state budget item in FY 1982 and FY 1983 is corrections. Thirty-nine states are now under federal court order or have litigation pending to improve prison facilities, and others face the need for new prisons to relieve crowded conditions and respond to public concern over crime rates.

Aid to Local Governments. Perhaps the most basic policy choice states have had to make is between funding for direct state government functions and funding for aid to local governments. More political conflict and interest-group lobbying has gone into this choice than any other. In several states, the competing forces have taken their case beyond the state budget and tried to protect their claims on fiscal resources through constitutional amendments or fundamental legislation.

In California, the state bail-out legislation that assisted localities in the wake of Proposition 13 contains a basic deflator. It specifies that if available state resources fall below certain levels, all of the shortfall will be absorbed through reductions in aid to localities. The combination of surplus erosion and recession-related revenue losses triggered the deflator. According to studies of the California legislative analyst's office, without a two-thirds legislative override, all of the $1.2 billion remaining in Proposition 13 aid to localities would perforce have come under suspension in FY 1983 by the terms of the deflator. Whether the state budget should be balanced in this manner became a principal item of dispute in California. In the end, action was taken to preserve much of the special aid. In Massachusetts, too, the state after much debate again augmented state aid to localities to help relieve the burden of adjusting to the state's local property tax limitation.

In Michigan, state-local relations are, if anything, still more complicated. Under the Headlee amendment to the state constitution, Michigan must devote at least 41.6 percent of its budget to local aid. This requirement has become a continuing source of conflict during economic downturns when state welfare obligations rise and total general revenues fall, squeezing the local aid commitment. Fiscal year 1982 was no exception. Michigan cut over $550 million in spending for both state and local purposes, partly to adjust to major revenue shortfalls and partly to fund unanticipated social welfare costs arising from the recession. Nearly all of these costs involve direct state funding of "state purposes.'' The state is completing an analysis to determine FY 1982 compliance with Headlee, and some observers believe Michigan may be one to two points under the mandated 41.6 percent as a result of its mid-year adjustments. What action the state will take in this event is unclear, but it could involve painful reallocation of limited resources.

Political Patterns in Budget Revisions. Some recurrent political patterns are discernible in the state budget adjustments. These resemble the lines of budget conflict drawn at the federal level. Republican governors and Republican legislatures, with few exceptions, have favored closing state budget gaps through stronger spending reductions and lesser tax increases than Democratic governors and Democratic legislatures. In the mix of taxation, Republican leaders have tended to resist increases in business and personal income taxation. Democratic leaders have favored these increases where additional tax revenues were needed. Differences in party attitudes toward aid to local governments, and even state social welfare spending, have been far less consistent than one might predict. Michigan, Ohio, Washington, and Wisconsin are all states where Republican governors have argued for preservation of the states' social welfare role during severe recession.

Conclusions

One of the principal distinguishing characteristics of the Reagan experiment is the crucial role it assigns to the states in changing domestic priorities. The administration has proposed relinquishing many program responsibilities for the states to assume at their discretion. It has embarked on a plan to cut back federal mandates and federal funding so that the states can determine their own priorities untouched by federal directives. A program grounded in this philosophy must be evaluated by the effects it has at all levels of government (and in the private sector), not by changes in federal policy alone.

This chapter has emphasized that the Reagan initiatives arrived at a special moment in the states' own fiscal history. They had just completed three years of unprecedented tax cutting, largely depleting their current and prospective fiscal reserves in the process. This history has made it difficult economically for the states to replace lost federal funds or take over programs that the federal government has relinquished, even if they desired to do so. Politically, it is difficult for the states to recant their own commitment to tax relief and endeavor to raise taxes in reaction to federal tax reductions. As a result, the Reagan initiatives are much more likely to produce *net* reductions in government activity today than would have been the case three or four years ago. It is not fanciful to speculate that if Ronald Reagan had been elected in 1976 and had implemented his proposed turnback at that time, much of the revolution in tax and spending reductions by state and local governments would have been preempted by federal initiatives, leaving a quite different mix of government activity.

Current constraints on the state and local sector make it less likely that the full set of New Federalism proposals will be put in place. Only if there is extremely strong economic growth between now and 1991 can the transfer of funding and program responsibilities that the administration proposes occur without large-scale tax increases or real spending reductions by state and local governments. The tension between the federal budget and state-local budgets is delicately balanced and dependent upon strong economic growth for its successful reconciliation.

The short-run signs of state budget reactions are consistent with this assessment. Most states have declined the opportunity to use state funds to increase program support under the new block grants. Often, the federal cuts have been passed on in state budgets without significant debate.

The states' primary attention is now focused on sorting out their own policy priorities. This has been made necessary by their tax restraints and budget gaps, but it is also being reinforced by changes in federal policies. One set of issues the states must resolve is their fiscal relations to the localities. Aid to local schools, property tax relief, and state controls over local tax and spending discretion all are receiving the reconsideration that tight budgets often produce. Another fundamental concern is what social welfare policies the states will pursue in the future. In both cases, federal program changes have altered the external inducements that states used to face. But the states' own desired policies are only now emerging from the budget debates.

There are signs that the administration will in the end retreat from a pure version of dual federalism as its objective in federalism reform. It has shown itself willing to discuss a uniform floor for AFDC payments, compensatory federal aid for states with low taxing capacity, and retention of federal program assistance for functions (like highways) that the states identify as of fundamental importance to them. Compared to the austerity of the New Federalism, these are important political concessions. Compared to the state of federalism that Ronald Reagan inherited in 1981, however, even the modified program would represent remarkable movement toward the president's goal of restoring an older model of federalism to the country.

APPENDIX: STATE BUDGET ADJUSTMENTS

This appendix summarizes budget developments and principal fiscal issues in twenty-eight states. These are the twenty-five states chosen as representative of the national distribution of states by population size, region, and fiscal condition, as well as three further states—Nebraska, Washington, and Wisconsin—added to provide information on states facing severe budget adjustments. States are grouped by budget condition, as presented in table 6-8 of the text.

Information was collected through state legislative fiscal officers and executive budget officers by The Urban Institute and National Conference of State Legislatures.

State	Budget Events	Tax Policies	Spending Priorities	Special Issues
POOR BUDGET CONDITION				
Michigan	Three executive orders cut $559 million (more than 12%) from FY 1982 budget. Emergency tax and revenue increases added $339 million to balance budget. These follow steep FY 1981 cuts. FY 1982 budget imbalance created by $681 million recession-related shortfall in revenues,	Adopted six-month increase of 1 percentage point in income tax. State has preserved all property tax relief programs.	1. State made decision not to restrict welfare eligibility in face of recession. Added $266 million in unbudgeted costs because of high unemployment rates. 2. Higher education absorbed largest FY 1982 budget reductions, though state has budgeted for restoration in FY 1983.	State is under continuing pressure from referenda initiatives to further reduce property taxes. Fall 1982 initiative proposes 75% reduction in property taxes levied for schools. Headlee amendment requires that aid to local governments not fall below 41.6% of state budget. This has con-

198

Minnesota

State made $1.0 billion in adjustments to $8.5 billion FY 1982-1983 biennial budget in addition to a $195 million cut in the previous biennium.

FY 1982-1983 biennium adjustments include:

Enacted temporary 7% income tax surcharge.

Expanded sales tax base.

Reduced coverage of homestead property tax relief.

Reduced indexing provisions of income tax.

$344 recession-related increase in social program costs, $90 million in extra interest on short-term borrowing.

Before June 1982 temporary income tax increase, FY 82 general fund revenues were below FY 1980 levels.

FY 1983 budget shows 3.4% spending increase.

3. AFDC grant increase for FY 1983 will be deferred. Medicaid cost containment given emphasis.

4. State reductions in school aid have raised local share of school costs. Special education aid cut more than basic aid.

5. Employee wages renegotiated downward. Mandatory days off.

There has been sustained conflict between Democratic Farm Labor (DFL) legislature and Republican governor over size of spending cuts *vs.* tax increases and composition of both.

DFL favored business tax increases, less spend-

For two successive biennial budgets, state has relied on postponing costs to balance budget. This practice has borrowed against future budgets. Legislature revised state's balanced budget requirement to permit balance over bien-

strained budget adjustments.

State	Budget Events	Tax Policies	Spending Priorities	Special Issues
Minnesota (continued)	• $402 million in spending cuts. • $348 million in tax hikes. • $268 million in spending deferrals or revenue acceleration.		ing reduction, preservation of local property tax relief. Governor vetoed budget-balancing bill in Dec. 1981 on grounds it should contain more spending cuts. Insisted income tax hike be temporary. Resisted business tax increases. Decision has been made to return part of school costs to local governments by cutting school aid, cutting school tax relief, relaxing conditions for school district increases in property tax rates. Health, welfare cut least of major budget categories.	nium rather than for each fiscal year.

Nebraska	Cut FY 1982 budget by 3%. FY 1983 budget less than that originally recommended for FY 1982 despite tax increases. State nearly exhausted $100 million balance because of revenue shortfall in FY 1982.	State has raised personal income tax (from 15% to 17% of federal liability), corporate income tax, general sales tax, and cigarette tax.		Nonpartisan, unicameral legislature. State board empowered to raise taxes without legislative action if necessary to balance budget.
Ohio	Between February and June 1982 more than $1.3 billion of adjustments made in $13.5 billion biennial budget. Approximately $500 million in spending cuts; $600 million in tax increases; the rest, spending deferrals and miscellaneous measures. Actions follow severe 1981 adjustments.	July 1981: Increased gas tax in two steps to yield extra $220 million in FY 1983. November 1981: Made permanent previously temporary 1¢ sales tax increase. March 1982: Gave effect to public utility and corporate franchise tax adopted conditionally in November. June 1982:	Five rounds of spending cuts since Dec. 1980. Most cuts have exempted public welfare programs, though Ohio starts from low base in welfare support. Basic education aid has received special protection in budget. Corrections spending also protected. Largest cuts (June 1982) distributed as follows:	State and voters exercise strict control over local tax revenues. Almost all levy increases require voter approval.

State	Budget Events	Tax Policies	Spending Priorities	Special Issues
Ohio (continued)		25% surcharge for last six months in 1982 and 12.5% surcharge for calendar 1983 on personal income tax, special increase in high-bracket tax rates.	Basic aid to schools cut by 4% and categorical aid to schools cut 7.9%. AFDC cut by $32 million in anticipation of reduced caseloads, but general relief and Medicaid increased by $124.2 million. All operating budgets cut 10%. Highway repair spending boosted by gas tax increase as part of capital preservation program.	
Oregon	At year end FY 1979, state had $285 million in general fund balances. Balance disappeared when state	Deferred indexing of income tax exemption. Increased cigarette tax. Accelerated income tax withholding.	Through first rounds of cuts, state preserved its strong property tax relief program. But in last rounds, it slashed maxi-	Tax relief and surplus return policies were adopted to defuse 1979 referendum initiative

- Returned surplus through one-time 9% income tax credit (1979 tax year).
- Passed law requiring return to taxpayers of revenue more than 2% beyond budgeted level.
- Adopted 30% property tax rebate program.
- Adopted income tax indexation.

For FY 1983 two special sessions:

- Cut appropriations $205 million.
- Raised taxes $154 million.
- Accelerated tax collections by $69 million.

Republican governor favored greater reliance on spending reductions to balance budget.

mum rebate under 30% relief plan from $800 to $215. Principle of property tax relief without household income limit has come under fire.

By far greatest reductions have been made in welfare programs. Eligibility for AFDC and Medicaid has been tightened. AFDC rolls down 15% despite unemployment; Medicaid rolls down more than 20% from 1979. Most of these adjustments are from policy changes initiated in 1980.

AFDC benefit levels reduced 20% by eliminating separate food, shelter, clothing allowances. Unemployed fathers program dropped.

modeled after Proposition 13.

State strictly controls local tax increases.

Electorate restrains taxes; has right within ninety days to place on ballot initiative to overrule any tax increase.

State	Budget Events	Tax Policies	Spending Priorities	Special Issues
Washington	State has made adjustments of more than $1.4 billion in biennial budget of $7.2 billion. Spending reductions: $631 million. Tax increases: $797 million. Governor can make across-the-board budget reductions without legislature's involvement.	December 1981: Raised sales tax 1¢. April 1982: Reimposed sales tax on food. Voters had removed this tax at referendum in 1978. In two steps state placed 4% surtax on all general fund taxes, additional 3% surtax on all except sales tax.	November 1981 cuts: School Aid: 1.7% Human Resources: 3.0% Higher Education: 6.2% General Government: 5.9% April 1982: Biggest cuts came from deferring employee salary raises. Local school aid cut 0.5%. Health and human services cut 0.6%. Rest of budget cut 3%. AFDC benefit levels increased by 8% despite cuts. June 1982: Governor convened another special session to	School districts have threatened suit that school aid cuts threaten "full funding of basic education" ordered by state courts. Block grants introduced for school aid. Remove targeting on special education pupils.

avoid across-the-board cuts of 8.2%, only type permitted by law without legislative action.

Once again, school aid received preferential treatment.

AFDC and Medicaid eligibility likely to be protected, spending cut less than rest of budget.

Democrats favor more business taxation.

Wisconsin	Made adjustments of $465 million in biennial budget, almost entirely through tax increases.
	
	Tax increases: $416 million.
	
	Expenditure reductions under $50 million:
	
	FY 1982: 2% across-the-board cut except local aid, property tax relief, state hospitals, and prisons.
	
	FY 1983: 4% cut with same exceptions.
		FY 1983:
		  Increased sales tax from 4¢ to 5¢.
		  10% surcharge on corporate income tax for 1982 and 1983.
		  Cigarette tax increased.
		
		Democratic legislature voted unitary tax on integrated oil companies; Republican governor vetoed.
			School aid and property tax relief are top priorities.
			
			Governor proposed using sales tax income for general fund in FY 1983, thereafter earmarking receipts for enlarged property tax relief plan.
			
			Legislature voted to allow sales tax to expire after FY 1983, but passed new tax relief program for FY 1984, and gave initial legisla-

State	Budget Events	Tax Policies	Spending Priorities	Special Issues
Wisconsin (continued)			tive ratification to state constitutional amendment to finance property tax relief from increased sales tax. Would be voted on by public—April 1983	
FAIR CONDITION				
Alabama	State uses system of "contingent" appropriations. Some budget appropriations are conditional upon adequate revenue receipts. These are first to be cut during shortfalls. 90% of budget consists of earmarked funds.	1980 gas, alcohol, and cigarette tax increases are the only tax increases in the last eighteen years.	1. Federal courts have found Alabama's prisons and mental health facilities inadequate. Ordered improvements. 2. Education has earmarked to it all of income tax and most of sales tax receipts—the most rapidly growing revenue sources. Governor has been unsuccessful in attempts to relax earmarking.	$500 million from sale of oil and gas leases used to create Heritage Trust Fund. Income only can be spent, except principal can be used to fund previous appropriations for prisons and mental health facilities.

Arizona	FY 1982 budget balanced by across-the-board 5% cut in operating budgets. Deferred capital spending. For FY 1983 governor proposed only 2.9% increase in spending.	No new taxes for FY 1983. Reduced and delayed implementation of gas tax increase. Legislature approved extension of income tax indexing to tax brackets. Food exempted from sales tax in 1981.	1. Property tax relief is top priority. State has broad rebate program, ceiling on local assessment growth, 2% per year limit on property tax revenue growth. School aid is tied to property tax relief. 2. Ten-year highway plan introduced in 1981, financed by lottery and gas tax hike. 3. State aid to schools raised greatly in 1981. Block grant form eliminates special education earmarking.	3. Welfare programs have most of contingent appropriations; will get heaviest cuts.	Property tax limits and relief were adopted in part to resist constitutional amendment in November 1980 election.
California	FY 1983 budget involves first absolute reduction in general fund spending (2%) since 1943.	Democratic legislative leadership favored tax increases to help balance budget, but June 1982 referenda mandated full	1. Existing legislation overridden to deny cost-of-living adjustments for AFDC, most other welfare benefits.		Republicans favored state aid to localities as budget priority. Democrats favored state social program spending.

State	Budget Events	Tax Policies	Spending Priorities	Special Issues
California (continued)	Pension contributions skipped and reduced to balance FY 1982 and FY 1983 budgets.	indexing, other tax reductions. Legislature abandoned tax increases as contrary to public will.	2. Medically indigent made state-county program; was solely state program. Number of measures to restrain Medicaid costs. 3. "Deflator" provision of Proposition 13 bail-out bill overridden by 2/3 vote. Would have required all of revenue shortfall to be made up by reductions in bail-out aid to local governments.	More tax and spending limit proposals to be on fall referenda ballot.
Florida	Small pro rata cut to balance FY 1982 budget.	State adopted 1¢ increase in sales tax ($760 million per year).	State share of sales tax (1/2¢) to be used primarily for elementary and secondary education and crime control. Governor and legislature in 1981 committed themselves to putting Florida in top quartile, nationwide, for	1980 TRIM statute mandates that local millage rates must not raise property tax revenues from previous year, except for new improvements. Up to 5% increase allowed with referendum approval.

State						
Idaho	Four-day work week imposed to balance FY 1982 budget. Republican legislature reduced Democratic governor's FY 1983 budget growth from 12.3% to 10.6%.	No major changes, except increased gas tax for highways.	Legislative cuts mostly in social programs. Protection of elementary and secondary education in face of local property tax limits has been state budget priority.	teacher salaries within five years. Other 1/2¢ of sales tax to be returned to localities, part tied to property tax relief, part discretionary. Highway financing a priority. Medicaid costs rising rapidly.	From FY 1979 to FY 1981 state had 1% property tax limit on counties. Counties above limit had property tax levies frozen. Law relaxed to allow 5% per annum growth in FY 1982. For FY 1983 House passed a bill allowing local option sales or income tax. Senate defeated bill but likely to appear again.	State greatly affected by federal reductions in refugee aid.

State	Budget Events	Tax Policies	Spending Priorities	Special Issues
Illinois	FY 1982 budget balanced by requiring agencies, except education, to keep a 2% reserve in operating budgets. Little spending growth in FY 1983 budget.	Has postponed remaining phase-out of sales tax on food.	Contain state spending at basically FY 1982 levels and refrain from cutting welfare and Medicaid benefits.	Proposed liquor tax to increase appropriations to education and mental health did not pass.
Indiana	Implemented $85 million in budget adjustments by accelerating withholding, delaying tax refunds, delaying last pay check for some workers to new fiscal year.	Reduced income tax rate modestly in 1981. Rate increase may be introduced in next year's legislative session.	Froze state employee salaries. Increasing spending on state and local roads. High growth for corrections spending.	Indiana has transferred many powers of localities to state. State Tax Commission must approve all local budgets. State had imposed freeze on local property tax levies, now relaxed to freeze property tax rates. State pays 20% of all individual/local property tax bills, half of the increase in local school costs from base year, 1972.

Kentucky	State had to balance FY 1982 budget with one of nation's most severe spending cuts—$236 million or 10% of annual budget plus $46 million of deferrals and other actions. Governor made cuts while legislature out of session.	FY 1983: Raised alcohol tax. New truck tax to finance highway program.	FY 1982 cuts: eliminate all new capital projects. ● 15% cut in all general fund programs, except ● Human resources and education cut 8%. ● State police and corrections, no cut. Two FY 1983 priorities: controlling rapid growth of Medicaid, highway finance.	State has 4% limit on local property tax levy growth. Legislature has challenged governor's right to reduce budget without legislative consultation.
Maryland	Small adjustments.	Governor proposed 4¢ gas tax increase in FY 1983, legislature approved 2¢ in 1983 and 2 1/2¢ in 1984.	Basic education protected by automatic inflation adjustments. Cuts come in special and vocational education.	
Massachusetts	Governor supported elimination of income tax surcharge. Legislature thus far has rejected.	Local aid has emerged as predominant issue. Legislature boosted local aid by $273 million in FY 1982 to offset	Proposition 2-1/2 limits property tax to 2.5% of full value, limits total levy growth to 2.5% annually, cuts	

State	Budget Events	Tax Policies	Spending Priorities	Special Issues
Massachusetts (continued)			Proposition 2-1/2's revenue losses. FY 1983 budget adds $133 million in further local aid, over governor's opposition; adopts allocation formula specifically tied to Proposition 2-1/2 losses. Governor favored tax cuts over increased local aid.	auto excise taxes. Sets schedule for towns to reduce taxes to allowable limit. Override provision added in FY 1982, but voters have rejected most override proposals.
Missouri	Reduced FY 1982 spending by $95.6 million to balance budget; postponed $100 million of spending to FY 1983.	Cigarette tax increase enacted to assist education. Gas tax increase to be put before voters.	Elementary and secondary education received additional funding due to tax increase.	Starting in FY 1982, growth in state revenues limited to growth in personal income. Local property tax growth limited to CPI. Limits have not as yet been a significant constraint.

		Governor's priorities	
New Jersey	Newly elected Republican governor ran on platform of reducing business taxes. Proposed cutting corporate tax, adding sales tax on motor fuels and cigarettes with revenues dedicated to highway maintenance and repair, prison improvements, respectively. Legislature rejected extension of sales tax to motor fuel by one vote in Senate.	Governor's priorities were: • Highway maintenance and upgrading • Prison facilities • School aid Growth in all these areas cut back when motor fuel tax rejected.	New Jersey has high degree of revenue dedication, diminishing budget flexibility. Lottery proceeds are earmarked for education and state institutions; casino revenue earmarked for elderly's services and property tax relief. State's 5% limit on municipal spending growth due for renewal or termination. State expenditure growth limited to growth in state personal income but not as yet a constraint.
New York	Governor refused to certify FY 1983 budget as "balanced" without new taxes or spending cuts. Legislature accepted governor's vetoes until he certified budget for Governor proposed 1¢ sales tax increase for "leveling up" school aid. Legislature rejected. Proposed gas tax increase for road rebuilding. Also rejected.	Governor's priorities: • State assumption of Medicaid costs. • Equalizing school aid. • Highway and infrastructure rebuilding.	State's highest court overruled lower courts, held equalization of school spending not necessary. Removes "court-pointed gun" for greater school aid.

State	Budget Events	Tax Policies	Spending Priorities	Special Issues
New York (continued)	spring borrowing. After borrowing was completed, it restored higher spending.		Willing to cut other forms of local aid. Legislature rejected taxes to finance new initiatives, boosted traditional and other local aid.	
Utah	Recent revenue estimates have held up well, making mid-term cuts unnecessary.	Since 1979, strong property tax relief bills have been passed (reduce local property tax rates by 4 mills; circuit-breaker; classification proposal on fall 1982 ballot). Governor proposed severance tax; legislature rejected.	Corrections and health, fastest growing budget areas. School spending continues rapid growth. State mandates uniform per pupil expenditures, and finances costs minus local revenues raised by a 23 1/4 mill property tax.	State now prohibited by constitution from local revenue sharing. Amendment will be on fall 1982 ballot. State spending growth limited to 85% of personal income plus population growth; but not implemented because legislature has not approved population estimates. Block granting of aid to local governments.

Vermont	About $2 million in adjustments.	Raised sales tax from 3¢ to 4¢. Raised piggy back rate of income tax from 23% of federal liability to 24%.	Both tax changes used to finance greater aid to education. Tied to hope of property tax relief.	State studying new forms of increasing local revenues.

GOOD CONDITION

Colorado	For years, legislature has greatly altered governor's budget recommendations. Joint budget committee of legislature develops legislative budget bill on own initiative. One percent general budget cut in FY 1982.	State has provided large reductions in most taxes. 20% income tax credit in FY 1981, 16% credit in FY 1982. Has fully indexed income tax system.	Governor recommended major program of capital improvements. Legislature rejected plan but designated half of lottery receipts to capital investment. Republican legislature appropriated less for social services and higher education than Democratic governor recommended; replaced less of federal grant reductions.	Property tax classification proposed as constitutional amendment. State's 7% growth limit on general fund spending has been binding, forced return of revenues to taxpayers.
Hawaii	No significant adjustments.	Income tax growth restrained by $100 per capita credit in FY 1982,	Education and economic development top priorities.	State constitution now requires state to return revenue to taxpayers

State	Budget Events	Tax Policies	Spending Priorities	Special Issues
Hawaii (continued)		$25 per capita in FY 1983.		whenever general fund ending balance exceeds 5% of general fund revenues for two years.
Kansas	No expenditure cuts have been required.	Governor proposed severance tax; legislature rejected by 2 votes in Senate after House passage. State has steadily removed items from sales tax base (drugs, farm equipment, utilities, sales...).	Severance tax revenues would have been dedicated to school aid; designed to prevent local property tax increases, estimated at $38 million. Severance tax also would have made possible general fund transfers to highway fund.	State controls per-pupil spending growth of local school districts—permits increases from 5% to 15% for high-spending and low-spending districts, respectively. This spending control plus state aid policy virtually determines local property taxes.
New Mexico	No budget adjustments.	Energy-related taxes have supplanted income and sales taxes in state budget. Income tax has been cut to yield less in FY 1982 than FY 1976.	Priorities: Educational spending to prepare skilled work force for economic development. State is rapidly increasing spending on elementary	Two permanent funds created from energy income are expected to reach $2.5 billion in FY 1983. Income from one used for education; other

State		Priorities	
Oklahoma	$294 million surplus. 53% of general fund revenue comes from severance taxes, lease sales or rentals, and interest on permanent funds. Increased personal income tax exemption from $750 to $1000 at a $37.2 million cost.	and secondary education, vocational education at secondary and higher level. Public safety and corrections (partly in reaction to state prison riots).	supports state capital projects. Despite block grant replacement, replacement funding has not been major issue. The state has ceased to fund the Department of Human Services with dedicated funds. General fund revenues are to be appropriated to the department to increase legislative control.
Texas	Governor's budget is never introduced in legislature. Joint legislative committee develops its own proposal from agency requests.	Priorities: • Highways and other capital projects. • Basic and higher education. Elementary and secondary education and junior colleges receiving priority. State under federal court order to improve prison facilities. Highway spending has been protected by automatic inflation adjustments.	State has constitutional ceiling on AFDC spending. Some pressure to lower ceiling. No effort to compensate for federal reductions in social welfare.

Chapter 7

THE NONPROFIT SECTOR

Lester M. Salamon
Alan J. Abramson

The truth is that we've let government take away many things we once considered were really ours to do voluntarily. . . .
—President Ronald Reagan, September 24, 1981

One of the central goals of the Reagan administration's Economic Recovery Program has been to reduce the role of government in American society and to increase reliance on private institutions to meet public needs. While much of the attention has focused on the implications of this goal for private businesses, the implications may, in fact, be even more profound for that vast assortment of organizations that constitute the voluntary, nonprofit segment of the nation's private sector.

Nonprofit organizations have long held a special place in American life. Though private in character, they are essentially public in function, providing

[We are indebted to James Cline and William Trautman for research assistance with this chapter. In addition to the general sponsors of this project, we are also indebted to the Rockefeller Foundation, Independent Sector, the National Society of Fund Raising Executives, the 50l(c)(3) Group, Equitable Life Assurance Society, and the General Electric Foundation for financial assistance that helped support parts of the work reported here. A more extensive version of the results reported here is available in Lester M. Salamon and Alan J. Abramson, *The Federal Budget and the Nonprofit Sector* (Washington, D.C.: The Urban Institute Press, 1982).]

a host of public goods and serving as the major vehicle through which private charitable resources and voluntary efforts are brought to bear on the solving of community problems. They are, therefore, among the most likely candidates to inherit many of the functions from which government is pulling back. Moreover, they are the apparent, chosen instrument of a policy that seeks, as candidate Reagan put it in accepting the Republican party nomination in 1980, "to restore in our time the American spirit of voluntary service, of cooperation, of private and community initiative."

Ironically, however, while opening new opportunities for voluntary activity, the Economic Recovery Program may have the effect of weakening many of the private, voluntary organizations through which such activity occurs. Nonprofit organizations are not simply an alternative to government; rather, they operate in many spheres as partners of government. As a result, the same policies that reduce the role of government—and, hence, increase the need for nonprofit organizations—also reduce the ability of these organizations to meet this need. In addition, nonprofit organizations are affected by changes in tax policy of the sort embodied in the Economic Recovery Tax Act of 1981 because of the sensitivity of charitable giving to tax rates and the tax treatment of contributions. As a consequence, nonprofit organizations may not be able even to maintain their existing levels of service, much less respond to new needs and opportunities.

Since the voluntary, nonprofit sector is so important to the Reagan administration's policy goals, it is therefore important to unravel these strands of impact and examine the overall consequences of the proposed changes to these critical organizations and those they serve. The first section of this chapter defines more fully what the nonprofit sector is and what role it plays in national life. The special position this sector holds in the theory underlying the Economic Recovery Program and the measures that have been proposed to advance that position are outlined in the second section. The third section examines some of the realities not sufficiently acknowledged by this theory and program and documents the resulting challenges the Economic Recovery Program poses to the nonprofit sector. The fourth section reviews the limited data available on the actual impact of the changes now under way on both the demand for nonprofit organizations' services and the ability of these organizations to respond. In the final section these strands of analysis are pulled together and some general conclusions are drawn about the probable evolution of these organizations in the light of the policy changes now underway.

What is the Nonprofit Sector?

The nonprofit sector is a vast and diverse segment of national life. It embraces organizations as amorphous as informal neighborhood associations and as highly structured as multimillion dollar hospital complexes. Legally, it includes mutual insurance companies as well as churches, museums as well as social service agencies, chambers of commerce as well as research institutes. These organizations share a set of characteristics that set them apart from the other two major sectors of national life: business and government. In particular, nonprofit organizations are privately controlled, usually by a volunteer board, yet do not exist to earn a profit.

However, nonprofit organizations have as many differences as similarities. In fact, it is possible to distinguish three, and possibly four, broad classes of these organizations. The first class comprises funding agencies, or fundraising intermediaries, which exist not so much to deliver services as to channel resources to those who do. Included here are private foundations, United Way organizations, Blue Cross and Blue Shield, and other federated funders. The second class comprises organizations that exist primarily to provide goods or services to their immediate members, rather than to society or the community at large. Included here are professional organizations, unions, trade associations, and the like. The third class is made up of organizations that exist primarily to serve others, to provide goods or services to those in need, or to contribute in other ways to the general welfare. Included here are educational institutions, cultural institutions, social welfare agencies, day care centers, nursing homes, hospitals, and so forth. The fourth category, which embraces religious organizations, may not be a separate class at all, but a part of the second or third. Yet churches and other primarily religious bodies have a distinct status that warrants separate treatment.

Because of the amorphousness of the nonprofit sector, formulating a clear view of its scale has been difficult. The Internal Revenue Service, which requires all incorporated nonprofit organizations to file for tax-exempt status, reports that approximately 846,000 such organizations existed as of 1980. For purposes here, however, only the charitable segment of this sector, the third group of organizations identified, is of interest. Although a clear picture of these organizations is still difficult to obtain, data recently collected in a special census survey provide a useful start. According to these data, which are recorded in table 7-1, the charitable nonprofit sector in the United States embraced almost 107,000 organizations as of 1977. Thirty-eight percent of

TABLE 7–1

THE CHARITABLE NONPROFIT SECTOR IN THE U.S., 1977

Type of Organization	Organizations		Expenditures (in $ billions)	Paid Employees Number
	Number	Percentage of Total		
Social services	40,983	38	8.3	676,473
Legal aid services	1,101	1	0.3	12,440
Civic, social, and fraternal organizations	34,121	32	3.6	255,924
Education and research	11,074	10	15.5	980,116
Health	12,307	12	44.0	2,431,015
Arts and culture	3,480	3	1.1	59,761
Other	3,725	4	1.1	44,231
Total	106,791	100	73.8	4,459,960

SOURCE: Adapted from U.S. Census, *1977 Census of Service Industries*, SC 77-A-53 (1981), p. 3.

these organizations are engaged in providing social services, and another 32 percent are civic, social, or fraternal organizations.

These organizations clearly constitute an important part of the nation's service delivery system. They account, collectively, for almost 5 percent of the Gross National Product. They employ five times as many workers as the automobile industry and account for one-third of the employment in the nation's rapidly growing service sector. In many fields of activity, in fact, they are the principal service providers. Thus, nonprofit organizations deliver most of the hospital care, much of the postsecondary education, and a considerable portion of the social services (such as foster care and family counseling) provided in this country. They are also a major presence in the fields of art, music, culture, and research, and are the principal channel for a host of civic-action and community-organization activities.

In addition to their specific functions and economic position, moreover, nonprofit organizations add an important quality to national life. They help encourage voluntary involvement. They offer a flexible device for cooperative action to serve community needs. They provide a vehicle for applying private resources to charitable ends. They therefore provide an important source of diversity and independence that helps sustain the distinctive character of American society.

The Economic Recovery Program and the Nonprofit Sector: The Theory

These features of the nonprofit sector may explain why this set of institutions has long been an object of affection for political conservatives interested in finding an alternative to government for serving human needs. In fact, a more or less explicit conservative theory on the role and character of these organizations has taken shape over the past several decades and, in turn, has influenced political action. This section outlines this theory and shows how it is reflected in the Reagan administration's policy.

The Theoretical Underpinnings

The theory underlying the Economic Recovery Program's treatment of nonprofit organizations has its proximate roots in the conservative reaction to the French Revolution. To conservatives like Edmund Burke, the French Revolution was so objectionable because of its impact on the social groupings that formed the heart of medieval society—the "little platoons" of family, church, and local community in which men and women lived much of their lives. For Burke and others, these institutions exerted a civilizing influence beyond anything the state could ever provide. They offered a source of order, a fabric for social life, and a basis for resisting the tyranny of majority rule. As Burke argued in his well-known *Reflections on the Revolution in France*:

> We begin our public affections in our families. No cold relation is a zealous citizen. We pass on to our neighborhoods, and our habitual provincial connexions. These are inns and resting places. Such divisions of our country as have been formed by habit, and not by a sudden jerk of authority, were so many little images of the great country in which the heart found something which it could fill. The love to the whole is not extinguished by this subordinate partiality. . . .[1]

While Burke and the European conservatives had in mind principally the ascriptive institutions of the medieval world—the family, the parish, the gild—their argument has been translated into modern form in the writings of sociologist Robert Nisbet. For Nisbet, the decline of community—the dissolution of the "intermediate associations" lying between the individual and the larger institutions of society—which was prefigured in nineteenth century conservatism, has become the central fact of the modern era. It has produced a deep sense of personal alienation and, by undermining organized barriers to state power, a fundamental threat to human liberty. Writes Nisbet:

> Only through its intermediate relationships and authorities has any State ever achieved the balance between organization and personal freedom that is the condition of a creative and enduring culture. These relationships begin with the family and with the small informal social groups which spring up around common interests and cultural needs. Their number extends to the larger associations of society, to the churches, business associations, labor unions, universities, and professions. They are the real sources of liberal democracy.[2]

With Nisbet, however, the defense of intermediate associations is explicitly joined to a more pervasive conservative hostility to government. In his view, the weakening of intermediate associations and the resulting decline of community in the modern world, which is so much to be regretted, can be laid directly at government's feet. As he puts it:

> The conflict between the central power of the political state and the whole set of functions and authorities contained in church, family, gild, and local community has been, I believe, the main source of those dislocations of social structure and uprootings of status which lie behind the problem of community in our age. . . .
>
> The real conflict in modern political history has not been, as is so often stated, between State and individual, but between State and social group.[3]

The rise of the state and the extension of its activities into areas formerly monopolized by the family, the church, the village, and other intermediate associations, by robbing these organizations of their "functional relevance" (in Nisbet's term), has virtually insured their demise as vibrant institutions. The relationship between government and these organizations is thus seen exclusively in terms of conflict and displacement, not cooperation or mutual support.

This line of argument has been further elaborated by Peter Berger, John Neuhaus, and their colleagues in their work on the interaction between public policy and "mediating structures," including neighborhood, family, church, and voluntary associations. For Berger and Neuhaus, too, the government's impact on nonprofit organizations has been largely negative. The tendency of the government, in their view, is "to establish a state monopoly over all organized activities that have to do with more than strictly private purposes."[4] Expanded government activity, they claim, leads to restrictions on private providers, robs private agencies of clients, drains private agencies of volunteer labor by substituting paid employment for it, and reduces the felt need for private charitable contributions. All this results in a crowding out of the private resources that voluntary organizations need to operate. As Neuhaus and Theodore M. Kerrine put it, "The logical conclusion of our present course is that the state eventually becomes the sole provider of all social services."[5]

From here it follows logically that if the expansion of government has weakened voluntary organizations and other mediating structures, the contraction of government should stimulate their rebirth. Support for intermediate associations does not, in this view, require a positive program of action. It requires, rather, only the contraction of the state.

Voluntary Organizations in the Economic Recovery Program

This line of reasoning is reflected in the major features of the Reagan administration's Economic Recovery Program. The 1980 Republican platform, which provides the intellectual backdrop for this program, speaks pointedly of the need to "restore the family, the neighborhood, the community, and the workplace as vital alternatives in our national life to ever-expanding federal power." Federal activity, according to the platform writers, had largely functioned to "elbow aside private institutions." The corrective, therefore, is to get the federal government out of the way.

The Economic Recovery Program's strategy for reviving "the American spirit of voluntary service" thus consisted of the same two basic elements judged necessary to revive the economy: budget cuts and tax cuts. Support for the nonprofit sector was to be the fortuitous by-product of the administration's general economic strategy. Eleven months into the first year of the administration, a third element was added to this program—a volunteer task force on private sector initiatives and a special White House office on voluntarism. These three elements form the heart of the administration's program for strengthening voluntary organizations. The remainder of this section examines how the administration intends these measures to work. The next section then analyzes some of the negative impacts these and other measures of the administration also seem likely to have on nonprofit organizations.

Budget Cuts. The budget cuts proposed by the Reagan administration form the central part of its strategy to restore the private, nonprofit sector. The central thesis underlying the administration's position is that the federal government has inappropriately moved into fields that historically have been the exclusive preserve of private, nonprofit institutions, that it has displaced and undermined the private organizations operating in these fields and induced "excessive dependence on the federal government,"[6] and that, as a consequence, service to those in need has suffered. According to this theory, therefore, reducing federal involvement in these fields will greatly expand the opportunities available for action by private, nonprofit organizations.

The size of the opportunities to be so created for nonprofit organizations by the administration's budget proposals are large indeed. As reflected in table 7-2, the federal government expended $165.7 billion in FY 1981 on programs in fields where nonprofit organizations are active. This amount represented slightly more than one-fourth of all federal outlays and about one-third of all nondefense outlays. About 40 percent of this amount was allotted to the area of health, about 25 percent to needs-tested income assistance, about 15 percent to social welfare (including social services, employment and training, and community development), and 15 percent to education and research.

The initial budget that President Reagan submitted to Congress in March 1981 proposed substantial cuts in many programs of interest to nonprofit organizations, a considerable number of which were accepted by Congress.

TABLE 7–2

FEDERAL OUTLAYS IN FIELDS WHERE NONPROFIT ORGANIZATIONS ARE ACTIVE,
FY 1981 OUTLAYS

| | Outlays in 1981 | |
Program Area	In $ Billions	Percentage of Total
Social welfare	26.0	15.7
Social services	7.6	4.6
Employment and training	9.2	5.6
Community development	9.2	5.6
Education and research	24.6	14.8
Elementary and secondary	7.0	4.3
Higher education	12.3	7.4
Research and development	5.3	3.2
Health	64.6	39.0
Health finance	59.4	35.9
Health services	5.2	3.1
Income assistance	41.6	25.1
Housing	6.9	4.2
Cash	16.7	10.1
Food	15.3	9.2
Other	2.7	1.6
International aid	7.5	4.6
Arts and culture	0.7	0.4
Environment	0.6	0.4
Total	165.7	100.0

SOURCE: Authors' analysis of federal FY 1981 outlays as reported in the president's 1983
          budget.

In addition, the administration proposed further reductions in these programs
in its 1983 budget submitted to Congress in February 1982. As noted in table
7-3, these cuts are expected to reduce federal spending on programs of interest
to nonprofit organizations in FY 1982 by $11.3 billion below their 1981
levels, after adjusting for inflation. The further reductions proposed for FY
1983-1985 are even more severe. The administration wants to reduce spending
on programs of interest to nonprofit organizations by a total of $117.7 billion
(expressed in constant 1981 dollars) over the four years FY 1982-1985.

The areas of social welfare, and of education and research, are particularly hard hit. In 1981 funds allocated for these two areas accounted for 30
percent of federal spending for programs in fields where nonprofit organizations are active. However, these areas are to absorb 60 percent of the cuts
in these fields. As a result, spending in these areas is projected to be cut in
half in constant dollar terms between FY 1981 and FY 1985.

TABLE 7-3

PROJECTED CHANGES IN FEDERAL SPENDING IN FIELDS WHERE NONPROFIT ORGANIZATIONS ARE ACTIVE, FY 1981–FY1985

(In 1981 $ billions)

Program Area	Actual FY 1981	Estimated Reductions FY 1982[a]	Proposed Cuts[a]			Total FY 1982–85	Percentage Change FY 1985 vs. FY 1981
			FY 1983	FY 1984	FY 1985		
Social welfare	26.0	– 5.0	– 10.8	– 11.9	– 12.6	– 40.4	– 48
Education and research	24.6	– 2.3	– 6.7	– 10.1	– 11.8	– 30.9	– 48
Health	64.6	– 2.2	– 5.7	– 7.6	– 8.9	– 24.4	– 14
Income assistance	41.6	– 1.7	– 4.6	– 6.6	– 6.8	– 19.7	– 16
International aid	7.5	—	—	—	– 0.3	– 0.2	– 4
Arts and culture	0.7	—	– 0.1	– 0.2	– 0.3	– 0.6	– 38
Environment	0.6	– 0.1	– 0.4	– 0.5	– 0.5	– 1.5	– 92
Total	165.7	– 11.3	– 28.2	– 36.9	– 41.2	– 117.7	– 25

SOURCE: Office of Management and Budget, *1982 Budget* and *1983 Budget*; authors' analyses. For further discussion of methodology, see Lester M. Salamon with Alan J. Abramson, *The Federal Government and the Nonprofit Sector: Implications of the Reagan Budget Proposals* (Washington, D.C.: The Urban Institute, 1981).

a. Deflation calculations use the economic assumptions in the president's 1983 budget. A special deflator, based on administration estimates of health cost growth, was used to deflate projected outyear Medicare and Medicaid spending.

To put these reductions in context and gauge the relative scale of the opportunity they provide to nonprofit organizations, it is useful to compare the proposed cuts with the overall levels of nonprofit organizations' activity in the relevant areas. As table 7-4 shows, voluntary organizations in the social welfare and community development fields would have to expand their existing levels of activity almost 30 percent in FY 1982 to fill the gap created by the federal cutbacks. In FY 1983, by the same measure, the expansions in nonprofit organizations' activity would have to be approximately 5 percent in arts and culture, 30 percent in education and research, and 60 percent in social welfare and community development. Even if these figures are discounted somewhat in view of claims about waste, fraud, and abuse, the fact remains that the gap to be filled by nonprofit organizations is quite substantial and a major challenge to the sector.

Tax Cuts. Against this backdrop, the tax proposals that were a critical part of the Economic Recovery Program's economic strategy take on special meaning. These proposals, which were enacted in August 1981, were designed primarily to increase savings, investment, and, ultimately, economic growth. To this end, individual tax rates were reduced by a total of 23 percent in stages over three years; the maximum tax on unearned income was reduced from 70 percent to 50; the taxation of estates was greatly eased; and liberalized depreciation rules were introduced that promise to reduce corporate tax obligations considerably.

Leaving aside for the moment the extent to which individual taxpayers actually will realize any real net tax reductions once inflation and scheduled increases in Social Security taxes are accounted for, administration spokesmen argue that the tax provisions will substantially increase charitable giving. It will do so, in this view, in two ways: first, by stimulating economic growth and thereby increasing before-tax incomes; and second, by reducing tax obligations and thereby increasing the share of this income that is retained by the taxpayer and therefore made available for charitable giving. Faced with the increased need for charitable giving created by the budget cuts, taxpayers will respond—so the administration assumes—with substantially larger charitable contributions and voluntary support.

Task Force on Private Sector Initiatives. Although the administration first assumed that the hoped-for, positive response to charitable needs might come forth automatically, subsequent consideration led to a decision to nudge this response along by a combination of presidential exhortation and organized action commissioned by President Reagan. Accordingly, the president has taken two formal steps in an effort to implement the administration's hopes for expanded voluntary action. First, a small White House office on private sector initiatives has been established to provide a focal point for adminis-

TABLE 7-4

REDUCTIONS IN FEDERAL OUTLAYS IN COMPARISON WITH NONPROFIT EXPENDITURES IN FIELDS OF INTEREST TO NONPROFIT ORGANIZATIONS IN FY 1982 AND FY 1983

(In 1981 $ billions)

Field	Nonprofit Expenditures 1981	Budget Cuts FY 1982	FY 1982 Budget Cuts as Percentage of Nonprofit Expenditures	Budget Cuts FY 1983	FY 1983 Budget Cuts as Percentage of Nonprofit Expenditures
Social welfare and community development	18.5	− 5.1	28	− 11.2	61
Education and research	23.5	− 2.3	10	− 6.7	29
Health	76.3	− 2.2	3	− 5.7	7
Arts and culture	1.7	—	—	− 0.1	6
Total	120.0	− 9.6	8	− 23.7	20

SOURCE: Nonprofit expenditure data extrapolated from *1977 Census of Service Industries*. Budget cut data from table 7.3 grouped to correspond with Census classification scheme.

tration and presidential action in this sphere. Second, in December 1981 the president named a task force on private sector initiatives, headed by Armco Steel Chairman C. William Verity, Jr. This task force includes forty-three other leaders of business, foundations, and voluntary agencies and a small staff of personnel volunteered by private businesses. With a self-imposed one-year lifetime, the task force has set as its task the creation of mechanisms for encouraging private action to meet national and community needs. These steps have included setting goals for philanthropic contributions by corporations, fostering the establishment of counterpart local task forces to encourage community partnerships between the public and private sectors, amassing a data bank of innovative private sector initiatives, and identifying legal and other barriers to charitable contributions and private, voluntary action.

The Economic Recovery Program and the Nonprofit Sector: The Realities

The notion that budget cuts, tax cuts, and presidential exhortation will help promote private voluntary organizations may be fully consistent with conservative political theory. This theory considers the relationship between government and such organizations as essentially competitive; it sees in the expansion of government the displacement of private organizations and the crowding out of charitable resources; and it views the impact of tax rates on private giving solely as a function of the amount of income left in private hands. In practice, however, the relationship between the government and voluntary organizations is considerably more complicated. As a consequence, many of the measures advanced by the Reagan administration in the hopeful expectation that they will have positive consequences for the nonprofit sector seem likely to have negative consequences of even greater magnitude, reducing the revenues these organizations receive from public sources and dampening the growth of private giving. To understand these consequences, it is necessary to look more closely at the interaction between government programs and nonprofit organizations' action, at the impact of tax changes on private giving, and at other administration actions likely to affect the affairs of nonprofit organizations.

Nonprofit Federalism

The political theory underlying the Economic Recovery Program's treatment of nonprofit organizations assumes that the federal government is a powerful monolith, systematically extending its reach into all spheres of life and replacing voluntary organizations, as well as state and local officials, with federal bureaucrats. Most of the scholarly literature on federal operations, by contrast, pictures a far more fragmented institution, heavily dependent on other power centers in the society to help define and carry out its responsibilities. In the domestic sphere, at least, the federal government does very little by itself. Rather, it relies on a vast array of third parties—states, cities, counties, research institutes, banks, universities, community organizations, social service agencies, and the like—to carry out its responsibilities. The result is an elaborate pattern of ''third-party government'' that is the central fact of federal domestic operations.[7]

Nonprofit organizations have been major beneficiaries of this pattern of ''third-party government.'' Far from displacing nonprofit agencies, the growth of government involvement has frequently broadened their role and stabilized their fiscal base.

Illustrative of this is the partnership that has developed between government and the nonprofit sector in the field of social services. During much of the nineteenth century, the provision of social services was a responsibility shared by the voluntary sector and state and local governments. State activities focused generally on institutional care for the blind, the deaf, and the mentally or physically handicapped, while private agencies handled home care and direct assistance. When pressures mounted for improved care of the poor during the latter nineteenth century and the early twentieth century, the flow of public funds into the social services area increased. However, because of the political pressures exerted by leaders of voluntary organizations, the pervasive moralistic approach to poverty then in vogue, and a widespread distrust of government machinery among Progressive leaders, much of this increased funding flowed to and through voluntary organizations.[8]

This pattern persisted when the federal government entered the social services field in the 1960s. Prior to this time, federal activity in the field of social welfare was limited to financial support to selected categories of needy persons (the blind, the deaf, the disabled, and dependent children) channeled through state and local governments. Not until the early 1960s, with the adoption of the ''services strategy'' to break the cycle of poverty, did the federal government become a significant factor in the field of social services. As it did so, however, it made specific provision—in the 1962 amendments to the Social Security Act and even more so in the 1967 amendments—for state agencies to utilize federal funds to ''purchase'' such services from nonprofit providers. By 1971, purchased services constituted 25 percent of the services expenditures under the programs that preceded enactment of the Social Services Block Grant program (Title XX) in 1972. Since then, the share of federal social service funds contracted to nonprofit organizations has increased further, reaching 70 or 80 percent in some jurisdictions and some service areas.[9]

This pattern of government support of nonprofit organizations has followed a similar course in other fields as well—in health care, education, research, housing, community development, the arts, and international relief. In some cases, in fact, government programs have even encouraged the creation of whole new classes of nonprofit organizations where existing institutions were lacking, thus expanding the basic structure and diversity of the sector. Examples are community economic development organizations, multicounty economic development districts, research institutes, community mental health centers, and the community action agencies fostered by the poverty program.

These arrangements are not new inventions. To the contrary, partnerships between government and nonprofit organizations are rooted deeply in American history. Some of the nation's preeminent private, nonprofit institutions— such as Harvard University, Yale University, Massachusetts General Hospital, and the Metropolitan Museum of Art—owe their origins and early sustenance to public support. "Through most of American history," writes Waldemar Nielsen, the foremost student of this subject, "government has been an active partner and financier of the Third Sector to a much greater extent than is commonly recognized." Concludes Nielsen: "Collaboration, not separation or antagonism, between government and the Third Sector. . . . has been the predominant characteristic. Such intimate association has also, on the whole, proven to be highly productive."[10]

In short, an elaborate set of partnership arrangements has developed between government and nonprofit organizations. As currently structured, these arrangements take three basic forms, although an infinite variety of combinations and permutations is possible. First, assistance flows directly from the federal government to nonprofit organizations, as is the case with research grants to private universities. Second, assistance flows from the federal government to nonprofit organizations through state or local governments; the Title XX Social Services Block Grant program is an example. Finally, federal assistance to the nonprofit sector can flow through individuals in the form of in-kind assistance payments; this route prevails for Medicare.

In part because of this complexity, however, the extent of this interaction between the federal government and nonprofit organizations has been difficult to gauge with precision. No data are systematically collected on federal aid to nonprofit organizations. To gain a sense of the extent of this aid, therefore, it is necessary to piece together estimates program by program, drawing on available research and the insights of program managers.[11]

Table 7-5 records the results of such an effort. It shows that federal financal support to nonprofit organizations totaled $46.1 billion in FY 1981. This means that federal support accounted for about 38 percent of the income of the sector. By contrast, total private giving, exclusive of giving for sacramental religious purposes, amounted to $28.8 billion that same year. In other words, a broad-gauged system of public philanthropy has taken shape side by side with the system of private philanthropy, and the public system now provides a larger share of the resources of nonprofit organizations than all of private giving combined, whether from individuals, corporations, or foundations.[12]

This pattern of public support to nonprofit organizations varies, however, by type of organization, as table 7-5 also shows. Based on data on total expenditures of nonprofit organizations drawn from the 1977 Census of Service Industries, with projections to 1981, federal support to the sector varies from about 18 percent of total expenditures in the case of arts and cultural organizations to over 50 percent in the case of social welfare and community development organizations.[13]

These figures on government support of the nonprofit sector do not take account of the encouragement provided to charitable activity through the tax code. In particular, the deductions that individuals and corporations can claim for charitable donations represent an implicit subsidy to the sector estimated at $10.8 billion in 1981. Most of this support flows to those types of orga-

TABLE 7–5

FEDERAL GOVERNMENT SUPPORT AS A SHARE OF TOTAL NONPROFIT REVENUES, EXCLUDING RELIGION, 1981

(In $ billions)

Type of Organization	*Federal Government Support*	*Total Expenditures*	*Federal Government as Percentage of Total*
Social welfare and community development	9.6	18.5	51.9
Education and research	6.2	23.5	26.4
Health	29.9	76.3	39.2
Arts and culture	0.3	1.7	17.6
Other	—	1.7	—
Total	46.1	121.7	37.9

SOURCE: For expenditure data, see notes for table 7–4. For the methodology used to calculate federal support for nonprofits, see Salamon with Abramson, *The Federal Government and the Nonprofit Sector.*

nizations that rely most heavily on private support and receive the least direct public revenues.

In short, an extensive and complex pattern of "nonprofit federalism" has evolved in this country, linking government and nonprofit organizations in partnership arrangements to serve human needs. Far from displacing nonprofit organizations, the federal government has come to rely on them extensively to carry out the functions the public has called on it to perform. To be sure, the resulting relationships are not without their tensions and strains. Involvement in government programs subjects nonprofit organizations to crosscutting federal regulations and fiscal controls. It also requires greater management control and probably contributes to bureaucratization. However, what little empirical research has been done on the issue does not support the view that involvement with government grossly distorts the agencies' goals or destroys their independence. One study of 155 agencies affiliated with the Greater New York Fund/United Way, for example, recorded little change in the agencies' core programs as a result of the acceptance of government funds.[14] A related study of voluntary social welfare agencies in California reached a similar conclusion: ". . . the impact of government funds in controlling voluntary social service organizations may be much less than is commonly believed. . . . Generally agencies did what they always wanted to do, but for which they previously lacked the means."[15]

In short, the tensions that exist in this set of relationships occur within a framework that also has much to recommend it. These relationships blend public purposes with private capabilities and put publicly generated resources at the disposal of private voluntary institutions to address democratically defined community needs. Thus, they represent one of the more innovative and important American contributions to the practice of government.

Nonprofit Federalism and the Reagan Budget

Viewed against this backdrop, the budget cuts intended to expand the opportunities for action by private, nonprofit organizations are likely to have another, far different, effect. They will reduce the resources that nonprofit organizations have available even to provide their existing levels of service. In fact, as shown in table 7-6, nonprofit organizations' revenues from federal sources are estimated to decline by $3.7 billion (in 1981 dollars) between FY 1981 and FY 1982. Moreover, based on the administration's budget proposals for subsequent years these revenue losses would accelerate, to the point that they would total $35.3 billion over the entire FY 1982-1985 period. Particularly hard hit by these cuts would be social service and community development organizations, which would lose the equivalent of about 60 percent

TABLE 7-6

PROJECTED CHANGES IN REVENUES OF NONPROFIT ORGANIZATIONS FROM FEDERAL SOURCES, FY 1981–FY 1985

(*In 1981 $ billions*)

Type of Organization	Actual FY 1981	Reductions Estimated FY 1982[a]	Proposed Cuts[a]			Total FY 1982–1985	Percentage Change FY 1985 vs. FY 1981
			FY 1983	FY 1984	FY 1985		
Social services	6.6	– 1.6	– 3.6	– 3.8	– 4.1	– 13.1	– 61
Community development	2.2	– 0.3	– 1.0	– 1.4	– 1.3	– 4.0	– 59
Education and research	6.2	– 0.6	– 1.3	– 1.9	– 2.2	– 6.0	– 36
Health	29.9	– 1.0	– 2.5	– 3.4	– 4.1	– 11.1	– 14
International aid	0.8	– 0.1	– 0.1	– 0.2	– 0.2	– 0.5	– 23
Arts and culture	0.3	– 0.1	– 0.1	– 0.2	– 0.2	– 0.5	– 61
Total	46.1	– 3.7	– 8.6	– 11.0	– 12.1	– 35.3	– 26

SOURCE: *1982 Budget* and *1983 Budget*; authors' analyses. For further discussion of methodology, see Salamon with Abramson, *The Federal Government and the Nonprofit Sector.*

a. Deflation calculations use the economic assumptions in the president's 1983 budget. A special deflator, based on administration estimates of health cost growth, was used to deflate outyear Medicare and Medicaid spending.

of their federal support between 1981 and 1985. As noted earlier, however, these types of organizations receive the largest shares of their income from federal sources. Thus, they face the greatest potential increase in demand for their services as a consequence of the overall budget reductions.

To put these proposed reductions in nonprofit organizations' revenues into even clearer perspective, it is useful to compare them with the existing levels of private charitable contributions and to ask what level of increase in private giving would be needed to compensate for the budget cuts and inflation and thus allow nonprofit organizations to maintain the same level of activity they achieved in 1981 over the subsequent four years. As shown in table 7-7, the rate of increase needed would be considerably higher than the highest increase to date—the 12 percent increase in nonreligious private giving in 1981. In fact, during the period 1983 to 1985 the rate of increase needed in private giving would be three to four times this record level.

In short, the reduction of federal activity has provided some new opportunities for nonprofit organizations in the fields in which they operate, but these opportunities are substantially offset by the severe revenue losses these organizations will experience in the process. As a consequence, many nonprofit organizations will have serious difficulty maintaining existing levels of activity, let alone taking advantage of expanded opportunities.

TABLE 7-7

LEVELS OF INCREASE IN PRIVATE GIVING REQUIRED TO HOLD NONPROFIT
ORGANIZATIONS AT 1981 SPENDING LEVELS AFTER TAKING ACCOUNT OF INFLATION
AND BUDGET CUTS, 1982–1985
(In $ billions)

	Private Giving in Previous Year[a]	Estimated Revenue Loss to Nonprofit Organizations	Percentage Increase in Private Giving Needed to Maintain Existing Value of Private Support and Offset Lost Federal Revenue[b]
1982	28.8	− 4.1	22.1
1983	32.3	− 10.2	37.6
1984	36.3	− 14.1	43.8
1985	40.8	− 16.7	45.6

SOURCE: Data on private giving are from *Giving U.S.A., 1982 Annual Report* (New York: American Association of Fund-Raising Counsel, Inc., 1982). For sources for data on revenue loss to nonprofits, see table 7–6.

  a.   Assumes giving will continue to grow at 1981 rate of 12.3 percent annually for nonreligious organizations.

  b.   Using economic assumptions in the administration's FY 1983 budget.

Taxes and Private Giving

Complicating the picture further is the fact that the administration's expectations about the positive impacts of its proposed tax cuts on private giving also overlook an important point: Levels of private giving are affected not only by the income that is available but also by the "cost" of contributing that income to charity.

Admittedly, the concept of the "cost," or "price," of giving is complex. But it is a familiar concept to tax lawyers and accountants and has been firmly established empirically through more than fifteen years of economic research.[16] The central notion is that because charitable contributions are tax deductible for taxpayers who itemize their deductions, the out-of-pocket cost of giving a dollar to charity for such taxpayers is really less than a dollar. How much less depends on the taxpayer's tax bracket. For a person in the 70 percent tax bracket, for example, the out-of-pocket cost of contributing a dollar to charity is really only 30 cents, since the government would have taxed 70 cents of the dollar anyway had the taxpayer not given it to charity. If the tax rate for that taxpayer were to fall to 50 percent, however, the out-of-pocket cost of contributing that same dollar to charity would then be 50 cents, or two-thirds higher.

To say that levels of giving are responsive to the tax-related "cost" of giving is not, of course, to say that other factors are not involved. After all, since giving still "costs" something even for persons in the highest tax brackets, other factors must be involved in decisions to give to charity—for example, feelings of attachment to particular institutions, a desire to do good, moral and religious convictions, and a host of other factors. However, a substantial body of research has established that price plays a role and cannot be ignored in any serious evaluation of the consequences of tax changes on private giving.

The 1981 Economic Recovery Tax Act has a number of features that raise the cost of giving in this way. These include a phased reduction of individual tax rates of 23 percent between October 1981 and July 1983, a reduction in the maximum tax on unearned income from 70 percent to 50 percent, a reduction in the capital gains tax rate, a thoroughgoing liberalization of estate taxation, and the effective lowering of corporation taxes through liberalized depreciation rules. At the same time, the act contained one provision lowering the cost of giving, in stages, for taxpayers who do not itemize deductions; it will permit them to claim deductions for charitable contributions even if they do not itemize their other deductions.

For a clear understanding of the impact of the 1981 tax act on private giving, therefore, it is necessary to take account of a number of different factors at once: the increased before-tax and after-tax income the act is supposed to create as a direct consequence of lower tax rates; the increase in the cost of giving these lowered tax rates will also produce; the gradual opening of an above-the-line charitable deduction for taxpayers who do not itemize deductions; and the fact that the number of taxpayers who itemize deductions increases as incomes rise.

Table 7-8 records the results of such an analysis, focusing on individual contributions, which make up 83 percent of all private giving. The table compares the probable levels of such giving under the 1981 law with what would have occurred had the old law remained in force.[17] This table shows that, compared with the previous law, the 1981 law is likely to dampen the growth of giving by private individuals, even under the optimistic economic assumptions originally advanced by the Reagan administration. Although giving by private individuals is projected to increase in absolute terms under the new law, the increase will be significantly slower than under the previous law, so that by 1984 nonprofit organizations will end up with contributions that are $18 billion less in actual dollar terms, and $10 billion less in constant 1980 dollar terms, than they would have been.

The 1981 tax law does not only affect the aggregate amount of private giving. Because the tax rate changes affect upper-income taxpayers more than lower-income ones, the act also seems likely to alter the distribution of charitable giving, increasing the share of lower- and middle-income taxpayers from 56 to 61 percent and reducing the share provided by upper-income taxpayers from 44 to 39 percent. Because taxpayers in different income brackets have different patterns of charitable giving, these shifts in the distribution

TABLE 7–8

PROJECTED PRIVATE INDIVIDUAL GIVING UNDER THE 1981 TAX LAW AND
PRE-1981 LAW, 1981–1984
(In $ billions)

	Actual Dollars			1980 Dollars		
Year	Pre-1981 Law	1981 Law	Difference	Pre-1981 Law	1981 Law	Difference
1981	45.0	44.5	− 0.5	40.8	40.5	−0.3
1982	52.4	49.1	− 3.3	43.4	41.3	−2.1
1983	60.2	54.7	− 5.5	46.0	42.9	−3.1
1984	70.5	61.5	− 9.0	49.9	45.5	−4.4
Total	228.1	209.8	−18.3	180.1	170.2	−9.9

SOURCE: Charles T. Clotfelter and Lester M. Salamon, "The Impact of the 1981 Tax Act on Charitable Giving," *National Tax Journal*, June 1982.

of the burden of giving are likely to affect different groups of recipients differently. In particular, lower- and middle-income taxpayers tend to give a higher proportion of each dollar of charitable contributions to religious organizations than do higher-income taxpayers. An increased share of total private individual giving provided by lower- and middle-income taxpayers thus translates into a larger than proportionate increase in giving to churches and a considerable slowing or reduction of giving to organizations traditionally supported more heavily by the wealthy, such as hospitals, educational institutions, and arts groups.

To be sure, the analysis presented here assumes that the relationships between income levels, the tax-related costs of giving, and giving levels that prevailed in the recent past will persist into the foreseeable future. In practice, however, these relationships could change in response to presidential exhortation or the realization that needs are greater as a result of the reduction in public sector support.[18] Nevertheless, the clear implication of the analysis presented here is that the optimistic assessments of the consequences of the 1981 tax act for charitable contributions must be tempered considerably to take account of the full impacts this act is likely to have. Consideration of other features of the law that are likely to discourage private giving, such as the liberalization of estate taxation and the easing of the "pay-out" requirement imposed in 1969 on private foundations would reinforce this view.

Postal Rates and the Combined Federal Campaign

In addition to the budget cuts and tax cuts analyzed, the Economic Recovery Program is also likely to affect nonprofit organizations in two other ways—by changing the rates on nonprofit bulk mail and by altering the "donor option" provisions in the important "Combined Federal Campaign" solicitation.

Postal Rates. Thanks to a special federal subsidy, nonprofit organizations pay lower rates than commercial organizations for second-class mail (periodicals), third-class mail (bulk advertising and solicitations), and fourth-class mail (books). Particularly important to nonprofit organizations are the lower rates for third-class mail because they apply to a large proportion of their mailings (about 8.6 billion of the 9.8 billion non-first-class pieces mailed by nonprofit organizations in FY 1981 were third-class mail) and because they directly affect their direct-mail fund raising.

As part of the budget package submitted to Congress in March 1981, the Reagan administration proposed to cut the subsidy for these reduced rates by 37 percent. As a result of congressional action on this request, the Postal Service was forced in January 1982 to raise the rates nonprofit organizations must pay for basic presorted third-class mail from 3.8 cents per piece to 5.9 cents, an increase of 55 percent.

For many nonprofit organizations, especially those that rely on direct-mail solicitations, the effect of this postal rate increase may be far greater than the effects of the budget cuts themselves. The March of Dimes, for example, spends about 8 percent of its budget on mailings. At a time of increased pressures on nonprofit organizations to raise funds from private sources, the postal rate hike adds another burden.

Combined Federal Campaign. A final impact of the Reagan admin-istration on the nonprofit sector, important for symbolic as well as for sub-stantive reasons, concerns a proposed change in the regulations governing the federal government's own work place charitable solicitation, the Combined Federal Campaign (CFC). Over the past decade, major inroads have been made by nontraditional charities representing minorities, women, environ-mental concerns, and other causes to secure eligibility to receive funds gen-erated through the CFC. The vehicle for this advance was an administrative arrangement that vested local control over the CFC in a group of four char-ities—United Way, National Health Agencies, International Services Agen-cies, and National Service Agencies—that allocated undesignated funds according to a formula based on past years' experiences and that allowed local independent agencies to participate in the CFC.

Under a draft executive order promulgated by the Office of Personnel Management in March 1982, however, these features of the CFC would change. First, authority for the local campaign would be vested in a single Principal Combined Fund Organization. In the vast majority of cases, this organization would be the United Way. Second, the undesignated funds would no longer be distributed according to formula but would be distributed on a discretionary basis by this Principal Combined Fund Organization. Finally, local independent charities would not be permitted to participate in the CFC unless they were affiliated with a national federation.

Because the Combined Federal Campaign is the largest single work place charity drive in the nation, these changes could have significant effects on a number of charities. More than that, opponents fear that they could set an unfortunate example for other work place drives, an example that runs counter to long-standing efforts to open work place solicitation to groups beyond the traditional ones normally embraced within local United Ways. Since many of these groups will be losing public funds, the argument is that they should have freer access, not more restricted access, to work place solicitations.

In final regulations issued as this book goes to goes to press, these changes have been somewhat modified. Nevertheless, the residue of ill-will created by this incident is likely to linger.

The Impact in Reality: Early Indications

The ultimate impact of these budget and tax changes on nonprofit organizations cannot, of course, be determined at this point. For one thing, advance funding and ongoing agency contracts have delayed somewhat the impact of the budget decisions already taken, while other decisions are still only pending. In addition, state and local governments are still sorting through the changes in federal funding levels and program structures, delaying further any clear sense of the impact on nonprofit organizations and those they serve. Finally, the talk of retrenchment and the limited evidence of impact to date has stimulated a willingness to try new approaches, to reach out to volunteers, to approach new funding sources, to develop joint service arrangements, and so on. In some places, these new approaches seem to be having a noticeable effect on agency operations, easing somewhat the effects of the funding cutbacks on agencies and their clients.

Although the full picture of the consequences of the Reagan administration's policies for nonprofit organizations is not yet clear, some early indications of the impacts are evident. For one thing, private funding sources in all parts of the country report a massive surge in applications from nonprofit organizations. Applications for funding at the Atlantic Richfield Corporation, for example, increased by 100 percent between 1980 and 1981. A request for proposals for research and action projects from the Department of Health and Human Services elicited some 8,000 responses, many of them from nonprofit agencies seeking aid to carry on their program activities.

Beyond this increase in the volume of proposals to private funding sources, the nonprofit sector has faced a steady diet of layoffs, reduced time, and belt tightening. Community arts organizations, which had relied heavily on CETA workers, were among the earliest affected directly by the cuts, but community-based organizations and many main-line social welfare agencies are now severely feeling the pinch as well. Finally, throughout the sector there is a pervasive and debilitating sense of uncertainty which has disrupted planning, demoralized staff, and left the viability of many agencies in serious question.

To be sure, these negative signs are countered by positive evidence of innovation, of closer ties to the private corporate sector, of greater local activism and concern, and of enhanced voluntary action. Impressive as they are, however, these positive signs do not approach in magnitude the financial impact on the sector resulting from the funding cutbacks already approved at the federal level or still under consideration.

Conclusions

Whatever its ultimate effect, the Economic Recovery Program has served the useful purpose of raising for public attention and debate the fundamental question of the appropriate roles of government and private voluntary agencies in serving human needs in the latter part of the twentieth century. The Economic Recovery Program is based on a political theory that posits a necessary conflict between government and private, nonprofit agencies. To encourage action by nonprofit organizations, therefore, the Economic Recovery Program proposes to reduce the federal government's presence.

What this approach overlooks, however, are the numerous ways in which government in the United States assists nonprofit organizations and contributes to their economic health. As a result, measures intended to aid these organizations may end up significantly weakening them instead. In particular, while increasing the need for nonprofit services, the Economic Recovery Program seems likely to reduce significantly the resources available to these organizations to meet their existing responsibilities. In the areas of social welfare and community development, in fact, the administration's budget would substantially dismantle the partnership arrangements that have been forged over several decades between the federal government and the nonprofit sector. To compensate nonprofit organizations for the resulting loss of government support would require a tripling or quadrupling of historic rates of private giving, something few close observers, even those most enthusiastic about the private sector, believe is likely. The 1981 tax act, far from encouraging private giving, seems likely, on balance, to restrain its growth, especially once the effects of indexation of tax rates takes hold in 1985. The prospect, in short, is for a period of significant fiscal strain for the sector, and for the crippling of important components of the sector—in particular, community-based organizations.

These strains could be relieved, of course, by a surge of voluntarism, by new approaches to service delivery and to the use of philanthropic resources, and by increased private support for nonprofit institutions. However, it will probably be necessary to rethink the issue: Is the dismantling of the government-nonprofit organization partnership really consistent with the long-run goals of the Economic Recovery Program? Perhaps it would be better to accept this partnership and seek ways to improve it, while preserving the essential private, voluntary character of these organizations. Such an approach is consistent with the conclusion of the Commission on Private Philanthropy and Public Needs (the Filer Commission) that ''government support for much nonprofit activity is an indisputable fact of life that must be lived with and reckoned with.''[19] Interestingly enough, moreover, it is also consistent with the view of John Neuhaus and Peter Berger, of the American Enterprise Institute, who criticize government for harming the sector, yet see the possibility for an enlightened and sensitive public policy "designed to enhance mediating structures and the pluralism that mediating structures make possible."[20] Finally, it is consistent with the position of President Reagan's task force on private sector initiatives, which has launched a concerted effort to encourage "community partnerships" involving the public as well as the private sectors to respond to community and national needs.

In short, the best approach to our national problems may not lie in the strict separation of the sectors. It may lie, rather, in improving the innovative partnership arrangements that have taken shape haphazardly and often sloppily over the past several decades, that are filled with strains and irrationalities, but that nevertheless have much to recommend them. Whatever else the Economic Recovery Program does, if the shock it has administered to these partnership arrangements serves to improve their basic structure and operation, it will have made a major contribution to the functioning of American society.

PART THREE

THE SHIFT IN SOCIAL POLICY

Chapter 8

EMPLOYMENT, TRAINING, AND ECONOMIC DEVELOPMENT

Marc Bendick, Jr.

The Reagan administration's initiatives in the fields of employment, training, and economic development have been among the most far-reaching of any aspect of domestic policy. If President Reagan's budget proposals for FY 1983 are accepted, employment and training will experience a 63 percent reduction in outlays between 1981 and 1986, the largest percentage cut in any category of domestic programs (see chapter 3, table 3-6). The administration's policy changes have included eliminating a Public Service Employment program serving more than 300,000 disadvantaged adults; proposing to cut federal expenditures for training by several billion dollars per year; cutting in half the activities of the federal-state Job Service; seeking to end regional development activities costing more than half a billion dollars per year; and proposing a market-oriented approach—called enterprise zones—for spurring growth in economically distressed locales.

These initiatives reflect the administration's belief that a healthy private economy is an effective substitute for direct government action in addressing social problems such as the labor market difficulties faced by low-skilled adults, disadvantaged youth, and residents of economically distressed areas. The administration has stated that one of its objectives is to ameliorate the high unemployment, low wages, and other labor market handicaps experienced by such groups. However, it believes that government programs often hinder rather than advance these objectives; thus, it proposes a fundamentally different strategy.

The purpose of this chapter is to describe the administration's proposed and actual changes in employment, training, and economic development programs and to consider their likely effects.[1] The first section of the chapter describes the nature of the structural employment problems these programs have been designed to address, and the second section examines the ability of the private economy to ameliorate them. A third section examines the effectiveness of three approaches used in the past to address these problems. The final section of the chapter provides some conclusions.

Those conclusions can be summarized as follows. First, although structural employment problems diminish during periods of general economic prosperity, this "trickle down" effect is by no means sufficient. Past experience teaches that economic prosperity and targeted programs must act as complements, not substitutes, to improve the situation of disadvantaged workers. Second, some of the changes proposed by the administration will reallocate resources in ways that should improve program performance. However, the major effect of these changes will be to reduce the level of resources devoted to these programs despite the fact that these resources were being used cost effectively. In reducing expenditures for employment, training, and economic development, the Reagan administration has adopted a strategy that seems oddly out of step with several important social goals. Some of these goals—such as increased earnings for low-income families—may not be important in the administration's list of priorities. But others goals—such as economic growth, full employment without inflation, and reduction of welfare dependency—stand high on the administration's agenda.

The Nature of Structural Employment Problems

Among the approximately 130 million persons of working age in the United States, there is a wide variation in both earnings capacity and employment opportunities. Some persons experience high wages and fringe benefits, job security, and fulfilling work activities. Others experience low wages; recurrent or sustained unemployment; work that is unpleasant, boring, or dangerous; and few opportunities for advancement.

To a large extent, such differences do not represent social or economic problems and do not call for a government response. To the extent that they reflect differences in native ability or work effort, for example, American society largely accepts such differences in rewards. But where the unfavorable experiences of workers reflect circumstances beyond a person's control, such as racial discrimination, or lead to unacceptably low incomes for workers and their families, resulting in welfare dependency, then differences in labor market outcomes may become matters of public concern.

Prominent Target Groups

Three partially overlapping groups have traditionally been thought of as overburdened by such labor market difficulties and have consequently been targets of government attention: low-skilled adults, disadvantaged youth, and residents of economically depressed areas.[2]

Low-skilled Adults. Some adults are handicapped in the labor market by their lack of job credentials, training, experience, and contacts, and, in some cases, by their lack of work habits and motivation. Such problems tend to be concentrated among members of minority groups, women, and persons with special handicaps (for example, physical disabilities or the inability to speak or understand English).

Estimates of the number of adults who experience serious and persistent labor market handicaps vary with the definitions used to identify them. However, the estimates in one recent study can be cited as typical of the orders of magnitude involved. In that study, it was found that about 5 percent of all male adult heads of families and 67 percent of all female heads of families were consistently in the lowest 10 percent of the male earnings distribution.[3] These numbers correspond to about 5 million individuals, or about 5 percent of the U.S. labor force.

This lack of labor market success can be considered a social problem for four reasons. First, low earnings typically mean that the worker and his or her family live at a socially unacceptable level of total income. For example, a family of three whose sole source of income is one worker employed at the federal minimum wage of $3.35 per hour will remain below the poverty line even if that worker is employed full time. When such a worker leaves the job market and must be supported by public assistance, costs are imposed on taxpayers. Employment programs are thus used, in part, to make public assistance a less attractive alternative. Second, there are additional costs to society because of the loss of production that the person would have generated if employed. Third, American society values work apart from the income and production it generates. Work, it is felt, makes individuals stable citizens, good role models for their children, and contributing members of society. Finally, many low-skilled adult workers are members of minority groups. In their case, discrimination, both past and present, is one reason for their lack of labor market credentials and labor market success. For them, adult employment and training initiatives are used to compensate for past and present injustices.

Disadvantaged Youth. Unemployment rates among teenagers and young adults have always been higher than those among adult workers, and younger workers' wages are substantially lower than those for adults. These differences are, for the most part, not serious problems because they tend to disappear as young workers mature and become more experienced. However, some groups of younger workers face more serious problems. For example, in 1980, when the unemployment rate among white teenagers was 16 percent, it was 23 percent among Hispanic teenagers, 39 percent among black teenagers, and 45 percent among black teenagers living in poverty sections of metropolitan areas. About 75 percent of the total weeks of unemployment experienced by all youth in 1977 was concentrated among only 8 percent of those seeking work. This group facing persistent unemployment represents about 2 million younger workers.[4]

The labor market difficulties of these youth have traditionally been a focus of social concern. If a young person fails to make a good initial connection with the labor market, a vicious circle may be set in motion. He or she may develop bad work attitudes and habits, as well as a poor work record, and become increasingly unemployable. Improved initial labor market experiences may therefore have a high payoff throughout the adult years. In addition, providing employment opportunities to that group is sometimes seen as a way to reduce street crime and social unrest. Finally, many employment problems of disadvantaged youth arise from the failure of the public schools to prepare them adequately for the world of work. Although the long-run solution to this problem may be to reform the school system, in the absence of such reform the employment and training system is called on to remedy these deficiencies.

Residents of Economically Distressed Areas. There are two types of locations in the U.S. where residents have difficulty finding employment because job opportunities are scarce. One is economically distressed inner cities; the other is regions experiencing long-term economic decline.

The federal government has made special job development efforts for residents of these areas for two reasons. First, many persons in American society—perhaps the majority—have deep roots in their home communities. An involuntary move away from family, friends, and familiar surroundings in search of employment may impose severe psychological, as well as financial, costs. Second, when workers do abandon locales of low opportunity, they leave behind underutilized capital infrastructure, both public and private, that must be duplicated in the new location. The costs of this duplication are one reason to reemploy workers where they currently live. Recognizing these circumstances, the federal government has become involved in "moving jobs to people" as an alternative to moving people to jobs.

The employment difficulties faced by these three groups of workers suggest a variety of rationales for government action. One is the failure of the private labor market to develop and utilize human resources efficiently. Another is concern about the distribution of income and employment opportunities. Still a third is the government's failure to solve recurring problems in areas of public responsibility such as education, income maintenance, or discrimination. All these reasons together make one point clear, however. The federal government has become involved because private labor market outcomes proved socially unacceptable. Each of these failures has to be considered in evaluating the assertion that a healthy private economy alone can effectively address the nation's structural employment problems.

To What Extent Can Prosperity Solve Structural Employment Problems?

Faith in the benefits of economic growth and prosperity is at the heart of the Reagan administration's approach to employment, training, and economic development programs:

> The past decade of deteriorating national economic performance has been accompanied by a rapid build-up of Federal grants and other subsidies designed to alleviate the effects of that deterioration on specific segments of the population and economy. Federal programs have thus been created and expanded in the name of stimulating growth, jobs, . . . and in other ways to alter and fine-tune the level and composition of national economic activity. Many of these programs, however, have served to distort the market economy and have thereby contributed as much to the problems they were intended to address as to their solution. . . . The President's budget and comprehensive economic plan approach the real problems associated with deteriorating economic performance from a fundamentally different premise. . . . The President's plan contemplates severe reductions in make-work job programs . . . and regional and community development subsidies, as well as a host of other misdirected spending and subsidy programs. In the context of a healthy expanding economy, stable financial markets and a revival of savings, investment, and entrepreneurship, normal market forces will be relied upon to achieve present program goals.[5]

To what extent can these "normal market forces" actually be relied on to redress the labor market difficulties catalogued?

The evidence is clear that, to some extent, a rising economic tide does lift all boats. That is, some of the benefits of general economic prosperity do "trickle down" to the lowest income groups and to those having difficulty in the labor market. During the period 1963 to 1975, when real per capita income increased by 31 percent, the proportion of households with total incomes below the poverty line declined from nearly 22 percent to just under 14 percent.[6] While some of the decline is attributable to the expansion in public transfer benefits, much of it resulted from the earnings gain of low-income workers.

One reason for such a decline is that hard-to-employ and disadvantaged workers benefit from the high employment rates that accompany economic prosperity. Approximately three-quarters of poor persons younger than sixty-five have some wage and salary income. A lower unemployment rate helps them directly by providing jobs for those who are unemployed and providing full-time jobs for those involuntarily employed part time. In the longer run, a tighter labor market provides additional benefits to these groups. It brings back into the labor force workers who, in times of high unemployment, are discouraged from looking for work. It raises wages, improves working conditions, and creates training and advancement opportunities as employers compete for workers. It allows workers to accumulate seniority and unemployment insurance coverage.

Indeed, several studies have shown that disadvantaged groups in the labor market have a larger proportional stake in the cyclical prosperity of the economy than do middle-class workers because disadvantaged workers are more vulnerable to firms' changing labor needs. It has been estimated that for every one percent change in the national unemployment rate, the unemployment rate for white males who are heads of families in poverty changes 1.3 percent, and the rate for black males who are heads of families in poverty changes 1.6 percent.[7] A one percent reduction in the national unemployment rate can bring about 1.5 million persons out of poverty.[8] A reduction in the national unemployment rate from 7 percent to 3 percent (a very low rate), would, according to one estimate, increase nonwhite median family income from 50 percent of the corresponding white income to 60 percent.[9]

However consistent these findings are with the administration's faith, the limitations of this approach must also be noted. One direct indication of the resistant nature of structural employment problems is their persistence throughout the business cycle. Even when the economy is in a period of high overall employment, rising wages, and general prosperity, the relative disadvantages described earlier do not disappear. Consider, for example, the unemployment experience of various groups in comparison to white males between the ages of thirty-five and forty-four. During the period 1948 to 1977, the nation experienced several periods of prosperity and recession. Even in periods of prosperity, the smallest difference ever observed between the unemployment rate of white males and that of minority males was 2.3

points. During the same period, the unemployment rate among minorities averaged about twice that of whites, with even larger differences for teenagers.[10] Moreover, there is evidence that the gaps between advantaged and disadvantaged groups may be widening over time, further insulating disadvantaged workers from the benefits of general prosperity.[11]

The reason that these differences do not disappear is that employers can incur additional costs when they hire structurally disadvantaged workers. Welfare mothers, low-income minority teenagers, and similar persons are often more expensive to train and supervise and are less productive than are more "mainstream" employees. Inner-city ghetto neighborhoods or isolated rural areas are less efficient places to locate plants and offices than are pleasant suburban locales. In light of their primary responsibility to corporate stockholders to minimize costs and generate profits, private employers generally are not willing to make employment decisions that threaten production efficiency, however important the social goal that might be promoted. Thus, firms hire mainstream workers first and disadvantaged workers only as a last resort in very tight labor markets.

But labor markets tight enough to offer extensive opportunities for disadvantaged workers also generate inflation. Economists now estimate that an unemployment rate as high as 7 or 8 percent may be necessary to prevent acceleration in the rate of inflation.[12] The current high unemployment rate is tolerated, at least in part, because it is viewed as a means of preventing price rises. Disadvantaged workers bear a disproportionate share of the costs associated with high unemployment, and government programs targeted to their labor market difficulties thus represent an attempt to improve their employment prospects without imposing inflation on society as a whole.

Finally, it should be noted that these estimates of gains associated with prosperity refer to changes that occur when the economy recovers from recessions. They do not refer to the effects of long-run economic growth, which is the focus of much of the Reagan administration's hopes for the poor and disadvantaged. What few estimates are available of the poor's stake in long-run growth indicate that it is, at best, proportionate.[13]

Another way to place in perspective the efficacy of the "trickle down" approach is to compare it to the effects of alternative policies targeted directly to disadvantaged workers. The impact of targeted initiatives is substantially higher than that of across-the-board macroeconomic stimulation. For example, one recent study compared the number of jobs created for long-term unemployed workers by an across-the-board tax cut generating general prosperity and by a government public service employment program targeted specifically to these workers. This comparison concluded that, per dollar of federal deficit, about twice as many jobs could be created for the long-term unemployed through direct government action as through jobs trickling down from aggregate prosperity.[14]

The truth about the stake of disadvantaged workers in national economic progress, however, is not to be found in analyses comparing aggregate growth and targeted government initiatives as alternatives. Ultimately, the two approaches are necessary complements. For example, general economic prosperity generates job opportunities for the graduates of government training programs, while the training programs ready workers for these opportunities. Similarly, government efforts to develop employment in distressed locales are difficult to initiate when even prosperous locales are experiencing recession; but without such efforts, recovery of the general economy tends to bypass the depressed areas. Thus, a high-employment, high-growth economy is something in which disadvantaged workers, as well as everyone else in the nation, have a stake. However, prosperity alone is not sufficient to ensure progress among persons at a competitive disadvantage in the labor market. Employment, training, and economic development programs form a necessary spout through which general prosperity trickles down to such people.

The Administration's Policy Initiatives

In its policies—as distinguished from its rhetoric—the Reagan administration has given some recognition to this complementarity. It has not attempted to eliminate all federal employment, training, and economic development initiatives. However, it has proposed (and, in large part, achieved) major reductions in their levels of funding and major changes in their structure and operations. Table 8-1 provides an overview of selected budgetary changes achieved by the administration for FY 1982 and proposed for FY 1983. The table indicates that, if the administration's proposals for 1983 were to be adopted, federal obligations for employment, training, and economic development would fall more than 60 percent over the administration's first two years. Because of inflation, the decline in real service levels would be even greater.

Following is a description and evaluation of these changes in three program areas: job creation, training and placement, and economic development.

Job Creation in the Public Sector

That the government should act as an employer of last resort for the unemployed is an idea with precedents from time immemorial. In Elizabethan England, for example, public workhouses for the poor were created to require

TABLE 8-1

FEDERAL OBLIGATIONS FOR SELECTED EMPLOYMENT, TRAINING, AND ECONOMIC DEVELOPMENT PROGRAMS
(FY 1981–FY 1983)

	Federal Obligations (In $ millions)			Percentage Change 1981–1983
	FY 1981 (actual)	FY 1982 (estimated)	FY 1983 (proposed)	
Employment and training				
Comprehensive Employment and Training	3,692.3	1,779.4	395.7	
Special programs for youth	1,695.4	1,695.4	237.2	
Other nationally administered programs	426.8	469.1	82.3	
Private sector programs	272.4	266.5	62.6	
Training grants to states (proposed)	a	a	900.0	
Job Corps	a	a	320.0	
Special targeted programs	a	a	180.00	
Employment service (grants to states)	781.4	428.89	408.5	
Community Service Program for Older Americans	267.0	58.2	.0	
Work Incentives (WIN) program	371.0	231.8	11.1	
Total	7,506.3	4,929.2	2,597.4	−65.4
Economic development				
Economic development grants	257.9	130.0	.0	
Loans and loan guarantees	86.1	.0	.0	
Local public works	82.8	60.4	30.0	
Regional Development Program	31.6	3.7	.0	
Appalachian Regional Commission[b]	95.1	72.6	4.0	
Urban Development Action Grants	675.0	440.1	440.0	
Total	1,228.5	706.8	474.0	−61.4

SOURCE: Office of Management and Budget, *Budget of the United States Government, Fiscal Year 1983* (Washington, D.C.: GPO, 1982), Appendix, part I, various pages.
a. Outlays in these years are reported within other programs.
b. Excluding highway programs.

labor from paupers in return for food and shelter. The concept became familiar in America during the 1930s, when a series of New Deal programs—including the Civil Works Administration (CWA), the Works Progress Administration (WPA), the Civilian Conservation Corps (CCC), and the National Youth Administration (NYA)—were created to provide employment opportunities for millions of the nation's jobless.

The Reagan administration inherited, as the current embodiment of this concept, the Public Service Employment (PSE) program under the Comprehensive Employment and Training Act (CETA).[15] This program provided temporary federally funded jobs to persons who were unemployed for cyclical reasons (Title VI) and also to those who were structurally disadvantaged in the labor market (Title II). At its peak, in March 1978, the program enrolled more than 750,000 persons, about 10 percent of all those unemployed at that time; total expenditures for PSE amounted to $5.66 billion in FY 1978. The program dwindled continually from that peak, and by the end of FY 1980 enrollment had shrunk to 328,000.

Early in its tenure the Reagan administration announced its intention to end the PSE program and, with congressional concurrence, did so by the following September. This action reduced federal outlays about $0.6 billion for FY 1981 and about $3.6 billion for FY 1982. Of the approximately 300,000 persons who were terminated from PSE jobs following this action, slightly fewer than half found alternative employment (about half of these in temporary or part-time jobs), while the remainder reentered the world of unemployment and, in many cases, increased dependence on public assistance. The Congressional Budget Office estimates that for every dollar of reduced federal outlays for PSE, the federal government initially suffers an increase in public assistance outlays and loss of tax revenues amounting to twenty-nine cents.[16]

Basic to the administration's opposition to public service employment is its belief that CETA's mission was to train disadvantaged workers to enable them to obtain unsubsidized employment and that PSE had not been effective in accomplishing that mission. Evaluation studies offer some support for this view. In the mid-1970s the average net cost to taxpayers of an enrollee in the Public Service Employment program was $4,692, while annual postprogram wage gains (assumed to last five years) were $661. When discounted to make these amounts comparable in time, the cost-effectiveness ratio that emerges is only .53 (table 8-2). Similar ratios in subsequent rows of table 8-2 show that other CETA activities serving similar clients generated higher ratios, indicating greater effectiveness.

Although these ratios provide some basis for evaluating the success of public service employment in enhancing postprogram earnings, the PSE program as originally designed had a second objective: providing financial as-

TABLE 8–2

THE COST EFFECTIVENESS OF VARIOUS CETA ACTIVITIES IN ENHANCING THE
POSTPROGRAM EARNINGS OF DISADVANTAGED ADULT WORKERS

CETA Activity[a]	Average Net Government Cost per Participant[b]	Average Annual Postprogram Wage Gains per Participant	Cost-Effectiveness Ratio[c]
Public service employment	$4,692	$661	.53
Adult work experience	5,844	243	.16
Classroom training	1,418	391	1.05
On the job training	2,636	774	1.11

SOURCE: Laurie J. Bassi, *CETA—Is It a Cost Effective Method for Increasing the Earnings of Disadvantaged Workers?* (Washington, D.C.: The Urban Institute, 1982).

a. Estimates are based on data from the Continuous Longitudinal Manpower Survey for CETA participants during 1975 and 1976 who met the 1978 criteria for eligibility.

b. Incorporates savings from reduced income maintenance expenditures and increased tax payments.

c. Wage gains are assumed to last for five years. Note that the numerator in this ratio presents benefits from the point of view of program enrollees, while the denominator presents costs from the point of view of the federal government. Therefore, the ratio can be used to measure the relative cost effectiveness of alternative programs but not to judge whether the benefits to society exceed the cost.

sistance to localities in need of public services. PSE workers were employed by local governments and nonprofit organizations in a variety of clerical, service, and maintenance roles. It has been estimated that about 20 percent of federal PSE expenditures served as "fiscal substitution," meaning that they paid for services that would have been provided in the absence of the program. The remaining 80 percent helped expand public services in such areas as park and street maintenance, school crossing guards and teachers' aides, social services outreach workers, and clerical staffing to allow government offices to stay open longer hours. There is no solid "market" basis for estimating these services' value to the public. Nevertheless, observers of the program have concluded that, if the services are perhaps not quite worth their entire cost of production, that cost is closer to a true estimate of their worth than is zero.[17]

To the extent that these observations are correct, the cost-effectiveness ratio presented in table 8-2 is misleading because it omits a major category of benefits. If these benefits are included, then the total value of the program could well be larger than that for the alternative CETA activities displayed in the table. Thus, a decision to end PSE, which at first seemed a matter of relative effectiveness in helping program participants, can also be viewed as a matter of judgment concerning the value of goods and services produced by the public sector compared with the value of goods and services produced by the private sector. The Reagan administration's general attitude is that public sector activities, at the margin, are less important to the American economy and society than are private sector activities. The administration's decisions on the CETA PSE program, which implicitly placed little value on the program's public sector outputs, reflected that attitude.

In implicitly placing small value on PSE's output, the Reagan administration was not alone. The Carter administration had also planned to curtail the program, and this decision met relatively little resistance from either Congress or the local governments directly affected. In part, this lack of enthusiasm reflected a growing consensus that more emphasis on training was appropriate. In part, the decision was a result of bad publicity the program had received—some of it justified—about waste, abuse, and mismanagement at the local level. And finally, the decision reflected program amendments adopted in 1978, partially in reaction to that publicity, that restricted eligibility to economically disadvantaged persons. By 1980, 99 percent of Public Service Employment enrollees met the program's criteria of economic disadvantage (table 8-3). Before these amendments were adopted, localities had been free to hire less disadvantaged employees. As the PSE work force became more exclusively disadvantaged, its perceived usefulness to local governments declined, and political support for the program waned.

Ultimately, then, the demise of the Public Service Employment program may have been due less to the program's perceived ineffectiveness than to lack of political support. A program that, in its final years, was targeted strictly to disadvantaged workers was no longer highly valued by local governments. In the absence of political opposition, the Reagan administration's fundamental drive to reduce the size of the public sector found in PSE a visible and vulnerable target.

Preparation for Unsubsidized Jobs

While rejecting the concept of federally funded jobs, the administration embraced an alternative strategy: training to enhance the attractiveness of workers to employers offering unsubsidized jobs, primarily in the private sector. However, as with other policies endorsed by the administration, this favorable opinion earned training programs only a vitiation of budget reductions, not stability or expansion. The administration has proposed that total federal training activities for adults and youth for FY 1983 be allocated at $1.8 billion, a reduction of about 44 percent from the FY 1981 allocation.

TABLE 8–3

CHARACTERISTICS OF PARTICIPANTS IN PROGRAMS UNDER THE COMPREHENSIVE EMPLOYMENT AND TRAINING ACT (CETA) (FY 1980)

	Participant Characteristics at Time of Application to Enroll (Percentage)				
	Economically Disadvantaged[a]	Unemployed or Underemployed	Receiving Public Assistance	Nonwhite	Female
Adult programs					
Public service employment	99	97	29	45	47
Classroom training	98	93	33	50	56
On-the-job training	96	95	19	37	36
Adult work experience	98	96	40	46	59
Youth programs					
Youth work experience	100	49	41	54	52
Summer youth employment program	100	31	48	71	49
Youth employment and training program	100	57	35	53	52
Youth community conservation and improvement program	100	80	24	48	26

SOURCE: Special tabulations from the CETA Management Information System, U.S. Department of Labor.

a. "Economically disadvantaged" is defined as belonging to a family receiving public assistance or whose income is less than the official poverty level.

Until the 1960s the federal government was not extensively involved in worker training, except to a small extent under vocational education programs. However, beginning with the Manpower Development and Training Act of 1962 and continuing under CETA, the federal government became active on a multibillion dollar scale in providing training to both adults and youth. Most of this activity was targeted to the disadvantaged, although small amounts have been spent on skilled workers unemployed in midcareer because of technological or other kinds of economic changes. In FY 1981, the last full year of activity under Carter policies, federal outlays for training totaled about $3.2 billion.

The administration's enthusiasm for training as a strategy for assisting disadvantaged workers stems, in part, from cost-effectiveness analysis of the type previously discussed. As table 8-2 indicates, classroom and on-the-job training for adults generates significantly higher postprogram earnings, per dollar of federal effort, than PSE or work experience. This pattern of greater effectiveness holds particularly for minorities and females, who generally benefit more from CETA participation than do white males.

Quantitative evaluations are not available for most federal training programs targeted to disadvantaged youth, with the exception of the Job Corps. The Job Corps offers comprehensive training and services to poor, unemployed, out-of-school youth aged sixteen to twenty-one. The program operates through approximately 100 residential training centers where enrollees receive remedial basic education, vocational skill training, extensive supportive services (such as health care), and general preparation for work. These centers are operated by sponsors ranging from for-profit contractors and trade unions to the U.S. Forest Service.

A careful evaluation of two years of the postprogram experience of Job Corps graduates, compared with the experiences of similar young adults who did not pass through the program, showed that Job Corps enrollment produced, on average, an increase in employment of more than four weeks a year; an increase in earnings of approximately $500 per year; a 4 percent increase in military enrollment rates; a 25 percent increase in the probability of earning a high school diploma; and a reduction of more than four weeks per year in recipiency of public assistance and unemployment insurance payments. Taken together, these benefits total $7,343 per enrollee (in present value terms), a figure that exceeds by 45 percent the average cost of the program—$5,070.[18] Moreover, these results were achieved with a population of severely disadvantaged youth, the population simultaneously most urgently in need of assistance and the most difficult to serve.

When the Reagan administration took office, the Job Corps was training 44,000 enrollees annually. The administration reduced this number to 32,000 for FY 1982 and has proposed a further reduction, to 22,000, for FY 1983. The latter reduction offers federal budgetary savings for FY 1983 of $85 million. However, if the cost-benefit analysis is correct, these cuts will ultimately cost society about $123 million in such forms as lost productivity and increased crime and welfare dependency.

One controversy surrounding the Reagan administration's reductions of federal training activities concerns the items to be cut. The administration has taken the position that one defect in current CETA training programs is that only 18 percent of total program expenditures is spent on training itself; 44 percent provides stipends for enrollees; another 18 percent covers supportive services (such as transportation and child care); and 20 percent supports program administration.[19] In the administration's proposals for federal training activities in FY 1983 and beyond, expenditures for stipends and supportive services would be forbidden, and expenditures for program administration would be reduced. Thus, more training would be provided than previously, even though program expenditures would be reduced.

In support of this position, the administration argues that, in an environment of fiscal constraint, stipends and other peripheral supports should command lower priority than training activities themselves. Furthermore, eliminating stipends removes a short-run financial incentive for enrolling in training and thereby will focus training on those most serious about long-run self-improvement. Opponents of the ban contend that, in the absence of stipends, many persons for whom training might work well would be unable to make a long-term investment in training and would instead be forced to accept "dead-end," minimum wage jobs. Firm evidence to resolve this controversy is not available. However, it is likely that, should stipends be eliminated, more enrollees would be drawn from the ranks of current recipients of public assistance (who receive income support from that program) and younger workers (who are supported by their families), and a smaller proportion would come from the ranks of low-skilled, working adults.

Finally, the administration has proposed major changes in the delivery system for federally supported training. When CETA expires in September 1982, the administration wants to replace the current system of local government control with a system involving more state and private control. Federal funds would flow to states via a block grant and from states to service deliverers via a system of Private Industry Councils (PICs), on which a majority of seats would be held by local business representatives. This approach reflects the administration's belief that, because the decisions of the

PICs would be controlled by these business representatives, the graduates of the programs would be better prepared to work in the private sector.

Empirical evidence suggests that this assumption could be wrong. Private Industry Councils have been operating on a limited scale as part of the current CETA program for several years (under CETA's Title VII), and their track record is mixed, at best. These councils are relatively new, and their effectiveness would probably improve as they gain experience. At the same time, however, existing CETA agencies ("prime sponsors") have been more successful in helping workers move into the private sector than has commonly been assumed. For example, of the 1976 training enrollees between 70 and 94 percent (depending on their characteristics and the type of training they received) were employed in the private sector in 1978;[20] that percentage is approximately the same proportion as the 80 percent of all jobs which are found in this sector. It is not obvious that the private sector-oriented PICs will be more effective on this score.

A final way in which the federal government promotes the movement of structurally disadvantaged workers into unsubsidized employment is through the federal-state employment service (in most states called the Job Service). In existence since the 1930s, the service operates on a large scale. In FY 1980, for example, 2,600 local offices throughout the United States registered 16.6 million job seekers, listed 8.3 million job openings, and placed 5.9 million workers.[21] The Job Service is also responsible for a variety of special services, such as enforcing work registration requirements in public assistance programs and screening CETA applicants.

Beginning in FY 1982, the Reagan administration sharply reduced funding for the Job Service, leading to the closing of several hundred local offices and a reduction of activities nationwide from 30,000 staff years in FY 1981 to 17,500 staff years in 1982. Further cuts, to 13,900 staff years, are proposed for 1983.

Despite its large scale of operation, the Job Service has never become a dominant labor exchange in U.S. labor markets. Its millions of placements each year constitute only a fraction of total placements. Furthermore, much of its responsibility for disadvantaged workers is of a regulatory or enforcement nature, and this function has distracted time and effort from counseling and placement assistance. The result has been widespread discontent with the Job Service's overall effectiveness.

Despite these limitations, the Job Service has traditionally served as a placement resource for many of the nation's disadvantaged workers. In FY 1980, minority workers accounted for 30 percent of all Job Service applicants, and nearly 1.4 million were successfully placed. Youth accounted for 31 percent of all applicants, and more than 1.7 million of them were placed.[22]

Women, the physically handicapped, migrant farm laborers, and other disadvantaged groups all receive disproportionate amounts of Job Service attention. Thus, the service is one public institution serving to link the opportunities created by general economic growth to the disadvantaged.

Economic Development

Seeking employment for disadvantaged workers in already established enterprises is one approach to employment problems. Another set of federal programs seeks to foster the development of private enterprises likely to hire them. When the Reagan administration took office, it inherited a range of geographically targeted federal economic development programs, lodged primarily in three agencies—the Economic Development Administration, the Appalachian Regional Commission, and the Department of Housing and Urban Development.[23]

The Economic Development Administration of the Department of Commerce has, since 1974, administered a variety of grants, loans, and loan guarantees to foster the development of private firms in localities, both urban and rural, of persistently high unemployment and large-scale outmigration. Some of this assistance goes directly to firms, and some goes to localities to create public infrastructure (such as sewers, roads, and industrial parks) to make the location attractive to firms. During FY 1981, outlays of the Economic Development Administration totaled nearly half a billion dollars.

The Appalachian Regional Commission is an independent agency that, since 1965, has provided grants to the thirteen Appalachian states for community development projects, economic development projects, and highway construction. During FY 1981, outlays of the commission (excluding highway projects) totaled $95 million.

The Department of Housing and Urban Development has, since 1974, administered the Urban Development Action Grant (UDAG) program, which provides discretionary competitive grants to local governments to be used, in conjunction with other public funds and private investment, for locally initiated economic development projects. During FY 1981, $697 million in new awards were made for 443 projects.

The administration proposed to eliminate all funding for the Economic Development Administration and the Appalachian Regional Commission. These programs both emphasize only government involvement in development projects. The Urban Development Action Grant program, on the other hand, provides public funds to leverage private investment. This program was allowed to continue, albeit at funding at about 35 percent below FY 1981 levels.

The administration lodged three specific complaints against the Economic Development Administration and similar federal initiatives:[24]

Lack of targeting—The original purpose of EDA was to provide special assistance to distressed areas, but now more than 80 percent of the nation has become eligible.

Lack of effectiveness—There is little evidence that these programs have induced job development that would not have occurred anyway. To the extent that jobs were induced in distressed localities, they were induced largely at the expense of jobs located elsewhere. That is, jobs were redistributed but not created.

Hindrance to efficiency—To the extent that the programs influenced the location of firms and jobs, they reduced the nation's productivity by inducing firms to locate where they could not be most efficient.

In addition to setting forth these criticisms, the administration also believes the programs are superfluous in an environment of general prosperity:

Economic expansion and job creation will be stimulated by the President's overall economic recovery program. . . . By 1986, the President's program is expected to create millions of new jobs. Improvements in overall economic conditions offer more hope to distressed areas than do the programs to be terminated.

The isolation of these economically distressed areas from the beneficial effects of aggregate prosperity has been discussed earlier in this chapter; that isolation is, in fact, the rationale for these programs. However, the specific weaknesses of the EDA programs identified by the administration echoed criticisms made long before the administration took office by those supportive of the concept of a federal economic development role. Expenditures by EDA have not been well targeted to areas of greatest need; many EDA projects have involved poorly located industrial parks and activities (such as local public works) with little or no potential to attract firms and jobs; and much of EDA's portfolio of grants and loans to firms has been of questionable financial soundness. EDA has survived and grown over the years less because of proven effectiveness in economic development than because it has provided attractive "pork barrel" opportunities for Congress. Perhaps largely for the same reasons, it survived the administration's proposal to abolish it.

In the case of Urban Development Action Grants, a recent evaluation of the program provides some basis for judging the administration's acceptance of it compared with the EDA approach.[25] In a sample of 80 recent UDAG projects, it was determined that approximately $5.50 of private investment was leveraged by each UDAG dollar; only one dollar in six of UDAG resources substituted for private investment that would have been made anyway; 90 percent of UDAG projects proved to be financially viable; and one new job had been "created" for each $11,570 of UDAG expenditures. The last figure compares favorably to costs of about $13,000 per job for the EDA Business Development Loan program and $60,000 per job for the EDA Local Public Works program.

While such evidence is impressive, caution is warranted in concluding that the administration's preferences are sound. The most important ground for concern is "creaming," the tendency of UDAG projects to be located in areas that, while not attractive without UDAG subsidy, are still less distressed than some of the locations in which EDA has tried to encourage development. Many UDAG projects, for example, are new hotel complexes in the downtown areas of large cities, while many EDA projects were attempts at industrial job creation in more distressed areas. The employment value of service jobs in downtown hotels is relatively limited because of low wages and the absence of advancement opportunities. Similarly, the fact that 90 percent of UDAG projects proved to be financially viable may suggest that many of the projects undertaken were almost feasible without subsidies. The criteria the administration has chosen to use in judging the relative effectiveness of these programs thus tend to be financial; such considerations as economic need or the quality of the jobs generated have largely been ignored.

Even assuming that programs should emphasize public-private cooperation (as in UDAG) rather than public action alone (as in EDA), there is no obvious basis for the administration's proposal to reduce funds for *both* types of efforts, other than its general search for federal budget reductions wherever they are to be found.

The administration has proposed one additional initiative to spur economic development: an experiment with enterprise zones. This approach embodies a sharp philosophical break with past federal initiatives. Rather than increasing government activity in local areas as a catalyst for change, the concept of enterprise zones is to create jobs and economic expansion by reducing such activities:

> The Enterprise Zone concept is based on utilizing the market to solve the problems of the Nation's economically depressed areas, relying primarily on private sector institutions. . . . This would be similar to the free trade zones established in other parts of the world, such as Hong Kong, which have been quite successful in stimulating the development of poor areas.
>
> Enterprise Zones are based on an entirely fresh paradigm of thought concerning economic growth and distressed areas. The old approach was based on two elements—subsidy and central planning. . . . The new approach is instead based on market processes. Instead of subsidy, it focuses on removing government barriers to economic growth, barriers which are preventing people from creating, producing

and earning their own wages and profits. The approach is to focus on what the government is doing that inhibits economic growth. . . . And instead of central planning, the new approach seeks to create a general climate of open markets where entrepreneurs and economic activity could flourish, relying on market forces to determine the course of redevelopment within the zones.[26]

The administration proposes to make available four types of economic incentives to firms in the zones. First, federal tax relief is to include an investment tax credit for capital investments, a 10 percent credit for increased payrolls, a 50 percent tax credit on wages paid to disadvantaged employees, elimination of capital gains taxation, and a 5 percent income tax credit to employees. Second, federal regulatory relief is to be available, at the request of the state and locality in which a zone is located. Third, state and local governments are expected to provide additional tax relief and regulatory relief from their own programs. Finally, state and local governments are expected to enhance the attractiveness of zones by improving public services and by focusing infrastructure investment, job training, and other development activities there.

Until Congress enacts specific legislation, the magnitude of incentives that will be involved is not known. Even then, there will be variation among zones because decisions in this proposed program are to be made primarily outside the federal government. States and localities will compete for selection as demonstration sites, and a key factor in this competition will be the extent and creativity of the incentives they offer. Nevertheless, the general level of effort being proposed appears to be modest. The administration has estimated that the annual foregone revenue from federal tax relief for a typical zone will be only about $1,240 per worker. Many important categories of federal regulations are excluded from potential regulatory relief; these include all regulations mandated by law (including the minimum wage) and all those affecting civil rights, public safety, health, and the environment. The federal government will not undertake infrastructure construction or special training programs in any zones, and while states and localities may undertake such expenditures, the funds available to them for such activities are likely to be extremely limited. Thus, enterprise zones as proposed may not bring dramatic change to distressed locales, in part because the value of incentives available to firms within the zone may be quite limited.

Firms will balance the potentially modest benefits from locating in a zone against the extra costs or risks of operating in these locations. To be eligible for designation as a zone, according to the administration's proposal, an area must be one of pervasive poverty, unemployment, and general economic distress. It must have an unemployment rate at least 50 percent above the national average, at least 20 percent of its residents must fall below the poverty line, or the locale must have lost at least 20 percent of its population over the last decade. In urban areas such places are heavily burdened by crime, dilapidated public infrastructure, crowded and old-fashioned factory buildings, and a low-skilled labor force. In rural areas such locales are generally characterized by inaccessibility to raw materials, markets, and skilled labor. In the past twenty years, the federal, state, and local governments have engaged in a variety of incentive programs to encourage firms to locate or expand in such areas or to hire particular categories of workers. The general record of these programs is that firms are highly unresponsive to modest incentives, being more concerned about the potential impact on profitability of the generally adverse conditions.[27]

Another reason for caution concerning the potential of zones is that many of the proposed incentives are not designed well enough to serve the development needs of business firms. A prime example is the fact that the proposed federal tax relief is nonrefundable. Thus, these tax incentives are largely useless to small firms and new firms, which typically have little or no tax liability against which to claim a nonrefundable credit. Yet such firms are important generators of employment. Moreover, no provisions are included for overcoming well-known barriers to the survival and prosperity of these firms. The federal government can take a number of actions to help such firms grow, such as facilitating access to capital markets via loan guarantees or providing developed plant sites.[28] The forms of assistance on which the administration has focused—tax relief and regulatory relief—seem to have been selected primarily because of their compatability with a philosophy of reduced government and not because of their value in meeting the needs of firms.

A final factor limiting the effectiveness of enterprise zones is their scope. The administration proposes to designate only seventy-five zones (twenty-five a year for three years), which means that the program would cover only about 4 percent of the 2,000 locales in the country that meet the proposed eligibility criteria. The administration's position is that this limited effort is appropriate for experimentation with a new and untried approach. That position seems sensible enough. Nevertheless, it leaves unanswered the question of what happens to the remaining 96 percent of distressed locales while the experiment is being conducted.

Conclusions

When the national economy grows and prospers, opportunities for disadvantaged workers improve, but only modestly. These workers still lack job skills and experience, still face discrimination, and still live in locales of little opportunity. Only when labor markets get extremely tight do employers dip extensively into the labor pool of disadvantaged workers. The fear of inflation means that tight labor markets do not occur often, and certainly not recently. The national unemployment rate has not dipped below 5 percent since 1973.

The Reagan administration has rejected many of the federal government's earlier programs to address the problems of structurally disadvantaged workers. It views these programs primarily as impediments to growth and their elimination as part of a comprehensive effort to reduce the size of the federal government. It believes that the higher levels of national prosperity resulting from such streamlining will improve the lot of disadvantaged workers. At the same time, the federal initiatives to be retained are to be reshaped to emphasize the role of the private sector.

This chapter has not examined all aspects of this strategy. In particular, it has not discussed the extent to which a reduction in government spending and taxes will or will not contribute to national prosperity. (On that subject, see chapters 2 and 4 of this volume.) Rather, it has concentrated on two topics: (1) the extent to which prosperity "trickles down" to structurally disadvantaged workers in the absence of federal initiatives and (2) the effects on these workers and on society at large of reducing, eliminating, and re-shaping employment, training, and economic development programs along the lines the administration has proposed.

Undoubtedly, some of the administration's proposed changes focus on programs where improvements in performance were long overdue. The Economic Development Administration, particularly its public works activities, and the Job Service, particularly its enforcement activities, present clear examples. However, many of the program changes the administration has endorsed seem to have been chosen primarily because they were a ready source of budgetary savings rather than because they were consistent with the administration's economic growth objectives—objectives that require some investment in human resources if they are to be achieved. Substantial cuts have been imposed on programs whose effectiveness in promoting these objectives was well documented. The cuts imposed will increase welfare dependency, reduce national productivity, and make more difficult the achievement of full employment without inflation. Thus, many of the administration's actions seem to run contrary to its announced objectives.

The programs that have been functioning effectively have served to forge important links between aggregate prosperity and disadvantaged workers. If the economy operates in the future much as it has in the past—and it is a bold assertion to suppose otherwise—then in the absence of these programs, prosperity alone will not suffice to integrate these groups into the labor market. In forming the spout by which prosperity trickles down, these programs constitute an essential complement to macroeconomic initiatives. The historical record weighs heavily against the administration's assertions that such efforts can be reduced without substantial cost both to those directly served and to society at large.

Chapter 9

HEALTH

Judith Feder
John Holahan
Randall R. Bovbjerg
Jack Hadley

For more than two decades, several administrations and both political parties have actively promoted better access to medical care. Many health policy makers saw the 1965 enactment of Medicare and Medicaid as a commitment to federal health financing that would culminate in national health insurance. But national health insurance never happened. Disagreements among proponents about how best to design it, concern about rising medical costs and a growing federal budget, and political disenchantment with federal programs prevented its passage. Still, throughout the 1970s, prominent spokesmen for both political parties advocated broader federal involvement in health care financing.

Commitment to expansion ended abruptly with the Reagan administration, whose philosophy is that the federal government should do less not more in the health care sector. Consistent with its broader aims, the administration's objectives for the health care sector are to reduce federal spending, minimize federal regulation, increase the responsibilities of the states and the private

[The authors gratefully acknowledge comments and suggestions from Robert Berenson, Rick Curtis, Paul Ginsburg, Philip Held, Jack Meyer, Diane Rowland, and Margaret Sulvetta.]

sector, and reform private as well as public financing to promote competition and efficiency in health care delivery.

As this chapter will show, the administration has successfully reduced spending in some federal programs, returned some responsibilities to the states and the private market, and eliminated some regulation. But the administration has not pursued the market-oriented reforms it believes necessary to promote efficiency and thereby slow health's growing absorption of people's incomes and governments' budgets. Despite spending cuts that will reduce service use and increase costs to public beneficiaries, the federal government's health care spending will continue to grow rapidly.

The next section describes the evolution of the federal role in health prior to the Reagan administration's taking office. The following two sections outline the administration's efforts to redefine that role and the likely consequences of those efforts. The discussion focuses on health care financing and service programs and on policies that affect the general market for medical care.[1]

Historical Review

The federal government's involvement in health financing grew enormously over the last decade and a half, as federal programs assumed responsibility for financing medical care to certain vulnerable populations--the elderly, the disabled, and many of the poor. Entitling these groups to "mainstream" medical care increased their use of services and improved their health. But at the same time, public along with private insurance fueled rapid increases in medical prices and the sophistication of medical care. Experts and politicians began to question whether more expensive service was worth its costs, and "cost containment" joined access improvement on the federal policy agenda of the 1970s. Side by side with 1972 legislation extending Medicare to the disabled and proposals for national health insurance from both Republican and Democratic administrations, the federal government adopted a multitude of policies aimed at controlling increases in health care spending. None of these policies had had much impact when the Reagan administration took office.

Expansion of the Federal Role in Health

Federal programs expanding access to medical care predate the major social legislation of the 1960s. Federal grants to state maternal and child health programs began with the 1935 Social Security Act; federal financing of medical care to state cash assistance recipients goes back to 1950; Hill-Burton construction loans supported hospital growth throughout the country following World War II; and tax policy has long fostered dramatic expansion of private health insurance as a tax-free fringe benefit.

The 1960s nevertheless brought a dramatic change in the federal government's role in health financing—the establishment of federally funded insurance programs for the elderly and many of the poor. In 1965 Medicare entitled the elderly to federally financed medical care, and Medicaid committed open-ended federal matching funds to state-run (but federally guided) entitlement programs for segments of the poor. Medicare was extended to the disabled and end-stage renal patients in 1972.

For some specific services and populations, federal policy makers found insurance programs insufficient. Simply enabling people to purchase service, they believed, would not assure service availability or adequate use. Special problems and their constituents received special attention during the 1960s and 1970s, as Congress enacted a multitude of grant programs to train many types of health professionals; support the development and operation of particular services, such as primary, emergency, and mental health care; and aid particular populations, such as migrant workers, the mentally ill, and victims of black lung and hypertension. Public health also received attention, with grants to states for general public health activities plus specific grants for immunization, fluoridation, rodent control, and prevention of lead paint poisoning and venereal disease.

Responsibility for new population groups after 1965 brought a substantial increase in the federal government's share of personal health care spending. The federal share doubled from 10 percent to 20 percent almost immediately after Medicare and Medicaid began operations and rose another 10 percent thereafter, through implementation of the 1972 Medicare expansion. The larger federal responsibility reduced consumers' responsibility for out-of-pocket payments from over half to less than a third of all spending.[2]

New federal programs did not mean that everyone had protection against the potentially catastrophic costs of illness. In 1976, about 30 percent of the population had public protection, about 60 percent had private, and about 10 percent had no protection at all. Low-income persons, young adults, and the unemployed were less likely than others to have insurance coverage. One-third of the privately insured population had only limited insurance protection and were still exposed to catastrophic risks. Medicaid covered only about half the poor—because of many states' below-poverty income standards and exclusion of even very poor able-bodied adults, aged 18 to 64. Medicare, supplemented by Medicaid, protected the poor elderly, though the near-poor and the better-off elderly continued to face sizable cost-sharing burdens.[3]

Despite these gaps, expansion of public programs meant more medical care and better health for the aged and the poor. Immediately after Medicare and Medicaid began, the elderly's use of hospitals increased 25 percent. Since then, the proportion of the elderly entering the hospital has continued to increase, though shorter hospital stays have kept overall use relatively steady.[4] Several surveys have shown that blacks and low-income persons have experienced substantial increases in their use of medical care.[5] Although many factors other than medical care affect people's health status, greater use of medical care has been accompanied by steady declines in mortality rates in the last 15 years, in sharp contrast with the preceding 15 years (1954-1968) of little change.[6]

Growth in Health Care Spending

These gains in health and medical care use have come at considerable cost. Federal spending on medical care rose twelvefold between 1965 and 1980 (see table 9-1). Categorical grant programs have grown substantially but remain a tiny proportion of the total. Over three-quarters of the federal health budget now goes to Medicare and Medicaid. These programs not only increased federal spending at their start, but continued to grow at rapid rates (over 15 percent per year from 1970 to 1980). Private spending also grew rapidly (fourfold) between 1965 and 1980, and both public and private health spending grew faster than government revenues and people's incomes. Federal health spending almost tripled its share of the federal budget between 1965 and 1980, rising from 4.5 to 11.8 percent. Health's share of state and local spending grew by about a third, from 6.9 to 9.3 percent, and health's share of private incomes rose by 23 percent, from 6 to 7.4 percent.[7]

Public and private spending rose for similar reasons—a combination of population growth, more service use per capita, more services per user, and greater "intensity" or resources per service. Medical price increases, which exceeded general price increases, accounted for more than half the spending increases between 1965 and 1980 and three-quarters of the increase between 1975 and 1980. Greater service use and intensity explain most of the remainder. Increases in intensity have been particularly significant for hospital care. Costs per hospital day have risen 12 percent per year since 1965, about 50 percent more than the increase in the prices hospitals pay for goods and services.[8]

Why do these spending increases occur? Partly because people value medical care, but also because neither consumers nor providers weigh the benefits of medical care against its full costs. Insurance coverage—public or private—reduces consumers' sensitivity to medical costs, and people use more and higher-priced care. Other practices insulate consumers from the impact

TABLE 9–1

THE FEDERAL HEALTH BUDGET: CALENDAR 1965–1980
(In $ billions)

	1965	1970	1975	1980	Average Annual Compound Rate of Growth 1970–1980
Medicare[a]	—	7.5	16.3	36.7	15.88%
Medicaid[b]	—	3.0 ⎫	7.9	14.6	15.18
Other public assistance for medical care	1.4 ⎬1.4	0.2 ⎭	} 3.2		
Veterans and Department of Defense[c]	2.0	3.6	6.3	10.0	10.22
Other personal health care[d]	0.3	0.8	2.1	3.0	13.22
Public health[e]	0.3	0.6	1.2	1.2	6.93
Research and construction	1.6	2.0	3.3	5.3	9.75
Total[f]	5.5	17.7	37.1	70.9	13.88
Total federal spending (FYs)[g]	118.4	196.6	326.2	579.6	10.81
GNP	691.0	992.7	1,549.2	2,626.1	9.73

SOURCES: Robert M. Gibson and David R. Waldo, "National Health Expenditures, 1980," *Health Care Financing Review*, September 1981, tables 2A-2F and 7A-7F; Mark S. Freeland and Carol E. Schendler, "National Health Expenditures: Short-Term Outlook and Long-Term Projections," *Health Care Financing Review*, winter 1981, table 1; U.S. Department of Commerce, Bureau of the Census, *Statistical Abstract of the United States*, table 416, "Federal Budget Receipts, Outlays and Debt 1940–1981" (Washington, D.C.: GPO, 1981).

a. Includes administrative and benefits costs; some funds come from beneficiaries' premiums.

b. Includes state payments for Medicaid eligibles to "buy into" Medicare coverage. Includes similar welfare medical care for 1965 and 1970.

c. Includes Veterans Administration, CHAMPUS, and retiree benefits.

d. Includes maternal and child health; medical payments for vocational rehabilitation, temporary disability, and workers' compensation; PHS and other federal hospitals; Indian Health Service; alcohol, drug abuse, and mental health; and school health.

e. Does not include environmental spending.

f. Totals may not match because of rounding.

g. Does not include "off-budget" spending (including Export-Import Bank before 1974) or "tax expenditures."

of rising service costs on insurance premiums. Employers contribute all or most of the insurance premiums for most of the population insured through the workplace. Taxes help finance and promote this insurance, since employers' contributions to premiums are excluded from employee taxable income. With the exclusion, each dollar an employer pays toward premiums buys an employee a dollar's worth of insurance coverage, while that same dollar paid in wages would be taxed and bring the employee less than a dollar

to spend. By reducing the price of insurance, this tax exclusion both encourages the expansion of insurance (even to cover predictable and manage-
able expenses—the "first dollar" of medical spending) and reduces the burden
of (and therefore resistance to) premium increases. In 1981, the tax exclusion
cost the federal government over $19 billion in forgone revenues. These tax
expenditures are larger than the federal share of the Medicaid program and
have grown much faster than either Medicare or Medicaid spending.[9]

In these circumstances, private insurers have felt little pressure to limit
what they pay providers, for the most part paying providers' costs or charges.
Medicare (and, to a lesser extent Medicaid) has followed suit, primarily to
assure beneficiaries access to care. More revenues have meant more sophisticated medical care, as providers pursue better medicine and personal or
institutional interests in new techniques and services.

Policies to Contain Medical Costs

As medical costs have risen, policy makers have come to question whether
medical costs are worth their benefits. The problem is not simply that medical
care costs too much (though budgetary problems are substantial). Rather the
problem is the absence of either market or political controls over decisions
on how much to spend.

Governments have recognized the medical cost problem since the early
1970s, but recognition of the problem did not bring agreement on what to do
about it. Congress enacted a variety of cost containment measures, most of
which substituted political controls for the market constraints on health spending that insurance had weakened. President Nixon retained wage-price controls
on the health care sector after removing them elsewhere. The 1974 National
Health Resources and Development Act required states to plan and regulate
capital investment in health care facilities. For Medicare and Medicaid, 1972
legislation required the establishment of local physician groups (Professional
Standards Review Organizations—PSROs) to review and control beneficiaries' use of services, imposed ceilings on Medicare payments to physicians,
and established some constraints on hospital payment.

The wage-price controls temporarily slowed health spending, but the
other measures had little impact.[10] This should not be surprising, since neither
PSROs nor capital expenditures regulation ("certificate of need") altered the
public and private insurers' willingness to pay providers' costs or charges for
most services. Medicare constraints on payments to hospitals and physicians
have also been weak and have failed to slow growth in program expenses.[11]

States have been most aggressive in breaking the tie between public
payments and provider charges or costs. Although state payment limits fre-

quently apply only to Medicaid, eight states have gone further, by limiting private as well as public payments to hospitals. These rate-setting programs, once well established, can slow hospital cost increases by two to four percentage points a year.[12]

National rate-setting has been considered but not adopted. President Carter made hospital revenue controls a high priority, but Congress rejected several versions of his proposal. Many factors led to its demise, including its complexity. But equally important were the hospital industry's opposition and the lack of vocal taxpayer support.

One 1970s cost containment program differed from the rest by attempting to revive market forces. The Health Maintenance Organization (HMO) Act promoted prepaid group practices and other physician groups that agreed to provide comprehensive services in return for a fixed fee per person. These prepayment arrangements (which date back to the 1930s) offer providers greater incentives to control costs than insured fee-for-service practice, in which providers earn more as they provide more services. Responding to a Nixon administration initiative, Congress enacted legislation providing funds for HMO development and requiring large employers to offer their employees HMOs (where available) as alternatives to their traditional insurance plans. The hope was that employees would see advantages to the HMO, and that their interest would pressure traditional providers to become more efficient to compete for business.

Implementation of this notion ran into innumerable obstacles and the original concept was never fully put into effect.[13] Also, it is unclear whether HMOs' lower costs come from efficiency or from enrollment of lower-risk people and the extent to which traditional practice responds to HMOs.[14] Moreover, although HMO enrollment almost doubled between 1974 and 1981, still only about 4.5 percent of the population are enrolled in HMOs. HMOs have not affected the bulk of the American public or its health care system.

Toward the end of the 1970s, proponents of competition advocated further stimulus to the market through tax and insurance reforms to increase consumers' sensitivity to insurance premiums and their interest in efficient service.[15] Reforms of this sort were included in Democratic and Republican national health insurance proposals and in independent legislation. But no action was taken.

The federal government's inability to contain either public or general medical costs reinforced general reluctance to increase federal spending and was an impediment to adoption of national health insurance during the 1970s. The Nixon, Ford, and Carter administrations introduced legislation, and Congress came close to enactment of some type of bill more than once during the decade. Policy makers of both parties believed that the federal government should provide insurance for the 10 percent who still lacked private or public coverage and should protect the privately insured against the potentially "catastrophic" costs many policies did not cover. Some argued that national health insurance was the best way to gain control over health spending, because it would force the federal government to decide how much should be spent. Others believed that more insurance coverage would simply exacerbate already unacceptable health spending increases. Concern about that prospect led President Carter to condition his support for national health insurance on prior enactment of hospital revenue controls. Neither national revenue controls nor national health insurance were enacted before President Carter left office, and the decade ended as it began, with health care absorbing a growing share of personal income and government budgets.

Budget Reductions and Program Changes

Access improvement disappeared from the health policy agenda when the Reagan administration took office. Consistent with its overall objectives, the administration committed itself to substantial reductions in federal health spending and greater reliance on state governments and the private market. To accomplish these goals, the administration has promised both budgetary cuts and broader reforms to revive market competition and thus slow growth in private as well as public health spending.

This section outlines the administration's budgetary reductions and related policy changes for Medicare, Medicaid, and health services grants. To date, budget cuts have been the administration's primary health care policy. One of their major effects will be to reduce service use by public beneficiaries. The most costly and fastest-growing program (Medicare), however, has suffered the smallest proportionate cuts, and, in the absence of financing reforms, these cuts will do little to slow overall growth in federal health spending.

Overview of Budget Reductions

The federal government's obligations to health spending when the Reagan administration took office and the cuts made by Congress in 1981 are shown in table 9-2. With no changes in federal health policy, projections indicate that total federal health spending (excluding Veterans Administration and Department of Defense spending) would have risen from $69.4 billion in 1981 to $132.1 billion in 1986, increasing as a share of federal spending from 9.7 percent to 12.8 percent. Medicare would absorb the bulk of that spending, more than doubling from $42.5 billion in 1981 to $91.1 billion in 1986.

TABLE 9–2

FEDERAL HEALTH EXPENDITURES: ESTIMATED EFFECTS OF CHANGES ENACTED BY THE 97TH CONGRESS

(In $ billions)

	FY 1981	FY 1982	FY 1983	FY 1984	FY 1985	FY 1986
Baseline outlays assuming policies as of January 1981						
Medicare	42.5	50.3	59.1	68.7	79.2	91.1
Medicaid	16.8	18.4	20.8	22.7	25.1	27.8
Other[a]	10.1	10.1	10.8	11.6	12.4	13.2
Total	69.4	78.8	90.7	103.0	116.7	132.1
Outlay reductions due to 1981 legislation						
Medicare		−0.6	−0.9	−1.0	−1.1	−1.3
Medicaid		−0.5	−0.7	−0.8	−0.9	−0.2
Other[a]		−0.7	−1.6	−2.0	−2.3	−2.5
Total		−2.5	−3.6	−4.2	−3.8	−4.3
Percentage change in baseline outlays due to 1981 legislation						
Medicare		(−1.2%)	(−1.5%)	(−1.5%)	(−1.4%)	(−1.4%)
Medicaid		(−2.7%)	(−3.4%)	(−3.5%)	(−3.6%)	(−0.7%)
Other[a]		(−6.9%)	(−14.8%)	(−17.2%)	(−18.5%)	(−18.9%)
Total		(−3.1%)	(−4.0%)	(−4.1%)	(−3.2%)	(−3.2%)
Total outlays assuming policies as of February 1982						
Medicare		49.7	58.2	67.7	78.1	89.8
Medicaid		17.9	20.1	21.9	25.1	27.6
Other[a]		9.4	9.2	9.6	10.1	10.7
Total		77.0	87.5	99.2	113.3	128.1

SOURCE: Authors' estimates based upon Congressional Budget Office's 1981 baseline projections and economic and technical assumptions as of February 1982.

a. All remaining health outlays, excluding Veterans Administration and U.S. Department of Defense and allowances and offsetting receipts.

Federal Medicaid expenditures are smaller and would have increased less rapidly. Service grants, health education, health research, and other health programs account for only a small share of the total in all years. Tax expenditures are larger than any federal health program except Medicare—$25.1 billion in 1981, projected to increase to $28.1 billion in 1983.[16]

Practical politics has heavily influenced the Reagan administration's budget reductions. Medicare and Medicaid are entitlement programs, obligated to pay for covered services used by eligible persons. Federal funds adequate for this purpose are permanently obligated and not subject to the congressional appropriations process. Powerful constituencies resist any changes in these programs—the elderly protecting their Medicare benefits, providers protecting their revenues, and states protecting their access to substantial federal funds. Furthermore, spending cuts in entitlement programs are not simple to make. They require changes in eligibility, benefits, or payment rules, which are both politically controversial and somewhat unpredictable in their effects.

In contrast, grant programs are politically vulnerable and readily controlled. As small programs directed to narrow constituencies, they lack the entitlement programs' strong political backing. Unlike entitlement programs, grant program spending is fixed by the appropriations process, where it competes with all other "discretionary" programs.

In its 1982 budget proposals, the administration avoided significant changes in Medicare, pressed states to change Medicaid, and made sizable cuts in grant programs. Medicare was deemed part of the social insurance "safety net" and thus was exempted from major cuts and policy changes. Medicaid fell outside the "safety net." The administration pushed states to cut spending with a proposal to cap federal contributions, and also proposed to give the states increased flexibility in setting Medicaid's eligibility, benefit, and payment rules. By far the largest proportionate proposed cut was the 25 percent reduction in the health services grant programs. The reduction was accompanied by a proposed shift from categorical funding, which allocates funds according to federal priorities, to block funding, which allows the states much greater spending freedom.

As shown in table 9-2, congressional action followed this ranking, but cut Medicare more and other programs less than the president had requested. Although Congress gave states somewhat more flexibility, it retained more federal control than the administration would have liked. Projected reductions in federal spending were 3.1 percent in 1982 and 3.2 percent by 1986. For 1982, projected Medicare spending was reduced by 1.2 percent, Medicaid by 2.7 percent, and other spending by 6.9 percent. (This latter reduction reflected a much larger cut in health grant programs.) By 1986 the relative size of the Medicaid cut will greatly diminish and cuts in the "other" category will become quite large.

TABLE 9–3

HEALTH EXPENDITURES: ESTIMATED EFFECTS OF CHANGES PROPOSED IN THE 1983
BUDGET
(In $ billions)

Baseline outlays, assuming policies as of February 1982	FY 1982	FY 1983	FY 1984	FY 1985
Medicare	49.7	58.2	67.7	78.1
Medicaid	17.9	20.1	21.9	25.1
Other[a]	9.4	9.2	9.6	10.1
Total	77.0	87.5	99.2	113.3
Outlay reductions proposed in 1983 Budget				
Medicare (with competition legislation)		−3.0	−6.0	−8.7
Medicare (w/o competition legislation)		−3.0	−4.0	−4.6
Medicaid		−2.0	−2.3	−3.7
Other[a,b]		.6	.7	.7
Total[c] (with competition legislation)		−4.4	−7.6	−11.7
Total[c] (w/o competition legislation)		−4.4	−5.6	−7.6
Percentage Changes Proposed in 1983 Budget				
Medicare (with competition legislation)		−5.1%	−8.9%	−11.1%
Medicare (w/o competition legislation)			−5.9%	−5.9%
Medicaid		−10.0%	−10.5%	−14.7%
Other[a]		*	*	*
Total[d] (with competition legislation)		−5.7%	−8.4%	−10.3%
Total[d] (w/o competition legislation)			−5.6%	−6.7%
Resulting Outlays From Changes Proposed in 1983 Budget				
Medicare (with competition legislation)		55.2	61.7	69.4
Medicare (w/o competition legislation)		55.2	63.7	73.5
Medicaid		18.1	19.6	21.4
Other[a,b]		9.8	10.3	10.8
Total[c] (with competition legislation)		83.1	91.6	101.6
Total[c] (w/o competition legislation)		83.1	93.6	105.7

SOURCE: Authors' estimates based on CBO economic and technical assumptions as of February 1982.

*Percentage change not calculated because of the transfer of WIC program to health.

a. All remaining health outlays, excluding Veterans Administration and U.S. Department of Defense allowances and offsetting receipts.

b. The administration has proposed transferring the women, infants, and children (WIC) nutrition program, classified as an income security program, to health to be included as part of an expanded maternal and child health block grant. The expenditures do not represent an increase in federal spending.

c. Total includes transfer of WIC program to health.

d. Total does not include transfer of WIC program to health.

The 1983 budget proposes further spending reductions, even larger than those made in the 1982 budget (see table 9-3). The administration would take more from Medicare than before, further reduce federal contributions to Medicaid, and incorporate more categorical programs into block grants with less total funding. If these proposals were all adopted, federal spending on these programs would be about 10 percent less in 1985 than under fiscal 1982 policies (and 12.9 percent less than spending projections when the administration took office). Spending would still increase rapidly, however—by 22.2 percent between 1983 and 1985. Moreover, half the projected Medicare savings and a third of total projected savings for 1985 are attributed to a competition initiative which has yet to be proposed. In its absence, spending is estimated to increase 27 percent between 1983 and 1985.

Changes in Medicare

As the biggest and fastest-growing federal health program, Medicare's costs are critical to federal health spending. Policy options to contain costs fall into three categories. First, federal policy could try to slow the rate of increase in general health care costs, which drive Medicare spending. Second, Medicare could try to use its dollars more efficiently, by changing beneficiaries' service use or the amount of payment for covered services. Third, Medicare could save money by reducing its benefits, shifting responsibility to beneficiaries by raising their service costs or reducing their service use, or by narrowing eligibility.

To date, policies to contain Medicare costs have been specific to Medicare. Although there has been no move to withdraw Medicare's universal eligibility for the elderly and disabled, a large share of the budget cuts have shifted financial responsibility to beneficiaries.[17] Cuts have also been made in physician and hospital payment. But, as described below, limits on physician payment will mean higher charges (more cost sharing) for beneficiaries, and reductions in hospital payments will not alter methods that support ever higher hospital costs per day. These per day costs are the overwhelming cause of increases in Medicare's hospital spending, which accounts for 70 percent of all Medicare spending.[18]

Increased cost sharing and benefit reductions accounted for more than half the $0.6 billion in projected 1983 Medicare savings from the 1981 congressional actions. Most of the remainder came from limits on payments to hospitals. The administration's 1983 budget is projected to save an additional $3 billion in 1983 through a variety of means, the most important of which are described below.[19]

Changes in Beneficiary Cost Sharing. Although President Reagan proposed no changes in cost sharing for fiscal 1982, Congress increased Medicare's cost-sharing requirements. Congress changed the method for calculating

Medicare's hospital deductible, raising it about 12 percent, and increased the physician deductible from $60 to $75. For 1983, the administration has proposed that the physician deductible rise with inflation (a proposal Congress considered and rejected in 1981) and that coinsurance be required on some services now without it (home health and hospital-based physicians). The administration has promised, but not yet proposed, to set a ceiling on all Medicare cost sharing in return for more cost sharing on hospital use until the ceiling is reached.

The 1983 budget would also raise cost sharing by reducing Medicare payments to physicians. Beneficiaries are now responsible for 20 percent of Medicare's "allowed" charge and for any charges above the allowed amount. The 1983 budget would tighten Medicare's allowable charge significantly. Experience suggests that physicians will respond by charging beneficiaries some or all of the amount the program denies.[20]

Higher charges to beneficiaries—through formal cost sharing and physicians' charge practices—come on top of already sizable out-of-pocket liabilities for Medicare beneficiaries. These liabilities reflect cost increases in the share of medical expenses that Medicare beneficiaries continue to pay. Although Medicare protects its beneficiaries relatively well against hospital costs, its protection against physician service costs has declined, as Medicare beneficiaries pay rising premiums for medical benefits, coinsurance, and charges above the amounts that Medicare allows. Excluding nursing home costs (which Medicare never intended to cover), the elderly now spend about 12 percent of their incomes on medical care compared to 13 percent in 1965.[21] Although the elderly receive better medical care, have a much lower risk of catastrophic spending for acute care, and have much higher incomes today, their medical liabilities remain substantial.

Higher cost sharing will probably reduce Medicare beneficiaries' use of services, particularly for those elderly not poor enough to qualify for Medicaid (13 percent of Medicare enrollees also receive Medicaid) or affluent enough to purchase private health insurance. Higher cost sharing will mean higher premiums for supplementary private insurance, which may reduce the number of elderly who purchase it.[22] Higher cost sharing also may affect use of physician services by beneficiaries with private insurance, since this insurance may not cover the deductible and rarely covers charges above amounts Medicare will pay. How much of any use forgone may be unnecessary is not known, although there is some evidence that use of physician services by beneficiaries with chronic conditions is only minimally affected by cost sharing.[23]

The administration's promised proposal to remove the current limit on covered hospital days and set a ceiling on Medicare cost sharing would address a major gap in current Medicare coverage. Although only a tiny proportion (less than half of one percent) of beneficiaries ever exhaust their hospital benefits, all beneficiaries face that risk. Similarly, open-ended cost sharing can impose substantial burdens on the very sick, particularly the poor or near-poor elderly without Medicaid or private insurance. The administration's suggested ceiling of $2,500 (about half the elderly's 1979 median cash income), however, would still expose this group to catastrophic risks. To promote efficient service use and afford adequate protection, cost sharing would ideally vary with income.

Changes in Hospital Payment. Medicare's agreement to pay the costs hospitals incur in delivering service has been criticized as inflationary from the start of the program. Intended to assure the access of beneficiaries to mainstream care, its effect has been to underwrite continual increases in hospital costs. Throughout the 1970s, the Congress and most administrations were reluctant to alter the payment method, fearful of antagonizing the hospital industry, uncertain of the design that would best promote efficiency and maintain access, and reluctant to shift burdens to other purchasers of hospital care. Aside from experimentation with alternative payment methods and efforts (stopped in the courts) to reduce some "extras" in the payment formula, the only restriction on hospital payment has been to deny payment for routine costs to hospitals egregiously out of line with their peers. The Reagan administration and the Congress have continued previous administrations' efforts along these lines but have not altered the payment system's basic approach.

The impact of these measures on Medicare liabilities is limited. First, ceilings on routine costs alone affect only about half of hospitals' costs and encourage hospitals to shift overhead costs to the open-ended category of ancillary services. Second, although ceilings tied to average costs can reduce Medicare liabilities for particularly high-cost hospitals, they may not alter the rate of increase in hospital costs over time. Continuing hospital expenditure increases are particularly likely if hospitals earn greater revenues from other payers to compensate for Medicare reductions.[24] The smaller Medicare's reductions are, the easier such compensations become.

On its own, Medicare cannot prevent hospitals from compensating for its payment limits with higher charges to other payers. But certain Medicare payment constraints would actively promote cost shifts to others, rather than cost reductions. For example, in its 1983 budget proposals, the administration proposed to reduce its payments to 98 percent of "allowable" cost. Under this approach (offered as an "interim" method, pending reforms), a hospital would be left with uncovered liabilities for Medicare beneficiaries regardless of its efficiency or the general appropriateness of its expenditures. Hospitals whose accounting systems did not already maximize Medicare's share of allowable costs could be expected to adjust their accounting to avoid a real loss. To the extent that this occurred, Medicare would save nothing. Without accounting adjustments, hospitals would be forced to seek financing from other payers. Hospitals with a small proportion of privately insured patients, especially public teaching hospitals, would be particularly hard hit by this approach.

Changes in Medicaid

To date, the administration's actions toward Medicaid reflect both its effort to reduce federal spending and its commitment to increase state responsibility and autonomy in financing health care for the poor. However, the administration's "New Federalism" initiative, announced with the 1983 budget, would reverse this direction by federalizing Medicaid in return for a greater state role in welfare and a multitude of smaller health and social programs. The governors initially proposed the Medicaid transfer, and the administration went along. Administration policy appears to reflect officials' belief that state absorption of welfare would be worth an increased federal role in health and that federal administrators would be more willing to control Medicaid spending than administrators in the states would be. Whatever its objectives, New Federalism is still on the drawing boards, and its adoption in any form is uncertain. This discussion will focus on the implications of the reduced federal role in the Medicaid program that is currently being pursued by the administration.

In its 1982 budget proposals, the administration sought to promote efficiency in Medicaid operation by "capping" the rate of increase in the federal share of Medicaid costs. As an "interim" measure, pending broader health care reforms, the administration proposed a flat "cap" of 5 percent on the growth of the federal Medicaid share for 1982 (to rise with the rate of increase in GNP thereafter), coupled with statutory changes allowing the states to better target limited dollars.

Responding to strong pressure from the governors, Congress rejected the administration's cap. House Democrats agreed to lower spending but designed their own cuts. Final congressional action retained open-ended matching, but reduced the federal share by 3 percent in 1982, 4 percent in 1983, and 4.5 percent in 1984. To reward efficiency, the law allowed states to offset the federal reduction, dollar for dollar, for any amount by which they held 1982 spending below 109 percent of the projected 1981 level. Congress also allowed states a one percentage-point offset to the reduction in federal matching payment for each of the following: an effective hospital rate-setting program already in operation; a state unemployment rate over 150 percent of the national average; and effective third-party collection and fraud-and-abuse programs.

Congress also altered Medicaid's rules for eligibility, benefits, and payment. By setting a ceiling on earned income for AFDC eligibility, Congress directly reduced the number of persons who automatically qualify for Medicaid benefits. States were given greater freedom to determine eligibility and benefits for certain groups, to make hospital payment less dependent on hospital costs, and to seek competitive bidding for some services. Finally, the legislation authorized the Department of Health and Human Services to waive a variety of statutory requirements to help states develop alternatives to fee-for-service medicine and long-term care services outside nursing homes.

The 1983 budget proposed more cuts in federal contributions with less attention to increased flexibility. Proposals include reducing federal matching rates for coverage of optional beneficiaries and services, eliminating federal matching grants for state payments to cover Medicare premiums and cost sharing for the elderly or disabled poor, and phasing out federal reimbursement for persons erroneously covered. The administration also proposed to require states to impose cost sharing on Medicaid services and to allow states to recover long-term care costs from beneficiaries' estates and relatives. Political opposition to federal cuts, particularly in the context of negotiation over New Federalism, makes enactment of many of these proposals unlikely.

For the most part, federal policy only sets the ground rules for Medicaid policy. Actual policy is made by the states.[25] The reductions in federal matching payments have had only a marginal impact on state behavior. Basically, they reinforced the far stronger pressure to reduce state spending that results from expenditure projections in excess of state revenues. Economic slowdowns, lost federal revenue sharing, and formal limitations on state and local taxes have reduced state revenues, while Medicaid costs have risen with medical cost inflation, recent increases in welfare caseloads because of unemployment, and increases in inpatient hospital utilization.[26]

Next to these pressures, the effects of the federal reductions were relatively small.[27] Many states expect to reduce the 3 percent federal cut to 2 percent through their third-party collection and fraud-and-abuse programs; the hardest-pressed states will receive the one percent offset because of unemployment; and seven states (accounting for about 30 percent of all Medicaid spending) are expected to receive the one percent offset for a hospital rate-setting program. Some states report that their spending will stay under 109 percent, in several cases because of restrictive measures taken before Congress passed the 1981 law. The ceiling on AFDC eligibility in the 1981 law also somewhat mitigated the financing cuts, as several states reported reductions in their Medicaid rolls from the eligibility change.

Although the FY 1982 federal cuts were small, federal policy changes are affecting the kinds of actions states take. These focus on eligibility for covered services, methods used to pay providers, and the scope of Medicaid benefits.

Eligibility. Medicaid eligibility is quite complex and varies across states. At a minimum, states must cover welfare recipients, and may include some persons potentially or actually eligible for welfare but not receiving it. States are permitted to cover the "medically needy"—persons whose age, disability, or family status falls within welfare categories and whose incomes exceed cash assistance levels but are nevertheless considered inadequate to cover medical bills. Regardless of income, able-bodied persons ages 18 through 64 and childless couples are not eligible for federally financed Medicaid benefits. Many states provide Medicaid-equivalent or other benefits at their own ("state only") expense to poor people not eligible for federal welfare payments.

The simplest way to limit Medicaid eligibility is to constrain eligibility for cash assistance. Over the years, most states have not raised AFDC standards to keep pace with inflation. As individuals' incomes rise, they leave the welfare and Medicaid rolls. States find that cutting eligibility by freezing income standards is politically more palatable than making actual cuts. But, over time, the impact of this approach has been substantial. Despite the rapid growth of low-income female-headed families, there were fewer Medicaid recipients in 1979 than there were in 1974.

Along with freezes on eligibility standards, several states are also eliminating Medicaid eligibility for some population groups. Now, as in the mid-1970s, state-only eligibles and unemployed parents are likely to be affected. Many states are also using the 1981 law's authority to drop coverage for young people aged 18 to 21, and, consistent with 1980 legislation, are tightening their enforcement of limits on the assets of persons entering nursing homes.

Overall, states' eligibility cuts have not been drastic. To date, states have not eliminated their "medically needy" programs (which account for almost half of Medicaid costs) and have not used new authority to set different eligibility standards for different groups. States' eligibility reductions are constrained for political and fiscal reasons. States are loath to risk the political consequences of reducing the elderly's coverage for nursing home care, which accounts for 40 percent of all Medicaid spending. For other groups, states fear that eligibility cuts would probably shift burdens to state or locally owned hospitals, as private providers refused service to the uninsured. State taxpayers would then bear the full cost of services, rather than just the state's share of Medicaid. Although freezes on eligibility impose this shift, and some states are indifferent to its occurrence, most see an advantage in federal participation in financing care to the poor.

Service Coverage and Payment Controls. States can also control Medicaid spending by limiting covered services or rates of payment. Federal law requires states to provide many medical services and allows states to cover others considered less essential. States can always choose not to cover optional services. Furthermore, the Medicaid statute has always allowed states to limit the scope or duration of any covered service, so long as "reasonable access" is maintained. The 1981 legislation made few significant changes in coverage provisions, but did allow states to provide different benefits to different eligibles.

Payment rates also affect total service use and service costs. Although the Medicaid law has always allowed states autonomy in setting physician fees and considerable flexibility in setting nursing home rates, federal oversight has inhibited state freedom in setting hospital payments. The 1981 changes greatly reduced federal oversight of hospital payment methods.

States are actively constraining Medicaid benefits and payments. Hospitals are a primary target, given the new payment authority and hospitals' importance (27.6 percent) in total Medicaid spending. Although the Medicaid law has allowed states to use an alternative to Medicare's method of cost reimbursement since the early 1970s, as of mid-1981, only thirteen states had adopted alternatives. The states' reluctance to pursue alternatives reflected the political power of the hospital industry, the perceived difficulty of meeting federal requirements for a satisfactory reimbursement system, and concern not only about access to care but also about the financial viability of public hospitals, which rely heavily on Medicaid revenues.

The 1981 law and its implementing regulations greatly reduced federal requirements on state systems, and some other concerns are being mitigated by fiscal pressure. Under the new law, state payments are less closely tied to hospitals' actual costs than previous law required. Although the courts will ultimately determine how much payment can deviate from costs, there is a strong likelihood that payment limits will become more stringent. By mid-1982, eighteen states had alternative systems[28] and almost as many states reported serious consideration of changes in hospital payment policy since passage of the 1981 law.

In addition to reimbursement changes, several states have introduced (or reduced) limits on the number of hospital days they will cover. These limits may reduce hospitals' willingness to accept Medicaid patients. They may also encourage patient transfers and the transfer of financial responsibility for Medicaid patients to other patients in a private hospital or to local taxpayers (if private hospitals transfer sicker patients to public institutions). Local governments' willingness and ability to support this care will vary from place to place.

Limits on Medicaid's hospital payments may also reduce private hospital service to Medicaid recipients and increase demands on public hospitals. The 1981 law authorizes special consideration in Medicaid rates for hospitals with a large proportion of Medicaid patients. Some states are using this provision to maintain federal participation in support of state or locally owned institutions as well as to assure the viability of providers of last resort.

State discretion over Medicaid payment to physicians has historically been much greater than that over payments to hospitals. While several states pay the same as Medicare, and some pay more, roughly half pay substantially less. Most of the largest states have fairly low fees and current fiscal pressure will keep them low. This policy may be having the unintended effect of reducing physicians' willingness to serve Medicaid patients, thus increasing Medicaid recipients' reliance on more expensive outpatient departments or inpatient care.[29] Independent of federal law, some states are trying to alter their fees to prevent this occurrence.

The 1981 law gave states greater flexibility to promote efficient alternatives to fee-for-service—including health maintenance organizations and less structured "case management" and "capitation networks." "Case management" involves paying fees to physicians for total management of a patient's care; "capitation networks" are prepayment arrangements with primary care physicians. Such plans are largely untried and face significant implementation problems. States are approaching these mechanisms with caution and few short-run savings can be expected.

Nursing homes, which account for over 40 percent of Medicaid expenses, have been only minimally affected by the 1981 legislation and are not a major target of current state efforts to cut Medicaid spending. Inactivity here largely reflects the considerable efforts of states to control nursing home growth in the past.[30] States have had the authority to constrain nursing home rates throughout Medicaid's history.[31] Nursing homes have never been paid as generously as hospitals, and states are appropriately concerned that further constraints on rates will mean less access to care and reduced quality of care for Medicaid recipients.

Congress may have alleviated access problems somewhat in 1981 by expanding Medicaid's coverage of long-term care services *outside* the nursing home. Congress hoped that expanding this coverage would save money by keeping people out of institutions when they required less extensive service than a nursing home provides. Experience suggests, however, that these new benefits may increase public expenses, since such services still are expensive and many more people are served than would otherwise enter nursing homes.[32] States must obtain federal approval or "waivers" for initiatives in this area, and federal regulations require assurances from states that Medicaid costs with the new benefits will not exceed costs without them. Assurances, however, are based on estimates and there is considerable room for manipulation. To many states, the new provision offers an opportunity to shift the costs of services they now fund at full or considerable state expense to the Medicaid program, with its relatively generous federal matching funds. By the summer of 1982, twenty-two states had applied for ''community care waivers,'' seven states had been approved, and many more were planning to apply.

States could also reduce Medicaid spending by eliminating coverage for intermediate-level nursing homes and other optional Medicaid benefits. With few exceptions, however, states have not eliminated coverage of major optional services. States began coverage of intermediate care facilities to reduce reliance on more expensive skilled nursing homes and to cover state-financed facilities providing less skilled nursing and personal care. In addition, states upgraded public facilities caring for the mentally ill and mentally retarded to meet Medicaid certification standards and earn Medicaid revenues. These optional services have been among the fastest growing items in Medicaid. They are not likely targets for cuts because states would then bear all, not just some, of these service costs. State costs would increase even if total costs fell. However, states have imposed limits on drugs and on minor optional services, such as those provided by dentists, chiropractors, and optometrists. These are considered less essential services and unlikely to result in a shifting of costs to fully state-financed sources.

Conclusions. States are actively seeking to limit Medicaid spending. However, state activity stems more from general fiscal problems than from changes in federal Medicaid policy. Major actions include freezes and some reductions in eligibility, reform of hospital payment, and limits on covered hospital days. The opportunity to limit hospital payment and some innovations in physician payment come from changes in federal law intended to enhance state flexibility. Other changes reflect the states' use of authority they have had all along.

The major impact of these changes will be to reduce payments made on behalf of the poor, thereby reducing their access to care. Many of the cutbacks may result in a shift of financial burdens to private providers or to local governments. States and their cities and counties will lose federal matching payments in the process, and areas will vary in their willingness and ability to support care.

One exception to retrenchment is the expansion of long-term care services outside institutions, authorized by the 1981 law. This expansion may compensate somewhat for limited access to nursing homes, but it may increase Medicaid costs. The federal government will bear the brunt of these costs, as states shift other programs for which funds have been cut to the Medicaid program, with its still open-ended federal matching funds.

While states are generally constraining the scope of their programs, there are clear limits on their willingness to do so. The poor and chronically ill are in need of some level of medical care and are unable to pay for it. Government support—whether federal, state, or local—is required. Maintaining some basic structure of Medicaid eligibility and benefits is attractive to states, despite the federal cutbacks, because the federal government matches state payments. Without Medicaid, state or local governments would bear these costs on their own.

Health Care Grants

The administration's efforts to realign governmental responsibilities have been most successful with respect to the multitude of health services grant programs. These grants have gone to state and local governments or to independent projects or organizations for diverse purposes, including public health, medical care to specific populations, and development of particular kinds of medical services. The kind and scope of program that grants have supported vary dramatically by program area and by region, and they defy simple classification. But all grants respond to perceptions of underservice of some kind, and many focus on poor populations. Through "categorical" grants, earmarked for specific purposes and subject to direct federal oversight, federal policy makers hoped to fill gaps they saw in the services provided by state and local governments or the private market.

The Reagan administration believes that decisions on the adequacy of service should be left to state and local governments. As a step in this direction, the administration's 1982 budget proposed combining twenty-five categorical health grants into two "blocks"—which would allow states considerable discretion in the use and allocation of funds. The blocks were to be funded at 75 percent of 1981 levels and allocated among the states in proportion to 1981 allocations of the former categorical grants.

Previous administrations had also proposed a shift toward health block grants, but had little success. The Reagan administration accomplished much, though not all, of its agenda. Congress gave the president more block grants than he had proposed, consolidating somewhat fewer categorical programs with more federal strings and lower spending cuts. Table 9-4 shows how Congress created four health blocks out of twenty-one programs, rather than two from twenty-five. (The precise number cited by different observers may vary because of how "program" is defined.) One "block," Primary Health Care, covered only the Community Health Centers program and retained so many requirements that it remained essentially categorical.

Despite the congressional changes, the new policy gives states far more discretion and far less federal money. Table 9-5 shows how total FY 1982 funds were cut 21 percent below FY 1981 levels and 28 percent below FY 1980. (Partly through mid-year rescissions of funds, the FY 1981 totals had

TABLE 9-4

BLOCK-GRANT STRUCTURE: PROPOSED VERSUS FINAL FORM

Two Blocks Proposed By The Administration	Old Categoricals	Four Blocks Enacted By Congress
Health Services (15 programs)	Community health centers Primary care research and development[a]	1. Primary care
	Maternal and child health grants to states SSI disabled children's services Hemophilia Sudden infant death syndrome	2. Maternal and child health (7 programs)
	Home health services Emergency medical services	3. Preventive health and health services (8 programs)
	Community mental health centers Alcoholism project grants and contracts Alcoholism grants to states Drug abuse project grant and contracts Drug abuse grants to states	4. Alcohol, drug abuse, and mental health (5 programs)
	Migrant health Black lung services	Not consolidated—they remain categorical programs

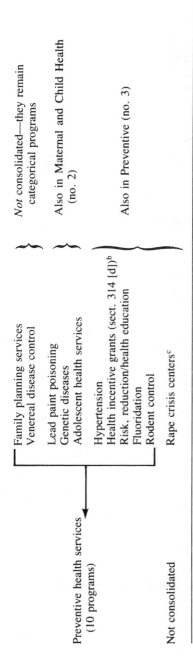

Preventive health services
(10 programs)

Family planning services
Venereal disease control

Lead paint poisoning
Genetic diseases
Adolescent health services

Hypertension
Health incentive grants (sect. 314 [d])[b]
Risk, reduction/health education
Fluoridation
Rodent control

Not consolidated—they remain categorical programs

Also in Maternal and Child Health (no. 2)

Also in Preventive (no. 3)

Not consolidated

Rape crisis centers[c]

SOURCES: Richard J. Price, *Health Block Grants*, Congressional Research Services, The U.S. Library of Congress, December 29, 1981. The original administration proposal included 26 programs, but the immunization program was withdrawn for consolidation after the initial announcement. The number of categorical programs affected varies according to the definition of ''program'' used. OMB's categorization for its *Catalog of Federal Domestic Assistance*, for example, counts 28 categoricals.

a. The R& D program was dropped in favor of a transitional planning grant to states for FY 1982 only, which was never funded.
b. Sect. 314(d) operated as a smaller block grant even before consolidation.
c. Not funded in FY 1981; originally created in 1980, outside Public Health Service.

TABLE 9-5

BLOCK GRANT SPENDING VERSUS PRIOR CATEGORICAL SPENDING

Block	FY 1980 Appropriations[a] (In $ millions)	FY 1981 Appropriations[b] (In $ millions)	FY 1980–81 Percentage Change	FY 1982 Appropriations[c] (In $ millions)	FY 1981–1982 Percentage Change	FY 1980–1982 Percentage Change
Preventive	169.9	93.1	−45.1	81.6	−12.4	−52.0
Alcohol, drug abuse, mental health	606.0	540.4	−10.8	428.1	−20.8	−29.4
Maternal and child health	432.8	454.4	+5.0	347.5	−23.5	−19.7
Primary care[d]	320.0	323.7	+1.1	246.3[d]	−23.9	−23.0
Total	1528.7	1411.6	−7.6	1103.5	−21.8	−27.8

a. Richard J. Price, *Health Block Grants* (updated 5/82 by telephone).
b. U.S. Department of Health and Human Services. Division of Health Budget Analysis, (7/82). Figures reflect mid-year rescissions in some cases.
c. Office of Management and Budget, *Budget of the United States Government, Fiscal Year 1983—Appendix* (corroborated by DHHS above). Figures reflect Congressional Continuing Resolution, in absence of final appropriations bill, and are significantly lower than the authorizations in The Omnibus Budget Reconciliation Act of 1981.
d. The Primary Care "block" will still operate categorically until at least FY 1983.

themselves already been lowered, notably for preventive services.) Over two years, preventive care suffered the most; maternal and child health and primary care suffered the least.

Block-grant proponents, especially within the administration, contend that spending cuts need not mean service cuts, since blocks allow offsetting administrative efficiencies—less "red tape," fewer reporting requirements, and more interprogram coordination and flexibility in program operations. Existing administrative spending, however, is much smaller than the cuts made.[33] Moreover, not all federal requirements have been ended, and states are moving to implement their own reporting and audit requirements to replace those that have been eliminated. For these reasons, almost all observers expect the ultimate consequence of budget reductions, even given the block grants' new flexibility, to be fewer and somewhat different services. The real issues here are whether more state control will achieve better value, even for less money, and whether states will get more of what people really want by changing the pattern of the (fewer) services delivered. This is impossible to determine as yet and is ultimately a value judgment. Any major progress in streamlining and improving programs will require more time, as well as considerable top-level attention, which is not readily available during the current fiscal crisis. These changes also will encounter resistance from multiple constituencies, including public employees.

It is too soon to predict where service cuts will occur and what their consequences will be. Almost all states have accepted the new block grants, in view of the immediate availability of funds, state officials' enthusiasm for increased discretion, and the administrative "fee" (up to 10 percent) the federal government would have charged for continuing to operate the categorical grants. But the first year of the health block grants, FY 1982, is really a transition period. States had almost no time to prepare for the block grants, and federal funding and regulations were still uncertain even as the fiscal year began. This uncertainty, reinforced by many states' inability to act without a legislature in session, postponed major state policy changes. In addition, many or most state programs cuts have been cushioned for most of FY 1982 because states still have in hand much of their 1981 categorical funds. The full extent of the federal reductions will not be felt until 1983 and beyond.

Partly because of these circumstances, states as yet have made relatively little use of their new discretion. They typically have retained existing program categories and have spread reduced 1982 funding pro rata across programs— at least for programs previously run at the state level. (Some federal funds previously went directly to local agencies and independent organizations or

projects. These are at greater immediate risk under state administration.)
Because states supplemented particular federal categorical grants to varying
degrees, pro rata cuts do not affect all services uniformly. Programs receiving
a small proportion of state funds (an indication of state priorities even under
the categorical programs) are hardest hit.

Although 1982 state activity is largely transitional, some trends are
emerging.[34] Most importantly, almost no state seems disposed to replace lost
categorical funds dollar for dollar. Some states are even requiring the same
proportionate cuts in any state matching funds that had previously been required under the old categorical grants. Some states have tried to cushion the
effects of cuts somewhat—in some cases by taking resources from less-valued
programs; in others, by shifting services previously funded under categorical
grants to other federal programs. Medicaid is the most attractive option, since
it still offers open-ended federal matching and can cover a variety of services,
such as family planning and long-term care, previously offered under categorical grants. A very few states have undertaken major reallocations.

How states will reallocate less money over the long run remains an open
question. But some predictions are possible, based on how programs fared
during earlier budget austerity. The main losers will surely be programs and
people most dependent on previous federal funding. These programs remained
"federal" initiatives and were of low priority to the state. State commitment,
budget inertia, and a sense of entitlement are likely to protect programs well
funded from state sources. Programs offering medical care to the sick will
probably fare better than preventive or public health, and mainstream medical
services that go beyond the poor (like crippled children's programs) will
probably do better than programs more oriented toward the poor. The political
appeal of a program's beneficiaries will undoubtedly weigh large. For example, mental health programs are usually viewed more favorably than sub-
stance abuse programs, and within the latter, alcohol programs are typically
favored over drugs.

It is hard to go much beyond these generalizations. But it is safe to say
that pressures for reallocation and more efficient management will increase.
In the administration's 1983 budget, several additional categorical programs
are proposed for consolidation into block grants—notably including family
planning, black lung, and migrant health. The very large Supplemental Nutrition Program for Women, Infants, and Children (WIC) is to be folded into
the maternal and child health block, with about a 30 percent cut in funding.
(WIC is now a Department of Agriculture program.) The administration is
determined to reduce the federal role in all these health programs, for both
philosophical and fiscal reasons.

Reforms to Promote Efficiency and Limit Health Costs

To the Reagan administration, rising health costs are not simply a budgetary or public problem. According to the 1982 *Economic Report of the President*, the growing share of private, like public, spending devoted to health reflects a health care financing system gone awry. Tax policy that insulates consumers from the full cost of health insurance (by excluding employer-paid premiums from taxable income) and insurance policies that insulate consumers from the direct cost of medical care (without substituting alternative constraints) "have frequently led consumers to purchase more medical care than they would have purchased if compelled to pay the costs."

To bring health care spending into line with health care's benefits, the Reagan administration promised to replace regulation with reforms to increase consumer sensitivity to insurance costs and thereby promote competition among insurers to improve efficiency in the use and delivery of medical services. Insurers could pursue greater efficiency in two ways, by increasing consumer incentives to weigh costs against benefits in using service (with higher consumer cost sharing, probably up to a ceiling) and by increasing providers' incentives to deliver only necessary services at minimal cost (by negotiating rates, giving preference to low cost providers, denying payment for "unnecessary" service use, and so on).

The administration has not pursued its reform strategy. Although it has been somewhat successful in reducing federal regulation, it has so far taken no initiative to enhance competition. The result of inaction has been continued medical cost increases, putting considerable pressure on the federal budget. In response to this pressure, the administration (or the Congress) may turn to the restraints on provider revenues that they initially rejected as "regulation."

Strategies to Enhance Competition

Although the administration has proposed no plan, the elements of a market strategy can be gleaned from its public pronouncements, options prepared for consideration, and legislative proposals.[35] The strategy would address public and private programs—the former through vouchers, the latter through tax reforms.

The private sector component has several facets. Most critical, in many people's view, is a ceiling on the amount of any employer-paid health insurance premium exempt from employees' taxable income. A cap of $150 per month now being discussed would affect about 40 percent of households insured through employment,[36] and encourage cost sensitivity in their insurance plans. To use that sensitivity to promote competition among insurers, most proposals would require or encourage employers to offer employees a choice among different types of health insurance plans, with employers making an equal dollar contribution to each plan, and, perhaps, rewards (including untaxed rebates) to employees choosing lower cost plans. This policy would depart from most current practice. Most employees (about 80 percent in 1977) now have no choice among plans; and where they do, the employer typically contributes more toward more expensive plans.[37]

Proposals differ in the requirements they would impose on employer offerings. Most proposals would impose minimum standards on all plans, addressing catastrophic coverage, information and advertising practices, and financial management. Some proposals would require specific offerings (plans with a specified amount of cost sharing or various types of health maintenance organizations), and some would try to prevent plans from competing for low-cost enrollees (by varying employer contributions with the employees' age, family, or health status; limiting the employees' freedom to switch plans; and restricting opportunities for plans to control enrollment).

The likely impact of proposed reforms on the private insurance and medical care market has been hotly debated. It will depend on the behavior of employers and employees and the pressure they put on insurers and providers to change patterns of service use and spending. Employer and employee lack of resistance to the rapid premium increases of the last decade and a half, even though cushioned by tax exclusions, makes many analysts question whether such policy changes would have a large effect. Health premiums amount to less than 6 percent of payroll costs, and health benefits are reportedly highly valued by employees.[38] Employers have been loath to tamper with these benefits in any way employees would construe as a reduction in benefits—including stringent utilization controls, restriction of benefits to specific providers, or limited payment. Further, both employers and unions have resisted choice among benefits plans as an interference in their prerogatives. If employees are offered a choice, they may prefer to "prepay" first-dollar expenses and avoid cost sharing or may be reluctant to join plans that require a change in providers.

On the other hand, there is growing recognition among employers that this administration will not remove their health cost problem through national health insurance or address it through regulation. Efforts to reduce the rate of growth in fringe benefits are reportedly spreading and include not only benefit reform but employer participation in community "coalitions" to contain local health care costs. Evidence about actual employee choices also suggests that consumers will weigh costs against benefits in their purchase of insurance. A recent study found that in 1977, among employees offered a choice, almost as many employees chose the lowest-cost option as the highest-cost option—despite employers' larger contribution and the tax advantage of the latter.[39]

There is also debate about the impact insurance changes would have on costs. Observers less optimistic about the success of such changes argue that insurer competition will focus more on enrolling good risks than on greater efficiency, that providers can avoid dealing with aggressive insurers, and that limited availability of capital, managerial talent, or provider and consumer interest will inhibit the growth of efficient delivery systems (like HMOs) as competitors to traditional fee-for-service providers. More sanguine observers argue that risk selection can be constrained, that empty hospital beds and a growing supply of physicians will make some providers willing to compete on the basis of costs, and that the action of some will put significant pressure on the rest.

Finally, there is heated disagreement about whether consumer choice is a desirable means of limiting health spending. Opponents believe that health care differs from other goods and services, that costs should not be an issue in the use of medical care, that all citizens should have comprehensive coverage, and that government should make decisions on the appropriate level of total spending. Proponents believe that different consumers value health care differently, that these values can guide service use without prohibiting access to needed care, and that allowing consumers to weigh costs against benefits will assure a better correspondence between total costs and benefits than would government decisions.

There is general agreement that a strategy of market reform will take time to be put into place and have any impact on health costs. In contrast, federal revenue gains from a change in tax policy could be immediate and substantial. Assuming an effective date of January 1, 1983, a tax cap of $150 per month would yield new federal revenues of $2.9 billion for 1983 and $7.9 billion by 1986.[40]

For public programs, enhancement of competition through choice entails a shift from publicly run to publicly financed insurance. Program participants would receive fixed-value vouchers to purchase insurance in the private market. The initial value of these vouchers would be the cost of an average beneficiary's medical care under the public system. As fixed-value vouchers encourage beneficiaries to pursue maximum value for their premium dollars, insurers are expected to effect efficiencies to compete for the voucher business. If beneficiaries' choices slow the rate of increase in overall program costs, government financers would save money over time.

There is reason to doubt that competition for Medicare and Medicaid beneficiaries' vouchers can lower public program costs. Medicare and Medicaid already pay providers lower rates than the private sector does. With rates constrained, it becomes difficult to set a voucher level sufficiently high to attract insurer and provider participation, without at least initially raising costs to the public program. Not only would private insurers probably have to pay providers more than Medicare or Medicaid (lacking their market share); they would incur marketing costs and financial risks not present in the public programs.

While overall savings are possible by reducing the reliance of Medicaid recipients' on high-cost hospitals and by reducing overall Medicare or Medicaid utilization rates, establishing mechanisms to achieve this goal is relatively complex. Innovations that enhance efficiency might occur in areas with large numbers of physicians and empty hospital beds. But competition for low-risk enrollees generally would be simpler and therefore seems more likely. If vouchers were offered on an optional basis, the result could be higher not lower public costs. People with below-average costs would get and use average-cost vouchers, while people with high costs would remain a public responsibility. If vouchers were mandatory, risk selection would still occur, but high-risk consumers, not government, would bear its costs. Government could save money by constraining the increase in voucher levels over time. However, if the increase were less than that in private medical care prices, the result would be reductions in the scope and quality of benefits for public beneficiaries.

Political Realities

Although the administration remains formally committed to reforms in the insurance market, its practical commitment has been quite limited. Initially, White House preoccupation with broader budgetary issues inhibited action, but, over time, other obstacles have emerged. Within the administration, it has been difficult to reach consensus on specific reform policies—particularly since many policies appropriate to the reform of health financing conflict with broader administration objectives. The administration's strong commitment to tax reductions impeded endorsement of the tax cap, and the administration's efforts to reduce federal regulation dampened enthusiasm for the active federal oversight that most reform proposals require.

Strong outside opposition to reforms has further weakened the administration's commitment. Most interest groups oppose the tax cap and the choice requirements. Business opposes any federal restriction on deductible business expenses or regulation of its fringe benefits. Labor perceives a reduction in valued benefits. Insurers resist the burdens and risks of competitive pressure. And providers fear the instability and potential financial pressure competitive reform could bring. The attractiveness of revenues from a tax cap may yet produce congressional action despite this opposition, but the administration has clearly relinquished the lead in promoting a competitive health care market.

The administration has been more aggressive in pursuing its promise to reduce federal regulation. In response to administration proposals, Congress authorized termination of federal funding for up to 30 percent of PSROs, if found ineffective. Following a review of PSRO performance, the administration eliminated approximately that proportion. The administration also proposed to eliminate federal requirements for state capital expenditures or certificate-of-need regulation by 1985, on grounds that restricting free entry and growth would interfere with the competitive process. Although Congress did not eliminate the federal mandate for state regulation in 1981, it did reduce federal requirements and federal funding. Further reduction of the federal role may occur in 1982. Reduced support for certificate-of-need regulation and PSROs is consistent with research evidence that neither has had much impact on hospital costs.[41]

Reduction of regulation without action to revitalize competition was never expected to slow spending for health care. There is growing concern among states and the administration that, without other reforms in the system, rejection of regulation could even stimulate expenditure growth. Health planners around the country report a substantial increase in applications for capital improvements and expansion. Although capital to support proposed investments is limited and costly, some investment analysts share the planners' view that an end to certificate-of-need regulation would mean an explosion in hospital spending.[42]

Whether or not prompted by deregulation, hospital spending grew especially rapidly in 1981, after slower growth in the preceding three years. Analysts attribute the earlier slowdown to the hospitals' "Voluntary Effort" to contain costs—a reaction to the Carter administration's hospital cost-containment proposal.[43] With this effort, the hospitals intended to defuse the pressure for congressional action. The renewal of hospital spending increases may reflect hospitals' compensation for earlier restraint or simply their desire to take advantage of a "breathing space" in public controls.

Fearful that the latter is the case, most states report that they will retain certificate-of-need regulation, even if federal requirements disappear.[44] More important, the administration has begun to rethink its opposition to Medicare payment limitations, previously rejected as too "regulatory." Congress is also pushing in this direction. As described earlier, there are two options for containing Medicare's hospital spending—slowing the overall rate of increase in hospital costs, to which Medicare payment is now tied, or breaking the tie between Medicare payment and hospital costs. Given its reluctance to promote competition as a means to slow overall growth (and given the fact that even aggressive pursuit of competition would take time to have an impact), the administration is apparently considering the alternative—the reform of Medicare hospital payment methods. Options include tightening ceilings on costs Medicare will pay (extension of the ceiling on routine costs to cover all hospital costs), setting Medicare rates independent of costs, allowing hospitals to bid for Medicare business, and requiring patients to pay more for more costly hospitals.

Rate restrictions of almost any sort can save Medicare money. Because Medicare's market share is large (about a third of nonprofit hospital revenues), significant reductions in its payments may slow all hospital spending if hospitals respond by cutting costs. Hospitals would undoubtedly try to compensate for Medicare cuts with higher charges to other payers, but the larger Medicare's cuts, the harder it becomes. Over time, different restrictions have different implications for cost increases, beneficiary access, and distribution of responsibility for financing hospital care. Tighter ceilings would save money for Medicare, because the program would reject costs above the allowed percentile of all hospital costs. But the ceiling would be tied to costs, and Medicare spending could continue to rise (particularly if hospitals get other payers to compensate for Medicare cuts). On the other hand, a commitment to keep rates tied to costs would help maintain beneficiaries' access to care.

Payments set independent of costs could allow greater control over Medicare spending but would encourage greater differentials between Medicare and other payers. Not only would hospitals attempt to raise charges to private patients to offset Medicare reductions, but refusal to serve Medicare patients would also become more likely.

Making Medicare business attractive to relatively low-cost hospitals (by such practices as promising a given volume of business or covering costs not otherwise paid) could save Medicare money while maintaining access. However, access would be limited to particular hospitals—a departure from current free choice, which Medicare beneficiaries value. An alternative would retain free choice and allow hospitals to charge patients more than what Medicare pays. Variation in charges would increase consumers' sensitivity to price and could encourage hospitals to compete for their business. However, given the elderly's predilection for supplementary insurance coverage and reliance on physicians with ties to particular hospitals, this competition may be less effective than it would be if hospitals negotiated directly with Medicare on rates and performance.

The likelihood that Medicare payment limits will reduce access to care for Medicare beneficiaries or shift costs to private purchasers is one reason that Congress and previous administrations have resisted payment reform (or, in the case of the Carter administration, proposed revenue controls affecting all payers). However, budgetary pressures are weakening this resistance both in the Reagan administration and the Congress. Some observers even see an advantage in shifting costs to private payers. Boosting costs for employers, in particular, may push them to seek low-cost providers or negotiate rates, thus promoting price competition even without tax reforms. Alternatively, higher costs may push employers (like many insurers) to advocate public rate regulation.

Conclusions

The Reagan administration proclaimed two major goals for federal health policy: (1) reduction of federal responsibilities and expenditures and (2) reform of public and private insurance mechanisms that promote rapid increases in health care costs. In its first year and a half in office, the administration's actions have been dominated by the budget; reforms have not even been formally proposed.

Budget cuts have affected all health programs, though to different degrees. The most dramatic changes came in health services grant programs, as block grants replaced most categorical spending and federal appropriations dropped by about 20 percent. It is too soon to ascertain exactly how states will respond to these changes and how beneficiaries will be affected. But early reactions indicate that states will not replace federal cuts dollar-for-dollar and that some programs will fare better than others as states allocate more limited funds.

Medicaid experienced smaller cuts. Legislation reduced only the amount federal spending would have grown. But this reduction, in combination with even more compelling general fiscal pressures, is leading many states to limit their Medicaid spending. Federal legislation tightened eligibility for cash assistance, which automatically induced Medicaid cutbacks. Under preexisting authority, states have constrained growth in eligibility standards and have imposed limits on covered services. Under newly legislated authority, some states have cut particular groups of eligibles from their welfare or Medicaid rolls and tightened specific eligibility standards. Many states are making hospital rates less dependent on hospital costs. These measures will reduce poor people's access to care and increase demands on public providers. Most states, however, have avoided dramatic cutbacks in eligibility or benefits. States are concerned that cuts would increase the dependence of the poor on sources of health care that are fully financed by state and local taxpayers.

Medicare's status as a social insurance rather than a welfare program has protected it from high percentage budget reductions. Nonetheless, in 1981 Congress increased the cost sharing required of beneficiaries, and the administration proposed further cost-sharing increases in its 1983 budget. New cost-sharing requirements raise already substantial patient cost-sharing liabilities and probably will affect service use, especially by the near-poor elderly who do not qualify for Medicaid. Although some cuts have been made in Medicare hospital payment, there has been no reform of the payment method that ties Medicare payments to hospital costs. Hence the rate of increase in Medicare spending will continue, albeit from a somewhat smaller base.

As long as federal health spending rises with general medical costs, budgetary cuts alone cannot control federal health spending. The administration has endorsed a market strategy for slowing all health cost increases, not simply to control public spending but to better align costs with benefits in the health care sector. This strategy would require tax reforms and other measures to increase the sensitivity of both private consumers and public program beneficiaries to the price of insurance and thereby increase insurers' incentives to promote efficient use and delivery of health care services. The success of such an approach is by no means certain, but problems in the strategy are less significant to the administration's performance than its failure to pursue its professed intent to promote competition. The administration has offered no legislation to implement the market strategy or any other strategy to limit health care costs. Maintenance of the tax exclusion for insurance premiums costs the federal government more than its share of the Medicaid program, yet no reduction in this subsidy has been proposed. With its inaction, the administration not only abandons its goals for greater efficiency, but also undermines its capacity to achieve overall budget control.

Inaction will entail several consequences for private consumers and public programs. Health costs will probably continue to rise at a rapid rate. For the roughly two-thirds of the privately insured population with comprehensive insurance, this will mean higher premiums, unless the private sector initiates cost-saving measures on its own. The other third will face a greater risk of catastrophic expenditures. Costs are always a problem for those without private or public insurance, but with economic recession and Medicaid cutbacks the number of people falling into this category is on the increase.

The failure to address Medicare costs will add to the pressure to make even further cuts in health services grant programs and to reduce federal contributions to Medicaid. Given the states' already considerable efforts to limit their spending, further federal cuts are more likely to mean reductions in service or higher costs to state taxpayers than to produce greater efficiency.

Reforms within the Medicare program to limit its growth would reduce the pressure to cut programs targeted to the poor. In the short run, well-designed constraints on hospital payment could save Medicare money while having a limited impact on beneficiaries' access to care. In the long run, Medicare can control its costs and maintain access to mainstream care only if private purchasers also pursue greater efficiency. Whether government or private purchasers take the lead, concern about rising health care costs promises to be high on public and private agendas throughout the 1980s.

Chapter 10

SOCIAL SERVICES

Michael F. Gutowski
Jeffrey J. Koshel

Income and in-kind transfers such as food, medical services, and housing are not the only needs of disadvantaged citizens. Nor is poverty the sole determinant of the need to look beyond one's own resources for assistance. The disoriented older person living alone, the pregnant teenager, the seriously disabled adult, and the abused or neglected child are examples of potential users of social services who can be found in all income classes.

Since the turn of the century, a broad array of social service programs has developed, funded by local, state, and federal governments, as well as by private organizations. Starting in the early 1960s, the federal government in particular expanded its financing role in this area. The changing domestic priorities of the Reagan administration are dealing a severe blow to publicly funded social services. If the president's FY 1983 budget proposals are accepted, inflation-adjusted federal financial support for social services will be reduced by almost 40 percent from FY 1981. Lower levels of government and private agencies will not be able to compensate for the loss. Each state and locality will have to decide how to respond to this cutback and which services to reduce or eliminate. These are difficult decisions, given the nature and purpose of social services programs.

Social services programs serve at least three major functions. First, they often provide the glue that holds together an array of federal, state, and local programs as well as the lives of the individuals who must cope with disabling problems. The vocational rehabilitation counselor, for example, develops a rehabilitation plan for a disabled client that often includes medical care, provided under Medicare or Medicaid, and referral to an appropriate income transfer program, such as Supplemental Security Income (SSI). Second, many social services authorized by federal legislation are intended to reduce or prevent unnecessary institutionalization. In the absence of publicly supported, community-based services, many physically disabled individuals, mentally retarded adults, or neglected children would have to rely entirely upon their family, friends, and voluntary organizations or be placed in public institutions. A third purpose of many social service programs is client advocacy. For example, the Older Americans Act specifically vested, within the Administration on Aging, an advocacy function on behalf of the elderly. The social caseworker or rehabilitation counselor generally "goes to bat" for the disadvantaged client. The public sector social services client typically does not have the knowledge, resources, or sophistication to confront the bewildering array of existing programs.

The first section of this chapter briefly reviews the historical trends in providing and financing social services and some of the reasons for these trends. The second section documents the changes in federal social services policy under the Reagan administration and speculates on some of their likely programmatic consequences. The final section discusses several concerns that are created by the changed circumstances.

Historical Developments in Social Services

An active federal role in support of social services did not develop until the first decade of this century. Prior to that time the responsibility for social services was assumed by state and local governments and charitable organizations. The federal role in social service programs has steadily expanded since then, with its primary emphasis on funding and technical support. The actual provision of social services has largely remained a function of state and local governments and private organizations.

The Expanding Federal Role in Social Services

Before the turn of the century, federal government participation in social services was minimal. The White House Conference on Dependent Children in 1909 marked the turning point toward active and continuing participation of the federal government in social services. The conference led to the formation in 1912 of the Children's Bureau, which still exists today as the federal agency responsible for promoting national policy on child welfare.

The National Civilian Rehabilitation Act of 1920 was another early key federal initiative in social services. It established the state-federal vocational rehabilitation program using the basic format of federal financing and state or local provision of social services that would become the predominant model. The New Deal ushered in an era of expanded federal involvement in social welfare programs, though most of the major initiatives were in income security, employment, and health. World War II brought with it a temporary federal commitment to day care programs to meet the needs of women working in the defense industry, with day care services provided to about 600,000 children. The postwar period saw little growth in social services except for a greatly expanded range of health, education, and social services for veterans.

The Public Welfare Amendments of 1962 initiated a period of rapid growth in federal financing of social services. These amendments provided for federal cost sharing (at a rate of 75 percent) with states for social services aimed at reducing or preventing the dependency of people on welfare. The law did not define clear limits on the types of services that were eligible for federal matching funds.

The extent to which states drew upon this new source of federal support for social services varied widely. Several states aggressively led the way in shifting the costs of social services to the federal government.[1] Between 1967 and 1971, federal funds made available under the 1962 amendments expanded from $242 million to $776 million. California alone absorbed between one-quarter and one-third of all federal funds during this time. It is somewhat ironic to note that this period coincides with President Reagan's first five years in office as governor of California. "California officials had a sophisticated grasp of the implications of the open-end in social services and the ways in which private as well as state and local public funds could be used."[2] They recognized the gains to be made from shifting services from programs with fixed budgets. They openly attempted to maximize federal matching grants. As Illinois, New York, and other states began adopting the same techniques, federal funding for social services continued to grow rapidly.

By 1972 Congress and the administration had decided to place limits on the growth of spending in social services. Between 1971 and 1972 federal grants for social services authorized by the 1962 amendments had more than doubled, to $1.688 billion. A national ceiling of $2.5 billion for social services expenditures under this program was enacted in 1972. Three years later a social services block grant program was created, under Title XX of the Social Security Act. Hailed as a "new federalism" initiative, Title XX substantially widened the latitude given to states in designing social services programs.

Clients eligible for services were expanded to include persons whose incomes were as high as 115 percent of the state's median income. The proportion of clients who were required to be categorically related (i.e., eligible for benefits under Aid to Families with Dependent Children (AFDC), Supplemental Security Income, or Medicaid) was reduced from 90 percent to 50 percent.

The 1960s and 1970s also saw the creation of several other major social services programs. A number of community-based service programs were funded by the Office of Economic Opportunity and its successor, the Community Services Administration. Most notable among these was Head Start, which provided comprehensive education and socialization services for disadvantaged preschool children. In 1965 the Older Americans Act was passed, which established a federal financing mechanism for locally based social services and nutrition programs for the elderly.

Although the 1970s saw the development of several new social services programs such as the ACTION volunteer program (1973) and the Legal Services Corporation (1974), there was no corresponding increase in the growth of resources for social services. Federal budget levels for some programs (e.g., rehabilitation services and Title XX services) continued to increase, but the rate of increase was less than that of inflation. Table 10-1 shows that federal support for major social services programs (adjusted for inflation) peaked in 1978. The decline in the real value of federal support between 1978 and 1981 was modest, but it set the stage for the more significant reductions under the current administration.

The rapid growth of federal funding of social services during the 1960s and 1970s was accompanied by steady, though less spectacular, growth in social services funding support by state and local levels of government. State and local spending for a broad range of social services programs increased from $722 million in 1960 to $4.2 billion in 1979.[3] This growth was far beyond that required to meet matching requirements for receipt of federal funds, suggesting that state and local governments perceived a strong need for such programs independent of federal encouragement. However, because of the more rapid increase in federal spending over the past several decades, the federal share of total public expenditures grew from 41 percent in 1955 to more than 60 percent in 1979.[4]

Factors Underlying the Expanding Public Role

The expanding role of the public sector in funding and providing social services can be traced to three principal factors, involving equity considerations, legal requirements, and economic concerns.

TABLE 10–1

FEDERAL FUNDING FOR MAJOR SOCIAL SERVICES PROGRAMS
(FY 1975–FY 1981)
FEDERAL OBLIGATIONS
(In 1981 $ millions)

	FY 1975	FY 1976	FY 1977	FY 1978	FY 1979	FY 1980	FY 1981
Title XX Social Services	3,259	3,297	3,468	3,868	3,672	2,887	2,490
Child Welfare[a]	246	278	288	318	293	341	524
Head Start	684	636	651	804	810	806	814
Administration on Aging[b]	386	398	612	656	684	788	749
Rehabilitation services	1,182	1,174	1,166	1,115	1,069	1,023	924
Community services	645	728	1,096	1,029	884	605[c]	527
Other services[d]	328	384	474	621	672	667	623
Total	6,730	6,895	7,756	8,412	8,084	7,118	6,651
Percentage change from previous year		+ 2.5	+ 12.5	+ 8.5	− 3.8	− 12.0	− 6.6

SOURCE: Office of Management and Budget, *Budget of the United States Government, FY 1977–FY 1983* (Washington, D.C.: GPO).

a. Includes other programs funded by the Department of Health and Human Services, Administration for Children, Youth, and Families, such as child abuse and runaway youth. Does not include Title XX funds for the same purposes.

b. Includes Department of Agriculture Support for Nutrition Program.

c. Does not include energy crisis assistance program.

d. Includes developmental disabilities, legal services, domestic volunteer (ACTION), juvenile justice and delinquency prevention.

Equity. The concern over equity has probably been the major reason why the funding levels and program emphasis of federal, state, and local social services expanded during the 1960s and 1970s. Increased funding reflected the normative judgment that the disadvantaged or poor should have equal access to specific services such as day care, family planning, and vocational training. Although such services have a well-organized private market, the poor or disadvantaged often cannot purchase such services without forgoing necessities.

Equity is typically discussed in terms of redistribution of income, but the traditional sense of justice extends equity beyond this narrow approach to embrace broader humanitarian principles. The abused child, the battered spouse, the pregnant teenager, the severely handicapped adult, and the disoriented older widow are examples of groups that most members of society express a desire to support with needed services regardless of the income level of their families. Active social services intervention in such cases will not typically yield positive results in a dollars-and-cents, benefit-cost calculus from a public sector perspective, but an overriding sense of public purpose has accompanied social services intervention in such cases.

The concern over equity was an important reason why the locus of financial responsibility for the indigent moved from communities to states and eventually to the federal government. Equal access to care of minimal quality across communities and states provided much of the impetus for state and, then, federal involvement in social services.

Legal Requirements. The legal system in our country tends to regard matters of equity as the province of the judicial system. There is growing documentation of the extent to which protection of the rights of welfare recipients, prisoners, mental patients, and other receivers of social services has served as a basis for direct judicial intervention in the provision of social services.[5] There is no question that the role of such intervention has grown stronger in recent decades.

The 1966 *Lake* v. *Cameron* case is a precedent-setting example of active judicial intervention in administration of social services programs.[6] Catherine Lake was an elderly woman found wandering in the streets of the District of Columbia. She later contested her commitment to the local public mental hospital. The federal court ordered that the district court should examine all alternatives to institutionalization, ranging from home care services to foster care. In Catherine Lake's case, no satisfactory alternative was found, so she remained at St. Elizabeth's Hospital. However, the decision was used as a precedent for later intervention. In the state of Maryland, for example, several judges take active roles in designing social services plans in all adult guardianship and civil commitment cases.

The combination of federal, state, and local judicial intervention in social services is likely to continue to play a major role in determining the level and allocation of public funds for social services. In many instances it may seriously constrain the options available to state and local officials to adjust to their changing fiscal situation.

Economic Factors. Some of the rationale for public financing of social services has been based on promoting market efficiency and reducing social costs. For example, many social services are aimed at reducing institutionalization. In some cases, home care, transportation, homemaker, meals on wheels, and other services can be effective in deferring or preventing costly institutionalization. Adolescent pregnancy prevention and family planning can lead to reduction in welfare and health service expenditures. Preventing or reducing the need for more expensive forms of care is a key "external benefit" of many types of social service programs. The federal government, in particular, has a strong financial interest in this objective, given its massive investment in noninstitutional care through programs such as Medicaid, Aid to Families with Dependent Children, Supplemental Security Income, and Social Security Disability Insurance.

Social Services within a Changing Federal Budget

The Reagan administration's policy toward social services is clearly motivated by its broad concerns about the need for budgetary restraint in domestic programs and the appropriate division of responsibility between federal and state governments. The president's FY 1983 budget requested another large reduction in social services funding on top of what he had exacted from Congress for FY 1982. Under his new federalism and block grant approach, states are given increased flexibility over the uses of the dwindling federal social services funds. This section discusses these broad policy directions and their more immediate consequences for major social services programs.

Broad Policy Directions

Congressional action on President Reagan's FY 1982 budget led to greatly reduced federal support for social services. The enacted legislation will reduce real spending levels by 20 percent between FY 1981 and FY 1983 (see table 10-2). Coupled with this reduction in federal support was a movement toward fewer constraints on state and local spending, as Title XX was converted to a less-restrictive block grant.

TABLE 10–2

CHANGES IN FEDERAL FUNDING FOR MAJOR SOCIAL SERVICES PROGRAMS UNDER THE REAGAN ADMINISTRATION
(Budget authority in 1981 $ millions)

	FY 1981 Actual	FY 1983 Current Services (incorporating changes enacted in 1981)		FY 1983 President's Budget (proposed)	
		Amount	Percentage Change from 1981	Amount	Percentage Change from 1981
Title XX Social Services	2,991	2,098	−30	1,690	−43
Child welfare[a]	502	429	−15	325	−35
Services to selected groups	2,599	2,441	−6	1,998	−23
Program funding:[b]					
Head Start	814	—	—	781	−4
Administration on Aging	760	—	—	558	−27
Rehabilitation services	924	—	—	534	−42
Community services	525	338	−36	89	−83
Other social services[c]	240	177	−26	159	−34
Total	6,857	5,483	−20	4,261	−38

SOURCE: Office of Management and Budget, *The Budget of the United States Government, Fiscal Year 1983*, Appendix and unpublished tabulations of current services estimates. Inflation ajustment for FY 1983 funding has been made by the authors.

a. Includes $328 million in FY 1981 program activities financed through AFDC foster care.

b. Program obligations of the Department of Health and Human Services and the Department of Agriculture; excludes activities financed through the Department of Education.

c. Includes domestic volunteer programs (ACTION), developmental disabilities, legal services, and juvenile justice and delinquency prevention.

The president's FY 1983 budget request entails further large reductions in social services that would lead to an overall real spending cut of 38 percent in FY 1983 from FY 1981 levels. The combination of enacted and proposed legislation would affect some areas of social services spending much more than others. Head Start, included as one of the "social safety net" programs, would be reduced by only 4 percent between FY 1981 and FY 1983. Community services, however, would be cut by 83 percent. The social services block grant funding level for FY 1983 would reduce by 43 percent the real spending financed through Title XX in 1981.

President Reagan's FY 1983 proposals also continue the movement toward program consolidation and increased state flexibility under block grants. A child welfare block grant would fund child welfare services and training, foster care, and adoption assistance at a real spending level 35 percent below that of FY 1981. A community services block grant would fund community-based antipoverty activities, with a drop in real spending of 83 percent from FY 1981. Finally, the administration's federalism initiative eventually would shift to the states full financing and administrative responsibilities for virtually all social service programs except, perhaps, Head Start.

Social Services Block Grant

The Omnibus Budget Reconciliation Act of 1981 renamed the Title XX program the Social Services Block Grant and made several key changes. The most significant changes were a sharp reduction in federal funding and elimination of state matching requirements. There were also some modifications in reporting requirements and more flexibility in allocation of funds for services to the states.

The Reagan administration had initially proposed consolidation of Title XX with several other social services programs, including child welfare and Community Services Administration programs, into a single Social Services Block Grant funded at $3.8 billion for FY 1982. This would have represented a 25 percent decrease from the $5.0 billion budgeted for the consolidated programs in 1981. The final reconciliation did not consolidate any other programs into the newly designated Social Services Block Grant.

For FY 1982 President Reagan requested that the $3.0 billion in budget authority for Title XX be reduced to $2.25 billion. The final figure in the reconciliation was $2.4 billion, about a 20 percent reduction from the previous year's appropriation. The president's FY 1983 budget requested another 18 percent reduction in the Social Services Block Grant to $1.97 billion.

The new block grant virtually eliminates federal reporting requirements. States will no longer be required to target assistance to SSI and AFDC recipients, and they will not have to adhere to federal income eligibility guidelines. States will be free to develop and design their own social services packages subject to minimal restrictions. Funds cannot be used for capital improvements, education, or medical care. Requirements for state plans and public participation in the social services planning process have been eliminated.

State and local officials appreciate the additional administrative discretion provided under the block grant; however, they are quite concerned about the sharp decline in federal funding support for social services. The 20 percent cut in federal nominal funding levels between FY 1981 and FY 1982, coupled with a nearly 10 percent reduction in the inflation-adjusted value of dollars, has already forced a number of administrative and programmatic changes. These include staffing reductions, service reduction or elimination, rate freezes on contracts with private providers of services, the shifting of some social services costs to Medicaid (e.g., adult home health) and AFDC (e.g., day care), and administrative "economies" (e.g., reduced staff travel, supplies, etc.).

A discussion of the experience in one state will illustrate some of the types of changes and effects stemming from the FY 1982 reductions. In Texas the federal Social Services Block Grant allotment was decreased from $176.3 million for FY 1981 to $149.8 million for FY 1982. Because of population growth, the Texas share declined by only 15 percent compared to the national decline of 20 percent. In addition to staff reductions and administrative "economies," the Texas Department of Human Services considered two major options for managing the decline in resources. One option was to apply the same 15 percent reduction to each program and administrative area in social services. The second was to allocate funds based on relative priorities of major program areas. The second option was adopted.

Table 10-3 displays the cuts in spending by major program area in Texas. Protective services directed toward children and the elderly fared better than adult and family services. The budget reductions have been estimated to have a significant impact on the number of clients served. For example, the child day care client annual caseload in Texas is expected to decline by about 19 percent, from 46,756 in 1981 to 37,940 in 1982. For the emergency family services program all services are being eliminated except for family violence and self-help projects. Emergency information and referral, arrangements for emergency food and shelter, and crisis counseling services are expected to decline by 26 percent. Community care services, which are designed to prevent or delay unnecessary entry into nursing homes, are expected to have only a token decrease in clients served (less than 2 percent decline). Interagency agreements, which are primarily Title XX-funded university training programs, were dropped.

TABLE 10–3

Effects of Omnibus Budget Reconciliation Act of 1981 on Texas Social
Services Budget
(Federal and state funds)

Service Area	Original 1982 Budget[a] (In $ millions)	Revised 1982 Budget[b] (In $ millions)	Percentage Cut from Budget
Protective	50.6	45.7	9.6
Day care	36.9	31.2	15.4
Family planning	17.5	14.7	15.8
Employment	2.6	1.9	24.4
Emergency	3.1	2.9	26.3
Social administration	4.3	3.6	17.7
Community care	82.6	74.9	9.3
Long-term training	3.3	0	100.0
Licensing	5.5	5.5	0
Agency administration	14.4	11.8	18.1
Fringe	13.2	12.0	9.0
Contingency fund	0	1.2	—
Total	234.0	204.9	12.4

Source: E. Durman, B. Davis, and M. Gutowski, *Texas Implementation of Changes in Entitlement Programs and Block Grants—Preliminary Report* (Washington, D.C.: The
Urban Institute, 1982).
 a.   Budget based on Title XX authorization level scheduled under prior law.
 b.   Budget based on Reconciliation Act authoriziation.

In the short term, the elimination of the 25 percent state and local matching requirements under the Social Services Block Grant will probably have little effect except in a few states. During the past few years most states spent more than required to match their federal share of social service dollars. All other things being equal, one would not expect state dollars for social services to decline but perhaps even to rise to offset the reductions in federal funds. However, states are faced with cutbacks in other federally funded programs and, in some cases, face recently legislated revenue or spending limitations that put severe pressure on their ability even to sustain their social services funding. One testimony to the priority given to social service programs is the decision by twenty states to transfer monies from the Low Income Energy Block Grant to the Social Services Block Grant under provisions contained in the Omnibus Budget Reconciliation Act.

The elimination of federal guidelines on eligibility and reporting requirements is not viewed as a significant change at the state level. States need more information than is currently provided to the federal government for their own management purposes. A number of states, such as Maryland and Illinois, are continuing with the development of new management information systems. The data previously reported to the federal government generally have been regarded to be of little value or validity. States have used their own reporting formats and service categories all along. The required federal reports never have been an accurate indicator of state social services behavior.

Child Welfare Services

As recently as June 17, 1980, Congress passed the Adoption Assistance and Child Welfare Act (P.L. 96-272), which sharply increased federal funding of state child welfare services programs. The act also created a strong federal presence guiding the nature and structure of state child welfare activities. A sharp increase in federal financial participation in child welfare for FY 1981 was followed by a modest decline in FY 1982 and a substantial 30 percent reduction as part of a Child Welfare Block Grant proposal for FY 1983.

Child welfare is a program area in which the current administration seeks to extend the principles of the ''new federalism'' despite a recent congressional initiative to induce states to adhere to federal program guidelines. P.L. 96-272 required states to redirect their efforts toward more permanency planning for children. The concern was that too heavy a reliance was placed upon extended use of foster care when the interests of both the children and the taxpayers would be served better by greater efforts to place the children in permanent homes. The increased federal support was directed toward subsidized adoption for hard-to-place children, family reunification, and in-home supportive services. The law requires states to conduct an inventory of children who have been in foster care for more than six months, implement a statewide information system on children in foster care, and implement a case review system for each child in foster care. States are also required to implement services designed to return children to their homes whenever possible. Clearly, the 1980 law and the 1981 budget brought an expanded federal presence into child welfare services.

The Omnibus Budget Reconciliation Act left the provision of P.L. 96-272 basically intact, though federal funding dropped below 1981 levels. The 1983 budget request folds adoption subsidy, foster care, and protective services into a Child Welfare Services Block Grant and cuts funding levels about 35 percent below the FY 1981 level.

Child welfare advocates contend that passage of the Child Welfare Block Grant would effectively repeal P.L. 96-272.[7] The movement toward permanent placement of children was predicated on federal financial incentives built into the law. Passage of the law rested on the notion that permanent placement was more cost effective in the long run than placing children in out-of-home care. Any short-run budget savings stemming from a block grant that resulted in fewer children leaving the foster care system would result in long-run cost increases.

The administration has countercharged that many states had begun movement toward more permanent planning well before passage of P.L. 96-272. It argues that the relative costs of in-home services and foster care vary widely among states, and that states can best define the most cost-effective approach to child welfare services delivery. The imposition of unnecessary federal reporting requirements increases the cost of the program.

The level of federal funding is another major issue. In FY 1981, federal child welfare program support was $524 million. In FY 1982, it dropped to $509 million, and the 1983 budget request is for $391 million. This decline, coupled with the reduction in the Social Services Block Grant funds, has caused significant changes in the availability of child welfare services. In Texas, for example, federal funding reductions resulted in the elimination of services to more than 40,000 children and youth. Although children in life- and safety-endangering situations are still being served, children at high risk of abuse and neglect are not. The state has also dropped services to unmarried and school-age parents. Thus, the child welfare budget reductions in Texas have been concentrated in prevention activities.

Head Start

The Head Start program is the major social services program that has received a continually increasing federal budget allocation through FY 1983. The administration has placed Head Start in the unique position among social services programs of being excluded from budgetary reductions. The reasons for this exception presumably stem from the strong political support the program enjoys as well as its success in meeting its program objectives.

Head Start relies on locally based and locally controlled prime sponsors and has a great deal of grass-roots community support. The program emphasis is on children from disadvantaged families, with a disproportionate representation of black and Spanish-speaking children served. Sponsoring agencies are primarily community action agencies (64.6 percent), with other nonprofit agencies (11.1 percent) and public school systems (10 percent) serving as the primary sponsor in most other cases. The program is intended to enhance the social and cultural competence of preschool children from low-income families in an attempt to enhance their capacity to deal with society and the school system as they grow older. It has been successful in raising the self-esteem of the children and better preparing them for elementary school activities.[8]

The Administration on Aging

In FY 1982 funding for the Administration on Aging (AoA) declined for the first time, going from $748 million to $720 million. The requested decrease for FY 1983 is sharper, to $652 million. Compared to most other social service programs, however, declines in AoA programs are recent and relatively modest.

The administration is committed to providing greater flexibility in AoA programs. Consistent with "New Federalism" initiatives, the administration has proposed greater latitude for states in allocating Older Americans Act funds. Key elements of the administration's legislation extending the Older Americans Act were repeal of the 50 percent requirements for access, in-home, and legal services (states and communities can continue to provide these services at their discretion); greater flexibility for state-operated ombudsman programs serving older residents of long-term care facilities; changes in state and area planning and reporting requirements to fit state needs; removal of specific budget subcategories for discretionary funding in order to provide the secretary of the Department of Health and Human Services with the flexibility to target funds of special need; and elimination of restrictions on the secretary's discretion to commingle certain funds with other departmental funds in support of projects benefiting the elderly.

State and local agency programs welcome the increased autonomy, but they are concerned about the declines in federal support for their activities in recent years and the larger planned reductions for FY 1983. The impact of these decreases cannot be determined at this time.

Vocational Rehabilitation

The state-federal vocational rehabilitation (VR) program is the federal social services grant program with the longest continuous history, dating back to the 1920s. It is also the first major social service program to experience real declines in federal support. It received relatively favorable treatment from the mid-1950s through the mid-1970s, but more recently inflation has eroded the value of federal funding.

Another source of funds for state VR agencies is expected to be curtailed substantially by federal regulation changes announced in October 1981 by the Social Security Administration. The costs of rehabilitation services for clients receiving Social Security Disability Insurance (SSDI) or Supplemental Security Income (SSI) were financed through the Social Security trust funds. Under these provisions, approximately $120 million per year was transferred to VR agencies to cover the costs of rehabilitating SSDI and SSI clients. The new regulations sharply limited the basis for reimbursing VR agencies. Reimbursement will not be made until the successful rehabilitation is demonstrated, and then only if the client is returned to performance of substantial gainful activity for a period of not less than nine months.

The regulations further stipulate that total reimbursement for an individual case must not be so high as to preclude savings to the trust fund, where savings are measured as Social Security benefits that will not have to be paid if the person is rehabilitated. The state agencies have the right of first refusal to participate in the program. If they elect not to participate, private profit or nonprofit organizations will be allowed to take part.

In FY 1979 the number of applicants accepted for rehabilitation services in the state programs was 1.2 million, and 324,000 clients were considered rehabilitated. By FY 1980 the number of applicants accepted dropped to just over 1.0 million, and the number of successful rehabilitations fell to 277,000. During the five-year period, real federal resources for rehabilitation fell 13.4 percent; the number of successful rehabilitations correspondingly fell by about 14 percent. If this pattern continues, successful rehabilitation can be expected to fall by more than 40 percent between 1981 and 1983. Few states have eliminated operating programs, but a substantial number have been reducing the number of clients served and have begun procedures to restrict eligibility for services. Most states have adopted and are continuing to develop new management practices to increase efficiency, but most state administrators predict decreasing returns to scale from such activities.

Virtually all states indicated that they have been compensating somewhat for reduced funding by trying to use resources from other community programs more effectively. But the tightening of eligibility requirements in other federally restricted programs, coupled with declining budgets in those areas, is beginning to close off optional sources of funding for disabled clients. For example, the New York Department of Social Services had been contracting with the state VR agency for services to the disabled, but transfers of funds to the New York VR agency have become one of the casualties of budget retrenchment in the state's social service programs.

Community Services Administration

The Community Services Administration (CSA) represents one of the remaining vestiges of the 1964 Economic Opportunity Act. It is the federal antipoverty agency in which local grantees, the community action agencies, often serve as sponsors of Head Start programs as well as recipients of grants from many other federal and state programs. The community action agencies represented an attempt to bring social services programs closer to the community. In a sense, the original intentions were similar to the goals of the

New Federalism. "The governments closest to the people--the state and local governments--are more responsive to the needs and desires of their citizens than is the federal government."[9] The community action agencies carried the theme a step further, reflecting the view that community-based organizations could respond more effectively to the needs of disadvantaged citizens than could even local governments. The real level of CSA expenditures declined modestly under the Carter administration.

The Omnibus Budget Reconciliation Act accelerated this trend, leaving CSA's 1981 funding at about one-third of its 1977 level of $1 billion, in real terms. The president's 1983 request calls for an additional major cut to below $100 million. The Reagan administration has shifted CSA to the Department of Health and Human Services. Its intent is to phase out entirely its activities by subsuming them under the Social Services Block Grant.

The sharp decline in CSA funds implies that the range of community services provided will of course be curtailed. In the Atlanta region, for example, CSA provided a broad range of social services to about 33,000 clients in FY 1981. The Atlanta Regional Commission estimates that the number of clients served in FY 1982 will fall to 16,500 and decrease even further in FY 1983.[10]

Issues

This review of the impact of recent federal activities suggests several major policy concerns involving social service programs. Although some effects of these changes are already apparent, others probably will not be noticeable for some time. Each issue discussed below will be the subject of further investigation as the analysis of changing domestic priorities continues over the next few years.

Impact on Social Welfare Effectiveness

According to Health and Human Services Secretary Richard Schweiker, the inability of the Reagan administration and Congress to agree on some method of controlling the growth of entitlement programs is squeezing the life out of discretionary programs such as social services.[11] The changing mix of social welfare spending is illustrated in table 10-4. The last column shows the ratio of federal expenditures for social services to those for income security and health over the past two decades. In 1982 the ratio of federal expenditures on social services to federal payments to individuals for all

TABLE 10–4

COMPARISON OF FEDERAL EXPENDITURES ON INCOME SECURITY AND HEALTH
PROGRAMS WITH FEDERAL EXPENDITURES ON SOCIAL SERVICES
(FY 1966–FY 1982)

Fiscal Year	*Income Security (In $ billions)*	*Health (In $ billions)*	*Social Services (In $ billions)*	*Ratio of Social Services Spending to Income Security and Health Spending (Percentage)*
1966	25.3	.3	.8	3.1
1967	27.2	3.8	1.5	4.8
1968	29.4	5.5	1.8	5.2
1969	32.5	6.9	2.0	5.1
1970	37.3	7.5	2.3	5.1
1971	48.3	7.9	2.7	4.8
1972	54.8	9.3	4.0	6.2
1973	64.1	10.0	3.7	5.0
1974	75.7	11.8	3.7	4.2
1975	99.4	15.4	4.4	3.8
1976	116.3	18.5	4.5	3.3
1977	125.4	22.4	5.1	3.5
1978	132.5	26.1	5.6	3.5
1979	145.2	30.2	6.6	3.8
1980	174.5	36.3	6.1	2.9
1981	204.1	43.8	6.5	2.6
1982	228.9	50.7	6.4	2.3

SOURCES: Office of Management and Budget, *Budget of the United States Government, Fiscal Year 1983*, Payments for Individuals (Washington, D.C.: GPO, 1982), table 3; Office of Management and Budget, *Federal Government Finances, 1983 Budget Data* (Washington, D.C.: GPO, 1982), table 7.

income security and health programs was only 2.3 percent. The level of federal support for social services relative to income transfers over the past three years is less than any time since the creation of Medicare and Medicaid in the mid-1960s.

As was noted earlier, social services can complement other cash or in-kind benefits and thereby increase the effectiveness of several programs beyond the sum of their individual contributions. As federal spending on social services programs is decreased relative to income security and health programs, some disproportionate reduction in the overall effectiveness of our societal investment in social welfare can be expected. The priority that states have attached to maintaining their social services funding is an indication of their growing concern over this changing mix of federal social welfare spending.

Replacing Diminished Federal Support

Social services agencies have been adjusting to eroding federal support since the late 1970s. Under the Reagan administration, the erosion of social services funds by inflation has been exacerbated by substantial cuts in dollar levels in almost all program areas. The efforts made by state and local administrators in recent years to reduce the costs of services and to target resources more effectively have had to be supplemented by significant changes in program financing strategy.

There are three basic methods that states and localities can use to replace federal dollars for social services programs. First, the financing of a few services can be shifted to entitlement programs with opened-ended federal matching funds or, as discussed in chapter 6, from other block grants. Second, states and localities can raise additional funds for social services beyond those needed to match federal dollars. Third, increased support for these programs can be sought from the private sector. These methods have had distinct limitations in the past and, in general, are likely to have even more constraining limitations over the next several years. However, the incentives for states to pursue these methods will be even greater due to fiscal pressures.

Shifting Federal Funding Sources. A few services can be shifted from traditional social services funding sources to open-ended entitlements: day care for children of AFDC families, home health care and personal care for individuals with functional limitations under Medicaid, and family planning services for persons eligible for Medicaid coverage. The potential for states to do this is limited but significant. Where it occurs it will increase the costs to the federal government and allow states to stretch their social services budgets further.

Federal regulations treat the cost of day care for children of working AFDC mothers in such a way as to compensate the mothers for their day care expenses. (In a few states this provision does not apply due to the complexities of their welfare payment schedules.) This public subsidy represented by the day care allowance can be provided through the AFDC program rather than the Social Services Block Grant mechanism for AFDC recipients who are working. In 1979 approximately 30 percent of social-services-funded day care went to such AFDC recipients in all states, representing $245 million.[12] Since 1979 a number of states have shifted from social-services-funded day care to AFDC-subsidized day care. Therefore, the amount that could be transferred today is limited, but some potential still exists.

Under Medicaid, states have always had the ability to provide home health services and the option of providing personal care services as well. In 1980 expenditures for such purposes totaled $358 million.[13] Until recently these services had to be prescribed by a physician and supervised by a nurse. The "medical" context of in-home care provided under Medicaid made it appear somewhat different to state officials than the in-home services funded under Title XX. With less money available under Title XX, some states (e.g., New York, South Carolina, Iowa, and Minnesota) decided that despite the "technical" differences, Medicaid could substitute for social services funds to cover home health and personal care.

The Omnibus Reconciliation Act gave states greater flexibility in using Medicaid for noninstitutional care. As long as a state can reduce its projected nursing home population, it can apply the projected savings to cover noninstitutional care.[14] The potential amount of social-services-funded noninstitutional care that could now be transferred to Medicaid under the Omnibus Reconciliation Act provisions could be significant. In 1980, for example, service expenditures for noninstitutionalized Supplemental Security Income recipients under Title XX totaled $640 million, about 21 percent of all Title XX expenditures for that year.[15]

Under Title XX, family planning services had been required to be provided by each state, although they also had to be offered under Medicaid. In 1980 approximately $81 million of family planning services were paid for by Medicaid.[16] As long as the state is willing to limit its family planning services to those recipients eligible for Medicaid, there is nothing to prevent them from transferring all the costs of family planning services to Medicaid from the Social Services Block Grant.

The ability of states to substitute AFDC and Medicaid funding for family planning and other services may be drastically reduced as a result of further efforts to decrease the federal budget deficit. The Reagan administration has proposed to cap the federal contribution to Medicaid and to transfer the AFDC program to the states. If either or both of these proposals are eventually accepted by Congress, states will not be able to offset their sharply reduced budgets for social services with other federal funds.

Increasing State and Local Financial Support. It is difficult to obtain a precise estimate of the level of support that states and localities provide for social services. Expenditure data on programs authorized by federal legislation, for instance, do not include certain social services funded by states and communities, such as services to dependent and neglected children who are not from AFDC families.

Using aggregate data compiled by the Social Security Administration, the best estimate that can be made of the relative share of funding between the federal government and the state and local governments for social services is 60 percent federal and 40 percent state and local for 1979.[17] The ability and willingness of state and local governments to expand their funding commitments in the face of the economic recession and general cutbacks in federal assistance are in serious doubt at present. Very few states are even attempting to offset reduced levels of federal support for social services with increased state support.

Increasing Private Sector Support. Charitable giving for social services was estimated at $4.35 billion for 1979.[18] This estimate covers the set of services typically supplied by United Way agencies. As such, it involves a broader set of services, such as Boy Scouts and Little League, than those funded by public sources. Nevertheless, private spending for social services represents a significant portion of spending for social services, probably accounting for 35 to 40 percent of the total.

Individuals and corporations are highly unlikely to make up for much of the reduction in federal support for social services.[19] The American Association of Fund-Raising Counsel reports that, over the last five years, the average annual rate of growth in charitable giving for social services has been about 11 percent.[20] The annual growth in charitable giving would have to increase to approximately 40 percent in order to offset the reduction in real federal spending for social services that is scheduled to occur between 1981 and 1983.

One other possible response from the private sector is an increase in in-kind contributions. Prior to the creation of the Legal Services Corporation, for example, legal services for poor families were"donated" by private lawyers. Although it is impossible to estimate precisely the effect of eliminating federal funding for legal services (except for those authorized by the Older Americans Act), withdrawal of federal support will probably return us to the situation of the early 1960s, when there was a widespread belief that the volume of donated legal services was insufficient to insure equal access for citizens of all income levels to the judicial system.

Client Advocacy versus Cost Reduction

The administration's desire to reduce the costs of social services will undoubtedly clash with the legislative intent of some major programs to advocate on behalf of their client groups. Advocating for particular clienteles involves, among other things, providing information and referral services to individuals who are entitled to specific benefits, either cash or in-kind transfers. Agencies on aging, vocational rehabilitation agencies, and developmental disability councils are just some of the social services organizational entities that are required by law to advocate on behalf of their service populations. Over time, it will be important to observe how such organizations attempt to fulfill this mandate in the face of drastically reduced resources. It would not be surprising if administrators choose to support direct services, such as emergency protection for the elderly, instead of advocacy or information and referral services.

Since the mid-1960s community action agencies and legal service agencies have also played a role in increasing participation rates in income transfer and health programs. They undoubtedly had an effect on increasing participation rates and assisting citizens in obtaining eligibility for some income transfer and medical entitlement programs. The reduced level of federal support for CSA and the scheduled elimination of federal support for legal services will, in all likelihood, result in a gradual decline in community awareness and advocacy for client entitlement to public programs.

Quality of Services

The changes made by local and state administrators of social services to cope with greatly diminished resources may very well have a deleterious effect on the quality of services provided. A brief review of the major modifications made by administrators provides prima facie evidence of this consequence:

1. Public agency monitoring of services provided by private contractors is being curtailed or eliminated in a number of areas.
2. Client caseloads of agency workers are being increased as a result of staff reductions.
3. Standards of care (e.g., licensing of providers) are being relaxed or eliminated.
4. Less-qualified people are being hired by state and local agencies in order to reduce the average staff salary.
5. Staff training is being postponed or eliminated.
6. Donated services for the private sector are being sought to replace those that had been purchased.
7. Maximum hours or months of particular services, such as homemaking, are being reduced.
8. Prevention services are being eliminated to concentrate on those currently in need of care.

Although no one of these actions may be sufficient to cause a deterioration in the quality of the services provided, together they strongly suggest that some reduction in the quality of care is inevitable.

Availability of a Social Safety Net

Social services can be seen as part of the social safety net that the administration has cited as necessary to provide care for truly needy people. Foster care and adoption services, for example, are clearly needed to protect one of the most dependent groups in our society—abandoned or abused children. As discussed earlier in this chapter, the ability of states and localities to provide such services is in jeopardy right now, and the funding cuts proposed for child welfare services in FY 1983 are likely to make it even more difficult to serve such children in the future. The same can be said for their ability to provide care for disoriented adults or severely handicapped individuals who are attempting to remain in noninstitutional settings.

In the past, the care of dependent people was generally provided in large institutions. For a variety of reasons, especially the availability of federal financial support, the locus of care for such individuals was eventually shifted to community-based facilities, such as foster care homes, group homes, and nursing homes. For community-based alternatives to work effectively, there must be an adequate range of community resources and social services programs. A movement back to large institutions may be one consequence of reductions in social services expenditures (except for individuals who are protected by federal or state statute, such as handicapped children).

As the full effects of the Reagan budget cuts begin to be felt over the next few years, it will be important to evaluate the adequacy of the social safety net in protecting vulnerable people, particularly those who most recently have received services in noninstitutional settings. It will be equally important to assess whether short-term federal budget savings in community services to the elderly, the handicapped, and other at-risk populations result, in fact, in increased costs to states to support such people in institutional arrangements.

Chapter 11

EDUCATION

June A. O'Neill
Margaret C. Simms

Education in the United States is heavily publicly funded and publicly operated. But it has been primarily state and local governments that have been responsible for this public support. During the 1970s the federal government contributed about 11 percent of the revenues of educational institutions; state and local governments contributed about 64 percent; and private sources the remaining 25 percent.

The relative importance of these funding shares and their historical evolution differs significantly by level of schooling. Local jurisdictions were at one time largely responsible for funding elementary and secondary education. Over time their role in funding, along with their autonomy, declined as primarily state and secondarily federal funding rose. At the end of the 1970s, state and local governments shared about equally in the funding of public elementary and secondary schools, while the federal share had grown from about 3 percent in 1950 to close to 10 percent. Private schools now account

[Margaret C. Simms is responsible for the elementary and secondary education portion of this chapter, and June A. O'Neill for the section on higher education. The authors gratefully acknowledge comments from Charles Benson, David Breneman, Denis Doyle, Thomas Glennan, and Susan Nelson, and assistance with data from Deborah Kalcevic.]

for about 11 percent of enrollments and resources at the elementary and secondary level.

The picture at the higher education level is very different. In 1950 about half of enrollments and resources in colleges and universities were in privately controlled institutions. More recently they have declined in relative importance with the enormous rise in state funded institutions. At the end of the last decade private institutions enrolled 22 percent of students and received about one-third of all higher education revenues. The sources of funding of private and public institutions, however, are not clearly divided by private and public origin since both receive considerable revenues from state and federal governments as well as from students and other private sources. Moreover, in recent years federal support has been going increasingly to college students directly, by-passing the institutions. Although this direct student aid has increased dramatically, federal giving to institutions has declined over the decade relative to other sources of higher education funding.

The Reagan administration has sought a significant change in the dollar contribution of the federal government to education in keeping with a change in the philosophy behind the federal role. President Reagan's 1983 budget expresses the belief that the "federal government's influence on parental, state, and local education decision making has been growing rapidly in recent years." The program changes are designed to reduce federal control, which is seen as exerting much more influence through the rules and regulations that accompany funding than the small level of funding would imply. These aims are to be achieved through substantial funding reductions and through other actions, such as the abolition of the federal Department of Education and the conversion of many categorical education programs for elementary and secondary schooling to block grants, which provide greater flexibility for state and local governments. The one proposed funding increase, the initiation of a tuition tax credit for parents with children attending private elementary and secondary schools, is intended to give parents more control and public schools more competition.

At the higher education level, funding cutbacks have been proposed along with some programmatic changes. These would mainly reduce the provision of student aid to middle- and upper-income students, while generally adhering to the recent trend of concentrating federal funds on student aid rather than on institutional funding. The changes proposed at the elementary and secondary school levels clearly involve a more profound change in direction. The major issue they raise is whether the reduced funding or diminished federal control will lead to signficantly diminished resources for low-income children and others who have been the target populations for the major compensatory education programs.

In his first year in office, President Reagan was partly successful in getting his proposed changes through Congress. Appropriations exceeded his requests while regulatory changes were more modest than requested. In spite of the reluctance of Congress to make radical changes in educational policy, the Reagan administration still proposes to cut the 1986 federal expenditures on education to half of their 1981 levels.

This chapter is divided into two major sections. The first discusses elementary, secondary, and vocational education while the second focuses on student financial aid for higher education. Each section reviews historical trends in educational programs, summarizes the changes in those programs that have been proposed and implemented under the Reagan administration, and discusses the likely impacts of these changes for students, schools, and governmental jurisdictions.

Elementary, Secondary, and Vocational Education

The provision of educational services at the elementary and secondary level has been and remains primarily the responsibility of state and local governments. However, the role of the federal government has grown significantly over the past three decades. Federal funding as a percentage of total elementary and secondary school revenues has increased from 2.9 percent in 1949-1950 to 4.6 percent in 1959-1960 and 9.8 percent in 1980-1981.[1] Federal mandates for state and local provision of special services have also increased, giving the federal government an influence over education that exceeds the proportion of funds provided.

The History of the Federal Role

The federal role in providing financial support for elementary and secondary education began in 1917 with the passage of the Smith-Hughes Act providing funds for vocational education. This intervention was directly related to labor shortages in the expanding industrial sector. Although there was interest in expanding aid to education beyond vocational programs, no major new initiatives were passed until the introduction of impact aid during the Korean War. This program was established to provide funds in lieu of taxes to local school districts where a substantial federal presence, such as a military base, increased school enrollment or reduced local tax revenues.

Additional funds for scientific, technical, and foreign language studies became available under the National Defense Education Act in 1958.

A major change in the level and direction of federal aid occurred in the 1960s. Because education was thought to be a major tool in eliminating poverty, federal support was directed toward the disadvantaged. These programs were developed both to provide for children in low-income states which could not afford to provide special services and to provide for disadvantaged children regardless of location on the assumption that many state governments were unwilling to provide these services. The Vocational Education Act of 1963 included provisions for targeting funds on disadvantaged groups. The most significant change, however, came with the passage of the Elementary and Secondary Education Act of 1965 (ESEA). The majority of the funds authorized under ESEA were accounted for by Title I, which provided aid to disadvantaged children. Amendments were added in later years to provide funds for handicapped and bilingual students. During the 1970s funds were authorized for districts undergoing desegregation (Emergency School Aid Act) and mandates were legislated for the handicapped (Education for All Handicapped Children Act).

The federal government has not provided funds to support private schools at the elementary and secondary levels. However, many of them are eligible for and have participated in federal programs targeted on the disadvantaged. A move to provide tuition tax credits to parents with children in private schools began in earnest in the late 1970s, but no law has passed both Houses of Congress.

Largely as a result of the increased number of programs, federal education expenditures increased from $490 million in 1960 to $3.2 billion in 1970. Even after adjusting for inflation, the increase in funding over the ten-year period was in excess of 300 percent. Between 1970 and 1979 federal funding for education doubled to $6.7 billion, but as a result of inflation, real expenditures increased less than 10 percent over the decade. In fact, during the last half of the decade, increases failed to keep pace with inflation.

The Status of Major Education Programs in FY 1981

In FY 1981 federal outlays for elementary, secondary, and vocational education were $7.0 billion. Over one-half of the funds went to programs for the disadvantaged, mainly under Title I. The second largest program was vocational education, followed by educational programs for the handicapped, and impact aid. These four programs constituted nearly 90 percent of all federal outlays at the elementary and secondary level (table 11-1).

TABLE 11–1

FEDERAL FUNDING FOR ELEMENTARY, SECONDARY, AND VOCATIONAL EDUCATION
FOR FY 1981
(In $ millions)

	FY 1981	
	Budget Authority	Outlays
Compensatory education for the disadvantaged	3,112	3,354
Other elementary and secondary education programs	614	735
Indian education	352	316
Impact aid	662	697
Education for the handicapped	1,052	1,035
Vocational and adult education	782	728
Other	166	178
Total	6,713	7,043

SOURCE: Office of Management and Budget, *Budget of the United States Government, Fiscal Year 1983* (Washington, D.C.: GPO, 1982).

Aid to the Disadvantaged. Funding for compensatory education for the disadvantaged (Title I) in FY 1981 was $3.4 billion. The congressional intent was to provide additional monies to school districts with large numbers of disadvantaged students; to provide special services to low-achieving children in schools with low revenue levels; and to subsidize programs that contributed to the cognitive, social, and emotional development of particular students.[2] Ninety-four percent of all school districts received some funds under Title I, but districts with large concentrations of poor children received larger per pupil allocations. This tendency was increased by the addition of concentration grants in 1978 which directed additional funds to districts where there were 5,000 or more poor children or where such children constituted over 20 percent of the student population.

Regulations governing the use of Title I funds have been extensive and accounting for the use of funds has involved substantial amounts of paperwork. In order to assure that the federal monies were being used to "supplement and not supplant" local expenditures, states and localities have been required to maintain their previous expenditure levels. Moreover, the local district had to show that it spent a comparable amount on Title I and non-Title I children exclusive of Title I funds. Although these regulations have elicited complaints from local districts, they appear to have resulted in well-targeted programs and have helped local officials resist pressure to use funds for tax relief or for general education purposes.[3] Even more importantly, studies indicate that

Title I programs have increased educational performance. For example, between 1970 and 1979 students attending Title I eligible schools improved their reading skills faster than comparable students attending non-Title I eligible schools.[4]

Other programs have been targeted on disadvantaged groups, including those for children of migrant workers, children with limited English-speaking ability, and Indian children. Most of these programs were highly targeted, and the majority distributed funds on a competitive or application basis. The sum of the outlays for these programs was small in comparison to Title I. Evaluations of program outcomes are either nonexistent or inconclusive.

Vocational Education. Although the federal vocational education program has been a substantial proportion of federal spending on education, it has constituted less than 10 percent of all funds spent on vocational education. States are required to match the federal contribution dollar for dollar. The fact that states provide far more funds than required suggests that the federal government has had little impact on the overall level of spending on vocational education. Rather, its primary influence has been on the composition of spending. The 1976 Vocational Education Act provided numerous set-asides for the use of federal funds. These set-asides required local districts to use a percentage of federal funds to provide services to special target groups, including 10 percent for the excess cost of vocational education for the handicapped and 20 percent for the excess cost of vocational education for disadvantaged groups. States were required to match these amounts. The act also established guidelines for sex equity in vocational training.

The bulk of all funds for vocational education are spent at the secondary level. Studies on the effectiveness of secondary vocational education indicate that it results in no net lifetime economic benefits.[5] However, the pattern of lifetime earnings differs for some of the vocational fields. For example, women in business and office training and men in industrial education tend to receive higher earnings than their academic curriculum counterparts immediately after graduation from high school. But over time they have somewhat lower growth in earnings. Women in home economics tend to receive consistently lower wages than women trained in other subjects. Vocational education may have some effect on high school dropout rates, thereby increasing the earnings of individuals because of an increase in educational attainment.[6] However, some analysts argue that vocational education reduces postsecondary school attendance, thereby depressing the earnings of some individuals who might otherwise attend college or other postsecondary institutions. There is no solid evidence to support either side of the argument.[7]

A small portion of vocational education funds are spent on postsecondary education. There do appear to be some gains from postsecondary vocational education, especially for blacks. However, the data on the effectiveness of postsecondary education are quite limited.[8]

Aid for the Handicapped. Programs for the handicapped have been of two types. The first involves a set-aside within a general program such as vocational education. The other type is the specially funded program. There are two such programs—one under Title I of ESEA which has supported pupils in state institutions, and one under the Education for All Handicapped Children Act which mandates an appropriate education for all handicapped children. Despite the federal mandate, these programs have covered only a small proportion of the costs of educating the handicapped. Thus, the major financial burden of the federal mandate has fallen on the states and localities. Outcomes from handicapped programs can be multidimensional, making an evaluation difficult to construct. To date most research has been confined to measuring compliance with regulations.

Impact Aid. The federal impact aid program has provided funds to local school districts that are affected by federal activity. It has included payments for children whose parents both live and work on federal installations (class A) and, at a lower level, for those whose parents either live or work on federal installations (class B). In recent years it has provided payments to approximately 4,400 school districts for over 2.5 million "federally connected" children. Since there are few restrictions on the use of impact aid, it is more like general aid than any other federal education program. This has made it very popular with school districts. However, federal policy makers have long been interested in reducing impact aid, primarily for class B recipients. The main argument for doing so has been based on the supposition that not all localities receiving aid have been adversely affected by the federal presence, since federal installations increase economic activity directly by providing civilian jobs and indirectly by increasing demand for private goods and services. Moreover, in the case of families that live or work outside of the installation, tax revenues are often generated that go into school district coffers.

Policy and Funding Changes under the Reagan Administration

Shortly after taking office President Reagan proposed a substantial reduction in the federal presence in elementary, secondary and vocational education, in conjunction with his 1982 budget amendments. This was to be achieved by consolidation of many programs and general reduction in outlays. As part of its broader effort to simplify the grants-in-aid system, the administration put forth a plan to consolidate forty-four elementary and secondary education programs into two block grants. The first was to assist states and localities in meeting special needs (such as programs for the disadvantaged and the handicapped), and the second was to improve the resources and performance of schools. The administration's proposal included a reduction of 25 percent in overall funding from FY 1981 policy, or baseline, levels for the individual programs. This was justified in part on the basis that the reductions in regulations and increase in state and local flexibility would reduce state and local program costs.

President Reagan also proposed reductions in other special population programs, vocational education, and impact aid starting in FY 1982. All cuts were 20 to 25 percent from the FY 1981 baseline levels, with the exception of impact aid. Here the president's recommendations paralleled the Carter administration's, calling for a 50 percent reduction from the amount necessary to maintain services at the FY 1981 level. This was to be achieved by totally eliminating payments to class "B" pupils.

All of the proposed cuts were in terms of budget authority or appropriations. These appropriations give the federal government the authority to enter into obligations for that fiscal year or future years. Outlays, on the other hand, represent the disbursement of funds based on present or previous years' authority. Consequently, a large reduction in budget authority will generally mean a smaller initial annual reduction in outlays, but one which will increase in size in subsequent years.

Congress accepted only part of the president's 1982 budget proposals. Under chapter 2 of the Education Consolidation and Improvement Act of 1981 (ECIA), over one-half of the proposed forty-four programs were put into one education block grant to improve the resources and performance of schools. However, the block grant consolidating special needs programs was not created. All of the large special needs programs described earlier remained categorical. Overall, the Reagan administration requested just under $5.6 billion in budget authority for elementary, secondary, and vocational education, 33 percent less than the amount needed to maintain programs at the FY 1981 level. Congress authorized $6.1 billion, still 26 percent less than the amount necessary to maintain the FY 1981 policy levels. However, because of the lag in outlay reductions, those for FY 1982 will be only 9 percent less than the baseline (table 11-2). By FY 1986 the outlay reductions will be nearly 30 percent relative to the FY 1981 policy levels.

Instead of being incorporated into a block grant, Title I was modified under chapter 1 of ECIA. Budget authority was set at $2.9 billion, a 27 percent cut from the FY 1981 baseline. Budget outlays for FY 1982 are estimated at $3.0 billion, down 13.5 percent relative to prior policy levels. In addition to the reduction in funds, regulations governing the use of funds

TABLE 11–2

FEDERAL FUNDING FOR ELEMENTARY, SECONDARY,
AND VOCATIONAL EDUCATION FOR FY 1982
(In $ millions)

	Funding Necessary to Maintain FY 1981 Policy Levels[a]		Actual Appropriations[b]	
	Budget Authority	*Outlays*	*Budget Authority*	*Outlays*
Compensatory programs for the disadvantaged[c]	3,961	3,475	2,886	3,006
Block grants for improving school programs[d]	681	NA	470	33
Indian education	379	367	333	328
Impact aid	866	837	456	645
Education for the handicapped	1,208	1,040	1,042	1,110
Vocational and adult education	1,022	930	733	977
Other	154	NA	223	650
Total	8,271	7,427	6,143	6,739

SOURCE: Congressional Budget Office (CBO).

a. Some minor rescissions to FY 1981 budget authority were sought by President Reagan and granted by Congress. These figures reflect the service levels prior to the rescissions.

b. Based on congressional action through 1981.

c. Chapter 1 of the Education Consolidation and Improvement Act of 1981 (ECIA).

d. Chapter 2 of ECIA.

were significantly reduced and reporting requirements were modified or eliminated.

The programs consolidated under chapter 2 of ECIA included numerous small programs such as Emergency School Aid, programs for the gifted and talented, support for innovation, libraries, and instructional resources. Total budget authority was $470 million, about 24 percent less than baseline.[9] Distribution of funds to states is based on the state's share of the school age population. States are required to pass on at least 80 percent of the funds to localities by a formula which includes need factors. Provisions are included to insure that private schools have access to the programs for which they are eligible.

Funds for impact aid were authorized at a level of $456 million, close to the Reagan request. This is approximately one-half of the prior policy levels. A three-year phase-out is provided for class "B" children.

Since most education programs are forward-funded, most of the changes enacted as part of the FY 1982 budget do not have any fiscal effect on states and localities until the 1982-1983 school year, which began in July 1982. Therefore the impact of the changes and the extent of state and local adjustments to the changes are not yet known.

President Reagan proposed additional large cuts in his 1983 budget for elementary and secondary education that would affect every major program area. His total request for elementary and secondary education FY 1983 budget authority was $4.4 billion, over $2 billion less than the authority necessary to maintain programs at the level which prevailed after the FY 1982 budget cuts. By FY 1986 both authority and outlays would be approximately one-half of the totals at the FY 1982 policy level. The largest reductions would again be for the special education needs and impact aid programs (table 11-3).

Major program changes were also proposed in the 1983 budget. These included once again a block grant for special education needs programs as well as others for vocational and adult education programs and for handicapped programs. Set-asides in the vocational and adult education programs for the handicapped and disadvantaged would be eliminated. The move toward lower levels of funding and more block grants, in combination with a proposal to reduce the Department of Education to a noncabinet level foundation, would greatly reduce the federal presence in education.

The Impact of Changes

The changes that have been proposed by the Reagan administration and those implemented by Congress involve both an overall reduction in funds

TABLE 11–3

FEDERAL FUNDING FOR ELEMENTARY, SECONDARY,
AND VOCATIONAL EDUCATION FOR FY 1983 THROUGH 1986
(In $ millions)

	Funding Necessary to Maintain FY 1982 Policy Levels		Administration Proposals in 1983 Budget	
	Budget Authority	Outlays	Budget Authority	Outlays
1983 Total	6,592	6,413	4,415	5,576
Compensatory education for the disadvantaged[a]	3,120	2,965	1,942	2,553
Block grant for improving school programs[b]	509	360	433	355
Indian education	355	340	308	314
Impact aid	475	558	287	403
Education for the handicapped[c]	1,125	1,076	846	877
Vocational and adult education[c]	799	755	500	601
Other	209	359	99	473
1984 Total	6,952	6,618	3,807	4,591
1985 Total	7,469	7,002	3,807	3,907
1986 Total	8,027	7,497	3,807	3,811

SOURCE: CBO.

a. Chapter 1 of ECIA.
b. Chapter 2 of ECIA.
c. Includes programs proposed for consolidation in FY 1983.

and a change in the regulations governing the expenditure of federal funds. These two categories should be distinguished in evaluating the impacts on the amount of funds flowing to different states and localities and on the services received by target group children.

General or Crosscutting Impacts. Budget cuts in education will affect virtually every state and locality in the country. The net effect on the level of spending for education will vary according to the willingness and ability of these jurisdictions to generate additional funds for education. While the overall percentage of education funds provided by the federal government prior to the 1982 changes was only 9 percent, some states and localities received significantly more. Among the states, the southeastern region was notable in terms of its receipt of federal funds, with Mississippi having received 24.8 percent of its total education revenues from federal sources in 1978-1979. In many cases the factors that generated the large federal funding, most notably a high concentration of low-income families and low revenue bases, make it exceedingly difficult for jurisdictions to replace revenue losses through their own sources. Even wealthier states like California will have difficulty replacing funds because of tax or expenditure limitations.

An examination of the distribution of federal funds indicates that the effect of the cuts will be different for different programs. Studies which have analyzed the distribution of federal funds in relation to district wealth, poverty concentration, and jurisdictional type (central city, suburb, nonmetropolitan area) have found significant differences in distributional patterns. Not surprisingly, Title I funds have been distributed disproportionately to districts with high concentrations of poor families, with those districts receiving per pupil allocations that were twice the national average. In contrast, impact aid has been more likely to go to suburban areas and has been less likely to be distributed to districts with high poverty concentrations.

The distribution of Title I funds by jurisdiction presents a mixed picture. The jurisdictions that have received large per pupil allotments under Title I were not necessarily property poor. In the more urban states the central cities, which often have high tax bases, have been major recipients because of high concentrations of poor children and higher per pupil expenditures. In the less urbanized states, the recipient districts were more likely to be low-wealth rural districts. Impact aid funds, especially class B payments, were more likely to go to medium-wealth and high-wealth districts than to low-wealth districts.[10]

The administration's rationale for the regulatory and structural changes was twofold. First, the administrative oversight and paperwork involved in monitoring and reporting on the use of federal funds was judged to be expensive. Reduction in the amount of regulation would produce administrative cost savings that would partially offset the budget cuts. In addition, many programs involve overlapping target groups. Consolidation of programs and modification of regulations would allow states and localities to choose the mix of programs that meets their needs.

The evidence in support of the cost-savings argument is mixed. A GAO study of thirty-one categorical programs in one region indicates that administrative costs for education programs can be significant, running as high as 18 percent of total expenditures in some areas.[11] However, the average cost was only 4 percent of total funds, much lower than the budget reductions. On the other hand, there is evidence to suggest that federal categorical programs with overlapping populations can come in conflict and produce undesirable results. A study of twenty-four elementary schools in eight school districts found that children who were eligible for more than one federal program were sometimes pulled out of the regular classroom so often for special programs (because localities felt it was necessary in order to comply with federal regulations requirements), that they never got the benefit of regular instruction.[12]

Programs for the Disadvantaged. Budget authority for these programs was cut 27 percent from the FY 1981 service level in FY 1982, and another 38 percent cut from this new level has been requested by the administration for FY 1983.[13] In addition to the funding cutbacks, regulations have been significantly reduced and may lead to less targeting and still lower overall levels of funding for the target populations. The Congressional Budget Office estimates that a 20 percent reduction in Title I funds translates into only a one percent reduction in total elementary and secondary education expenditures in a typical district. However, it can represent 6 or 7 percent of total expenditure in the poorest districts, where Title I has been as much as one-third of the total budget.[14] Since several studies indicate that Title I is effective in raising achievement, a funds reduction which is not replaced by states or localities could mean impaired educational outcomes for disadvantaged children. If there is a link between educational achievement and socioeconomic status, the nation may be achieving short-run savings at a significant cost in terms of both equity and efficiency.

Vocational Education. Overall program cuts are not likely to result in significant reductions in vocational programs because of the large state overmatch of federal funds. However, a block grant approach that would eliminate set-asides for target groups would tend to blur the focus of federal programs in this area. The target groups—the disadvantaged, the handicapped, those with limited English-speaking ability, and women in nontraditional fields—have previously been slighted by vocational programs. If the federal government is going to maintain any role in vocational education, an alternative and perhaps more appropriate strategy would be to eliminate nontargeted vocational aid and maintain a focus on the target populations who seem to benefit from various vocational programs.[15]

Aid to the Handicapped. Consolidation of handicapped programs may improve program efficiency. However, the consolidation will not necessarily lead to administrative cost reductions that are sufficient to offset the budgetary reductions. Since federal aid to the handicapped only covers a small part of the total cost of educating this group, the states argue that budget cuts, in the absence of changes in legislative mandates, are imposing additional costs that they should not have to bear.

Impact Aid. Cuts in impact aid seem to be consistent with a strategy of withdrawing from areas where there is no federal purpose. Impact aid is a general aid program and is not targeted in terms of student need. Moreover, payments to class "B" students do not, for the most part, go to low-wealth districts, which would indicate the availability of resources to replace cuts in federal aid.

Public Support for Private Schools

While the Reagan administration has implemented changes that will reduce federal support for public education, it has proposed a program that will increase federal support for private education. The proposal will take the form of a tuition tax credit for parents who enroll their children in private schools. This approach is consistent with the Reagan philosophy of increasing reliance on private markets. The administration argues that the tax credit will increase parental choice and will provide increased competition for public schools, forcing them to improve their performance. The result will be increased efficiency in both sectors.

The tuition tax credit that President Reagan has proposed would be phased in over three years. It would be limited to students enrolled in private elementary or secondary schools that do not engage in discriminatory practices. The credit would be equal to 50 percent of tuition costs with a maximum credit of $100 in 1983, $300 in 1984, and $500 in 1985 and beyond. The credit would not be refundable for those with tax liabilities that are less than one-half of tuition costs. Parents with incomes between $50,000 and $75,000 would get only a partial credit. Those with incomes over $75,000 would receive no credit. The estimated cost to the Treasury in lost tax revenues would be $100 million in 1983, but would reach $1.4 billion by 1986, assuming little or no change in enrollment patterns.[16] Since this tax reduction is an alternative to increases in education expenditures, consideration of its equity and efficiency effects is important.

Approximately 18 percent of all elementary and secondary schools in the United States are under private control. They enroll about 11 percent of all children in grades K-12. This percentage has been relatively constant over the past decade. The vast majority of private school students are enrolled in religious schools, 64 percent in Catholic schools, and 21 percent in other church-affiliated schools in 1978-1979. Only 15 percent were enrolled in nonaffiliated schools.[17]

While private schools enroll children from all socioeconomic backgrounds, their distribution by race and income differs from that of the public sector. Enrollment in private schools is weighted toward upper-income groups. Ten percent of private secondary school enrollment consists of children from families earning less than $12,000 compared to 20 percent for public schools. Twenty-five percent of these private school children are from families with over $38,000 in annual income as opposed to 11 percent of public school children.[18] Below family income levels of $20,000, blacks are only one-half as likely as whites to be in private schools.

This review of enrollment characteristics indicates that a tuition tax credit, in the absence of enrollment changes, would provide more benefits to upper-income groups than to lower-income groups and more to whites than to blacks. This tendency would be compounded by the nonrefundable nature of the credit. Only families with taxable income would benefit from the credit and only those with a tax liability equal to or greater than the tax credit would get the full benefit of the credit. This excludes the poor and those who receive the bulk of their income from nontaxable transfer payments.

In order for the tuition tax credit to increase efficiency and competition, parents have to be willing and able to exercise choice. That is, there would have to be shifts in enrollment. Since parents without taxable income receive no benefit it does not effectively increase the choices available to them. And it is their children who are most likely to be in the worst public schools. With a tuition tax credit higher-income parents may move their children from public to private schools because the cost of private school enrollment will drop. However, it is not clear that schools will accept more students as opposed to raising tuition.

In fact, based on the assumptions underlying their cost projections, policy makers in the administration do not expect the tax credit to result in significant enrollment shifts. Thus, it largely would provide windfall benefits to those who currently have their children enrolled in private school. While some of them may be families with moderate incomes who send their children to moderate tuition parochial schools, the bulk of the benefits will go to higher-income groups.

Net Effect of Reagan Policy Changes

The Reagan administration has proposed stringent cutbacks in federal funding for public elementary and secondary education. If they are fully implemented FY 1984 funding would be approximately one-half of actual FY 1981 funding levels and one-third of FY 1981 policy levels. The cuts in programs such as Title I that are distributed in a way that favors central cities or poor rural areas are likely to have an adverse effect on overall funding for education in those jurisdictions since they are unlikely to be able to replace lost funds. The net effect of program modifications (funds reductions, regulatory changes, and conversion to block grants) will mean increased flexibility for states but will probably also mean reduced levels of educational resources available to the disadvantaged, the handicapped, and other groups that the federal government has sought to protect in the past. As a result, the federal government would not be providing a significant proportion of funds for elementary and secondary education, nor would it have a clear purpose in its funding. This seems to make sense only if viewed as an interim step on the road to the total elimination of such federal aid.

While the federal role in public education may be reduced or eliminated, Reagan's proposal for a tuition tax credit would provide tax relief for families who have children enrolled in private schools. By 1986 this tax expenditure would be nearly 40 percent of the administration's projected expenditures for the support of public elementary, secondary, and vocational education programs, resulting in a marked shift in the balance of federal support for elementary and secondary education from public to private schools and from the disadvantaged to higher-income groups in the population.

Higher Education

Federal programs providing aid to college students have been marked for sharp cutbacks in the Reagan administration budget for FY 1983, following a round of FY 1982 budget trimming under the Reconciliation Act of 1981 and the continuing resolution. These programs had grown dramatically during the latter part of the 1970s; expenditures more than doubled between 1978 and 1981. Moreover, a good part of the increase was attributable to program changes extending benefits to middle- and upper-income students. The character and size of the program growth made it a ripe target for budget cutters. While the 1981 changes essentially held federal expenditures level, the proposed FY 1983 changes would reverse all of the growth from 1978 to 1981 and then some. As a result, a large proportion of college students and their families are threatened with deep cuts in benefits they had come to expect.

The changes in the budget already made and those proposed have not gone unnoticed. The press has regularly recorded the protests of parents, students, college presidents, and lobbyists. In fact, in response to the milder program trimming enacted in 1981, one reporter in discussing the "new era in paying for college" noted that "students and their families are digging deeper into savings, cutting back on vacations, turning to computers to seek out esoteric scholarships and reconsidering not only the type of college they will attend but also, in some cases, whether they will go at all.''[19] Congress appears to have heard the outcry, and the cuts proposed in the 1983 budget may not materialize, or at least not to the extent requested.

This section addresses the issues involved in the federal funding of higher education with a focus on student aid. The arguments dealing with a federal role in funding higher education are assessed in the light of what is known about the significance of higher education to individuals and to society, and about the possible effects of government subsidies on student enrollment patterns. The recent trends in federal funding of postsecondary education are reviewed and then the enacted and proposed budget changes are assessed.

Benefits and Costs of Higher Education and the Federal Role

A college education is desired for two reasons. One is that a college education can broaden interests and add to the enjoyment of everyday living. If these life enhancing aspects of college were all, however, it would probably not assume the importance it does. The second reason for valuing college is that it can have significant effects on earnings subsequent to college—in other words, it has a strong investment component.

A college student incurs direct costs—tuition, fees, books, and extra living expenses. In addition, although often overlooked, the student incurs opportunity costs in the form of earnings foregone while in school. The average high school graduate eighteen to twenty-four years of age currently earns about $12,000 a year working full time; and this amount (less any summer and possible part-time earnings), which represents what the college student could have earned, adds significantly to the real total costs of a college education. In return for this investment college graduates can expect to earn substantially more over their lifetimes than high school graduates. In 1979 the earnings of college graduates at ages twenty-five to thirty-four exceeded those of high school graduates by 30 percent, and, at older ages, by more than 60 percent.[20] A number of studies have used information on direct and opportunity costs and on the projected stream of higher earnings over the lifetime tu calculate the expected rate of return to an investment in college training. Typically a sizable return has been found.[21]

Since investment in college education seems to provide a substantial private payoff in terms of higher earnings and, possibly, other less tangible sources of satisfaction as well, it is appropriate to ask why college students should be subsidized by the federal government. Three main reasons have been given to justify public subsidies in this area.

One argument alleges that the private gain to individuals does not capture the full social return; therefore individuals will invest less than an optimum amount in college in the absence of a subsidy. The social return is said to exceed the private return because of effects that enhance the income and well-being of society as a whole. Measuring these is not easy, however. As a first step to measuring a social rate of return, researchers have included as part of the return the higher taxes paid by college graduates over their lifetimes. However, social costs also exceed private costs because of the subsidies to higher education that enable students to pay much less out of pocket than the full instructional costs of their training. These extra costs have been estimated to somewhat more than offset the returns from higher taxes; so a social rate of return that takes account of full social costs and additional taxes is slightly lower than the private return.[22]

What of other externalities? It is possible that in various elusive ways an increase in college education increases the rate of advancement in knowledge or technology, which in turn increases national income. If all of the increase in the productivity of labor and capital realized in the 1940s and 1950s were attributable to college education, the social rate of return to such an education would be twice the private rate.[23] This would be an upper limit measure of externalities based on the most extreme assumptions. It is more plausible that any "advancement in knowledge" effect derives from research activites, many of which are conducted at universities, rather than from the routine instruction of students. It also should be noted that during the 1970s the rate of productivity advance has slowed sharply; applying the same procedure as above to this period would indicate that virtually no increment could be attributed to higher education.[24]

It is sometimes stated that higher education produces social benefits of a nonmonetary nature, but these have been even more difficult to pin down than the monetary social benefits. For example, a college education may lead to appreciation of the arts and humanities. While this may be true, it is hard to see how it would have any significant benefit to those who do not go to college but who would be asked to pay the bill for those who do. Similarly, better attitudes and good citizenship have been cited as examples of social benefits from a college education, but college campuses have also fostered extremist groups that have been disruptive of widely accepted social norms.[25]

On balance, the case for subsidizing college attendance based on sizable externalities is far from solid. These comments, it should be stressed, apply to the subsidization of college attendance at the federal level for all income levels. As noted, a stronger case could likely be made for the federal subsidization of research on the basis of externalities. Moreover, at the state level, particular kinds of social benefits may well exist. States may find it to their advantage to sponsor state institutions of higher education in order to provide technical expertise in their industries, to attract educated and re-sourceful residents, or simply to foster state pride. For these reasons, it is not surprising that the bulk of state spending on higher education should be through the provision of aid to state-run institutions rather than the granting of direct aid to students to be used in any school.

The second reason often given for providing public support to higher education stems from the difficulties inherent in financing an investment in "human capital," which unlike an investment in physical capital provides no ready collateral to back up a loan. Private lenders cannot easily obtain a lien on future earnings gains. Moreover, the earnings gains are likely to be subject to a wide range of risks. In short, unsubsidized loans by students in private markets would likely bear exorbitantly high interest rates relative to the average market rate. The effects of these capital market problems do not fall equally on all students. Those whose parents are affluent enough to self-finance the investment through prior savings or current income are obviously more fortunate than others. There is little controversy that government loan programs of some type are desirable to remove barriers to schooling arising from capital market limitations. Because of the desirability of providing fi-nancing that is portable across state lines, such assistance is more naturally a federal role. The extent to which such loans should be subsidized, however, is a more controversial topic and subject to the same arguments about exter-nalities as other student aid.

The third reason for government intervention in the financing of higher education is to provide equality of opportunity to young people whose parents cannot provide them with a sufficient endowment to finance the training of their choice. This line of reasoning suggests that a program of public subsidies for youth from low-income families is a legitimate function of government. But should it be a federal function? As suggested, it is in the interest of state and local governments to provide subsidies by charging below cost in state and locally run institutions. A large proportion of students now have access to such a subsidized school. Tuition charges, however, may still be prohibitive for some students. Moreover, the available public institution may not fit the educational needs of the student. An affluent society may therefore choose to provide low-income youth with funding that enables them to have a wider choice over institutions, including those in other states. The federal govern-ment is an appropriate source of such funding.

Are there any drawbacks to an active federal role in financing higher education? One concern is that freedom of thought and action may be impaired by a large governmental role on college campuses particularly at the federal level. In the United States the financing of higher education has been char-acterized by diverse funding sources, which should provide a safeguard against government interference. In 1979 state and local governments provided 35 percent of the revenues of institutions of higher education, the federal government 15 percent, student tuition and fees 21 percent, private philanthropy and endowments 7 percent, and school enterprises (such as hospitals) and other sources provided 23 percent.[26] These proportions have changed over time with the growth in state supported institutions, the relative decline in the importance of private institutions, and the erratic but generally growing role of the federal government. The effect of these changes on the free functioning of colleges and universities would be difficult to document. A desire to guard against government intrusion is one factor, however, behind a preference for providing federal funds directly to students rather than to institutions.

Another concern is that government may not intervene in the right way and may produce unintended results that make things worse than they were before. Thus, one may question subsidies that result in income transfers from the poor, who do not attend college, to the middle classes who do, or that bias the choice between one type or another of schooling or training in what may be an inappropriate direction.[27]

Effects on Enrollments

The arguments for government support of higher education are based on the premise that cost is an important factor determining college attendance. However, if enrollments are not very responsive to subsidies, the justification for such government spending is considerably weakened. The government expenditure in this case would be a windfall for those who would attend college in any event. Since college students come disproportionately from high-income families, such a transfer would be of questionable merit on equity grounds, particularly if distributed in equal amounts to students at all income levels.[28] Empirical research investigating the response of enrollment to changes in college costs indicates that enrollments do respond, although the effect seems to be quite small for the average person of college age. A 10 percent cut in tuition leads to a one percentage point increase in the enrollment rate of eighteen to twenty-four year olds.[29] However, the response is considerably greater for those from lower-income homes, while those at middle- and upper-income levels appear to respond quite weakly.[30]

Factors other than direct college costs have been shown to have substantial effects on college attendance. Student ability (as measured by test scores and grades in high school) and parents' education both have strong positive effects on college attendance. So does family income, though seemingly to a lesser extent.[31] Estimates of the expected gain in earnings resulting from college attendance, and of opportunity costs, would be expected to influence enrollments, but they have less frequently been taken into account.

In sum, direct student costs are one of many factors affecting college enrollment. Students at lower-income levels, however, are more greatly affected by cuts in costs (through direct aid or tuition reduction). Governmental support for higher-income youth is more likely to be a windfall with little effect on school attendance, while support for low-income youth has a greater effect on attendance.

Have college enrollment trends been substantially affected by student aid? Over the entire period 1960 to 1980 there has been an increase in college attendance among those age eighteen to twenty-one years (table 11-4). Women have increased their attendance much more sharply and steadily than men, however, and are currently more likely than men to be enrolled at ages eighteen and nineteen. The pattern for men makes sense only if one takes account of the draft during the Vietnam War. This appears to have had the effect of inducing a large jump in college enrollment among men, which subsequently subsided once the war ended. In the latter half of the 1970s enrollment rates did not rise for men and increased for women at a much slower rate than previously, despite large increases in federal student aid programs. This does not necessarily mean that student aid was ineffective, however, since offsetting factors may also have operated. Stagnating real family incomes and a declining rate of return to college would have dampened the demand for higher education.

More sophisticated analysis is clearly needed to fully explain the enrollment patterns of the past twenty years. However, the evidence from studies on the effect of changes in tuition on student enrollment suggests that increased aid in the magnitudes available would not have a large effect on overall enrollments. Since no surge in enrollments occurred in the 1970s, the trend is compatible with the studies.

Programs and Policies

Although government subsidy of higher education is widely endorsed, the magnitude of support and the form it should take have been widely debated. During the 1960s, federal expenditures on higher education were largely confined to institutional support, mainly for research, and for traineeships and fellowships. What little student aid was provided did not go directly to students but was given to institutions to dispense. One exception was the GI bill program, which at various times has provided substantial aid for support of veterans returning to school. During the early 1970s a pronounced shift was made towards student aid and away from institutional funding. Between 1972 and 1980 federal spending on research in higher educational institutions

TABLE 11-4

PERCENTAGE OF MEN ENROLLED IN COLLEGE AND IN THE ARMED FORCES
AND PERCENTAGE OF WOMEN ENROLLED IN COLLEGE, BY AGE[a]

Calendar Year	Men				Women	
	18–19 Years		20–21 Years		18–19 Years	20–21 Years
	In College	In Armed Forces	In College	In Armed Forces	In College	In College
1960	28.4	14.0	21.5	18.5	22.5	12.5
1965	35.9	10.4	28.9	19.8	30.3	18.9
1966	36.5	12.7	29.2	26.8	30.7	19.9
1967	35.9	12.8	29.9	29.6	31.5	22.6
1968	38.7	10.6	30.4	30.3	33.1	20.6
1969	39.1	11.2	32.3	27.8	34.4	24.0
1970	36.6	8.9	31.3	23.4	34.6	22.3
1971	37.9	8.0	31.2	17.4	34.4	25.7
1972	34.4	8.7	31.2	13.2	34.3	25.6
1973	31.9	8.4	29.5	12.2	31.1	25.1
1974	30.6	8.3	30.3	10.3	33.0	25.3
1975	33.8	7.9	30.8	9.3	36.7	26.6
1976	32.6	7.3	29.1	9.1	36.9	29.4
1977	32.8	6.8	30.2	8.9	36.2	27.9
1978	32.6	6.7	28.0	8.8	36.1	26.2
1979	31.3	6.2	27.8	8.5	35.9	27.7
1980	32.1	6.4	29.0	8.5	37.6	28.2

SOURCE: *School Enrollment—Social and Economic Characteristics of Students: October 1979*, Current Population Reports. Series P–20. no. 360. U.S. Bureau of the Census.

a. College enrollments and armed forces as a percentage of total noninstitutional population in the age group.

grew modestly (by 16 percent in real terms) and other institutional spending fell by 42 percent in real terms. Direct student aid payments, on the other hand, have increased substantially, largely as a result of the expansion of the Basic Education Opportunity Grants program (BEOGS) and Guaranteed Student Loans (GSLs). From 1974 to 1981, all student aid including Social Security benefits and the GI bill rose by 35 percent after adjusting for inflation and by 294 percent excluding these two programs (table 11-5). By 1981 total student aid expenditures had reached $10 billion.

It was not surprising, therefore, that Congress and the president should begin to take a close look at the programs. Some cutbacks were proposed in the Carter budget for 1981 and were retained in the initial Reagan budget and implemented by Congress. Funding cuts were enacted as part of the Reconciliation Act of 1981 and the 1981 continuing resolution. The resulting program levels essentially maintain the Department of Education's student aid programs at their FY 1981 levels in real terms through FY 1985. (They would rise in current dollars as shown in table 11-5). The Social Security student benefit, however, will be virtually phased out by FY 1985. President Reagan's 1983 budget proposes significantly deeper cuts in the Department of Education aid programs. The remainder of this section reviews the recent history and discusses the details of the enacted and proposed legislative changes of the Reagan administration with respect to the major student aid programs.

Basic Grants. The Basic Educational Opportunity Grants program, now known as Pell grants, was established by the Education Amendments of 1972. The program was intended to aid low-income students and initially provided a maximum grant of $1400. The provisions for determining a student's eligibility and the size of the grant award are based on a formula for assessing need costs that rivals the income tax for sheer complexity. The eligibility formula is based on the family income of the student adjusted for taxes and certain deductions—such as medical expenses, private school tuition for children, a family size offset, and an employment cost offset. Family assets are also taken into account. An assessment rate is applied to this adjusted family income to determine the amount the student's family is expected to contribute. Further adjustment is made for the college costs of other members of the family enrolled in postsecondary school. The specifics of the formula differ for students who are independent of their parents with additional distinctions for the student's marital status.

The amount the student actually receives depends on eligibility level as determined by the needs analysis as well as on the costs of attending college and the student's enrollment status. The grant cannot exceed half of college costs. As a result of these various components the level of income at which a student may qualify for a grant, and the size of the grant obtained, varies

TABLE 11-5

FEDERAL OUTLAYS ON STUDENT ASSISTANCE FOR HIGHER EDUCATION
(FY 1974–FY 1985)

	Actual			Baseline Projections[a]			President's FY 1983 Budget[b]	
	FY 1974	FY 1978	FY 1981	FY 1982	FY 1983	FY 1985	FY 1983	FY 1985
	Current Dollars in Billions							
Department of Education Programs								
Basic grants	.0[c]	1.6	2.5	2.3	2.3	2.7	2.0	1.4
Guaranteed loans	.3	.5	2.3	3.0	3.7	4.2	3.4	3.2
Campus-based[d]	.5	.8	1.4	1.2	1.1	1.2	1.0	.0[c]
Total	.9	2.9	6.2	6.5	7.1	8.1	6.4	4.6
Social Security	.8	1.4	2.0	1.4	.8	.1	.8	.1
Veterans	2.6	2.7	1.8	1.5	1.2	.7	1.2	.7
Total Aid	4.3	7.0	10.0	9.4	9.1	8.9	8.4	5.4

Constant (1982) Dollars in Billions[e]

Department of Education Programs								
Basic grants	.1	2.2	2.7	2.3	2.1	2.2	1.9	1.2
Guaranteed loans	.6	.7	2.5	3.0	3.4	3.5	3.2	2.6
Campus-based	.9	1.1	1.5	1.2	1.0	1.0	.9	.0[c]
Total	1.7	4.1	6.7	6.5	6.6	6.7	6.0	3.8
Social Security	1.5	2.0	2.2	1.4	.7	.1	.7	.1
Veterans	4.8	3.8	1.9	1.5	1.1	.6	1.1	.6
Total Aid	8.0	9.8	10.8	9.4	8.5	7.3	7.8	4.4

SOURCES: U.S. Department of Education, Congressional Budget Office, and Office of Management and Budget.

a. Assumes the policies incorporated in the Omnibus Budget Reconciliation Act of 1981 and the continuing resolution for FY 1982. CBO estimates based upon CBO's economic and technical assumptions.

b. CBO reestimates of the president's 1983 budget proposals.

c. Less than $0.05 billion.

d. Includes supplemental opportunity grants, work study, direct loans, and state student incentive grants.

e. Based upon the implicit GNP price deflator for personal consumption expenditures.

considerably. A student who is attending a high cost institution and who is from a large family with several siblings also attending high cost institutions could conceivably qualify at levels far in excess of what might in other circumstances be considered needy.

The original BEOGS legislation restricted eligibility to lower-income students by applying a higher needs assessment rate to parents' adjusted incomes (20 percent of the first $5,000 of discretionary income and 30 percent of all remaining discretionary income). The Middle Income Assistance Act of 1978 (MISAA) expanded the program to reach more middle-income students by reducing the assessment rate to 10.5 percent. The maximum grant was also increased. As a result of these changes the program reached 47 percent more students, mostly from middle-income families.[32] In 1979-1980, 41 percent of dependent students came from families with more than $15,000-a-year incomes (23 percent from families with more than $20,000 incomes).[33]

Participation is relatively greater for students attending private rather than public institutions. In 1979-1980 almost half of all undergraduates attending private institutions were receiving basic grants.[34] Many grant recipients attend proprietary vocational schools, however. Confining the calculation to private four-year colleges and universities reduces the proportion to 37 percent. The comparable figure for public institutions is 26 percent. The provision that the grant cannot exceed 50 percent of education expenses undoubtedly increases access to private institutions which have higher costs, because they typically rely more on tuition for revenue.

What effect has the program had on college enrollments? It is estimated that 41 percent of the low-income students (family income of less than $16,000) receiving basic grants would not have enrolled in postsecondary schools without the program.[35] However, the program can be credited with only 17 percent of the enrollments of middle-income recipients and 6 percent of the enrollments of high-income students. Since 40 percent of BEOG expenditures on freshmen in 1979 were received by middle- and upper-income students, the program seems to provide a substantial windfall to the families of college students.

The Reagan administration requested an appropriation in basic grants for FY 1982 of between $300 and $700 million below the existing policy level.[36] The maximum grant was to have been increased and family-size offsets and the cost of attendance were to have been adjusted for inflation. At the president's request these changes were not made. Thus, the provisions of the Education Act of 1980, which stipulated these increases, were rescinded. In addition, across the board cuts of $80 per grant were made to bring the program's costs within budget. Overall spending totals, however, were kept fairly constant in real terms.

The president's 1983 budget proposes deeper cutbacks which would reduce the FY 1985 program levels to about 50 percent of their FY 1982 levels. These cuts would be achieved in part by raising the needs assessment rate, which would eliminate most middle-income students from the program. Presumably the effective income cutoffs would revert to the standards prior to MISAA. The retargeting would be an efficient way to reduce program costs if the results of the studies reviewed are correct; changes in enrollments of middle-income students should be minimally affected. However, further reductions in the maximum grant are proposed (from $1,670 in FY 1982 to $1,600 thereafter), which in real terms would be an even larger cut. Since lower-income students are affected by small changes in subsidies, their enrollments are likely to drop. Because the traditional age college population will be declining in number during the 1980s, it should be possible to reduce program costs and maintain inflation-adjusted benefits for low-income students if at the same time the program were retargeted by reducing the eligibility of middle-income students.

Guaranteed Student Loans. The GSL program addresses a problem that government, in principle, clearly can play a role in solving—that of access to markets for financing a college education. GSL was first authorized as part of the Higher Education Act of 1965 with the intent of providing an incentive to private lenders to make loans to students. Loans were limited to students with family income below $15,000. The federal government was obligated to pay the interest charges while the student was in school and to guarantee the lender against default. Both of these federal obligations result in federal costs. In addition, in order to assure lender participation, Congress later provided for a "special allowance" to be paid to the lender by the government when the statutorily set interest rate charged to borrowers falls below the market rate of return. The creation of the Student Loan Marketing Association (Sallie Mae) in 1972—a private corporation authorized to provide a market for student loan obligations—was also intended to encourage lender participation. In 1976 the special allowance was automatically tied to quarterly changes in the rate for 91-day Treasury bills.

The enormous growth in the program in recent years is attributed in large part to the sharp rise in market interest rates that soared above the interest rate paid by students. The student rate had been fixed at 7 percent by legislation since 1968 and was only raised to 9 percent by 1980 legislation, effective January 1981. The divergence between market and GSL interest rates alone would have increased costs; but it also greatly enhanced the attractiveness of program participation.

Another significant change contributing to program growth was the removal of any income ceiling for borrowers in GSL under the 1978 legislation

(MISAA). Program growth was further enhanced when the maximum cumulative amounts that students could borrow were raised to $12,500 for undergraduates and $25,000 for graduates, and when eligibility for borrowing was extended to parents of students. The number of borrowers increased from 1.5 million in 1979 to 3.5 million in 1981. As a percentage of all students this was an increase from about 15 percent to 33 percent. The total volume of loans increased from $3 billion in 1979 to $7.7 billion in 1981. Federal program outlays associated with this loan volume were $500 milllion in 1978 and reached $2.3 billion in 1981.

It is not known what effect the liberalization of the GSL program had on student enrollments. Based on estimates of the effects of subsidies on the college attendance patterns of middle- and upper-income youth, one would expect little induced change in enrollments—that is, the additional funding most likely went to those who would have enrolled anyway. One piece of evidence suggests that the income of loan takers rose sharply. In the state of Virginia the proportion of borrowers with family incomes above $40,000 increased from 10 percent in 1979 to 20 percent in 1980.[37]

Such escalating program growth attracted considerable attention from budget cutters. President Carter's 1982 budget proposed a series of program changes designed to cut program costs (by $878 million in 1982). An income ceiling was to be reintroduced by means of a needs assessment; the in-school interest subsidy was to be eliminated; loans to parents were to be offered at essentially nonsubsidized market rates. These proposals were adopted by the incoming Reagan administration but were amended by Congress. Instead of eliminating the in-school subsidy, an "origination of fee" of 5 percent was imposed on all new loans, which essentially covers half of the first-year interest costs. The needs test requirement was imposed only on families earning more than $30,000 a year. Because of the way college costs are taken into account, it is still possible for families with incomes well above $30,000 to receive a loan. These changes went into effect in August 1981, too late to affect student loans substantially for the 1981-1982 school year. The full effects will be first felt for the 1982-1983 school year.

The Reagan budget for 1983 proposes some old and some new ideas for GSL cuts. The "origination fee" would be increased to 10 percent; the needs analysis would be applied to all students including those with family annual incomes under $30,000; graduate students would be allowed to borrow only from an auxiliary loan program which charges close to the market rate; special allowance payments would be limited to a prescribed period. Despite the significant cutbacks, GSL program costs would remain high through 1985 because of existing loans.

The very size of the program and its middle-class clientele make it politically difficult to trim. Although it has not been funded at such generous levels for long, GSL quickly became extremely popular. As noted at the outset, a loan program is desirable to ease market imperfections which might lead to exorbitant market rates for college investments. Enabling students to pay at the market rate may therefore be viewed as a prudent way to insure student access. Providing subsidized loans to all students regardless of income is not an efficient use of federal funds.

Campus-based Programs and State Incentive Grants. The Supplemental Education Opportunity Grants program (SEOG) and the National Direct Student Loans program (NDSL) are campus-based versions of basic grants and student loans respectively. Federal funds are allocated to colleges and universities by means of a complex formula. The funds are offered to the students by the schools so that in effect they enable schools to attract the students of their choice by means of lower tuition. Private institutions appear to gain more from campus-based aid than do public institutions when their share of aid is compared to their share of enrollment.[38] Available information suggests that this aid is somewhat less narrowly targeted on the poor than is direct student aid, such as basic grants. In 1976, 44 percent of dependent students receiving campus-based aid in private institutions were from families with $12,000 income or more; in four-year public institutions this proportion was 32 percent; in two-year public schools it was 21 percent.[39] In 1981, expenditures on SEOG were $405 million and on NDSL $345 million.

College Work Study (CWS) is the third campus-based program. It is the largest of the campus-based programs, spending $583 million in 1981. Unlike the others, it is a type of public employment program. Colleges receive funds to employ students who are expected to work at the minimum wage. If the students do in fact perform useful work for the school, it would be more appropriate to fund it out of the research or other activity that generates the employment. If the jobs are "make work" jobs, it would be more efficient to provide the subsidies directly to the students rather than circuitously through the work study program.

The State Student Incentive Grants (SSIG) is a small ($78 million in 1981) program designed to encourage states to provide scholarships to students by providing matching funds up to a fixed allotment. The existence of the fixed allotment at relatively low levels, however, limits the program's usefulness.[40]

Although the campus-based aid and SSIG programs have been funded for 1982 at real levels comparable to those of 1978-1979, they are slated for near elimination under the 1983 Reagan budget. Proponents of campus-based aid stress that it expands student choice since, in the competition with publicly subsidized schools, private institutions may not survive. Direct aid to students is said to give them access to a wider array of existing schools, but indirectly it also helps to insure a diversity of institutions since its recipients have free choice as to which institutions they attend. Furthermore, direct aid can be much more readily targeted. Thus, the case for campus-based programs is not very compelling.

Social Security and Veterans Benefits. Payments to students by the Social Security Administration and the Veterans Administration (the "GI bill") are not education programs per se, although they have often provided a considerably larger volume of funds to students than the Department of Education programs. The current GI bill has not been affected by 1982 or 1983 legislative proposals. The program of Social Security benefits for students is being phased out under the Reconciliation Act of 1981. These benefits are obtained by children of deceased, retired, or disabled workers insured under Social Security. In 1979 the average benefit received by students was $194 a month.

The merits of the Social Security program for students had long been questioned for several reasons. Benefits were given without a means test. Moreover, since the size of the benefit is tied to the parent's Social Security entitlement, the higher the earnings of the parent, the higher the benefit. While many recipients do have low incomes, it does not seem equitable to provide a large benefit to those qualifying under Social Security while other equally needy young people cannot qualify. Finally, under Social Security a payment to dependent children is only made after age eighteen if the dependent attends school (up to age twenty-two). Therefore, those children who leave school to work do not qualify. With the introduction of the basic grants program, the Social Security benefit for students seemed to many to be superfluous. The phasing out or reduction of the student benefit had been sought in the past (for example, by Presidents Carter and Ford). However, many of those who were counting on the Social Security benefit may be faced with unanticipated problems in financing their college educations, particularly since the basic grants and loan programs have also been trimmed.

Conclusions and Issues for the Future

The Reagan administration took office after several years of exceptionally large increases in federal funding for student aid programs. Moreover, the expansion mainly served to increase aid to middle- and upper-income students. It was clearly a time to take stock of program changes and evaluate the federal role in higher education. The changes effected by the administration and

Congress in 1981 essentially prevented any further increases in the federal higher education budget—future levels of spending in real terms were held at their FY 1981 level. The Reagan 1983 budget proposes major additional cutbacks in funding that would more then reverse the expansion caused by the Education Act of 1978 (MISAA).

The general direction of these cuts follows lines that many economists have long advocated for federal funding of higher education. Direct aid to students is emphasized relative to aid to institutions; the programs are to be targeted on low-income persons, and loans will continue to be available at market rates to all students. More questionable, however, is the overall amount of funding that would be available to low-income students. The maximum grant in the basic grants program was initially $1,400 when BEOGS was legislated in 1972. Because of inflation, $1,400 in 1972 is equivalent to about $3,400 in 1983 dollars. The proposed maximum of $1,600 is, therefore, only half of what was originally envisioned as the suitable maximum. This does not necessarily mean that the original standard was correct. But what the standard should be clearly requires more careful consideration of what the program aims to achieve.

Issues concerning the loan program are intertwined with basic grants. If basic grants addressed the needs of low-income students, then there would be no compelling reason to provide larger subsidies in the loan program. However, other terms of the loan could be better tailored to the future earnings of college graduates. For example, the length of pay-off period could be increased.

A large number of factors makes the outlook for colleges and universities rather uncertain for the coming decade. Because of the coming decline in the number of youth in the traditional college ages, enrollments are not likely to increase as they have in the past, under any circumstances. State and local governments are undergoing more financial stress than they have in the past, and this could put pressure on them to raise tuition and fees. Lower tax rates could reduce philanthropic contributions. Pressure for more federal aid to institutions is likely to grow. It will be important to evaluate carefully whether the federal government should step in to provide such assistance, and if so, to what extent and in what form.

Chapter 12

INCOME SECURITY

James R. Storey

Since 1935 the federal government has played a major role in assuring a degree of financial security for most Americans. This income security function has been realized through two quite distinct approaches. The broader of the two is aimed at the partial replacement of wages lost due to the retirement, death, disablement, or unemployment of a breadwinner. The primary federal activities included here are the major cash social insurance programs, Social Security and unemployment compensation, and various tax provisions and regulation of fringe benefits in the private sector. The second approach provides assistance or welfare that is means-tested or conditioned upon family income. Programs of this type provide both cash assistance, such as Aid to Families with Dependent Children (AFDC); Supplemental Security Income (SSI) for the aged, blind, or disabled; and in-kind assistance such as Food Stamps and housing subsidies.

This varied assortment of activities has developed over four decades in response to a great many social and economic concerns. However, the preponderance of public policies for income security has evolved in reaction to two major policy objectives. First, government has attempted to encourage the development of a fair and adequate retirement income system through a combination of public benefit entitlements, regulation of private pension plans, favorable tax treatment of income in old age, and tax incentives for retirement

saving. Second, for persons of working age who experience economic deprivation—particularly those who are heads of families with children—public
policy has struggled with two interrelated concerns: (1) how to design welfare
programs that are equitable and meet a family's needs without unduly disrupting the family head's work incentives; and (2) how to structure federal
and state roles in welfare programs so that the degree of cost sharing and
program control is acceptable to both levels of government.

These major policy issues have come to be dominated in recent years
by an overriding policy consideration—the need for greater budgetary control
and restraint. Spending for income security purposes (which is defined exclusive of health insurance programs in this chapter) now exceeds all other
components of the federal budget, and the annual growth in such spending
generally accounts for over one-third of all nondefense program spending
increases. Slowing this normal growth in income security outlays is difficult
politically because it requires changes in legal entitlements that affect the
current or future incomes of virtually everyone. Thus, the budgetary control
objective collides with other policy goals. Its pursuit shapes significantly the
possible directions for initiatives aimed at rationalizing retirement income
systems or restructuring welfare programs.

An essential part of the Reagan administration's budgetary policy is to
reduce the growth in income security outlays that would have occurred under
the laws in effect in 1980. Sizable reductions were achieved in congressional
actions on the 1982 budget, and the president has proposed further large cuts
for 1983 and beyond. The reductions in programs directed to the low-income
population have been substantial and generally involve lowering benefit amounts
for recipients with earnings. Increased state control over welfare policies is
also emphasized and is formally embodied in President Reagan's ''New Federalism'' initiative.

The budget cuts in social insurance programs to date have been proportionately much smaller and have had only a mildly restraining effect on long-
run growth rates. However, movement toward a new policy on retirement
income is evident. The Reagan administration is less inclined than its predecessors to use pension plan regulation as a means of changing policy.
Instead, greater personal retirement saving is being encouraged through expanded tax subsidies for that purpose. Major changes in Social Security were
proposed but rejected by Congress. The president has established a commission on social security reform in an effort to build a consensus for significant
change in this area.

This chapter examines the Reagan administration's policy initiatives in
income security and their implications. It begins with a summary of major
policy developments prior to 1981 and the most important issues confronting

President Reagan when he took office. The next section discusses the specific changes that have already been implemented or proposed by the president. The third section assesses the immediate and likely longer-term consequences of these changes. The chapter concludes with speculation about future policy implications.

Policy Development Prior to 1981

The Social Security Act of 1935 established the basic framework of income security programs that persists today: the federal Social Security system; the state unemployment insurance system; and federal grants to states for public assistance to certain categories of needy people. Spawned in reaction to the Great Depression, these programs were greatly expanded during the 1950s and 1960s with that period's economic growth and the burgeoning popularity of Social Security. The 1960s and early 1970s saw a proliferation of aid programs for the needy as the War on Poverty and Great Society initiatives focused public attention on those people not benefiting sufficiently from economic growth.

The increased costs of income security benefits were a growing concern by the mid-1970s as economic stagnation took hold. The need to constrain costs, coupled with other concerns, led to major attempts to improve and simplify the welfare system and to rationalize the provision of retirement income. Although many improvements resulted from these reform efforts, the 1970s ended with the central purposes of reformers still out of reach and heightened concern about mounting program costs. The problem of budgetary control, dissatisfaction with the welfare system, and unresolved concerns about Social Security and pensions were paramount on the agenda of the incoming Reagan administration.

Trends in Income Security Spending

Between 1935 and 1980, federal outlays for income security programs[1] grew from less than $1 billion to $217 billion, or 8 percent of the Gross National Product (GNP). Their current 37 percent share of the federal budget is the largest of any functional area. Programs that operate as federal grants to state governments account for a significant part of overall nonfederal spending as well—39 percent of all state spending on public welfare and 6 percent of total state expenditures for all purposes.

The pattern of growth in income security spending is shown for major programs in table 12-1. Income security's share of the federal budget has

TABLE 12-1

FEDERAL OUTLAYS FOR INCOME SECURITY PROGRAMS, 1935–1980

(In $ billions)

Program	1935	1945	1955	1965	1970	1975	1980
Social insurance and related programs							
Social Security (OASDI)	—	0.2	4.3	16.6	29.7	63.6	117.1
Income security for veterans (excl. non-service-connected pensions)	0.5	0.8	2.3	2.2	3.8	5.1	8.1
Federal employee retirement and disability	0.1	0.2	0.8	2.8	5.6	13.3	26.8
Unemployment compensation	—	a	0.1	0.2	3.4	13.5	18.0
Other programs[b]	—	0.1	0.6	1.1	1.6	4.1	6.5
Subtotal	0.6	1.3	8.1	22.9	44.1	99.6	176.5
Low-income assistance programs							
Aid to Families with Dependent Children (AFDC)	—	a	0.4	1.0	2.1	5.1	7.3
Supplemental Security Income (SSI)	—	0.3[c]	1.0[c]	1.7[c]	1.9[c]	4.8	6.4
Veterans non-service-connected pensions	a	0.1	0.8	1.9	2.3	2.7	3.6
Earned income tax credit	—	—	—	—	—	—	1.3
Low-income energy assistance	—	—	—	—	—	—	1.6
Other cash assistance	—	a	a	a	0.1	0.2	0.7
Food Stamps	—	—	—	a	0.6	4.6	9.1
Other food programs[d]	0.2	a	0.3	0.7	1.0	2.0	4.9
Housing assistance	a	a	0.1	0.2	0.5	2.1	5.5
Subtotal	0.2	0.4	2.6	5.5	8.5	21.5	40.4
Total	0.8	1.7	10.7	28.4	52.6	121.1	216.9

Addendum							
Total as a percentage of							
Gross National Product (GNP)	0.3	0.3	2	4	5	8	8
Total personal income	1	1	3	5	6	10	10
Federal budget outlays	12	2	16	24	27	37	37

SOURCE: Data for 1935 through 1965 are from *Social Welfare Expenditures, 1929–1966*, Social Security Administration Research Report No. 25 (Washington, D.C.: GPO, March 1968); Data for 1970 through 1980 are from various *Budgets of the United States Government* (Washington, D.C.: GPO); Data in addendum are from various *Budgets of the United States Government* and *Economic Reports of the President* (Washington, D.C.: GPO).

a. Less than $50 million.
b. Includes railroad retirement system and benefits for disabled coal miners.
c. Figures prior to 1975 are for the old program of assistance to the aged, blind and disabled that SSI replaced.
d. Includes child nutrition programs and distribution of surplus commodities.

tripled since 1935 and more than doubled since 1955. These benefits have quadrupled as a share of GNP since 1955, and their proportion of total personal income rose from 3 to 10 percent. The expansion and maturation of Social Security was the largest factor behind this growth. However, these relative measures of spending magnitude remained level from 1975 to 1980 as program expansions all but ceased and Social Security approached maturity. Still, large year-to-year dollar increases in spending arise due to rising numbers of eligible beneficiaries, benefit increases for new beneficiaries due to increases in the wages upon which benefits are based, and cost-of-living benefit increases for current beneficiaries.

Although the number of need-related programs proliferated in the 1960s and 1970s and their spending in 1980 was more than seven times the 1965 level, the share of income security benefits devoted to this type of aid has actually been less since 1965 than before. About 25 percent of total benefits were spent on aid to the needy before 1965, but this proportion has since ranged between 15 and 20 percent.

The $96 billion increase in federal income security outlays from 1975 to 1980 consisted of a $77 billion growth in social insurance benefits ($54 billion from Social Security alone) and a $19 billion rise in need-related aid. Only a quarter of the latter increase resulted from growth in the traditional cash aid programs (AFDC, SSI, veterans pensions). Most of the growth in low-income aid resulted from increased Food Stamp participation and benefit levels that rose with food prices (24 percent), new commitments for subsidized housing (18 percent), and enactment of new forms of aid (15 percent).

Income security programs are also significant on the revenue side of the federal budget since Social Security and several others have their own dedicated revenue sources. The payroll taxes collected at the federal level now amount to 30 percent of all federal revenues.

Furthermore, the income tax code contains numerous exemptions, deductions, and credits that serve an income security purpose (table 12-2). Most of these tax expenditures are associated with the exclusion of social insurance benefits from taxation and tax incentives for retirement saving. Retirement saving incentives are now the largest tax expenditures associated with income security.

This huge growth in government's income security role resulted from a complex of economic factors, demographic change, and significant shifts in public opinion regarding social policies. The remainder of this section provides an overview of major income security policy developments of the past several decades, first for the social insurance systems and then for low-income assistance.

TABLE 12–2

SELECTED TAX EXPENDITURES FOR INCOME SECURITY PURPOSES, 1970–1980
(In $ billions)

Tax Expenditure	CY 1970	FY 1975	FY 1980
Tax expenditures related to social insurance			
Exclusion of benefit payments			
Social Security (retirement)	3.0[a]	2.7	6.9
Social Security (disability)	0.1	0.3	0.7
Social Security (dependents, survivors)	a	0.4	1.0
Unemployment compensation	0.4	2.3	2.5
Workers compensation	0.2	0.5	1.2
Veterans compensation	0.6[b]	0.5	1.0
Net exclusion of pension contributions and earnings			
Employer plans	3.1	5.2	12.9
Other plans	0.2	0.4	2.1
Exclusion of insurance benefits	0.5	0.8	1.6
Additional exemptions and credits for blind and elderly	a	1.2	2.1
Tax expenditures related to low-income assistance			
Exclusion of benefit payments			
Public assistance	0.1	0.1	0.4
Veterans pensions	b	c	0.1
Earned income tax credit	—	—	0.4

SOURCE: Congressional Budget Office, *Tax Expenditures: Current Issues and Five-Year Budget Projections for Fiscal Years 1982–1986* (Washington, D.C.: GPO, Sept. 1981), table 1.

a. For 1970, data for Social Security (dependents, survivors) and additional exemptions and credits for blind and elderly are included with Social Security (retirement).

b. For 1970, the veterans pension figure is included in the veterans compensation figure.

c. Less than $50 million.

Development of Social Insurance Policies

Enactment of the Social Security Act in 1935 heralded a major turning point in federal intervention to protect individuals against precipitous financial loss. Two major systems of social insurance were created. Unemployment insurance has changed little in terms of basic structure and purpose between 1935 and 1980. Social Security, on the other hand, expanded greatly and now has many features not included in the original law. The federal role in retirement income provision also underwent a major change with enactment of the Employee Retirement Income Security Act (ERISA) in 1974.

Unemployment Insurance. The only major structural change in unemployment benefits prior to 1970 was a provision adopted in the 1960s to extend benefits to unemployed workers for an additional thirteen weeks whenever the unemployment rate exceeded a threshold level. The 1970s saw much more change as the economy reached its worst condition since the Great Depression. Coverage of state and local employees, farm workers, and domestic workers was expanded, and a temporary twenty-six-week extension of benefits was in force during the 1975 recession. A new program of trade adjustment assistance was established to aid unemployed workers in industries adversely affected by U.S. trade policy, and its coverage was liberalized substantially after the initial implementation.

Social Security. The expansion of Social Security occurred in a long series of amendments that began before anyone actually retired under the system and continued through 1972. The system was broadened by adding new categories of beneficiaries—survivors of covered workers, the dependents of retirees and survivors, disabled workers, and early retirees aged sixty-two to sixty-four. Coverage of the work force expanded to include virtually all privately employed workers and many government employees.

Benefit entitlements were also modified frequently. First, benefits directly proportional to wages were discarded in favor of a progressive formula that replaced a considerably larger share of earnings in retirement for lower-wage workers. Second, benefit amounts were increased over time by Congress as economic growth continually presented the system with an unplanned surplus of payroll tax revenues. Third, Congress continually liberalized the "retirement test"—the provision for reducing benefits according to a beneficiary's earnings—so that those who worked could realize larger total incomes.

The 1972 amendments, which included a 20 percent benefit increase, marked the end of the expansion of Social Security coverage and benefits. Ad hoc benefit increases gave way to automatic adjustments linked to the Consumer Price Index (CPI), an approach adopted (also in 1972) in part as a means of constraining costs. In 1977 Congress selectively trimmed future benefit costs and increased payroll taxes, and it was recognized that further benefit savings or revenues might be needed to meet long-run commitments. This abrupt turnaround from expansion to retrenchment was caused by a combination of circumstances. The trust fund reserves became dangerously low as inflation drove up benefits and a stagnant economy did not produce the expected payroll tax revenues. The long-run funding outlook also turned sour as fertility and mortality projections proved wrong. Despite the 1977 legislation, by 1981 the short-run funding outlook was once again problematic due to the state of the economy.

Regulation of Private Pensions. Even though Social Security benefits have risen dramatically, the system has always been regarded as a floor under retirement income that should be supplemented by pension benefits and personal savings. During the 1970s Congress also became concerned about the pension component of this retirement system and enacted the Employee Retirement Income Security Act of 1974 (ERISA) to improve private pension coverage and funding and protect the pension rights of plan participants.

After a long period of growth in pension plans, coverage had stagnated far short of universality in the 1970s, with about one-half of private, nonfarm jobs covered by plans. Only about one-fourth of Social Security retirees were also receiving a private pension. Even many of these retirees had financial difficulties. They usually retired with adequate incomes, but the real value of the pension was often severely eroded over time since pensions are almost never fully adjusted for inflation. Finally, poor funding and management of some pension plans jeopardized the retirement security of millions of workers with private coverage.

ERISA dealt with some of these concerns by setting minimum standards for employee participation and vesting, funding, and rules of fiduciary conduct. The Pension Benefit Guaranty Corporation was established to protect the benefit rights of workers and pensioners when plans are terminated. These reforms have been beneficial to many workers, although the new requirements imposed by ERISA were probably a factor in the decline in the number of plans that occurred soon after enactment.

Efforts to extend ERISA to public pension plans have not succeeded, and a recommendation of President Carter's Pension Policy Commission to mandate minimum universal pension coverage found little support. Thus, the momentum for further improvement in retirement income through pension regulation had waned shortly before the Reagan administration took office.

Low-income Assistance

The Social Security Act provided for federal matching grants for state assistance to needy persons who were aged or blind and to families with dependent children with a deceased, absent, or incapacitated parent. Prior to 1960 the only major change in this program was the addition in 1950 of a fourth category of recipients (the permanently and totally disabled) eligible for such federal matching. Subsequently, however, low-income assistance changed considerably as public policy focused on the problems of poverty in the 1960s and then sought in the 1970s to rationalize and improve the numerous, ill-coordinated programs that had developed.

The War on Poverty. Prior to the 1960s there had been little systematic federal policy concerning poverty and its alleviation. Rather, the focus had been on society's insuring against the primary risks of income loss faced by

working people and on ameliorating the plight of the "deserving poor"—
that is, the categories of needy people that society did not expect to be self-
sufficient. As the politics of the 1960s led to a new awareness of chronic
regional economic problems, other structural labor market problems, and past
civil rights violations, the prior notion of a "deserving poor" category began
to break down. The idea that a wealthy nation should attempt to pull everyone
up to at least a minimal living standard took root and grew. Efforts to improve
direct aid for the needy resulted in higher federal matching for state welfare
payments, enactment of the Medicaid program, and the extension at state
option of AFDC to two-parent families where one parent was unemployed.

Steps also were taken both to require and to encourage AFDC families
to move off the welfare rolls. These efforts were spurred not only by the
antipoverty crusade but also by a growing opinion that many nonworking
AFDC mothers should be in the labor force. This changing opinion was
grounded in part in the fact that more women generally were working, but it
also reflected a fear that AFDC was creating a "welfare class" of families
with no breadwinners to serve as role models for their children. Legislation
was enacted to increase job-related services, require mothers without preschool children to work, and provide AFDC recipients with a positive incentive to work. Whereas previously any earnings resulted in a equivalent reduction
in benefits, a 1967 law disregarded the first $30 of monthly earnings and one-
third of any excess over $30 plus work expenses.

New programmatic approaches were also developed to assist needy persons not covered by the public assistance categories and to supplement the
benefits of those who were. The Food Stamp program was initiated in 1964
and was greatly expanded in the late 1960s. New forms of subsidized housing
assistance for low-income families were established, not only for renters but
also for home buyers. A longstanding policy of providing a federal subsidy
for elementary and secondary school meals was augmented to provide a deeper
subsidy for meals served to children from low-income families.

The Welfare Reform Era. This surge in benefit expansion was followed
by major attempts at systematic reform that spanned the Nixon, Ford, and
Carter years. The impetus for welfare reform originated in 1969, when advocates of the poor who wanted to eradicate the remaining poverty gap formed
an alliance with Nixon administration officials who sought to restructure
welfare programs. The goals were to (1) establish a federal benefit floor more
generous than that paid in the poorest states; (2) reduce the inequity between
the "working poor" not eligible for welfare and the welfare eligibles; (3)
step up efforts to move into jobs those able-bodied AFDC parents not caring
for preschool children; (4) begin a resorting of roles between the federal and
state governments, with the federal government running a streamlined national

income maintenance system; and (5) head off the proliferation of new aid programs.

The reform efforts of Nixon, Carter, and various members of Congress never realized their central purpose of replacing AFDC with a federal income maintenance system. This failure stemmed largely from two difficulties. First, to provide both adequate benefit levels for the penniless and substantial incentives for recipients to work at an acceptable program cost proved to be impossible. The combination of a reasonable benefit level and only a partial reduction of benefits for earnings results in a large eligible population. Second, it was feared that a federal benefit floor high enough to replace AFDC in a large number of states would create political and economic problems in states where wages for unskilled labor were quite low.

The welfare reform effort did spawn a series of important initiatives, however. The state programs of aid to the aged, blind, and disabled were replaced with the federal Supplemental Security Income (SSI) program. Major improvements in Food Stamps fashioned the program into a "funny money" version of the national income floor President Nixon had sought as a replacement for AFDC. Enactment of a refundable earned income tax credit provided a wage subsidy to working poor heads of families with children.

Several other major program expansions occurred during the 1970s independent of the welfare reform effort. Commitments to subsidized housing rose substantially, child nutrition assistance took on new forms, and rising oil prices led to special aid to low-income households to help pay their fuel bills.

The overall incidence of poverty had declined significantly during the 1960s (from 22 to 13 percent of the population) with economic growth and expanded social insurance and low-income assistance. The leaner years of the 1970s saw little further poverty reduction (one percentage point); however, increased benefits resulted in further improvement for the neediest groups. The poverty rate among the aged fell from 24 to 15 percent, and for female-headed families from 37 to 33 percent.

Income Security Issues When Reagan Took Office

The Reagan administration took office with restraint of federal spending as one of its main objectives. Thus a key item on the agenda was to reduce the normal growth in income security outlays in ways that were in harmony with other income security policy goals. However, this budgetary objective had to be sought in the context of the policy developments just discussed. Welfare programs were widely regarded as inequitable among states and recipient groups, and the combinations of multiple benefits were thought to result in inadequate work incentives. A dozen years of attempts to gain more national control over the system, better coordinate the various programs, and improve their management had succeeded only partially.

The situation of Social Security seemed even more critical. Unforeseen economic and demographic trends had already halted the once common use of the program as a vehicle for improving the social welfare; now even its fiscal integrity was in doubt. Regulatory efforts to fashion pension benefits into a more predictable partnership with Social Security in providing a decent retirement income had left basic issues of coverage and benefit protection unresolved. Lost pension credits due to job mobility and the effects of inflation on benefit values were particularly troublesome. The third component of retirement income, personal savings, was not a major income source for most elderly, and the saving rate nationally for the years 1977 through 1980 was at its lowest level since the late 1940s.

Policy Changes under President Reagan

The income security area would pose a series of difficult choices for any administration in the early 1980s but particularly for one committed to domestic budgetary restraint. If policy goes unchanged, income security outlays will continue to rise, driven by rising prices and wages, growth in eligible recipients, and, in recessionary periods, by rising unemployment. These outlay increases limit any flexibility to reorder budget priorities or alter the size of government. However, to change policy requires enactment of legislation that will affect the personal incomes of potentially millions of people who fall mostly into categories of great social concern. Policy changes also upset existing federal-state fiscal arrangements and the distribution of federal grants. Alterations in public retirement systems may have substantial repercussions for the private pension industry. Phasing in policy changes over long time periods—while mitigating such problems—totally eliminates short-term budgetary flexibility.

The Reagan administration has approached income security with three apparent major goals: (1) to reduce the short-term growth in spending that would otherwise occur by making a variety of changes in entitlements that can be implemented quickly; (2) to turn over greater responsibility for welfare assistance to the states; and (3) to promote greater reliance by individuals on their own resources through work and asset accumulation and lessen dependence on public benefits.

Budgetary Restraint Measures

Generally speaking, the actions the Reagan administration proposed in conjunction with the 1982 budget revisions and 1983 budget request reflect a short-run view that policy changes should result in immediate budgetary savings. The impacts of such changes have to be politically acceptable to Congress based on current effects on constituents. Therefore, cuts enacted in 1981 in social insurance and related programs were limited to the most questionable benefits. Many of the welfare cuts were designed to avoid reducing benefits of the poorest recipients; savings were also sought based on evidence of need for administrative improvements. For the most part, the administration's 1983 proposals follow the pattern established for 1982.

The major failures of Reagan's 1982 budget proposals in Congress resulted where short-term income losses would have hit politically favored groups. Elimination of the minimum floor on Social Security benefits was accepted only after Congress agreed to apply it solely to new beneficiaries. Major Social Security proposals that would have immediately reduced early retirement benefits for new beneficiaries were never seriously considered by Congress.

Viewed as a one-time budgetary action, the administration's attempt to reduce income security spending was amazingly successful. (However, as indicated in the next section, enacted measures may not be as significant in curbing long-term trends.) President Reagan proposed income security entitlement cuts rising to an estimated $17 billion by 1984. He obtained the enabling legislation to achieve about three-quarters of such savings. Many recent presidents had proposed savings in income security entitlements, but rarely was the necessary legislation enacted. In fact, such savings proposals were often regarded as one of several budget "gimmicks" to disguise the real outlay and deficit implications of overall budget requests.

The expected outlay savings in 1984 arising from 1981 actions ($12.8 billion) are about 4 percent of projected income security spending under previous policies, or about half the normal yearly increase in income security outlays. The extent of the cuts varies greatly among program areas (table 12-3). Nearly 60 percent occurred in low-income assistance programs, although these account for only 18 percent of income security outlays. Within this category, the cuts fell most heavily on programs offering aid for specific consumption goods (food, housing, fuel) rather than general cash assistance. These in-kind programs sustained nearly half the income security cuts, though they comprise only a tenth of all income security spending. AFDC and unemployment compensation were also reduced in size by amounts greater than a pro rata reduction would have yielded.

TABLE 12-3

BASELINE INCOME SECURITY OUTLAYS AND ENACTED SAVINGS PROJECTED TO 1984, BY PROGRAM

Program	Baseline Outlays (In $ billions)	Percentage of Total	Estimated Outlay Savings (In $ billions)	Program Savings as Percentage of Baseline	Program Savings as Percentage of Total Savings
Social insurance and related programs					
Social Security (OASDI)	194.1	58.6	3.1	1.6	24.2
Income security for veterans (excl. non-service-connected pensions)	12.0	3.6	0.1	0.8	0.8
Federal employee retirement and disability	42.9	12.9	0.7	1.6	5.5
Unemployment compensation	18.4	5.6	1.2	6.5	9.4
Other programs[a]	5.8	1.8	0.2	3.4	1.6
Subtotal	273.2	82.4	5.3	1.9	41.4
Low-income assistance programs					
Aid to Families with Dependent Children (AFDC)	9.2	2.8	1.5	16.3	11.7
Supplemental Security Income (SSI)	8.4	2.5	0.1	1.2	0.8
Veterans non-service-connected pensions	4.2	1.3	0.0	0.0	0.0
Earned income tax credit	1.0	0.3	0.0	0.0	0.0

Low-income energy assistance	2.9	0.9	1.0	34.5	7.8
Other cash assistance	1.2	0.4	0.1	8.3	0.8
Food Stamps	12.9	3.9	2.4	18.6	18.8
Other food programs[b]	6.8	2.1	1.7	25.0	13.3
Housing assistance	11.6	3.5	0.7	6.0	5.5
Subtotal	58.2	17.6	7.5	12.9	58.6
Total	331.4	100.0	12.8	3.9	100.0

SOURCE: Unpublished projections, Congressional Budget Office, July 28, 1981 and August 6, 1981.

NOTE: Detail may not add to totals due to rounding.

a. Includes railroad retirement system and benefits for disabled coal miners.

b. Includes school lunch and other child nutrition programs.

The president's 1983 budget proposals again sought substantial savings in income security benefits--$9 billion in 1984, rising to $11 billion in 1986. Almost 80 percent of the 1984 savings would fall on the low-income aid programs. Most of the remainder would come from limits on federal retiree benefit adjustments.

Cuts in Low-income Assistance Programs

The savings already enacted in low-income assistance programs fall into three categories. First, benefit amounts were reduced for welfare recipients with earnings by lowering AFDC and Food Stamp income eligibility limits and partially or totally eliminating certain allowable deductions from countable income. These actions were by far the most profound from a policy viewpoint, as they reversed past efforts to increase recipients' financial incentives to work. Such changes reduced outlays by $2.0 billion. These enacted provisions and further changes proposed in the president's 1983 budget are listed in table 12-4.

Substantial savings were also realized through reductions in funding levels of several programs administered at the state or local level. Low-income energy assistance and the Puerto Rico Food Stamp program were both con-verted to block grants and reduced by a total of $1.3 billion. Another major saving ($1.7 billion) was achieved by reducing the federal subsidy for school meals. The administration's 1983 budget proposed further block grants for food programs, various savings in AFDC, and an eventual turnover of AFDC and Food Stamps to state control. (Reduced spending for housing assistance is described in chapter 13.)

The third category of savings is related to administrative efficiency. Congress changed the procedure for income accounting in the AFDC, SSI, and Food Stamp programs so that income is now measured retrospectively. Prospective income accounting, while more sensitive to recipient needs, re-sults in greater overpayments. These changes saved $0.8 billion.

The administration's welfare cuts were designed to avoid reducing the benefits of recipients with the least income. However, a 1983 budget proposal would deny new SSI recipients the existing $20 monthly income disregard. Since most SSI eligibles have income from Social Security or elsewhere, dropping this disregard would be tantamount to lowering the federal income floor for the needy aged, blind, and disabled by $240 a year.

Cuts in Social Insurance and Related Benefits

With one exception, enacted reductions in social insurance benefits were not large relative to pre-Reagan spending. That exception is unemployment

TABLE 12–4

POLICY CHANGES AND PROPOSALS TO REDUCE BENEFITS FOR WELFARE RECIPIENTS
WITH EARNINGS

Program	Changes Enacted in 1981	1981 Administration Proposals Not Enacted	1982 Administration Proposals
AFDC	Limitations on child care and work expense deductions from countable income		
	Cap on gross income allowed for eligibility		
	Limitation on "$30 + 1/3" monthly earnings disregard to first 4 months as recipient		
	Option for states to run "workfare" programs[a]	Require states to have "workfare" programs[a]	Require states to have "workfare" programs[a]
	Eligibility for unemployed-parent families restricted to those where primary earner is the person unemployed		Limit unemployed-parent eligibles to those participating in "workfare" program
			Delete benefit for parent who deliberately quits job, reduces hours, or refuses job
Food Stamps	Cap on gross income allowed for eligibility		
	Limit indexing of income deductions and repeal newly enacted deductions		
	Reduce earnings disregard from 20 percent to 18 percent of wages		Eliminate earnings disregard
			Increase benefit reduction rate to 35 percent of countable income

a.   "Workfare" refers to the Community Work Experience program in which certain categories of welfare recipients are required to work without pay for a number of hours sufficient to offset the cost of the welfare benefit.

compensation, where 1982 budget savings of $1.2 billion (6.5 percent of baseline outlays) were achieved, mainly from a narrowing of benefits for long-term unemployment. A more restrictive trigger was adopted for the thirteen-week extension of unemployment benefits that occurs when unemployment is high, and eligibility for trade adjustment assistance (TAA) was drastically curtailed. (A 1983 budget proposal would eliminate TAA.) These changes are consistent with Reagan administration objectives to limit government interference in the market economy and to induce able-bodied people to depend less on public benefits.

Social Security savings of $2.5 billion in the 1982 budget were obtained from a variety of provisions, none of which affected the basic entitlements of retired workers. The Social Security minimum benefit was dropped for beneficiaries coming on the rolls after December 31, 1981. Social Security dependents' and survivors' benefits to college students are being phased out. A cap was placed on total public disability benefits equal to 80 percent of final wages. Implementation of a planned liberalization in the Social Security retirement test was delayed. Death benefits under Social Security (and also veterans programs) were eliminated for certain cases.

The changes made in Social Security did not deal with the system's funding problems, although the major benefit reductions rejected by Congress would have done so. Social Security still could become insolvent as early as 1983 unless Congress acts to increase the system's revenues or reduce its costs. Because of its political sensitivity, the administration has chosen to defer major initiatives on these questions until 1983 while awaiting recommendations from a new National Commission on Social Security Reform due to report by the end of 1982. It also has abstained from any new initiatives to address the principal long-run issues—the Social Security trust fund deficit anticipated in the next century, and the need to rationalize public and private retirement programs into a more sensible and equitable overall system.

Changes in Tax Expenditures

While benefit savings were being achieved through the budget review process, tax expenditures for the purpose of encouraging retirement saving increased dramatically (table 12-5). This increase was due in part to provisions of the 1981 Economic Recovery Tax Act but also to the growth in earnings of pension fund assets. On the other hand, the income tax rate reductions had the effect of slowing growth in preexisting tax expenditures associated with the exclusion of income security benefits from taxable income. The major tax expenditure for low-income families--the earned income tax credit--actually declined in value because eligibility limits and maximum amounts were not adjusted for inflation.

TABLE 12–5

Estimated Income Security Tax Expenditures for Fiscal Years 1981 and 1983 and Percentage Change, for Selected Tax Expenditures

Tax Expenditure	Estimated Revenue Loss (In $ billions)		Percentage Change in Revenue Loss
	FY 1981	FY 1983	
Tax expenditures related to social insurance			
Exclusion of benefit payments			
Social Security and railroad retirement	11.8	13.8	+ 16.7
Unemployment compensation	2.0	2.7	+ 36.5
Veterans compensation and pensions	1.4	1.5	+ 8.9
Net exclusion of pension contributions and earnings			
Employer plans	23.4	27.5	+ 17.6
Keogh plans, IRAs, other	2.2	3.8	+ 73.3
Additional exemptions and credits for blind and elderly	2.4	2.5	+ 5.2
Tax expenditures related to low-income assistance			
Exclusion of public assistance benefits	0.4	0.4	–4.4
Earned income tax credit	0.6	0.5	–18.9

Source: Office of Management and Budget, *Budget of the United States Government, Fiscal Year 1983* (Washington, D.C.: GPO, February 1982), Special Analysis G, Tax Expenditures.

Because of the broadening of individual retirement account (IRA) eligibility to include all wage earners and their nonworking spouses and an increased contribution limit for both IRAs and Keogh plans, the tax expenditures for these exclusions are expected to rise by 73 percent over the two-year period. By 1983 they are expected to amount to more than a tenth of all pension-related tax expenditures.

Tax expenditures associated with exclusion of public benefits are generally rising more slowly than the benefits themselves. In fact, the revenue loss due to excluding public assistance will actually fall by 4 percent because of both tax rate reductions and cuts in benefits for those on welfare who work. The revenue loss from the earned income credit will decline by nearly a fifth over the two years.

Consequences of the Policy Changes

The changes made in 1981 have already had an impact on program recipients. Immediate effects on available benefits can be determined. However, the longer-term consequences of these policy changes cannot yet be fully measured since they depend on responses by individuals, state and local governments, and private organizations. This section first presents an analysis of the immediate effects of selected benefit changes for the group most affected—welfare recipients who also have wage income. It then discusses several longer-term implications regarding the national commitment to a "social safety net," the efficiency of policies aimed at the working poor, the likely future course for the retirement income system, and the impact of budget cuts on future growth in program spending.

Short-term Effects of Welfare Savings

The magnitude of the Reagan welfare cuts has been widely discussed by the media in budgetary terms, and the impacts on typical families have been shown. However, information has not been available on how important the cutbacks are as reductions in total family income, how the relative impact varies among different kinds of families, and the numbers of people so affected. A study by the Congressional Budget Office (CBO)[2] (summarized in chapter 16) analyzed the distribution of benefit cuts by income class, but it did not distinguish the relative impacts within the lowest income bracket ($10,000 and below) or among family types. This section reports on a more detailed analysis of a national sample of families conducted by the author using a computer model that simulates the AFDC and Food Stamp program changes and measures their consequences for individual family incomes.[3]

Three comparisons between old law and new law benefits were made based on (1) actual 1979 income data, (2) income projected to 1984 using CBO's low economic growth scenario, and (3) 1984 projections using CBO's high economic growth scenario.[4]

The average changes in income that would have occurred had the 1981 welfare cuts been in effect in 1979 are shown in table 12-6 for various recipient groups. The income of families receiving AFDC but no other welfare benefit would have been reduced by an average of 2 percent ($194) a year. AFDC families also receiving Food Stamps would have lost $231 in benefits. (Actual total losses to AFDC families are greater than shown here since some families lost Medicaid eligibility, some now pay more than before for school lunches, and some who live in public housing now pay higher rents.) SSI recipients

TABLE 12-6

CHANGES IN MEAN 1979 INCOME, PROGRAM ELIGIBILITY, AND POVERTY STATUS DUE TO WELFARE BENEFIT REDUCTIONS, FOR SELECTED RECIPIENT GROUPS

Eligibility Group	Mean Pretax Posttransfer Annual Family Income, 1979[a] ($)	Change in 1979 Mean Income		Change in Number of Eligible Families		Change in Number of Families in Poverty	
		($)	(%)	(Number)	(%)	(Number)	(%)
Eligible for							
Any transfer payment	13,764	−24	−0.2	−135,029	−0.4	+137,156	+1.5
AFDC only	9,898	−194	−2.0	−31,446	−1.3	+74,477	+6.2
AFDC and Food Stamps	7,989	−231	−2.9	−47,164	−4.5	+15,271	+4.0
SSI and Food Stamps[b]	5,582	−11	−0.2	−1,566	−0.2	+2,111	+0.9
AFDC, SSI and Food Stamps	10,576	−97	−0.9	−1,685	−1.3	c	c

SOURCE: Urban Institute simulations of policy changes using the TRIM model and the March 1980 Current Population Survey.

a. Income data include the value of Food Stamps as well as cash income. The data on income and changes in income use the family as the unit of analysis. Since welfare-eligible units will differ somewhat from the family definition because of program rules, the income data generally are higher than the incomes for the welfare-eligible units.

b. There is no change in income for SSI-only cases that could be measured in the TRIM model. The only programmatic change was the switch from prospective to retrospective income accounting.

c. Sample size is too small.

who received Food Stamps would have experienced a small average loss of $11 in benefits.

Within these recipient groups, as expected, the losses are greatest for recipients with earnings. For example, AFDC-Food Stamp families with working female heads would have lost an average of 6 to 7 percent of annual income. For two-parent families with a male earner, the reductions would have been smaller (less than 2 percent) because welfare benefits are a smaller part of their total family income.

The administration's 1983 budget proposals would deepen these losses. The proposed cuts again would affect primarily benefits for recipients with earnings. However, unlike the enacted cuts, the proposed savings would affect substantially most Food Stamp recipients, all new SSI beneficiaries, and AFDC family units that share a household with other individuals.

The number of families losing eligibility for various combinations of benefits or falling below the poverty level because of the enacted cuts is substantial. Nearly 5 percent of the AFDC-Food Stamp cases lose their combined eligibility, most becoming AFDC-only cases. Even so, the number of AFDC-only families declines because of lost eligibility. The welfare cuts move an estimated 137,156 families below the poverty level, a 1.5 percent increase in the number of poor families. Most of this increase occurs in the AFDC-only population, whose poverty rate increases by 6 percent.

Projections of the enacted welfare changes to 1984 indicate that the effects will be smaller relative to gross family incomes than in 1979. That is, in both the low- and high-growth scenarios, mean family incomes are estimated to rise faster than will the benefit reduction amounts caused by the policy changes. For example, the $231 average reduction found in 1979 for AFDC-Food Stamp families would rise to $247 in 1984 (low growth path), but this latter amount would be a smaller part of gross income (2.3 percent in 1984 compared to 2.9 percent in 1979).

Long-term Welfare Policy Issues

The administration argues that the long-term implications of its policies are favorable for those persons now on welfare. The objective of strong economic growth, if realized, will benefit everyone through greater job opportunities and faster wage growth. (See chapter 16 for further discussion on this point.) Officials anticipate that steps taken to reduce welfare eligibility and implement state "workfare" projects will promote greater work effort by low-income family heads. This section deals with the implications of benefit changes in a welfare policy context.

The welfare changes enacted thus far, while important, are relatively modest in scope and do not depict accurately the profound policy redirection set in motion by the administration. Two basic tenets of welfare policy have been called into question. What responsibility does the federal government bear to assure that a "safety net" is in place for those who find themselves in need of financial help? How should welfare assistance be provided to those who can work but have wages insufficient to meet family needs?

The "Safety Net" and the Federal Role in Income Support. When the Reagan administration announced its Program for Economic Recovery in February 1981, it established "preservation of the social safety net" as the first among nine criteria used in revising the Carter administration's fiscal 1982 budget. Although the rhetoric about the safety net was subjected to a wide range of interpretations, the February document did identify a set of "social safety net programs":[5] "social insurance benefits for the elderly; basic unemployment benefits; cash benefits for dependent families, elderly and disabled; and social obligation to veterans." These descriptive labels were not formal program titles; instead, they were general characterizations of the parts of programs that the administration did not seek to change.

The adjectives in the above quotation took on more definition in light of subsequent administration proposals. Exempted from proposed 1982 budget cutbacks were Social Security age sixty-five retirement benefits; unemployment benefits for the first thirteen weeks of unemployment; cash welfare aid to eligibles with no other source of income; and the major veterans programs. Thus, the "safety net" did not in fact include early retirees, disabled workers or retirees' dependents under Social Security; workers unemployed longer than thirteen weeks; the typical welfare recipient (who has income other than welfare); and recipients of noncash aid regardless of their income. "Safety net" proved to be a term that categorized people neither by their degree of current financial need nor by their vulnerability to future economic insecurity. Rather, it appears to have been used primarily to delineate and protect the benefits of those for whom cutbacks would likely have aroused the strongest reaction in Congress. The proposed savings for the 1983 budget mostly abide by the safety net concept that evolved in the 1982 budget, though greater savings are being sought than before in veterans benefits.

The confusion over what a safety net should include highlights the fact that a national income floor has never actually been adopted. The closest approximation is provided by the Food Stamp program, which supplements cash income with food coupons scaled to income according to a nationally uniform schedule for all people who meet the needs test. Ironically, this program has been treated most harshly under President Reagan.

The administration's New Federalism proposal would transfer to state control a number of federal programs, including AFDC and Food Stamps. In its most extreme form this would constitute a complete turning away from any federal responsibility for an income floor for all but the aged and disabled.

While state-run welfare systems could be required to meet minimum federal standards, strong standards might be rejected or circumvented and would make little sense in any case under the New Federalism concept.

Thus far, the states have not been willing to accept this federalism proposal. A majority seem to favor the idea that there is a need for federal responsibility for an income floor. Their argument is based on the nationwide impact of economic change and the fact that states with serious economic problems usually experience simultaneously a rising welfare burden and declining tax revenues. Given the president's twin emphases of welfare cost reductions and transfer of authority to state government, the most basic questions about the safety net have gone unasked. Is the current protection afforded the neediest Americans adequate, and is this income floor fair in its variation among states, localities, and population groups?

Reversal of Past Policy on the Working Poor. However the battle of state versus federal roles is resolved, the direction of policies regarding the working poor has already been reversed from that of the 1960s and 1970s. Through actions taken at the president's request in 1981, Congress moved away from the notion that low-income people are to be encouraged to work through positive financial incentives. To illustrate how the changes in AFDC and Food Stamps alter disposable incomes and financial work incentives, it is helpful to focus on a single parent with two children (the most common AFDC family).[6] Disposable income for such a family whose head has earnings typical of AFDC eligibles has declined in 1982 in every state compared to prior law. In some states the degree of decline is substantial—for example, from $731 to $534 a month in Connecticut, a 27 percent drop. In low-payment states, the decline tended to be less in degree but perhaps more severe in terms of the hardship that may result—for example, from $449 to $371 (67 percent of the poverty level) in Louisiana. The 1981 changes result in a nonworking AFDC parent and two children being better off than the example family with a working parent in twelve states.

These policy changes also altered dramatically the marginal gain to AFDC recipients from working an extra hour or seeking a higher wage. For example, in California a recipient formerly could keep about 30 cents of an extra dollar of wages over a wide earnings range ($100 to $450 a month). Now that same recipient would realize almost no gain over the $100 to $350 range and would lose income at the margin by earning more than $350.

Prior to 1981 presidential welfare initiatives had placed strong emphasis on lowering effective tax rates (taxes plus benefit offsets) applied to wages of low-income family heads and on eliminating precipitous loss of large benefits due to minor increases in earnings. Supporting arguments emphasized both work incentives and equity (i.e., that families of low-income workers should end up with greater total income than is available to comparable families without working members). In deciding to reverse this policy, the Reagan administration had several arguments in its favor. First, if federal welfare spending had to be cut, the most humane way may be to reduce benefits for the least poor recipients (i.e., the working poor). Such action necessarily reduces financial work incentives for those still eligible for assistance. Second, there has been great public resentment surrounding the extension of welfare eligibility to persons with five-figure earning levels, even though such cases are a small proportion of the caseload. This circumstance is necessitated by a program design that combines payment amounts based on both need standards related to family size and benefit reduction rates well below 100 percent.

A third administration argument—that the marginal tax rate is not an important determinant of work effort for lower-income people—is one that will be long debated. This incentives question was studied extensively in the 1960s and 1970s using both AFDC program experience and specially designed field experiments.[7] The analytic evidence is imprecise, but a general conclusion of the experiments is that the variation in work response to different benefit levels and reduction rates was modest. The studies are based on circumstances not exactly the same as those facing today's AFDC families. For instance, implicit tax rates on earnings greater than 100 percent and a possible loss of Medicaid eligibility were not analyzed. Still, existing evidence does generally support the administration view in two respects. Eliminating the "$30 plus one-third" disregard will probably lower program costs, and the work effort of those affected will not be greatly reduced. One well-regarded study of AFDC data concluded that "liberalized work incentives may encourage current recipients to increase labor supply, but these increases will be more than offset by work reductions of former nonrecipients who are now attracted onto the program."[8] Also, some sociological research suggests that economic incentives are not the only important consideration in a person's decision to work, since work itself has been found to have an intrinsic value independent of income.[9]

Whatever the effects of marginal tax rates, there is a way in which the nominal work incentive for a welfare eligible can indisputably be increased without lowering the payment level or the benefit offset rate. This approach is to increase the personal cost to eligibles of applying for and continuing to receive benefits. Several administration AFDC proposals have this effect. The prime example is the proposed mandatory "workfare" program to require certain AFDC family heads to "work off" their benefits. (Congress thus far has left this program a state option.) It is thought that such measures serve to deter would-be recipients from applying for benefits, perhaps more than offsetting any caseload increase that might result from the reduced financial work incentives. Administration officials have argued that those so deterred are not really in need of assistance by definition, for a person in dire need would not hesitate to apply.

Critics of the administration's policy on work incentives have countered with several arguments. First, they argue that welfare applicants should be served, not hassled, by the bureaucracy and thus should not be subject to provisions aimed at deterring applications. Second, there is an equity argument in favor of having substantial financial work incentives for welfare recipients; that is, persons with incomes low enough to qualify for welfare should still be able to reap financial gain from working just as any other worker would expect. Third, the idea that low-income people will not respond to positive work incentives, whether or not an accurate notion, runs counter to the supply side theory that greatly increased economic activity will flow from lowered tax rates. This contradiction in policy may add to the perception held by many that the administration has treated poor people relatively harshly.

The fourth argument against this administration policy direction is one of feasibility. To make workfare programs perform well in providing relevant work experience to all eligibles may involve program costs much larger than the benefits will justify. While programs designed to move welfare recipients into jobs have a long history, none has been applied to all eligibles statewide, and until recently states could not restrict remuneration of job program participants to cover only their welfare benefits. The demonstrations of workfare for AFDC recipients that occurred in several states prior to the Reagan administration generally have been judged ineffective.[10] Similar tests for persons receiving Food Stamps or local general assistance have been successful in some instances. However, this success is probably because the clientele involved (single individuals and male family heads) were different than those of the AFDC program.

One major problem in previous AFDC workfare projects has been resistance by local administrators. The new round of workfare tests will benefit from the strong support and encouragement of the administration, and that fact may mitigate problems of implementation. However, acceptance of the community work experience program advocated by the administration will ultimately hinge on actual state experience. The problems they will encounter are predictable: potentially large administrative costs with unknown and perhaps immeasurable results; problems in enforcing work force discipline; resentment of those who desire public service jobs but are not eligible for them; a reduction in the incentive of public agencies to improve productivity; and taxpayer irritation with the provision of public services by a poorly trained and perhaps unmotivated welfare work force.

These problems will have to be weighed against several redeeming factors: the provision of job experience to unskilled people who may benefit from even the most limited work opportunities; a positive feeling among local taxpayers that they are getting a tangible service in return for the taxes paid to otherwise idle neighbors; and the availability of workers for local projects for which no other funds are available.

Long-term Implications for Retirement Policy

Although public retirement benefits have largely escaped budget cuts, the immediate and long-term funding problems of Social Security suggest a continued focus by policy makers on retirement issues. Administration initiatives are discussed below with respect to two key questions: Will society come to rely more on personal savings in retirement? Will a major restructuring of Social Security be attempted?

The Potential for Privatization of Retirement Income. Public benefits have become increasingly important as a source of income in old age. For example, in 1978 Social Security benefits accounted for 38 percent of all cash income for persons age sixty-five and over, up from 3 percent in 1950 and 30 percent in 1962. They amount to at least half of the income of more than half of the elderly and comprise 90 percent or more of the income of nearly a quarter of the elderly.[11] Wages and asset income accounted for 23 and 19 percent, respectively, of the income of the elderly in 1978. These two sources totaled 79 percent in 1950 and 46 percent in 1962. Pension plans accounted for 14 percent in 1978, up from 9 percent in 1962.

Despite this large and growing role of public benefits, we may soon be at a turning point that eventually will result in a greater proportion of income in old age flowing from wages and assets. The likelihood of this occurrence stems largely from the financial limitations on the Social Security system. The Social Security funding problem may result in reductions in scheduled future benefit levels. Further, the administration, several key members of Congress, and two recent government commissions have urged changes in Social Security designed to delay retirement age and increase the labor force activity of older people.

Another factor that may encourage greater reliance on work and savings is that, during a period of rapid economic change, employees cannot count on improvements in the value of their future pension benefits relative to wages. Many people retiring today will do better than earlier cohorts because of past pension gains. But a young or middle-aged worker today must plan under the assumption that spells of unemployment are more likely and, for many, a change in career, firm, or industry is a real possibility. Since the majority of workers cannot take their pension credits with them when they change jobs, they lose those credits or see them reduced in value by inflation before reaching retirement age. This lack of portability of credits when workers change jobs cannot be corrected without major federal intervention. Such action would fly in the face of the current trend toward deregulation of private businesses.

While most older workers may be able to retire for some years to come with more adequate incomes than their predecessors, many younger workers may be forced to consider the possibility of, at best, stagnation in the availability and adequacy of retirement income and, at worst, a substantial reduction in Social Security benefits. Thus, it is logical that these employees may work longer and save more to improve their financial prospects in old age. Two new measures—one enacted, one proposed—will act to support such behavior.

The measure enacted in 1981 provides an added incentive for personal retirement saving by changing the tax law to permit all wage earners a tax-deferred $2,000 annual contribution to an individual retirement account (IRA). If large numbers of people take advantage of this provision and keep the funds intact until retirement age, there could be a major increase in the asset income available in old age. Should IRAs prove popular, Congress may increase allowable contribution levels over time. Such a step might strengthen a trend toward privatization by encouraging less federal regulation of pension plans or a reduced role for Social Security.

There are three principal stumbling blocks to a greater reliance on IRAs in their present form. First, the higher a person's tax rate, the higher the incentive to save through an IRA. The incentive is weakest for low-income workers who are the least likely to have pension coverage. Thus, for many workers IRAs may not serve well as an alternative to an employer pension plan. A second problem is that any voluntary saving program will inevitably result in a substantial number of people who fail to take advantage of it. This can create a social problem if Social Security is cut back. Third, the flexibility of personal control over IRA funds increases the risk of poor management of one's retirement assets. Again, a major social problem could result.

A 1982 proposal by President Reagan to prohibit mandatory retirement rules would serve to delay the time of retirement for some older workers. Currently, employers can compel workers to retire at age seventy. Elimination of such rules would have two effects. First, an estimated 5 percent of older workers would continue working beyond the ages at which they now retire.[12] Second, employers would be pressured to provide pension credits for work past the "normal retirement age" (usually age sixty-five). A good many pension plans provide little or no credit for delayed retirement, thereby inducing employees to retire earlier than they might otherwise.

The Need for Long-term Social Security Reforms. A potential insolvency of the Social Security trust funds in 1983 due mainly to poor economic conditions will force Congress to address the system's financing. But a long-term funding issue also requires attention since actuarial projections indicate that the system's financing cannot cover fully the expected benefit costs when the post-World War II "baby boom" generation retires in the next century. Legislated payroll taxes are at historically high levels, and there seems to be little interest in Congress in raising them further. Thus, if the projections prove to be correct, either the system will have to be pared back and provide fewer benefits, or it will have to tap new revenue sources and leave fewer funds for other public purposes or for private investment.

Adjustments in revenue sources and tax rates can be made with little lead time, though other budgetary factors and tax considerations may limit what can be done in any one year. Measures to reduce costs, on the other hand, have to be phased in over a long period to avoid undesirable effects on people who are too near retirement age to alter their behavior. There is no scarcity of ideas for achieving long-range savings since this topic has been addressed by several governmental studies and legislative proposals. However, the Reagan administration, despite its emphasis on reducing the size of government, failed to capitalize on a potential opportunity in 1981 to enact long-term cost-saving Social Security reforms. Proposals were offered in May 1981 that would have greatly reduced long-term spending, but they were poorly conceived and politically infeasible. Any political momentum for such initiatives that may have existed in 1981 has declined sharply only a year later.

Administration failure to mount an effective reform effort can be attributed to the top priority assigned to short-term budget cuts and the attention that execution of the budget plan required. Short-term Social Security benefit cuts through structural changes are hard to achieve, as the administration has now learned. The May proposals were guided too much by the logic Budget Director David Stockman applied to such issues in William Greider's *Atlantic Monthly* article: "I'm just not going to spend a lot of political capital solving some other guy's problem in 2010."[13]

Of course, it is the year 2010 or thereabouts when the sharp rise expected in the aged population will occur and the beginning of a substantial funding shortfall is projected. This shortfall may not materialize, in fact, since many long-range assumptions are involved in such estimates. Furthermore, even if it does, Congress may well choose to devote more resources to benefits for the elderly as the society grows older. However, if curbing the system's cost is to remain an option to meet the projected long-run constraints, then action in the near term is advisable. This would allow a long phase–in time for any benefit reduction measures and facilitate long-range individual career and financial planning. Whether the bipartisan National Commission on Social Security Reform will propose long-term reforms—and how effective its report will be in persuading Congress—remains to be seen.

Implications of Budget Cuts for Future Budgetary Growth

When the Reagan administration revised the Carter 1982 budget, it sought income security savings amounting to 10 percent of outlays in 1984 and a one-third reduction in outlay growth from 1982 to 1986. The actual result was a 4 percent outlay saving and a lowering of the growth rate by one-fifth. Although congressional inaction is partly responsible for the lesser figures, the main reason is the much poorer economic performance than the administration expected.

It was noted earlier that the 1982 budget reductions were proportionally far greater for low-income assistance (13 percent) than for social insurance and related programs (2 percent). A similarly large differential is found when these reductions are viewed in terms of the restraint this introduced on long-term budgetary growth. The income security budget data presented in chapter 3 indicate that without the Reagan cuts the annual growth rate in outlays from 1982 to 1986 would have been 7.4 percent. Taking the cuts into account, the expected annual growth rate is 6.0 percent. For low-income assistance, the spending growth rate was slashed by more than half, from 5.9 to 2.7 percent. However, the growth rate for social insurance spending was reduced by only one percentage point, from 7.6 to 6.5 percent.

Although the potential for curbing growth in low-income assistance is significant, the actual experience could prove to be less dramatic. Because changes in AFDC and Food Stamps raised the rate at which benefits decline with earnings, benefits will rise more rapidly as earnings fall. Thus, the present recession may result in greater welfare costs than have been predicted. Another factor that may undermine the assumed reduction in welfare spending growth is the unknown work response of recipients to the higher offset rates. If, as some observers predict, large numbers of people quit work because they are now better off on welfare, spending will be higher than expected.

Social insurance spending growth will still be determined largely by factors the president's budget reduction measures did not seriously confront: cost-of-living increases, the normal growth in entitled individuals, and real benefit increases due to the rising wage base upon which benefits are computed. Some small cuts were made that address each of these factors, but spending growth will still depend heavily on such uncontrollable factors as economic performance and the numbers and longevity of Social Security retirees.

In one case, unemployment compensation, the administration did succeed in reducing the sensitivity of spending to economic performance. In July 1981 the Congressional Budget Office estimated that a one-percentage-point increase in the unemployment rate would add $5.9 billion to unemployment benefit outlays. In February 1982, after enactment of the cutback in the thirteen-week extended benefit program, CBO estimated an outlay increase of only $4 billion for a one-point rise in unemployment. Thus, the present recession is raising these outlays by about $2 billion less per point of unemployment than would have occurred without the cuts. Of course, this change attenuates one original purpose of the program, which is to support consumer demand automatically in an economic downturn.

Conclusions

The Reagan administration's first year brought a change in direction for certain income security policies and substantial budget reductions. These reductions affected low-income assistance proportionately much more than social insurance programs. Benefit cuts were greatest for those low-income people who work. The effectiveness of the cutbacks as a restraint on long-term spending growth was minimal since the annual growth rate for the large social insurance systems was reduced by only one percentage point. The administration sought substantial income security savings in its 1983 budget request, with the cuts again falling most heavily on the low-income assistance programs. Any major initiative to change Social Security has been deferred until the commission established by President Reagan reports its recommendations in late 1982.

The administration has launched a redirection of welfare policy on two fronts. A devolution of responsibility for income support to the states is being sought, and steps have already been taken to change welfare recipients' work incentives and work requirements. The first of these initiatives is most evident in the New Federalism proposal to turn over to the states complete responsibility for the AFDC and Food Stamp programs. Lengthy negotiations with the states over this proposal are likely. State officials are concerned about the financial impacts of economic change on their populations and budgets and the potential for adverse effects from welfare policies in neighboring states. Thus, any politically viable plan probably will have to impose some national standards on program rules and provide a federal guarantee against costs exceeding a ceiling.

Two new developments regarding welfare recipients and work experience will receive close scrutiny. The benefit cuts for recipients with earnings, enacted in 1981, have become a primary focus of those concerned about welfare policy. If evidence on the subsequent behavior of recipients indicates that they are less likely to work, then the recent curtailment of financial work incentives will become a major issue. The second development is the state experimentation with "workfare" projects. Whether or not "workfare" becomes a significant factor in welfare policy, as the administration advocates, should hinge on a critical assessment of the initial demonstration efforts now getting underway.

Less attention has been given to the reductions in income security benefits that affect a middle-class clientele, mainly because the effects are being felt more slowly. However these cuts—the Social Security minimum and college student benefit phase-outs, the administrative review of disability claims, the limitations on unemployment benefits, the drastic reduction in trade adjustment assistance, the cuts in federal subsidies for school meals—need to be analyzed to capture their overall impacts on beneficiaries' well-being and to inform future debate on proposals for further reductions in social insurance and related benefits.

The reaction of wage earners to the liberalized IRA rules will be crucial in determining future retirement policy developments. If participation is at a high level across a broad spectrum of the eligible population, then policy makers may want to consider measures to promote greater reliance on private retirement saving relative to public benefits. A key question will be the extent to which IRA contributions represent net additional saving that would not have occurred without the provisions of the 1981 tax law.

A major debate over Social Security reform will likely begin in 1983 after the commission reports. It appears that a consensus for any action either to reduce the system's costs or increase its revenues will require strong presidential leadership. How President Reagan decides to respond on this issue will be a key factor in income security policy for the remainder of his term in office.

The president's position on Social Security will also be a major determinant of the extent to which his budget policy will limit growth in federal spending. If the most conservative president since before the New Deal chooses to leave the future growth of these entitlements largely untouched, the continued strength of public support for Social Security will be affirmed. The long-term implication of such an eventuality is that either the federal government will become larger relative to the total economy, or its role in other areas ultimately will have to be reduced.

Chapter 13

HOUSING AND COMMUNITY DEVELOPMENT

Raymond J. Struyk
John A. Tuccillo
James P. Zais

The hallmark of the housing and community development policies of the federal government in the past quarter century has been an expanding list of objectives and the tools to accomplish them. Today one can list at least seven separate objectives of federal housing policy, each supported by an economic rationale and a group of programmatic tools (see table 13-1).

Alternatively, one can characterize federal housing activities by the more commonly used organization in discussions of the federal budget. *Housing assistance* policies aim at providing adequate and affordable housing for those who could not otherwise afford it. *Housing finance and tax* policies promote the availability of affordable credit to housing suppliers and home purchasers and implement favorable treatment for housing in the federal income tax code in order to reduce its cost. Finally, *community development* policies are geared to upgrading the physical attributes of neighborhoods to make them more attractive as residential or commercial locations. The policies in these three

[The authors gratefully acknowledge the help of Margery Austin Turner and Thomas Thibodeau in preparing this chapter. Martin Levine and Howard Sumka provided very helpful comments on a draft.]

TABLE 13–1

OBJECTIVES OF U.S. HOUSING POLICY, RATIONALE, AND ASSOCIATED PROGRAMS

Objective	Economic Rationale for Government Intervention	Programmatic Tool
Ensuring availability of adequate and affordable housing, especially to low-income households.	Earmarked income redistribution. Allocation: Supply imperfections, partially caused by government housing codes.	Interest rate, demand, and tax subsidies for construction of new units; also, mortgage insurance and financing for new units; leasing existing units meeting minimum standards.
Increasing residential construction; reducing cyclical instability in the construction industry.	Stabilization: improved industry efficiency from lower amplitude of the business cycle.	Mortgage insurance; tax expenditures for home ownership and rental properties; interest rate reductions for purchase of new homes in periods of high interest rates; variety of credit institution regulations.
Increasing the availability of mortgage credit.	Allocation: perhaps to offset market imperfections, including discrimination.	Mortgage insurance; purchases of mortgages by government or quasi-government agencies; tax and regulatory advantages to mortgage originating institutions.
Encouraging homeownership.	Perhaps some income distribution.	Tax expenditures for mortgage interest and property tax deductions; increased mortgage availability; mortgage insurance; regulation of financial institutions.
Insuring equal housing opportunities.	Offset allocation failure; insure horizontal equity.	Insuring equal access to government housing assistance programs; enforcement of antidiscrimination statutes.

TABLE 13–1 (continued)

Objective	Economic Rationale for Government Intervention	Programmatic Tool
Providing housing to persons with special needs, such as age or disability.	Allocation: price signals are not clear; income redistribution via earmarked grants.	Various subsidies for construction or modifications to create dwellings with special features; subsidies to augment families' housing demand.
Encouraging neighborhood preservation and revitalization.	Allocation: price signals are not clear; modest amount of income redistribution.	Upgrading of infrastructure; subsidies for housing rehabilitation; rent subsidies; sometimes use of subsidized new construction as part of strategy; mortgage insurance.

areas can be both complementary and conflicting, as the following examples indicate.

First consider the use of various policy tools to stabilize a "fragile" residential neighborhood. Under federal credit policies, the Federal Housing Administration (FHA), by insuring mortgages, makes sure mortgage funds are available in areas from which private financial institutions have withdrawn. Federally sponsored community development grants are used to repair the neighborhood's streets and to upgrade the capacity of the storm sewers to prevent the recurrence of localized flooding. Meanwhile, the city uses federally funded housing assistance to provide rent supplements to a few dozen households to buoy landlords' rent rolls. Finally, the city may also consider constructing a small multifamily housing project on a vacant land parcel, with the cost of the project reduced by use of favorable tax provisions and direct subsidies.

But look at this same process within a larger context. Attempts to stabilize inner-city neighborhoods can be seriously undermined by continued construction of new units in the suburbs, especially in metropolitan areas where the number of households is constant or growing slowly. Thus all of the activities listed in the prior paragraph can be thwarted by federal credit policies that pump mortgage funds into suburban development and by federal assistance programs targeted to new construction. Viewed both in this light and against the need for greater investment in other sectors, many have questioned the rationality of federal housing and community development policies.

The Reagan administration has two apparent broad reactions to the breadth of the federal involvement in housing and community development. First, it believes that the federal government's housing assistance and housing finance activities have been too expansive. Second, it believes that the task of any needed coordination of housing and community development policies is best allocated to local actors with a minimum of federal oversight. One of the president's early acts was to appoint a housing commission to report in April 1982 to recommend ways to redirect and limit federal activity. Meanwhile, the regulatory changes implemented since January 1981 and the administration's budgets for FY 1982 and FY 1983 are consistent with the themes just stated. So too have been the public pronouncements of the leadership at the Department of Housing and Urban Development (HUD) and the Office of Management and Budget (OMB). Likewise, the mood of the Congress is in harmony with the administration's, at least as indicated in the legislation enacted in 1981.

Somewhat more specifically, in addition to budget savings, the administration has identified four objectives for its housing program. Its actions and proposals can be judged against these objectives.

1. Whenever possible, use the more efficient and less costly approach in pursuing an objective.
2. Place greater emphasis on the private sector in the implementation of government policy.
3. Target assistance more sharply to those most in need.
4. Decentralize decision making and program implementation to the maximum degree possible.

The administration has been especially energetic in applying these standards in the assisted housing and housing finance areas.

The balance of this chapter discusses and, to a limited extent, evaluates the impacts of the Reagan initiatives. It is important, however, to place these recent actions in historical context. The next section provides this background. The following section, then, enumerates the major actual and proposed changes in each area and discusses their implications and impacts. The final section provides an overall summary.

Selected Developments, 1974–1980

Federal involvement in the housing sector is a creation of the Great Depression. The 1930s witnessed the initiation of the public housing program with its multiple objectives of generating employment, upgrading the housing stock, and providing low-cost living accommodations. It also saw the establishment of the FHA and the federal agencies that control the federally chartered thrift institutions. Until recently there was greater experimentation and evolution in federal housing assistance and community development policies than in housing finance policy. This section provides a background for interpreting the Reagan initiatives by briefly reviewing the 1970s, concentrating on the trends that emerged during that decade and the significant policy events occurring in its second half.

Housing Assistance and Community Development

The Housing and Community Development Act of 1974 is a landmark in U.S. housing policy. It created a new housing program (Section 8), replaced seven categorical grant programs with the Community Development Block Grant (CDBG) program, and for the first time provided a mechanism for coordinating housing and community development activities, the Housing Assistance Plan (HAP).[1]

The Section 8 program consists of two major program components, one for leasing existing housing units and one for developing new or substantially rehabilitated units. Both leave ownership and management up to private landlords and investors; both require assisted households to contribute only a fixed proportion of their incomes toward rent; and both obligate the federal government to make up the difference between tenant contributions and a reasonable market rent. Both programs also established the maximum income for households of four persons eligible to participate at 80 percent of the local area median family income, or about 200 percent of the poverty line.

The major trend in housing assistance during the Carter years was the steady rise in the share of housing assistance provided through new construction. Table 13-2 shows the number of assistance commitments made (i.e., the number of additional units for whose subsidy Congress appropriated funds) and the unit mix for fiscal years 1976–1982. A large number of additional units were added to the stock of assisted units in the early years, and then a gradual decline occurred throughout the Carter years. Contemporaneously there was a steady rise in the share of units specified for new construction until an abrupt change took place in FY 1981. The rise in the importance of new construction is attributable in part to the lags in the implementation of any new housing construction program, but after 1977 it also reflects the preferences of the HUD leadership in favor of new construction.

The decline in the total number of incremental units is related to the rise in the share specified as new construction. As the new unit mix was shifted

TABLE 13–2

NUMBER OF ASSISTANCE COMMITMENTS MADE AND PROGRAM MIXES,
HUD HOUSING ASSISTANCE PROGRAMS
(FY 1975–1982)

Section 8/ *Public Housing*	*1976* *and TQ[a]*	*1977*	*1978*	*1979*	*1980*	*1981*	*1982[d]* *(Estimate)*
Assistance commitments made (in thousands)	517	388	326	325	206	178	202
Percentage distribution New construction[b]	39	52	55	61	63	43	35
Existing housing[c]	61	48	45	39	37	57	65

SOURCE: Martin Levine, *Federal Housing Assistance: Alternative Approaches* (Congressional Budget Office, 1982), table 5.
   a.   Includes three-month transition quarter (TQ) between the July-to-July and October-to-October fiscal years.
   b.   Includes substantial rehabilitation.
   c.   Includes moderate rehabilitation.
   d.   Estimate assumes use of all funding provided in appropriations acts passed during the first season of the 97th Congress plus budget authority carried over from 1981.

toward new construction, fewer total units could be assisted with a given amount of budget authority, since a new unit requires about four times the budget authority of an existing unit.[2] For example, the HUD FY 1981 budget requested an additional 300,000 units with 60% new units and 40% existing units. If the same budget authority had been applied to the FY 1977 52-48 split, 389,000 units could have been added, a 30 percent increase. In fact, however, budget authority increased sharply over the FY 1977–FY 1980 period, as the per unit cost of new units accelerated and the unit mix shifted.

The 1974 act required that the mix of new construction and existing units proposed each year by the administration in its budget submission be based on the locally prepared Housing Assistance Plans. The plans themselves were a statement of each local government's strategy for improving the housing situation of its poor using housing assistance and community development resources in concert. When Congress considered the FY 1981 budget in 1980, based primarily on cost considerations, it finally overrode the HAP-based figure and specified a 50-50 new-existing unit mix. Actual execution resulted in the 43-57 split shown in table 13-2. This action had the unfortunate effect of sharply reducing the incentive to local governments of developing a serious housing strategy.

As noted, the 1974 act created the CDBG program, which replaced seven categorical programs and distributed most of the funds directly to local governments using a formula based on needs. The most dramatic shift embodied in the legislation was the increase in local discretion.[3] Activities funded need only be predominantly for physical improvements, that is, "bricks and mortar" as opposed to services, and be consistent with the program's multiple objectives: help for low- and moderate-income households, elimination and prevention of slums and blight, conservation and expansion of the housing stock, and expansion and improvement of community services.

Significant changes in federal involvement in community development also occurred during the Carter administration. First, HUD moved to tighten both planning for the use of CDBG and housing assistance funds and the reporting on their actual use. Within a month of taking office, the Carter administration announced its central theme of greater targeting—a greater concentration of CDBG program benefits to low- and moderate-income households and a sharper geographic concentration of resources so that demonstrable changes in neighborhood conditions would take place in a few years.

Two developments also led to greater federal use of neighborhoods as the unit for intervention in community development. The Neighborhood Reinvestment Corporation Act of 1978 reorganized an ongoing activity, the Urban Reinvestment Task Force, into a quasi-public corporation to develop neighborhood rehabilitation programs and to identify, test, and replicate local private partnerships for neighborhood preservation. Under the main program to foster housing rehabilitation, a local corporation, Neighborhood Housing Services, has been established. It is distinguished by the requirement that various local actors must be actively involved, including residents (usually represented by neighborhood organizations), governmental officials, and financial institutions. By the end of 1980, there were 121 Neighborhood Housing Services operating in 95 cities.

Another element in the growing "neighborhood movement" was the establishment within HUD in 1977 of an office to promote the role of neighborhood organizations in the urban revitalization process—a tribute to the effects of opening up the system through CDBG. In 1979 a Neighborhood Self-Help Development program was created to further encourage neighborhood entities as delivery agents.

A major new program was launched in these years: Urban Development Action Grants (UDAG). Under UDAG, grants are awarded on a competitive basis to local governments to provide economic development to distressed areas. The program increased the infusion of federal resources to distressed areas, but these resources were often uncoordinated with other housing and community development activities.

Federal Involvement in the Housing Finance System

The current federal involvement in the housing finance system began as the result of the financial collapse that ushered in the Depression. In the wake of massive defaults on owner-occupied housing that followed the crash of 1929, the federal government created a group of institutions and instruments designed to shield the housing sector from any similar future occurrence.

The regulatory system worked well as long as the economy remained stable. In the mid-1960s, however, the economy began to display some erratic behavior and the essential weaknesses of regulation emerged. In the 1970s historically unprecedented rates of inflation drove up interest rates and increased the uncertainty present in the financial system. One manifestation of this uncertainty was the rise of short-term interest rates relative to long-term rates, which proved to be a disaster for mortgage lenders. The bulk of their liabilities were in short-term instruments, the cost of which increased with the market. On the other hand, their assets were concentrated in long-term mortgages carrying lower rates from earlier times. Rising inflation and interest rates began to squeeze these institutions and exacted a cost for their specialization in mortgage lending in the form of lower profits and declining net worth. Moreover, competing institutions, such as money market mutual funds, with few regulatory restraints, were responding to the new economic situation with instruments designed to appeal to a public that was becoming more financially sophisticated.

By 1980 the need for reform in housing finance was patent, and it was finally launched by the passage of the Depository Institutions Deregulation and Monetary Control Act (DIDMCA). This bill effectively broadened the powers of mortgage lending institutions to bring them in line with their more lightly regulated competitors. Further, it provided for the gradual removal of interest rate ceilings on all classes of deposits. In response, the financial regulatory agencies, particularly the Federal Home Loan Bank Board, have been moving to increase the asset powers of mortgage lenders so that they can become viable in the environment of volatile interest rates.

Mortgage instruments also continued an accelerating transformation over this period. Beginning in 1976 federal agencies began to authorize the use of alternatives to the standard level payment mortgage. The Federal Home Loan Bank Board granted authorization to issue variable rate mortgages to federally chartered institutions in California in 1977; this move was followed by national authorization in 1979. FHA began experimenting with a graduated payment mortgage that has become a substantial part of FHA's business. Finally, the Federal Home Loan Bank Board began in 1979 to issue regulations specifying a number of newly allowable mortgage instruments, including adjustable rate mortgages (a very limited variable rate mortgage), renegotiated rate mortgages, and shared appreciation mortgages (the lender's return is enhanced through the establishment of an equity position in the collateral property). The use of alternative instruments has also been encouraged by secondary market agencies, particularly the Federal National Mortgage Association (FNMA).

Federal tax policy over the period consistently provided strong incentives to individuals to become homeowners through property tax and mortgage interest deductions and favorable capital gains treatment. The size of these tax expenditures is an unforeseen consequence of the original 1913 tax law. During the postwar years these benefits blossomed to unimagined size, the vast bulk of which are enjoyed by higher-income households. On the other hand, in recent years the tax advantages to developers of rental housing have been eroded through several rounds of tax legislation.

Federal Activity in FY 1981

An examination of the 1981 federal housing and community development budget is helpful in obtaining an overall picture of the size and scope of these activities just prior to the Reagan administration's taking office. For housing assistance and community development, the relevant figures are outlays and total obligations. The latter are the total resources committed by Congress— new budget authority plus other sources, such as repayments of prior loans. For the subsidized housing programs, *total obligations* are funds committed to add units to the inventory of assisted units, either through new construction or leasing of existing units. Associated subsidies are contracted for up to 40 years. For 1981 alone new total obligations for this purpose were $29 billion (table 13-3). Accumulated but unspent budget authority from past years as well as 1981 totaled a staggering $250 billion. *Outlays*, or actual spending, on the other hand, totaled $5.7 billion; these are the subsidy payments from appropriated budget authority, predominantly from prior years.

In community development the CDBG program took the lion's share of the budget, with budget authority of $3.6 billion. Action grants were second with $0.7 billion, and the other major activities accounted for less than $100 million each. Total outlays for housing assistance and community development combined were large by any measure: $11.3 billion, or $150 for every household in the country.

For the federal housing credit programs, the germane information is the amount of credit provided or insured (in the case of FHA loans) rather than budget authority and outlays. The appropriations are often small amounts because little or no subsidy is being provided. The loan-insuring activities of FHA for homes, rental properties, and home improvement loans and the Government National Mortgage Association (GNMA) mortgage-backed security programs are clearly very large items. The figures for these programs can be better understood once one realizes that nationally each year about

TABLE 13–3

SUMMARY OF FEDERAL HOUSING AND COMMUNITY DEVELOPMENT FINANCING IN
FY 1981
(In $ millions)

A. Housing and Community Development		
	Total Obligations[a]	Outlays
Housing assistance		
Subsidized housing programs	28,799	5,746
Low-income housing (Section 8)	19,357	3,114
Public housing	7,322	1,472
Homeownership and rental housing[b]	2,109	861
Public housing operating subsidies	1,071	929
Community development		
Community Development Block Grants	3,574	4,042
Urban Development Action Grants	694	371
Rehabilitation Loan Fund[c]	91	60
Urban Renewal	78	144

B. Housing Credit		
	Direct Loan Obligations	Guaranteed Loan Commitments
Rural Housing Loan Program	3,487	d
Federal Housing Administration	414	23,635
GNMA—mortgage-backed securities	--	42,150
Housing for elderly and handicapped[e]	873	--
GNMA—Special Assistance Fund (Tandem)[f]	3,074	5,008

C. Tax Expenditures	
Expenditure	Amount
Excess bad debt reserves for financial institutions	$ 325
Deductibility of mortgage interest on owner-occupied housing	20,145
Deductibility of property taxes on owner-occupied housing	9,125
Exclusion of interest on state and local housing bonds for owner-occupied housing	685
Deferral of capital gains on home sales	1,160
Exclusion of capital gains on home sales for persons age 55 and over	450
Expensing of construction period interest and taxes	755

  a. Total obligations is budget authority plus offsets to financing requirements from other services, e.g., carryover of prior year's budget authority.
  b. Section 235 and 236 programs.
  c. Section 312 program.
  d. Less than $10 million.
  e. Outlays were $817 million.
  f. Outlays were $1,303 million.

$150 billion in residential mortgage loans are made. The federal activities in table 13-3 cover some $78 billion. Although there is substantial double counting in these figures because GNMA handles FHA-insured paper, these agencies are nonetheless important actors in the residential mortgage market.

One must also include various tax expenditures to get an accurate picture of federal budget outlays (see panel C of table 13-3). As suggested above, most of these accrue to higher-income homeowners, directly or indirectly. Thus, even if all outlays for housing assistance and community development were directed to lower-income households, federal housing policy—as reflected in expenditures—would have to be labeled as one dominantly benefiting middle- and higher-income families.

Change during the Reagan Administration

Various aspects of the federal role in housing assistance, finance, and community development were redirected in the early months of the Reagan administration, and even greater changes are proposed. The record through mid-1982, however, is uneven. In both housing finance and assistance, some sharp departures will occur if Congress follows the lead of the administration. In housing finance the administration is pressing for a dramatic reduction in the activity of federal agencies in mortgage credit. In the assistance area, the prescription is for radical surgery: no additional households are to be assisted; assistance will be targeted to the poorest families; and there will be a virtual end to government-supported new construction. The continuation of the major community development programs seems reasonably secure, albeit at lower spending levels. On the other hand, there has been a sharp return to greater local discretion in the CDBG program.

Housing Finance

The Reagan administration appears to have two primary goals for housing finance. The first is to reduce federal housing credit activities. This action is consistent with the administration's general thrust to reduce greatly the size and influence of the federal government in credit markets. The second goal is to accomplish a restructuring of the mortgage lending industry to reduce its insulation from other credit demands and to improve its ability to weather interest rate fluctuations. To accomplish these goals the president offered several proposals in his 1983 budget: authorization for GNMA mortgage-backed securities is to be reduced by about $20 billion, to approximately $48 billion; tandem mortgage purchase activities will terminate as of 1982; FHA activities are to be targeted to those not currently served by the private market and the system made more efficient through the use of a single insurance fee charged at the outset of the loan; FHA mortgage rates are to be deregulated and will thus move with the market; and budget authorization for the Farmers Home Administration (FmHA) for new direct loans is to be reduced from $2.6 billion in the 1982 budget to $1.1 billion. In addition, reductions in outlays are projected for the Federal Deposit Insurance Corporation (FDIC) and Federal Savings and Loan Insurance Corporation (FSLIC), such that both insurance funds will be net recipients of funds by 1984.

These proposals, coupled with administration actions in the regulatory area, mean a departure from the past course of federal credit programs. However, they reinforce the existing trend toward deregulation of the housing finance system programs. There is another continuity as well: the administration has advanced no proposals to limit the enormous tax expenditures. This is clearly at odds with its rhetoric on improved targeting and efficiency.

With respect to regulation, the Reagan administration has moved aggressively to implement both the spirit and the letter of the Depository Institutions Deregulation and Monetary Control Act of 1980 to allow thrifts to become more competitive with other financial institutions. Between June 1981 and June 1982, the Federal Home Loan Bank Board and the Federal Deposit Insurance Corporation passed on and approved more than 200 mergers and acquisitions, including several that crossed state and industry lines. In addition, the Federal Home Loan Bank Board has consistently expanded the asset and liability powers of savings and loan associations, most recently approving the sale of money market mutual funds from savings and loan portfolios. In addition, the board has authorized a variety of mortgage instruments that are effectively negotiable between borrower and lender within wide bands. It has also issued regulations changing the accounting treatment of savings and loan losses in a way that will facilitate the merger of failing institutions with successful ones.

The Reagan administration visualizes a future housing finance system in which the providers of mortgage credit will be indistinguishable from the providers of credit to any other segment of the economy. Because there will be a closer match between the interest rates on thrifts' assets and liabilities, there will be smaller swings in the availability of mortgage funds from these institutions. This will mean a moderation of the cycles that have occurred in housing (relative to general economic activity). But it also means mortgage interest rates will be higher, because housing will no longer receive the preferential treatment it has historically enjoyed among the demanders of credit.

This future, however, will not come about immediately. During the transition many more mortgage lending institutions will disappear. To reduce the speed and pain of this transition, the administration agreed to the creation of the All-Savers Certificates to help thrifts recoup some of their lost deposits. Even with this assistance, however, the insuring institutions will face a strong drain on their funds because of lending institutions' failures. For this reason the administration's optimistic projections for inflows of reserves to the FDIC and FSLIC in the future appear unwarranted.

The initiatives of the Reagan administration to reduce federal housing credit programs run directly counter to the strong expansion in the past several years in these activities—especially the growth in GNMA's mortgage-backed securities program. A "competition" justification has been used to reduce the authorization for GNMA guarantees. The administration believes that GNMA has blocked the development of private sector instruments for the sale of mortgages. It argues that GNMA has occupied a monopoly position in the mortgage-backed securities market and has used that position to keep competitors out by lowering its price. More specifically, it argues that GNMA sets its fees on the basis of its cost and not on the basis of the value of the federal guarantee that its securities carry. Running somewhat counter to this monopoly view is the fact that GNMA deals only in FHA and VA mortgages, leaving 80 percent of the secondary market to others.

The administration probably envisions the abolition of GNMA through direct elimination, its sale to the private market, or a gradual increase in the price charged for the guarantee to the point where GNMA is outbid by the private market. This abolition would reduce the amount of the government's mortgage insurance obligations by removing the motivation for at least part of FHA's lending activities. Because FHA serves low-income homeowners to a greater degree than do other mortgage insurers, the availability of affordable mortgages to marginal homebuyers would be disproportionately affected by the demise of GNMA.

The overall situation with FHA is somewhat less clear. Although the administration would probably like to see FHA eliminated and private firms filling most of its functions, it has not yet proposed this directly. Rather, the role of FHA is being narrowed until it serves only persons neglected by the private market, especially lower-income home purchasers. The proposals to allow the FHA interest rate to float and to charge insurance fees up front, however, work in the opposite direction because they effectively increase the costs of the FHA loan.

The main point is that if the administration is successful in carrying out its initiatives, the federal role in the residential mortgage credit market will be dramatically altered. The effects of these changes on the availability of mortgage funds, and, hence, interest rates and the affordability of housing, will depend on the extent to which private institutions fill the vacuum that is created.

Housing Assistance

A number of legislative actions taken in 1981 based on the administration's 1982 budget proposals, coupled with the president's FY 1983 proposals, provide a clear picture of the administration's philosophy about housing assistance. It wants to halt the growth in the number of households receiving assistance, target the available assistance to poorer households, reduce benefits, and emphasize use of the existing stock over building new housing projects.

Program Size. The administration has taken the position in its FY 1983 budget that holding the number of households receiving housing assistance to 3.8 million—the number that should be receiving assistance at the end of FY 1983—is "essential to the administration's effort to control long-term federal government spending."[4] In 1981, as the administration looked at some $250 billion in unspent but appropriated budget authority to be spent over the next 30 years, it decided that housing assistance already had received its slice of the shrinking federal domestic pie. This position is at sharp variance with the actions of Republican and Democratic administrations dating back at least twenty-five years. A major implication of this policy is that housing assistance will remain a "limited entitlement" program, that is, fewer households will receive assistance than would if program "slots" were available for all who qualified for such help.

The administration began moving toward this objective by convincing Congress to appropriate funds dominantly for existing housing for FY 1982, although still sufficient to support a 200,000-unit program. The president's 1983 budget, including proposed rescissions (i.e., not spending some already appropriated funds), calls for a *net reduction* of assisted units by the end of FY 1983 compared to the number for which funds had been appropriated through FY 1982.

The effect on the HUD-subsidized housing budget is very large indeed. Requested FY 1983 budget authority is $23 billion lower than that in the FY 1981 current services budget. By contrast, only $0.5 billion in outlays is saved because of the long lead time for new construction projects. In future years outlays would fall further compared to actual FY 1981 outlays as cheaper programs are substituted for more expensive forms of assistance.

The proposals for the FmHA FY 1983 budget are equally drastic. From FY 1982 to FY 1983 the overall budget is slashed by two-thirds. For the main homeownership program (Section 502), the expected number of assisted units falls from 67,500 to 20,100.

The 3.8 million units expected at the end of FY 1983 also may not be sustained in future years. Costly public housing projects are to be retired, and others may be withdrawn, if operating subsidies are insufficiently funded. Moreover, the administration's intentions are unclear for replacing the budget authority for currently assisted units when appropriations are exhausted.

Sharper Targeting and Reducing Benefits. In 1981 Congress enacted several important changes to the housing assistance programs. The purposes of these changes were better targeting of limited resources, greater equity among participants in public housing and other housing assistance programs, and greater equity between participants in housing programs and nonparticipants. At the same time, however, the new rules may have adverse implications that were not fully anticipated. Three changes were enacted: (1) the contribution by a tenant receiving housing assistance was increased from 25 to 30 percent of his or her income;[5] (2) eligibility for assistance was restricted by limiting the share of all recipient households who have incomes between 50 and 80 percent of area median incomes (adjusted for family size) to 10 percent of the units available for occupancy[6] (other recipients must have incomes below 50 percent of the area median, which is about 133 percent of the poverty line on a national basis; and (3) the definition of income used in computing the tenant's contribution was made uniform for the Section 8 and public housing programs. In the past local public housing authorities had wide latitude in defining incomes; now more income will be counted by some authorities.

The practical gains in targeting from lowering the income ceiling for eligibility are modest when interpreted as a share of program participants. It appears that no more than 20 percent of the recipients of assistance in the public housing and Section 8 programs have incomes above the 50 percent of area median level.[7] There is no doubt, however, that "very low income households" (i.e., those with incomes below 50 percent of local median income) have more severe housing problems than other households. In 1977 renter households with very low incomes spent 40 percent of their incomes on average for housing, compared with 25 percent for households in the 50 to 80 percent of median group. Likewise, 20 percent of renters with very low incomes live in units classified as needing rehabilitation, compared with 12 percent of those with 50 to 80 percent of median.[8]

Changes enacted to achieve greater equity are, by themselves, on the mark. Participants have had to pay substantially less for housing because of the subsidies in comparison to nonrecipients with equivalent incomes and quality of housing. (The number of potentially eligible families who can participate is determined by the fixed budget, unlike entitlement programs,

such as AFDC, which are openended.) In 1977, for example, about 80 percent
of unsubsidized very low income renter householders spent more than 30
percent of their incomes on housing. Subsidized renters, on the other hand,
were required to contribute only 25 percent of their incomes for housing. The
1981 changes will narrow the differential between subsidized and unsubsidized
households.

As part of the FY 1983 legislative package, the administration proposed
further reducing rental subsidies by counting the value of Food Stamps as
income in determining a participant's contribution to rent. Because the size
of the Food Stamp subsidy varies inversely with income, poorer households
will suffer greater reductions in their total resources. This is clearly at odds
with most concepts of a target efficiency.

Raising the share of income required of participants will probably have
much greater effects on the profile of participants than will the eligibility
restrictions. The higher contribution rate reduces benefits and lessens interest
in the program of households who formerly would have participated. Beneficiaries will be increasingly impoverished.

Analysts at HUD have estimated the likely effect on tenant profiles in
public housing of full implementation of that part of the 1981 legislation that
raises tenant contributions to 30 percent of income. The results of these
calculations for participants with incomes of greater than 50 percent of local
area median show that three of four current participants in this group—some
116,000 households—are expected to leave public housing. They will account
for 81 percent of all households leaving public housing. Thus, the higher
rental contribution would increase the degree of targeting significantly in
public housing. Similar effects can be anticipated in the Section 8 program.

An important implication of shifting the profile of participants in housing
assistance programs to lower-income groups is that management of housing
projects will become more difficult. The vast majority of the 1.2 million
public housing units are in projects, as are the units in the other production
programs. It is generally believed that maintaining a given level of services
becomes both more costly and challenging as the incidence of single-parent
and extremely poor households in a project increases.[9] Congress well may
have to accept less targeting to insure the continued utilization of the existing
projects and to avoid costly defaults.

Emphasizing Use of the Existing Stock. Extending a pattern initiated
by Congress in 1980, both the executive branch and Congress have continued
to deemphasize new construction. The FY 1982 housing budget has a mix of
65 percent existing and 35 percent new construction and substantial rehabilitation. In the FY 1983 budget the administration proposes to go much further—to a 92 percent existing and an 8 percent new construction mix. The

shift in unit mix, combined with shorter contract periods and reduced benefit levels, results in the requested dramatic cuts in the budget authority noted earlier. Moreover, the president has proposed, through rescission of appropriations, to forgo two-thirds of the units to be constructed with FY 1982 appropriations.

The main justification for building fewer new units to house low-income households is the great expense of these units. In the early 1970s it cost about twice as much to provide a unit month of housing services from a federally assisted newly built unit than it did to lease a privately owned existing unit.[10] On efficiency grounds, existing housing dominates, as long as it is in adequate supply. A second argument is that there is a sufficient supply of adequate housing available in most markets. The results of the housing allowance supply experiment in which open enrollment programs have been operated for five years in two metropolitan areas suggest that leasing a few more existing dwellings with federal funding would have no effect on market prices.[11]

The broader question is whether or not there will be sufficient housing for low-income nonrecipients in the absence of the new construction programs. The available research indicates that most subsidized new construction substitutes for private building, so the net impact on availability seems small in any event.[12] However, the administration's only plan to stimulate residential construction is by lowering interest rates via macroeconomic policy. Until such policies take effect and the filtering process works itself out, there likely will be spot shortages, and the poor may well pay a greater share of income for their housing.

Another aspect of the "adequate supply" argument is the administration's assertion that the housing problem of the poor is now primarily one of affordability and not of housing quality. There is no question that in the postwar period housing quality in this country has improved dramatically.[13] However, we know that in 1977 two-thirds of very low income renter households were spending over 30 percent of income on housing, while 20 percent of them were living in units needing rehabilitation. Affordability certainly affects more households, but substandard housing remains a problem. Furthermore, the incidence of substandard housing for the permanently poor is very high, 40 percent, about double that of the transiently poor.[14] Emphasizing the affordability problem in program implementation, while structuring housing assistance to serve a fixed number of recipients using the existing stock, can be expected to have little impact on housing quality.

There is an important implication of the combination of employing the existing stock and fixing the number of assisted households at 3.8 million. It might be thought of as a neglected opportunity. The lower per unit subsidy of using the existing stock and raising participant contributions to 30 percent

of income means that for the first time serving all of income-eligible households who want to participate is possible. There are about nine million income-
eligible renters when a 50 percent of median income limit is used. Of those,
3.4 million will be served by the end of FY 1983, assuming there are still
0.2 million recipients in the 50 to 80 percent of median income group. (The
other 0.2 million are assisted homeowners.) From the experience in the open
enrollment housing allowance supply experiment, one would expect about
2.2 million of the remaining 5.6 million eligible households to participate if
given the opportunity. The balance could be served in six years if 365,000
households were added annually. The national objective of assisted housing
would have been achieved, and housing assistance could be administratively
integrated with the other income support programs.[15] Here it could be argued
that the administration's objectives of program rationalization and reduced
spending are in conflict.

Finally, the administration has proposed in its FY 1983 budget to modify
the Section 8 existing program significantly. The resulting "housing voucher"
program[16] embodies two types of change. One type will make the program
more efficient; changes are based on favorable experiences in the experimental
housing allowance program.[17] The effects of the second type are less clear,
but they may make the program less successful. These modifications would
affect the fair market rent (FMR), the rent upon which the government's
subsidy is based. The FMR would be lowered across the board and then fixed
at its first-year level for every participant for the five-year length of the contract
or until the household quits the program. Both of these changes reduce the
benefits to participants, over time possibly dramatically. Coupled with the
increase in the first year's tenant contribution to 30 percent of income and
the proposed counting of the subsidy value of Food Stamps in income, these
provisions might make benefits insufficient to induce families living in dwellings failing the program's physical standards to relocate to a unit that would
pass. In short, the program may not be capable of achieving its primary
objective.

Combined Effect of Proposed and Enacted Changes. The changes
from the benefit levels of the Section 8 existing program (as constituted in
1980) by the 1981 legislative amendments and those proposed by the Reagan
administration in the FY 1983 budget are large by any standard. Estimates
of their combined effects on subsidies previously provided to some typical
households are shown in table 13-4. For elderly individuals, for example,
benefits decline by 15 percent because of the change enacted in 1981 that
increased the participant's contribution to rent from 25 to 30 percent of
income.[18] The proposed lowering of the FMRs by itself would reduce benefits
to the same group on average by *an additional* 23 percent. Counting the

TABLE 13–4

ESTIMATED PERCENTAGE REDUCTIONS IN SUBSIDIES TO CURRENT HOUSING PROGRAM PARTICIPANTS FROM CHANGES ENACTED IN 1981 OR PROPOSED FOR ENACTMENT IN 1982[a]

Household Type	Increased Participant Rent Share, .25 to .30 (1981 Law)	Count Subsidy Value of Food Stamps (Proposed)	Lower Fair Market Rents (Proposed)	All Changes Combined
Husband and wife with two children	− 18	− 5	− 25	− 48
Elderly couples	− 19	− 5	− 26	− 51
Elderly individuals	− 15	− 5	− 23	− 44
All households[b]	− 14	− 6	− 22	− 44

SOURCE: Simulations using aged Current Population Survey data by the Urban Institute.

a. 1980 rules for the Section 8 program were applied to all renter households living in subsidized housing regardless of program to get base subsidy figure. Households included in this analysis are only those who would receive a positive subsidy payment after all changes were implemented.

b. Includes other household types besides those listed earlier in the table.

subsidy value of Food Stamps drops benefits *on average* by only 5 percent. (However, the effects on poorer households are much more deleterious since the subsidy value of their Food Stamps is much greater than average.)

The combined effects of the changes enacted in 1981 and those proposed in the FY 1983 budget would be to reduce the benefits of the typical elderly individual by 44 percent. For elderly couples the figure is 51 percent. Translated into dollars, the average benefit reduction for elderly couples is from $2,055 to $1,009 on an annual basis. For the average two-parent family with two children the benefit cut is nearly 50 percent, from $2,804 to $1,459.

Community Development

In many ways, the major programs in community development already were consistent with the philosophy of the Reagan administration on the proper role of federal government. Central to the programs are the block grant approach, leveraging of private investment, federal provision of technical assistance, and local decision making. Indeed, once the budgetary battles of 1981 were over, the administration appeared to adopt the view in its FY 1983 budget that these programs were worthwhile.

Nevertheless, the administration, both alone and together with Congress, made significant changes in the community development programs during its first year in office. The CDBG program has two main components. These are the small cities portion, in which the smaller jurisdictions in each state compete against each other for funds from a separate allocation of CDBG monies, and the entitlement part, under which large cities and populous urban counties receive funds determined on a formula basis. Both components have been substantially altered as a result of legislative and regulatory changes.

States were given the option of administering the small cities segment of the program as of October 1981, thus relieving HUD of this function. Thirty-seven states have said they will take on this responsibility. States will receive funds, once their applications are reviewed by HUD; and then they can make the awards themselves. In exchange for being able to allocate these funds, the states must engage in planning for community development programs and provide some level of technical assistance to localities. Perhaps most significantly, states must themselves provide funds equal to 10 percent of the amount available from HUD for community development under the small cities program, although they can deduct 50 percent of the administrative costs of handling the program.[19]

The legislation is silent on how individual small cities must use their funds. Although draft regulations tacitly gave extreme latitude in this regard, the final regulations at congressional insistence retain some key targeting provisions. For example, "maximum feasible priority" is to be given to benefiting low- and moderate-income residents and to preventing slums and blight. For the entitlement communities' portion of the program, which accounts for 70 percent of expenditures, Congress eliminated the seventy-five day review period and the possible veto of applications. In effect, this moves CDBG much closer to general revenue sharing.

The administration has also moved through regulatory powers to modify the entitlement portion of the program. The most important change is in the nature of the Housing Assistance Plan that is required. The extent of detailed information necessary to complete these forms has been dramatically reduced. In effect, attempts to tie performance to future funding have been dropped. Together these changes reverse the actions of the Carter administration. As recently as 1980, communities seeking CDBG funding for economic development were required to specifically describe the activities they proposed to fund. The application also had to take into account the effect of community development activities on involuntary displacement of low- and moderate-income persons.

The effects of these changes on the targeting of program resources remain to be seen. However, reduced reporting requirements and the slashed budget of HUD's program evaluation office may combine to make the answer to this key question unobtainable.

The administration has a more mixed record for its approach to utilizing the neighborhood as a point of intervention. On the one hand, Congress cut funding for several programs used by neighborhood groups, including grants administered by the Economic Development Administration's Office of Special Projects. It also eliminated HUD's fledgling program to help neighborhood groups stabilize and revitalize their areas—the Neighborhood Self-Help Development grant program. On the other hand, the neighborhood-based programs of the Neighborhood Reinvestment Corporation continues to be supported. One possible rationale for this different treatment is that the first program involved direct federal grants, whereas the second involves primarily technical assistance. Yet both encourage grass-roots participation in community development. The elimination of the former appears to be philosophically inconsistent with continued support of the latter.

The administration has advanced several ideas of its own for an expanded federal role in community development. One of these is the notion of "urban enterprise zones." The administration supports this concept as a free market approach to urban problems. It claims to focus on the real problems of distressed areas by providing tax and regulatory relief at the federal, state, and local levels to a zone within a distressed city. Under the administration's proposal, HUD could designate up to twenty-five such zones each year for up to three years on a competitive basis. Once designated, tax incentives related to investment, payroll, employee income, and capital gains would encourage activity in the zone. Furthermore, activities would benefit from relaxed regulations.[20]

The second proposal is a "rental rehabilitation grant" that would be applied to multifamily rental units. Such grants could provide up to 50 percent of the cost of rehabilitation and would also be linked, at least initially, to the modified Section 8 certificate program discussed earlier. Funds would be distributed on a formula basis. The rationale for this categorical program appears to be that it would be a complement to the voucher program to make more acceptable housing available to the poor. Such a grant program would be viewed as more efficient than the Section 312 rehabilitation loan program and the Section 8 moderate rehabilitation program, which it replaces.[21]

Summary

A broad overview of the intentions of the Reagan administration for the federal government's role in housing can be provided with the assistance of two devices. The first is a summary of the effects of the Reagan proposals on federal housing credit activities and on federal budgets, beginning in 1982 and extending to 1987. The second is a comparison of the changes proposed against the goals the administration set for itself.

The budget figures underscore the administration's priorities: dramatic reductions in housing assistance, cuts in community development and credit programs, and expansion of subsidies to homeowners. The immediate emaciation of incremental housing assistance activity is clearly evident in the budget authority figures (table 13-5). The negative figures for 1983 and 1984 reflect the recapture of formerly appropriated funds. By contrast, outlays continue to rise because of inflation and because of units in the "pipeline" reaching occupancy. Even so, outlays in 1987 are $2.5 billion below what they would be under the OMB current services estimate. In general, however, these figures mask the most significant change advanced by the administration: a halt in the expansion of the number of households to be assisted.

The sharp reduction in the level of federal activity in housing lending is also clear in table 13-5. Direct loan guarantees are estimated to fall by over one-half between 1981 and 1983 and are sustained in current dollars thereafter at this lower level. The future of the GNMA mortgage-backed securities program is unspecified after 1983, as is that of guaranteed loan commitments generally. By comparison community development programs are relatively unaffected; no further reductions in nominal funding levels after 1982 are proposed.

In sharp relief to all of the foregoing, however, are tax expenditures, which are slated to rise steadily over the period. Indeed, between 1981 and 1987 they will more than double. This pattern, coupled with fixed housing assistance program size and lower benefits per recipient, means that housing policy is being tilted further to serve middle- and upper-income Americans.

As part of the introductory remarks to this chapter, four objectives that the Reagan administration established to guide its agenda for action were enumerated. As part of this summary it seems reasonable to sort through the welter of enacted and proposed changes and ask how they compare with these objectives. Is the administration being true to itself? Since some of these objectives (e.g., greater efficiency) are widely accepted, they provide some measure of the administration's early achievements.

A summary scoring is given in table 13-6. The actions are scored as consistent (C) with the objective, inconsistent (I), unclear (?), or neutral (-). A glance at the table suggests that most actions have been neutral with respect to most objectives. For the nonneutral cases the administration gets generally high marks for consistency. There are several cases, however, in which the effects of the actions may turn out to be either consistent or inconsistent with the objectives. Three of these involve changes in the regulations of the CDBG program. Outcomes here depend on the targeting of program funds by lo-

TABLE 13–5

SUMMARY OF CHANGING FEDERAL HOUSING ACTIVITIES, FY 1981–FY 1987

(*In $ millions*)

	Fiscal Year							Change	
	1981	1982	1983	1984	1985	1986	1987	81–83	83–87
HUD housing assistance									
Budget authority	24,840	5,217	-5,221	-3,478	890	-1,627	1,728	-30,061	6,949
Outlays	5,747	6,726	7,352	7,831	8,401	8,867	9,205	1,605	1,853
Community development[a]									
CDBG	3,695	3,456	3,456	3,456	3,456	3,456	3,456	-239	0
Urban development grants	675	440	440	440	440	440	440	-235	0
Enterprise zones[b]	—	—	—	310	620	930	930	—	930
Housing credit									
Direct loan guarantees[c]	3,901	4,110	1,456	1,451	1,474	1,466	1,456	-2,445	0
Guaranteed loan commitments[d]	65,785	76,609	73,400	f	f	f	f	7,615	—
Housing tax expenditures[e]	32,645	37,695	42,755	46,640	51,935	59,905	69,095	10,110	26,340

SOURCE: *Major Themes and Additional Details* (Washington, D.C.: GPO); Office of Management and Budget, *Budget of the United States Government, Fiscal Year 1983* (Washington, D.C.: GPO, 1982), table G-2; and Joint Committee on Taxation, U.S. Congress, *Estimates of Federal Tax Expenditures For Fiscal Year 1982 and 1987* (Washington, D.C.: GPO, 1982), table 1.

a. Budget authority.
b. Outlay equivalents of tax expenditures.
c. Includes Farmer's Home Administration and the Federal Housing Administration.
d. Includes Federal Housing Administration and GNMA mortgage-backed securities program.
e. Includes items listed in table 3, plus exclusion of interest on certain savings certificates.
f. Mortgage-backed securities program activity not specified in the budget.

TABLE 13–6

SUMMARY OF THE CONSISTENCY OF MAJOR ACTIONS OR PROPOSALS
WITH FOUR OBJECTIVES

Actions	Improved Efficiency	Greater Private Sector Involvement	Target Benefits	Decentralized Decision Making
Housing finance				
Regulatory changes	C	-	-	-
GNMA credit limits	?	C	-	-
FHA refocus	?	C	-	-
Housing assistance				
Limited program size	I	-	-	-
Redefined eligibility				
and reduced benefits	I	-	C	-
Emphasis on existing				
housing	C	C	-	-
Community Development				
Block Grant				
State administration of				
small cities program	?	-	?	C
Regulatory revision in				
entitlement portion				
of program	?	-	I	C

NOTE: C = actions are judged to be consistent with objective.
      I = actions are judged to be inconsistent with objective.
      ? = effect of actions is unclear; could be consistent or inconsistent with objective.
      - = action is neutral with respect to objective.

calities when the extent of federal oversight has been sharply reduced. For entitlement communities, however, less targeting is expected, given the strenuous efforts of the previous administration in this area.

The attainment of improved efficiency from the restrictions proposed on GNMA and FHA activities is also ambiguous. Here the outcome depends on whether or not private institutions fill the void created and, if they do, whether they are more efficient than their federal counterparts.

There are two cases within housing assistance in which the administration's action well may be inconsistent with the objective of improved efficiency. In proposing to limit the number of households to be assisted, the administration is continuing both an ad hoc approach to housing assistance policy and an inability to integrate fully housing assistance with other social welfare programs. The second case involves the reduction of benefits to program participants that stems from several rather independent actions. These are particularly acute in the housing voucher program as proposed and may make it impossible for the program to achieve its housing objectives. This possibility is especially disturbing because this is to be the main vehicle for providing housing assistance in the future.

The administration has proposed a fundamental redirection in U.S. housing policy, upon which the nation has already embarked. Government priorities are shifting away from the poor. The building industry and thrift institutions are to become more dependent on pure market outcomes. Whether the nation will continue to follow this strong lead remains to be seen.

Chapter 14

TRANSPORTATION

Ronald F. Kirby
Carol T. Everett

Transportation represents one of the nation's most important economic sectors; annual expenditures for transportation total close to one-fifth of the Gross National Product. Historically, investment in canals, railroads, highways, and other forms of transportation has been a key factor responsible for periods of rapid economic development. Currently the maintenance and modernization of the transportation system are seen as essential for future growth and development.

The evolution of the nation's transportation system has been guided and influenced by all levels of government. However, the relative roles of the federal, state, and local governments have gradually changed over time. While the federal government concentrated initially on national and international transportation, over the last two decades it has expanded its involvement into state and local transportation as well as into areas which were previously the exclusive domain of the private sector.

Over the past decade, the major emphasis in the transportation sector has shifted away from new capital expenditures and toward maintenance and rehabilitation of existing infrastructure. During this period, the deteriorating

[The authors would like to thank George Eads of the University of Maryland and Pat McCann of the Congressional Budget Office for their comments and advice.]

condition of existing transportation systems and its implications for future
growth have become a matter of national concern.[1] Concurrently, the nature
and scope of federal financial involvement have come under increasing scrutiny.

Against this background, the Reagan administration has proposed major
changes in the financing responsibilities of the various levels of government
and of transportation users. This chapter examines the proposed changes in
financing arrangements. It does not discuss equally important changes in
regulatory policy, but some of these are addressed in chapter 5. The chapter
begins by reviewing the issues concerning the current federal role in financing
transportation. It then examines the Reagan initiatives and early reactions to
them. Finally, the chapter discusses the implications of these proposals for
the future condition and operation of the nation's transportation system.

Issues in the Federal Financing of Transportation

The federal government currently contributes in excess of $20 billion
annually to the financing of the nation's transportation system. More than 60
percent of this federal funding is provided to help construct, rehabilitate, and
maintain transportation facilities such as highways, transit systems, airports,
and waterways. A substantial portion of the remainder is devoted to federal
services such as air traffic control and the U.S. Coast Guard. The federal
government also provides substantial operating assistance to urban mass transportation and Amtrak passenger rail services. Table 14-1 shows the breakdown
of major transportation expenditures by level of government in FY 1980
(excluding funds expended under human services and revenue-sharing programs).

When the Reagan administration took office, the level of federal financial
involvement in the transportation sector had been increasing steadily for several decades. Citing excessive government regulation of free enterprise as a
deterrent to economic growth, and believing that much of the federal taxing
and decision-making power should be returned to state and local governments,
the Reagan administration has undertaken a major effort to cut back federal
involvement in the transportation sector.

The general steps President Reagan has proposed to restructure financial
responsibilities for transportation can be grouped into three categories: (1)
those designed to place more reliance on state and local governments; (2)
those designed to place more reliance on user fees (instead of general revenues)
where a federal transportation service "provides special benefits to identifiable
recipients above and beyond those which accrue to the general public"; and
(3) those designed to place more reliance on private sector provision of
transportation.[2] These steps are based on the convictions that state and local

TABLE 14-1

GOVERNMENTAL EXPENDITURES ON TRANSPORTATION
(FY 1980)

Expenditure Category	Amount (In $ millions)	
	Federal Government	State and Local Governments
Highways	9,891	23,854
Urban mass transportation	3,238	3,008[a]
Airports and airways	3,183	1,888
Water transport and terminals	2,110	1,168
Coast guard	1,598	—
Rail freight	628	36[b]
Amtrak	823	9

SOURCES: U.S. Department of Commerce, Bureau of the Census, *Governmental Finances in 1979–80* (Washington, D.C.: GPO, 1981). Office of Management and Budget, *The Budget of the United States Government:* 1981 (Washington, D.C.: GPO, 1980), Appendix; American Public Transit Association, *1981 Transit Fact Book* (Washington, D.C.: 1980).

a. Includes operating and capital assistance only; assumes state and local expenditures on capital are one-fourth the federal share.

b. Includes local rail service assistance only; assumes state and local governments contributed a 30 percent match to the federal dollars authorized for local rail service assistance in FY 1980.

governments should be responsible for programs with primarily state and local benefits; that users should pay for transportation except where there is some overriding national interest; and that the private sector is a more efficient provider of transportation services than the public sector.

The history and extent of federal financial involvement in the transportation sector vary greatly across the different forms of transportation. For highways and waterways, for example, the federal government has played a major financing role virtually since the inception of connected, well-defined road and waterway systems. For mass transportation and airports, on the other hand, major federal financing has been introduced only over the last two decades. User fee contributions to federal financing also vary greatly: highways, airports, and waterways are financed to differing degrees through earmarked user taxes, while other federal financing for other forms comes almost entirely from general revenues. The role of the private sector in providing transportation services has been reduced as federal financing has permitted public takeover of certain unprofitable services considered essential by policy makers.

Intergovernmental Responsibilities

There are certain aspects of the transportation infrastructure that have the characteristics of a natural monopoly and, for national security, safety, and administrative reasons, have been considered the responsibility of the federal government. The interstate highway system, the national waterway system, and the national air traffic control system are primary examples, though the existence of major toll roads demonstrates that highways need not be federally financed. In many western countries national railroad networks are also under federal ownership and control, though, for the most part, they are privately owned in the United States.

Some activities currently supported by the federal government could be supported by state and local governments. Airport development, urban roads, and urban mass transportation are three good examples. The rationale for federal involvement in these activities has been that the federal government can more easily collect and administer funds, as in the cases of airports and roads, or that needs exist which state and local governments are unable or unwilling to meet, as in the case of mass transportation. The federal role in these areas has been controversial and provides an obvious target for the Reagan administration's review of the size and influence of the federal government in the transportation sector.

Two major issues have developed regarding the role of different levels of government: the appropriateness of federal influence over matters which could, and perhaps should, be the domain of state and local governments; and the distortional effects of federal funding on state and local spending. The urban portion of the interstate highway program is an example of the former issue, and the urban mass transportation program is an example of the latter.

Federal cooperation with states to finance highway development began in 1916 with formula-based grants and culminated in 1956 when Congress designated a set of federal user taxes for the Highway Trust Fund to finance the interstate highway program.[3] While the interstate program generated substantial benefits for intercity passenger and goods movement, the urban portion did not live up to expectations. Key segments were never completed because of the undesirable side effects of massive highway construction in developed areas. Those portions that were completed did not seem to the general public to significantly reduce traffic congestion.[4] The disruptive effects of highway construction on residential neighborhoods were much greater than had been expected, as were the levels of economic activity lured from central areas to the suburbs.[5] In retrospect, many believe that greater attention should have been paid to local concerns in this portion of the interstate program, with state and federal objectives playing a lesser role.[6]

In their preoccupation with road expansion during the 1950s, public officials paid little or no attention to the growing problems of public transit systems. With few exceptions, U.S. cities insisted that, despite rapidly declining ridership, transit systems should maintain extensive services and cover their costs from farebox revenues. As revenues began to fall short of the full costs of service provision in the late 1950s, transit operators postponed replacement of capital equipment and encountered increasing difficulty in maintaining adequate services.

The early 1960s brought public acceptance of the view that federal assistance to transit was warranted for capital replacement and expansion, though it was still firmly believed that operating costs should be recoverable from the farebox. With the enactment of a program of federal capital assistance in the Urban Mass Transportation Act of 1964 there began an era of extensive transit capital replacement and expansion. In most large cities new public transit authorities were formed to purchase assets of private bus companies, all with the understanding that public financial assistance would be limited to capital purchases.

Eventually, declining ridership, increasing costs, and public insistence on both extensive and low-fare service combined to create operating deficits which grew from a national total of $11 million in 1965 to $288 million in 1970 and $1.7 billion in 1975.[7] In 1974 Congress enacted a new section of the Urban Mass Transportation Act to fund up to 50 percent of transit operating deficits, subject to a limit for each urbanized area based on population and population density. State and local governments provided funds to match the federal program, and by the late 1970s, 57 percent of transit operating expenses were covered by public subsidies: 17 percent by federal, 13 percent by state, and 27 percent by local sources.

The federal capital assistance program did not achieve its objectives of providing a long-term cure for the ills of mass transit. Indeed, by making new equipment relatively inexpensive to local governments, the program created incentives for transit operators to retire vehicles prematurely and to incur excessive capital expenses.[8] When growing political support for transit finally led in 1974 to the provision of federal operating assistance, the new program was separated legislatively and administratively from the earlier capital assistance program. Though this assistance has been supported strongly by the nation's cities, it has encouraged excessive cost inflation in transit operations.[9] Thus, although it has stimulated substantial improvements in mass transit services, federal assistance has had the undesirable side effect of undermining transit efficiency.

User Responsibilities

There is no uniform policy with respect to recovering the costs of federal services from transportation users. For example,[10]

- Barge operators and other users of the inland waterway system pay only a small fraction of system costs, whereas users of the federal highway system pay for all federal financial assistance through user fees.
- Almost all the services rendered by the U.S. Coast Guard to the maritime community are provided without user charges.
- Receipts from aviation user fees historically have covered only about half of the federal expenses attributable to air carriers and general aviation.

The issue of user fees for transportation services has been a controversial one for decades. Although every president since Franklin D. Roosevelt has advocated the imposition of user fees on the barge industry, Congress refused to take action until President Carter tied a waterway user fee proposal to a popular public works bill. And even though road users cover the aggregate costs of road construction, maintenance, and operation, the allocation of these costs between different classes of road users has been debated continually.[11] In the spring of 1982 the Reagan administration sent to Congress a new report on the allocation of highway costs that recommends higher user charges for heavy trucks.[12] The recommendation has been opposed vigorously by certain segments of the trucking industry.

The different levels of federal cost recovery through user fees have had the effect of providing differential federal subsidies to competing forms of transportation. Heavily subsidized waterborne freight service competes with less heavily subsidized rail service, for example, and with virtually unsubsidized pipelines.[13] Early in 1982 President Reagan's Secretary of Transportation, Drew Lewis, pointed out the long-term competitive distortions caused by differential user fees:

> There probably never has been a time in which the competitive interrelationships among the surface freight modes have not been skewed in one direction or another by federal subsidy policy (or regulatory or tax policies for that matter).[14]

Experience suggests, however, that politically, attempting to remedy these distortions by legislating increased user fees will be an extremely difficult undertaking.

Public versus Private Sector

As discussed earlier, the urban transit industry has gradually passed from the private to the public sector with growing federal, state, and local financial involvement. The other areas of public takeover are certain passenger and freight rail services.

Intercity passenger rail services receive federal financial assistance through the National Railroad Passenger Corporation (Amtrak), created by the Rail Passenger Service Act of 1970. Originally intended to be a for-profit corporation, Amtrak has had to rely on federal assistance throughout its existence. The number of trains and routes operated by Amtrak has declined gradually throughout the 1970s, even though over 50 percent of Amtrak's operating costs are covered by federal funds. The greatest demand for Amtrak services currently lies along corridors connecting major cities in the Northeast and on the West Coast. Proposals have been entertained for the development of high speed "bullet" train services along these and other selected corridors, but to date neither the federal government nor private sources have been willing to make the major investments required.

The principal objective of federal financial involvement in the rail freight industry has been to preserve and improve rail freight service while maintaining private sector involvement. The Regional Rail Reorganization Act (or 3R Act) of 1973 led to the restructuring of some of the bankrupt northeastern railroads into the Consolidated Rail Corporation (Conrail), and appropriated funding for rail lines excluded from Conrail in the same region.[15]

The Railroad Revitalization and Regulatory Reform Act of 1976 (or 4R Act) expanded federal assistance to financially distressed railroads throughout the entire nation in the form of federal loan guarantees and federal government purchase of redeemable preference shares. Assistance to rail lines under the 4R Act can be used either for the continuation of rail service or for the provision of substitute service. The federal financing share declined gradually from 90 percent in FY 1977 to a maximum of 70 percent in FY 1980, reflecting the intent of Congress to gradually shift the full responsibility for rail line assistance to state and local governments.

The growth in governmental financing of transportation has been accompanied by a growth in public ownership and operation of transportation services. Urban mass transportation systems are now almost entirely publicly owned and operated, and the formation in the 1970s of Amtrak and Conrail represented steps in the direction of public ownership of passenger and freight railroads. These steps have been taken reluctantly, and only when there appeared to be no other short-range alternative for insuring that important services would be maintained. Proponents of a stronger role for the private sector have continually challenged the desirability of expanding public ownership. They have offered a number of alternatives, including relaxation of economic regulation, more carefully targeted public subsidies, and greater use in subsidy programs of competitive procedures involving the private sector.[16]

The Reagan Initiatives

On taking office, the Reagan administration proposed significant cutbacks and structural changes in federal transportation programs. Congress largely ratified the proposed budget cutbacks in the Omnibus Reconciliation Act of 1981 but to date has not acted on the administration's proposals for major structural changes such as increases in user fees and shifts to state and local governments of selected functional responsibilities.

Shifting Responsibilities to State and Local Governments: Changes Enacted to Date

The transportation budget reductions affecting state and local governments mostly were in highways and mass transportation.[17] In highways, the Reagan administration proposed a major reduction for the federal highway program that assists states to construct and improve interstate, primary, secondary, and urban highway systems.[18] Generally, over the last five years, Congress has increased the obligational authority for this program. In the Omnibus Reconciliation Act of 1981, however, Congress voted to reduce the obligation limit for FY 1982 to $8.2 billion (from the Congressional Budget Office baseline level of $9.6 billion) and to set the FY 1983 limit at $8.8 billion. Out of the more than $13 billion then available from new and past authorizations, the appropriations committee approved only $8 billion for highway obligations in FY 1982.

Table 14-2 shows the final impact of congressional actions in calendar year 1981 on budget authority for several transportation programs, including three grants-in-aid programs. After budget authority is provided (through the appropriations process in the case of urban mass transportation, Amtrak, and Conrail; through the authorizing committees in the case of highways and airports), actual obligations under the different programs for each year are constrained by congressional limits. These limits have reduced the funding actually available for the programs for FY 1982 and beyond. Because there is a long lead time before some committed projects are implemented, however, the effect of cuts in obligation limits on actual outlays (see table 14-3) may not be felt for several years. For highways, for example, the Congressional Budget Office (CBO) has estimated that outlays in FY 1982 will drop by only 3 percent, even though Congress enacted a 17 percent reduction in the 1982 obligation limit.

In mass transportation, the Reagan administration proposed to continue capital assistance at reduced levels and to phase out operating assistance over a three-year period. Congress chose not to act on the president's proposal for

TABLE 14-2

PROPOSED AND ACTUAL CHANGES IN FEDERAL BUDGET AUTHORITY FOR SELECTED TRANSPORTATION PROGRAMS

(*In $ millions*)

Program	Actual FY 1981	FY 1982	FY 1983	FY 1984	FY 1985	FY 1986	FY 1987
Highways							
1981 baseline[a]	9,048	7,854	8,600	9,320	9,955	10,610	—
After 1981 budget process		8,279	9,265	9,635	10,075	10,540	11,005
Reagan's FY 1983 proposal			7,800	8,225	8,225	8,225	8,225
Mass transportation							
1981 baseline	4,615	5,090	5,507	5,914	6,274	6,623	—
After 1981 budget process		3,495	4,011	4,311	4,603	4,919	5,227
Reagan's FY 1983 proposal			3,150	2,976	2,976	2,976	2,976
Airports							
1981 baseline	570	789	872	942	996	1,046	—
After 1981 budget process		450	489	529	568	604	636
Reagan's FY 1983 proposal			450	450	450	450	450
Amtrak							
1981 baseline	881	1,048	1,139	1,241	1,331	1,443	—
After 1981 budget process		735	788	850	915	986	1,057
Reagan's FY 1983 proposal			600	500	525	550	575
Conrail							
1981 baseline	500	560	500	300	300	300	—
After 1981 budget process		85	0	0	0	0	0
Reagan's FY 1983 proposal			0	0	0	0	0

SOURCES: Congressional Budget Office (CBO) and the Office of Management and Budget.

a. The 1981 baseline is the 1981 CBO current services projection.

TABLE 14-3

PROPOSED AND ACTUAL CHANGES IN FEDERAL OUTLAYS FOR SELECTED TRANSPORTATION PROGRAMS
(In $ millions)

Program	Actual FY 1981	FY 1982	FY 1983	FY 1984	FY 1985	FY 1986	FY 1987
Highways							
1981 baseline[a]	8,350	8,285	9,000	9,700	10,700	11,500	—
After 1981 budget process		8,065	8,100	8,800	9,420	10,060	10,720
Reagan's FY 1983 proposal			8,026	7,998	8,150	8,220	8,235
Mass transportation							
1981 baseline	3,950	4,090	4,340	4,450	4,588	4,907	—
After 1981 budget process		3,869	4,155	4,249	4,199	4,215	4,622
Reagan's FY 1983 proposal			3,155	2,996	2,934	3,004	2,971
Airports							
1981 baseline	524	674	770	842	914	974	—
After 1981 budget process		482	484	488	495	553	590
Reagan's FY 1983 proposal			374	467	683	538	468
Amtrak							
1981 baseline	750	930	1,140	1,244	1,311	1,425	—
After 1981 budget process		800	755	808	907	978	1,048
Reagan's FY 1983 proposal			610	500	525	550	575
Conrail							
1981 baseline	500	460	500	300	300	300	—
After 1981 budget process		85	0	0	0	0	0
Reagan's FY 1983 proposal			0	0	0	0	0

SOURCES: Congressional Budget Office (CBO) and the Office of Management and Budget.
a. The 1981 baseline is the 1981 CBO current services projection.

structural changes in FY 1982 but instead agreed to a large across-the-board cut in budget authority for all Urban Mass Transportation Administration (UMTA) programs. The reconciliation and appropriation processes combined reduced UMTA's FY 1982 budget authority by 31 percent (see table 14-2). This represents a dramatic change by Congress which in FY 1980 and FY 1981 increased UMTA's budget authority by 36 percent and 45 percent, respectively. As with highways, UMTA's outlays will not reflect this change immediately because close to one-half of UMTA's budget is for capital grants. CBO predicts only a 7 percent reduction in FY 1982 outlays, even though there will be a 31 percent reduction in FY 1982 budget authority.

The Reagan administration has combined these shifts in financing responsibility with shifts in regulatory responsiblity. The most notable example has been in the area of transit accessibility for the handicapped. Under President Carter the federal government issued a rule requiring that all conventional transit services supported by federal funds be made fully accessible to wheelchairs.[19] This rule preempted local authority and imposed expensive retrofit requirements on many transit systems. Six months after President Reagan took office, the Department of Transportation (DOT) issued an interim final rule which withdrew the full accessibility requirement and allowed each community to make its own decision on services for the handicapped.[20] The revised rule returns to earlier requirements dictating that handicapped persons receive services which are "reasonable in comparison" to those available to the general public.

DOT has taken other administrative steps to reduce federal regulatory involvement in local transit matters. In early 1982 the secretary issued a notice declaring the agency's intent to end mandatory use of the *White Book* rules on federally financed bus purchases. Up until this point local transit companies have had to conform to federal vehicle specifications when procuring buses with federal funds. Removal of this requirement would allow local jurisdictions more flexibility in bus procurement decisions.

Shifting Responsibilities to State and Local Governments: Proposed Changes

President Reagan's FY 1983 budget submission proposes short-term and long-term policy changes that continue his administration's efforts to shift decision making and responsibility for a variety of policy, budgetary, and regulatory matters to state and local governments.

Short-term Proposals. The short-term recommendations for transportation include focusing federal highway funds on rehabilitating existing interstate and primary highways; phasing out transit operating assistance by

1985; and concentrating transit capital assistance on modernizing and rehabilitating existing proven systems. The proposals would also phase out assistance to states for rail transit planning and for rehabilitation of low-traffic
branchlines by 1983; require states to pay the full costs for special state Amtrak
routes; and phase out grants-in-aid to the nation's largest airports.[21]

Tables 14-2 and 14-3 show the president's FY 1983 budget proposal for
four of these transportation programs. In each case, the budget authority and
outlays proposed are dramatically lower than those for FY 1982.

In translating these policy proposals into legislative changes, the administration has made only limited progress. Because of difficulties encountered in revising highway user charges, no new highway legislation had been
submitted to Congress by mid-1982. Legislation dealing with financing for
airport development was under discussion with Congress in mid-1982, but
no specific bill had been agreed upon.

In mass transportation, however, the administration has sent to Congress
a bill to implement the president's short-term recommendations. The proposed
Transit Assistance Act of 1982 would transform transit capital assistance from
a discretionary grant program into largely a formula grant program. Under
the new formula, capital assistance would be allocated to communities on the
basis of state and local financial commitments to transit (including farebox
revenues). New rail starts and extensions would be ineligible for federal
funding. In line with the administration's desire to phase out federal operating
assistance by 1985, the bill reduces the amount of operating funds for FY
1983 by 38 percent from their FY 1982 level, and by a similar percentage
again from 1983 to 1984 (using 1982 as the base). The bill also shifts more
responsibility for decisions about transit operations to the local level. Transit
systems receiving federal operating funds would be allowed more flexibility
in considering public comment prior to implementing service changes and
would no longer be required to charge half-fare rates to the elderly and
handicapped during the off-peak hours.

Long-term Proposals. The president's FY 1983 budget submission also
included his New Federalism initiative, or "long-term proposal for a sorting
out of responsibilities between the federal government and the states."[22]
Among the 124 federal grant programs targeted for turnback under this proposal are 13 transportation programs budgeted at over $11.2 billion in FY
1984.[23] The programs include grants-in-aid for airports; noninterstate highway
programs (primary, rural, urban, bridge, construction safety, and highway
safety); the interstate transfer program (which allows urban transit capital
projects to be substituted for a previously approved portion of the interstate
highway system in an urban area); the Appalachian highway program; and
urban mass transportation assistance (capital and operating).

As presently conceived, the turnback component of the federalism initiative would mean that, starting in FY 1988, states would have full responsibility for the costs and administration of these and 111 other nontransportation programs currently administered by the federal government. To help states adjust to this new fiscal relationship, the president's federalism initiative proposes a $28 billion trust fund that would be financed by a portion of the revenues from the oil windfall profits tax and from federal excise taxes on a number of items. Included would be the revenue generated from two of the four cents of the federal gasoline tax.

A state could use its share of the trust fund monies[24] in two ways for transportation. First, it could reimburse DOT for grant costs if it wanted to continue receiving grants under one or more of the thirteen programs designated for turnback. Second, it could treat the trust fund monies like revenue-sharing funds and spend them for any transportation purpose it saw fit. Under the second option, a certain percentage of the trust fund monies would have to be passed through to local governments.

In 1988 the initiative calls for DOT to drop the thirteen categorical grant programs, and for the federal government to start a synchronized four-year phase-out of both the federalism trust fund and the federal excise taxes going to finance it. At this point states would be in full control of all aspects of the thirteen transportation programs and could choose to adopt the relinquished federal taxes if they wished.

Increasing User Fees

The administration has proposed new or increased user fees for several federally provided transportation services. It also has proposed legislative changes that would allow state and local governments more flexibility to raise funds to support locally provided transportation services receiving limited federal funding.

For example, in the area of air transportation the administration has proposed increased federal aviation user fees to finance modernization of the federally owned air traffic control system. Under the administration's first proposal, federal user fees for general aviation would have been increased significantly. Transportation analysts have consistently argued that aviation users, especially general aviation, do not bear the full costs that they impose on the aviation system. According to the Reagan administration general aviation users in 1981 paid only about 5 percent of their FAA allocable costs.[25] Because of strong opposition from general aviation groups, the administration's first user fee proposal was scaled back.

As part of its New Federalism initiative the administration has proposed to reduce federal financial involvement in the nation's largest airports. To help state and local governments find new revenue sources, the administration has proposed that local airport authorities be allowed to charge airlines user fees as a means of raising airport development funds.

Another administration user fee proposal has been to double inland waterway user charges. At Senate hearings on the results of a congressionally mandated study of the impact of existing waterway user fees, Secretary of Transportation Drew Lewis expressed the administration's long-term interest in shifting full costs for waterway improvements from the general taxpayer to the users. Congressional Budget Office Director Alice Rivlin testified that federal subsidies to the waterway industry currently amount to one-fourth of the industry's total shipping costs, and that this is the largest subsidization of any of the freight modes. CBO estimates that doubling current waterway user fees would increase the average waterway operator's total costs by about 16 percent in 1990.[26]

In the area of ports, the administration has submitted a proposal similar to that for airports. It shifts the responsibility for financing offshore port improvements and maintenance to local port authorities and recommends that port authorities be given the right to charge commercial vessels user fees adequate to raise the necessary funds.

The Coast Guard presently finances almost all its services through general revenues. The administration believes that there are easily identifiable beneficiaries of Coast Guard services who should be assessed the full costs that they impose on the federal government. An early administration proposal to initiate fees for licenses, inspections, navigation aids, and search and rescue services was rejected by Congress because of adverse reaction from recreational boaters. A revised proposal significantly reduces most of the charges in the earlier fee schedule.

The secretary of transportation has proposed a five cent increase in the federal gasoline tax[27] to help finance highway and transit capital projects. While acknowledging critical highway needs, the president has decided to defer consideration of the proposal until preparation of the FY 1984 budget.

Increasing Private Sector Involvement

The Reagan administration has taken several steps to return what it considers private transportation functions to the private sector. The most notable example is Conrail. Shortly after taking office, President Reagan expressed his desire to terminate federal subsidies for Conrail and to sell off the rail freight system as soon as possible to the private sector. In the Omnibus

Reconciliation Act of 1981, Congress and the administration worked out a framework for returning Conrail to the private sector. Congress added provisions to help the railroad become profitable and thus avoid a piecemeal sale.[28]

The Reagan administration has shown an interest in increasing private sector involvement in other transportation areas as well. The administration-sponsored Transit Assistance Act of 1982 encourages participation of private providers of mass transportation services by exempting them from the labor protection provisions of the Urban Mass Transportation Act.

Responses to Date

Most of President Reagan's program still is in the proposal stage, and those aspects that have been put into effect are so recent that their impact has yet to be fully felt. This section reports on some early reactions to the Reagan proposals.

Intergovernmental Responsibilities

State and local governments are negotiating with the administration on President Reagan's federalism initiative. Their major concerns are whether the size of a federalism trust fund would be adequate to support the responsibilities returned to the states, and whether the fiscal impacts of the initiative would be distributed equitably. These mirror state and local concerns with the cuts made to date in transportation.

The transportation interest groups generally have reacted negatively to the president's efforts to shift more responsibilities to the states and localities. For the most part, these groups believe that decentralizing transportation funding would lead to a proliferation of inconsistent rules and regulations across states as well as to less than optimal levels of funding.

Some interest groups have predicted that fewer federal dollars will mean a deterioration in transportation services or even a complete loss of services. The American Public Transit Association (APTA), a trade association representing the urban mass transit community, testified before the House Committee on Public Works and Transportation that a phase-out of transit operating assistance would mean the demise of up to 25 percent of the nation's transit systems, especially in small- and medium-sized communities.[29] This was just one of the conclusions of an APTA survey, done in December 1981, of the impacts of cutbacks in federal operating assistance. Other findings based on responses from 116 transit systems were that 67 percent would reduce service;

89 percent would raise fares; 79 percent would require increased state and local assistance; and 56 percent would require new taxes. Thirty-seven percent would have base fares climb over one dollar (more large than small communities would experience the dollar plus fare).

Some transportation analysts are more optimistic about the consequences of fewer federal funds. As noted, many federal aid programs, through their inconsistent matching ratios and formulas, have distorted state and local decision making. The Urban Mass Transportation Act, for example, has biased local expenditures toward capital by requiring smaller local matching shares for capital (one local dollar for every four federal dollars) than for operating expenses (one local dollar for each federal dollar). Some observers believe that transit funding cutbacks will force transit operators to replace their least productive fixed route segments with more efficient forms of mass transportation, such as carpools and vanpools, shared taxis, subscription buses, and jitneys.[30] The extent of such improvements in transportation efficiency will almost certainly depend, however, on whether the administration is as willing to tackle the distorting incentives in current programs as it has been to reduce overall funding levels.

User Responsibilities

To date, President Reagan's user fee proposals have not been well received by either Congress or affected user groups. As Senator Domenici pointed out in hearings on the impact of existing inland waterway user fees, "the issue of user charges is one that lacks any real constituency, other than sound government. . . . Clearly anyone with a subsidy wants that subsidy to continue."[31] The limited support that does exist for user fees comes primarily from two groups. One is federal decision makers who rely on the revenues from user fees to support steady levels of transportation expenditures. Another is freight transporters who always support increased user fees for their competitors. The Association of American Railroads has been a consistent advocate of higher road user charges for heavy trucks, for example.

Because of strong opposition to its first user fee proposals for air and water transport services, the administration has softened the magnitude of increases in revised proposals. Affected user groups complain that the proposals underestimate the size of public benefits from these services, overprice the services, and include charges for services which aren't used. They also are concerned that most of the revenues generated will be used to reduce budget deficits rather than to supplement the accounts supporting the services.[32]

Unlike air and water transport user fees, there has been wide support for increased highway user fees. Recent studies show that there has been significant deterioration in highway system performance and that there is an urgent need for increased highway expenditures.[33] Secretary of Transportation Drew Lewis's proposal for a five cent increase in the federal gasoline tax would have raised about $5.5 billion dollars per year, a substantial increase in financing capability. The president's decision to defer consideration of a federal gasoline tax increase has dismayed many highway and transit interest groups (the secretary's proposal earmarked one cent of the tax increase for mass transportation).[34] Because of this decision Congress probably will pass one-year extensions of the current highway and mass transit programs and delay consideration of new legislation until the president is prepared to deal with the financing question.

Public versus Private Sector

Responses to the administration's efforts to increase private sector involvement have been mixed. Some groups wonder how the private sector can be expected to perform well where it failed before.[35] They point to failed urban bus companies and the Penn Central as examples to support their thesis. Private businesses, on the other hand, are excited about the prospects for involvement. The International Taxicab Association (ITA), for example, a nonprofit organization representing the nation's taxicab industry, favors DOT's attempts "to redefine the federal government role in transportation matters and to place greater reliance on the private sector to provide transit services."[36]

Some transportation analysts also are advocating a larger role for the private sector in providing transportation. A recent Urban Institute study considered the "reprivatization" of some portions of urban public transportation and concluded that more competitive market conditions would promote greater diversity in types of service offered and lower average costs for these services.[37]

Conclusion

The Reagan administration has proposed a number of far-reaching changes in the allocation of financial responsibilities for transportation. In its first year in office, the administration convinced Congress to make significant reductions in obligation limits and budget authority for almost all federal transportation programs. However, for capital-intensive programs such as highways, there will be a delay before these cuts will translate into significant reductions in federal outlays. In addition to the budget cuts enacted to date, the administration proposes a gradually reduced federal role in financing highway systems, urban mass transportation, airport and seaport development, and passenger rail services. Conrail services are slated to be transferred completely to the private sector, and it is proposed that both the water and air transport systems be financed to a greater extent through user fees.

The administration's outstanding proposals are receiving close scrutiny from several quarters. Transportation interest groups are naturally concerned about a reduced federal role and, with the exception of some highway and transit interest groups, are balking at actions that would increase user fees. State and local governments are particularly anxious about the president's proposal to shift to them a major share of the funding responsibility for transportation. The nation's transportation infrastructure is decaying at a rapid pace, and state and local governments are facing large and urgent capital replacement needs. At the same time, states and cities are finding that their fiscal capacity is shrinking because of a depressed economy, high interest rates, and taxing limitations.

President Reagan's unwillingness to support a five cent increase in the federal gasoline tax has postponed any congressional plans to deal with highway and transit financing problems in the near term. With virtually no prospect of higher gasoline tax revenues, the Congress seems likely to extend current legislation for one more year rather than develop new multiyear legislation. This will delay federal action on one of the nation's most pressing infrastructure problems: the repair and rehabilitation of major highways and mass transit systems. The historically important role of a well-financed and efficient transportation system in economic development suggests that the administration's transportation policies may be inconsistent with its goals for reviving economic growth. The failure of the administration to come to grips with these long-term needs is probably the single greatest shortcoming in its transportation policy making to date.

Closely associated with the level of federal financing for transportation is the structure of federal transportation programs. In the past, restrictions of federal assistance to expenditures on new facilities and equipment has been partly responsible for overcapitalization, inadequate maintenance, and overextension of transportation facilities. In general, the Reagan administration is planning to continue this restriction of federal funds to capital expenditures, though to some degree it has shifted federal priorities away from new projects and toward rebuilding dilapidated systems. Past experience suggests that, unless other changes are also made, this policy will continue to promote inappropriate state and local choices between building new facilities, maintaining existing facilities, and supporting operating expenditures. This issue should be given careful attention as the administration's specific legislative proposals are considered by Congress.

If the administration's proposals are adopted they will have major impacts on the demand for and supply of transportation services. Some of the proposed changes such as increased user fees and greater private sector involvement have been recommended by transportation experts for years. Based on past analyses, changes resulting from these proposals can be expected to produce more rational and more efficient transportation services. The impacts of the proposed shifting of additional financial responsibilities to state and local governments are less clear. Limitations on fiscal capacity at the state and local levels and the distorting incentives still embedded in the structure of federal financing programs could frustrate efforts to deal with the deteriorating condition of the nation's transportation system.

PART FOUR

IMPACTS ON PEOPLE AND PLACES

Chapter 15

REGIONAL IMPACTS

Thomas Muller

Economic growth rates and the level of economic activity vary considerably across the states and regions of the country. While most of the variation is caused by private sector forces, federal tax and expenditure policies contribute to regional differences. The federal impact occurs as a result of an imbalance between the revenues the federal government collects from a region and the federal expenditures made in that region. This imbalance can affect regional employment and income levels. Historically, federal policies have operated to redistribute income from the wealthier, more industrialized regions of the country to areas with lower levels of income and economic activity.

For the most part, the geographic pattern of federal tax and expenditure policies is not an explicit consideration when programs are adopted or changed. Tax policies are based on a rough notion of ability to pay and the desire to stimulate certain activities. Therefore, federal revenues tend to be drawn disproportionately from regions with the highest levels of economic activity, income, and wealth. Federal expenditures are motivated by an even more diverse set of circumstances. A handful of programs, such as the Appalachian Regional Commission, are designed to aid a specific region. Certain others, such as unemployment insurance, welfare, and revenue sharing, are skewed toward individuals and governments with the lowest incomes. However, the

vast bulk of federal expenditures do not have a regional redistributional objective. Reclamation and flood control spending is concentrated in areas with
certain geographical and topographical characteristics. Defense spending occurs where there are military facilities and industries that produce military
goods and services; nondefense federal employment expenditures are concentrated near the nation's capital and in various cities where the federal
government maintains regional offices. Social Security and Medicare payments are concentrated where the nation's elderly live.

Despite the lack of an explicit regional bias in federal policies, the impact
of the federal government on regional economic growth became a major
political and economic issue during the 1970s with the "Sunbelt-Frostbelt"
debate. The erosion of the industrial base of the northern and central regions
of the country, the rapid growth of the South and West, and the boom in the
energy producing states heightened interest in whether federal policies inadvertently were hurting the declining states and further boosting economic
growth in those regions with the healthiest economies.

Interest in this issue is likely to intensify with the massive shift in federal
priorities called for by the Reagan administration. This chapter provides a
preliminary assessment of the differential impact that the domestic program
cuts, the build-up of defense spending, and the tax reductions are likely to
have on the regional pattern of federal revenues and expenditures—and therefore on economic activity, employment, and income levels in the various
regions.

The results of the analysis described in this chapter indicate that both
the tax cut and expenditures shifts will be unequally distributed among regions
and states. The tax reductions will benefit higher income states the most, in
particular those in the "Sunbelt" region. The defense outlay increases will
be concentrated among a small group of states. The largest per capita losses
due to the domestic program reductions will be borne by the Northeast and
by low-income southern states. The net result generally will be to widen fiscal
and economic disparities between the more affluent and growing regions of
the country, on the one hand, and the poorer and less economically vital
regions, on the other hand.

This chapter first summarizes the regional patterns of federal taxes and
expenditures that ended during the last half of the 1970s. Next, the chapter
provides estimates of the changes in the pattern of federal expenditures implied
by the Reagan policies along with a similar analysis of the shifts in revenue
burdens. The third section of the chapter discusses employment and income
effects that are likely to accompany this shift in net federal expenditures.
Conclusions   summarize   the   major   findings   and   their   implications.

Regional Fiscal Flows in the Pre-Reagan Period

During the post-World War II period, northern industrial states contributed a disproportionate share of total taxes collected by the Treasury. Since expenditures were more equally distributed among regions than taxes, there was a net outflow from the North to the South and West.

Federal Taxes

Since the 1930s, federal tax collections per capita have been consistently higher in the Northeast and the Great Lakes regions than in the balance of the nation.[1] This pattern arises because the federal tax system is mildly progressive and the income and wealth of these regions historically have been above the national average. During the post-World War II period, and particularly during the 1970s, this disparity moderated. A combination of rising social insurance receipts, directly linked to employment growth in the South and West, and rising income in these regions gradually reduced the tax burden differentials that had been present since the Great Depression. Total tax collections continued to be marginally higher in the North compared to the West and South until 1980. However, the rising wealth of energy-rich Texas, its immediate neighbor states, and the Pacific states raised their tax burdens closer to the national average. Since 1980, tax contributions from the "Sunbelt" have comprised more than half the national total, although on a per capita basis, tax payments remain slightly higher in the North. At a more disaggregated regional level, variations in tax contributions remain substantial, ranging in 1980 from $2,604 per capita in the Pacific states to only $1,767 per capita in the East South Central region.

Federal Outlays

Per capita nondefense outlays during the 1970s tended to exceed the national average in both sparsely populated western and industrial northeastern states. In the western states, low population density, large federal land ownership, Indian reservations, and topographic characteristics contributed to above average funding for reclamation projects, economic development, highway construction, forest protection, and federal payments in lieu of property taxes. In the Northeast, the states receiving high per capita federal assistance were characterized by above average transfer payments and large federal grants to states and localities.

States with the lowest nondefense spending, such as Indiana, Ohio, North Carolina, and Texas, are states with low transfer payments, education aid, and employment assistance. This reflects state policies which substantially restrained public sector outlays, resulting in low state tax burdens, and consequently less federal general revenue sharing funds. In Indiana and Ohio, low federal spending for pensions to veterans and retired civil servants reflects outmigration of the retired population to the "Sunbelt," particularly Florida. Somewhat surprisingly, total federal spending in to Florida, despite pension-related transfer payments, has been consistently close to the national average.

As in the case of taxes, regional differentials in per capita federal outlays narrowed somewhat during the mid- and late 1970s. Nevertheless, disparities remain. These are caused primarily by differences in defense outlays, which ranged in 1980 from $290 per capita in the Great Lakes region to over $1,000 in the Pacific region. This great variation in the geographic distribution of defense outlays is a relatively new development. In the 1940s and 1950s, when over one-half of the federal budget was devoted to defense outlays, they were fairly balanced regionally, with procurement contracts concentrated in the North and most of the defense payroll in the South and West (a pattern evident for close to a century). In the post-Korean War period, however, there has been a slow but steady shift in procurement contracts to the South and West, primarily as a result of changes in weapon systems.

Net Flows

During the early 1970s, all but five of the twenty-nine southern and western states—Delaware, North Carolina, Idaho, Oregon, and Nevada—received more federal dollars than their tax contributions. The largest net dollar inflow accrued to California, which although ranking near the top nationally in per capita income, consistently received a larger share of all federal outlays than the fraction of taxes paid by its residents and business firms. On the other hand, per capita federal inflows in northern regions exceeded the national average only in Connecticut, Kansas, Maine, Rhode Island, and the Dakotas. The two industrial states, Connecticut and Rhode Island, were in this group as a result of military shipyard activity. Net outflows were the largest from Illinois, Michigan, and Ohio, which collectively received only two dollars from federal agencies for every three dollars paid to the Treasury.

The pattern observed in the early 1970s remained relatively stable during the last half of the decade. The direction of net fiscal flows resulting from federal activities in FY 1980, which is shown in table 15-1, reveals that three regions redistribute a considerable share of their personal income to the balance of the nation. The combined effect of large tax contributions by northern industrial states, the more regionally equal distribution of nondefense federal funds, and the concentration of defense outlays in the South and West resulted in a steady flow of federal dollars from northern regions to other areas. Most

TABLE 15–1

TOTAL AND PER CAPITA FEDERAL REVENUE AND EXPENDITURE FLOW IN FY 1980

| | Taxes | | Outlays[a] | | | | Net Flow | | |
| | | | Defense | | Nondefense | | | | |
Region	Total ($ billions)	Per Capita ($)	Total ($ billions)	Per Capita ($)	Total ($ billions)	Per Capita ($)	Total ($ billions)	Per Capita ($)	Percentage of Per Capita Income
New England	30.4	2,462	9.9	800	21.9	1,776	1.4	113	1.1
Middle Atlantic	91.4	2,485	15.5	422	65.7	1,785	-10.2	-277	-2.7
East North Central	102.6	2,462	12.1	290	65.7	1,577	-24.8	-595	-6.1
West North Central	39.5	2,299	6.1	354	32.9	1,915	-0.5	-29	-0.3
South Atlantic[b]	77.9	2,109	29.4	795	70.6	1,912	22.1	598	6.8
East South Central	25.9	1,767	6.7	456	26.6	1,816	7.4	504	6.8
West South Central	52.8	2,224	13.1	550	34.2	1,441	-5.5	-232	-2.6
Mountain	25.1	2,208	7.9	694	19.6	1,721	2.4	211	2.3
Pacific	82.8	2,604	32.0	1,007	53.8	1,693	3.0	94	0.9
Total U.S.	528.4	2,332	132.7	585	391.0	1,726	-4.7	-21	—

SOURCE: Community Services Administration, *Geographic Distribution of Federal Funds in Fiscal Year 1980* (Washington, D.C.: GPO, 1982). The distribution of outlays for some programs have been modified to reflect the incidence of activity at the state level. Subcontract distribution has been included in defense outlay allocation.

a. Excludes interest payments on national debt.
b. Includes the District of Columbia.

notable is the massive net outflow from the Great Lakes Region, equaling 6 percent of that region's total personal income. On a per capita basis that region received fewer defense dollars than any other and lower than average levels of nondefense dollars but paid higher than average taxes to the Treasury.

The South—outside the Texas/Oklahoma/Louisiana "energy pocket"—continued to be the biggest beneficiary of federal fiscal activities. The net inflow of funds accounted for 7 percent of its total personal income. In several southern states, such as Arkansas, net federal dollar inflows are attributable to low tax contributions, while in others, including South Carolina and Georgia, a combination of military facilities and below average tax payments is the cause of the fiscal surpluses. To a lesser extent, the West and New England are also net beneficiaries of federal activities, largely as a result of defense outlays.

Federal tax and expenditure patterns generally continued to serve an income equalization function between the higher-income industrial states and low-income states with large rural populations such as Mississippi, Arkansas, Maine, South Carolina, and the Dakotas. However, federal outlays in some instances contributed to greater rather than reduced regional income concentration. Energy rich Alaska and California, both among the top five states in per capita income, have been net recipients of federal dollars for decades. The geographic pattern of defense outlays, which are unrelated to population or income characteristics, is the major factor explaining such deviations from the otherwise income-equalizing role that the federal government has played historically among regions and states.

The Change in Regional Fiscal Flows under the Reagan Administration

Chapter 3 discussed the federal tax and spending changes proposed by the Reagan administration. In his Program for Economic Recovery and subsequent 1982 and 1983 budget proposals, President Reagan outlined an agenda which, relative to the policies he inherited, would result by FY 1986 in an annual tax reduction of over $200 billion, an increase in military expenditures of over $70 billion, and a reduction in nondefense spending of well in excess of $100 billion. Such changes would result in a major shift in net federal fiscal flows among regions and states.

The 1981 tax cut and subsequent congressional actions on the FY 1982 budget granted the president most of what he initially requested. The multiyear tax cut is estimated to reduce revenues by $39 billion in FY 1982, growing to $244 billion by FY 1986. This will benefit the more affluent and faster growing states most. The first in a series of expenditure cuts reduced non-defense programs by an estimated $31.6 billion in FY 1982, growing to $54.8 billion by FY 1986. States historically most dependent on federal funds for social programs will absorb a disproportionate share of these reductions. Finally, the first in a series of planned defense increases raised estimated outlays for FY 1982 by $7.3 billion, growing to $33.1 billion by FY 1986.[2] Much of these will flow to states with existing aircraft and shipbuilding facilities.

These estimates provide a basis for projecting both immediate and longer-term effects on federal dollar flows among regions that result from the changes in federal policy occurring in the first year and a half of the Reagan administration. It is also possible to speculate about the effects of likely subsequent changes. Such projections are discussed below for nondefense spending reductions, defense outlay increases, and tax reductions—first separately, and then in combination. In each case the incremental changes in dollar flows are shown both for the nine regions described earlier and for a set of eight states selected for the diversity of consequences they illustrate.

Domestic Program Reductions

While most federal domestic programs were reduced by the administration below their prior policy levels, a small group accounts for over one-half of the estimated $31.6 billion outlay reductions during FY 1982. Reductions exceeding $1 billion occurred in each of the following areas: Social Security, government employee retirement (civilian, military, railroad), student financial assistance, trade adjustment assistance, Food Stamps, child nutrition, Aid to Families with Dependent Children (AFDC), farm price supports, and employment and training programs. Reduced outlays for these and another fourteen programs account for over 90 percent of the reductions.

If these cuts are allocated on the basis of region and state funding distributions during FY 1980 and FY 1981, per capita program cuts exceed the national average in each northern region.[3] Reductions are below the national mean in all other regions. The West South Central states, dominated by Texas, absorb the smallest reduction, $119 per capita, while estimated losses in the agricultural West North Central (Plains) states, estimated to be $151 per capita, exceed other regions. Reductions among the eight selected states range from $103 per capita in Texas to $160 per capita in New York (table 15-2).

An examination of all fifty states (table A-9) reveals that two distinct groups of states absorb the largest per capita reductions: (1) those affected most by the sharp curtailment of a specific program and (2) those affected by a large number of program cuts. States in the first category include Alaska, (school assistance in federally affected areas); Michigan (trade adjustment

TABLE 15–2

REGIONAL DISTRIBUTION OF REDUCTIONS IN DOMESTIC PROGRAMS, FY 1982

Area	Total ($ millions)	Percentage of U.S. Total	Per Capita ($)
Regions			
New England	1,800	5.7	145
Middle Atlantic	5,500	17.5	149
East North Central	6,100	19.3	146
West North Central	2,600	8.2	151
South Atlantic	4,800	15.2	127
East South Central	2,000	6.3	136
West South Central	2,900	9.2	119
Mountain	1,500	4.8	128
Pacific	4,300	13.6	133
Total U.S.	31,600[a]	100.0[a]	138
Selected States			
Arkansas	351	1.1	153
California	3,143	9.9	130
Colorado	397	1.3	134
Iowa	407	1.3	140
New York	2,822	8.9	160
Ohio	1,515	4.8	141
Texas	1,528	4.8	103
Vermont	65	0.2	127

SOURCE: U.S. Department of the Treasury, Federal Aid to States, Fiscal Year 1981 (Washington, D.C.: GPO, 1982); Community Services Administration, Geographic Distribution of Federal Funds in Fiscal Year 1980.

a. May not sum because of rounding.

assistance to automobile workers); North Dakota and Nebraska (agricultural subsidies); and New Mexico (energy programs). A number of other states are disproportionately affected by sharp reductions in particular programs. For example, reduced payments to low-income households to offset high fuel bills, not surprisingly, have a greater impact in Vermont than in Texas. Reduced urban transit aid affects New York, with its large mass transit network, more than other states, while reduced highway construction grants have their largest per capita impact in low population density western areas.

The second group of states includes New York, where per capita reductions exceeded the average in eight out of ten large programs, and Massachusetts and Arkansas. These states have had relatively high federal social welfare payments and have imposed high tax burdens in part to finance their contributions to these programs.

At the other end of the spectrum is a group of geographically dispersed states with per capita program losses one-third or more below the national average. The one characteristic shared by these states, which include New Hampshire, North Carolina, Texas, and Utah, is their fiscal conservatism. The per capita taxes raised from their own sources in all four of these states are substantially below the national average. New Hampshire and Texas are among the few states in the nation without state income taxes. Program reductions in Wyoming are also below average because Wyoming receives a low level of federal funding for social services.

The program reductions are not trivial relative to state personal income. In FY 1982, program reductions will equal 1.4 percent of personal income nationally, and range from one percent of personal income in Texas, to 2 percent in neighboring Arkansas.

Defense Expansion

The regional distribution of military outlays related to the Reagan defense build-up differs significantly from the regional distribution both from the FY 1980 base and the defense increase that would be expected from a continuation of existing trends. In the overall defense budget, procurement and research and development account for less than one-third of total outlays, while employee compensation accounts for about 43 percent. During the late 1970s, nearly one-half of all prime contracts (for equipment, supplies, services), but only a fifth of all DOD payrolls, accrued to northern states. Western states typically obtained 28 percent of DOD payrolls and a slightly higher percentage of prime contracts.

The expanded portion of the defense budget resulting from Reagan priority changes is dominated by weapon systems acquisition and research and development. These account for close to 70 percent of the total increment in FY 1982 and 76 percent of the increment in the following years. Table 15-3 compares the regional distribution of defense contracts in FY 1979 and FY 1980 with the actual and likely distribution of contracts under the initial stage of the administration's defense build-up that Congress granted in the FY 1982 budget.[4] Relative to past patterns, the Pacific, New England, and East North Central regions tend to gain the most, while the Middle Atlantic and South Atlantic regions will see their past share decline substantially. These estimates include adjustments for the regional flow of subcontracts which total up to half of each prime contract dollar. Historically, northern manufacturing states with only a few large defense contractors have benefited from the subcon-

TABLE 15–3

REGIONAL DISTRIBUTION OF DEFENSE CONTRACTS AND SUBCONTRACTS

Region	Actual FY 1979 (%)	Actual FY 1980 (%)	Projected[a] FY 1982 Increment (%)
New England	9.2	11.2	15.9
Middle Atlantic	15.5	15.4	9.4
East North Central	12.4	10.6	14.1
West North Central	6.7	5.8	3.2
South Atlantic	18.8	15.2	9.3
East South Central	3.1	3.9	5.7
West South Central	3.6	7.9	4.3
Mountain	3 9	3.3	1.6
Pacific	26.8	26.7	36.5
Total U.S.	100.0	100.0	100.0

SOURCES: U.S. Department of Defense, *Military Prime Contracts By State 1979 and 1980*, (Directorate of Information, 1979 and 1980) and author's calculations. Subcontracts flows from unpublished U.S. Department of Defense data.
   a.   Includes only incremental contracts attributable to administration add-ons during 1981. For references, see footnote 3.

tracting process, while states with large defense firms, such as Mississippi (shipyards), Connecticut (submarines), and Missouri (aircraft), issue more subcontracts to out-of-state firms than they receive.

The estimated distribution of the total increase in defense outlays above the prior baseline, including increased weapon systems procurement, service contracts, and payroll is shown in table 15-4.[5] While the Middle Atlantic, Mountain, and particularly the southern regions' share of the expanded military budget will drop, New England and the North Central states will increase their former share. A few states, such as Vermont, should benefit from sub-contracting, since a thriving electronics industry has developed in the state in recent years. The big winner will be the Pacific region, which will receive roughly one-third of the added defense outlays in FY 1982 and subsequent years. Most of this gain will be garnered by California, the unquestioned giant in the defense industry, which already receives twice the national per capita defense spending average.

Tax Reductions

The geographic distribution of the tax reductions will depend on the level and growth of personal income and capital investment growth within various regions. During the early 1980s, more than half the nation's personal income

TABLE 15–4

REGIONAL DISTRIBUTION OF INCREASED DEFENSE OUTLAYS, FY 1982

	Total Outlays ($ millions)	Percentage of U.S. Total	Per Capita Outlays ($)
Regions			
New England	900	12.3	73
Middle Atlantic	600	8.2	16
East North Central	900	12.3	21
West North Central	400	5.5	23
South Atlantic	1,000	13.6	27
East South Central	400	5.5	27
West South Central	500	6.8	21
Mountain	200	2.7	18
Pacific	2,400	32.9	75
Total U.S.	7,300	100.0	32
Selected States			
Arkansas	14	0.2	6
California	1,904	26.1	80
Colorado	60	0.8	21
Iowa	35	0.5	12
New York	436	6.0	25
Ohio	356	4.9	33
Texas	456	6.2	32
Vermont	28	0.4	55

SOURCES: National total from chapter 3. Distribution by state and region from *The Reagan Defense Market* (Greenwich, Conn.: DMS Corporation, 1981) and U.S. Department of Defense, *Program Acquisition Costs by Weapon System* (February 1982).

and over 60 percent in new nonresidential construction was generated in the South and West. While the administration projects that most tax benefits will accrue to northern state residents, there is no evidence that this indeed will be the case. If income and investment growth follow past trends, and if the migration patterns observed during the late 1970s continue, the "Sunbelt" will reap the largest share of the savings from the tax reductions. This will probably be true as well on a per capita basis by 1986.

The FY 1982 tax savings of regions and selected states are shown in table 15–5. On a per capita basis, residents of the Pacific region will accrue the largest benefits, an average $201, or 17 percent above the national average. Those residing in northern manufacturing states will accrue benefits close to the national average. Tax savings in the rural and southern states outside the energy pocket will be less than three-quarters of the national average.

TABLE 15–5

REGIONAL DISTRIBUTION OF ESTIMATED TAX REDUCTIONS, FY 1982

	Personal Income Tax ($ millions)	Corporate and Other Taxes ($ millions)	Total ($ millions)	Per Capita ($)
	Regions			
New England	1,600	600	2,200	178
Middle Atlantic	4,600	1,700	6,300	171
East North Central	4,800	2,100	6,900	166
West North Central	1,900	900	2,800	163
South Atlantic	4,100	1,900	6,000	162
East South Central	1,200	500	1,700	123
West South Central	3,100	1,500	4,600	194
Mountain	1,400	700	2,100	185
Pacific	4,300	2,100	6,400	201
Total U.S.	27,000	12,000	39,000	172
	Selected States			
Arkansas	162	88	250	109
California	3,175	1,566	4,741	200
Colorado	405	175	580	201
Iowa	310	167	477	164
New York	2,122	839	2,961	169
Ohio	1,269	527	1,796	166
Texas	1,998	950	2,948	207
Vermont	44	18	62	121

SOURCE: National totals from Congressional Budget Office. State distribution of personal income tax reductions based on the 1978–1980 individual tax payment trends by state.

Net Regional Flows

The net regional and state fiscal flows arising from the Reagan administration's tax and spending policy shifts are presented in table 15-6. Estimates are provided for FY 1982 and for the FY 1986 implications based on policy changes enacted in 1981. Without further spending cuts or tax increases the Treasury will incur large deficits in both years from these policies because the tax cuts enacted in 1981 were larger than the spending cuts initiated in the FY 1982 budget. These deficits mean that every region will experience a net inflow.

REGIONAL FISCAL FLOWS ATTRIBUTABLE TO CHANGES IN TAX AND SPENDING POLICIES, FY 1982 AND FY 1986

	New Flow ($ millions)		Per Capita Flow[a] ($)	
	FY 1982	FY 1986	FY 1982	FY 1986
Regions				
New England	1,300	14,300	104	1,149
Middle Atlantic	1,400	31,700	38	860
East North Central	1,700	38,500	41	924
West North Central	600	10,800	35	627
South Atlantic	2,200	33,700	58	893
East South Central	100	9,000	7	611
West South Central	2,200	26,700	90	1,071
Mountain	800	11,300	68	966
Pacific	4,500	45,700	139	1,408
Total U.S.	14,800	221,200	65	965
Selected States				
Arkansas	$ −87	—	−38	—
California	3,502		145	
Colorado	243		82	
Iowa	105		36	
New York	575		33	
Ohio	637		59	
Texas	1,876		127	
Vermont	25		48	

SOURCE: Tables 15–2, 15–4, 15–5 and other estimates by author.
a. Based on July 1, 1981 population.

The largest per capita net inflow of federal funds in FY 1982 will occur in western and southwestern states. Collectively, the Sunbelt will receive close to two-thirds of the total net flow resulting from policy shifts of the Reagan administration. California will accrue $3.6 billion, or $151 per capita, which is more than the net surplus it received from all federal spending and taxing activity in FY 1980. Texas will accrue $1.9 billion, offsetting its pre-Reagan net loss from all federal spending and taxing policies. California and Texas, which together account for over one-third of the total FY 1982 net inflow, should improve their economic bases relative to most other states as a result of the Reagan policies.

Arkansas presents a striking contrast to Texas. In this state, the third poorest in the nation, program reductions will exceed the gains from the tax cut and the military build-up. Arkansas is among the low-income group of states that includes Mississippi, South Carolina, and New Mexico, which historically have benefited from federal programs with substantial net inflows.

By FY 1986 the impact of the tax cuts passed in 1981 will dwarf the effects of the defense build-up and the reduction in social spending that the Congress passed in 1981. The sharp rise in defense outlays will continue to benefit primarily California, Connecticut, Maine, Massachusetts, Mississippi, and Virginia. Defense outlays in FY 1986 will exceed domestic program cuts in New England by a small amount and in the Pacific states by several billion dollars. Thus, even in the absence of a tax cut, changes in expenditure priorities from social to defense expenditures will benefit several states.

The net regional inflow of $221.2 billion projected for FY 1986 in table 15-6 is unlikely to materialize. To reduce the deficit, policies will be enacted that both raise revenues and reduce spending. In particular, if there were no deficit in FY 1986, the net regional inflow would be zero and all regions and states faring worse than the average would experience a net outflow. Future deficit reduction policies will probably have regional impacts that will differ somewhat from the policies enacted during 1981. For this reason the ultimate geographic impact of the shift in priorities brought about by the Reagan administration is still an open question. However, preliminary actions by Congress on the FY 1983 budget suggest that the pattern of relative shifts in net fiscal flows resulting from the 1981 actions is a good indicator of likely future shifts.

Personal Income and Employment

Fiscal flows provide useful information on how a particular state or region fares in its interactions with the federal government. But the ultimate interest in such an analysis is the impact such flows have on state and regional economies, employment, and income. The direct employment and income effects of federal program reductions or a new defense contract are easy to estimate. However, the indirect employment and income effects resulting from the overall degree of fiscal stimulus represented by the changes in net flows of federal funds must be estimated using economic models. The application of such models suggests that despite the deficit spending projected for FY 1982, the policy changes enacted in 1981 should act to lower personal income the first year.[6] Experience shows that domestic program reductions are quickly translated into lower consumer expenditures, while personal and corporate tax cuts take a longer time to increase consumption and investment. The short-run personal income losses attributable to the Reagan policies will be somewhat greater in northern states than in the South and West. After a year or so the positive effects of the tax cuts will have worked their way through the economy, while the adverse effects associated with domestic program reductions will have been mitigated.

The shift in spending priorities is having a direct impact on employment. According to the Department of Commerce, reductions in the Comprehensive Employment and Training Act (CETA) programs resulted in a loss of 100,000 public service employment jobs in calendar 1981, which were not offset by non-CETA public job expansion at the state and local level. In the absence of job substitution, the FY 1982 CETA reductions could reduce employment by 300,000, with the largest relative losses occurring in the Northeast and low-income southern states.

On the other side of the ledger, based on the CBO baseline data, the Reagan defense build-up will result in a net gain of less than 100,000 jobs during 1982. Most of those new jobs will be located in a dozen or so metropolitan areas. Among the seven states which will share half or more of all new prime contracts during the next several years, only one has unemployment levels exceeding the national average. The defense industry is generating new jobs in high-wage engineering, technical, and skilled blue collar occupations. These openings will encourage migration to defense industry centers since unemployment rates in most centers are currently below the national average.

Slightly fewer jobs will be lost in the Southwest and West as a result of domestic cutbacks than in other regions. In only a handful of states, however, can defense job gains be expected to offset domestic program job losses.

Conclusions

The policy changes occurring under the Reagan administration will affect various regions and states in different ways, reflecting the relative importance to the areas of domestic spending programs, the defense industry, and tax liabilities. The domestic program reductions will have the greatest per capita adverse impact on three groups of states: the Northeast, since this region has been a major beneficiary of federal social programs; the low-income southern and northern rural states, many with unemployment rates substantially above the national average; and the Midwest where several states are dependent on agricultural subsidies. In general, the southwestern and western states will experience below average reductions in federal spending for domestic programs.

Increases in defense outlays will partially offset the domestic program losses in FY 1982. As the production of new ships, aircraft, and other military hardware accelerates during the mid-1980s, the increased defense outlays are likely to fully offset domestic program cuts only in the Pacific region and several New England states. While increased military outlays will be concentrated in California, Connecticut in the Northeast and Virginia in the South are among the states that will benefit as well. Economic activity generated by these outlays will be more geographically concentrated than previously committed DOD funds, with the New England and Pacific regions receiving about half the added military budget, while southern states, dependent on DOD payrolls, will receive a smaller share of the expanded budget than in previous years.

Both historical trends and the positive regional fiscal flows resulting from the policy changes discussed in this chapter, suggest that the residents of southwestern and western states should benefit more from the tax cuts than those in other regions. However, households in such high-income northern states as Connecticut, New Jersey, and Illinois will also receive substantial tax reductions.

It is not possible at this time to gauge the economic impact of the tax cuts since they are causing unprecedented peacetime deficits. It is also premature to estimate the effects of new taxes, fees, and spending cuts that will be enacted in FY 1983 and beyond to reduce the deficit. Therefore, one cannot currently determine whether the adverse effects of such deficit spending will offset benefits associated with increased consumption. Similarly, income and employment effects are also difficult to estimate empirically beyond 1983. While most regions will be retaining more in the way of tax relief and added defense spending than program cuts take away, the higher deficits will require additional borrowing and thus higher interest payments, reducing funds for other federal programs. In the short run, the aggregate effect of shifting tax and spending policies will be to reduce both personal income and employment. In the longer run, both should rise, holding other factors constant.

On the whole, President Reagan's policies will widen economic and fiscal disparities between wealthy and growing states, on the one hand, and less affluent and economically vital states, on the other hand. Policy changes will increase the economic and fiscal disparities between western and southwestern states and those east of the Rockies, including some of the nation's poorest areas, such as the Appalachian region. There are, as one would expect, numerous exceptions to this East-West pattern. Oregon, for example, will experience more adverse effects than its neighbors, while Connecticut will benefit more from added defense outlays than other states. However, on balance the changes add further fuel to the "Sunbelt-Frostbelt" debate and raise more fundamental questions about the extent to which federal policy should more explicitly take into account its regional fiscal impacts.

Chapter 16

THE ECONOMIC WELL-BEING OF FAMILIES AND INDIVIDUALS

Lee Bawden
Frank Levy

The Reagan administration came to office with three major domestic policy objectives: stimulating economic growth, reducing the role of the federal government, and reducing dependence on government transfers. These were to be accomplished without reducing federal support to the truly needy—those who cannot (or are not expected to) work. As important as the agenda itself was its timetable. All three goals of the president's program were to be achieved in a relatively short period of time. The president acknowledged that his program would require immediate sacrifices by many, but he argued that these sacrifices would quickly be ameliorated by the gains of economic growth.

When a program works quickly, it is judged by its ends; but when a program works slowly, the means to achieve the ends become more important. Had the economy responded as rapidly and favorably to the Program for Economic Recovery as the administration initially predicted, the equity of the president's program might be moot. But because the economy entered a

[The authors are grateful to Dick Michel, Clara Hager, and Randy Webb who conducted the simulations reported later, and to Sheldon Danziger, June O'Neill, Margaret Simms, Gene Smolensky, and Jim Storey who made valuable comments on earlier drafts.]

recession and the prospects for recovery are still uncertain, issues of equity and fairness have become more important.

This debate may be ephemeral. If unemployment declines, inflation continues to subside, and sustained economic growth occurs—and if the prosperity is widely shared—public opinion will surely judge the program a success. But if the gains from economic growth do not offset the economic losses the policy changes have caused for some, particularly those with low incomes, the issues of equity and fairness are likely to remain center stage.

This chapter examines the likely effects on the economic well-being of families and individuals of both the president's tax and spending changes and the longer-run growth his overall Program for Economic Recovery is intended to produce. First, changes in the level and distribution of income over the past two decades are reviewed to provide a context for the likely effects of the Reagan administration's policy actions. Economic growth has been the primary determinant of rising standards of living during the past twenty years; both it and the expansion of income transfer programs have reduced the proportion of the population living in poverty. However, because of major changes in the demographic composition of the lower-income population, the poor cannot be expected to benefit as much from economic growth in the future as they have in the past.

Second, the reductions in social programs and personal income taxes proposed by the Reagan administration and enacted by Congress are briefly reviewed. The majority of the program reductions are in benefit payments to individuals and grants to state and local governments which, along with the tax cuts, will have a direct impact on the economic status of families and individuals. The nature of the program and tax cuts suggests that the lower-income population, particularly those with a strong attachment to the labor force, will fare least well from the more immediate effects of the policy changes, while those with higher incomes will gain most.

The third section of this chapter reports on quantitative analyses of the effects of the tax cuts and benefit reductions in selected income transfer programs which confirm the hypothesis just stated. Also discussed is the importance of responses to the policy changes by individuals, state and local governments, and charitable organizations and how these responses might influence ultimate outcomes. Finally, the role future economic growth might play in ameliorating the impact of these program and tax changes is considered. Under assumptions of growth slightly more optimistic than the administration's January 1982 projections, the purchasing power of the average family will be 6 percent higher in 1984 than in 1980. However, if economic growth is more modest, the average family's purchasing power will be no higher in 1984 than it was in 1980. Although the gains due to high economic growth accrue to families in all income classes, including the poor, increased earnings are not likely to offset the negative consequences of program changes for some families, particularly many AFDC recipients with earned incomes.

The chapter concludes by noting that the long-run consequences of the administration's domestic program depend importantly on how much economic growth occurs by 1984 and beyond, and how the gains from that growth are shared among the population.

Recent Trends in Living Standards and Income Distribution

Economic growth has always been an important determinant of family well-being. The economy grew steadily from the early 1960s to the early 1970s, and the living standard of the typical family rose substantially while the proportion of the population with incomes below the official poverty line declined almost by half. During the 1970s, however, average living standards increased only slightly while the proportion of the population in poverty remained roughly constant. These broad trends in income were the consequence of several more specific factors, of which three were most important. First, two-parent family income gains generally mirrored the overall performance of the economy, rising rapidly with the sustained economic growth from the early 1960s into the early 1970s and stagnating thereafter as the economy experienced periods of simultaneous high unemployment and high inflation. Second, the number of families headed by single women, often with low incomes, rose dramatically. And third, public transfers grew rapidly, raising many people—especially the elderly—out of poverty.

However, official statistics on the shape of the income distribution remained deceptively constant in the 1960s and 1970s. Female-headed families merely took the place of many male-headed and aged families in the bottom fifth of the income distribution. Also, much of the increase of government transfers in this period was for in-kind benefits, such as Food Stamps and Medicaid, that are not counted in the official income statistics. If these are counted as income, the degree of income inequality and the size of the poverty population both are reduced more, especially during the 1970s.

Changes in Incomes

Government statistics on family income refer to before-tax income and exclude the value of in-kind benefits. Between 1960 and 1970 median family income (corrected for inflation) rose by 34 percent (table 16-1). This large increase contrasts sharply with the 1970 to 1979 period during which real median income rose by less than 7 percent. The distribution of family income over the two decades showed little change. The share of total family income received by each one-fifth of families in 1979 was within one percentage point of its share in 1960.

In a rough sense, the proportion of the population in poverty is equivalent to the lower tail of the income distribution, but the two concepts differ in several respects. The poverty count is based on all persons, including those who live alone, while the income distribution statistics refer to families. In addition, the poverty standard against which a family's income is measured depends on family size. This means that some large families not in the lowest quintile will be counted as poor while some small families who are in the lowest quintile will not. Most important, poverty standards are adjusted for inflation but not for changes in real standards of living, so the official poverty standard is an absolute concept. As a result, the proportion of families in poverty tends to shrink during a period of economic growth while the proportion of families in the lowest quintile remains constant by definition.

Since real dollar incomes rose rapidly in the 1960s and modestly in the 1970s, the poverty standard for an urban family of four fell from 54 percent of median family income in 1960 to 40 percent in 1970 and 38 percent in 1979. The proportion of the population below the poverty line fell from 22.4 percent in 1960 to 12.6 percent in 1970 but declined only one additional percentage point, to 11.6 percent, by 1979.

Together, these statistics support the simple explanation that absolute standards of living rose rapidly in the 1960s and were stagnant in the 1970s due primarily to overall economic conditions. But, as shown by the following statistics, the influence of demographic factors—especially changes in family structure—were also important in determining these changes in median family income.

Historical information on the distribution of families, classified by the characteristics of the head and, where applicable, the labor force status of the wife, are shown in table 16-2. There was a sharp increase from 1960 to 1979 in the proportion of families headed by a nonaged female (from 7 to 12 percent) and an equally sharp increase in the proportion of two-parent, two-earner families (from 30 to 39 percent).

An example of the impact of these demographic changes on median income statistics is illustrated in table 16-3 by the comparison of black and white family incomes over the 1970s. The aggregate statistics suggest that black families lost ground over the decade, not only relative to white families but in absolute terms as well. Median family income for whites increased by over $1,200 while median family income for blacks declined by $93. How-

TABLE 16–1

THE DISTRIBUTION OF FAMILY INCOME FOR 1960, 1970, AND 1979

(In 1979 $)

Income Divisions	1960 Share of Total Family Income (%)	1960 Income Level at Upper End of Quintile ($)	1970 Share of Total Family Income (%)	1970 Income Level at Upper End of Quintile ($)	1979 Share of Total Family Income (%)	1979 Income Level at Upper End of Quintile ($)
1st quintile	4.8	6,823	5.4	9,533	5.3	9,830
2nd quintile	12.2	11,765	12.2	15,553	11.6	16,220
3rd quintile	17.8	15,598	17.6	21,121	17.5	22,985
4th quintile	24.0	21,568	23.8	29,032	24.1	31,590
5th quintile	41.3	—	40.9	—	41.6	—
Top 5 percent	15.9	33,176[a]	15.6	45,331[a]	15.7	50,286[a]
Addendum						
Median family income		13,744		18,444		19,661

SOURCE: Bureau of the Census, *Current Population Reports,* Series P-60 (Washington, D.C.: GPO).

a. This is the lower income bound for the top 5 percent.

TABLE 16–2

DISTRIBUTION OF FAMILIES BY TYPE,
1960–1979

Family Type	Percentage of All Families		
	1960	1970	1979
Male or female head over 65	13	14	15
Female head under 65	7	9	12
Male head under 65 with nonworking wife	47	42	31
Male head under 65 with wife in the paid labor force	30	31	39
All others[a]	3	3	2
Total	100	100	100

SOURCE: *Current Population Reports*, various issues.
NOTE: In this and subsequent tables in this chapter, totals may not add due to rounding.
a. Includes, in particular, families headed by an unmarried male under age 65.

TABLE 16–3

SELECTED STATISTICS ON MEDIAN FAMILY INCOMES
(In 1979 $)

Family Type	Median Family Income		Annual Growth Rate (%)
	1970 ($)	1979 ($)	
All white families	19,255	20,502	0.7
All white male-headed families	20,122	21,824	0.9
All white female-headed families	10,760	11,452	0.6
All black families	11,737	11,644	–0.1
All black male-headed families	14,610	16,887	1.6
All black female-headed families	6,685	6,906	0.4
All families	18,444	19,661	0.7

SOURCE: *Current Population Reports*, various issues.

ever, the disaggregated data indicate that the median income for both male-headed and female-headed black families actually rose over the period—the former almost twice as fast as for white male-headed families. But the income of black female-headed families started from a much lower level and rose only modestly. Thus, the overall decline in black median family income was caused by a shift in family structure toward female-headed families rather than a reduction of incomes to male- and female-headed families per se.[1]

The large increase in government benefit programs has also worked in combination with demographic shifts to substantially change the nature of the poverty population. Throughout the 1970s, incomes of the elderly gained from increases in Social Security benefits and from the replacement of the state-run income support program for the elderly by the federal Supplemental Security Income (SSI) program. The impact was dramatic. Real median income for all families rose in the 1970s at an average rate of 0.7 percent per year. By contrast, the median income of households headed by someone aged sixty-five or more rose by 2.1 percent per year. The substantial increase in income transfers improved the position of the elderly in the overall income distribution and, in particular, sharply reduced the chances that an elderly family would have an income below the poverty line. The proportion of elderly who were poor declined from 25 percent in 1970 to 15 percent in 1979 (table 16-4).

Despite this improvement in incomes of the older population, the proportion of the entire U.S. population in poverty remained stable because, while elderly families were leaving poverty, newly formed female-headed households were entering. In 1960 roughly two-thirds of the poverty population lived in households headed by a man less than sixty-five years old. The economic expansion of the 1960s reduced the poverty population largely by increasing the incomes of these nonaged, male-headed families. By 1970 a slowly growing number of poor female-headed households comprised a rapidly growing share of a declining poverty population. Between 1970 and 1979 a more rapid increase in female-headed households combined with the increase in elderly incomes caused the composition of the poverty population

TABLE 16–4

STATISTICS ON THE POVERTY POPULATION FOR 1960, 1970, AND 1979
(Percentage)

Poverty Measure	1960	1970	1979
Proportion of the total population in poverty	22.4	12.6	11.6
Composition of the poverty population			
Household head 65 or over	13.8	18.5	14.1
Female household head less than 65	21.2	28.4	43.7
Male household head less than 65	65.0	53.9	42.2
Total	100.0	99.8	100.0
Incidence of poverty by household type[a]			
Household head 65 or over	35.2	24.5	15.1
Female household head less than 65	50.0	37.4	33.3
Male household head less than 65	17.8	7.6	6.6

SOURCE: *Current Population Reports*, various editions.
  a. Incidence refers to the proportion of a group who are poor.

to change further but left the size relatively constant. By 1979 the proportion of the poverty population living in female-headed households had risen to 44 percent, more than double their representation in 1960.

The figures cited above have been pretax money income, the measure used in official government statistics. A more complete measure of income, adjusted for in-kind benefits and taxes paid, would have produced somewhat different results. Examining after-tax income, rather than pretax income, would have produced somewhat lower rates of income growth (particularly over the 1970s) and would have resulted in a slightly more equal distribution of income. Counting Food Stamps, the insurance value of Medicaid and Medicare, and other similar in-kind benefits in income statistics would have substantially increased the incomes of persons at the low end of the income distribution. One recent study indicates that when these benefits are treated as income, the proportion of the population in poverty in the late 1970s falls from its official value of 11 to 12 percent to a range of 6 to 9 percent.[2]

The Effects of Rising Transfers

These recent trends are both heartening and disturbing. They suggest that over the 1970s the country made continued progress in raising living standards of the poorest families. But these increased living standards have come about through increased government benefits rather than increased self-sufficiency on the part of low-income individuals. More generally, the late 1960s and 1970s contain two major trends: a rapid growth of government benefit programs and a rapid growth in the population dependent on government benefits for their incomes. The simultaneous occurrence of these trends raises serious questions about the effects of these growing public transfers. Do they make work less attractive for some families? Do they encourage formation of particular kinds of families which are prone to dependence, such as female-headed households? Do they displace private means of support such as charity?

The first question has received the most analytical attention. The evidence indicates that the answer is generally affirmative; the expansion of government benefit programs has caused a modest reduction of work effort in the population—about 5 percent according to the most recent study reviewing the relevant literature on this issue.[3] However, the degree of this work reduction varies considerably across different age groups and family types, with those workers having the closest attachment to the labor force (such as prime age males) exhibiting the least sensitivity to transfer payments, and those having less labor force attachment (such as female heads of families and those near retirement or with physical ailments) exhibiting the most. For example, evidence indicates that allowing partial Social Security benefits to be paid upon retirement before age 65 was an important cause of the rapid decline in the labor force participation of men sixty to sixty-five years of age. Extended unemployment benefits and liberalizations in the federal disability insurance program have had similar effects on other groups.

Public transfer programs may have contributed modestly to the increasing number of female-headed households. This can occur in two ways. First, the availability of benefits could reduce the cost of separation and divorce for a woman and so facilitate marital break-up. Second, once a family is receiving benefits the level of benefits could inhibit remarriage. Empirical studies provide mixed support for the family break-up theory and somewhat firmer support for a modest inhibition of remarriage.[4] Few studies have examined why large numbers of elderly no longer live with their children in extended family situations, but most researchers would agree that the increase in Social Security and SSI benefits has been a contributing factor.

The third issue—the effect of government programs on private support mechanisms—has been widely discussed but has received little empirical attention.[5] However, what evidence there is—some of which is presented in chapter 7—does not suggest that government programs have significantly displaced private charity.

One can conclude from a review of the evidence on all three of these issues, then, that increased government benefits probably have increased the dependence on transfer programs slightly. But, at the same time, the programs have resulted in sizable net increases in the incomes of the recipients.

Some Implications

This review provides a context for the examination of the effects of President Reagan's policies on income and its distribution in two respects. First, the administration argues that high tax rates and increased transfers have led to a reduction in work effort by families at both ends of the income distribution, but that the administration's policies will reverse this trend. The evidence suggests that a significant increase in transfers to individuals over the past ten to fifteen years has led to only modest declines in work effort; thus a reduction in these programs will not lead to a major increase in earnings for low-income families. Similarly, a review of the literature in chapter 3 on the effect of income tax rates on work effort concludes that the work response of prime age males is fairly insensitive to changes in tax rates (though the decision to retire may be affected). The work effort of wives may be affected more, but the response cannot be very large given the dramatic increase in the number of working wives during the 1970s in the face of rising real tax rates. Thus the reduction in marginal income tax rates is not likely to have a significant effect on the earnings of families, though the tax deduction for the second family earner enacted in 1981 could have a modest effect on the work effort of married women.

Second, the administration's policy changes are intended to produce a healthy economy, benefiting families in all income classes. The evidence cited for the 1960s, when the economy was relatively prosperous, suggests that real economic growth does raise the entire income distribution. On the other hand, the changing composition of low-income households in the 1970s toward those with less earning potential suggests that economic growth in the 1980s will have less effect on the earnings of low-income households then it did during the 1960s because of the large decline of nonaged, male-headed families among this group.[6]

Policy Changes

The program and budget changes enacted by Congress in 1981 and those proposed in the president's 1983 budget are detailed in earlier chapters. This section summarizes these changes, focusing on those that will directly affect the economic status of individuals and families, and discusses their rationale.

Major Domestic Policy Changes

Probably the most significant changes enacted in 1981 involved the tax system. Personal income tax rates were lowered in three steps beginning in 1981 with a cumulative reduction of 23 percent by 1984. Rates on unearned income were reduced from 70 percent to 50 percent beginning in 1982—thereby decreasing the maximum tax on capital gains from 28 to 20 percent. Business taxes were reduced, primarily by allowing more rapid depreciation of plant and equipment, and estate, gift, and excise taxes were cut back as well.[7]

Reductions in expenditures were enacted in 1981 for most domestic programs. As documented in chapter 3, the largest percentage cuts were in discretionary grants to state and local governments. These account for over one-quarter of the $31.6 billion in total reductions in domestic programs in FY 1982 and a growing share in succeeding years. Most of these state and local grants have been used to provide employment, education, training, health, or social services to individuals and families. Of the projected savings in these grants of $14 billion in FY 1984, the largest reductions were for employment and training, compensatory education, urban mass transit, and

Environmental Protection Agency construction grants. About $8 billion of this $14 billion reduction occurred in programs heavily targeted on low-income individuals, and another $2 billion was in programs moderately targeted on this population.[8]

Nearly half of the cuts in expenditures for domestic programs were in direct benefit payments for individuals and families. Changes enacted in 1981 are estimated to reduce federal expenditures for such cash and in-kind benefits by $15.8 billion annually by FY 1984. This represents on average a 4 percent reduction from the expenditure levels implied by prior policy. However, the degree of reductions varied considerably from program to program. The largest percentage cuts were in programs targeted on the low-income population. In percentage terms, these cuts were two and one-half times larger than those in the other programs (table 16-5). Among the low-income assistance programs, nearly 60 percent of the dollar savings come from three areas—Food Stamps, child nutrition programs, and Aid to Families with Dependent Chil-

TABLE 16–5

ESTIMATED REDUCTIONS IN FY 1984 OUTLAYS FOR PAYMENTS TO INDIVIDUALS AND FAMILIES RESULTING FROM 1981 CONGRESSIONAL ACTIONS

Program, By Type	FY 1984 Baseline Outlays (In $ billions)	Change In 1984 Outlays	
		(In $ billions)	(%)
Social insurance and others			
Social Security (OASDI)	189.5	− 3.7	− 2.0
Unemployment compensation	23.3	− 2.4	− 10.3
Trade adjustment assistance	0.7	− 0.5	− 71.4
Medicare	67.7	− 1.0	− 1.5
Guaranteed student loans	4.9	− 0.8	− 16.3
Subtotal	286.0	− 8.4	− 2.9
Low-income assistance			
Food Stamps	14.6	− 1.6	− 11.0
Child nutrition programs	5.0	− 1.4	− 28.0
AFDC	9.8	− 1.3	− 13.3
Student financial aid	4.8	− 1.2	− 25.0
Medicaid	22.9	− 1.0	− 4.4
Low-income energy assistance	2.9	− 0.8	− 27.6
Housing assistance	11.5	− 0.3	− 2.6
Veterans income security	15.4	− 0.1	− 0.6
Supplemental Security Income	8.0	0.3	3.8
Subtotal	94.9	− 7.4	− 7.8
Total	381.0	−15.8	− 4.1

SOURCE: Authors' estimates based on methodology described in chapter 3.

dren (AFDC). The reductions in social insurance and other programs also will affect households below the median income level more than those above, since two of the major savings come from eliminating the minimum benefit for future Social Security retirees and curtailing extended unemployment insurance benefits.

The remaining domestic budget reductions occurred in other federal operations, ranging from environmental protection to law enforcement, whose benefits rarely can be traced to specific individuals.

The administration's 1983 budget proposals called for even larger domestic program reductions than those enacted by Congress in 1981. Their distribution across programs is roughly similar to the prior year's, with the greatest reductions in benefit programs for individuals and deep cuts once again in discretionary grants to state and local governments.

The Rationale

Any administration's policies involve a reconciliation of diverse points of view. Nonetheless, there are some common philosophical beliefs underlying these policy shifts. One of these beliefs is that government benefit and tax policies have evolved in ways that discourage work effort, particularly of the poor and the rich. It is argued that at the low end of the distribution the increasing availability of benefits has made unemployment attractive vis-a-vis low-wage work; in higher ranges of the distribution, high marginal tax rates have reduced take-home wages to the point where individuals have little reason to choose additional earnings over more leisure.

Taken by itself, this view suggests a simple remedial policy: lower marginal income tax rates and reduce benefit programs. Across-the-board cuts in benefit programs, however, conflict with the administration's desire to provide a safety net for those recipients who could not be expected to work, the truly needy. Thus, program expenditure cuts were generally achieved by reducing benefits for actual or potential recipients with earned incomes. Typically these reductions take the form of tightened eligibility criteria that sharply increase the rate at which benefits will be reduced as earnings increase. Thus, basic benefits were maintained in both the AFDC and Food Stamp programs, but benefit reduction rates were increased, thereby reducing income eligibility levels. Benefit reduction rates were also increased for housing assistance and child nutrition programs and were reinstated for guaranteed student loans.

It has been pointed out by critics of the administration that these higher "tax rates" on the earnings of welfare recipients are inconsistent with the administration's policy at the upper end of the income distribution. There, income tax rates were reduced to further reward and stimulate productive economic activity. However, the administration's apparent view is that work among potential welfare recipients is best encouraged by tightening eligibility or through regulation. Thus, stiffer work requirements were proposed for those receiving benefits. States were encouraged to begin workfare programs requiring beneficiaries to "work off" their benefits at the equivalent of minimum wages. The administration has proposed that workfare be required in all states in 1983, and that the unemployed receiving extended unemployment benefits must accept any job paying the minimum wage or better, rather than a "suitable" job.

Three other factors undoubtedly came into play in the selection of program changes. The first is simply that if sizable reductions in domestic programs are required, there is little choice but to cut substantially those programs providing benefits to individuals, either directly by the federal government or indirectly through state and local governments. This is because they constitute such a large share of all domestic program outlays. Second, an argument for reducing eligibility levels rather than basic benefits is that income-tested programs provided assistance to some families who were not truly needy or poor, as well as raising the incomes of some poor families considerably above the poverty line.[9] A final factor in determining which programs were cut and by how much was the political clout of the beneficiaries. The small reductions in programs for older people and for veterans are surely cases in point.

These conditions have led to the biggest reductions being proposed and enacted in programs for the nonaged, low-income population. And the choice of which of these programs to reduce and how to reduce them will probably have the greatest effect on incomes of working poor and near-poor families.

Effects on Economic Well-being

Some important immediate consequences of the administration's policy changes on the economic status of households can be captured by examining the incidence of the tax and benefit reductions. Ultimate impacts are much more difficult to predict. This is because they will depend not only on the tax and benefit changes but also on changing economic conditions and the responses of individuals, state and local governments, and charitable organizations to the policy shifts. This section first discusses these issues and then presents some analysis of the effects on household incomes of the changes in income taxes and selected transfer programs. Both immediate impacts and those possible by 1984 under two different economic growth scenarios are considered.

General Issues and Evidence

A current preoccupation of the media is to highlight those families adversely affected by the program cuts. This is only one part of the broader question of who are the immediate gainers and losers from the policy changes, and by how much do they gain or lose. These questions are quantitatively addressed for some programs later in this section.

To fully address the effects of the policy changes in the longer run, at least four questions must be answered. One, will President Reagan's Program for Economic Recovery result in a stronger economy and higher overall incomes than otherwise would have been the case? Two, how will the gains due to economic growth be distributed across households at different income levels? Three, what will be the ultimate magnitude and distribution of the changes in total public spending and taxes? And four, will increases in earnings due to economic growth and other private sector responses compensate for the immediate losses experienced by households adversely affected by domestic program cuts? How much economic growth might result from the administration's policy changes is unknown at present (see chapters 2 and 4 for a discussion of this issue). Answers to the remaining questions depend importantly on behavioral responses to the policy changes by individuals, state and local governments, and charitable organizations.

The administration expects that reduced marginal income tax rates and reduced income-tested benefits to individuals will stimulate increased work effort. The evidence cited earlier suggests that this response will be relatively small. Less is known about the likely response of state and local governments and nonprofit organizations to the administration's changes in domestic policies. Two types of responses are of particular interest. First, will the reductions in federal grants be partially offset by increased state and local governmental and charitable expenditures? Or, will the financial conditions of these entities result in reductions in expenditures from their own revenue sources, thus exacerbating the effects of the reductions in federal funds? Second, how will states, localities, and nonprofit organizations distribute more limited resources to potential recipients? Will they target the services more on those with the very lowest incomes, thereby denying services to those most affected by the cuts in federal benefit programs, or will the reductions in services be across-the-board?

Information from a detailed survey and analysis of a sample of states is reported in chapter 6. It indicates that states by and large are not moving to replace large portions of the reduced federal grant funds with their own revenues. Many states still have not formulated their full response to the 1982 federal budget reductions, let alone the additional ones that will result from congressional action on the 1983 budget. However, as a result of their own recent tax relief and spending limitation programs and the poor performance of the economy, few states appear likely in the foreseeable future to be able to compensate more than very partially for the loss in federal funds.

It was noted earlier that the federal budget reductions in income-tested transfer programs primarily affect the less poor recipients. States have not generally taken steps to alter this distributional impact of the reductions in entitlement programs. Less can be said about the targeting practices of states and localities in response to the more limited discretionary program funds. As noted earlier, the federal budget reductions in this area are concentrated in programs primarily serving the low-income population. However, particularly in light of the increased flexibility they are being given for the expenditure of federal funds, states and localities can shift remaining program funds to favor different groups within the low-income population. It is too soon yet to determine how much this will occur.

The administration has argued that the private sector will fill some of the gap in needs being created by the withdrawal of the federal government. The major actor in any such private sector response would be charitable organizations within the nonprofit sector. The impacts of the administration's overall Program for Economic Recovery on this sector are analyzed in chapter 7. There it is argued that nonprofit organizations not only are unlikely to be able to compensate much for the general reduction in federal funds for social welfare purposes, but that they will have to struggle greatly just to prevent a decline in the scope of their own activities. This is because the very federal grants that are being reduced are their primary source of financial support and the change in tax laws is likely to have an adverse impact on their private revenue sources.

Finally, existing evidence is inadequate for assessing either the short-run or long-run effects of some policy changes because the beneficiaries of certain policies are largely unknown. For example, actions taken by Congress in 1981 will reduce business taxes far more than benefit programs for individuals, yet the ultimate distribution of this tax cut among income classes is not known. While stockholders are more concentrated in the higher income brackets, some of the gains may also be passed on to consumers through lower prices, or to workers via higher wages. Estate and gift taxes were also reduced substantially, and although these gains will accrue more to higher than to lower-income households, the income levels of recipients of gifts and inheritances are not known.

Given all the important unknowns, any analysis of the effects of federal policy changes under the Reagan administration on the income and broader economic status of families and individuals must be regarded as preliminary and partial. However, the more general information discussed can be supplemented with more precise estimates of the magnitude and distribution of the income effects of the changes in personal income taxes and certain transfer programs.

Static Analyses

Two studies are reported here which have analyzed the distributional implications of the federal policy changes in taxes and transfers. The first, performed by the Congressional Budget Office (CBO), broadly examines a large number of policy changes. The second, performed by the authors, is a more detailed analysis of a selective set of policy changes.

CBO Study. CBO estimated the effect on household income by income class of the changes in federal personal income taxes and virtually all cash and in-kind transfer programs enacted in 1981 (table 16-6). According to this analysis, by 1984 households on average can expect to gain over $1,000 in income and benefits after taxes. The average household will lose $200 in transfers but gain $1,280 from the tax cut.

This gain is not evenly distributed across income classes, however. Households under $10,000 actually lose income on average because the benefit reductions more than offset the tax reduction. At the other extreme, households with very high incomes lose only negligible amounts of transfer benefits and gain significantly from the tax cuts. Gains are more modest in the other income classes, and grow as a percentage of income as income rises.

While this analysis is helpful to understanding the effects of the 1981 federal tax and transfer program changes on different income groups, it has

TABLE 16–6

CHANGE IN HOUSEHOLD INCOME DISTRIBUTED BY TYPE OF POLICY CHANGE, BY INCOME CLASS, CY 1984

Income Class (In 1982 $)	Federal Income Taxes ($)	Cash Transfers ($)	In-Kind Transfers ($)	Total ($)	Change In Cash Income[a] (%)
Below 10,000	170	−290	−100	− 220	−1.2
10,000–20,000	590	−130	− 90	370	1.9
20,000–40,000	1,280	− 70	− 50	1,160	3.8
40,000–80,000	2,520	− 50	− 70	2,400	5.6
Over 80,000	19,350	− 70	− 50	19,230	7.9
Average	1,280	−130	− 70	1,080	3.9

SOURCE: Congressional Budget Office, "Effects of Tax and Benefit Reductions Enacted in 1981 For Households in Different Income Categories," Special Study, February 1982, tables 11 and 12.

a. Excludes the change in benefits in-kind because they are not included in the income base.

two major limitations. First, the analysis was largely conducted by using aggregate models to estimate total changes in revenues and outlays by program and then allocating those changes across broad income classes according to what is generally known about the distribution of program benefits and taxes. This method yields less accurate estimates than using data on individual households and program rules and then aggregating across households. Furthermore, it does not permit analysis of the effects of the policy changes on particular population groups.

The second major limitation of the CBO estimates is that the changes in personal income taxes might be considered misleading because they were measured by comparing the new law with tax burdens that would have occurred had there been no change in the 1980 tax laws through 1984. This is not necessarily the most appropriate comparison since bracket creep due to inflation and real income growth would have pushed tax revenues to extremely high levels by 1984, and further increased progressivity of the tax system. Taxes would almost certainly have been cut by Congress under any president. How they would have been cut is unknown, however, and deciding on a proper reference point for measuring the effects of the Reagan tax changes is problematic.

Urban Institute Study. Because of these limitations in the CBO study, we conducted our own analysis of the tax changes and a limited set of program changes using data on individuals and families from the March 1980 Current Population Survey (CPS). These data were combined with a computer program developed and refined over the past decade and embodying detailed parameters of tax and transfer programs and appropriate assumptions about participation of eligible families in the AFDC and Food Stamp programs.[10] This permits a simulation of the policy changes on individuals and families, given their particular characteristics, and then aggregation of these effects over certain population groups.

The issue of an appropriate reference point for measuring the effects of the tax changes was addressed first. Estimates were first made of the effects on household incomes of the change in personal income taxes using two different reference points for measuring the change. The first reference point, like the CBO study, assumes no change in the tax structure through 1984; the second holds constant from 1980 through 1984 the tax burden faced by households at given levels of income after adjusting for inflation.[11]

As might be expected, the measured effects of the 1981 personal income tax changes are quite different between the two reference points. This is true both for the average effects and for their distribution across income classes (see table 16-7). Assuming no change in the pre-Reagan tax structure through 1984, income taxes for the average household are reduced by the 1981 tax

TABLE 16-7

EFFECT OF ECONOMIC RECOVERY TAX ACT (ERTA) ON TAXES PAID BY HOUSEHOLDS IN 1984, BY INCOME CLASS, UNDER TWO
ALTERNATIVE MEASURES
(In 1980 $)

Income Class[a] ($)	(1) Taxes Paid if No Change in Old Law ($)	(2) Tax Reduction Measured Relative to No Change in Pre-ERTA Law / Tax Reduction Under ERTA ($)	(3) (2) as Percentage of (1)	(4) Tax Reduction Measured Relative to Constant Real Tax Burden, 1980–1984 / Taxes Paid if Real Tax Burden Constant ($)	(5) Tax Reduction Under ERTA ($)	(6) (5) as Percentage of (4)
Household Average	3,924	−1,155	−29.4	3,244	−476	−14.7
Below 11,350	412	−129	−31.3	260	0	0.0
11,350–22,700	3,061	−899	−29.4	2,335	−331	−14.2
22,700–34,050	7,723	−2,284	−29.6	5,849	−831	−14.2
34,050–45,400	14,689	−4,335	−29.5	11,299	−1,802	−15.9
45,400–56,750	21,024	−6,117	−29.1	16,964	−2,939	−17.3
Over 56,750[b]	36,858	−10,064	−27.3	29,984	−5,361	−17.9

SOURCE: Urban Institute TRIM2 simulations.
a. Income is net after federal income taxes, FICA taxes, cash transfers, and Food Stamps.
b. Earned incomes are capped at about $57,000 ($50,000 in 1979 dollars) for each individual earner in the household.

changes by 29 percent.[12] However, compared to a base of constant real tax burdens through 1984, the Reagan income tax changes reduce these taxes for the average household by only 15 percent. All income classes receive about the same percentage reduction in taxes when compared to the old law. The second reference point, however, demonstrates that by the time it is fully implemented in 1984, the 1981 tax cut will not reduce the real tax burden of the average lower-income household from its 1980 level. (This is because the standard deduction, personal exemptions, and provisions of the earned income tax credit, which benefit only low-income households, were unchanged through 1984. With prices assumed to rise by 34 percent from 1980 to 1984, this inevitably will lead to higher real tax burdens for many low-income households with constant real income levels despite the rate cuts.) On the other hand, real tax burdens are reduced for all other income classes, in a mildly regressive pattern.

The second measure is used in the remaining analysis for two reasons. First, the assumption of constant real taxes is neutral and avoids the obvious bias of the unrealistic assumption that the tax structure would have remained unchanged through 1984. More importantly, this measure is probably the most meaningful for the majority of taxpayers because it indicates whether those with the same real incomes will be paying more or less taxes in 1984 than in 1980.

The combined effect of the personal income tax reductions and cuts in AFDC and Food Stamp benefits are shown in table 16-8 for families and unrelated individuals (hereafter referred to simply as families). Families, on average, realize a small gain in income after taxes and transfers of about 3 percent. Low-income families are estimated to experience a small decline in income since they pay slightly more taxes and lose some AFDC and Food Stamp benefits. As income rises the benefit losses are dominated by the tax reductions. The higher a family's income the greater is its percentage increase in after-tax income due to the tax cut. Thus the general picture that emerges from this analysis is similar to that of the CBO analysis, despite the differing methods employed, though the magnitudes of the effects are different.

The results indicate the effects on typical families at various income levels. However, they mask considerable variation in the effects of the policy changes on low-income families. Some have little or no earned income and are unaffected by the tax changes, and others receive no AFDC or Food Stamp benefits and are therefore unaffected by the cuts in these programs. Table 16-9 shows data similar to table 16-8, but only for families who would have received AFDC benefits sometime during the year in the absence of the program changes and whose incomes after taxes and transfers are estimated to be below twice the poverty threshold. Two-fifths of these families have

TABLE 16–8

EFFECT OF 1981 CHANGES IN PERSONAL INCOME TAXES, AFDC, AND FOOD STAMPS
ON THE INCOMES OF FAMILIES BY INCOME CLASS
(In 1980 $)

Income Class[a] ($)	Number of Families[b] (1,000)	Changes in Family Income Due to Changes in				
		Taxes ($)	AFDC ($)	FS ($)	Total ($)	Total (%)
Below 3,750	6,207	−6	−3	−2	−11	−0.5
3,750– 7,500	13,803	−21	−12	−3	−36	−0.6
7,500–11,250	13,736	40	−15	−7	18	0.2
11,250–15,000	12,521	188	−9	−3	176	1.3
15,000–18,750	11,184	366	−2	−1	364	2.2
18,750–26,250	17,003	549	0	0	549	2.5
26,250–37,500	11,198	1,088	0	0	1,088	3.5
37,500–52,500	4,236	2,277	0	0	2,277	5.3
Over 52,500[c]	822	4,694	0	0	4,694	7.4
Average	90,711	460	−7	−2	451	2.7

SOURCE: Urban Institute TRIM2 simulations.

   a.   Income is net after federal income taxes, FICA taxes, cash transfers, and Food Stamps.

   b.   The numbers include both families and unrelated individuals.

   c.   Earned incomes are capped at about $57,000 ($50,000 in 1979 dollars) for each individual earner in the household. Thus average income from all sources less taxes and transfers for this group is $63,758.

no earnings and are thus unaffected by the changes in either taxes or the AFDC and Food Stamp programs.[13] Most of the AFDC families with earnings lose AFDC and Food Stamp benefits, and many pay more personal income taxes.

Among families with earnings, those with the highest incomes and smallest AFDC payments lose the largest amount of benefits. For example, families with incomes between 1.25 and 2.00 times the poverty line lose from $300 to $375 in AFDC benefits, while payments to those below the poverty line are reduced by about $150. This, of course, is a result of how the AFDC program was changed—by increasing the benefit reduction rate, or the "tax" on earnings, while retaining the basic benefit. The pattern is similar for Food Stamps, although the decreases are much smaller.

Tax burdens increase the most for near-poor families with incomes below 150 percent of the poverty level. As family income approaches twice the poverty level, rate reductions more than offset the real tax increases caused by the lack of inflation-adjustment of the earned income tax credit, personal exemptions, and standard deduction; and families realize lower real tax burdens. Thus the largest relative declines in income resulting from the combined

TABLE 16–9

EFFECT OF 1981 CHANGES IN INCOME TAXES, AFDC, AND FOOD STAMPS ON AFDC FAMILIES, BY POVERTY LEVEL
(In 1980 $)

Earnings and Poverty Level (PL)ᵃ Status	Average Income ($)	Number of Families (1,000)	Pre-Reagan AFDC & FS Benefits ($)	Change in Benefits		Total Change in Benefits (%)	Change in Income Due to Taxes ($)	Change in Income Due to Both Taxes and Benefits	
				AFDC ($)	FS ($)			($)	(%)
No earningsᵇ	5,406	1,372	4,324	0	0	0.0	0	0	0.0
Some earnings									
Below 1.00 PL	5,449	897	2,622	–153	–6	–6.1	–41	–200	–3.7
1.00–1.25 PL	8,648	430	3,257	–263	–24	–8.8	–113	–400	–4.6
1.25–1.50 PL	10,074	307	2,887	–372	–32	–14.0	–148	–551	–5.5
1.50–1.75 PL	11,937	216	2,446	–301	–29	–13.5	–96	–426	–3.6
1.75–2.00 PL	13,506	149	1,975	–315	–15	–16.7	18	–312	–2.3

SOURCE: Urban Institute TRIM2 simulations.

a. The urban poverty level for a "typical" AFDC family—a mother and two children—was about $8,350. For a mother and three children it was about $6,600 in 1980.

b. All families below twice the poverty line.

effects of the tax, AFDC, and Food Stamp changes are for working AFDC families with incomes just above the poverty level. Their incomes after taxes and transfers decline by as much as $550, or 5.5 percent. Poor families with earnings lose less—$200 or 3.7 percent of their incomes on average—due to the policy changes.

Conclusions. The results of the CBO and Urban Institute analyses of effects of the changes in taxes and selected transfer policies enacted in 1981 can be summarized as follows. The broad middle class will realize modest reductions by 1984 in their real tax burdens, resulting in a small increase in their after-tax real incomes. Substantial gains will accrue to higher-income families, while the 46 million families with incomes below $15,000, in the aggregate, will have no significant change in their real after-tax income. However, this latter result masks the consequences of the policy changes for those families most adversely affected, namely the 2 million AFDC families with some earnings and with incomes below 1.75 times the poverty line. As a group, their real income levels will decline over 4 percent, with the greatest relative losses accruing to those with incomes just above the poverty line.

These are not large changes in income for most groups, though a 4 to 5 percent loss in real income by poor and near-poor AFDC recipients will surely be felt, and the annual gain of those in the highest income bracket is substantial. The direct short-run effects of the policy changes are to the advantage of the rich and to the disadvantage of the poor (more so than these analyses have shown because many reductions in benefits for low-income families are excluded) and have modestly benefited the middle class.

The Effects of Economic Growth

The administration's initial claims for its own economic program—almost immediate and sustained economic growth—were not realized. Rather, the economy fell back into a recession in mid-1981, with a recovery of uncertain strength and duration apparently beginning in mid-1982. Most observers would now agree that the feasible options from mid-1982 through 1984 are bounded on the up side by continuous but unspectacular economic growth, and on the down side by a stop and start growth path that will be hard pressed to raise real income levels above their 1980 levels.

The static analysis just reported did not consider any possible effects of different rates of economic growth on the level and distribution of family incomes. This is now done. The examination explores the implications of different rates of economic growth by using the January 1982 CBO high and low economic projections through 1984. The most optimistic projection—the "high growth path"—assumes that the unemployment rate rises from 7.1 percent in 1980 to a peak of about 9 percent in 1982 and then declines to 6.6

percent in 1984. Aggregate real wages are assumed to rise by 8.1 percent from 1980 to 1984. Given the economic conditions prevailing through mid-1982, these projections are very optimistic. The pessimistic economic projection—CBO's low growth path—assumes that the unemployment rate will be 8.4 percent in 1984 and real aggregate wages will rise by only 1.7 percent from 1980 to 1984.[14] The estimates that follow are based on the 1980 Current Population Survey aged to 1984 under these two growth scenarios.

Effects on All Families. Whether high or low economic growth is attained will have a considerable effect on the average income of families and individuals in 1984. As shown in table 16-10, real earnings are estimated to be 2 percent less in 1984 than in 1980 if low growth occurs, but 6.5 percent more if high growth is achieved.[15] Even high growth will raise average real earnings only to their 1979 level (not shown in table), which indicates how far the economy declined in 1980 and 1981.

The policy changes improve average incomes after taxes and transfers in 1984 primarily because the tax cuts through 1984 are much larger than the expenditure reductions enacted to date. But the effect on incomes of achieving high versus low economic growth through 1984 are about twice as large as

TABLE 16–10

Effects of Growth Assumptions and 1981 Policy Changes on the Average Real Incomes of Families, 1980 to 1984

(In 1980 $)[a]

Type of Income	Average Income ($)	Change From 1980 to 1984 (%)
Average earnings		
1980[b]	15,858	—
1984—low growth	15,540	–2.0
1984—high growth	16,892	6.5
Average income after taxes and transfers[c]		
1980[d]	16,249	—
1984—low growth, pre-Reagan policies	15,925	–2.0
1984—low growth, Reagan policies	16,270	0.1
1984—high growth, pre-Reagan policies	16,781	3.3
1984—high growth, Reagan policies	17,230	6.0

Source: Urban Institute TRIM2 simulations, except as noted below.

a. Estimates are for both families and unrelated individuals.

b. Calculated from the TRIM2 simulations, adjusting for the increase in families and individuals and the decrease in real aggregate wages from 1979 to 1980.

c. Transfers include Social Security, government and private pensions, unemployment compensation, workers compensation, alimony, child support, SSI, general assistance, AFDC, and Food Stamps. Taxes include personal federal income and FICA taxes.

d. Calculated from the TRIM2 simulations, adjusting for the increase in families and individuals, the decline in real aggregate wages, and the rise in taxes from 1979 to 1980.

the effect of the policy changes. Under the low growth scenario, benefits from the tax cut just offset the loss of earnings due to poor performance of the economy—incomes in 1984 after taxes and transfers are estimated to be about the same as in 1980.

Effects on Low-income Families. The simulations of the relative effects of high and low growth scenarios through 1984 suggest that low-income families have a modest stake in the extent to which economic growth is achieved. Low growth would slightly increase the number of families in poverty in 1984 over 1980. However, 8 percent fewer families (about one percent of all families) would be in poverty if high growth is achieved than if this low growth path prevailed.

The gains from economic growth are limited by the fact that an increasing proportion of poor families are aged or headed by females with limited earnings potential. It is nonaged, two-adult, low-income families who benefit the most from declining unemployment rates.[16] By historical standards, then, this is a rather modest percentage decline in the number of poor families in response to a substantial decline in unemployment.[17]

Over 90 percent of AFDC families, those affected most by the policy changes, are headed by women and are not expected to reap much benefit from economic growth. Some of those with earnings do benefit from a more prosperous economy, however, resulting in a reduction in the number of AFDC families by 4 percent under high growth compared with the low growth scenario. Those remaining on AFDC whose earnings are increased by high growth, however, will experience little change in their net incomes because AFDC benefits will be reduced by a comparable amount.

Responses to Changes in Work Incentives. Our estimates presented in this section assume no change in work behavior by individuals due to either the decline in marginal tax rates or the increase in benefit reduction rates in transfer programs.[18] The possible impacts of taxes and transfer programs on work were discussed earlier in this chapter, and the specific response of AFDC recipients to changes in the AFDC program and the initiation of workfare are discussed in chapter 12. These reviews suggest that any changes in work behavior due to altered work incentives caused by the policy changes will be quite modest.

Conclusions

Evidence available to date suggests that in the short run the 1981 policy changes will provide modest income gains (after taxes and transfers) for the average household. However, the gains to families in the upper income brackets are quite large and, on average, low-income families will experience a small net loss. Working poor and near-poor families, particularly AFDC recipients, will be the most adversely affected.

Analysis of the effects of economic growth on family income shows that under high growth assumptions average income (after taxes and transfers) in 1984 will be about 6 percent higher than in 1980. If low growth prevails, family income is estimated to be about the same in 1984 as it was in 1980. While the administration's tax and transfer policies increase the number of families in poverty, high growth would more than offset this effect. The gains to growth are not large for this population, however, because of the declining proportion of nonaged, two-parent families among the poor.

These assessments are preliminary for several reasons. First, the effects of changes in several major programs (e.g., Medicaid, unemployment insurance, and grants to states and localities) are not examined. Second, the tax cuts enacted through 1984 will require further reductions in program expenditures which may dwarf the program cuts enacted in 1981. Which programs are reduced in the future and how they are reduced will significantly affect how gains and losses are distributed across the population. Third, responses of individuals, state and local governments, and charitable organizations to the policy changes are uncertain and will influence the final consequences of the policy changes for the economic well-being of families and individuals. Finally, the administration's horizon extends well beyond 1984. It may be that recent and future policy changes will shift the economy to a new, higher growth path that will bring about unprecedented prosperity after 1984.

However, it is clear that the changes introduced thus far make the distribution of income less equal and require some sacrifices by low-income families while granting large tax cuts to high-income families. The pre-Reagan distribution of income was not sacrosanct, and some would regard this redistribution as an achievement in itself. But polls indicate that the majority of the population, while wanting to reduce taxes and eliminate public aid to those who can but will not work, are concerned with the fairness of the short-run policy changes. A prosperous economy that made almost everyone absolutely better off, even though the relative gains were unequally distributed, would mitigate these concerns.

The linchpin of the administration's domestic program is economic growth, and the success of the program will be judged in large part on the degree of growth achieved. Available evidence suggests that economic conditions in 1984 will not be substantially improved over 1980, and that the fairness of program changes, which were justified primarily to stimulate economic growth, will remain an issue by which the Reagan administration will continue to be judged.

APPENDIX

FEDERAL OUTLAYS AS A PERCENTAGE OF GROSS NATIONAL PRODUCT,
(FY 1956–FY 1981)

			Outlays Excluding Net Interest	
Federal Fiscal Year	*Total Outlays, Current Dollars*	*Total Outlays, Constant (FY 1972) Dollars*	*Constant (FY 1972) Dollars*	*Constant (FY 1972) Dollars, High-employment*
1956	17.1	18.8	17.6	17.6
1961	19.2	20.2	18.9	17.4
1966	18.6	19.0	17.7	18.0
1971	20.4	20.2	18.8	18.2
1976	22.7	22.3	20.7	18.9
1981	23.7	22.6	20.3	18.9
Increase from FY 1956 to FY 1981	6.6	3.8	2.7	1.3

SOURCES: 1. For total outlays (including budget and off-budget amounts) in current and constant dollars and GNP by fiscal year: Office of Management and Budget, "Federal Government Finances," February 1982, pp. 60–63, 66–70, and 72–75. (Off-budget outlays were converted to constant dollars using the implicit GNP price deflator for federal nondefense purchases of goods and services.)

2. For high-employment budget expenditures in current dollars and for potential GNP in current dollars: Frank de Leeuw and Thomas M. Holloway, "The High-Employment Budget: Revised Estimates and Automatic Inflation Effects," *Survey of Current Business,* April 1982, pp. 21–33. (High-employment adjustment to actual budget outlays was made in constant dollars using the implicit GNP price deflator for personal consumption expenditures, consistent with OMB constant dollar tabulations. High-employment GNP was converted to constant dollars using the implicit price deflator for total GNP.)

TABLE A-2

FEDERAL OUTLAYS BY DOMESTIC PROGRAM AREA
(FY 1966–FY 1981)

	Billions of Dollars				Percentage of GNP			
	FY 1966	FY 1971	FY 1976	FY 1981	FY 1966	FY 1971	FY 1976	FY 1981
Income security	28.7	54.7	124.9	218.2	4.0	5.3	7.6	7.6
Low-income assistance	(3.2)	(7.8)	(20.1)	(35.9)	(0.4)	(0.8)	(1.2)	(1.3)
Social insurance and other	(25.5)	(46.8)	(104.8)	(182.2)	(3.5)	(4.5)	(6.4)	(6.4)
Health	2.6	13.5	31.5	66.0	0.4	1.3	1.9	2.3
Education	2.5	5.1	7.6	15.1	0.3	0.5	0.5	0.5
Social services	0.8	2.7	4.5	6.5	0.1	0.3	0.3	0.2
Employment and training	1.1	2.1	6.6	9.8	0.2	0.2	0.4	0.3
Housing and community development	2.6	2.2	6.5	12.7	0.4	0.2	0.4	0.4
Transportation	5.8	8.1	13.5	23.5	0.8	0.8	0.8	0.8
Veterans benefits	5.9	9.8	18.4	23.0	0.8	1.0	1.1	0.8
Revenue sharing	0.3	0.5	7.2	6.9	0.0	0.0	0.4	0.2
Other domestic programs	16.8	21.3	30.1	54.4	2.3	2.1	1.8	1.9
Total	67.1	120.0	250.8	436.1	9.3	11.6	15.3	15.3

SOURCE: Office of Management and Budget, "Federal Government Finances," February 1982, pp. 27–49, 73–75. See notes to table 3–6 for explanation of the domestic program areas.

TABLE A–3

FEDERAL TAXES, OUTLAYS, AND THE BUDGET DEFICIT
(FY 1956–FY 1981)

Federal Fiscal Years	Federal Tax Receipts		Federal Budget Deficit (Percentage of GNP)
	Percentage of GNP	Percentage of Budget Outlays	
1956–1960	18.0	98.5	0.3
1961–1965	18.2	95.9	0.8
1966–1970	19.2	95.6	1.1
1971–1975	18.6	91.4	1.8
1976–1980	19.3	88.8	2.4
1981	21.0	91.2	2.0

SOURCE: Office of Management and Budget, "Federal Government Finances," February 1982, pp. 4–5, 11–12, 72–75.

NOTE: The multiyear entries are computed as the average of the corresponding five fiscal years.

TABLE A-4

CONGRESSIONAL BUDGET OFFICE BASELINE BUDGET PROJECTIONS, BY MAJOR BUDGET CATEGORY, JULY 1981

	FY 1981 Outlays		FY 1986 Outlays		Annual Rate of Growth, FY 1981 to FY 1986	
	Billions of Dollars	Budget Share (%)	Billions of Dollars	Budget Share (%)	Nominal (%)	Real (%)
National defense	159.6	24.2	254.0	26.7	9.7	3.2
Benefit payments to individuals	316.1	47.9	484.0	51.0	8.9	2.6
Low-income assistance	(66.6)	(10.1)	(95.8)	(10.1)	(7.5)	(1.4)
Social insurance and other	(249.5)	(37.8)	(388.2)	(40.9)	(9.2)	(3.0)
Other grants to state and local governments	56.9	8.6	71.3	7.5	4.6	−2.5
Net interest	66.1	10.0	59.1	6.2	−2.2	−7.7
Other federal operations	61.1	9.3	81.5	8.6	5.9	−0.6
Total	659.8	100.0	949.9	100.0	7.6	1.2

SOURCE: Congressional Budget Office, *Baseline Budget Projections: Fiscal Years 1982–1986* (Washington, D.C.: GPO, 1981), pp. 38, 82. Real rates of growth for nondefense categories were computed on the basis of implicit deflators in OMB tabulations. See Office of Management and Budget, "Federal Government Finances," March 1981, pp. 67, 75.

TABLE A-5

TOTAL TAX RECEIPTS AS PERCENTAGE OF GROSS DOMESTIC PRODUCT, OECD MEMBER COUNTRIES, 1955–1980

	Ranking Order 1955	1955	1965	1975	1977	1980	Ranking Order 1980	1980 Minus 1955 (Percentage Points)
Germany	1	30.8	31.6	35.7	37.9	37.2	8	6.4
Italy	2	30.5	27.3	29.0	30.9	30.1[a]	15	-0.4
Austria	3	30.0	34.6	38.5	39.4	41.5	6	11.5
United Kingdom	4	29.8	30.8	36.9	35.5	35.9	9	6.1
Norway	5	28.3	33.2	44.8	47.2	47.4	2	19.1
New Zealand	6	26.8	24.3	30.0	32.7	31.7	12	4.9
Finland	7	26.8	30.1	36.2	39.5	34.5	10	7.7
Netherlands	8	26.3	35.5	45.8	46.3	46.2	3	19.9
Sweden	9	25.5	35.6	44.2	50.8	49.9	1	24.4
Belgium	10	24.0	31.2	41.1	42.8	42.5	5	18.5
United States	11	23.6	26.5	30.2	30.3	30.7	14	7.1
Denmark	12	23.4	30.1	41.1	41.3	45.1	4	21.7
Australia	13	22.6	23.8	29.1	29.7	29.8[a]	16	7.2
Ireland	14	22.5	26.0	32.5	35.4	37.5	7	15.0
Canada	15	21.7	25.9	32.9	31.8	32.8	11	11.1
Switzerland	16	19.2	20.7	29.6	31.6	30.7	13	11.5
Japan	17	17.1	18.1	21.1	22.6	25.9	18	8.8
Portugal	18	15.4	18.6	24.8	27.5	29.8	17	14.4
Average		24.7	28.0	34.6	36.3	36.6		11.9

SOURCE: Organization for Economic Cooperation and Development, *Long Term Trends in Tax Revenues of OECD Member Countries, 1955–1980* (Paris: OECD, 1981).

NOTE: Countries have been ranked by the 1955 figures.

a. 1979 figures.

TABLE A–6

DISTRIBUTION OF PERSONAL INCOME TAX RETURNS, BY MARGINAL RATE OF TAX,
1961 AND 1979

Marginal Tax Rate Bracket	1961		1979	
	Percentage of All Returns	Cumulative[a] Percentage	Percentage of All Returns	Cumulative[a] Percentage
0	20.8	20.8	21.3	21.3
14	—	20.8	7.9	29.2
15	—	20.8	—	29.2
16	—	20.8	6.6	35.8
17–18	—	20.8	12.8	48.6
19–20	46.3	67.1	4.0	52.6
21–22	23.2	90.3	11.7	64.3
23–24	0.4	90.7	10.9	75.2
25–28	5.9	96.6	8.6	83.8
29–34	2.3	98.9	8.7	92.5
35–38	0.4	99.3	2.8	95.3
39–44	0.2	99.5	2.6	97.9
45–53	0.4	99.9	1.2	99.1
54–60	—	99.9	0.7	99.8
61–80	0.1	100.0	0.2	100.0

SOURCE: Eugene Steuerle and Michael Hartzmark, *Individual Income Taxation 1947–79*, table
           A–5.
   a.   Returns taxed at or below highest marginal rate in bracket.

TABLE A-7

Changes in Tax-exempt Levels of Income Compared to the Poverty Threshold, by Filing Status and Number of Dependents, 1948–1984

| | Single Taxpayers | | Tax-Exempt Level of Income — Married Couples (Joint Returns) | | | | | |
| | | | Zero Dependents | | Two Dependents | | Four Dependents | |
	Tax-exempt Income (Dollars)	Percentage of Poverty Line	Tax-exempt Income (Dollars)	Percentage of Poverty Line	Tax-exempt Income (Dollars)	Percentage of Poverty Line	Tax-exempt Income (Dollars)	Percentage of Poverty Line
1948	667	54.5	1,333	85.5	2,667	103.6	4,000	122.1
1954	667	48.8	1,333	76.6	2,667	97.3	4,000	109.3
1960	667	44.3	1,333	69.5	2,667	88.3	4,000	99.1
1966	900	54.6	1,600	76.1	3,000	90.4	4,400	99.6
1972	2,050	96.5	2,800	103.3	4,300	100.6	5,800	101.9
1978	3,200	96.6	5,200	123.0	7,200	108.1	9,200	103.6
1980	3,300	78.8	5,400	100.7	7,400	87.9	9,400	83.5
1981	3,300	71.4	5,400	91.2	7,400	79.7	9,400	75.7
1984	3,300	58.9	5,400	75.2	7,400	65.7	9,400	62.4

SOURCES: Tax-exempt levels are from Eugene Steuerle, "The Tax Treatment of Households of Different Size" (Paper presented at American Enterprise Institute conference, *Taxing the Family*, Washington, D.C., October 1981), table 1. Poverty thresholds for nonfarm families and individuals were indexed by the CPI for years before 1960 and for 1981 and projected by the administration's CPI assumptions for 1984. The poverty threshold used is that defined by the Social Security Administration in 1964 and revised by a Federal Interagency Committee in 1969. It is adjusted each year for changes in the CPI and therefore corresponds to approximately the same standard of living in each year.

TABLE A–8

EFFECTIVE TAX RATES ON DEPRECIABLE ASSETS USED IN NONRESIDENTIAL
BUSINESS, 1952–1979
(Percentage)

	Maximum Statutory Tax Rate	Tax Rate on New Capital			Average Effective Tax Rate on Corporate Profits
		Total	*Equipment*	*Plant*	
1952	52.0	62.2	64.0	57.5	49.0
1953	52.0	60.2	61.8	56.2	49.0
1954	52.0	55.3	56.3	52.5	46.0
1955	52.0	53.1	53.9	51.0	45.0
1956	52.0	52.7	53.5	50.7	45.0
1957	52.0	54.4	55.4	51.9	45.0
1958	52.0	54.6	55.6	52.0	46.0
1959	52.0	55.4	56.5	52.6	45.0
1960	52.0	54.8	55.8	52.2	46.0
1961	52.0	53.1	53.9	51.0	46.0
1962	52.0	41.7	39.3	47.8	44.0
1963	52.0	41.4	39.1	47.4	44.0
1964	50.0	29.0	23.0	44.5	42.0
1965	48.0	27.7	21.9	42.8	40.0
1966	48.0	36.7	33.7	44.5	40.0
1967	48.0	36.3	33.0	44.7	40.0
1968	52.8	43.3	40.3	51.0	43.0
1969	52.8	56.5	57.2	54.7	45.0
1970	49.2	54.1	55.1	51.7	44.0
1971	48.0	37.5	33.1	48.7	42.0
1972	48.0	37.5	33.1	48.7	40.0
1973	48.0	40.0	36.2	49.8	39.0
1974	48.0	45.0	42.3	51.8	37.0
1975	48.0	40.4	36.3	50.9	37.0
1976	48.0	39.8	35.6	50.7	36.0
1977	48.0	39.3	34.9	50.5	35.0
1978	48.0	39.9	35.6	50.7	35.0
1979	46.0	38.4	34.3	49.0	33.0

SOURCE: Hulten, Robertson, and Davies, unpublished.

TABLE A-9

DISTRIBUTION OF NONDEFENSE PROGRAM REDUCTIONS, BY REGION AND STATE,
FY 1982
(In $ millions)

	Payments to Individuals[a]	All Other[b]	Total	Per Capita
New England	1,126	537	1,663	134
Maine	116	45	161	142
New Hampshire	63	32	95	101
Vermont	46.0	19	65	126
Massachusetts	573	281	853	148
Rhode Island	102	36	138	145
Connecticut	226	124	350	112
Middle Atlantic	3,873	1,629	5,502	149
New York	2,038	784	2,822	160
New Jersey	716	323	1,039	140
Pennsylvania	1,119	522	1,641	138
East North Central	4,354	1,740	6,094	146
Ohio	1,036	479	1,515	141
Indiana	586	207	793	145
Illinois	974	516	1,490	130
Michigan	1,328	363	1,691	184
Wisconsin	430	175	605	128
Plains	1,947	689	2,636	153
Minnesota	439	166	605	148
Iowa	300	107	407	140
Missouri	551	221	772	156
North Dakota	98	26	124	188
South Dakota	92	27	119	173
Nebraska	219	57	276	175
Kansas	248	85	333	140
South Atlantic	3,191	1,613	4,804	127
Delaware	64	22	86	144
Maryland	379	230	609	143
District of Columbia	112	60	172	273
Virginia	419	208	627	115
West Virginia	169	80	249	128
North Carolina	428	212	640	108
South Carolina	268	163	431	136
Georgia	493	209	702	126
Florida	859	429	1,288	126
East South Central	1,305	747	2,052	139
Kentucky	330	176	506	138
Tennessee	322	324	646	140
Alabama	392	150	542	138
Mississippi	261	97	358	141

TABLE A–9 *(continued)*

DISTRIBUTION OF NONDEFENSE PROGRAM REDUCTIONS, BY REGION AND STATE,
FY 1982
(In millions)

	Payments to Individuals[a]	All Other[b]	Total	Per Capita
West South Central	1,864	1,013	2,877	118
Arkansas	266	85	351	153
Louisiana	372	203	575	133
Oklahoma	240	183	423	136
Texas	986	542	1,528	103
Mountain	881	658	1,539	132
Montana	80	35	115	145
Idaho	86	66	152	158
Wyoming	25	22	47	96
Colorado	239	157	396	134
New Mexico	69	155	224	169
Arizona	232	99	331	118
Utah	101	60	161	106
Nevada	49	64	113	134
Pacific	2,870	1,446	4,316	133
Washington	348	253	601	143
Oregon	221	124	345	130
California	2,128	1,015	3,143	130
Alaska	76	17	93	226
Hawaii	97	37	134	137
Total U.S.	21,411	10,072	31,483	137

SOURCE: State and local distribution from Community Service Administration, *Geographic Distribution of Federal Funds in FY 1980* (Washington, D.C.: GPO, 1982).

a.   Includes farm price supports; Food Stamps; school lunches; CETA; Social Security retirement and disability insurance; Medicare; Medicaid; AFDC; railroad, civil service, and military retirement benefits; grants to low-income persons for college tuition and energy costs; unemployment insurance; trade adjustment assistance; educational impact assistance; and educational assistance under Title 1.

b.   Includes urban mass transit assistance, community development block grants, urban development action grants, highway construction, and nonmilitary Department of Energy programs.

NOTES

NOTES TO CHAPTER 1

1. Presidential Message to the Congress, February 18, 1981. See *America's New Beginning: A Program for Economic Recovery* (Washington, D.C.: GPO, February 18, 1981), p.1.

2. *Economic Report of the President* (Washington, D.C.: GPO,1982), p. 92.

NOTES TO CHAPTER 2

1. With more adults at work, there were fewer hours to devote to home, family, and leisure time activities, and per capita income gains were achieved, in part, because people devoted less time to these activities.

2. Arthur M. Okun, *Prices and Quantities: A Macroeconomic Analysis* (Washington, D.C.: The Brookings Institution, 1981).

3. Francis M. Bator, "Fiscal and Monetary Policy: In Search of A Doctrine," *Economic Choices: Studies in Tax/Fiscal Policy* (Washington, D.C.: Center for National Policy, 1982), p. 35; and Alan S. Blinder, *Economic Policy and the Great Stagflation* (New York: Academic Press, 1979), pp. 102-103.

4. *Economic Report of the President* (Washington, D.C.: GPO, 1982), p. 23; hereafter referred to as *Economic Report of the President, 1982.*

5. The annual growth rate of real output per hour worked in private business declined from 3.2 percent for 1948-1965, to 2.3 percent for 1965-1973, and to 1.1 percent for 1973-1978. For the past three years productivity growth (at 0.2 percent) has almost ceased. See J. R. Norsworthy, Michael J. Harper, and Kent Kunze, "The Slowdown in Productivity Growth: Analysis of Some Contributing Factors," *Brookings Papers on Economic Activity* 1979:2.

6. William D. Nordhaus, "Policy Responses to the Productivity Slowdown," *The Decline in Productivity Growth*, Federal Reserve Bank of Boston, Conference Series No. 22, June 1980.

7. *Economic Report of the President, 1982*, chapter 2.

8. The president's message at the beginning of the *Economic Report of the President, 1982* states that the proposed tax reductions will have "a powerful impact on the incentives for all Americans to work, save and invest" (p. 7), but the evidence reviewed in a later chapter (chapter 5) leads the Council of Economic Advisers to a more cautiously worded conclusion.

9. In an interview with Hedley Donovan, reported in *Fortune* (September 21, 1981, p. 70), President Reagan stated: "From my own study of economics—that's where I got my degree, not that I was a great scholar or anything—I've always had a feeling we've underestimated the psychological factor."

Or as David Stockman put it: "The whole thing is premised on faith, on belief about how the world works. The inflation premium melts aways like the morning mist. It could be cut in half in a very short period of time if the policy is credible. That sets off adjustments and changes in perceptions that cascade through the economy. You have a bull market in '81, after April, of historical proportions." As quoted in William Greider, "The Education of David Stockman," *The Atlantic Monthly*, December 1981, p. 29.

Notes to Chapter 2 (continued)

10. Text of President Reagan's address to a joint session of Congress on February 18, 1981, as reprinted in *Congressional Quarterly*, February 21, 1981, p. 361.

11. Text of President Reagan's March 10 message to Congress transmitting revisions to the 1982 budget, as reprinted in *Congressional Quarterly*, March 14, 1981, p. 485.

12. Text of President Reagan's July 27, 1981, televised speech as reprinted in *Congressional Quarterly*, August 1, 1981, p. 1403.

13. A similar question in a *Time*/Yankelovich survey in January 1981 elicited only 52 percent in favor of "the incoming administration's" tax proposal. Either the president did a good job in selling the program between the two dates or differences in the wording of the question account for the different responses. See *Opinion Outlook*, March 9, 1981, p. 2.

14. William Greider, "The Education of David Stockman,' *The Atlantic Monthly*, December 1981, p. 32. To prepare the alternative forecast, Stockman first turned to Alan Greenspan but after the Townsend-Greenspan model failed to produce results consistent with the administration's economic theories, John Rutledge of the Claremont Economics Institute in California was called in to assist in their preparation.

15. Rudolph G. Penner, "Budget Assumptions and Budget Outcomes," *American Enterprise Institute Economist*, August 1981.

16. This range represents a 90 percent confidence interval, based on repeated simulations using the DRI model. Uncertainty with respect to assumed policy parameters and predicted economic performance was allowed to introduce uncertainty regarding the deficit outcome. The cited confidence interval implies that in one out of ten simulations, the model would yield a deficit estimate outside of this range. The simulations incorporate all of the budget policies enacted during 1981 but assume adoption of less than one-half of the deficit reduction measures in President Reagan's FY 1983 budget. This material was prepared by Otto Eckstein for the Conference on Current Economic Policy, sponsored by the National Academy of Sciences and The Urban Institute on June 3-4, 1982.

17. This book went to press before the 1982 midyear update of the administration's economic assumptions became available. The estimates for the two years following the date they were made represent a short-term forecast. The longer-term estimates do not represent forecasts of economic conditions but are "projections consistent with the economic policy objectives of the administration" (*1983 Budget*, pp. 2-4).

18. See, for example, Herbert Stein, "Another New Economics," *The American Enterprise Institute Economist*, April 1981. "Reagan Readies the Ax," *Newsweek*, February 16, 1981, and A. F. Ehrbar, "A Strong Start on the Economy," *Fortune*, March 23, 1981. A typical comment from Karl Bruner, a leading monetarist at the University of Rochester, was: "It looks as though one group was working on real growth, another on monetary policy, and a third on inflation. When you put the numbers together, they don't make sense." (A. F. Ehrbar, "A Strong Start on the Economy," *Fortune*, March 23, 1981, p. 480).

19. "Why Economists Want Reagan to Raise Taxes," *Business Week*, October 5, 1981, p. 116.

20. *Economic Report of the President, 1982*, p. 64.

21. The Program for Economic Recovery states that "the economic scenario assumes that the growth rates of money and credit are steadily reduced from the 1980 levels to one-half those levels by 1986." Since M1-B adjusted was growing at a rate of 6.7 percent in 1980, this implies about a 3.4 percent rate of growth *by 1986*. Yet M1-B adjusted was growing less rapidly than this in 1981.

22. William Fellner, "On the Merits of Gradualism and on a Fall-back Position If It Should Nevertheless Fail: Introductory Remarks," *Essays in Contemporary Economic Problems: Demand, Productivity, and Population*, 1981-1982 edition, William Fellner, project director (Washington, D.C.: American Enterprise Institute, 1981), p. 3.

23. Timothy B. Clark, "Fed's Tight Money Policy May Collide With Reagan's Huge Budget Deficits," *National Journal*, February 20, 1982, pp. 327-330.

24. *Economic Report of the President, 1982*, p. 48.

25. Testimony of Representative Henry S. Reuss before the Senate Budget Committee, March 15, 1982.

26. *Economic Report of the President, 1982*, p. 74.

27. Donald D. Hester, "Innovations and Monetary Control," *Brookings Papers on Economic Activity*, 1981:1; Albert M. Wojnilower, "The Central Role of Credit Crunches in Recent Financial History," *Brookings Papers on Economic Activity*, 1980:2; Henry Kaufman, "Reaganomics," *Challenge*, September/October 1981.

28. Economists in favor of this alternative include (among others) James Tobin (Yale University) and Herbert Stein (American Enterprise Institute).

29. *Economic Report of the President, 1982*, p. 63; Statement of Treasury Under Secretary for Monetary Affairs, Beryl Sprinkel, before the Joint Economic Committee's Subcommittee on Monetary and Fiscal Policy, April 8, 1981, p. 7.

30. Timothy B. Clark, "Fed's Tight Money Policy May Collide With Reagan's Huge Budget Deficits," *National Journal*, February 20, 1982, p. 328.

31. Bennett T. McCallum, "Rational Expectations and Macroeconomic Stabilization Policy: An Overview," *Journal of Money, Credit and Banking*, November 1980.

32. Francis M. Bator, "Fiscal and Monetary Policy: In Search of a Doctrine," *Economic Choices: Studies in Tax/Fiscal Policy*, (Washington, D.C.: Center for National Policy, 1982), p. 27.

33. If the growth of velocity drops (people choose to hold more money)—as normally occurs in a period when nominal interest rates are falling—then nominal GNP will rise still more slowly unless the Federal Reserve accommodates the increased demand for money.

34. *Economic Report of the President, 1982*, pp. 58-61.

35. The first estimate is from *Economic Report of the President, 1982*, p. 76 and from Beryl Sprinkel's testimony before the Joint Economic Committee's Subcommittee on Monetary and Fiscal Policy, April 8, 1981, p. 14; and the second is from Shadow Open Market Committee, *Policy Statement and Position Papers*, September 21-22, 1980, University of Rochester, Graduate School of Management, p. 6. Two of the monetarists in the current administration (Sprinkel and Council of Economic Advisers Member, Jerry Jordan) were both members of the committee at the time this statement was prepared.

36. *Economic Report of the President, 1982*, table B-25, p. 295. In addition, the exchange value of the dollar increased substantially over this period, reducing the prices of imported goods.

37. Data on businessmen's price expectations are collected by the Commerce Department and can be found in the *Survey of Current Business*, January 1982, vol. 62, no. 1, pp. 21-22. Data on consumer price expectations are collected by the University of Michigan's Survey Research Center and can be found in *Economic Outlook U.S.A.*, various issues.

38. For further data and discussion of recent wage developments, see Wayne Vroman, "Recent Wage Inflation and Prospects for Its Deceleration," The Urban Institute, April 1982.

39. The employment cost index is a better measure of underlying wage rate trends than the hourly earnings index because it is less contaminated by changes in the skill mix of the labor force over the business cycle. On the other hand, it is not seasonally adjusted. Since most nonunion wage increases are concentrated in the first quarter of the year, the second quarter figures (not available at the time this was written) may show a still more substantial drop in the index.

40. Arthur Sackley, "Wage Increases Moderate in 1981," *Monthly Labor Review*, May 1982, vol. 105, no. 5, p. 6.

41. These simulations have been done by Robert J. Gordon using a model explaining the fixed-weight GNP deflator with coefficients estimated for the period 1954:I through 1980:4. During the first five quarters that the current administration was in office, the annualized unemployment rate was 2.3 percentage points above its "full-employment" level which would, according to these simulations, cause inflation to fall by almost 2 percentage points. When one adds in the indirect effects of tight monetary policy on prices (through its impact on the value of the dollar and the relative price of food, energy, and imports), the model is capable of fully

Notes to Chapter 2 (continued)

predicting the recent decline in the fixed weight deflator. For more details, see Robert J. Gordon and Stephen R. King, "The Output Cost of Disinflation in Traditional and Vector-Autoregressive Models," *Brookings Papers on Economic Activity*, 1982:1.

42. Estimated by assuming an Okun's Law coefficient of 2 and a full-employment unemployment rate of 6 percent.

43. Robert J. Gordon and Stephen R. King, "The Output Cost of Disinflation in Traditional and Vector-Autoregressive Models," *Brookings Papers on Economic Activity*, 1982:1, p. 43.

44. If the rate of inflation depends on the *rate of change* in the unemployment rate as well as its *level* then an expansion of output and reduction in unemployment, even from a high level, will be somewhat inflationary. For evidence to this effect, see George L. Perry, "Inflation in Theory and Practice," *Brookings Papers on Economic Activity*, 1980:1, p. 229; and Charles L. Schultze, "Some Macro Foundation for Micro Theory,' *Brookings Papers on Economic Activity*, 1981:2, p. 552.

45. With a nonaccommodative monetary policy, there would have to be an increase in velocity to permit this stimulus to operate. After taking into account the secondary effects of this amount of stimulus on the economy, nominal GNP would rise by perhaps 3.5 to 4.0 percent, most of it going to increase real output and reduce unemployment. The multiplier used in this calculation is based on Congressional Budget Office estimates. See *The CBO Multipliers Project: Methodology for Analyzing the Effects of Alternative Economic Policies*, August 1977 and *Entering the 1980s: Fiscal Policy Choices*, January 1980. These multipliers assume that the Federal Reserve holds the path of unborrowed reserves constant.

46. Lyle E. Gramley, Statement before the Subcommittee on Domestic Monetary Policy of the Committee on Banking, Finance, and Urban Affairs, U.S. House of Representatives, October 27, 1981 (reprinted in *Federal Reserve Bulletin*, November 1981, p. 833).

47. Statement of Treasury Secretary Donald Regan before the House Appropriations Committee, February 9, 1982, p. 99.

48. Author's calculations based on administration's savings and deficit assumptions.

49. Author's calculations based on 1970's savings rate and CBO projections of the deficit assuming administration's 1983 budget proposals are not adopted.

50. Peter K. Clark, "Investment in the 1970s: Theory, Performance, and Prediction," *Brookings Papers on Economic Activity*, 1979:1, p. 104.

51. Martin Feldstein, "Inflation and the American Economy," Harvard Institute of Economic Research, Discussion Paper no. 856 (November 1981), p. 21. Because nominal interest costs are tax deductible, real after-tax interest rates have fallen sharply over the past twenty-five years, according to Feldstein. This has probably encouraged all types of investment but especially investment in owner-occupied housing and in consumer durables since the "income" (services) from these assets are not taxed. Corporate income, in contrast, tends to be overstated and thus overtaxed during an inflationary period, reducing the real net return on business investment, as well as interest costs, and encouraging a shift in investment from business to consumer uses. Some would argue that the appropriate solution to this problem is reform of the tax system, selective credit controls, or a reduction of inflation rather than a tight monetary–easy fiscal policy mix.

NOTES TO CHAPTER 3

1. Whenever a budget year is mentioned, it is the federal fiscal year that now ends on September 30 of the year in question. All budget data cited in the text and tables are in current dollars by federal fiscal year, unless otherwise specified.

2. Federal outlays are of course only one, albeit major, indicator of the size and scope of federal government activity. Other indicators often cited include tax expenditures, regulatory activities, and credit activities. Commonly employed measures of these others show parallel, if not greater, federal growth over the past twenty-five years.

3. Furthermore, most of the recent increase in federal expenditures has been in the form of benefit payments for individuals and interest payments on the public debt. To the extent that such outlays constitute a transfer of purchasing power from one population segment to another, they do not reduce the amount of goods and services available for private consumption.

4. The "social insurance and other" category includes benefit outlays that are primarily conditioned upon prior contributions, rather than upon current financial need. Many of these programs are financed through trust funds, as with Old Age and Survivors Insurance, Disability Insurance, Medicare, unemployment compensation, and Civil Service retirement. While such programs are not specifically targeted on the poor, they do serve substantial numbers of low-income persons.

5. "Total grants to state and local governments," shown as an addendum in table 3-2, includes that portion of all benefit payments that flow through state and local budgets, in addition to the amount of "other" federal grants. The major programs are AFDC and Medicaid.

6. See Congressional Budget Office, *An Analysis of President Reagan's Budget Revisions for Fiscal Year 1982* (Washington, D.C.: GPO, 1981), p. xxiii. See also chapter 2 of this volume for a discussion of the economic assumptions underlying the administration's budget projections.

7. CBO did assume changes in economic policy, particularly a tax cut, in order to derive its economic assumptions. However, the revenue and spending estimates were still based on the current tax and spending policies in order to provide an appropriate baseline.

8. Details on these tax cuts and their rationale are in chapter 4.

9. See *America's New Beginning: A Program for Economic Recovery* (Washington, D.C.: GPO, February 18, 1981), pp. 12-27.

10. The president's 1983 budget proposals are a better reflection of his long-term spending priorities than are his 1982 budget proposals. This is because the 1983 budget specifies reductions that the president had earlier indicated he would seek but had not included in his 1982 budget proposals. His 1983 budget proposals also reflect additional cuts that he was seeking in light of the first year's experience. The major proposal of the president that is lost by this focus on the 1983 budget is in the Social Security area. In response to congressional pressure to clarify some of the cuts that were planned but not included in the 1982 budget proposals, the president proposed in May 1981 a major reduction in Social Security benefits, which he estimated would save $3.8 billion in 1982, growing to $9.6 billion in 1984. This was immediately and unanimously rejected by the Senate, in part because it provided for no phase-in to allow those near retirement an opportunity to adjust their plans. The president subsequently withdrew the proposal and suggested the creation of a bipartisan commission to recommend Social Security reforms.

11. As a share of GNP, defense would rise to 7.1 percent in 1986 from 5.7 percent in 1981. This would be roughly the same as in 1965, before the Vietnam War build-up, and again in 1972 when its level was dropping rapidly from the Vietnam War high of 9.4 percent in 1968.

12. As indicated in table 3-5, spending on other federal operations is the net effect of program outlays and undistributed offsetting receipts (the government's contribution to employee retirement plans, rents and royalties on the Outer Continental Shelf (OCS), and surplus property disposal). The president's 1983 budget proposed a doubling of undistributed receipts from 1981 to 1986, largely through surplus property disposal and accelerated leasing on the OCS. Thus, a sizable portion of the decline in such spending was in the form of increased receipts and not decreased outlays.

13. The long-term effects of the extreme reductions proposed in housing are actually far greater than reflected in table 3-6, since it takes thirty years for cuts in housing budget authority to be fully translated into outlay reductions.

14. President Reagan also proposed reductions in off-budget outlays of $4.7 billion and increases in receipts through user charges of another $2.6 billion for a total nondefense deficit reduction of nearly $49 billion, by the administration's estimate.

15. The estimates of 1982 and 1986 spending changes are the authors' own. Background information on their derivation is contained in an appendix that will be provided upon request.

16. In brief, the budget baseline was estimated by revising CBO's July 1981 baseline projections to reflect CBO's more recent (February 1982) economic assumptions with respect

Notes to Chapter 3 (continued)

to unemployment, inflation, interest rates, and real GNP growth. Adjustments were also made to reflect updated technical reestimates and to exclude questionable savings. Among such excluded savings were those associated with the strategic petroleum reserves, Medicare, disaster loans, and federal employee pay raises. We are indebted to John Ellwood for identifying many of these questionable reductions.

17. This estimate differs from the earlier-cited 6.4 percent reduction in "nondefense programs" because "domestic program" spending does not include international affairs outlays, allowances, or offsetting receipts.

18. See chapter 13 for more details on this.

19. For further discussion of the economic consequences of large deficits, see chapter 2.

20. For example, the February 1982 CBO baseline projections show that, despite reductions in 1986 of over $20 billion in benefit payments for individuals, such outlays are estimated both to grow as fast from 1982 to 1986 and to reach a higher level in 1986 than shown in the July 1981 baseline projections.

21. Even these CBO reestimates accepted the administration's figures for several substantial savings that were viewed as highly questionable at best.

22. The question of what would be an appropriate deficit in 1986 from an economic point of view has no easy answer. However, most economists would agree that the deficit, if any, should be truly small by then, given the assumption of a strongly growing economy and an unemployment rate approaching 6 percent. See chapter 2 for discussion of the economic effects of deficits.

23. The absence of an analogous discussion of tax increase options does not reflect a preference toward spending cuts as a deficit reduction strategy. Since tax policy is discussed in chapter 4, this chapter focuses on spending.

24. Congress rebutted the president's May 1981 Social Security proposals largely because of the immediate impact they would have had on early retirees. The president then proposed a bipartisan commission to consider future changes in the program and to submit its report after the November 1982 elections. As a result, the president's 1983 budget contained no Social Security proposals.

On the other hand, the 1983 budget did propose substantial Medicare savings through structural reforms. However, these were assumed to come largely from lower overall medical costs through the enactment of measures promoting competition in the health care sector. This plan now appears stalled within the administration because of its politically controversial nature (see chapter 9).

NOTES TO CHAPTER 4

1. The limits voters placed on state taxes, and the foreshadowing this provided of the federal tax limitation movement, is explored in depth in chapter 6 of this volume.

2. *1981, Changing Public Attitudes on Governments and Taxes*, A Commission Survey (Washington, D.C.: Advisory Commission on Intergovernmental Relations).

3. When the income tax was initiated in 1913, less than one percent of the population was covered and the tax was about 0.1 percent of personal income. Richard Goode, *The Individual Income Tax*, rev. ed. (Washington, D.C.: The Brookings Institution, 1976), p. 4.

4. A decline in family size was also a contributing factor. In 1960 there were 2.9 personal exemptions per tax return; in 1978 there were 2.5 exemptions per return. Although exemptions for persons 65 years and over increased per return, they were far outweighed by the decline in exemptions for dependents, which fell from 1.5 dependents per return in 1960 to 0.8 dependents per return in 1978. (U.S. Internal Revenue Service, *Statistics of Income*, Individual Income Tax Returns, various years.)

5. Charles R. Hulten, James W. Robertson, and Sally Davies, "A History of Effective Tax Rates on Income from Capital: 1952-80," Working Paper 1485-01 (Washington, D.C.: The Urban Institute, June 1981). For an alternative set of estimates using a different set of assumptions, see Dale W. Jorgenson and Martin A. Sullivan, "Inflation and Corporate Capital Recovery," in Charles R. Hulten, ed., *Depreciation, Inflation, and the Taxation of Income from Capital*, (Washington, D.C.: The Urban Institute Press, 1981), pp. 171-237.

6. The average tax rate concept used in this paper is *not* adjusted for inflation by removing the inflation-induced rise in inventory profits. Specifically, our measure of corporate profits—which is based on the U.S. *National Income and Product Accounts*—does not include the inventory valuation adjustment or the capital consumption adjustment. When these adjustments are made, the resulting average tax rate behaves much the same as the average rate of figure 4-1 before 1974 but has a huge rise in 1974 to a peak of 66 percent. After 1974 the modified average rate stays at or above the statutory rate.

It is also important to note that the *marginal* tax rates in figure 4-1 refer to the corporate tax alone. The combined burdens of the individual and corporate taxes are, of course, much larger. Unfortunately, it is difficult to estimate a combined marginal rate, but if this were done, the result would likely show the effects of bracket creep during the 1970s.

7. U.S. Department of the Treasury, Internal Revenue Service, *Depreciation Guidelines and Rules*, Publication 456 (Washington, D.C.: GPO, 1962), revenue procedure 62-21.

8. The ITC initially reduced the amount of the equipment cost that could be depreciated. The "basis step-down" was repealed in 1964 and since then equipment receiving the ITC can be fully depreciated.

9. Inflation also led to a substantial increase in nominal inventory profits, which had the effect of increasing tax liabilities even though no increase in real income had occurred. Working against this effect, however, was the inflation-induced gain from low-interest debt obligations. Corporations that had issued low-interest debt in preinflationary times experienced untaxed implicit capital gains at the expense of their creditors when interest rates rose dramatically.

10. The capital gain provision was made effective for all sales or exchanges occurring after June 9, 1981.

11. U.S. Department of the Treasury, Office of Industrial Economics, *Business Building Statistics* (Washington, D.C.: GPO, August 1975); and Charles R. Hulten and Frank C. Wykoff, "Economic Depreciation and Accelerated Depreciation: An Evaluation of the Conable-Jones 10-5-3 Proposal," *National Tax Journal*, vol. 24, no. 1 (March 1981), pp. 45-60.

12. See Emil Sunley, "Acceleration of Tax Depreciation: Basic Issues and Major Alternatives," in Charles R. Hulten, ed., *Depreciation, Inflation, and the Taxation of Income from Capital* (Washington, D.C.: The Urban Institute Press, 1981) for a detailed discussion of the various proposals for tax reform advanced in 1980, including that by Alan J. Auerbach and Dale W. Jorgenson, "Inflation-Proof Depreciation of Assets," *Harvard Business Review*, vol. 58, no. 5 (September-October 1980), pp. 113-118.

13. Congressional Budget Office, *Baseline Budget Projections for Fiscal Years 1983-1987* (Washington, D.C.: GPO, 1982), table 12, p. 32.

14. Congressional Budget Office, *An Analysis of the Roth-Kemp Tax Cut Proposal* (Washington, D.C.: GPO, 1978), p. 37.

15. The second-earner deduction does not provide full equity. Married couples with higher earnings and a more equal division of income between them will receive the least relief, although they now pay the largest marriage penalty. Others (those with a very unequal division of income between them) will receive a larger marriage bonus than before. For a discussion of this and alternative proposals see June O'Neill, "Family Issues in Taxation" (paper presented at conference, Taxing the Family, Washington, D.C.: American Enterprise Institute, October 1981); and Joint Committee on Taxation, "The Income Tax Treatment of Married Couples and Single Persons," A Report of the Joint Committee on Taxation (April 2, 1980).

16. For a discussion of the arguments concerning the personal exemptions, see Eugene Steuerle, "The Tax Treatment of Households of Different Size" (paper presented at American Enterprise Institute conference, Taxing the Family, Washington, D.C., October 1981).

17. For a description of The Urban Institute's simulation model, see chapter 16.

18. This effect is partly due to the inclusion of Social Security taxes, which are a large portion of total federal taxes at lower income levels and were, of course, not reduced by ERTA.

19. The problems of measuring income include the poor reporting of nonwage income (such as income from dividends, interest, rent, and transfers) and imperfect data on the receipt of earned-income tax credits and capital gains. Furthermore, the effects of several provisions of ERTA could not be estimated and so were omitted, the most important of which is the corporate income tax cut. The omission of the corporate income tax is potentially significant: If the incidence falls on the owners of capital, as many believe, the combined burden of the individual and corporate income tax before ERTA would have been more progressive than the burden of the individual income tax alone, but the corporate tax cut would also have disproportionately benefited higher-income individuals. It is also important to recognize that the tax burdens reported in this chapter do not take into account the impact of changes in provisions on before-tax income. As a result of the tax cut, people may in fact move their income from tax-sheltered or tax-preferred sources with lower returns to formerly more heavily taxed sources with higher returns. Such shifting would tend to increase both income and taxes and restore some lost revenues. These "supply-side" effects may be important but could not be estimated.

20. J. R. Norsworthy, Michael J. Harper, and Kent Kunze, "The Slowdown in Productivity Growth: Analysis of Some Contributing Factors," Brookings Papers on Economic Activity, no. 2 (Washington, D.C.: The Brookings Institution, 1979), pp. 387-421.

21. The effects of a tax increase are actually more complex. An increase induces a reduction in hours of work because of the reduction in the return to work versus leisure, a "substitution effect." But the lower wage also reduces income and this "income effect" may encourage more work. However, since the wage reduction in this case is due to a tax increase, people may not perceive their income to go down if they receive additional utility from the increased government expenditure. Income effects may not be important, therefore, in evaluating the effects of tax changes.

22. Labor force participation rose because of a large increase in female participation that offset a slight decline in male labor force participation. The decline in the real income of men over this period combined with increasing opportunities for women accounted to a large extent for the rise in women's employment. See June O'Neill, "A Time-Series Analysis of Women's Labor Force Participation," American Economic Review, vol. 71, no. 2 (May 1981), pp. 76-80.

23. See, for example, the collection of articles in Glen C. Cain and Harold W. Watts, eds., Income Maintenance and Labor Supply (Chicago: Institute for Research on Poverty Monograph Series, Rand McNally, 1973). See also Sheldon Danziger, Robert Haveman, and Robert Plotnick, "How Income Transfers Affect Work, Saving and the Income Distribution," Journal of Economic Literature, vol. 19, no. 3 (September 1981), pp. 395-1028.

24. See Jerry A. Hausman, "Labor Supply," in Henry J. Aaron and Joseph A. Pechman, eds., How Taxes Affect Economic Behavior, (Washington, D.C.: The Brookings Institution, 1981) and Hausman's Income and Payroll Policy and Labor Supply, Working Paper no. 610 (Cambridge, Mass.: National Bureau of Economic Research, 1981).

25. See, for example, Harvey Rosen, "Taxes in a Labor Supply Model with Joint Wage-Hours Determination," Econometrica (May 1976), pp. 485-507.

26. Daniel Feenberg, "The Tax Treatment of Married Couples and the 1981 Tax Law" (Paper presented at American Enterprise Institute conference, Taxing the Family, (Washington, D.C., October 1981).

27. These points are elaborated by Harvey Rosen in "What is Labor Supply and Do Taxes Affect It?" American Economic Review (May 1980), pp. 171-176. The direction of the effect on human capital is not clear. Foregone earnings that constitute a major part of human capital investments are not taxed—and this would make human capital investments more attractive than physical capital investments. Also, the tax tempers the riskiness of the investment. However,

the progressive tax makes a long work life less attractive—a factor that cuts into the rate of return. Rosen has recently done some empirical work suggesting that investment in on-the-job training is on balance *increased* as marginal tax rates increase, resulting in possible overinvestment.

28. Michael J. Boskin, "Taxation, Saving, and the Rate of Interest," *Journal of Political Economy*, vol. 86 (April 1978), pp. S3-S27.

29. Lawrence H. Summers, "Taxation and Capital Accumulation in a Life Cycle Growth Model," *American Economic Review*, vol. 71, no. 4 (September 1981), pp. 533-544.

30. Philip E. Howrey and Saul H. Hymans, "The Measurement and Determination of Loanable-Funds Saving," Brookings Papers on Economic Activity, no. 3 (Washington, D.C.: The Brookings Institution, 1978), pp. 655-705.

31. The question of whether output affects swamp tax incentives in determining the demand for investment has been actively debated with little resolution. In a recent article Lawrence H. Summers notes: "While there is agreement as to the inadequacy of business fixed investment, there is little agreement as to the causes of the shortfall. For example, in a recent proceedings volume of the *American Economic Review*, Alan Blinder concludes with Robert Hall that 'The principal source of inadequate capital formation has been our failure to do anything about recessions, not our active use of anti-investment stimulative policies,' while Martin Feldstein (1980) argues that the interaction of inflation and taxation accounts for much of the decline in corporate capital accumulation that has taken place over the last decade." Summers, "The Effect of Economic Policy on Investment," in Laurence H. Meyer, ed., *The Supply-Side Effects of Economic Policy*, cosponsored by The Center for the Study of American Business at Washington University, St. Louis, Missouri, and The Federal Reserve Bank of St. Louis (Hingham, Mass.: Kluwer Boston, 1981), p. 115; and references therein.

The difficulty in sorting out the relative importance of various investment determinants is also discussed by Peter K. Clark, "Investment in the 1970s: Theory, Performance and Prediction," Brookings Papers on Economic Activity, no. 1 (Washington, D.C.: The Brookings Institution, 1979), pp. 73-124.

32. For a more detailed discussion, see David F. Bradford, "The Economics of Tax Policy Toward Saving," in George M. von Furstenberg, ed., *The Government and Capital Formation* (Cambridge, Mass.: Ballinger, 1980), pp. 11-71.

33. See Patric H. Hendershott and James D. Shilling, "The Impacts on Capital Allocation of Some Aspects of the Economic Recovery Tax Act of 1981," NBER Working Paper No. 825 (December 1981). The Hendershott and Shilling study finds that the tax treatment of business fixed investment under ACRS is brought more into line with the treatment of residential housing.

34. See Don Fullerton and Yolanda Kodrzycki Henderson, "Long-Run Effects of the Accelerated Cost Recovery System," NBER Working Paper No. 828 (December 1981). The Fullerton-Henderson simulation model finds substantial efficiency gains associated with ACRS but also finds that intrasectoral efficiency could be significantly increased by shifting to a more neutral tax.

35. Alan J. Auerbach and Dale W. Jorgenson, "Inflation-Proof Depreciation of Assets," *Harvard Business Review*, vol. 58, no. 5 (September-October 1980), pp. 113-118.

36. Don Fullerton, "Can Tax Revenues Go Up When Tax Rates Go Down?" OTA Paper 41, (September 1980), Office of Tax Analysis, U.S. Department of the Treasury.

37. David F. Bradford, "The Economics of Tax Policy toward Saving," in George M. von Furstenberg, ed., *The Government and Capital Formation* (Cambridge, Mass.: Ballinger, 1980), p. 16.

38. See Otto Eckstein, statement in "Forecasting the Supply Side of the Economy," Hearings of the Joint Economic Committee, Congress of the United States (May 21, 1980), pp. 24-39.

39. One important reason is that Congress is currently considering tax increases to shrink the size of the federal deficit. The size and composition of these tax increases are likely to affect the ultimate success of ERTA in meeting its three objectives.

NOTES TO CHAPTER 5

1. See, for example, Edward F. Denison, *Accounting for Slower Economic Growth: The United States in the 1970's* (Washington, D.C.: The Brookings Institution, 1979).

2. *The Economic Report of the President Together with the Annual Report of the Council of Economic Advisers* (Washington, D.C.: GPO, January 1980), p. 87. This figure compares with William Nordhaus's "consensus" estimate of 0.2 percentage points used in his apportionment of causal factors reported in chapter 2. It converts to a different *percentage* figure because Nordhaus put the *total* slowdown in productivity at 2.5 percentage points, of which cyclical factors were responsible for 0.3 percentage points. The CEA estimate of the cyclically adjusted decline was, as noted, about 1.5 percentage points.

3. Ibid.

4. The term "social" regulation has come to be used to identify regulations concerned with improving health, safety, and public welfare. The most common regulatory instrument used is standard setting. The term "economic" regulation is commonly used to identify regulation that deals with prices charged by individual industries and with controls on the entry of new firms into these industries. Economic regulation's objective is to assure that such prices are "reasonable" and that service is "adequate." In practice these two categories cannot be so sharply distinguished: "economic" regulation, in its broadest sense, is aimed at improving the public welfare; "social" regulation often affects entry and even prices in achieving its ends. But the terminology has become so common that we will adopt it.

5. David Stockman, "Avoiding a GOP Dunkirk," December 1980, U.S. Office of Management and Budget.

6. *The Economic Report of the President Together with the Annual Report of the Council of Economic Advisers*, February 1982, chapter 2, p. 42.

7. Stephen Breyer, *Regulation and Its Reform*, (Cambridge, Mass.: Harvard University Press, 1981).

8. See "Regulators and the Polls," *Regulation* November/December 1978, p. 10.

9. The controls over petroleum prices, the demise of which President Reagan speeded up in January 1981, were a legacy of the Nixon wage-price program.

10. Presidential Message of October 8, 1975, to the Congress of the United States.

11. Presidential Message of May 19, 1975, to the Congress of the United States.

12. Presidential Message of November 13, 1975, to the Congress of the United States.

13. *Executive Order 12291 on Federal Regulation: Progress During 1981* (Washington, D.C.: Executive Office of the President, Office of Management and Budget, April 12, 1982), p. 33.

14. Press Release, the Vice President, Office of the Press Secretary, December 30, 1981.

15. Total *Federal Register* size will also be influenced by the elimination of "special" volumes, such as the recently eliminated *Calendar of Federal Regulations*.

16. Fact Sheet, "President Reagan's Initiatives to Reduce Regulatory Burdens," February 18, 1981, the White House.

17. The order applies only to executive department agencies, not to independent agencies. The independent agencies are guided by commissions composed of five to nine officials, not by a single individual as executive department agencies are. Although the members of independent commissions are appointed by the president, they hold office for a fixed term and are not legally accountable to the president.

18. Major rules are defined to include any rule likely to result in (1) an annual effect on the economy of $100 million or more; (2) a major increase in costs or prices for consumers; individual industries; federal, state, or local agencies; or geographic regions; or (3) significant adverse effects on competition, employment, investment, productivity, innovation, or on the ability of U.S.-based enterprises to compete with foreign-based enterprises in domestic or export markets. Categories (1) and (2) track the definition of "major" rule employed by the Carter administration (see notes 2 and 14). Category (3) was added by Executive Order 12291.

19. See note 17.

20. "The Decision Makers," *National Journal*, April 25, 1981, p. 785.

21. For example, it has been reported that fifty-one employees, including twenty-eight lawyers, were forced from the Department of the Interior's solicitor's office in March 1981. Less than two months later the department advertised for six new lawyers—theoretically in different skill areas. Another example was the secretary of the interior's attempt to transfer the Office of Surface Mining's technical services division from Denver, Colorado, to Casper, Wyoming. The move was stopped after congressional hearings revealed that it would impose hardships on industry as well as agency employees, many of whom had already resigned to avoid the transfer. See "How Interior is Changing, from the Inside," *Washington Post*, January 8, 1982, pp. 19-21.

22. Office of Management and Budget, *Budget of the United States Government, Fiscal Year 1983* (Washington, D.C.: GPO, 1982), appendix.

23. "Administration Says It Merely Seeks A 'Better Way' to Enforce Civil Rights," *National Journal*, March 27, 1982, p. 539.

24. Ibid.

25. "U.S. Relaxing Enforcement of Regulations," *Washington Post*, November 15, 1981, p. A-15.

26. "EPA, Citing State Deferrals, Asks Justice to Drop 49 Enforcement Cases," *Inside EPA*, November 13, 1981.

27. "U.S. Relaxing Enforcement of Regulations," *Washington Post*, November 15, 1981, p. F-1.

28. Ibid.

29. Ibid.

30. "U.S. Fund Cuts Reduce Nursing Home Checkup," *New York Times*, March 5, 1982, p. A-16.

31. Crosscutting rules have been described as "generally applicable requirements imposed on grants across the board to further various national social and economic policies." An example would be the Civil Rights Act of 1964. See generally, David Beam, "Washington's Regulation of States and Localities: Origins and Issues," *Intergovernmental Perspective*, summer 1981, p. 8.

32. See T. Moore, "Regulation—The First Year," "Transportation," *Regulation*, January/February 1982, p. 28.

33. "Retreat from Competition—Trucking Regulation at the ICC,"*Report of the Joint Economic Committee of the United States Congress*, January 3, 1982. See also, "Re-regulating at the ICC: 'The Congress Made Me Do It!'"*Regulation*, November/December 1981, pp. 5-9. See, American Trucking Associations, Inc. v. ICC, 659 F.2d 452 (5th Cir. 1981).

34. 47 *Federal Register* 11875, March 19, 1982.

35. See, Vermont Yankee Nuclear Power Corp. v. National Resources Defense Council, Inc., 435 U.S. 519 (1978).

36. Christopher Demuth, Remarks at the Announcement of EPA's Emissions Trading Policy, April 2, 1982.

37. Stewart Baker, "The Deregulation That Wasn't," *Washington Post*, July 19, 1981, p. C-2.

38. T.R. Reid, "The Disparity Between Rhetoric and Reality," *Washington Post*, February 1, 1982, pp. A-11, 15.

39. 46 *Federal Register* 46755, September 21, 1981.

40. State Farm Mutual Auto Insurance Co. v. Department of Transportation et al., Appeal No. 81-2220 (U.S. Court of Appeals for District of Columbia Circuit, June 1, 1982).

NOTES TO CHAPTER 6

1. Office of Management and Budget, *Budget of the United States Government, Fiscal Year 1983* (Washington, D.C.: GPO, 1982), p. M22.

2. This chapter draws heavily on an original survey of twenty-five states conducted by The Urban Institute in collaboration with the National Conference of State Legislatures. States

Notes to Chapter 6 (continued)

were chosen to be representative of the regional distribution, size, and fiscal condition of all states. Information on tax and budget changes was obtained from interviews with state budget officers, the chairmen and staffs of legislative fiscal committees, and gubernatorial aides. Where no other references are given for state-specific information, it is drawn from these interviews and from state budget documents.

3. On a national income and product accounts basis, federal aid in 1980 was 24.7 percent of state and local outlays. U.S. Department of Commerce, *Survey of Current Business, April 1982* (Washington, D.C.: GPO), table 3.3.

Statistical discrepancies among different data sources frequently confuse state and local fiscal studies. There are three common sources of confusion. (1) The three basic sources of data for federal grants-in-aid use different definitions of grants to the state and local sector. The sources are the federal budget, the Bureau of the Census reports on governmental finances, and the national income and product accounts. Differences are explained and reconciled in Office of Management and Budget, *Budget of the United States Government, Fiscal Year 1983* (Washington, D.C.: GPO, 1982), Special Analysis H, pp. 25-26. (2) State fiscal data are sometimes provided for calendar years, sometimes for federal fiscal years (October 1 to September 30), and sometimes for state fiscal years (variable, but most often July 1 to June 30). (3) Contributions to the state and local sector's social insurance (pension) funds and the surpluses in these funds are treated differently by different analysts. Unfortunately, no single data concept is fully satisfactory for all purposes. This chapter draws upon different data sources but identifies the data concept used in each case.

4. The year 1934 marked the first watershed in federal grant policy. Federal grants to state and local governments jumped more than ninefold between 1933 and 1934, mostly for temporary emergency relief programs. The first permanent shift in the character of federal aid came with the Social Security Act of 1935. In 1935, social welfare programs accounted for only 1.3 percent of federal grants to state and local governments; by 1938, they were 46.2 percent. See Advisory Commission on Intergovernmental Relations (ACIR), *Categorical Grants: Their Role and Design* (Washington, D.C.: GPO, 1978), pp. 18-19.

5. The following table summarizes the adoption of new statewide tax or spending limits since 1977. The first row indicates the number of states adopting measures that restrict state government revenues or expenditures. The second row indicates the number of states adopting measures that restrict all localities of a class within the state (e.g., all school districts or all cities). Some states have adopted measures affecting both levels of government.

Level of Government Subject to Limitation	1977	1978	1979	1980	1981	1982 (Jan.-May)	Total No. of Different States
State government	2	5	6	3	1	0	17
Local government	1	6	7	4	1	0	16
Total no. of different states	3	10	10	6	2	0	25

Source: Urban Institute, National Conference of State Legislatures survey.

6. With one year's exception, the property tax between 1972 and 1978 was selected annually as "the worst tax . . . that is, the least fair" in the annual public opinion polling conducted by the Advisory Commission on Intergovernmental Relations (ACIR) and Opinion Research Corporation. By May 1979, after approval of Proposition 13, the federal income tax gained the "worst" ranking and remained there through 1981. See ACIR, *Changing Public Attitudes on Governments and Taxes, 1981* (Washington, D.C.: ACIR, 1981), table A-1.

7. Roy Bahl, "State and Local Government Finances and the Changing National Economy," in Joint Economic Committee, *Special Study on Economic Change*, vol. 7, *State and Local Finance* (Washington, D.C.: GPO, December 1980), pp. 60-66.

8. Estimates of net revenue gained from tax-rate changes are derived by subtracting from actual tax revenue growth the growth that would occur with a fixed-rate tax structure. This latter is estimated by applying tax elasticities for different taxes, as found in the economics literature, to each year's tax receipts. Estimates are taken from Robert W. Rafuse, Jr., "The Outlook for State-Local Finance under the New Federalism" (Paper presented at a conference sponsored jointly by the New York State Legislative Commission on State-Local Relations and the Nelson A. Rockefeller College of Public Affairs and Policy, State University of New York at Albany, April 27, 1982). Although Rafuse's assumed elasticity for state and local income taxes—1.6— is somewhat higher than most estimates, the weighted elasticity of approximately 1.0 for all taxes agrees with standard estimates.

9. Federal outlays for the three economic stimulus grants (local public works, temporary employment assistance, and antirecession fiscal assistance) fell from $9.2 billion in FY 1978 to $5.0 billion in FY 1979, $2.2 billion in FY 1980, and $1.2 billion in FY 1981.

10. David Stockman, director of the Office of Management and Budget, testimony before the House Subcommittee on Manpower and Housing, April 28, 1981.

11. In a July 30, 1981, speech to the National Conference of State Legislatures, President Reagan asserted:

This nation has never fully debated the fact that over the past forty years federalism—one of the most essential and underlying principles of our Constitution—has nearly disappeared as a guiding force in American politics. My administration intends to initiate such a debate.

12. Morton Grodzins, "The Federal System," in *Goals for Americans: Programs for Action in the Sixties*, Report of the President's Commission on National Goals (New York: Prentice-Hall for the American Assembly, Columbia University, 1960), p. 265.

13. Even the term "dual federalism" revives the language used by the Supreme Court in 1936 to reject the constitutionality of New Deal legislation. James T. Patterson, *The New Deal and the States: Federalism in Transition* (Princeton, N.J.: Princeton University Press, 1969).

14. Claude E. Barfield, *Rethinking Federalism* (Washington, D.C.: American Enterprise Institute, 1981), pp. 69-73; Walter Guzzardi, Jr., "Who Will Care for the Poor?" *Fortune*, June 28, 1981. Also, Wallace E. Oates, "The New Federalism: An Economist's View" (Paper prepared for the Cato Institute, May 1982).

15. "Public Receptive to New Federalism," *Gallup Report No. 193*, October 1981, p. 2. Although there is little doubt that public opinion on federalism has moved toward the president's position, the extent of the reported shift differs markedly by poll and by the exact nature of the question asked. The ACIR-Opinion Research Corporation surveys, for example, ask the question, "From which level of government do you feel you get the most for your money—Federal, State, or Local?" Each year from 1972 through 1978, the federal government ranked first in public responses, but then was supplanted by local government. States remained third-ranked over the entire period, though they have improved strongly relative to the federal government. ACIR, *Changing Public Attitudes*, 1981, p. 5.

16. Quoted in Steven V. Roberts, "Budget Ax Becomes a Tool for Social Change," *New York Times*, June 21, 1981.

17. Surveys repeatedly have shown that those voting in state tax and spending limitation referendums favor across-the-board spending cutbacks only in "welfare" programs. Jack Citrin, "Do People Want Something for Nothing: Public Opinion on Taxes and Government Spending," supplement, *National Tax Journal*, May 1979; Paul Courant, Edward M. Gramlich, and Daniel L. Rubinfeld, "Why Voters Support Tax Limitation Amendments: The Michigan Case," *National Tax Journal*, March 1980; Helen S. Ladd and Julie Wilson, *Proposition 2-1/2* (Washington, D.C.: National Institute of Education, 1981).

18. Rafuse, "The Outlook for State-Local Finance."

19. A congressional supplement in February 1982 augmented the funds finally available for low-income home energy assistance.

Notes to Chapter 6 (continued)

20. Edwin L. Harper, deputy director of the Office of Management and Budget, testimony before the Senate Subcommittee on Intergovernmental Relations, May 13, 1981.

21. *Federal Register,* October 1, 1981, p. 48582.

22. Gene Durman, Barbara Davis, and Michael Gutowski, "The Implementation of Block Grants in Texas: Initial Developments," Urban Institute report to Department of Health and Human Services, February 1982.

23. General Accounting Office, *Federal Assistance System Should Be Changed to Permit Greater Involvement by State Legislatures* (Washington, D.C.: GPO, 1980); Carol S. Weissert, "State Legislatures and Federal Funds: An Issue of the 1980s," *Publius,* summer 1981, pp. 67-83.

24. The Primary Care Block Grant and the Elementary and Secondary Education Block Grant did not become effective until FY 1983. The state-administered portion of the Community Development Block Grant and the Community Services Block Grant supersede programs formerly funded through local governments or nonprofit organizations. Information on replacement funding cannot be obtained from state budgets alone.

25. Subsequent investigation was made of four other states in "good" fiscal condition: Alaska, Montana, North Dakota, and Wyoming. Of these, Alaska and Montana have budgeted for substantial replacement, Wyoming plans to take up the issue at a special legislative session, and North Dakota plans no replacement.

26. The most extreme case of state tax relief is offered by Alaska. The state has used its oil royalties to abolish the state income tax and create the Alaska Permanent Fund. In June 1982 the fund made "dividend" payments of $1,000 to every person who had lived in Alaska for six months. Annual distributions of half the fund's interest earnings are planned for the future.

27. States making general rate reductions in the personal income tax were Alaska, Delaware, Indiana, Maine, Minnesota, Montana, Nebraska, New Mexico, New York, North Dakota, Utah, Vermont, and Wisconsin. In 1978 all of these states except Indiana and North Dakota had state and local tax burdens (measured as percentage of personal income) above the state median.

States indexing personal income taxes were Arizona, California, Colorado, Iowa, Minnesota, Montana, Oregon, South Carolina, and Wisconsin. Only Iowa and South Carolina had 1978 state and local tax burdens below the state median.

28. National Governors' Association and National Association of State Budget Offices, *Fiscal Survey of the States, 1981-82,* Preliminary Report (Washington, D.C.: National Governors' Association, 1982).

29. The states ending FY 1981 with general fund balances in excess of 15 percent of general fund revenues, with the severance tax share of general fund revenues for FY 1982 shown in parentheses, are Alaska (88.7 percent with leases and royalties), Hawaii (0), Louisiana (42.5 percent with leases and royalties), Montana (24.0 percent), New Mexico (33.3 percent with leases and royalties), North Dakota (22.8 percent), Oklahoma (26.8 percent), Texas (27.8 percent), and Wyoming (22.4 percent).

30. Decisions to conform to or decouple from ACRS have been even more closely tied to state budget condition than state grants-in-aid replacement decisions. All five of the states listed in "good" condition in table 6-8, which have corporate income taxes, conform to the federal changes. Of the five states which have corporate income taxes and are categorized as in "poor" budget condition, three decoupled and the other two adopted ACRS but raised their tax rates to offset several losses.

NOTES TO CHAPTER 7

1. Edmund Burke, *Reflections on the Revolution in France* (1790).

2. Robert A. Nisbet, *Community and Power,* second edition (New York: Oxford University Press, 1962), p. 268.

3. Ibid., pp. 98, 109.

4. Peter L. Berger and Richard John Neuhaus, *To Empower People: The Role of Mediating Structures in Public Policy* (Washington, D.C.: American Enterprise Institute, 1977), p. 35.

5. Theodore M. Kerrine and Richard John Neuhaus, "Mediating Structures: A Paradigm for Democratic Pluralism," *The Annals of the American Academy of Political and Social Sciences*, vol. 446, Nov. 1979, p. 18.

6. Office of Management and Budget, *Budget of the United States Government, Fiscal Year 1983* (Washington, D.C.: GPO, 1982), part 5, p. 104.

7. For further elaboration of this point, see Lester M. Salamon, "The Rise of Third-Party Government," *The Washington Post*, June 29, 1980; and Lester M. Salamon, "Rethinking Public Management: Third-Party Government and the Changing Forms of Public Action," *Public Policy*, Summer 1981, pp. 255-275.

8. Ralph Kramer, *Voluntary Organizations in the Welfare State* (Berkeley: University of California Press, 1981), pp. 61-62.

9. Bill Benton et al., *Social Services: Federal Legislation vs. State Implementation* (Washington, D.C.: The Urban Institute, October 1978); U.S. Department of Health and Human Services, *Social Services U.S.A* (Washington, D.C.: GPO, 1981).

10. Waldemar Nielsen, *The Endangered Sector* (New York: Columbia University Press, 1980), pp. 14, 47.

11. For a fuller elaboration of these estimates and of the approach that led to them, see Lester M. Salamon with Alan J. Abramson, *The Federal Government and the Nonprofit Sector: Implications of the Reagan Budget Proposals* (Washington, D.C.: The Urban Institute, 1981).

12. This finding is consistent with the estimates developed by the Commission on Private Philanthropy and Public Needs (the Filer Commission). According to these estimates, all public support to the nonprofit sector (including state and local as well as federal government) totaled $23.1 billion in 1974, compared with nonreligious private giving of $13.6 billion. Gabriel Rudney, "The Scope of the Private Voluntary Charitable Sector," *Research Papers Sponsored by the Commission on Private Philanthropy and Public Needs* (Washington, D.C.: U.S. Department of the Treasury, 1977), pp. 135-42.

13. This finding is consistent with data generated by United Way of America from member United Way agencies across the country. These data indicate that government support represents as much as 70 to 80 percent of total revenues for agencies engaged in such functions as community/neighborhood development, child welfare, and services for the aged. United Way of America, *United Way Allocations, 1981*.

14. Nelly Hartogs and Joseph Weber, *Impact of Government Funding on the Management of Voluntary Agencies* (New York: Greater New York Fund/United Way, 1978), pp. 8-9.

15. Kramer, *Voluntary Organizations*, pp. 160, 163.

16. See, for example, Michael K. Taussig, "Economic Aspects of the Personal Income Tax Treatment of Charitable Contributions," *National Tax Journal*, vol. 20, March 1967, pp. 1-19; Robert A. Schwartz, "Personal Philanthropic Contributions," *Journal of Political Economy*, vol. 78, November-December 1970, pp. 1264-91; Martin Feldstein, "The Income Tax and Charitable Contributions: Part I—Aggregate and Distributional Effects," *National Tax Journal*, vol. 28, March 1975, pp. 81-100; Lawrence B. Lindsey, "Alternatives to the Current Maximum Tax on Earned Income," paper presented at the Conference on Simulation Methods in Tax Policy Analysis, National Bureau of Economic Research, January 1981; James N. Morgan, Richard F. Dye, and Judith H. Hybels, "Results from Two National Surveys of Philanthropic Activity," in Commission on Private Philanthropy and Public Needs, *Research Papers*, vol. 1 (Washington, D.C.: U.S. Department of the Treasury, 1977), pp. 157-323; Charles T. Clotfelter and E. Eugene Steuerle, "Charitable Contributions," in Henry Aaron and Joseph Pechman, eds., *How Taxes Affect Economic Behavior* (Washington, D.C.: Brookings Institution, 1981), pp. 403-66.

17. For a fuller discussion of this analysis, see: Charles T. Clotfelter and Lester M. Salamon, "The Impact of the 1981 Tax Act on Charitable Giving," *National Tax Journal*, June 1982; and Charles T. Clotfelter and Lester M. Salamon, *The Federal Government and the Nonprofit*

Notes to Chapter 7 (continued)

Sector: The Impact of the 1981 Tax Act on Individual Charitable Giving (Washington, D.C.: The Urban Institute, 1981).

18. The evidence reviewed by Susan Rose-Ackerman does not support the view that reduced government grants will stimulate increased private donations. Indeed, it suggests that such grants may encourage giving. See Susan Rose-Ackerman, "Do Government Grants to Charity Reduce Private Donations?" in Michelle J. White, ed., *Nonprofit Firms in a Three Sector Economy*, COUPE papers in Public Economics, pp. 95-114.

19. Commission on Private Philanthropy and Public Needs, *Giving in America* (Washington, D.C.: U.S. Department of the Treasury, 1978), p. 96.

20. Berger and Neuhaus, *To Empower People*, p. 45.

NOTES TO CHAPTER 8

1. Because of space limitations, this chapter does not address other important topics, notably changes in public regulation of private employment in such matters as minimum wages, equal employment opportunity, and occupational safety and health.

2. Workers dislocated by economic change—such as those laid off in the declining automobile and steel industries—represent another structural problem receiving increased attention. Again because of lack of space, they are not discussed here. See Marc Bendick, Jr., and Judith Radlinski Devine, "Workers Dislocated by Economic Change: Do They Need Federal Employment and Training Assistance?" in *Seventh Annual Report: The Federal Interest in Employment and Training* (Washington, D.C.: National Commission for Employment Policy, 1981), pp. 175-226.

3. Richard B. Freeman, "Troubled Workers in the Labor Market," in *Seventh Annual Report*, pp. 112 and 116.

4. Ralph E. Smith, "Groups in Need of Employment and Training Assistance," in *Seventh Annual Report*, pp. 46-49.

5. *America's New Beginning: A Program for Economic Recovery* (Washington, D.C.: Executive Office of the President, February 18, 1981), p. 21.

6. Peter Gottschalk, "Transfer Scenarios and Projections of Poverty into the 1980s," *Journal of Human Resources* vol. 16, no. 1 (Winter 1981), p. 44.

7. Edward M. Gramlich, "The Distributional Effects of Higher Unemployment," *Brookings Papers on Economic Activity* no. 2 (1974), p. 312.

8. Robinson G. Hollister and John L. Palmer, "The Impact of Inflation on the Poor," in Kenneth E. Boulding and Martin Pfaff, eds., *Redistribution to the Rich and the Poor* (Belmont, Calif.: Wadsworth, 1977), pp. 371-372.

9. Lester C. Thurow, *Poverty and Discrimination* (Washington, D.C.: The Brookings Institution, 1969), p. 61.

10. *Employment and Training Report of the President, 1980* (Washington, D.C.: GPO, 1980), pp. 249-256.

11. Ronald G. Ehrenberg, "The Demographic Structure of Unemployment Rates and Labor Market Transition Probabilities," in Ronald G. Ehrenberg, ed., *Research in Labor Economics*, vol. 3 (Greenwich, Conn.: JAI Press, 1980), p. 241.

12. Isabel V. Sawhill, "The Full Employment Unemployment Rate," Working Paper (Washington, D.C.: The Urban Institute, 1981).

13. Alan S. Blinder,*The Truce in the War on Poverty: Where Do We Go From Here?* (Washington, D.C.: National Policy Exchange, 1982), pp. 10-14.

14. Martin N. Bailey and James Tobin, "Inflation Consequences of Job Creation," in John L. Palmer, ed., *Creating Jobs* (Washington, D.C.: The Brookings Institution, 1978), p. 51.

15. See Richard P. Nathan et al., *Public Service Employment, A Field Evaluation* (Washington, D.C.: The Brookings Institution, 1981). The administration also inherited smaller job creation programs not discussed here, including the Young Adult Conservation Corps and the Community Service Program for Older Americans.

16. *Effects of Eliminating Public Service Employment* (Washington, D.C.: Congressional Budget Office, 1981) and *Implementation of the Phaseout of CETA Public Service Jobs* (Washington, D.C.: U.S. General Accounting Office, 1982).

17. Nathan et al., chapter 4.

18. Charles Mallar et al., *Evaluation of the Economic Impact of the Job Corps Program: Second Follow-up Report* (Princeton, N.J.: Mathematica Policy Research, 1980).

19. *Statement by the Secretary of Labor* (Washington, D.C.: U.S. Department of Labor, March 10, 1982).

20. Special tabulation, Continuous Longitudinal Manpower Survey, covering persons enrolled in CETA classroom training or on-the-job training during FY 1976.

21. *Employment and Training Report of the President, 1981* (Washington, D.C.: GPO, 1981), p. 47.

22. *Employment and Training Report, 1981* p. 48.

23. The largest federal support for economic development is actually not any of these programs but the federal tax exemption for interest on state and local industrial development bonds, which cost the federal treasury about $1.8 billion in FY 1982. The administration had proposed to restrict that program as well.

24. *Budget of the U.S. Government, Fiscal Year 1983: Major Themes and Details* (Washington, D.C.: GPO, 1982), p. 95.

25. *An Impact Evaluation of the Urban Development Action Grant Program* (Washington, D.C.: U.S. Department of Housing and Urban Development, 1980), pp. i-vi and p. 64.

26. *The Administration's Enterprise Zone Proposal: Fact Sheet* (Washington, D.C.: Office of the White House Press Secretary, March 23, 1982). Other enterprise zone proposals and proposed bills preceded President Reagan's official endorsement of the concept. The philosophy of the various proposals is similar, although details differ from those listed here.

27. See Roger Schmenner, *The Location Decisions of Large, Multiplant Companies* (Washington, D.C.: U.S. Department of Housing and Urban Development, 1981).

28. See David Rasmussen, Marc Bendick, Jr., and Larry C. Ledebur, "Evaluating State Economic Development Incentives from a Firm's Perspective," *Business Economics* vol. 17, no. 3 (May 1982), pp. 23-29.

NOTES TO CHAPTER 9

1. Notable exclusions are financing programs for veterans, the military, and federal employees; biomedical research; and food and drug regulation.

2. Data on national health expenditures come from Robert M. Gibson and Daniel R. Waldo, "National Health Expenditures, 1980," *Health Care Financing Review*, vol. 3 (September 1981), pp. 1-54.

3. See U.S. Congress, Congressional Budget Office, *Profile of Health Care Coverage: The Haves and Have-Nots"* (Washington, D.C.: GPO, March 1979); *Catastrophic Health Insurance* (Washington, D.C.: GPO, January 1977); and *Medicaid: Choices for 1982 and Beyond* (Washington, D.C.: GPO, June 1981), p. 13.

4. U.S. Department of Health and Human Services, Health Care Financing Administration, Office of Research Demonstrations and Statistics, "Ten Years of Short-Stay Hospital Use and Costs Under Medicare: 1967-1976," *Health Care Financing Research Report*, August 1980; and Charles R. Fisher, "Differences by Age Groups in Health Care Spending," *Health Care Financing Review*, vol. 1 (Spring 1980), p. 71. In contrast to hospital use, Medicare beneficiaries' use of physician services outside the hospital has remained relatively stable over time.

5. The Robert Wood Johnson Foundation, *Special Report*, no. 1, "America's Health Care System: A Comprehensive Portrait," 1978.

6. The Robert Wood Johnson Foundation, *Annual Report 1981*, pp. 11-12. For a detailed analysis of medical care's contribution to health, see Jack Hadley, *More Medical Care, Better Health?* (Washington, D.C.: The Urban Institute, 1982).

7. Computed from Robert M. Gibson and Daniel R. Waldo, "National Health Expenditures, 1980," tables 1, 2, and 3; and *1981 Statistical Abstract of the U.S.*, tables 423, 479,

and 713. Intergovernmental transfers are excluded from state and local spending. Private spending is presented here as a share of after-tax income, but because about half that spending is paid for through insurance, which is largely purchased with untaxed dollars, the out-of-pocket burden is somewhat less than shown.

8. Computed from American Hospital Association, *Hospital Statistics, 1981 Edition* (Chicago: American Hospital Association, 1981), table I, p. 5; and from hospital input price index provided by the Health Care Financing Administration.

9. Gail R. Wilensky, "Government and the Financing of Health Care, *American Economic Review*, forthcoming.

10. For a summary and comparison of the effects of cost containment measures, see Bruce Steinwald and Frank A. Sloan, "Regulatory Approaches to Hospital Cost Containment: A Synthesis of the Empirical Evidence," in Mancur Olson, ed., *A New Approach to the Economics of Health Care*, A Conference Sponsored by The American Enterprise Institute for Public Policy Research (Washington, D.C., 1981), pp. 274-308. On hospital rate setting, see Frank A. Sloan, "Regulation and the Rising Cost of Hospital Care," *Review of Economics and Statistics*, vol. 63 (November 1981), pp. 479-487. On PSROs, see U.S. Congress, Congressional Budget Office, *The Effect of PSROs on Health Care Costs: Current Findings and Future Evaluations* (Washington, D.C.: GPO, June 1979); and U.S. Congress, Congressional Budget Office, *The Impact of PSROs on Health Care Costs: Update of CBO's 1979 Evaluation*. (Washington, D.C.: GPO, January 1981). On regulation of capital expenditures, see U.S. Congress, Congressional Budget Office, *Health Planning: Issues for Reauthorization* (Washington, D.C.: GPO, March 1982).

11. Ceilings on hospital payment apply only to routine costs and in 1980 affected only an estimated 12 percent of hospitals. The Carter administration tightened the ceiling for 1981, extending its impact to an estimated 18 percent of hospitals. As described below, however, some of the costs above ceilings may be shifted to unregulated ancillary cost centers or recovered through higher charges to other purchasers. Ceilings on physician payment affect a larger proportion of physicians (about 50 percent overall, more for some specialties). But physicians offset the effects of ceilings by charging patients rates higher than the ceilings and increasing the volume and intensity of services for which they bill the program. See Lynn Paringer, "The Medicare Economic Index: Impact on Program Costs and Beneficiary Liability" Working Paper 1306-01-03. (Washington, D.C.: The Urban Institute, June 1981); "The Effect of the Medicare Economic Index on Reasonable Fees: Evidence from California," Working Paper 1306-01-04 (Washington, D.C.: The Urban Institute, July 1981); and Margaret Sulvetta, "Analysis of Changes in Physicians' Medicare Revenues," Working Paper 1250-04 (Washington, D.C.: The Urban Institute, August 1981).

12. Frank A. Sloan, "Regulation and the Rising Cost of Hospital Care."

13. Lawrence D. Brown, *Politics and Health Care Organizations: HMOs vs. Federal Policy*. The Brookings Institution, forthcoming.

14. For an assessment of HMOs' performance and their effect on fee-for-service providers, see Harold S. Luft, *Health Maintenance Organizations: Dimensions of Performance* (New York: Wiley-Interscience, 1981). Harold S. Luft, "Health Maintenance Organizations, Competition, Cost Containment, and National Health Insurance," in Mark V. Pauly, ed., *National Health Insurance: What Now, What Later, What Never?*, (Washington, D.C.: The American Enterprise Institute for Public Policy Research, 1980), pp. 283-306; and U.S. Congress, Congressional Budget Office, *Containing Medical Care Costs Through Market Forces*, (Washington, D.C.: GPO, May 1982).

15. For elaboration of this concept see Alain Enthoven, *Health Plan: The Only Practical Solution to the Soaring Cost of Medical Care* (Reading, Mass.: Addison Wesley, 1980).

16. About three-quarters of these tax expenditures result from the exclusion from income and payroll taxes of employer contributions to employees' insurance premiums. Other tax expenditures include itemized deductions of personal health insurance premiums and medical expenses, health-related charitable contributions, and exclusion of interest on state and local hospital bonds. Estimates come from the Office of Management and Budget.

17. There is, however, a more intensive administrative review of current disability claimants' continued eligibility. The result may be termination of Medicare as well as termination of cash disability benefits for some beneficiaries.

18. For most of the 1970s, Medicare hospital days and out-of-hospital physician visits remained relatively stable. Furthermore, between 1974 and 1979, increased enrollment accounted for only 2.8 percentage points of an 18 percent average annual rate of increase in Medicare spending. Hence increases in price and intensity of service account overwhelmingly for Medicare spending increases.

19. Almost a third of the projected federal savings would come from increased revenues rather than lower spending.

20. Paringer, "The Medicare Economic Index" and "The Effect of the Medicare Index on Reasonable Fees"; and Sulvetta, "Analysis of Changes in Physicians' Medicare Resources."

21. Calculated from Fisher, "Differences by Age Groups in Health Care Spending," table A (expenses for Medicare physician premiums are added to the expenditures Fisher reports); and Bureau of the Census, *Current Population Survey*, "Money Income of Persons and Families in the United States."

22. Over 60 percent of the elderly have private hospital insurance; over 40 percent have in-hospital physicians coverage; and 27 percent have coverage for physicians office visits. Marjorie Smith Carroll and Ross H. Arnett III, "Private Health Insurance Plans in 1978 and 1979," *Health Care Financing Review*, vol. 3 (September 1981), p. 56.

23. Charles R. Link, Stephen H. Long, and Russell F. Settle, "Cost Sharing, Supplementary Insurance, and Health Services Utilization among the Medicare Elderly," *Health Care Financing Review*, vol. 2 (Fall 1980), pp. 25-32.

24. On public-private payment differentials, see Health Insurance Association of America, "Hospital Cost Shifting: The Hidden Tax," (Washington, D.C.: Health Insurance Association of America, 1982) p. 4.

25. This discussion of state actions draws heavily on Lawrence Bartlett and Claudia Hansen, *Catalogue of State Medicaid Program Changes* (Washington, D.C.: State Medicaid Program Information Center of the National Governors Association, May 1982) as well as interviews with several state Medicaid directors. Data on specific Medicaid expenditures and rates of growth come from Health Care Financing Administration, *The Medicare and Medicaid Data Book*, 1981 (Washington, D.C.: U.S. Department of Health and Human Services, April 1982). An elaboration of the discussion presented here can be found in Randall R. Bovbjerg and John Holahan, *Medicaid in the 1980s: More State Control, Less Federal Money* (Washington, D.C.: The Urban Institute, forthcoming).

26. Linda E. Demkovich, "For States Squeezed by Medicaid Costs, The Worst Crunch Is Yet to Come," *National Journal* (January 10, 1981), pp. 44-49. Also, see chapter 6 of this book for a discussion of the fiscal pressures on state governments.

27. The effort required to compensate for federal cuts would vary inversely with federal matching rates. The federal government contributes more to Medicaid costs in low-income states. A low-income state with a federal match of 75 percent would have to raise its own spending 9 percent to offset a 3 percent federal cut. In contrast, a high-income state with the minimum 50 percent match could offset a 3 percent cut with a 3 percent increase.

28. Of the five states adopting alternative systems after enactment of the 1981 Omnibus Reconciliation Act, one (Alabama) originally applied and had its system approved under the old law. Some states that already had alternatives amended their systems following enactment of the new law. California's change is now under litigation.

29. Although substitution of hospital for physician care has not been demonstrated, evidence on the influence of fees on physicians' willingness to participate in Medicaid is quite strong. See Jack Hadley, "Physician Participation in Medicaid: Evidence from California," *Health Services Research*, vol. 14 (1979), pp. 266-280; Frank Sloan, Janet Mitchell, and Jerry Cromwell, "Physician Participation in State Medicaid Programs," *Journal of Human Resources*, vol. 13 (Supplement 1978), pp. 211-245; and Philip J. Held, John Holahan, and Cathy Carlson, "The Effect of Medicaid and Private Fees on Physician Participation in California's Medicaid Program," Working Paper 1306-02-01 (Washington, D.C.: The Urban Institute, March 1982).

Notes to Chapter 9 (continued)

30. Judith Feder and William Scanlon, "Regulating the Bed Supply in Nursing Homes," *Milbank Memorial Fund Quarterly/Health and Society*, vol. 58 (Winter 1980), pp. 54-88.

31. A 1972 amendment, implemented in 1977, for the first time established federal requirements on Medicaid payments to nursing homes. Rates were to be "reasonably cost-related," and the federal government had to approve the states' payment methods. This requirement reduced but did not eliminate state discretion in setting rates. In 1980, Congress removed requirements for federal oversight, leaving judgments as to cost-relatedness to the states and the courts.

32. William Weissert, "Toward a Continuum of Care for the Elderly: A Note of Caution," *Public Policy*, vol. 29 (Summer 1981), pp. 331-340; and Margaret Stassen and John Holahan, *Long-Term Care Demonstrations Projects: A Review of Recent Evaluations*, Working Paper 1227-02 (Washington, D.C.: The Urban Institute, February 1981).

33. Congressional Budget Office, *An Analysis of President Reagan's Budget Revisions for Fiscal Year 1982* (Washington, D.C.: GPO, March 1981), p. A-54.

34. This discussion draws on conversations with numerous state officials as well as groups which have conducted surveys of the states, notably the National Governor's Association and George Washington University's Intergovernmental Health Policy Project.

35. Discussions of competition drawn on here include the Congressional Budget Office, *Containing Medical Care Costs*; Mancur Olson, ed., *A New Approach to Economics of Health Care*; William Roy, ed., *Effects of the Payment Mechanism on the Health Care Delivery System*, Proceedings of a Conference November 7-8, 1977, National Center for Health Services Research; "A Special Symposium: Market-Oriented Approaches to Achieving Health Policy Goals," *Vanderbilt Law Review*, vol. 34 (May 1981); and "Special Issue: Competition and Regulation in Health Care Markets," *Milbank Memorial Fund Quarterly/Health and Society*, vol. 59 (Spring 1981).

36. Personal communication from the Congressional Budget Office.

37. Pamela J. Farley and Gail R. Wilensky, "Options, Incentives, and Employment-Related Health Insurance Coverage," unpublished paper presented at the Annual Meeting of the American Economic Association, Washington, D.C., May 1, 1982, pp. 7, 19-20.

38. For a discussion of employer attitudes, see Harvey M. Sapolsky et al., "Corporate Attitudes Toward Health Care Costs," Final Report NCHSR Grant No.: 1R 03 HS 034 47-01S1, December 1980 (unpublished).

39. Pamela J. Farley and Gail R. Wilensky, "Options, Incentives, and Employment-Related Health Insurance Coverage," p. 18.

40. Congressional Budget Office, *Containing Medical Care Costs Through Market Forces*, p. 35.

41. See the citations in note 3.

42. Statement on Health Planning prepared for the Subcommittee on Health and Environment of the House Committee on Energy and Commerce, U.S. House of Representatives by Harry P. Cain II, Executive Director, American Health Planning Association, March 22, 1982; and Linda E. Demkovich, "Reagan's Ideological Gamble—Eliminating Hospital Cost Review," *National Journal* (March 14, 1981), pp. 440-443.

43. U.S. Congress, House of Representatives, "Increase in Hospital Costs and the Effect of the Voluntary Effort," Hearing Before the Subcommittee on Health and Environment of the Committee on Energy and Commerce, December 15, 1981; and Frank A. Sloan, "Regulation and the Rising Cost of Hospital Care."

44. Intergovernmental Health Policy Project, *State Health Notes*, no. 22, December 1981.

NOTES TO CHAPTER 10

1. Martha Derthick, *Uncontrollable Spending for Social Services Grants* (Washington, D.C.: The Brookings Institution, 1975).

2. Ibid., p. 31.

3. Ann Kallman Bixby, "Social Welfare Expenditures, Fiscal Year 1979," *Social Security Bulletin*, vol. 44, no. 11 (November 1981) pp. 3-12.

4. Ibid, pp. 5-6.

5. See, for example, Nathan Glazer, "Should Judges Administer Social Services?" *The Public Interest*, winter 1978, pp. 64-80.

6. Ibid., p. 80.

7. Children's Defense Fund, *A Children's Defense Fund Budget: An Analysis of the President's Budget and Children* (Washington, D.C.: Children's Defense Fund, 1982), p. 43.

8. Eugene C. Royster et al., *A National Survey of Head Start Graduates and Their Peers* (Cambridge, Mass.: ABT Associates, 1978).

9. Office of Management and Budget, *Major Themes and Additional Budget Details, Fiscal Year 1983* (Washington, D.C.: GPO, 1982), p. 11.

10. Atlanta Regional Commission, "Preliminary Assessment of the Impact of Federal Health and Social Service Budget Reduction on the Atlanta Region" (Atlanta: Atlanta Regional Commission, July 1981).

11. See testimony of Richard Schweiker, Secretary of Health and Human Services, before Senate Labor, Health, and Human Services and Education Appropriations Subcommittee on April 14, 1982.

12. Office of Human Development Services, *Social Services, U.S.A., FY 1979* (Washington, D.C.: GPO) p. 2-23.

13. Health Care Financing Administration, unpublished data provided by Medicaid Program Data Branch and state Medicaid agencies.

14. Each state attempting to make this transfer must first receive a Medicaid waiver from the secretary of the Department of Health and Human Services (see chapter 9, "Health").

15. Office of Human Development Services, unpublished data from *Social Services, U.S.A., 1980.*

16. Health Care Financing Administration, unpublished data provided by Medicaid Program Data Branch and state Medicaid agencies.

17. Bixby, *Social Security Bulletin*, pp. 5-6.

18. *1981 Annual Report-Giving U.S.A.* (New York: American Association of Fundraising Counsel), p. 49.

19. See chapter 7 for a broad discussion of the effects of recent federal policy changes on the nonprofit sector and its ability to offset the reductions in public spending.

20. *1981 Annual Report-Giving U.S.A.*, p. 49.

Notes to Chapter 11

1. Advisory Commission on Intergovernmental Relations, *Intergovernmentalizing the Classroom: Federal Involvement in Elementary and Secondary Education* (Washington, D.C.: GPO, 1981), p. 5; and National Center for Education Statistics, *The Condition of Education: 1981* (Washington, D.C.: GPO, 1981), p. 98.

2. U.S. Department of Health, Education and Welfare, National Institute of Education (NIE), *The Compensatory Education Study: Executive Summary* (Washington, D.C.: GPO, 1978), p. 1.

3. See NIE, *The Compensatory Education Study*, pp. 4 and 11, Iris C. Rotberg, "Federal Policy Issues in Elementary and Secondary Education" ed. Robert A. Miller, *The Federal Role in Education: New Directions for the Eighties* (Washington, D.C.: Institute for Educational Leadership, 1981), pp. 23-26; U.S. Department of Health, Education and Welfare, *Annual Evaluation Report on Programs Administered by the U.S. Office of Education: FY 1979* (Washington, D.C.: GPO, 1980).

4. National Assessment of Educational Progress, "Has Title I Improved Education for Disadvantaged Students? Evidence from Three National Assessments of Reading," (Denver, Colo.: April 23, 1981).

5. Robert H. Meyer, "The Labor Market Effects of Vocational Education" (Washington, D.C.: The Urban Institute, August 1981).

6. John T. Grasso and John R. Shea, *Vocational Education and Training: Impact on Youth* (Washington, D.C.: Carnegie Foundation for the Advancement of Teaching, 1979).

Notes to Chapter 11 (continued)

7. This issue is discussed by Robert H. Meyer in "The Effect of Vocational Education on Postsecondary School Choices" (Washington, D.C.: The Urban Institute, August 1981); and "The Effect of Academic and Vocational Training on Lifetime Income: A Theoretical Analysis," Working Paper (Washington, D.C.: The Urban Institute, April 1982).

8. For a summary of studies on the effectiveness of vocational education see National Commission on Employment Policy, *The Federal Role in Vocational Education* (Washington, D.C., September 1981), chapter 1.

9. Several programs that are scheduled to be phased into the block grant over the next two years received separate funding in FY 1982. These programs are sometimes included in the totals for chapter 2, thereby increasing the appropriation figures.

10. Alan L. Ginsberg and J. Neil Killakea, "Patterns of Federal Aid to School Districts," *Journal of Education Finance* (winter 1977), pp. 380-395. Also, NIE, *Title I Funds Allocation: The Current Formula* (Washington, D.C.: GPO, 1977); and U.S. Department of Health, Education and Welfare, *Annual Evaluation Report*.

11. Congressional Budget Office, "An Analysis of President Reagan's Budget Revisions for Fiscal Year 1982," Staff Working Paper, March 1981.

12. Jackie Kimbrough and Paul T. Hill, *The Aggregate Effects of Federal Education Programs* (Santa Monica, Calif.: The Rand Corporation, 1981).

13. This does not include Indian education or bilingual education, which were also cut by smaller amounts.

14. Congressional Budget Office, *Analysis*, p. A-39.

15. See Congressional Budget Office, *Reducing the Federal Budget: Strategies and Examples, Fiscal Years 1982-1986* (Washington, D.C.: GPO, 1981), p. 104; or National Commission on Employment Policy, *A Vocational Education Policy for the 1980s* (Washington, D.C., March 1982).

16. Harrison Donnelly, "Little Hope Seen for Tuition Tax Credit Plan," *Congressional Weekly*, April 24, 1982, pp. 911-13.

17. Roy C. Nehrt, *Private Schools in American Education* (Washington, D.C.: National Center for Education Statistics, 1981).

18. James Coleman et al., *Public and Private Schools* (Washington, D.C.: National Technical Information Service, Preliminary Report, March 1981,: U.S. Department of Commerce, Bureau of the Census, *School Enrollment—Social and Economic Characteristics of Students: October 1979*, Current Population Reports Series, p. 20, no. 360 (Washington, D.C.: GPO, 1981).

19. Edward B. Fiske, *After the Federal Cutbacks, A New Era in Paying for College*, The New York Times Fall Survey of Education, November 15, 1981.

20. These percentages refer to men who worked full-time year-round. Women college graduates earned 37 percent more than women high school graduates at ages 25-34 years and about 53 percent more at ages 35 to 54—a greater increment than men at younger ages and a lower one at older ages. Because older groups belong to different cohorts and because successive cohorts of women have changed so radically with respect to their lifetime work patterns, it is particularly difficult to predict what will in fact happen to returns to college as the younger women age on the basis of these cross-sectional data. Earnings data are from Bureau of the Census, *Money Income of Families and Persons in the United States: 1979*, Current Population Reports Series p. 60, no. 129, Nov. 1981, table 53. (Washington, D.C.: GPO, 1981), table 53.

21. For various years between 1939 and 1961 the rate of return has been shown to be about 12 percent. See Gary S. Becker, *Human Capital*, second edition, published by National Bureau of Economic Research, distributed by Columbia University Press, New York, 1975, chapter 4 and chapter 6, section 2. A lower return, however, has been found for the early 1970s, but the measure and interpretation of this estimate are uncertain. See Richard B. Freeman's, *The Over Educated American*, (New York, N.Y.: Academic Press, 1976); and "Overinvestment in College Training?" *Journal of Human Resources* 10 (Summer 1975) 287-311.

22. See Becker, *Human Capital*, pp. 194-198.

23. Ibid., pp. 196-197. Becker's estimate was derived by assuming that all of the unexplained "residual" in accounting for economic growth (after accounting for the contribution made by the increases in capital, labor, and other measurable factors) is due to college education. Becker took an estimate of the residual and of the contribution of education to growth made by Edward Denison in *Sources of Economic Growth in the United States* (Washington, D.C.: Committee for Economic Development, 1962).

24. See J.R. Norsworthy, Michael V. Harper, and Kent Kunze, "The Slowdown in Productivity Growth: Analysis of Some Contributing Factors," *Brookings Papers on Economic Activity*, no. 2 (1979), pp. 387-421.

25. This point and others are made by Richard B. Freeman in "On Mythical Effects of Public Subsidization of Higher Education" in Lewis C. Solomon and Paul J. Taubman, eds., *Does College Matter?* (New York, N.Y.: Academic Press, 1973). On the existence and importance of externalities also see in the same volume the papers by Robert W. Hartman, David S. Mundel, Kenneth E. Clark, and W. Lee Hansen.

26. W. Vance Grant and Leo J. Eiden, *Digest of Educational Statistics, 1981*, National Center for Education Statistics (Washington, D.C.: GPO, February 1981), table 127. This underestimates federal support and, to a lesser extent, state support, and it overestimates students' contributions since students receive direct aid from the federal and state governments which is used to pay tuition and fees.

27. There has been considerable debate in the economics literature whether the provision of low (or free) tuition public institutions results in a transfer from the poor to the rich, since college attendance is highly selective of students from higher-income families. See W. Lee Hansen and Burton A. Weisbrod, *Benefits, Costs, and Finance of Public Higher Education*, (Chicago, Ill.: Markham, 1969) for the argument that college redistributes from poor to rich, and see the counterargument by Joseph A. Pechman in "The Distributional Effects of Public Higher Education in California," *Journal of Human Resources*, vol. 5, (summer 1970) pp. 361-70. For a discussion of these and other findings see David W. Breneman and Susan C. Nelson, *Financing Community Colleges, and Economic Perspective* (Washington, D.C.: Brookings Institution, 1981).

28. In 1979, 46 percent of dependent college students (18 to 24 years of age) came from families with incomes of $25,000 a year or more, whereas only 23 percent of dependent 18 to 24 year olds who had never attended college had families at that income level. Thirty-one percent of youth with no college training were from families with less than $10,000 in income while only 12 percent of college students had such low family incomes. (Calculated from Bureau of the Census, *School Enrollment-Social and Economic Characteristics of Students: October 1979*, Current Population Reports Series, p. 20, no. 360, April 1981, table 38.

29. This result was derived by Michael S. McPherson on the basis of a number of studies. See his "The Demand for Higher Education" in David W. Breneman and Chester E. Finn, Jr., eds., *Public Policy and Higher Education* (Washington, D.C.: Brookings Institution, 1978). It may be an overestimate. See the discussion in Arthur Padilla, "States and Private Higher Education," paper presented at the American Association meeting, December 30, 1981.

30. See John Bishop, "The Effect of Public Policies on the Demand for Higher Education," *Journal of Human Resources*, vol. 12 (summer 1977) pp. 285-307.

31. See the analysis of the determinants of postsecondary school attendance, pp. 299-301 in Robert H. Meyer and David A. Wise, "High School Preparation and Early Labor Force Experience," in Richard B. Freeman and David A. Wise, eds., *The Youth Labor Market Problem: Its Nature, Causes and Consequences* (Chicago, Ill.: University of Chicago Press, 1982).

32. Congressional Budget Office, *Federal Student Assistance: Issues and Options* (Washington, D.C.: GPO, March 1980), p. 17.

33. U.S. Department of Education, *Basic Grants, End of Year Report 1979-80* (Washington, D.C.: GPO, May 1981), table 6B.

34. U.S. Department of Education, *Basic Grants, End of Year Report 1979-80*, table 14A.

35. The results in this paragraph are from Winship C. Fuller, Charles F. Manski, and David A. Wise, *The Impact of the Basic Educational Opportunity Grant Program on College Enrollments*, Discussion Paper Series, John F. Kennedy School of Government, Harvard University,

Notes to Chapter 11 (continued)

July 1980. Also see their *New Evidence on the Economic Determinants of Post-Secondary Schooling Choices* in the same series.

36. The larger estimate is Congressional Budget Office's; the lower estimate is the administration's.

37. *The Guaranteed Student Loan Program: Options for Controlling Federal Costs While Preserving Needed Credit for College*, The Washington Office of the College Board, May 1981, p. A-4.

38. Breneman and Nelson, *Financing Community Colleges*, table 4-6.

39. Ibid., table 4-5.

40. See the discussion of State Student Incentive Grants and a proposal for an alternative in Robert W. Hartman, "Federal Options for Student Aid," in David W. Breneman and Chester E. Finn eds., *Public Policy and Private Higher Education*.

NOTES TO CHAPTER 12

1. The federal programs discussed in this chapter include several that are not in the income security function in the federal budget. The additional programs are military retirement, veterans income security programs, Coast Guard retirement, and Public Health Service officers' retirement. Budget data for housing assistance are included in this chapter, but issues are discussed in the context of housing policy in chapter 13.

2. Congressional Budget Office, *Effects of Tax and Benefit Reductions Enacted in 1981 for Households in Different Income Categories* (Washington, D.C.: CBO, February 1982).

3. The immediate effects of other income security cuts (e.g., in unemployment benefits, Social Security, and child nutrition) could not be analyzed at this level of detail in the time available for the study due to the limitations of the simulation model used.

4. The methodology used in the simulation and the economic assumptions are discussed in chapter 16.

5. *America's New Beginning: A Program for Economic Recovery* (Washington, D.C.: GPO, 1981), table 6, p. 14.

6. Information for this example is drawn from Tom Joe, "Profiles of Families in Poverty: Effects of the 1983 Budget Proposals on the Poor" (Washington, D.C.: Center for the Study of Social Policy, February 1982).

7. For a review of the experimental studies, see Robert A. Moffit, "The Effect of a Negative Income Tax on Work Effort: A Summary of the Experimental Results," chapter 11 in Paul M. Somers, ed., *Welfare Reform in America: Perspectives and Prospects* (Boston: Kluwer-Nijhoff Publishing, 1982). Studies of AFDC are reviewed in Sheldon Danziger, Robert Haveman, and Robert Plotnick, "How Income Transfer Programs Affect Work, Savings, and the Income Distribution: A Critical Review," *Journal of Economic Literature*, vol. 19 (September 1981), pp. 975-1028.

8. Frank Levy, "The Labor Supply of Female Household Heads, or AFDC Work Incentives Don't Work Too Well," *Journal of Human Resources*, vol. 14, no. 1 (winter 1979), p. 76.

9. For example, see Leonard Goodwin, *Do the Poor Want to Work?* (Washington, D.C.: The Brookings Institution, 1972).

10. Prior experience is summarized in Demetra Smith Nightingale, "Workfare and Work Requirement Alternatives for AFDC Recipients: New Priority on an Old Issue" (Paper presented at the 1982 Annual Forum of the National Conference on Social Welfare, Boston, Mass., April 26, 1982).

11. U.S. Department of Health and Human Services, Social Security Administration, *Income of the Population 55 and Over, 1978* (Washington, D.C.: GPO, 1981), p. 49.

12. James R. Storey, "The National Age Discrimination in Employment Act Studies: Results and National Policy" (Paper presented at the 34th Annual Meeting of the Gerontological Society of America, Toronto, Ontario, November 10, 1981).

13. William Greider, "The Education of David Stockman," *Atlantic Monthly*, December 1981, p. 43.

NOTES TO CHAPTER 13

1. For a more comprehensive discussion of U.S. housing policy, see R. Struyk, J. Tuccillo, and J. Zais, "Housing Policy in the First Two Years of the Reagan Administration, " Working Paper 3123-1 (Washington, D.C.: The Urban Institute, 1982).

2. Budget authority is the product of contract authority (the maximum expenditure permitted in the first year of the commitment) and the length of the contract. Contract authority for a new unit has been about twice that of an existing unit, and the length of the contract of a typical new unit is thirty years, while that of an existing unit in Section 8 is fifteen years.

3. For more on this, see Paul Dommel et al., *Decentralizing Urban Policy* (Washington, D.C.: The Brookings Institution, 1982), p. 224.

4. Office of Management and Budget, *Major Themes and Additional Details, Fiscal Year 1983* (Washington, D.C.: GPO, 1982), p. 110.

5. This is to be phased in over a five-year period for current participants. This change was foreshadowed by congressional action in 1979 that gave HUD authority, which was not used, to charge moderate-income households 30 percent of income instead of 25 percent.

6. For units made available for occupancy after October 5, 1981, the limit is 5 percent.

7. A 1979 survey of Section 8 new construction projects in Standard Metropolitan Statistical Areas (SMSAs) found that 75 percent of occupants were very low income households, i.e., incomes were below 50 percent of area median. For Section 8 existing, a national survey conducted in late 1976 showed 82 percent of recipients to be very low income households. Supporting data are in J. Wallace, Jr., S. Bloom, W. Holshouser, S. Mansfield, and D. Weinberg, *Participation and Benefits in the Urban Section 8 Program* (Cambridge, Mass.: Abt Associates, 1981); and M. Drury, O. Lee, M. Springer, and L. Yap, *Lower Income Housing Assistance Program: Nationwide Evaluation of the Existing Housing Program* (Washington, D.C.: GPO, 1978).

8. Supporting figures are in M. Levine, *Federal Housing Assistance: Alternative Approaches* (Washington, D.C.: Congressional Budget Office, 1982).

9. R. Struyk and J. Blake, *Determining Who Lives in Public Housing* Project Report 3009-2 (Washington, D.C.: The Urban Institute, 1982).

10. S. Mayo, S. Mansfield, D. Warner, and R. Zwetchkenbaum, *Housing Allowances and Other Rental Housing Assistance Programs—A Comparison Based on the Housing Allowance Demand Experiment, Part 2: Costs and Efficiency* (Cambridge, Mass.: Abt Associates, 1979).

11. C.L. Barnett, "Expected and Actual Effects of Housing Allowances-Housing Prices," *AREUEA Journal,* vol. 7, no. 3 (1979).

12. M. Murray, "Subsidized and Unsubsidized Housing States, 1961–77" (Washington, D.C.: U.S. Department of Housing and Urban Development, 1979). J.C. Weicher, *The Relationship Between Subsidized Housing Production and Loss Rates Within Metropolitan Areas,* Project Report 1484-1 (Washington, D.C.: The Urban Institute, 1982).

13. The President's Commission on Housing, *Interim Report* (Washington, D.C.: GPO, 1981), chapter 2.

14. S. Newman, R. Struyk, and D. Manson, *Poverty, Housing Deprivation, and Housing Assistance* Project Report 3089-1 (Washington, D.C.: The Urban Institute, 1982).

15. J. Khadduri and R. Struyk, "Housing Vouchers for the Poor," *Journal of Policy Analysis and Management,* vol. 1, no. 2 (1982).

16. This term is ours, not the administration's; they call the revised program "Modified Section 8." Our title derives from the fact that most of the changes come from the experience with the experimental housing allowance program and that "voucher" is now the generally accepted way of referring to housing allowances.

17. In particular, the changes would cease treating the FMR as the maximum for which a unit could rent and still be in the program (although the subsidy would be calculated using the FMR), and increase the incentive to participants to occupy units renting for less than the FMR. For the evidence in support of these changes, see E.O. Olson and D.R. Rasmussen, "Section 8 Existing: A Program Evaluation," *Occasional Papers in Housing and Community Affairs,* vol. 6 (1979), pp. 1–32.

18. In these computations an applicable Section 8 existing payment for 1983 was computed for each household receiving rental assistance in 1979 whose income was below 50 percent of

Notes to Chapter 13 (continued)

the area median. Then new payments were computed for the 1981 changes and for each of the proposed changes in the administration's budget, and then all changes were combined. Any household that no longer received a positive payment for the all-changes-combined calculations was dropped from the population of households being analyzed. Thus the figures in the table are for those households that would still be receiving a positive subsidy payment under the most restricted set of benefit rules. Also note these calculations *exclude* the effects of inflation pushing up rents at a higher rate than incomes. Thomas Thibodeau, *Modeling Alternative Housing Voucher Programs*, Contract Report 3087-2 (Washington, D.C.: The Urban Institute, 1982).

19. The amount of the deduction cannot exceed 2 percent of the total allocation.

20. See chapter 8 for further discussion of urban enterprise zones.

21. The Section 312 program was eliminated in the 1981 legislation, and the Section 8 moderate rehabilitation program is proposed for elimination in the FY 1983 budget.

NOTES TO CHAPTER 14

1. U.S. House of Representatives, Subcommittee on Surface Transportation, Committee on Public Works and Transportation, *The Status of the Nation's Highways: Conditions and Performance, Report of the Secretary to the United States Congress* (Washington, D.C.: GPO, 1981).

2. Office of Management and Budget, *Themes and Additional Budget Details for Fiscal Year 1983* (Washington, D.C.: GPO, 1982).

3. National Transportation Policy Study Commission, *National Transportation Policies through the Year 2000* (Washington, D.C.: GPO, 1979), p. 49.

4. John Meyer and Jose Gomez-Ibanez, *Autos, Transit, and Cities* (Cambridge, Mass.: Harvard University Press, 1981), chapter 1.

5. Tom Muller, Kevin Neels, John Tilney, and Grace Dawson, "The Economic Impact of I-295 on the Richmond Central Business District," Contract Report No. 5068-01 (Washington, D.C.: The Urban Institute, 1977).

6. A. Q. Mowbray, *Road to Ruin* (Philadelphia, Pa.: J. B. Lippincott Company, 1969).

7. Alan Altshuler, *The Urban Transportation System: Politics and Policy Innovation* (Cambridge, Mass.: The MIT Press, 1979), chapter 2.

8. John Meyer and Jose Gomez-Ibanez, *Autos, Transit, and Cities*, chapter 3.

9. Ibid.

10. Office of Management and Budget, *Themes and Additional Budget Details*, pp. 215-218.

11. Kiran Bhatt, Robert McGillivray, Michael Beesley, and Kevin Neel, *Congressional Intent and Road User Payments* (Washington, D.C.: The Urban Institute, 1977).

12. "DOT Sends Congress Report on Highway Cost Allocation," U.S. Department of Transportation Press Release (May 13, 1982).

13. National Transportation Policy Study Commission, *National Transportation Policies through the Year 2000*, p. 240.

14. "Administration Witnesses Take Offensive in Battle Over Waterway User Fee," *Traffic World* (February 15, 1982), p. 89.

15. The 3R legislation directed that these funds be used to finance the continuation of crucial rail services or for the systematic phase-out of rail services.

16. Ronald Kirby and Ulrich Ernst, "Involving Private Providers in Public Transportation Programs: Administrative Options," Working Paper 1199-1-5 (Washington, D.C.: The Urban Institute, 1981).

17. A provision in the Omnibus Reconciliation Act of 1981, which allows Conrail to divest itself of passenger commuter operations, is another transportation change which should be mentioned even though it will affect only one region of the country. As a result of this provision, five transit authorities in the Northeast must decide whether to assume operation of the Conrail lines or to contract with Amtrak for services. The act provides funds to buy out Conrail's capital equipment and supplies, and to help the affected transit authorities to plan for a transfer. The act provides no funds, however, to cover operating costs.

18. John Ellwood, Charles Cameron, Catherine Eschbach, John Gunther-Mohr, and Rita Seymour, "Background Material on FY 1982 Federal Budget Reductions" (Princeton, N.J.: Princeton Urban and Regional Research Center, 1982). The budget history on highways and mass transportation is based on information provided in this report, which is a background document for the first round of a field network evaluation study of the Reagan domestic program.

19. *Federal Register* (May 31, 1979), p. 31442.

20. *Federal Register* (July 20, 1981), pp. 37488-37494.

21. Office of Management and Budget, *Themes and Additional Budget Details*.

22. Ibid.

23. The $11.2 billion was calculated using data from the Congressional Budget Office.

24. Each state's share of the trust fund would be based on its 1979-1981 share of the federal grants designated for turnback. There would be an adjustment for gains or losses resulting from the Medicaid-welfare swap.

25. Office of Management and Budget, *Themes and Additional Budget Details*, p. 229.

26. "Administration Witnesses Take Offensive in Battle over Waterway User Fee," *Traffic World*.

27. Drew Lewis's proposal actually is for a five cent equivalent increase in the gasoline tax, meaning that all highway user fee taxes, not just the gasoline tax, would be increased to make up the five cents.

28. To help Conrail become profitable the Congress added provisions which allow it to divest itself of passenger commuter operations and to establish new scaled-down labor protection benefits. The act specifies that, until June 1984, Conrail must be sold as a complete system as long as it is deemed profitable.

29. U.S. House of Representatives, Subcommittee on Investigations and Oversight, Committee on Public Works and Transportation, *Hearings on the Financial and Productivity Problem of Urban Public Transportation* (Washington, D.C.: GPO, 1981), p. 517.

30. Neal Peirce and Carol Steinbach, "Cuts in Transit Aid May Hurt But Could Have a Silver Lining," *National Journal* (April 4, 1981), pp. 568-572.

31. "Administration Witnesses Take Offensive in Battle over Waterway User Fee," *Traffic World*, p. 88.

32. Judy Sarasohn, "Members of Congress, Trade Groups . . . Are Wary of Reagan's Full User Fees," *Congressional Quarterly Weekly Report* (November 7, 1981), pp. 2186-2187.

33. U.S. House of Representatives, Subcommittee on Surface Transportation, Committee on Public Works and Transportation, *The Status of the Nation's Highways*.

34. Rochelle Stanfield, "The New Federalism Is Reagan's Answer to Decaying Highways, Transit Systems," *National Journal* (June 12, 1982), pp. 1040-1044.

35. Damon Stetson, "Public Worker Unions Question Private Contracts," *The New York Times* (November 30, 1981).

36. U.S. House of Representatives, Subcommittee on the Department of Transportation and Related Agencies Appropriations, Committee on Appropriations, *Hearings on the Department of Transportation and Related Agencies Appropriations for 1982* (Washington, D.C.: GPO, 1981), part 7, p. 784.

37. Michael Kemp, Carol Everett, and Frank Spielberg, "The Future Economic Structure of Urban Public Transportation," Working Paper 3025-1 (Washington, D.C.: The Urban Institute, 1982).

NOTES TO CHAPTER 15

1. The regions of the United Stats are defined as follows:

North (Frostbelt)

  Northeast

    New England: Maine, New Hampshire, Vermont, Massachusetts, Rhode Island, Connecticut

    Middle Atlantic: New York, New Jersey, Pennsylvania

Midwest (North Central)

    Great Lakes (East North Central): Ohio, Indiana, Illinois, Michigan, Wisconsin

    Plains (West North Central): Minnesota, Iowa, Missouri, North Dakota, South Dakota, Nebraska, Kansas

Notes to Chapter 15 (continued)

South/West (Sunbelt)
  South
    South Atlantic: Delaware, Maryland, District of Columbia, Virginia, West Virginia, North
        Carolina, South Carolina, Georgia, Florida
    East South Central: Kentucky, Tennessee, Alabama, Mississippi
    West South Central: Arkansas, Louisiana, Oklahoma, Texas
  West
    Mountain: Montana, Idaho, Wyoming, Colorado, New Mexico, Arizona, Utah, Nevada
    Pacific: Washington, Oregon, California, Alaska, Hawaii.
    2. The spending estimates in this paragraph, which also underlie the calculation reported
in the remainder of this section, are taken from chapter 3. The revenue estimates are from
Congressional Budget Office, *Baseline Budget Projections for Fiscal Years 1983-1997* (Washington, D.C.: GPO, February 1982).
    3. For grant programs, the distribution is based on state funding shown in U.S. Department
of the Treasury, *Federal Aid to States, Fiscal Year 1981* (Washington, D.C.: GPO, 1982).
Nongrant program distribution is based on state outlays shown in Community Services Administration, *Geographic Distribution of Federal Funds in Fiscal Year 1980* (Washington, D.C.:
GPO, 1982). Outlay reduction totals for the nation are taken from chapter 3. Program reductions
which cannot be distributed by state (for example, contributions to international organizations),
or those which are minor, are allocated on a per capita basis. A list of programs included to
estimate cuts by region and state is shown in table A-9.
    4. The distribution of defense contractors in FY 1982 and future years is based on data
from several sources. Additional 1982 funding and prime contractor data for specific weapon
systems was obtained from *The Reagan Defense Market* (Greenwich, Conn.: DMS Corporation,
1981). Additional data on contractors and expected weapon systems acquisition costs in FY 1982
and FY 1983 were derived from U.S. Department of Defense, *Program Acquisition Costs By
Weapon System* (February 1982). Information on incremental obligational authority for FY 1982
and FY 1983 was derived from data provided by the Office of Assistant Secretary of Defense
(Public Affairs), February 1982. Since added weapons acquisition costs in FY 1982 exceeded
incremental outlays in FY 1982, acquisition costs were scaled down to reflect outlay levels. The
subcontractor adjustment process is described in Thomas Muller, *Regional Effects of Federal
Activities 1931-1981* (Washington, D.C.: The Urban Institute Press, forthcoming), Appendix C.
The allocation is based on estimated subcontract flows between states in FY 1979 and FY 1980.
    5. Incremental service contracts and payroll are distributed on the basis of their state share
in FY 1980. Procurement contracts are distributed as described in footnote 4.
    6. Albert A. Hirsch, "Policy Multipliers in BEA Quarterly Model," *Survey of Current
Business*, June 1977.

NOTES TO CHAPTER 16
    1. Gordon Green and Edward Welnick at the Bureau of the Census have reached similar
conclusions in forthcoming work.
    2. Timothy M. Smeeding, *Alternative Methods for Valuing Selected In-kind Benefits and
Measuring Their Effect on Poverty*, Technical Paper 50, U.S. Department of Commerce, Bureau
of the Census, March 1982.
    3. See Sheldon Danziger, Robert Haveman, and Robert Plotnick, "How Income Transfer
Programs Affect Work, Savings, and the Income Distribution: A Critical Review," *Journal of
Economic Literature*, vol. 19, no. 3 (September 1981), pp. 975-1028.
    4. For one example of such studies, see R. M. Hutchins, "Welfare, Remarriage, and
Marital Search," *American Economic Review*, June 1979, pp. 369-379.
    5. See Nathan Glazer, "The Limits of Social Policy," *Commentary Magazine*, September
1971, pp. 51-58.
    6. A recent study estimates that, given the current composition of the poverty population,
a 10 percent decline in the unemployment rate will reduce the number of families in poverty by

only 3 percent. See Peter Gottschalk, "Transfer Scenarios and Projections of Poverty in the 1980s," *Journal of Human Resources*, vol. 16, no. 1 (Winter 1981), pp. 41-60.

7. For a more complete discussion of tax changes, see chapter 4.

8. Congressional Budget Office, "Effects of Tax and Benefit Reductions Enacted in 1981 for Households in Different Income Categories," Special Study, February 1982, pp. 14, 31, 34, and 35.

9. Herbert Stein, "Curriculum for Economics 1981: Poverty and the Budget," *AEI Economist*, October 1980, pp. 5-6.

10. For additional information on the TRIM2 microsimulation model, see Randall Webb et al., "TRIM2 Reference Manual," Working Paper 3069-01 (Washington, D.C.: The Urban Insitute, March 1982).

11. This is achieved by indexing all of the tax parameters by the CPI. This includes the maximum standard deduction, personal exemption, the dividend exclusion, and the earned income tax credit maximum and phasedown—as well as the tax brackets.

12. While the magnitude and distribution of tax cuts under the first assumption in table 16-7 are roughly comparable to those estimated by CBO (using the same reference point), the results cannot be strictly compared because the CBO household income breaks are in 1982 dollars while these are in 1980 dollars, and because the CPS (which we used) caps earned incomes for individuals above $57,000 (in 1980 dollars). The latter biases downwards our estimated tax savings for the average household, as well as for those with incomes above $57,000.

13. Some of these families would not be on AFDC (or Food Stamps) the entire year; thus, some families can, for example, be on AFDC in the first part of the year but have sizable earnings (and be ineligible for benefits) in the second half of the year. This mainly explains why 60 percent of the families in table 16-8 have some earnings while a snapshot of AFDC recipients shows that only about 15 percent of the female heads work at any particular time. Part of this difference is also attributable to earnings by other family members.

14. Compared to the CBO high growth projection for 1984, the administration assumes a slightly higher unemployement rate but lower inflation and nominal wage growth, resulting in a slightly smaller increase in real wages (7.1 versus 8.1 percent). On balance, however, the administration's projection for 1984 is much closer to CBO's high growth path than to its low growth path.

15. These per family earnings figures differ from the aggregate earnings projections by CBO because the number of families and individuals are projected to increase from 1980 to 1984.

16. This literature is reviewed in chapter 8. See also an unpublished paper by Edward M. Gramlich and Deborah A. Swift, "*Ex Post* and *Ex Ante* Burden Sharing in a Recession," (mimeographed), December 1980.

17. The responsiveness of the number of poverty level families to economic growth is slightly larger here than suggested by Gottschalk's research cited earlier. He estimates that a 10 percent decline in the unemployment rate reduces the poverty population by 3 percent, while we show a 21 percent decline in the unemployment rate (from 8.4 percent under low growth to 6.6 percent under high growth), reducing the number of families and individuals in poverty by 8 percent.

18. The CBO growth projections used in deriving these estimates, however, contain some assumptions about changes in work behavior due to the policy changes.

ABOUT THE AUTHORS

Alan J. Abramson is a research associate in the Public Management and Economic Development Center of The Urban Institute. Mr. Abramson is currently working on a study of the nonprofit sector and has participated in a project analyzing the efficiency of various forms of federal governmental actions—direct loans, loan guarantees, insurance programs, tax subsidies, government corporations, regulations, and grants-in-aid. Mr. Abramson has been on the staff of the National Academy of Public Administration where he examined management problems of the American presidency. He is coauthor of "The Federal Government and the Nonprofit Sector: Implications of the Reagan Budget Proposals."

Lee Bawden is director of the Human Resources Policy Center at The Urban Institute. Dr. Bawden has conducted research on the causes and consequences of poverty, income transfers for the poor and the elderly, and employment and training policy. Prior to coming to The Urban Institute, he was professor of agricultural economics and economics at the University of Wisconsin and a fellow of the Institute for Research on Poverty. Dr. Bawden is the author of numerous professional publications.

Marc Bendick, Jr. is a senior research associate of the Human Resources Center at The Urban Institute. Dr. Bendick specializes in employment, economic development, and human resources development issues and evaluation of federal programs serving the poor and disadvantaged. He is coauthor of *Housing Vouchers for the Poor: Lessons from A National Experiment.*

Randall R. Bovbjerg is a lawyer and senior research associate in the Institute's Health Policy Center. His recent research has concentrated on state and local health policy shifts in an era of fiscal limitations and state reactions to federal health block grants and Medicaid changes. Before joining The Urban Institute he was a state insurance regulator in Massachusetts. Mr.

525

Bovbjerg's publications include articles on competition and regulation for the *Vanderbilt Law Review* and on competition and Medicare for *Seminars in Nephrology*.

George C. Eads is a professor in the School of Public Affairs at the University of Maryland, College Park, and a consultant to The Urban Institute. He has been a member of the President's Council of Economic Advisers, on the staff of the Council of Wage and Price Stability, and directed the research program in Regulatory Policies and Institutions at The Rand Corporation. Dr. Eads has written extensively on the subject of government regulation. Recent publications include "Harnessing Regulation: The Evolving Role of White House Oversight" and "Research in Regulation: Past Contributions and Future Needs."

Carol T. Everett is a research associate in the Transportation and Community Impact Center of The Urban Institute. Since joining the Institute Ms. Everett has been doing research on alternative approaches for providing public transportation services. She has worked on transportation issues for the Wisconsin Legislature and the Wisconsin Department of Transportation.

Judith Feder is senior research associate in the Health Policy Center at The Urban Institute. Dr. Feder's research has focused on the consequences of various health programs' design for cost and access to medical care. She has analyzed the implementation of Medicare, the structure of public and private health insurance for the elderly, hospital payment strategies, alternative designs for national health insurance, and public policies toward long-term care. Dr. Feder is coeditor of *National Health Insurance: Conflicting Goals and Policy Choices* and coauthor of *Insuring the Nation's Health: Market Competition, Catastrophic and Comprehensive Approaches*.

Michael Fix, a lawyer, is a research associate in the Transportation and Community Impact Center at The Urban Institute. Mr. Fix has conducted research on the impact of federal regulations on municipal expenditures, analyzed the effects of federal, state, and local regulations on housing costs, and examined legal constraints to the issuance and guaranteeing of local government debt.

Michael F. Gutowski is a senior research associate at The Urban Institute. Mr. Gutowski's research activities include analysis of housing policies, social services programs, and the special needs of both the disabled and elderly populations. His recent research has focused on the roles of private profit-making and nonprofit organizations in the delivery of human services.

Jack Hadley is a senior research associate in the Health Policy Center at The Urban Institute. Dr. Hadley's recent research includes an analysis of the implications that alternative national health insurance approaches would have on the supply and distribution of physicians, studies of the structure and financing of graduate medical education, and analyses of physicians' participation in the Medicaid program, including their price and output decisions. Dr. Hadley's most recent book is *More Medical Care, Better Health?*.

John F. Holahan is director of the Health Policy Center at The Urban Institute. He has recently completed a major study of physician services provided to Medicare and Medicaid patients and has coordinated a project which examined a wide variety of problems in implementing national health insurance. He is coeditor of *National Health Insurance: Conflicting Goals and Policy Choices,* and coauthor of *Insuring the Nation's Health: Market Competition, Catastrophic and Comprehensive Approaches.*

Charles Reid Hulten is a senior research associate in The Urban Institute's Public Finance Center. His research has dealt with productivity growth and capital formation and the role of federal tax policy in encouraging economic growth. Dr. Hulten is the editor of *Depreciation, Inflation, and Taxation of Income from Capital.*

Ronald F. Kirby is director of The Urban Institute's Transportation and Community Impact Center. Dr. Kirby's most recent work has been concerned with the federal role in the financing of urban highways and mass transportation. He also consults with the World Bank on transportation problems in developing countries. Dr. Kirby is the senior author of *Para-Transit: Neglected Options for Urban Mobility.*

Jeffrey J. Koshel is director of The Urban Institute's Social Services Center. He has conducted and supervised major studies of programs and policies affecting vulnerable population groups, including dependent and neglected children, the disabled, and the elderly. Mr. Koshel previously served as chief of the Human Resources Cost Analysis Unit at the Congressional Budget Office.

Frank Levy is a professor at the University of Maryland's School of Public Affairs and a senior research associate at The Urban Institute. His research interests include the distribution of income and earnings, welfare policy, and local public finance. His papers, "How Big is the American Underclass?" and "What Ronald Reagan Can Teach the United States About Welfare Reform" have been used extensively in recent discussions of welfare and poverty policy.

Gregory B. Mills is research associate at The Urban Institute, working on the "Changing Domestic Priorities" project of which this volume is part. His prior research has focused upon federal policies to improve welfare administration, especially in the Aid to Families with Dependent Children (AFDC) program. Prior to joining the Institute Dr. Mills served as an economist in the Department of Health and Human Services. He has been a research assistant at the John F. Kennedy School of Government, Harvard University.

Thomas Muller is a principal research associate in the Transportation and Community Impact Center of The Urban Institute. Dr. Muller has conducted numerous studies on the causes and effects of urban growth and decline, with emphasis on fiscal issues associated with economic expansion and contraction at the local and regional levels. Education finance, regional development, economic effects of population distribution, central city migration, and employment have been the focus of his recent reports.

June Avis O'Neill is principal research associate in the Human Resources Center of The Urban Institute. Dr. O'Neill's current research interests include the determinants of women's earnings and occupations, the determinants of child support, higher education finance, and issues in taxation. Prior to joining the Institute, Dr. O'Neill served as a member of the Senior Staff of the President's Council of Economic Advisers and chief of the Human Resources Cost Estimates Unit of the Congressional Budget Office. Dr. O'Neill's publications include *Sources of Funds to Colleges and Universities,* "Productivity Trends in Higher Education," *Resource Use in Higher Education, Trends in Output and Inputs,* and "The Tax Treatment of Married and Single Taxpayers."

John L. Palmer is codirector of The Urban Institute's "Changing Domestic Priorities" project of which this volume is part. His current research interests include economic, social, and budget policy. Dr. Palmer has been an assistant professor of economics at Stanford University, a senior fellow in the Economic Studies Program of The Brookings Institution, and an assistant secretary for the Department of Health and Human Services. He is the author or editor of numerous articles and books including *Inflation, Unemployment and Poverty; Creating Jobs; Toward an Effective Income Support System;* and several chapters in the annual Brookings Institution's *Setting National Priorities* volumes.

George E. Peterson is director of The Urban Institute's Public Finance Center. His research has dealt with the financing of state and local governments and includes recently completed studies of state and local pension systems, public capital financing, and the grants-in-aid system. Dr. Peterson is a member of the National Urban Policy Committee of the National Academy of Sciences. He is the senior author of the series of volumes, *America's Urban Capital Stock,* and general editor of the series, *Papers on Public Economics,* published in conjunction with the Committee on Urban Public Economics.

Lester M. Salamon is director of the Center for Public Management and Economic Development at The Urban Institute. His recent work has focused on alternative instruments of government action, on the processes of policy formulation and implementation, and on the impact of recent federal policy changes in the nonprofit sector. Dr. Salamon is currently directing a major Institute project that is analyzing the structure and role of private, nonprofit organizations. He has been deputy associate director of the Office of Management and Budget and associate professor of policy sciences at Duke University. Dr. Salamon is the author of numerous books and articles. His most recent publications are *The Illusion of Presidential Government;* "Rethinking Public Management: Third-Party Government and the Changing Forms of Government Action"; "The Federal Government and the Nonprofit Sector: Implications of the Reagan Budget Proposals"; and "The Federal Government and the Nonprofit Sector: The Impact of the 1981 Tax Act on Individual Charitable Giving."

Isabel V. Sawhill is codirector of The Urban Institute's "Changing Domestic Priorities" project, of which this volume is part. Dr. Sawhill's areas of research include human resource and economic policy. She has served as director of the National Commission for Employment Policy and chairman of the Department of Economics at Goucher College. She recently coedited *Youth Employment and Public Policy* and coauthored *Time of Transition: the Growth of Families Headed by Women.*

Margaret C. Simms is a senior research associate in the Human Resources Center at The Urban Institute. Her fields of research include education and training issues and state and local public finance. In addition Dr. Simms is director of the Institute's Minorities and Social Policy Program and served on the congressionally mandated Advisory Panel on Financing Elementary and Secondary Education. Prior to coming to the Institute, Dr. Simms was an associate professor and chairperson of the Department of Economics at Atlanta University. She is the author of many publications including "Fiscal Retrenchment: Toward What End?" "The Urban Fiscal Crisis: Proposed Solutions and the Impact on Isolation," and "Causes of Inequity in the Allocation of School Resources."

James R. Storey is director of the Income Security and Pension Policy Center at The Urban Institute. His current research includes studies of mandatory retirement policy, state and local pensions, financial incentives for retirement, and other retirement and welfare issues. Mr. Storey has been director of the Human Resources staff of the Senate Budget Committee, and senior economist of the Subcommittee on Fiscal Policy, Joint Economic Committee. He has written several papers and articles concerning welfare reform and issues related to income and employment of the elderly.

Raymond J. Struyk is director of the Housing and Community Development Center of The Urban Institute. Dr. Struyk is currently involved in a wide range of research projects on urban problems, housing markets, and public policies toward housing. He has served as deputy assistant secretary for research at the Department of Housing and Urban Development. Dr. Struyk is the author of numerous articles and several books in the housing area, including *Housing Vouchers For the Poor: Lessons from a National Experiment, A New System for Public Housing,* and *Improving the Elderly's Housing.*

John A. Tuccillo is a senior research associate in the Housing and Community Development Center of The Urban Institute. Dr. Tuccillo's research interests focus on the impacts of federal credit institutions on housing and the interaction of the tax system and housing investment. He has been a Brookings fellow at the Department of Housing and Urban Development, a staff member of the President's Commission on Housing, and consultant to HUD, GAO, the American Bankers Association, the Comptroller of the Currency, and Congress on mortgage markets and financial reform. He is the author of *Housing and Investment in an Inflationary World* and coeditor of *House Prices and Inflation.*

James P. Zais is a senior research associate in The Urban Institute in the Housing and Community Development Center. Much of his work has involved analyzing housing voucher programs. Dr. Zais has also been principal investigator for a major study of the impact of urban revitalization on the elderly. Previously he was an assistant professor at State University of New York/ Buffalo. His most recent publication is *Housing Assistance for Older Americans: The Reagan Prescription.*